OSCAR WILDE
The works of a conformist rebel

NORBERT KOHL
Professor of English Literature
University of Freiburg im Breisgau

Translated from the German by
DAVID HENRY WILSON

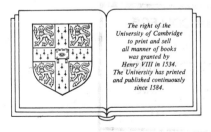

*The right of the
University of Cambridge
to print and sell
all manner of books
was granted by
Henry VIII in 1534.
The University has printed
and published continuously
since 1584.*

CAMBRIDGE UNIVERSITY PRESS
Cambridge
New York   Port Chester   Melbourne   Sydney

Published by the Press Syndicate of the University of Cambridge
The Pitt Building, Trumpington Street, Cambridge CB2 1RP
40 West 20th Street, New York, NY 10011, USA
10 Stamford Road, Oakleigh, Melbourne 3166, Australia

Originally published in German as *Oscar Wilde: Das literarische Werk zwischen Provokation und Anpassung*
by Carl Winter Universitätsverlag 1980
and © 1980 Carl Winter Universitätsverlag, gegr. 1822,
GmbH., Heidelberg. ISBN 3-533-02851-8/3-533-02852-6

First published in English by Cambridge University Press 1989 as
Oscar Wilde: The works of a conformist rebel

English translation © Cambridge University Press 1989

Printed in Great Britain at the University Press, Cambridge

British Library cataloguing in publication data

Kohl, Norbert
Oscar Wilde: The works of a conformist rebel – (European studies in English literature)
1. English literature. Wilde, Oscar, 1854–1900 – Critical studies
I. Title   II. Series
828′.809

Library of Congress cataloguing in publication data

Kohl, Norbert, 1939–
[Oscar Wilde. English]
Oscar Wilde: the works of a conformist rebel / Norbert Kohl: translated from the German by David Henry Wilson.
    p.   cm. – (European studies in English literature)
Translation of: Oscar Wilde. 1980.
Bibliography: p.
Includes index.
ISBN 0 521 32463 7
1. Wilde, Oscar, 1854–1900 – Criticism and interpretation.
I. Title.   II. Series.
PR5824.K5613   1989
828′.809--dc19   88-34830 CIP

ISBN 0 521 32463 7

CE

126 783

European Studies in English Literature

Oscar Wilde

This is the most complete study of Oscar Wilde's work yet undertaken. Its aim is to · gain a new understanding of his literary and critical *œuvre* by fully analysing each of his works on the basis of a textually orientated interpretation, also taking account of the biographical and intellectual contexts.

Professor Kohl's starting-point is the thesis that Wilde's identity – both personal and artistic – can only be adequately described in terms of a conflict between two opposing forces: individualism and convention. This conflict colours not only Wilde's use of romantic and Victorian images and motifs, but also his modern portrayal of the individual's alienation from society, the loss of transcendent values, the sovereignty of subjectivity and autonomous art, and also his formal experiments with language.

This penetrating and highly readable account of Wilde as a 'conformist rebel', published in German in 1980, is now available for the first time in English.

European Studies in English Literature

SERIES EDITORS
Ulrich Broich, Professor of English, University of Munich
Herbert Grabes, Professor of English, University of Giessen
Dieter Mehl, Professor of English, University of Bonn

Roger Asselineau, Professor Emeritus of American Literature, University of Paris-
    Sorbonne
Paul-Gabriel Boucé, Professor of English, University of Sorbonne-Nouvelle
Robert Ellrodt, Professor of English, University of Sorbonne-Nouvelle
Sylvère Monod, Professor Emeritus of English, University of Sorbonne-Nouvelle

This series is devoted to publishing translations into English of the best works written in European languages on English literature. These may be first-rate books recently published in their original versions, or they may be classic studies which have influenced the course of scholarship in their world while never having been available in English before.

To begin with the series has concentrated on works translated from the German; but its range will expand to cover other languages.

TRANSLATIONS PUBLISHED
Walter Pater: The aesthetic moment by Wolfgang Iser
*The Symbolist Tradition in English Literature: A study of Pre-Raphaelitism and
    'Fin de Siècle'* by Lothar Hönnighausen
The Theory and Analysis of Drama by Manfred Pfister
Oscar Wilde: The works of a conformist rebel by Norbert Kohl

TITLES UNDER CONTRACT FOR TRANSLATION
Studien zum komischen Epos by Ulrich Broich
Redeformen des englischen Mysterienspiels by Hans-Jürgen Diller
Die romantische Verserzählung in England by Hermann Fischer
*Studien zur Dramenform vor Shakespeare: Moralität, Interlude, romaneskes
    Drama* by Werner Habicht
*Die Frauenklage: Studien zur elegischen Verserzählung in der englischen Literatur
    des Spätmittelalters und der Renaissance* by Götz Schmitz
Das englische Theater der Gegenwart by Christian Werner Thomsen
*Anfänge und gattungstypische Ausformung der englischen Strassenballade,
    1550–1650* by Natascha Würzbach

La Dupe Elisabéthaine by Christiane Gallenca
Shakespeare et la Fête by François Laroque
L'Etre et l'Avoir dans les Romans de Charles Dickens by Anny Sadrin

for Willi Erzgräber

Contents

Preface

This book was originally published in Germany in 1980 by the Carl Winter Universitätsverlag, Heidelberg, under the title *Oscar Wilde. Das literarische Werk zwischen Provokation und Anpassung*. For this new, English edition I have taken the opportunity to up-date the text in accordance with the latest research, but otherwise there has been only one substantial change, which concerns the bibliography. In the German edition this comprised a detailed, annotated list of some 1,800 titles, but for reasons of space it has had to be cut to the bare essentials of primary and secondary literature.

When I first began work on this study during the late 1960s, it was common practice in literary criticism to devote as much attention to the person of the author as to his work, and my approach ran directly contrary to this tendency. In interpreting Wilde's literary and critical writings, I put text analysis first, while incorporating those elements of biography and literary and social history that seemed directly relevant. This is an approach with which I still identify, and through which I hope to have achieved a clear and balanced view of Wilde's work.

During the many years of research and writing, I have incurred debts to a large number of people. First and foremost, I must thank Professor Dr Willi Erzgräber, who provided the initial inspiration for this study, and accompanied it throughout with expert counsel. Long discussions with Dr Helmut Winter, who also read through the original manuscript, had a very positive influence on its final form. Ursula Fischer's inexhaustible enthusiasm helped me to overcome many moments of despair, and she also undertook the arduous tasks of reading proofs and compiling the index for the original German edition. Ilse Dexheimer, Christine Holtz and Heidi Winter also read the German proofs, and Marie-Luise Santangelo and Christa Völcker provided an immaculate German typescript. For the original bibliography I was indebted to countless librarians, and the services of the Deutsche Bibliothek and the Stadt- und Universitätsbibliothek in Frankfurt am Main, and the British Library in London, were truly indispensable. I am particularly grateful to the Deutsche Forschungsgemeinschaft, whose generosity in the form of a two-year research grant as well as subsidies for travel and printing costs, provided the material basis both for the writing and the publication of the book.

For this English edition my special thanks and deep appreciation are due to David H. Wilson, not only for his meticulous and fluent translation, but also for the critical and creative talents he has brought to bear on the work, smoothing out uneven arguments, compressing Germanic long-windedness, and generally sharpening the focus: 'the artist as critic as translator'! I am also most grateful to the Cambridge University Press for commissioning the translation and including the book in their series of European Studies in English Literature. In particular my thanks go to Kevin Taylor, the Press editor, and to Christine Lyall Grant for her thoroughness in preparing the text for publication. Thanks also to Jenny Wilson, who compiled the English index.

Frankfurt am Main   N.K.

Introduction

Any critic dealing with the life and works of Oscar Wilde will realise right from the start that his subject was not only an author but, to his contemporaries and also to succeeding generations, an outstanding personality on the English cultural scene of the late nineteenth century. He was ostracised and forced into exile by the guardians of tradition, cast by the liberals in the role of the martyred artist, victimised by puritan prudes and Pharisees, dismissed by literary historians as a brilliant epigon caught between the Victorian Age and modern times, and smugly classified by the critics as a first-class representative of the second division. And yet his works are always in print, his books are bought and read, and his plays are continually being produced. All this would seem to confirm his own judgment that 'I was a man who stood in symbolic relations to the art and culture of my age.'[1] He remains a symbol of the conflict between the middle-class values of the nineteenth century and the artist's need for freedom, and his name will always be linked to the attempt to reconcile the individual's desire for self-realisation with public pressure to conform to social convention.

Seldom has any author provoked such controversy both among the critics and among the public at large. Some saw him as the champion of aesthetics against a materialism that was swiftly casting off the threadbare cloak of religion; in his fight to liberate art from its philistine bondage, he was viewed as the figurehead of the *l'art pour l'art* movement. Others, however, regarded him as a publicity-seeking poser who was not to be taken seriously, and who merely substituted artifice for art and decoration for literature. He created a kind of symbiosis of art and life in which it was often difficult to tell which of the elements was the more real and the more significant. It is a situation again best summed up by himself, in words he is said to have spoken to André Gide: 'J'ai mis mon génie dans ma vie, je n'ai mis que mon talent dans mes œuvres'[2] [I have put my genius into my life, and have put only my talent into my works].

Indeed this famous quotation appears to underlie the approach of a good many Wilde critics,[3] whose research is directed principally towards illuminating the life and personality of this eccentric Irish Londoner. The biographies written by the generation that followed Wilde are mainly in the form of memoirs of friends or acquaintances, and are a mixture of

1

sympathy and antipathy, sentimentalism and sensation, sometimes offering a defence, and sometimes directly confirming his own claim that 'Every great man nowadays has his disciples, and it is always Judas who writes the biography.'[4] This aphorism however, cannot be applied to Robert H. Sherard, who in several books – for example, *Oscar Wilde. The Story of an Unhappy Friendship* (1902), and *The Life of Oscar Wilde* (1906) – wrote with touching, almost naive fidelity (though when necessary also with aggressive determination) about the legend of this revered writer so badly misunderstood in England and so fittingly appreciated on the Continent; according to Sherard, Wilde never did anything wrong, but was 'the purest man in word and deed'.[5] By contrast the memoirs of Lord Alfred Douglas, *Oscar Wilde and Myself* (1914),[6] read like a manifesto, mixing attack on the 'opposition' with vain self-glorification. Most of what he says about his former friend is so shot through with inflated pride and personal justification that one can only view his account with the utmost scepticism. The same must be said of the most famous of the early Wilde biographies, despite its many reprints: this was Frank Harris's *Oscar Wilde. His Life and Confessions* (1916) which occasionally offered revealing psychological insight into Wilde's personality and into the society in which he lived, and was also written with some panache, but was for the most part a kind of improvised entertainment with very little distinction between fact and fiction.[7] Later biographies, for example those by Hesketh Pearson (1946), Philippe Jullian (1967) and H. Montgomery Hyde (1976), have helped to rid Wilde's life story of its spurious embellishments, but what has long been lacking is an account that would combine the facts with sensitive characterisation and insight into the social and historical background. The foundations for such a critical synthesis were already laid in 1962, when Rupert Hart-Davis published his excellent edition of Wilde's letters, which he followed up with a supplementary volume in 1985.

Interest in Wilde's dramatic life story has had its effect not only on the voluminous biographical literature but also on the methods used to approach his works. It is, in fact, a two-way approach – in the one instance, his writings are used to illuminate the personality of the author, and in the second the personality is regarded as the key to understanding the work. Such biographically orientated interpretation is based on the premise that Wilde had neither a 'negative capability' in the Keatsian sense, nor an aesthetic leaning towards the 'impersonal poetry' venerated by T. S. Eliot. Wilde himself always stressed the importance of the personality in art, and such works as *The Picture of Dorian Gray*, *De Profundis*, and *The Ballad of Reading Gaol* seem scarcely to disguise the link between life and literature.

The biographical approach as outlined above dominated Wilde criticism until the 1950s. W. W. Kenilworth (1912) set out to achieve 'an understanding of the man through a consideration of his literature',[8] Arthur Ransome (1912) considered it necessary 'to look at books and life together as at a portrait of an artist by himself',[9] and Boris Brasol (1938) adhered to the thesis that Wilde's genius was 'the outgrowth of his personality'.[10] But when a writer's work is linked so closely with his life, and the individuality of his work is viewed only as a reflection of his singular personality and his singular way of life, the danger is bound to arise that his art itself will be relegated into the background, and his writings will be seen as fragments of a great confession[11] the unity of which lies not in the art but in the author. Logically such a standpoint must elevate the personality above the art, and indeed Arthur Symons's *Study of Oscar Wilde* (1930) took precisely this grave step, much in line with the comment already quoted from Wilde's conversation with André Gide. He drew a portrait of his contemporary which continues to influence people's views even today, and was to hinder more profound research into the works themselves: 'for the most part, he [Wilde] was a personality rather than an artist'.[12] In fact he went even further:

Without being a sage, he maintained the attitude of a sage; without being a poet, he maintained the attitude of a poet; without being an artist, he maintained the attitude of an artist. And it was precisely in his attitudes that he was most sincere. They represented his intentions; they stood for the better, unrealised part of himself.[13]

This damaging description of Wilde as a poser who was only credible in his poses is a delayed, rhetorically pointed and effective confirmation of the old Victorian prejudice, implying the very same insincerity that was attacked in earlier reviews of his work. Although elsewhere Symons does concede that Wilde was possessed of reason and that his wit revealed logical thinking, otherwise he sees the style of the author of *Intentions* as being merely 'a bewildering echo of Pater or of some French writer',[14] the fantasy of Wilde's much-loved fairy-tales as superficial, and the poetry of *The Ballad of Reading Gaol* as being almost completely without 'purely poetical quality'.[15] The resultant portrait is as crude as it has proved long-lasting: less an artist than a personality, less a personality than a poser.

Such prejudices placed the biographical study of Wilde's work in a virtual cul-de-sac, which was blocked still further by the fact that certain aspects of his life – especially his homosexuality – were regarded either as a taboo subject or, at best, as a regrettable aberration caused by excessive alcohol. When the taboo was, so to speak, lifted in the 1930s, it was an important step towards a less prejudiced, less moralising approach, but the mere succession of chapters dealing first with biography and then with works, as was so often the format, could only offer an unsatisfactory and superficial answer to the question of how real-life experiences were transmuted into literature. It was not until the 1930s and 1940s that two French authors released Wilde research from its straitjacket of apology, polemics and mystification into the area of critical analysis and interpretation. These authors were Léon Lemonnier and Robert Merle. Later scholars have tended to ignore their achievement, which above all lies in the fact that they abandoned the largely dilettante biographical method and replaced it with one that was psychologically orientated but concentrated first and foremost on the works themselves. At last Wilde's work was viewed as a whole and set in the context not only of his life but also of his art. The problems of a married Victorian who was also a homosexual are seen not as ends in themselves, but as motifs transmuted into literature.

Léon Lemonnier's monograph (1938) is certainly not a psychological study of the works in the strictest sense, but the individual chapters continually refer back to Wilde's homosexuality and the resultant feeling of guilt which Lemonnier regards as a prime impulse throughout Wilde's work. As early as 'Charmides', the most successful of the longer pieces in the *Poems* of 1881, the sterile lust of the young Greek and the link between love and death are themes that look forward to *Salomé* and *The Sphinx* and that reveal the 'sens du péché'[16] which runs like a single thread throughout the canon. The many fairy-tales may reflect the 'vie conjugale et régulière'[17] of the author as paterfamilias, but the relationship between the fisherman and the mermaid in 'The Fisherman and his Soul' clearly shows elements of abnormality and even perversion which might be interpreted as expressing a different *sensibilità erotica*, as well as suggesting that family life was not entirely trouble-free. In characters like Wainewright ('Pen, Pencil and Poison') and Dorian Gray, Lemonnier sees embodiments of the same 'notion ... de péché',[18] expressing a growing need for public confession of what Wilde regarded as a guilty perversion. And finally Lemonnier points to the recurrent motif of the secret in the comedies, as indicating Wilde's 'impuissance à s'échapper à soi-même'.[19] Wilde's work, then, is seen as a progressive, literarily coded emancipation of the personality from the repressions and restrictions of bourgeois Victorian morality, and also a hidden process of release from the torment of guilt – which, one might add, was to be followed by public atonement through trial and imprisonment. It is a thesis which in fact offers a remarkably consistent bond between a basic conflict in Wilde's life and some of the *idées obsédantes* of his work.

Ten years later, Robert Merle's comprehensive and highly stimulating thesis (1948)[20] seizes on Lemonnier's psychological-cum-literary approach, modifies it, and develops it on a broader base. Merle interprets both life and work by way of the author's neurosis, which he claims was the result not of a *'perversion refoulée'*[21] but, on the contrary, of a *'perversion satisfaite'*.[22] Wilde's awareness of his sexual 'perversion' in direct conflict with the established sexual morality of his time, directed his critical thinking towards negativity and nihilism, which manifested itself in an 'horreur du Réel'[23] and makes his writings appear as a large-scale attempt to escape from the tyranny of facts by elevating form over content, thought over action, and art over life:

> C'est [sa pensée critique] une tentative cohérente pour amener la vie à se passer de l'action, la société à se passer d'organisation, la critique à se passer d'analyse, l'art à se passer du réel.[24]

[It (his critical thought) is a coherent attempt to make life dispense with action, society dispense with organisation, criticism dispense with analysis, art dispense with reality.]

This nihilistic attitude towards the established social and moral order, together with the anti-realism of his aesthetics, makes it very easy to understand why the paradox – as a means of undermining the validity of conventional beliefs – was one of Wilde's favourite literary devices. Furthermore, the surprising importance that Wilde attached to style, together with his endless desire for story-telling and the mythical, poetical fantasy of his tales, all point to what Merle calls 'évasion'. At least as strong as his instinct for escape – perhaps even stronger – was his narcissistic urge for self-presentation, which in his case amounted to public confession of his feelings of guilt. Thus everything that he wrote after the 'phase de régression' was characterised by a two-way movement, *'une tendance à l'aveu et une volonté de secret'*.[25] The narrow range of his themes – for example narcissism, sin, secrecy, suffering, forgiveness and death – may be taken as a sign of the influence exerted on his art by his traumatic experiences as a homosexual outsider. As he was imprisoned by his 'Moi autarcique'[26] [autarchic self], which for him was the only true reality, change and novelty were only possible by means of form – as evinced by the many genres and the many styles he used – while the substance of his work remained basically the same, with its few recurrent characters, situations and motifs:

> Le seul caractère que Wilde ait créé – Dorian Gray – c'est lui-même. La seule situation dramatique qu'il ait décrite – le pécheur menacé par le châtiment – c'est la sienne. La seule thèse morale qu'il ait sérieusement soutenue – la nécessité du pardon – est la seule qui intéresse son propre cas. Le seul dénouement qu'il ait prévu à son angoisse – la déchéance et la mort quasi volontaire – c'est son propre destin. D'où, dans son inspiration, *une certaine monotonie qui, assez curieusement, explique et conditionne l'extrême variété extérieure de son œuvre.*[27]

[The only character that Wilde created – Dorian Gray – is himself. The only dramatic situation that he described – the sinner threatened by punishment – is his own. The only moral thesis that he seriously upheld – the necessity for forgiveness – is the only one that is of interest to his own case. The only denouement that he foresaw for his anguish – downfall and quasi-voluntary death – is his own destiny. From which arises, in his inspiration, a certain monotony that curiously enough explains and conditions the extreme external variety of his work.]

This recognition of contradictory traits in Wilde's character was expanded by George Woodcock in *The Paradox of Oscar Wilde* (1949) into the thesis that the contrasts actually sprang from a 'split personality'.[28] Woodcock constructs a whole series of contradictory traits: paganism/Christianity; aesthetic clown/creative critic; social rebel/social snob; playboy/prophet etc., which he uses as categories for his study of the works, at the same time continually drawing on biographical facts and on statements made by Wilde's contemporaries. In his concluding chapter, he takes Wilde's individualism to be the solution: 'The Contradictions Resolved':

And, in the last analysis, when we have considered all his various acts and attitudes, it is here that Wilde's real value remains, in his consistently maintained search for the liberation of the human personality from all the trammels that society and custom have laid upon it. All the rest is intentions, the intentions of a man struggling to realise his own greatness, and finding it completely only in failure.[29]

Woodcock believes that Wilde failed to reconcile the contrasting elements of his character and also to synthesise them in his work. For this reason, despite his talent as a conversationalist and a dramatist, he did not achieve true literary greatness. He was – in accordance with the traditional conclusion – 'a greater personality than a writer'.[30]

The studies by Lemonnier, Merle and Woodcock all contributed a great deal to our understanding of Wilde's work and its links with his life and personality. But, like so many other critics, they did not altogether avoid the biographical fallacy. Merle's insistence that Wilde's characters, dramatic situations, conflicts and solutions merely reproduce his own central moral dilemma – his guilty feelings about his homosexuality and his longing for expiation – inevitably suggest the same misleading conclusion offered by Woodcock.

The biographical approach to interpretation, concentrating on the influence of historical reality on the composition of a work, was from the very beginning complemented by attempts to link Wilde's writings to the literary traditions that he followed. In these comparative studies, the critics were concerned both with the conventions of style and form that Wilde used, and with the origins of his aesthetic and philosophical views. A classic example of this comparative and historical approach is Bernhard Fehr's *Studien zu Oscar Wilde's Gedichten* (1918). Following the tenets of positivism, in which the principle of cause and effect also applies to literature, Fehr saw himself as a kind of literary detective, following Wilde's tracks through the poems. Instead of focusing on the work itself and its links with the author, he set out to discover the external conditions that might have given rise to the work. Wilde himself was classified simply as 'geschickter Nachempfinder der verschiedensten Stilarten"[31] [skilful imitator of a great variety of styles]. Thus he writes of the poem 'Humanitad':

Er [Wilde] wirft rasch ein paar Blumen hin, die teilweise aus – Arnolds Garten stammen ..., lässt ein leises Shelleyisches Blumenläuten erklingen ... und betritt dann den schwierigen Weg ins Labyrinth der Ideen. Es handelt sich darum, auf schnellen Windungen Swinburne zu erreichen.[32]

[He swiftly throws in a few flowers, partly taken from Arnold's garden ... lets out a soft Shelley-like tinkle of flowers ... and then steps onto the difficult path to the labyrinth of ideas. It is a matter of making quick twists and turns in order to get to Swinburne.]

Similar methods (though admittedly not always in the same vein as the above) were used by Eduard J. Bock[33] to elucidate Wilde's links with Pater, by Ernst Bendz[34] to trace the stylistic influence of Pater and Matthew Arnold on Wilde's prose, and by Gerda Eichbaum[35] to tackle the problem of Wilde's relationship with James McNeill Whistler. Kelver Hartley, *Oscar Wilde. L'Influence française dans son œuvre* (1935), seeks to establish the French connection. After that, the old style of historical study, searching for sources, became more and more rare, although as late as 1971 the attempt (unsuccessful) was made to prove that Alfred de Musset's *Il ne faut jurer de rien*[36] was a source for *The Importance of Being Earnest*.

Such quests for source material, however, undoubtedly had their value. They showed how very closely acquainted Wilde was not only with the English but also with the French literature of his time, as well as how receptive he was to his predecessors' conventional modes of expression and aesthetic concepts, which he was able to absorb and use in his own way. It was a method that demanded an extraordinary degree of learning from the critic, and sensitivity to style together with a sharply discerning judgment. But just as the biographical approach tended to see the works as continual manifestations of vital events and traumatic psychological experiences, so the source-hunting approach ran the risk of interpreting every similarity or parallel between themes and devices as being straightforward 'influences'. Thus the creative element of the work was ceaselessly devalued, and Wilde tended to be dismissed as a mere imitator drawing on multifarious sources. The result of such studies has been the labelling of Wilde as an epigon, adorning himself with borrowed plumes.

More recent critics have abandoned the point-for-point comparative study of influences, and instead have sought to interpret the substance of the work in accordance with specific aesthetic and philosophical traditions. Edouard Roditi's monograph of 1947 set out 'to indicate the central position that Wilde's works and ideas occupy in the thought and art of his age, and in the shift of English and American literature from established and aging romanticism to what we now call modernism'.[37] Roditi sees Wilde as a precursor of modernism, exercising profound influence on such authors as Gide, Stefan George and Hofmannsthal. This influence consisted less in matters of literary form than in the vitality of his aesthetics and his theory of individualism. Roditi even goes so far as to place Wilde's critical writings on a par with those of S. T. Coleridge and Matthew Arnold. He sees Wilde's moral, aesthetic and political ideas as being united in the philosophy of dandyism, exemplified in the novel *The Picture of Dorian Gray*, which he calls an *'Erziehungsroman* of dandyism',[38] though its hero was 'a fallen dandy'[39] who falsified Lord Henry's 'philosophy of inaction'[40] and therefore had to fail.

It is disputable whether Wilde himself came anywhere near the ideal of the dandy, as embodied by Beau Brummell and depicted by Baudelaire. The early ostentatiousness of his 'aesthetic garb', and his constant self-advertisement, scarcely fit in with the refined elegance and unobtrusive dignity so essential to the true dandy. The search for the perfect form, stress on the autonomous personality, intellectual detachment from reality, the conviction that art was superior to nature – all these were not so much basic principles of Wilde's philosophy of life as norms applicable to his theory of art, a theory developed in his essays and given fictional form in *Dorian Gray* and in the comedies. It is well known that his aesthetic opposition to the Victorian bourgeoisie was indebted both to the French movement of *l'art pour l'art* and to English aestheticism, especially that of Swinburne, Pater and Whistler. It must therefore have seemed a promising avenue of exploration to trace the links between Wilde's aestheticism and these movements, and thereby determine more precisely his position in the history of ideas. As early as the 1930s Albert J. Farmer and Louise Rosenblatt wrote detailed studies – at virtually the same time – laying the base for a better understanding of the Aesthetic Movement and its literary-historical roots.[41] Then in the mid 1950s Aatos Ojala made aestheticism the cornerstone of his two-part book on *Aestheticism and Oscar Wilde* (1954/55). His aim was 'to show how far aestheticism underlies his personality, penetrates his philosophy, determines his art, and gives his style its colour and cadence'.[42] Ojala follows up Merle's thesis of 1948 with a psychological interpretation based on Wilde's narcissism, which he regards as a source of Wilde's homosexuality and which he also sees as underlying Wilde's art, which in turn is 'self-expression in the truest and the most subjective sense of the word'.[43] His study of Wilde's style is undoubtedly more productive; he uses a vast amount of statistical material to prove the extent to which Wilde's aesthetic philosophy imprinted itself on his use of language.

Ojala's detailed study of Wilde's style pointed the way to a change of direction which was apparent in the 1950s and, more especially, in the 1960s. After all the preceding biographical, historical, aesthetic and philosophical studies, the need was now for closer inspection of the individual works and the artistic methods that Wilde had used. The hope was that by concentrating on the texts, one might be able to reach a more objective judgment both of the works and of Wilde's literary status,[44] which had hitherto been unfairly affected by the findings indicated earlier. It is somewhat surprising to note that very little progress was made in this respect by German critics, for next to Shakespeare, Byron and Shaw, Wilde is one of the best known of English authors in Germany. Apart from Peter Funke's meritorious introduction *Oscar Wilde in Selbstzeugnissen und Bilddokumenten* (1969), there was a long gap from the 1920s onwards – indeed after the studies by Felix Paul Greve (1903), Carl Hagemann (1904, rev. 1925), Hedwig Lachmann (1905), and Philipp Aronstein (1922).

The change in critical focus during the 1950s and 1960s – particularly noticeable in the growing number of work-orientated essays published in literary journals – made its presence felt above all in the reception of the comedies. Apart from a few exceptions, such as Maximilian Rieger's dissertation[45] in the 1920s, the plays were only dealt with in monographs or in histories of drama (and then only cursorily). Examples of the new development are to be seen in the essays of Alan Harris (1954),[46] Arthur F. Ganz (1957),[47] Ian Gregor (1966),[48] Hélène Catsiapis (1978),[49] and Regenia Gagnier (1982)[50] on the comedies in general, and Cleanth Brooks's and Robert B. Heilman's structural analysis of *Lady Windermere's Fan* (1948),[51] as well as different studies of *The Importance of Being Earnest* by Richard Foster (1956),[52] E. B. Partridge (1958),[53] Arthur Ganz (1963),[54] Harold Toliver (1963),[55] and David Parker (1974).[56] Interest grew not only in the literary work but also in the critical, as evinced by publications edited by Richard Ellmann (1968)[57] and Stanley Weintraub (1968),[58] and studies by Guido Glur (1957),[59] Hilda Schiff (1960),[60] Robert E. Rhodes (1964),[61] Richard Ellmann (1966),[62] Wendell V. Harris (1971),[63] Herbert Sussman (1973),[64] and Michael S. Helfand and Philip E. Smith II (1978).[65]

Not until 1967 did a critic – Epifanio San Juan, Jr – dare to take on the task of reinterpreting Wilde's work in its entirety. Unlike most of his predecessors, his approach was orientated by text analysis, his starting-point being the following correct appraisal of the critical situation:

What is needed above all is a critical scrutiny of the individual works and an appreciation of the vision of truth embodied in forms which are significant and enduring. This study is written with that aim in mind.[66]

San Juan analyses the poems, *Dorian Gray*, the aesthetic and literary criticism, the plays and *The Ballad of Reading Gaol*. He traces a development in the poems from the early epigonic style through the voluptuous sensuality of *The Sphinx* to the plain and simple expressiveness of the *Ballad*. One must perhaps regard as questionable his assertion that Wilde sought to depict 'complex experience in a mode of lyrical intensity that would successfully unify multiple ways of feeling and thinking in a meaningful totality',[67] for there can be no doubt that few of the early poems were inspired by personal experience or by a profound involvement in intellectual problems. The *Dorian Gray* chapter is altogether more convincing. San Juan is one of the first critics to note the importance of space and time in the structure of the novel, the main problem of which is to depict the hero's 'lucidity of discrimination'[68] in his search for 'unity of self'.[69] San Juan sees the comedies as a mixture of the 'comedy of manners'[70] and the 'sentimental comedy',[71] with the former tending to be predominant. The thematic structure of the plays is determined mainly by the problem of identity, the motif of self-knowledge, and the conflict of 'feeling *versus* logic'.[72] The concluding interpretation of the *Ballad* also points to the theme of identity, and San Juan regards the poem as 'a mode of understanding the value of experience in the effort to realize one's identity'.[73] The value of this study lies in the detailed individual analyses, particularly of *Salomé*, *The Picture of Dorian Gray*, and *The Ballad of Reading Gaol*, though there is no unifying standpoint to link the various divergent interpretations together.

Wilde research during the 1970s reinforced the text-orientated approach, although attempts were still made to interpret the works as before from a biographical or historical point of view. Christopher S. Nassaar based his *Into the Demon Universe. A Literary Exploration of Oscar Wilde* (1974) on the following thesis:

Conscious of his place at the end of the century, he [Wilde] elevated the demonic to the status of a religion and tried to terminate the nineteenth century with a religion of evil, an unholy worship of evil beauty.[74]

No matter how sceptical one may be over such a thesis, one cannot deny that the author drew attention to an aspect of Wilde's work that had hitherto been badly neglected. But by dogmatically insisting on this valuable point as the keynote of his thesis, Nassaar forces all the works into the procrustean bed of his own concepts. Karl Beckson, in reviewing Nassaar's book, rightly suggests that the thesis of a 'demon universe' would be more suitably applied to such authors as Poe, Baudelaire and

Dostoevsky, who all set a completely different value on evil.[75] What Nassaar considers to be a metaphysical category is often no more than a literary convention – for instance, the *femme fatale* in *Salomé*. An interpretation of Wilde's work solely in moral terms such as 'innocence', 'evil' or 'demonic' can only lead to distortion and imbalance.

Apart from various introductory volumes,[76] Nassaar's study has been joined by three monographs which, from different standpoints, have greatly enriched our understanding of Wilde and his work. Rodney Shewan's *Oscar Wilde. Art and Egotism* (1977) concentrates on 'Wilde's relationship with literature'.[77] Shewan interprets Wilde's writings in terms of the tension between his personal need for expression and his aesthetic search for the perfect form. In the close link between art and life that was characteristic of Wilde, there are clear conflicts between emotion and intellect, self-fulfilment and the expectations of society, artistic design and the artist's own ideals, and these conflicts find expression in the 'patterns of self-projection and self-objectification'[78] within his work. These patterns can be seen in the three main characters of *Dorian Gray* – here Shewan refers to the well-known identification of Wilde with Basil, Lord Henry and Dorian – and also in the contrast between the individualism of the dandies and the moral conformity of the female 'Puritans' in the comedies. The inclusion of new material gleaned from manuscripts in the Clark Library, the many cross-references with which Shewan seeks to evaluate the position of each text within the canon and in literary tradition as a whole, and the generally convincing tone of the arguments enable this study to offer many penetrating insights into Wilde's literary art. This judgment is not affected by certain reservations that many readers and critics have expressed concerning the somewhat unbalanced emphasis[79] – for instance, Shewan devoted twelve pages to 'The Portrait of Mr W.H.', but little more than six to *The Importance of Being Earnest*.

J. E. Chamberlin, in his *Ripe Was the Drowsy Hour. The Age of Oscar Wilde* (1977), aimed at 'a clearer assessment of Wilde's career, of its place in the nineteenth-century scheme of things, and of the art and intellectual life of the period itself'.[80] His concern is therefore not with social history, but with the history of ideas, and he examines various philosophical and aesthetic concepts alluded to by Wilde or incorporated into his works. Chamberlin interprets decadence, aestheticism and symbolism as forms of the artist's alienation from his social environment. Only in art or in an aesthetically glamorised life was it still possible for him to create an identity for himself beyond the bourgeois code of values. The link between beauty and death or decay, between joy and suffering, was perhaps '*the* major theme of the age of Oscar Wilde'.[81]

Philip K. Cohen, in *The Moral Vision of Oscar Wilde* (1978), starts out from the belief that Wilde's work was 'a process of self-creation'[82] which fictionalised and reflected the development of the author's morally orientated view of reality. He argues that Wilde's lasting reputation is based neither on his aestheticism nor on his dandyism but – surprising as it may sound – his 'morality'. Sin and atonement, and the contrast between Old Testament severity and New Testament love of one's neighbour – these mark the parameters of Wilde's subject-matter. They find expression through the conflict between the sinner – loaded down with guilt – and the self-righteous puritan, between the individual's quest for self-realisation and the moral norms that so often block his path. The preferred solution to the problem lies not in punishing the guilty, but in the possibility of Christian forgiveness. If one accepts this moral perspective – which should in no way be confused with literary criteria – then Cohen's argument that the real or radical individualists are not the 'rebellious experimenters with evil', but the 'regenerate sinners',[83] seems plausible. The critical reader may, however, already entertain some doubts about this thesis, and when one takes into account the sentimentality with which Wilde depicts in particular the fallen women of his comedies, the doubts are sure to grow, especially when this thesis leads Cohen to conclude that *The Importance of Being Earnest* is nothing but 'an attempt to escape moral consider-ations through the trivialization of experience'.[84] Cohen's almost inci-dental treatment of Wilde's best play throws into question the methodolo-gical validity of his approach, for he seems to take a single (though admittedly important) aspect of Wilde's writing and make it the focal point for his interpretation of all Wilde's work. Notwithstanding these objections, however, Cohen's book forms a noteworthy complement to Shewan's study.

In addition to these comprehensive, thesis-orientated monographs, the 1970s and 1980s have produced several studies of individual works or groups of works. Alan Bird, *The Plays of Oscar Wilde* (1977), and Katharine Worth, *Oscar Wilde* (1983), both deal with the plays, while Manfred Pfister has written an excellent introduction to *The Picture of Dorian Gray* (1986).[85] Alan Bird, in the introduction to his book, states that 'Wilde's life is less important and less absorbing than his work',[86] and this rejection of previous trends in Wildean research is symptomatic of a new critical approach. Of course the shift of focus onto the texts themselves has not always been advantageous to individual works. *The Picture of Dorian Gray*, *The Importance of Being Earnest* and the critical writings have earned the greatest esteem, whereas *Salomé* is now deemed to have been overestimated, and interest has waned in *De Profundis*. Wilde's personality still fascinates, and so do the drama of his life and the atmosphere of his time, as is evident from the various biographies written in the 1970s and 1980s,[87] but in general there is now a far more sober and objective view of his literary qualities and of his artistic position at the crossroads between Victorian and modern times. But despite this welcome proliferation of work-orientated studies – a clear indication of the seriousness with which Wilde's writing is now taken – a major gap in Wildean research still waits to be filled: a critical edition of his works.

The present study sets out to integrate the various approaches of the past – biography, source-history, and history of ideas – in an overall interpretation of the works based first and foremost on analysis of the texts. The aim is to attain an understanding of their literary and artistic substance, and unlike most previous studies, it focuses squarely upon the individuality of the work and not upon that of the author. We must, however, bear in mind the fact that, in Arnold Hauser's words, 'für das Kunstwerk ausserkünstlerische Anregungen von entscheidender Bedeutung sind'[88] [for the work of art, stimuli from outside the world of art are of vital importance], and art can only be explained as the product of contrasting, non-artistic data from the real material and social world processed by formal, aesthetic, 'spontanen und durchaus schöpferischen Bewusstseinsakten'[89] [spontaneous and totally creative acts of consciousness]. Therefore even an interpretation based on textual analysis must incorporate the literary traditions inherited by the author, and the social reality in which he lived and to which he reacted. We shall be concerned with the themes, motifs, and conventions of form and style that Wilde took over from the past, and the ways in which he changed or renewed them. We shall also examine the links between his own concepts of art and those of the romantics and the Victorians, and we shall see what influence his ideas had on the literature of the modern age. In assessing the links with traditions, we shall not be imposing any positivistic concept of art that might set the individual work within a chain of cause and effect, and so reduce aesthetic and historical complexity to an empirically measurable and explicable system. We shall proceed, rather, from the idea of productive reception, for an artist's absorption of tradition will result in creative adaptation, setting in motion a process of renewal which in turn will bring about different aesthetic forms and contexts. With the split identity of Dorian Gray, for instance, Wilde took a familar theme from romantic literary tradition and gave it a totally new slant by using it as a means of expressing the conflict between art and morality. In the past Wilde was all too often denigrated as a mere imitator, shamelessly pretending that the ideas of his predecessors were his own, but such a view ignores the productive and creative processing of those ideas, and one need only think of the style of his comedies and his critical essays to realise the degree of originality with which he transmuted whatever material he had inherited.

Just as it is impossible to exclude literary traditions from a text-orientated analysis, so too must we keep in mind the fact that the artist's

individuality cannot be separated from consideration of his social existence. It would be as wrong to ignore the biographical background as it
was to make it the sole focal point. Dorian Gray's split identity, the
upper-class ambience of the comedies, and the ballad on the execution of a
soldier are certainly not unrelated to Wilde's own *doppelgänger* existence,
his snobbery, and his humiliating experiences in Reading Gaol – although
they must not be regarded as the inevitable consequences of
his real life. If we were to adopt an historical approach such as New
Criticism, or Russian Formalism, or the German 'Werkinterpretation',
and refrain from all reference to the author's biography or to his attitudes
towards the social reality of his time, we should be forced to exclude
whole dimensions of the works themselves.

The structure of this book is chronological, and follows the main
literary developments of the author from the early poems and plays
through to *The Ballad of Reading Gaol*. There are, however, individual
sections – for instance, that on Wilde's aesthetics – where it is necessary to
refer back to earlier phases of his concepts of art and literature. When
either form or content seemed to warrant it, works have been dealt with
together in a single chapter, even if they are of different genres. There are,
for instance, close formal and thematic links between *Salomé* and *The
Sphinx*, as well as between *De Profundis* and *The Ballad of Reading Gaol*,
both of which are reactions to Wilde's social downfall. In order to avoid
repetition, the individual comedies are also dealt with *en bloc* in accordance with their various themes and characters, but *The Importance of
Being Earnest*, which must have pride of place amongst Wilde's plays, has
a chapter all to itself.

Postscript: The wheels of academic research never cease to turn. Since
the completion of this edition, more studies of Oscar Wilde have
appeared, most notably Richard Ellmann's biography. Regrettably it was
no longer possible to include a discussion of this masterly work.

1   Epigonic experiments.
The early poems and plays

Poems (1881)

Wilde's literary career began during his student days in Oxford with the metric translation of various Greek choruses. He translated the chorus of cloud maidens from Aristophanes' *Nephelai*, the chorus of the captured Trojan women from Euripides' *Hecuba*, and a passage from Aeschylus' *Agamemnon* in which Cassandra ominously speaks of the forthcoming death of the Greek prince. Later he occasionally published poems in various magazines such as *The World*, *The Irish Monthly*, *Dublin University Magazine*, and *Kottabos*. In 1881 he put together most of these published poems along with several that had not been published, and they were printed by David Bogue in London in a single volume called simply *Poems*. Wilde paid for the publication himself. The letter that he wrote in May 1881, trying to interest the publisher in his juvenilia and ending with the self-confident claim that 'Possibly my name requires no introduction',[1] apparently did not have the desired effect, since it did not deter Bogue from soberly calculating the commercial possibilities. The success of the book, however, which went to almost five editions in a single year, appeared to confirm the audacious self-advertisement of its author; the purchasers may well have been attracted less by the quality of the contents than by curiosity about the first poetic utterances of this exponent of the Aesthetic Movement.

This view is strengthened by the fact that the comparatively encouraging sales of *Poems* were in grotesque contrast to the negative reception by the press. The author was criticised for having no 'distinct message'[2] and no 'genuine lyrical feeling',[3] his language was said to be 'inflated and insincere'[4] and his poems were full of 'profuse and careless imagery'.[5] Particularly galling was the rejection of a copy of *Poems* that Wilde sent to the library of the Oxford Union. Normally little attention was paid to such gifts, and they would certainly not be refused, but on this occasion there was a veritable explosion. Oliver Elton, who was later to make a name for himself as a literary historian, was already, at the age of twenty, so well read as a student that he was able to identify the innumerable allusions in Wilde's poems to earlier literary works, and he protested vigorously against acceptance of the volume. He based his objections on

15

the argument that Wilde was not the real author, but that the poems had been written by Shakespeare, Sidney, Donne, Byron, Morris, Swinburne 'and by sixty more'.[6] As a result, the book was rejected and sent back to the author.

As depressing as the rejection of *Poems* by his Alma Mater was the satirical review that appeared in *Punch* on 23 July 1881, contrasting the aesthetically appealing appearance of the book with its miserable content. Under the heading of 'Swinburne and Water', it reads:

The cover is consummate, the paper is distinctly precious, the binding is beautiful, and the type is utterly too. *Poems by Oscar Wilde*, that is the title of the book of the aesthetic singer, which comes to us arrayed in white vellum and gold. There is a certain amount of originality about the binding, but that is more than can be said about the inside of the volume. Mr WILDE may be aesthetic, but he is not original. This is a volume of echoes – it is SWINBURNE and water, while here and there we note that the author has been reminiscent of Mr ROSSETTI and Mrs BROWNING.

The sharpness of this judgment perhaps requires further explanation. It is clear that neither *Punch* nor the various other journals would have taken much notice of the poems – or they would at least have excused the excesses as a *péché de jeunesse* – had their author been unknown. But Wilde, with his eccentric appearance – long hair and 'aesthetic garb' – and the provocative radicalism of his gospel of beauty, had already drawn attention to himself as a leading figure in the Aesthetic Movement. Just a few months before the publication of the poems, in February 1881, a comedy called *The Colonel*, written by F. C. Burnand, the editor of *Punch*, had parodied this movement, and it was followed on 23 April by the première of Gilbert and Sullivan's comic opera *Patience; or Bunthorne's Bride*, whose main characters Archibald Grosvenor and Reginald Bunthorne were also caricatures of the aesthetes. In addition to these satires, there were George du Maurier's cartoons in *Punch*, which treated this very current and very controversial movement in such a negative light that they were bound to instil prejudices into a reading public which was already, by and large, somewhat negatively disposed towards the aesthetic cult. It must also be borne in mind that memories of Swinburne's *Poems and Ballads* (1866) and D. G. Rossetti's *Poems* (1870) – both of which had been condemned by the critics as blasphemous, immoral and obscene – were still fresh. Even if the *Punch* reaction to Wilde's poems was not quite as vicious as its reception of *Poems and Ballads* – the suggestion was made that Swinburne should change his name to 'SWINE-BORN'[7] – and there was no equivalent to Robert Buchanan's notorious article 'The Fleshly School of Poetry', nevertheless the association with this tradition of poetry was sufficient to re-awaken old prejudices.

There can be no denying that the extra publicity enjoyed by the

'Professor of Aesthetics and Art Critic' (as he dubbed himself), and which he now sought to exploit, was not justified by the quality of his writings. This gulf between pretensions and achievements had disastrous consequences, for it strengthened the suspicion that the 'upstart crow' was nothing but a poser. The impression was subsequently reinforced and resulted in the image of the insincere 'showman' so frequently to be found in twentieth-century criticism of Wilde.

The accusation of imitation and plagiarism permeated the reviews and most later studies, which then devoted themselves to corroborating this often justified reproach by means of detailed comparisons.[8] This narrowing of the perspective to a simple hunt for 'influences' often led to over-emphasis on the imitative traits, and neglect of other aspects. A typical example of this tendency is Bernhard Fehr's historical survey of Wilde's sources, *Studien zu Oscar Wilde's Gedichten* (1918). For instance, he summarises the many literary allusions in the poem 'Humanitad' with the following 'equation':

Humanitad = Matthew Arnold + Shelleys Sensitive Plant + Paters Schlusswort [Conclusion] + Swinburnes Dolores + Hesperia + Eve of Revolution + A Song of Italy + Siena + Halt before Rome + Super Flumina Babylonis + Perinde ac Cadaver + Morris' Anti Scrape Society + Paters Winckelmann + Swinburnes before a Crucifix + The Hymn of Man + Hertha + Baudelaires Héautontimorouménos. Damit hat man alles gesagt.[9] [That's all there is to say.]

Whether that really is 'all' is very dubious. This extreme example of a poem being reduced to a sort of mathematical formula is based on the positivistic view of literature, which masquerades as scientific objectivism, claims that all phenomena are absolutely explainable, and so looks on poetry as one more link in the chain of cause and effect, as if literature can be analysed in exactly the same way as the natural sciences analyse objects in the everyday world.

Fehr's book, for all its distortion and one-sidedness, confirms that imitation is one of the most striking features of Wilde's poems. If this observation is pertinent to and detracts from the artistic quality of the *Poems*, then there may well seem to be little point in a 'study of the poems as formal aesthetic objects'[10], as Epifanio San Juan described his own approach, for what could there be to gain from detailed analysis of the aesthetic structure of second- or third-rate poems? The study that follows, however, has a completely different starting-point. Without in any way denying the epigonic and eclectic nature of these poetic juvenilia, its central question concerns the themes Wilde dealt with in his poems, their relation to his own life – as revealed in his letters – and to contemporary conditions, and any thematic and stylistic links with his later writings. First and foremost, the analysis will deal with the attitude of the poet to his subject, and although formal elements such as language and metre will not be totally ignored, they will only be of secondary importance.

Themes and construction

The list of contents in the 1881 edition of *Poems* as well as in the Methuen edition of 1908 shows that the poems are grouped in sections of different sizes. If we follow the heading 'The Fourth Movement',[11] we may conclude that there are four parts to the volume. With the *transposition d'art* so popular since Théophile Gautier's *Symphonie en Blanc Majeur*, Wilde evidently wished to indicate that his book was structured along musical lines – that is, the four movements of a symphony. The individual movements are held together by the more or less similar nature of the poems they contain. 'Eleutheria' deals with political subjects, 'Rosa Mystica' with religious. The third group is itself divided into three: 'Wind Flowers', 'Flowers of Gold', and 'Impressions de Théâtre', combining bucolic motifs with a markedly impressionistic technique of construction. 'The Fourth Movement' brings together passion and a mood of *taedium vitae*. In between these thematically very different groups are five longer poems: 'The Garden of Eros', 'The Burden of Itys', 'Charmides', 'Panthea', and 'Humanitad'. The collection begins with the poem 'Hélas', and concludes with 'Glykyprikos Eros'.

It would be quite wrong to take the sequence of these sections as reflecting the different phases of the poet's spiritual development, especially since the division was not chronological. The poems in the 'Eleutheria' group are relatively late – between 1880 and 1881 – while the next section, 'Rosa Mystica', can be dated between 1876 and 1879. In many cases, Wilde actually split up some of his longer poems, revised individual parts of them, gave them new titles and put them in different sections.[12] 'Lotus Leaves' is one example: it originally appeared in *Irish Monthly* in 1877; Part 2 became 'Impression – Le Réveillon' in 'The Fourth Movement', Part 3 became 'Impressions: 2 La Fuite de la Lune' in the third group, and the remainder, under the same title, was left out of the 1881 edition altogether. Clearly, then, there is little significance in the division and the sequence.

The variety of motifs to be found in the poems corresponds to the speaker's fluctuating attitudes towards his subject-matter. This ambivalence can be sensed in the 'Eleutheria' poems, particularly the 'Sonnet to Liberty'. In the battle for freedom from oppression and tyranny, there is less emphasis on the revolutionary goal – namely, the establishment of democracy – than on the release of unbridled passion. The spirit of revolution in terror and anarchy is experienced as a reflection of the speaker's own rebellious soul:

... the roar of thy Democracies.
Thy reigns of Terror, thy great Anarchies,
Mirror my wildest passions like the sea
And give my rage a brother − ! Liberty![13]

Thus the idea of liberty is largely de-politicised, and enjoyed as the private emotion of the 'discreet soul'.[14] The speaker is untouched when despots destroy their subjects' rights with 'bloody knout' or 'treacherous cannonades',[15] and he has only limited sympathies with:

These Christs that die upon the barricades,
God knows it I am with them, in some things.[16]

He withdraws from any moral responsibility for the development of the common good, renounces any active participation in the struggle, and retreats into his own private sphere of experience. His dissatisfaction with the existing political order thus leads him logically to escapism and isolationism. In a mood of nostalgia he contrasts Cromwell's republic ('To Milton') with the modern, materialistic state which can no longer fulfil its function as imperial protector of the oppressed ('Quantum Mutata'). Presumably there is an allusion here to the attitude of Disraeli towards the Bulgarian freedom-fighters who rose up against the Turks in May 1876. The rebellion was savagely crushed by Turkish troops, who then massacred the civilian population.[17] These atrocities were initially played down by Disraeli, partly through ignorance of the facts and partly for political considerations, but in due course they became public knowledge through reports in the English press and through Gladstone's famous pamphlet *Bulgarian Horrors and the Question of the East* (1876). Wilde reacted with his 'Sonnet on the Massacre of the Christians in Bulgaria', which was inspired by Milton's sonnet 'On the Late Massacher in Piemont'. But even this poem lacks the revolutionary fervour which, for instance, is to be found in the militant essays and patriotic verses of his mother, who in the 1840s had written under the name 'Speranza', vehemently propagating the aims of the Irish Liberation Movement. Wilde is content to invoke a *deus absconditus*, who in the face of the evil in the world should at last reveal himself, 'Lest Mahomet be crowned instead of Thee!'[18]

The isolation of the poetic self from social development, and his refusal to try to change things, leads finally to a withdrawal into the ivory tower of art, though Wilde himself was certainly 'a man of the ivory megaphone rather than of the Ivory Tower'[19]:

Come out of it, my Soul, thou art not fit
For this vile traffic-house, where day by day
Wisdom and reverence are sold at mart,
And the rude people rage with ignorant cries

Against an heritage of centuries.
It mars my calm: wherefore in dreams of Art
And loftiest culture I would stand apart,
Neither for God, nor for his enemies.[20]

It is worth noting that his discontent with the present does not arise solely from the increasing commercialisation of the age, as in 'Quantum Mutata', but is also caused by 'rude people' raging against the 'heritage of centuries'. How is one to reconcile this distrust of the *vulgus profanum* with the democratic sentiments that mark the end of 'Louis Napoleon' and 'Ave Imperatrix'? One can sense the same reservations about the revolutionary potential of the proletariat as is to be found in Matthew Arnold's *Culture and Anarchy*. But while Arnold is at pains to overcome anarchic tendencies by establishing a new and classless principle of authority, Wilde is lacking both in serious political involvement and in any reformist zeal to find alternative solutions. The speaker's ambivalent attitude, preaching democracy and yet using its possible consequences as grounds for rejecting it ('Libertatis Sacra Fames'), may arise from the fact that Wilde was basically conservative with aristocratic ambitions, feigning a republican disposition that had no emotional roots whatsoever but was grounded in the uncommittedness of a modish intellectualism. The term 'freedom' in the 'Eleutheria' poems does not denote the freedom of the people and their self-determination, but the freedom of the unpolitical individual, the *theoretikos*, from state restrictions and social responsibilities, so that he can devote himself undisturbed to his 'dreams of Art / And loftiest culture'.[21]

These verses reveal a political passiveness that typifies late romantic aestheticism and Wilde's own personal attitude. Awareness of belonging to an elite cultural minority is combined with arrogance towards the lower classes and a rejection of the narrow-minded materialism of the middle classes, and together these make up a protest that denotes resignation rather than a desire to bring about reform. The anti-bourgeois revolt is lacking in revolutionary fervour. In this position of the *theoretikos*, compensating for his lack of social and political influence through his 'dreams of Art / And loftiest culture', and glorifying his rejection of practical engagement by assuming the role of the misunderstood guardian of cultural traditions in a time of philistinism, there were never any basic changes even in Wilde's later work. The greater emphasis he was to lay on hedonistic principles does not denote any fundamental change of direction, but can simply be seen as a degeneration of the aesthetic, with the sensual form of art taking over from its ideal content. The feeling that art has no social value, predominant in the poem 'Theoretikos', and forcing the wounded self to play the part of the self-sacrificing outsider, does not evolve into any form of aggressive opposition, but instead leads to an ideology of hedonistic self-fulfilment *sub specie artis*, the failure of which is brought to vivid life in *The Picture of Dorian Gray*. The attempt to make life merely a substratum of aesthetic emotions proves to be impossible, for it produces a split in the individual, whose identity is thus fatally undermined. The ethic of aesthetic hedonism in *Dorian Gray* has its political counterpart in the anarchic liberalism that Wilde offered as his contribution to social reform under the misleading title *The Soul of Man under Socialism*. Typically in this tract Wilde's solution to the problem lies not in curtailing the interests of the individual for the benefit of the community, but on the contrary in promoting the individual's interests above those of society.

Wilde's detachment from contemporary commercial and utilitarian norms, interlinked with his dismay at the devaluation of art in the public consciousness, reaches a peak in the long intermediate poem 'The Garden of Eros'; here he questions the progress of civilisation, which he holds responsible for the fact that the nymphs run weeping from the trees, and the naiads can no longer find refuge 'mid English reeds'[22]:

> Methinks these new Actæons boast too soon
>   That they have spied on beauty; what if we
> Have analysed the rainbow, robbed the moon
>   Of her most ancient, chastest mystery,
> Shall I, the last Endymion, lose all hope
> Because rude eyes peer at my mistress through a telescope!
>
> What profit if this scientific age
>   Burst through our gates with all its retinue
> Of modern miracle! Can it assuage
>   One lover's breaking heart? what can it do
> To make one life more beautiful, one day
> More godlike in its period ...?[23]

The poet's fear that the world will lose its myths and hence its poetry in the face of scientific and technological progress – a favourite theme of the romantics – has its historical roots in the eighteenth century with Rousseau, who warned against the corrupting influence of civilisation on the *vie simple*. The mention of the rainbow in the first verse quoted above may hark back to Keats, in whose poem *Lamia* the demystification of the rainbow exemplifies the irreconcilability of poetic and scientific observation:

> Do not all charms fly
> At the mere touch of cold philosophy?
> There was an awful rainbow once in heaven:
> We know her woof, her texture; she is given
> In the dull catalogue of common things.
> Philosophy will clip an Angel's wings

> ...
> Unweave a rainbow.[24]

The conflict between the poet's truth and that of the scientist is a problem to be found not only in romantic poetics but also even in our own times, and Macaulay's pessimistic claim that 'as civilisation advances, poetry almost necessarily declines'[25] may now seem somewhat premature. The advance of technology begun in the nineteenth century – particularly in medicine and industry – has undoubtedly raised the quality of life, even allowing for the problems and dangers that have arisen from unrestricted growth, and in *The Soul of Man under Socialism* Wilde himself discerned the positive aspects of mechanisation, especially the opportunity for 'cultivated leisure'.[26]

Christian idealism and philhellenism

In the late nineteenth century, technological progress and spiritual crisis went hand in hand. The passion for art was not an adequate substitute for religion and could not satisfy longings for faith, as is evident from the 'Rosa Mystica' poems that were amongst the earliest to be written. In June 1875 Wilde had travelled to Italy for the first time, visiting Milan, Venice, Padua, Verona and Florence, among other towns, though not going to Rome. Seeing the various religious monuments appears to have strengthened his interest in Catholicism. The rather vague hints in the poems concerning a possible conversion are borne out by some of his letters from that time, as well as by the remarks of friends:

> For lo, what changes time can bring!
>   The cycles of revolving years
>   May free my heart from all its fears,
> And teach my lips a song to sing.
>
> Before yon field of trembling gold
>   Is garnered into dusty sheaves,
>   Or ere the autumn's scarlet leaves
> Flutter as birds adown the wold,
> I may have run the glorious race,
>   And caught the torch while yet aflame,
>   And called upon the holy name
> Of Him who now doth hide His face.[27]

The cautiousness of these lines betrays the undecidedness of the speaker, who sees the Catholic faith as just one possibility that may open up in the course of time. The uncertainty and the vagueness of the statement have made many critics doubt the sincerity of Wilde's contemplation of Catholicism. J. D. Thomas, in his essay 'Oscar Wilde's Pose and Poetry',[28] considers the 'Rosa Mystica' group 'most open to the charge of insincerity'[29] and questions whether the young student had felt anything more of the faith than 'the pomp and ceremony of the Church'.[30] He supports his scepticism with a quotation from *De Profundis*: 'Religion does not help me'.[31] However, it can scarcely be true to the principles of literary criticism to set parts of poems written in the late 1870s beside a statement made in a letter of the 1890s and thence to draw conclusions about the sincerity or otherwise of an attitude expressed in the earlier works. The fascination that Catholicism held for Wilde cannot be wholly explained by the aesthetic charm of the buildings, robes and ceremonies. It must be remembered that in his student days Wilde underwent a process of spiritual orientation which – for an Oxford student in the 1870s – was almost bound to lead him towards Catholicism. The influence of Cardinal Newman and the Oxford Movement was still extremely strong on the younger generation, and many followed him on the path to Rome, including Wilde's student friend David Hunter-Blair, who was converted in 1875. To be converted or not to be converted was a problem that most undergraduates had to face sooner or later.

The question of conversion aroused in the young Wilde no deep need for faith, but rather an intellectual curiosity during a phase in which he was experimenting with various life styles and attitudes. He also went through periods of spiritual crisis in which the church seemed to offer a place of inner peace and sanctuary. His feelings at the time are made clear by the following extract from a letter to his student friend William Ward:

I have dreams of a visit to Newman, of the holy sacrament in a new Church, and of a quiet and peace afterwards in my soul. I need not say, though, that I shift with every breath of thought and am weaker and more self-deceiving than ever.

If I *could hope* that the Church would wake in me some earnestness and purity I would go over *as a luxury*, if for no better reasons. But I can hardly hope it would, and to go over to Rome would be to sacrifice and give up my two great gods 'Money and Ambition'. Still I get so wretched and low and troubled that in some desperate mood I will seek the shelter of a Church which simply enthrals me by its fascination.[32]

It is interesting to note that as grounds for possible conversion Wilde adds to 'quiet and peace' the desire for 'earnestness' and 'purity', which would seem to indicate his awareness of some threat to his moral integrity. The motifs of guilt and atonement occur repeatedly in the poems. In 'San Miniato' the speaker appeals to the Virgin Mary:

> O listen ere the searching sun
> Show to the world my sin and shame.[33]

This plea to the 'Virginal white Queen of Grace'[34] may perhaps be regarded as a conventional element of late romantic religious poetry, such as is to be found in E. A. Poe ('Catholic Hymn'), D. G. Rossetti ('Ave'), and Francis Thompson ('Assumpta Maria'), but the further confession of guilt in 'E Tenebris', taken in conjunction with the passage quoted from the letter, certainly strengthens the suggestion that the idea of conversion went together with Wilde's hope that he might be freed from the nagging feelings of guilt that oppressed him during this period.[35] It would be premature to assume that these were caused by homosexual practices, even if in his later works the recurrent motifs of sin and guilt point to the homosexuality which morally he was never able to overcome.

Although Wilde never totally freed himself from his fascination with the Scarlet Woman, religious dogma remained as alien to his anti-authoritarian principles as the supernatural doctrine of salvation was alien to his earthly goals of 'money and ambition'. His vacillating views of the world in these years come out clearly in the two long poems 'Panthea' and 'Humanitad' which quite brazenly put together the most disparate ideas in a quite chaotic structure. Pater's philosophy of the moment stands next to Darwin's theory of evolution; Swinburne's idealisation of Mazzini, one of the leading representatives of the 'risorgimento' (the Italian liberation movement) accompanies bucolic *carpe-diem* invocations such as might be found in Fitzgerald's *Rubáiyát of Omar Khayyám* (1859). The realisation that 'man is weak; God sleeps; and heaven is high; / One fiery-coloured moment: one great love; and lo! we die'[36] develops in 'Panthea' into a strange hope for a mystic unification with a 'Kosmic Soul'[37] that will guarantee immortality. The heart of the speaker beats excitedly at the thought of a 'grand living after death / In beast and bird and flower'.[38] In the face of such lines, Bernhard Fehr could not resist stylising the adventurous metamorphoses of the poetic 'I' into a caricature of the poet:

Man denke sich den dicken Wilde, der aus der Kehle des Zaunkönigs wieder zu singen beginnt und mit seiner Geliebten als bunt schillerndes Schlangenpaar über sein früheres Grab läuft oder als Tigerpaar die gelbäugigen Löwen des Dschungels zum Kampf herausfordert![39]

[One can imagine the fat Wilde beginning to sing again from the throat of the wren and running with his true love as a brightly shining pair of snakes over his earlier grave, or as a pair of tigers challenging the yellow-eyed lions of the jungle to come and fight!]

'Panthea' speaks less of pantheism in the sense of God being everything than of a monistic all-is-one-ness, a sort of cosmological panpsychism:

> We are resolved into the supreme air,
>   We are made one with what we touch and see,
> With our heart's blood each crimson sun is fair,
>   With our young lives each spring-impassioned tree
> Flames into green, the wildest beasts that range
> The moor our kinsmen are, all life is one, and all is change.[40]

25

The trauma of transience is to be overcome by belief in an endless
process of transformation relating to all existence, animate and inanimate. Viewed in such a way, death is not a country 'from whose bourn no
traveller returns', but simply denotes the point at which one stage of
existence passes into another. The metaphysical order is indicated, with
help from Darwin's theory of evolution: 'From lower cells of waking life
we pass / To full perfection',[41] and when this can no longer cover Wilde's
ideas, he unhesitatingly invokes neo-Platonic concepts: '... mighty waves
of single Being roll / From nerveless germ to man'.[42]

In the midst of this eclectic tangle of ideas there is an almost tangible
longing to overcome the great split between life and death, man and
Nature, in a mystic oneness that finds its expression in the poem
'Humanitad'. The speaker bewails the loss of harmony with Nature, and
wishes to recreate the unity between body and soul – a theme that is taken
up in the *doppelgänger* motif of *Dorian Gray* and indeed forms a focal
point of the narrative. The vague and scattered longings for faith that were
to be found in the 'Rosa Mystica' group have no part in this poem, for
'That which is purely human, that is Godlike, that is God.'[43] This is a sort
of humanistic atheism such as Swinburne had proclaimed in his 'Hymn to
Man' and in 'Hertha', where ultimately man and goddess are identical.

The outer cause of a profound inner change in Wilde, which manifested
itself in 'Panthea' and 'Humanitad' and brought about the final breakthrough of ideas he had absorbed mainly from Keats, Swinburne and
Pater, was the second journey to Italy which Wilde undertook in March
and April 1877. At the suggestion of his former tutor John Pentland
Mahaffy, Professor of Ancient History at Trinity College, Dublin, this
journey did not end in Italy but, unexpectedly, took him off on an
excursion to the classical sites of Greece. The significance that Wilde
attached to his planned visit to the *urbs aeterna sacra* can be gauged from
a short letter to his friend Reginald Harding, in which he writes:

I hope to see the golden dome of St Peter's and the Eternal City by Tuesday night.
This is an era in my life, a crisis. I wish I could look into the seeds of time and see
what is coming.[44]

If Macbeth's wish had been granted, he might well have curbed his own
ambitions, but Wilde would certainly not have wished his vision of
Athens, Mycenae and Olympia to be undone. The spiritual affinity
between the former winner of the Berkeley Gold Medal for Greek and
Mahaffy, author of *Social Life in Greece from Homer to Menander*
(1874) and *Rambles and Studies in Greece* (1876) – an affinity based on
their mutual admiration of the Greeks – made this experience an indelible
one for the young Wilde. The extent of his enthusiasm can be measured by
the fact that he did not return to Oxford until a month after the start of

term, thereby incurring a fine of £47 10s – which was half his yearly allowance – and being banned from studies for the rest of the term. His explanation for missing the start of term is convincing: 'Mr Mahaffy is such a clever man that it is quite as good as going to lectures to be in his society';[45] it was not, however, convincing enough to counter the petty bureaucracy of the college.

The after-effects of this Greek trip are clearly to be seen in the poems that were written at this time. Wilde's attitude towards Christianity has become more distant and more critical. In 'Easter Day' the speaker points out the contrast between the pomp and circumstance surrounding the Pope and the simplicity of the Galilean, to whom was given no 'place of rest'.[46] This new attitude is expressed quite bluntly in the 'Sonnet Written in Holy Week at Genoa', whose last verse reads:

> Ah, God! Ah, God! those dear Hellenic hours
>   Had drowned all memory of Thy bitter pain,
>   The Cross, the Crown, the Soldiers and the Spear.[47]

During the years that followed, Wilde's academic interest in classical art and culture ripened to a conviction that the pagan way of life, with its emphasis on the sensual and its balance between the needs of the body and those of the soul, was preferable to the inner life of Christianity. It was a view that was never to undergo any basic change, even after the humiliating experience of his imprisonment. It was only shortly before his death that he was converted, apparently having no objections to dying with the blessings of the Church, though never having been seriously prepared to live according to its commandments. André Gide once remarked that the wittiest sayings that Wilde wove into his conversation, most of them now lost for ever, always concerned the contrast between 'naturalisme païen' and 'idéalisme chrétien'.[48]

'Charmides' and the metamorphoses of love

Wilde's philhellenism finds its expression not only in his abundant – perhaps even excessive – use of classical nomenclature, but also in his long poem 'Charmides', whose uniformity of message and tone certainly makes it the most successful of the five long poems.[49] The first part tells of the Greek youth Charmides, who breaks into the temple of Pallas Athene, and hides there until night falls, because he wants to be near the statue of the goddess. He loosens her robes and kisses her cold breast. The revenge of the violated goddess is not long in coming – she appears to the transgressor at sea, and with a cry of 'I come'[50] he hurls himself into the waves and dies. At the beginning of Part Two, a sympathetic sea-god brings the dead body back to the Greek shore, where sirens take charge of it, wash it and anoint it in sweet-scented oils. A dryad, 'thirsty with love's drouth',[51] comes close, runs her fingers through his hair and kisses him, in the hope of waking him from his slumber. Thereupon the goddess Artemis kills this insubordinate servant with an arrow. In pity Venus asks Proserpina to intercede with the god of the underworld, so that the nymph's passion may at least be fulfilled in Hades. This wish is granted. The third and final part of the poem ends as follows:

> Enough, enough that he whose life had been
>   A fiery pulse of sin, a splendid shame,
> Could in the loveless land of Hades glean
>   One scorching harvest from those fields of flame
> Where passion walks with naked unshod feet
> And is not wounded, – ah! enough that once their lips could meet
>
> In that wild throb when all existences
>   Seemed narrowed to one single ecstasy
> Which dies through its own sweetness and the stress
>   Of too much pleasure, ere Persephone
> Had bade them serve her by the ebon throne
> Of the pale God who in the fields of Enna loosed her zone.[52]

The 110 verses of this poem, with a metric scheme based on Shakespeare's *Venus and Adonis*, contain a variety of motifs that are not to be found anywhere else in the *Poems* and some of which do not appear again in Wilde's work until much later, in *Salomé* and *The Sphinx*. The lasciviousness of the youth, whose sterile passion is enhanced by the sacrilegious nature of his deed as he uncovers the statue of the goddess in order to feast his eyes on her nakedness and to satisfy his lust on her cold limbs, looks forward to the perverse coupling of the sphinx with griffins, tragelaphs and the chimera. The behaviour of the love-crazed nymph, who stroked Charmides' corpse in pleasurable anticipation and 'with hot lips made havoc of his mouth',[53] has its parallel in *Salomé*, when she holds the severed head of John the Baptist in her hands and wishes to bite its lifeless lips. The similarities go even further: the erotic frenzy of both Salomé and the nymph is only satisfied when the partner is dead, and it is concentrated on a single moment of pleasure: 'narrowed to one single ecstasy'.[54] In both cases, the initiative stems from the female, whose sensual activities assume androgynous features. The motifs of love and death are tightly interwoven. However, in *Salomé*, *The Sphinx* and 'Charmides' the theme of love has degenerated into a form of eroticism which remains curiously sterile. It has something unnatural and even perverse about it, which the speaker feels to be sinful – Charmides' life is called 'A fiery pulse of sin, a splendid shame',[55] a description which, despite the positive quality of the adjectives, clearly offers a negative moral judgment. Wilde's morbid streak, which most scholars have not detected till *Dorian Gray* or the essays, is in fact already to be seen in this early poem. The moral comment at the end, however, as is so often the case with Wilde, contradicts his own theoretical precepts, for he condemns 'ethical sympathies' in art as 'an unpardonable mannerism of style.'[56]

The other love poems are for the most part little more than acts of homage to famous actresses and beauties of the time. 'Phèdre' is for Sarah Bernhardt, and 'Portia', 'Queen Henrietta Maria' and 'Camma' are for Ellen Terry. 'Sen Artysty; or, The Artist's Dream' came from the Polish actress Helena Modjeska, was first published in October 1880 in *The Green Room. Routledge's Christmas Annual*, and is assumed to have been translated by Wilde into English. He was, however, particularly smitten with Lily Langtry, who was regarded as one of the most beautiful women of the time and posed for many painters, including Whistler, Watts, Burne-Jones, Leighton and Millais. He called her 'The New Helen', and inscribed a copy of his poems which he sent to her: 'To Helen, formerly of Troy, now of London'.[57] The poems of *The Fourth Movement* do not have any of the passion and sensual ecstasy to be found in parts of 'Charmides'. Instead they often express feelings of satiety, separation and unrequited love. In 'Apologia' the speaker consoles himself after being rejected: 'But surely it is something to have been / The best belovèd for a little while'.[58] He feels himself to be 'sorrow's heritor'[59] and cherishes the 'barren memory / Of unkissed kisses'.[60] Parting and rejection are balanced by the comfort of short-lived happiness. The intellect searches for reasons that will make the pain of separation more bearable, and in 'Glykyprikos Eros' and 'To L.L.' there is a very definite emotional detachment. For all his disappointment, the speaker can announce: 'I have found the lover's crown of myrtle better / than the poet's crown of bays'.[61]

Decorative style and impressionistic imagery

The fact that the poet's subject-matter varies from political engagement to philosophical speculation, from religious longings to feelings of love, admiration and ennui testifies to a disposition that is without ties and is open to new impressions and influences. Corresponding to the multiple views of reality is an extraordinary multiplicity of forms and styles. Wilde uses couplets in the 'Ballade de Marguerite (Normande)', *terza rima* with a rhyme scheme of aab in 'The Harlot's House', Tennyson's *In Memoriam* stanza-form in 'Impressions. 2 La Fuite de la Lune', and sestets in all the longer poems, with each line consisting of five iambs except the last, which is an alexandrine. As well as sonnets, of which there are several in the *Poems*, and ballads – for example, 'The Dole of the King's Daughter (Breton)' – he also follows a fashion of the time and uses the *villanelle*, a difficult French form, which in 'Pan' he extends to a *double villanelle*. This form consists of nineteen lines with two recurrent rhymes. The first line of the poem is repeated as the sixth, twelfth and eighteenth, while the third line reappears as the ninth, fifteenth and nineteenth. This experimentation with form has its roots in the Pre-Raphaelites' predilection for medieval themes and archaic styles, as used especially by William Morris and D. G. Rossetti. This later romantic medievalism is nowhere near as marked in Wilde – he was much too enamoured of the Greeks – but it left its traces in the 'Ballade de Marguerite (Normande)' and 'The Dole of the King's Daughter (Breton)'.[62] The atmosphere of a chivalrous age is particularly noticeable in the first of these, with medieval-sounding names like Hugh of Amiens, Dame Jeanette and St Denys, and archaic turns of phrase or spelling, such as 'tapestrie', 'gramercy', 'countrie', and 'chapelle'.

Generally, Wilde's poetic diction runs along conventional lines. The occasional medieval and biblical allusions play a considerably less important part than the obtrusive alliteration – so typical of Swinburne – personifications, synaesthesia, mythological nomenclature, detailed lists of flowers, and a marked preference for colour. Wilde's tendency to overdo the use of particular devices – as in the preponderance of epigrams in the comedies – is already evident in the *Poems*. In reading the long intermediate poems, one cannot escape the impression that the poet regarded his lists of flowers as an essential prerequisite for 'intensive' nature poetry. The fact that he occasionally makes mistakes in his botany strengthens the suspicion that his knowledge came from sources other than observation of nature. The critic in the *Saturday Review* pointed out that 'meadow-sweet' and 'wood-anemone' do not flower at the same time.[63] Bernhard Fehr complained that the time of year in 'The Garden of Eros' – a night in June – would make the blossoming of the flower-carpet which is spread out during the first part of the poem 'höchst unbequem'[64] [extremely uncomfortable]. This devotion to flora, then, in no way denotes a particular love of the plant-world, but is rather an indication of Wilde's conforming to the conventional clichés of romantic nature poetry, as well as striving to create a decorative effect.

It is not only the 'nature' sections of the poems but also the incorporation of innumerable mythological names and allusions – often a quite unnecessary ballast of scholarship – that point to a distinct lack of artistic discipline. Their frequency is not due simply to Wilde's predilection for resonant names, but also to his desire to create the atmosphere of an Arcadian dream world, complete with gods and nymphs and shepherds, as far removed as possible from the real world. And yet there are also poems such as 'Requiescat',[65] 'On the Sale by Auction of Keats' Love Letters',[66] and 'To My Wife' that show Wilde to be capable of quite simple, unaffected diction. In particular 'Requiescat', with its predominantly dactylic rhythms, strikes home through the simplicity of its language, which corresponds perfectly to the grief Wilde felt at the death of his sister Isola. Among the experiments in form, the most notable poems are those in which Wilde tries to expand the literary medium by adding the dimension of another art – painting. This method seemed to guarantee that poetry would not fall into the 'heresy of the didactic', thus producing work devoid of any practical purpose that could draw its effect not from its content, but from its decorative form. This trend towards the picturesque and the colourful is most striking in 'Impression du Matin', 'In the Gold Room: A Harmony', 'A Symphony In Yellow', 'Fantaisies décoratives', and the other poems entitled 'Impression'. A vivid example of Wilde's impressionistic technique is to be found in 'Impression du Matin', which may well have been inspired by Whistler's *Nocturne in Blue and Gold: Old Battersea Bridge* and his other *Nocturnes*:[67]

> The Thames nocturne of blue and gold
>   Changed to a Harmony in grey:
>   A barge with ochre-coloured hay
> Dropt from the Wharf: and chill and cold
>
> The yellow fog came creeping down
>   The bridges, till the houses' walls
>   Seemed changed to shadows and St. Paul's
> Loomed like a bubble o'er the town.
>
> Then suddenly arose the clang
>   Of waking life; the streets were stirred
>   With country waggons: and a bird
> Flew to the glistening roofs and sang.
>
> But one pale woman all alone,
>   The daylight kissing her wan hair,
>   Loitered beneath the gas lamps' flare,
> With lips of flame and heart of stone.

The aesthetic attraction of this poem lies in its combination of visual and acoustic images that build up the impression of morning. The fog creeping over the houses and over St Paul's changes the normal shapes of the Thames landscape into an almost unreal dream setting, full of a strange and fascinating indeterminacy. Then this 'unreal' landscape is disturbed by the rattle of the waggons, heralding the town's awakening and bringing a note of dissonance into the harmony of the dawn. The reader's attention is then drawn to the woman beneath the gas lamp, and abruptly moral values are introduced into the decorative atmosphere, their conventionality having no small effect on the originality of the poem.

Quite different from the 'Impression du Matin' and other impressionistic poems, 'The Harlot's House'[68] draws its special effect from the manner in which its form and content alienate the given situation. In this variation on the theme of the dance of death, Wilde prefers suggestion through sounds and strange poetic diction. He creates an atmosphere of the macabre and the uncanny, rather like Poe's 'The Haunted Palace'. The dancers inside the harlot's house are compared to 'mechanical grotesques' and 'wire-pulled automatons'. Sometimes a 'horrible marionette' leaves the house and smokes a cigarette, 'like a live thing'. The representation of the dance, which suggests something living, is made in a style that brings out the mechanical nature of the movements, so that everything is transformed into a ghostly unreality and the characters seem like puppets obeying someone else's will instead of their own. The predominance of short vowels in the stress syllables (e.g. mechanical grotesques, fantastic arabesques, silhouetted skeletons) and of voiceless consonants – especially st/ts (stanzas 3–5) – makes the dance movements seem hard and staccato. In this poem there is less of the purely decorative impressionism that marks several of the other poems, and a greater tendency towards symbolism. It is not only the suggestiveness of the language, with its macabre and fantastic associations, but also the transformation of the beloved from a concrete figure to an abstract type (stanza 10) that denotes this change. The link between eroticism and death that is made by the dance of death taking place in the harlot's house – a link that typifies the literature of *décadence* – was already to be found, though in different form, in 'Charmides'. It is a theme that Wilde was to vary once more in *Salomé*, and to take up again in *The Ballad of Reading Gaol*.

Eclecticism and the reduction of the poetic self

The *Poems* reproduce momentary impressions, passing moods and thoughts in a poetic diction that has, to a greater or lesser degree, assimilated stylistic elements ranging from Shakespeare through Keats and Matthew Arnold and right up to Swinburne and D. G. Rossetti, and it is this range of expression that gives them their highly epigonic and experimental character. The poetic self, often identical to the biographical self, oscillates between political, religious and philosophical problems just as unpredictably as he veers from one poetic and artistic model to another. Thus Keats' philhellenism goes side by side with Swinburne's passion for Italy and Whistler's predilection for colourful patterns. This eclecticism, however, which is not unrelated to the time in which Wilde lived, should not lead to the false conclusion that the *Poems* are merely 'Swinburne and Water', or the work of a 'Keats gone mad'.[69] The impression one gains is that Wilde was continually giving shape to personal tensions and conflicts, but deliberately choosing a diction that only rarely conformed to the nature of the statement he wished to make. This discrepancy between subjective content and objective linguistic form explains not only the accusation of insincerity, but also the contradictory criticisms that, on the one hand, there is 'over-emphasis of the personal element',[70] while on the

other the poems are 'strangely impersonal'.[71] It often seems that the poet
has no direct contact with reality – as if it has never made its mark on him
through experience. Access to reality appears to be more a matter of
intellectual observation than of emotional experience. In Wilde a humanistic education and a remarkable 'awareness of all cultural history'[72] do
not merge into a unified poetic style as they do, say, in Ezra Pound or T. S.
Eliot. Even when one might have expected a direct emotional engagement,
as in the poet's reactions to the atrocities committed by the Turkish troops
in Bulgaria, the feelings are not given any original form but are set down in
the artificial pattern supplied by an existing work – Milton's sonnet 'On
the Late Massacher in Piemont'. It may even be that Wilde's 'Sonnet on
the Massacre of the Christians in Bulgaria' was not inspired by the events
themselves but by his reading Milton and the Gladstone pamphlet
mentioned earlier.

An example of the close link between poetic and biographical personae
is to be found in 'Hélas', which introduces the collection:

> To drift with every passion till my soul
> Is a stringed lute on which all winds can play,
> Is it for this that I have given away
> Mine ancient wisdom, and austere control?
> Methinks my life is a twice-written scroll
> Scrawled over on some boyish holiday
> With idle songs for pipe and virelay,
> Which do but mar the secret of the whole.
> Surely there was a time I might have trod
> The sunlit heights, from life's dissonance
> Struck one clear chord to reach the ears of God:
> Is that time dead? lo! with a little rod
> I did but touch the honey of romance –
> And must I lose a soul's inheritance?

This loss of wisdom and control and the chance to strike a 'chord', and
indeed the overall theme of 'wasted days'[73] is a central experience of the
poetic self. Time and again the longing for a clear and firm way of life
breaks through. But opposed to this desire 'To burn with one clear flame,
to stand erect / In natural honour'[74] is the confession of failure and total
lack of orientation:

> 'Tis I, 'tis I, whose soul is as the reed
>   Which has no message of its own to play,
> So pipes another's bidding, it is I,
> Drifting with every wind on the wide sea of misery.[75]

Without doubt this passive, drifting attitude – also inherent in the
thematic eclecticism of the *Poems* – mirrors Wilde's personal state of
mind during his years at Oxford. It is, incidentally, worth noting the word

'passion' in the first line of "Hélas', for in Wilde's language this does not only denote a state of violent emotion but also frequently carries the connotation of sin. The troubled conscience of the poetic self, fearing the loss of 'a soul's inheritance', foreshadows a theme that runs right through the collection of poems and indeed the later works.

This link between the *Poems* and Wilde's subsequent writings can be extended in other directions, too. In addition to sin there is the idea of the primacy of art, the special position of the artist as *theoretikos*, and the longing for a unity of body and soul. A recurrent topic in the *apologues* is the contrast between Christianity and Hellenism, while the poet's love of sonorous words, colourful epithets and classical names anticipates his preoccupation in the 1890s with the use of language as a tool of irony, paradoxical alienation or decorative effect rather than a means of communication and intercourse.

Clearly the *Poems* do not yet offer a clear picture of the basic tension between provocation and conformity that was such a vital element of Wilde's work and character. The passive imitation of traditional forms is still too dominant, and one might even say paradoxically that the provocative aspects of the poems – for example the sensuality of 'Charmides' – constitute conformity to the 'Fleshly School of Poetry' rather than any genuine innovation. Even though the poems do touch on themes that are later to be of prime importance, they do not reveal those qualities that are to characterise his major works – the critical intellect revealed in the essays, the ironic wit of the comedies, and the narrative gifts apparent in the fairy-tales and stories.

Vera; or, The Nihilists

Parallel to the publication of *Poems* in 1881 was Wilde's attempt to make a name for himself as a dramatist – partly from the necessity to open up new sources of urgently needed income, and partly to gain more publicity backed up by writings that would gain him access to artistic and literary circles. Apart from a very good degree and the self-awarded title 'professor of aesthetics and art critic',[76] the young Oxford graduate had very little of note to facilitate a successful entry into London society. The initial success of his persistent self-advertising can be gauged from the fact that just two years after leaving Oxford he became the target of the satirical magazine *Punch*, which lampooned him in the shape of the poet Jellaby Postlethwaite and the painter Maudle. There are also features of Archibald Grosvenor and Reginald Bunthorne in Gilbert and Sullivan's opera *Patience* – a satire on the Aesthetic Movement – which people associated with Wilde. In the long term his push for publicity had certain undesirable effects: the discrepancy between his eccentric self-promotion and his meagre achievements in the world of art – which he was always invoking – led to him being widely regarded as a poser who did not take himself seriously, and therefore did not need to be taken seriously by others.

Wilde's ever-lively sense of surprise was evident not only from his sensational dress and behaviour but also in his choice of scene and subject for his first play *Vera; or, The Nihilists*, with which he hoped to conquer the London theatre world. One might have expected this expert on classical literature, art and culture to base his first tragedy on the ancient myths of Greece or Rome. Instead he took on a contemporary theme from Russia: the uprising of the nihilists, an opposition party mainly composed of intellectuals, against the tyranny of the Tsars. What attracted him most to this revolutionary movement was presumably its anti-authoritarianism and its aim to restore individual freedom.[77] Wilde's political attitude, which at this time was a modish Republicanism, and his preoccupation with democratic ideas can also be found in the *Poems* (1881), for instance in the 'Eleutheria' group. Furthermore, in the 1870s Russia's military embroilment with England during the second Afghan war (1878) and its constant resistance to the spread of British colonialism had made it a very current subject of conversation, while additionally the exotic setting of a foreign country that had been screened from western civilisation should have been particularly attractive to the English public.

The direct inspiration for Wilde's play appears to have been an historical event whose connection with *Vera* has up to now been ignored by scholars: in March 1878 Vera Zasulič attempted to assassinate the commandant of Petersburg, General Trepov, who had had a political prisoner flogged before the latter had been legally found guilty. There was a sensational public trial which revealed countless injustices in the penal system and in turn developed unexpectedly into a tribunal against the autocratic rule of the Tsar. The trial ended with the acquittal of the accused, which amounted to a moral condemnation of the Tsarist system.[78] The similarity between the historical Vera Zasulič and the fictitious Vera Sabouroff lies not only in the names but also in the revolutionary motives that underlay the two women's actions.

It may be assumed that reports in the English press had given Wilde a general insight into the internal problems of Russia during the 1870s.[79] Particularly in 1877/78 there was a series of trials involving opponents of the regime, and these led to a radicalisation of political resistance centred upon the revolutionary organisation Zemlja i volja (Land and Freedom) founded in 1876. This opposition movement rapidly developed into a terrorist band whose attacks were directed against state oppression and the secret police. The attention with which these events were followed in England can be gauged from the number of articles that appeared in various respected magazines – for instance, a series of essays by Karl

Blind, 'Conspiracies in Russia', in the *Contemporary Review* of 1879,[80] and an article by the same author on Vjera Sassulitch (Zasulič) in the *Dublin University Magazine* of 1878.[81]

Vera was published privately in 1880. A few months later, in March 1881, it took on a macabre topicality through the murder of Tsar Alexander II. In December of the same year it was to be given a matinee performance with Mrs Bernard Beere in the title role. The production was supposed to take place in the Adelphi Theatre, but the plan fell through for reasons reported in *The World* (on whose staff Oscar's brother Willie worked for a while):

considering the present state of political feeling in England, Mr Oscar Wilde has decided on postponing, for a time, the production of his drama *Vera*.[82]

The reference was probably to the feelings of the Prince of Wales, whom Wilde did not wish to offend with the pro-nihilist tone of his play, since the wife of the new Tsar (Alexander III) was the prince's sister-in-law.

On 24 December 1881 Wilde left for America on a lecture tour, and he took his new play with him in the hope that he might find someone willing to put it on. He negotiated with Marie Prescott, an actress, who was willing to take the main part, but discussion over the production dragged on and, together with other unexpected obstacles, resulted in the premiere being put off until the following August, when Wilde went to America a second time to supervise rehearsals.[83] In the meantime, he had revised the text, adding several passages and a prologue, and had published this revised edition in 1882. Astonishingly the new version altered the dates and set the play in the years 1795 and 1800. Stuart Mason's bibliography gives the time of the action as 1880, as had been specified in the now very rare first edition printed in the same year. This new date for a drama set against the historical background of Russia in the 1870s naturally led to innumerable errors and at times absurd anachronisms which we shall return to later. The change of date was presumably due to Wilde's desire not to offend the royal family, for by setting the play at an earlier time he could draw the political sting from its message.

Vera at last received its premiere on 20 August 1883 in New York's Union Square Theatre. It was not a success, and after just one week was withdrawn from the repertoire. Most reviews were scathing. The *New York Times* called Wilde's first play 'unreal, long-winded, and wearisome',[84] the *New York Daily Tribune* described it as a 'fanciful, foolish, highly peppered story of love, intrigue, and politics',[85] while the critic of the *New York Herald* dismissed it as 'long-drawn, dramatic rot'.[86]

Before we discuss the causes of this negative reception, generally confirmed by Wilde critics,[87] let us summarise the plot:

Peter Sabouroff's inn is the setting for the prologue. Sabouroff is worried about his son Dmitri, who left home a few months ago to study law in Moscow and has not been heard of since. Dmitri's sister Vera is also worried about the fate of her brother. The conversation is suddenly interrupted by the arrival of a troop of soldiers taking eight prisoners to Siberia. They wish to make a short stop at the inn. Amongst the prisoners, who are described as nihilists, Vera recognises her brother, who manages secretly to pass her a note with an address in Moscow. She swears to avenge her brother and take his place in the revolutionary movement.

Between the prologue and Act I five years have passed. Vera has joined the nihilist movement and has become one of its leaders. The news that the next day the Tsar intends to impose martial law over the whole of Russia accelerates the revolutionaries' plan to assassinate him. Alexis, a member of the group, seems to know too much about the Tsar's palace and is suspected of being a spy. He is only rescued from further attacks by the unexpected arrival of a party of soldiers, led by General Kotemkin – the commander from the prologue – in search of conspirators. Vera tries to save the situation by pretending that all these masked people have met to rehearse a play for a touring theatre. When this attempt fails, Alexis reveals that he is the Tsar's eldest son, and he manages to deceive the general over the 'actors'' true intentions. In this way he regains the trust of the revolutionaries.

In the council chamber at the palace, the tsarevitch tries to persuade his anxious and insecure father – who seems to be very much under the evil influence of the cynical Prince Paul, his premier – to abandon the introduction of martial law. In his zeal he even goes so far as to reveal that he is a nihilist, but in this perilous situation he is rescued by chance – his father steps out onto the balcony and is shot, and he himself is instantly named successor.

One of his first official acts is to dismiss Prince Paul, who promptly joins the nihilists. Vera, whose affection for Alexis now comes more to the fore, asks that the new Tsar should be given a week to prove himself, but the group decide that he must die and they draw lots to decide who should kill him. Vera is chosen.

Unnoticed she makes her way into the Tsar's bedroom, but she cannot carry out her task, for at the critical moment Alexis wakes up and uses the occasion to tell her that he loves her. The only way in which Vera can resolve the conflict between her love for Alexis and her duty towards the revolution is to kill herself. She hurls the bloodstained weapon out of the window, to prove to her waiting colleagues that she has killed the Tsar, and she dies with the words 'I have saved Russia!'[88]

The conflict, then, is between Vera's revolutionary aims and her love for Alexis, but if this conflict between love and duty were to take on truly tragic dimensions, the two themes should have been so developed during the first three acts that their irreconcilability would have made clear the idea that the death of the heroine was the only possible solution. This is not the case. The relationship between Vera and Alexis is never properly developed, and indeed only comes to the fore after Act 3, when the otherwise cold-blooded revolutionary indulges in a semi-hysterical ranting over Alexis' non-appearance at a meeting of the nihilists:

> Oh, will he never come? Will he never come? ... Oh, he will come yet! ... Alexis! Why are you not here? ... O God, will he never come? ... Oh, why is Alexis not here?[89]

This series of interjections cannot conceal the absence of any convincingly portrayed passion, and the scene is certainly more melodramatic than tragic.

Vera initially defends Alexis by rightly drawing attention to his oft-declared love for the people and his liberal attitudes. But when her fellow revolutionaries have reminded her of her oath, and Michael, one of her co-conspirators, has recalled the fate of her banished brother in Siberia, she is all too swiftly convinced of the necessity of assassinating the new ruler. Clearly her obligation to her brother is stronger than her love for Alexis. In this climate of fanatical hatred against Tsarist authority, the question never arises as to whether this former colleague and courageous champion of nihilism, whose loyalty is now thrown into doubt only by the fact that he has taken over his father's office and thus broken the conspirators' oath, should actually be asked what his political views are. The equally obvious idea of testing the young Tsar's desire for reform by asking him to release her brother never even occurs to Vera. What conclusions can one possibly draw from the fact that, having just proclaimed the new ruler's love of freedom, Vera is chosen by lot to assassinate him and at once feels herself possessed by the spirit of Charlotte Corday and with a cry of 'on thy altar, O Liberty'[90] is prepared to save Russia from the supposed tyranny? Then she gives up her life out of love for Alexis and because she feels she must atone for her disloyalty to her friends. The oath 'that Russia shall be saved',[91] which she swears at the end of Act 3 in preparing herself to murder the Tsar, undergoes an unexpected and ironic reversal at the end of the play when, having not killed him, she cries 'I have saved Russia!'[92] Alexis lives on, as representative of a liberal policy, and so may be regarded now as the guarantor of a free even if monarchic state. Vera's suicide is in fact an illogical solution to the problem, since Alexis had just assured her: 'There shall be liberty in Russia for every man to think as his heart bids him; liberty for men to speak as they think.'[93] As this promise has already been borne out by various reforms, the political motive for the assassination loses all conviction and seems no more than an anarchistic act of blind hatred. Alexis is not a tyrant, as his father clearly was, and Vera's ideas of reform are basically no different from his, since both are concerned to re-establish a liberal society. For the play to be effective, Wilde would have to bring out contrasts and irreconcilable differences between the protagonists instead of emphasising their common ideas of freedom.

The characterisation of Alexis also suffers from the author's vacillation between political and emotional motivation of his characters. The young tsarevitch is presented as a keen and dauntless champion of liberalism, unshakably opposed to the tryanny of his father. He justifies his participation in the nihilist plot with the somewhat naive hope that this tyranny may be overthrown without bloodshed. He loves the people – an attitude that is corroborated by Michael and Vera. And yet in Act 4 he announces quite unexpectedly that his reason for taking the crown is his love for Vera: 'Vera, it is for you, for you alone, I kept this crown.'[94] Even more confusing for the reader or spectator is his spontaneous offer to Vera to renounce the Tsardom once he has realised that he cannot persuade her to become his wife and share with him the responsibility for Russia's destiny. One cannot help wondering how seriously he takes his new task and his concern for the welfare of his people when he is so ready to snuff out his own reformist zeal for purely personal reasons. Both Alexis and Vera begin by being politically motivated, and without any adequate dramatic preparation they both renounce their aims on emotional grounds: Vera cannot kill Alexis because she loves him, and Alexis is ready to give up the throne in order to marry her. The political idealism of the new Tsar and the revolutionary fanaticism of the nihilist fade away in sentimental declarations of love.

According to a letter that Wilde wrote to Marie Prescott – probably in July 1883 – he wanted to express a cry for liberty, but passion was to be the dominant theme:

As regards the play itself, I have tried in it to express within the limits of art that Titan cry of the peoples for liberty, which in the Europe of our day is threatening thrones, and making governments unstable from Spain to Russia, and from north to southern seas. But it is a play not of politics but of passion. It deals with no theories of government, but with men and women simply; and modern Nihilistic Russia, with all the terror of its tyranny and the marvel of its martyrdoms, is merely the fiery and fervent background in front of which the persons of my dream live and love. With this feeling was the play written, and with this aim should the play be acted.[95]

But instead of the intended conflict between politics and emotions, there is unfortunately nothing but a sentimental descent towards a melodramatic suicide, and the 'fiery and fervent background' is unhappily reduced to a totally unhistoric setting. The cardinal blunder was to transplant the nihilists from 1880 to 1795 though the movement did not even develop until the 1860s. The term 'nihilist' was coined by Turgenev in his novel *Fathers and Sons* (1862), which depicts the conflict between the idealism of the fathers and the more radical materialism of the sons. It is doubtful whether Wilde would even have regarded Russian nihilism as an alternative to Tsarist tyranny if he had known more about the basic philosophy of the nihilists. Just as he was attracted by the anti-authoritarianism and the emphasis on the freedom of the individual proclaimed by this movement, so too would he have been repelled by their radical rejection of traditional values, their one-track adherence to the natural sciences, and their gross materialism, reminiscent of Stirner and Feuerbach.

Alongside the error in the dating of nihilism, there is a whole collection of mistakes and oversights that reveal a serene disdain for historical accuracy. In the prologue, the commander berates Vera and the other guests as follows: 'You peasants are getting too saucy since you ceased to be serfs.'[96] The serfs were not freed until 1861, under Tsar Alexander II. Peter Sabouroff's reiterated exclamation: 'Let God and Our little Father the Czar look to the world'[97] should have been addressed to our little Mother the Czarina, namely Catherine II, who was still on the throne in 1795, the date of the prologue. The fictitious Tsar in the play can only be Paul I, who reigned from 1796 to 1801, but in Act 2 the Tsar asks:

Shall I banish him [Alexis]? Shall I (*whispers*) ...? The Emperor Paul did it. The Empress Catherine there (*points to picture on the wall*) did it.[98]

Somewhat premature is the grim advice which the new Tsar Alexis gives to his despotic ministers: 'If you value your lives you will catch the first train for Paris.'[99] No matter how much value they had put on their lives, these gentlemen could not have obeyed the injunction, but would have been forced to take a horse or a coach, since the first passenger train did not run till 1830 – and then it was between Liverpool and Manchester. The first Russian railway was built in the reign of Nicholas I in 1837 – the Tsarskoje Selo Line from Moscow to Pavlovsk.[100] Equally premature is Prince Paul's use of the word 'Communist'[101] to describe the doctrine that property should be divided equally. In this sense the word did not gain currency until the 1840s, in particular after the publication of Marx's *Communist Manifesto* in 1848. Of course, Wilde could have spared his reader a good deal of irritation if he had stuck to the original date of his play, but he never changed it back. In view of these blunders and various other weaknesses, it is extraordinary that such a seasoned critic as G. Wilson Knight can make the following judgment:

Scene on scene has power; characterization is excellent, rhetoric is adequate, the dialogue often crisp and the romance moving. Without sentiment or propaganda a full consciousness of European politics and sociology is felt to be in control.[102]

The weaknesses in characterisation and plot construction that are caused by the author's uncertain sense of direction and his inexperience as a dramatist are supplemented by a somewhat embarrassing amount of tragic language taken over from the Elizabethans, and particularly from Shakespeare. For instance, Vera's comparison between the mighty and the ordinary people is extremely reminiscent of Shylock's famous speech comparing Jews and Christians:

VERA: ... Are they [these crowned men] not men of like passions with ourselves, vulnerable to the same diseases, of flesh and blood not different from our own?[103]

SHY: ... hath not a Jew hands, organs, dimensions, senses, affections, passions? Fed with the same food, hurt with the same weapons, subject to the same diseases.[104]

Vera steels herself to kill the Tsar in much the same way as Lady Macbeth prepares herself to influence her husband to kill Duncan:

VERA: I am no woman now. My blood seems turned to gall.[105]

LADY M: Come, you spirits
        That tend on mortal thoughts, unsex me here ...

        Come to my woman's breasts,
        And take my milk for gall ...[106]

And just like Lady Macbeth she believes that 'One blow and it is over, and I can wash my hands in water afterwards.'[107] The fact that during the last meeting she thinks she hears a nightingale scarcely enhances the poetic quality of the passage, though again it awakens memories of the incomparable play it mimics.

Perhaps it would be unfair to regard these occasional Shakespearian echoes as deliberate imitations. This was Wilde's first attempt at tragedy, and at this time he had not yet freed his language and dramatic technique from the great tragic tradition he had inherited – one need only think of the many asides, the monologues and the frequent recurrence of the revenge motif. But in this play there is one character whose language anticipates the dandies of the later social comedies, and that is Prince Paul Maraloffski. He is cynical about the people's rights, hated and feared as prime minister, the most influential adviser to the Tsar, a flexible opportunist when the changes of political fortune necessitate a switch of allegiance, a smooth talker who is never lost for a witty turn of phrase, and one of whom the tsarevitch says: 'He would stab his best friend for the sake of writing an epigram on his tombstone.'[108] In fact some of his epigrams return later in the comedies – for instance: 'Experience, the name men give to their mistakes', which Dumby echoes with virtually the same words in *Lady Windermere's Fan*.[109] Many critics, including Frank Harris and Hesketh Pearson, see the importance of this play as lying mainly in its 'revelation of the future wit and critic'.[110]

Vera is a tragedy that is not tragic. Wilde takes material from Russian history and handles it unhistorically. The actions of the characters are dictated by the demands of the plot and not by the characters themselves. The language often degenerates into clichés which mimic passion without ever representing it. The conflict between love and revolutionary duty is not properly worked out, and therefore seems like an incomplete construction. As for the lighter passages of dialogue, to be found in the scenes with Prince Paul, these do not have the function of comic relief – as Wilde would have intended, following the Shakespearian example – but rather undermine the seriousness of the political intrigue.[111] But despite the failure of this 'péché de jeunesse', Wilde was to turn a second time to the genre of the tragedy with *The Duchess of Padua*, and for a second time he failed to do justice to his own genuine talent.

The Duchess of Padua

'Written by me, acted by you, and set by Steele Mackaye, this tragedy will take the world by storm.'[112] With such unbounded optimism young Wilde wrote in October 1882 to the American actress Mary Anderson, who had shown interest in the play after looking over an outline of the plot. A contract was agreed whereby the author was to receive 1,000 dollars to begin the work, and another 4,000 dollars on its completion provided that the actress liked the play and was satisfied that she could perform it.[113] Wilde fulfilled his part of the agreement by sending the completed play to Mary Anderson in March 1883, but she rejected it. This rebuff not only ruined Wilde's financial calculations, but must also have done considerable damage to his self-confidence. However, he remained perfectly composed when he received the bad news, as Robert H. Sherard reported:

Wilde opened it [Mary Anderson's telegram] and read the disappointing news without giving the slightest sign of chagrin or annoyance. He tore a tiny strip off the blue form, rolled it up into a pellet, and put it into his mouth. Then he passed the cable over to me, and said: 'Robert, this is very tedious.' After that he never referred again to his disappointment.[114]

The play was not performed in the 1880s, but in 1891 Lawrence Barrett presented it in New York at the Broadway Theatre under the title *Guido Ferranti*, at first anonymously but then with Wilde's name. It ran for three weeks and, in the words of the *New York Tribune*'s critic, was a 'success of esteem'.[115] Later productions in Germany in 1904 and 1906 were unsuccessful, and there was no production in England until 1907, when a single copyright performance was held at St James's Theatre. In a letter dated 19 July 1898, the author himself gave expression to his rather tardy insight into the fact that: '*The Duchess* is unfit for publication – the only one of my works that comes under that category.'[116]

Before we analyse the causes of this failure, we should outline the plot of Wilde's tragedy:

In an anonymous letter Guido Ferranti, a young man who has never known his father, is promised information about his origins if he goes to Padua market-place at about midday. There the anonymous letter-writer reveals himself as Count Moranzone who, as he explains at once, was a close friend of Guido's late father. Moranzone gives him details about the fate of his father, the former Duke of Parma, who was delivered into the hands of his murderers by the treachery of a friend. This traitor, who has also robbed Guido of his rightful inheritance – the dukedom of Parma – is the present Duke of Padua, Simone Gesso. Guido swears revenge, but Moranzone wishes him to delay the moment until he sends him a dagger as a signal. Guido accepts the stranger's advice unconditionally, takes a job in the royal household, leaves his friend Ascanio Cristofano, and resolves to devote his whole life to avenging his father: '. . . from this same hour I do forswear / All love of women, and the barren thing / Which men call beauty.'[117] The difficulty he will have in keeping his oath is immediately apparent when he sees Beatrice, the Duchess of Padua, leaving the Cathedral and is so smitten that he drops his dagger.

The symbolic significance of this action soon takes on a concrete form when he meets Beatrice in the palace, promptly declares his love, and receives an equally prompt and positive response. These declarations of mutual love are rudely interrupted by the arrival of a parcel from Moranzone containing the dagger which is both sign and instrument of the revenge that is now to be carried out. Guido leaves Beatrice, who then contemplates suicide; humiliated by the behaviour of her tyrannical husband and now abandoned by her lover, she does indeed seem to have little hope for the future.

In spite of pressure from Count Moranzone, Guido is in a state of Hamlet-like uncertainty, reluctant to carry out the revenge as planned because of his feelings for Beatrice. Instead he would like to place the dagger on the sleeping Duke's bed, together with a letter informing him when he awakes 'who held him in his power / And slew him not'.[118] This he considers to be the noblest form of revenge. In the meantime however, Beatrice, wrongly assuming that the main obstacle to her love is her husband, has killed the Duke. Although she has just unwittingly fulfilled her lover's original purpose, Guido is horrified by this deed which, as she keeps telling him, she has only done for love of him. Beatrice now seems to him like an 'angel fresh from Hell!'[119] and he renounces her. Thereupon she has him seized by the palace guards as the suspected assassin of the Duke.

A trial follows, in which Guido is accused of the murder. After an initial silence, he makes a false confession in order to save Beatrice from the death penalty. Previously she had attempted several times to prevent him from making a statement for fear that he would accuse her. But the court had rejected this interference in the process of law.

Shortly before Guido's execution, the conscience-stricken Beatrice slips masked and unrecognised into his cell to help him to escape, but he rejects her offer. So strong are her feelings of guilt that she drinks the poison which the prisoner had been given – because of his noble birth – as a means of choosing his own death. Guido then kills himself with a dagger.

While the problem in *Vera* was the conflict between political and emotional motives, and the revenge theme was only secondary, *The Duchess of Padua* is built on the conflict between love and revenge. As in *Vera* the political theme consists in the oppression of the people by a tyrannical ruler. In the first play, however, it is the tyranny of the Tsar that sparks off the revolutionary activities of the nihilists and so plays an integral part in the structure of the plot, whereas Gesso's brutal behaviour in *The Duchess* is only significant for the characterisation, bringing out his own cruelty and Beatrice's sympathy for the suffering people.

The task of avenging his murdered father is given to Guido by Moranzone, who thus has a similar dramatic function to that of the Ghost in *Hamlet*. Unlike Hamlet, though, Guido shrinks from the act of vengeance not because of 'conscience' which 'doth make cowards of us all', but because of love:

> ... loving her,
> My Lady, my white Beatrice, I begin
> To see a nobler and holier vengeance
> In letting this man live.[120]

Beatrice's reaction is exactly the opposite: her love for Guido drives her into killing the man who stands between them. But when Guido rejects her for moral reasons, she takes her revenge on him. Her actions would certainly have been more credible if Wilde had used Gesso's brutal treatment of her as a motive for the repulsive assassination, as Shelley for instance had justified the murder of Count Francesco Cenci in *The Cenci* (1819). The political reason – freeing the people from the oppressor –

might also have offered a convincing motive, especially in view of his cynical attitude towards his subjects as revealed at the beginning of Act 3.

There are also certain inconsistencies in the characterisation of Beatrice.[121] At the beginning of Act 2 she is very sensitive to the injustices committed against the people, and even decides to distribute 100 ducats from her 'private purse'[122] among the poor; but in Act 4 in the trial scene she can say with the cynical arrogance of power:

> We are not bound by law,
> But with it we bind others.[123]

Even if the reader or spectator may still have a degree of sympathy for her after the murder of her husband, this will certainly have disappeared by the end of Act 4 when her false accusation has resulted in the innocent Guido being condemned to death. Her almost petty desire for revenge on her former lover, which she justifies with the claim: 'I am what thou hast made me',[124] can scarcely be said to pave the way for her grand and spontaneous gesture of atonement when she drinks the poison.

In terms of dramatic construction and logical development, once again the play suffers from the author's inability to make the action flow from the characters' motives, interests and personal conflicts. Instead one has the impression that they are marionettes merely dancing on the strings of the plot. A typical weakness is the lack of adequate preparation for important scenes. For instance, Guido's blind obedience to the stranger Moranzone, even accepting the indefinite postponement of revenge, seems unmotivated in a character described as 'impulsive, ready to take oaths, to forget the past, to realise the moment only'.[125] His later hesitancy to kill the Duke is quite unexpected, especially since one might have assumed that his love for Beatrice would give him an added stimulus. And Beatrice's murder of the Duke is equally unexpected and under-prepared.

Another indication of the way Wilde presses his characters into a prefabricated frame is the abruptness of the transitions between different stages of the action. As soon as Guido has been given the task of revenge by Moranzone, he separates from his close friend Ascanio Cristofano without any apparent reason; he simply speaks somewhat nebulously of a 'bloody legacy'[126] which makes it impossible for their friendship to continue. Beatrice's passionate declaration of love for Guido is just as abrupt. In their very first conversation she says:

> Guido, though all the morning stars could sing
> They could not tell the measure of my love.
> I love you, Guido.[127]

Wilde's suspect dramatic technique and love of surprise effects are particularly evident at the end of an act, where romantic drama, especially

Victor Hugo's, and the nineteenth-century melodrama exert a strong influence. Guido's solemn renunciation of the 'love of women' and 'beauty'[128] at the end of Act 1 is immediately followed by the entrance of Beatrice, the sight of whom makes him falter in his oath. The end of Act 3 is even more of a shock. Beatrice, having killed her husband, throws the blame on Guido: 'This way went he, the man who slew my lord.'[129] At this time Wilde clearly believed that the effectiveness of the curtain depended on the degree to which the audience was taken by surprise. In a long letter to Mary Anderson, which was meant as a kind of introduction to the play, he refers to the end of Act 3: *suspense is the essence of situation, and surprise its climax*.[130] Clearly the young dramatist had somewhat superficial ideas as to the reasons for a play's effectiveness.

Wilde's desire to move his audience through powerful emotions on the stage can be seen from his directions. The final moments of Act 5 are a striking example:

They [Guido and Beatrice] *kiss each other now for the first time in this Act, when suddenly the* DUCHESS *leaps up in the dreadful spasm of death, tears in agony at her dress, and finally, with face twisted and distorted with pain, falls back dead in a chair.* GUIDO, *seizing her dagger from her belt, kills himself; and, as he falls across her knees, clutches at the cloak which is on the back of the chair.*[131]

One wonders whether perhaps there might not have been a simpler and more convincing way of portraying the lovers united in death? Shakespeare, who avoided such melodramatic gestures, certainly achieved more lasting effects with more economical means, for instance in the death scene of *Romeo and Juliet*, of which the above passage is obviously a rather poor imitation.

Wilde's attempts, at the beginning of the fourth and fifth acts, to relieve the seriousness of the situation by interpolating passages of comic dialogue involving the citizens of Padua and the prison guards are another reminder of Shakespeare, who used comic relief as an integral component of his tragedies. But Wilde's dialogue remains very much at the level of a Dogberry, Dull or Elbow:

MORANZONE: Is the Duke dead?
SECOND CITIZEN: He has a knife in his heart, which they say is not healthy
   for any man.
MORANZONE: Who is accused of having killed him?
SECOND CITIZEN: Why, the prisoner, sir.
MORANZONE: But who is the prisoner?
SECOND CITIZEN: Why, he that is accused of the Duke's murder.
MORANZONE: I mean, what is his name?
SECOND CITIZEN: Faith, the same which his godfathers gave him: what else
   should it be?[132]

In this dialogue the influence of Shakespeare is all too obvious. One might add that the uncertainty of touch in these low comedy scenes must also stem from the fact that Wilde was considerably more at home with the language and mentality of the Mayfair aristocracy than he was with the crude slang of the East End.

Wilde's dependence on existing dramas is even greater in this play than it was in *Vera*. Kelver Hartley has shown Wilde's debt to Victor Hugo, in particular *Lucrèce Borgia* (1833) and *Angelo, tyran de Padoue* (1835). A comparison between the names of the characters in *Duchess* and in *Lucrèce Borgia* will reveal parallels that can hardly be coincidental:

The Duchess of Padua	Lucrèce Borgia
Maffio Petrucci	Maffio Orsini
Jeppo Vitellozzo	Jeppo Liveretto
...	Oloferno Vitellozzo
Ascanio Cristofano	Ascanio Petrucci

There are clear similarities between Guido and Gennaro, a 'brave capitaine d'aventure',[133] who believes himself to be the son of a fisherman but is in reality a nobleman. His father has also been murdered, and just like Wilde's hero he plans revenge. As for Guido's relationship with Beatrice, it is strongly reminiscent of Rodolfo's with Catarina Bragadini, the wife of Angelo, the eponymous hero of Hugo's above-mentioned play. In fact Hugo frequently uses the plot of a conflict-ridden relationship between a young man – usually of unknown or of low-class origin, though often in reality of noble birth – and a higher-ranking and generally married woman: examples are Didier and Marion de Lorme in *Marion de Lorme* (1829), Hernani and Doña Sol in *Hernani* (1830), Gennaro and Lucrèce in *Lucrèce Borgia* (1833) and Fabiano Fabiani and Mary Tudor in *Marie Tudor* (1833). Mary Tudor's revenge on her favourite Fabiani, whom wrongfully she has thrown into the Tower because of his unfaithfulness, but whom she later – with newly enkindled love – wishes to set free again, runs parallel to Beatrice's wrongful accusations against Guido and her subsequent attempt to free him.

The romantic dramas of Victor Hugo were not the only models on which Wilde drew. The plot is also strongly influenced by the Elizabethan revenge tragedy, which was a genre all of its own during that rich period of theatre. Amongst the most famous examples are Thomas Kyd's *Spanish Tragedy* (1587), John Marston's *Antonio's Revenge* (1600) and *The Malcontent* (1604), Shakespeare's *Hamlet* (1603–4), *The Revenger's Tragedy* (1606) attributed to Cyril Tourneur, and the two Italian tragedies of John Webster, *The White Devil* (1612) and *The Duchess of Malfi* (1614). Some critics regard Webster as a strong influence,[134] particularly the latter play – perhaps because of its title – but there is no concrete evidence that Wilde borrowed anything from him. The trans-formation of Bosola from 'tool-villain' to avenger against his masters, and the brothers' plot against their sister the Duchess, of whose marriage to the steward Antonio they disapprove, have no parallel in Wilde. But the genre itself, with delayed revenge providing possibilities for the build-up of dramatic tension, must have influenced the composition of *The Duchess of Padua*.

Wilde's ambitious attempt to fuse elements of the Elizabethan revenge tragedy and the romantic drama into a great verse tragedy must be regarded as a failure.[135] As in *Vera*, the artistic execution suffers from the author's uncertain orientation, as his revenge play develops into a tragic love story. The actions of the heroine stem from the plot rather than from character, and indeed the sudden twists and turns in the behaviour of both main characters do not result from the pressures of inner conflicts but spring rather from the author's inability to link the different phases of his plot organically together. While the mixture of love and revenge themes remains firmly embedded in the Elizabethan tradition, the stock char-acters belong equally firmly to the romantic drama: Simone Gesso, the wicked Renaissance prince; Guido, the high-minded young man who wants to avenge his murdered father; Beatrice, the wicked ruler's un-happily married wife, who promptly falls in love with the young man; Moranzone, the embodiment of the revenge motif, his sights set on the death of the Duke; Ascanio, the faithful friend of the young hero. In the presence of so many theatrical clichés, the crude emotional shock effects, which are meant to stimulate the audience's attention by the unexpected switches in the plot, are scarcely likely to make the spectator feel genuinely involved in the action. Alongside these clumsy attempts at effect, there is the often excessive emotionality of the language in the love-scenes. Indeed excess is a word that applies to many aspects of this play, which has been described as 'blanker than its blank verse':[136] Guido's love, leading him to confess to a murder he did not commit; Beatrice's revenge, making her willing even to twist the law in order to attain her ends; The Duke's cynicism, leading him to say to Guido, in a monstrous parody of Polonius's advice to his son Laertes, 'that popularity / Is the one insult I have never suffered'.[137] The lack of artistic discipline, and the continual effort to highlight the play with striking effects, correspond to the personality of the author himself, who since his Oxford days had sought continually to draw attention to himself through his extravagant appear-ance and his unending self-advertisement, and whose creative flair depended to a great extent on the public's response to himself and his works.

In trying to place these two early tragedies in the context of Wilde's dramatic writings, one is bound to say that they contain precious few of the qualities of his later work and considerably more of the weaknesses which even increased experience did not altogether overcome. It may seem at first sight as though the two periods had nothing in common, but these first clumsy experiments do nevertheless contain certain features of Wilde's dramatic style that are to recur, sometimes in an improved form, in his later work. It must be remembered that the latter did not consist only of social comedies – even if these are the plays that are best known – but also of serious work such as *Salomé* and the two fragments 'La Sainte Courtisane' and 'A Florentine Tragedy'.

The tragedies of the 1890s and the serious passages in the social comedies all contain abrupt and often seemingly gratuitous twists of plot. One might quote the end of Act 3 of 'A Woman of No Importance' as an example, or Bianca's behaviour in 'A Florentine Tragedy'. 'Plot' is perhaps an inapposite term as regards the plays with exotic settings, such as *Salomé* and 'La Sainte Courtisane'; under the influence of symbolist aesthetics, the 'plot' is largely undramatic, having been basically reduced to a static succession of stylised, decorative dialogues.

A further similarity between the earlier dramas and the later works lies in the choice of characters. It has already been pointed out that Prince Paul in *Vera* anticipates the dandies of the comedies. There is also the disappointed woman who believes her love to be unrequited, or her wishes betrayed, and so vows vengeance: this theme is to be found with variations in *Vera* (Vera), The *Duchess of Padua* (Beatrice), *Salomé* and Isabel in the outline Wilde wrote for 'Ahab and Isabel'. Wilde's ability to plant and nourish conflicts in the characters themselves remains as dubious in the later plays as it was in the earlier. This has been noted many times. He tends to subordinate the clash of feelings and interests to functions of the plot, so that the characters lack psychological conviction and thus make it difficult for the reader or spectator to become involved.

The most radical change is to be noticed in Wilde's use of language. The dialogue in the earlier plays is mainly determined by the demands of the plot, or at least the theme being dealt with at the time, and is generally very bombastic; in the genuinely comic parts of the social comedies, this gives way to irony and paradox, often reduced to a series of epigrams arranged in stichomythic form; the more serious sections, however, are still dominated by a moralising, excessively emotional tone. Wilde's inability to master the language of passion is as marked as his success with the intellectually constructed language of the dandies. As far as the exotic dramas are concerned, the dialogue becomes totally stylised, full of decorative images, so that communication almost gives way to the creation of a poetic atmosphere.

The selfish and the selfless.
   The fairy-tales and stories

The fairy-tales

The publication in May 1888 of Wilde's first collection of fairy-tales, *The Happy Prince and other Tales*, must have come as a surprise to all those who had known him only as the notorious figurehead of aestheticism and the author of epigonic poems and sentimental dramas. The little book was dedicated to Carlos Blacker and illustrated by Walter Crane and Jacomb Hood, and the critics gave it a favourable reception. The *Athenaeum* said it contained 'charming fancies and quaint humour',[1] while the *Saturday Review* detected an underlying current of satire.[2] The author was sufficiently encouraged to send copies to friends and such prominent figures as Gladstone, Ruskin and Pater. He had the satisfaction of soon receiving a letter from his revered teacher at Brasenose College, Oxford, to say how 'delightful'[3] he had found the stories. Heartened by these positive reactions, Wilde published a second collection three years later, in November 1891, under the title *A House of Pomegranates*, illustrated by Charles Ricketts and C. H. Shannon and dedicated to his wife. These tales, of which 'The Young King' and 'The Birthday of the Infanta' had already appeared separately, were each dedicated to ladies of high society – a gesture not unconnected with his work as editor of the magazine *The Woman's World* from 1887 to 1889. Unlike the first collection, *A House of Pomegranates* attracted little attention initially. The relatively high price (one guinea) may well have been a deterrent, and the unsatisfactory reproduction of the illustrations, which according to Stuart Mason was due to a technical fault in the printing process, had a damaging effect on the appearance of the book.

Origin and reception

Along with *The Picture of Dorian Gray* and the comedies, Wilde's fairy-tales are probably the works with which most people would link his name most readily. In German-speaking countries alone the two collections (or at least one of them) appeared – often together with *Lord Arthur Savile's Crime and other Stories* – in more than twenty different translations between 1902 and 1976.[4] The two collections were first translated by Johannes Gaulke and Else Otten between 1902 and 1904, and soon afterwards came Rudolph Lothar and Frieda Uhl's version for the first complete German edition of Wilde, published by Wiener Verlag between 1906 and 1908. Insel-Verlag brought out another edition by Felix Paul Greve and Franz Blei in 1910, with illustrations by Heinrich Vogeler, and between 1910 and 1925 this version alone sold some 132,000 copies.[5] The 1920s saw at least seven translations, and between 1945 and 1948 there was a new one each year. This extraordinary accumulation in times of economic stringency – the late 1920s and just after the Second World War – is probably no coincidence, for many readers would have felt the need for a dream-world in which, after all their trials and tribulations, at last good would conquer evil. It is impossible to calculate exactly how many copies of Wilde's tales have been sold on the German market, but the extent of their popularity may perhaps be gauged from the fact that the Insel paperback edition first published in 1972 had by 1987 sold some 180,000 copies. A part of this success is certainly due to the tales being a particular favourite in schools, and if the countless school editions are added to the total, the sales in German-speaking countries must amount to hundreds of thousands.

Critics have not paid a great deal of attention to these stories, but when occasionally they have asked what led Wilde to write them, the usual answer has been along biographical lines. Hesketh Pearson thought Wilde was 'emotionally undeveloped',[6] but this explanation, though it might perhaps help us to understand certain weaknesses in the comedies as regards plot and characterisation, is perhaps a little too facile, especially since it ignores the time at which Wilde decided to embrace the genre. In this respect, Robert Merle's observations are rather more helpful, for he draws attention to Wilde's situation as husband and father of two children, as well as to his homosexual tendencies. The first collection of tales reveals Wilde as 'apaisé, détendu, heureux autant qu'il pouvait l'être'[7] [calm, relaxed, as happy as he could ever be], while *A House of Pomegranates* is a symbolic expression of his sexual ambivalence. Within this psychological frame of reference Merle, together with Léon Lemonnier, interprets the fisherman's relationship with a creature half-woman and half-fish ('The Fisherman and his Soul') as symbolising renunciation of 'normal' sexual behaviour; similarly the ugliness of the dwarf ('The Birthday of the Infanta') and of 'The Star-Child' represents a physical image of the 'disgrâce de l'inverti'[8] [disgrace of the invert] of which he was all too aware, since his homosexuality was a taboo subject in the society of his day. Against this background, the autoeroticism of the star-child takes on added significance, for Freud maintained that male homosexuality is characterised by a strong element of narcissism. Merle considers that Wilde's cruel rejection of his mother may be seen in conjunction with his growing estrangement from his wife, 'l'épouse que deux maternités successives avaient déformée'.[9]

Reading the tales like a psychoanalyst deciphering his patient's dreams may be fascinating, but it is also risky,[10] for no one really knows for sure when Wilde's homosexuality first began to dominate his sexual leanings, and in any case the psychological, psychoanalytical approach to literature is fraught with methodological difficulties. Apart from its indisputable merit of: 'Kunst aus dem Bann des absoluten Geistes herauszuholen' [releasing art from the power of the absolute spirit] and offering 'Glieder konkreter Vermittlung zwischen der Struktur von Gebilden und der gesellschaftlichen'[11] [elements of concrete mediation between the structure of [artistic] creations and society], its ahistorical reductionism constantly runs the inherent risk of cutting down origin, themes and structure to the mere dimensions of objective correlatives of the author's psychological experiences, thus completely ignoring, for instance, the effects of literary traditions and the conventions of his chosen genre. The fantastic transformation of the star-child from a beautiful boy into an ugly one, seen by Merle as a reference to Wilde's relationship with his wife, is a commonplace motif in fairy-tales and, in Vladimir Propp's terms, is one of the conventional and indeed basic functions of protagonists in this genre.[12] However interesting and sometimes revealing it may be to interpret literary texts as reflections of their author's subconscious mind, the critic's first line of argument must surely concern the author's artistic development, as he describes the form, content and effect of a text, analysing and evaluating it, as well as setting it in the context of the author's work as a whole.

Wilde himself made various comments on the tales, and these show how close was the link between their artistic conception and his general ideas about aesthetics. It is well worth remembering that shortly after the publication of *The Happy Prince* etc., he published one of his most important essays, 'The Decay of Lying'. There he emphatically denounced the emergence of an all too factual naturalism in nineteenth-century literature, declaring the true aim of the artist to be 'the telling of beautiful untrue things'.[13] Art begins with 'purely imaginative and pleasurable work dealing with what is unreal and non-existent'.[14] These theoretical utterances run parallel to the comments he made about the tales. In a letter to G. H. Kersley he calls them 'studies in prose, put for Romance's sake into a fanciful form',[15] and of 'The Happy Prince' he writes:

The story is an attempt to treat a magic modern problem in a form that aims at delicacy and imaginative treatment: it is a reaction against the purely imitative character of modern art – and now that literature has taken to blowing loud trumpets I cannot but be pleased that some ear has cared to listen to the low music of a little reed.[16]

It is clear from these remarks that the tales did not owe their existence merely to the chance circumstances of his personal or family life, but that they were the product of a deliberate artistic decision: their fantastic form resulted from his anti-realistic concept of art being put into creative practice. The fact that he chose the genre of the fairy-tale may be due in part to its attraction of magic and a heightened unreality, but also to the dynamic, almost mythical force that drove him into story-telling. From this point of view even *The Picture of Dorian Gray* – at least as far as its main theme is concerned – contains elements of a modern fairy-tale.

In neither *Dorian Gray* nor the tales, however, is the link between aesthetic theory and narrative practice as tight as it may at first appear. Primarily the gaps are due not to any shortcomings in textual structure or thematic motivation, but to unresolved problems in Wilde's aesthetic theory. He proclaimed the autonomy of art, preferring the imaginative to the imitative ideal and separating art from life and from all moral purposes, but paradoxically it was even more difficult for him to conform to these principles in the tales than it was in the novel. For in spite of their apparent detachment from the real world, they are inevitably imbued with their own special imagery which refers back to the reader's experience of reality, and indeed can only take on its meaning through such reference. Wilde's awareness of the problem was evident during the controversy over *Dorian Gray*, which he described as 'a story with a moral'.[17] Similarly, at the end of 'The Devoted Friend' the linnet confesses to having told a 'story with a moral',[18] to which the duck replies: '... that is always a very dangerous thing to do' – an observation confirmed by the authorial narrator: 'And I quite agree with her.'[19]

Structures, themes and style of the tales

Despite the variety of their themes, the tales – apart from 'The Fisherman and his Soul', the scope and complexity of which make it exceptional – have several structural features in common, and these are well worth analysing. They all have as their starting-point some kind of deficiency, which may be manifested in one of two ways: either the characters have no proper understanding of themselves and their surroundings, or they are lacking in love and consideration for their fellow creatures. In both cases, tensions arise between asocial egotism and social responsibility, between selfishness and thought for others, and it is these tensions that give the action its springboard and its direction. At first the (un)happy prince and the young king know nothing of the people's suffering, the ugly dwarf mistakes amusement for admiration, the student does not understand the nightingale's sacrifice, the supercilious rocket talks only about himself and regards his companions merely as a background for his own self-display, the selfish giant drives the children out of his garden and builds a wall round it, the narcissistic star-child pitilessly sends his weeping mother away, and the egotistical miller exploits poor Hans with false promises. The development of the action in all these stories depends on whether the initial moral defect or lack of insight is overcome – thus leading to a change in the character's behaviour – or continued to the end. Thus there are two types of dénouement: if the character passes his test and the fault is corrected, the ending is positive, in the form of a reward – often through some kind of Christian transformation, as in 'The Happy Prince', 'The Young King', and 'The Star-Child'; if the character persists in his self-deception and egotism, the ending is negative – a kind of unreconciled fade-out, as in 'The Remarkable Rocket', The Nightingale and the Rose', and 'The Devoted Friend'. In the tales with a positive ending, love of one's fellows, sympathy and self-sacrifice are rewarded, but in those with a negative ending the unenlightened or unpurified hero is punished: little Hans must die because he does not realise that he is only an object of exploitation for the miller; the rocket explodes unnoticed; the sacrifice of the nightingale, which presses its breast against the thorn of a rosebush so that its blood will be absorbed and bring forth a red rose, is senseless because the world around her, especially the student, does not appreciate it. Little Hans, the supercilious rocket, and the self-sacrificing nightingale have remained trapped in their illusions, unaware of the true nature of themselves or of others. An exception, though, is the ending of 'The Birthday of the Infanta', where the dwarf's insight into himself brings about his death. In view of these different categories of ending, it is hard to subscribe to Christopher S. Nassaar's thesis that: 'The fall from the world of innocence and subsequent attainment of a higher innocence is the governing principle of Wilde's fairy tales.'[20]

Moral purification, in the form of the change from selfish to selfless conduct – as manifested in the tales with a positive ending – requires both insight and a readiness for self-sacrifice.[21] The prince – who is only happy in the eyes of the mayor and town councillors – has no pangs of conscience until he learns from his exalted position about ugliness and misery. So long as he remained inside the palace of Sans-Souci, which was cut off from the world by a high wall, he had no idea what went on outside. Now he is ready to give up his gold so that he and his friend, the helpful swallow, may relieve the suffering of the poor and needy. When God asks his angel to bring the two most precious things in the city, these turn out to be the leaden heart of the prince, and the dead bird. There is a similar situation in 'The Young King'. There the king has three dreams, in which he sees three different people who are living in misery and have to slave away in order to supply the robes and jewels for his coronation, and only then does he become aware of the suffering that exists outside his resplendent palace Joyeuse. At once he renounces his royal pomp, takes his old worn-out clothes from the chest, puts a crown of briar on his head and rides off, despite the mockery of the courtiers and the people, to the coronation in the cathedral. It is not the bishop who places upon him the insignia of his earthly power, but God Himself, miraculously transforming him and dressing him in 'the raiment of a king'.[22] In both tales, the hero's change of attitude is stimulated by insight into the suffering around him and is rewarded by divine intervention.

It is, however, dangerous to draw premature conclusions from the social implications of these two stories as, for example, George Woodcock does with reference to 'The Young King':

This ['The Young King'] is a parable on the capitalist system of exploitation as severe as anything in William Morris, and it can stand beside the grimmest passages of Marx as an indictment of the kind of horrors which, Wilde was fully aware, were inflicted on the toilers in this world for the benefit of the people he satirised in his plays.[23]

To set Wilde beside Morris and Marx is surely going a little too far, and the socialism inherent in his gentle fairy-tale seems far more geared to aesthetic effect than to political propaganda. If these tales are indeed 'wry pieces of social and moral commentary',[24] as one critic suggests, then it must be said that the commentary contains little insight into or analysis of the social causes and effects of poverty. Instead, there is a series of snapshots: in 'The Happy Prince' we have the worn-out seamstress with her sick son, the starving writers, the weeping matchgirl; in 'The Young King' we see the gaunt weavers in their attic, the exploited galley-slave, and the toilers searching the dried-up river bed for rubies. This is poverty seen from outside – the scenery against which the main characters are to perform their actions. Beside the severity of Morris and the grimness of Marx, their tone is rather that of a 'modischen Sozialsentimentalismus'[25] [fashionable social sentimentalism] such as emerged from the organised philanthropy of the many charities that sprang up during the nineteenth century.

In 'The Happy Prince' and 'The Young King', the ignorant heroes are purified by their new awareness of social misery; in 'The Selfish Giant' and 'The Star-Child', the egotistic heroes are transformed under somewhat different circumstances. The giant drives the children out of his garden, which then suffers continual winter until one day the children come back through a hole in the wall. Then the trees blossom, the grass grows, the birds twitter, and it is spring again. The giant realizes that the prolonged winter had been caused by his selfishness, and so he repents and resolves to tear down the wall and make his garden into a children's playground for ever. He helps a child to climb the one frost-covered tree, which blossoms at once. In this story, the conflict and the solution are clear: the giant's asocial egotism, symbolised by the winter cold, is overcome by an act of unselfishness and love. The initial impetus for this transformation, however, comes from outside: the rhythm of nature is broken, and is only restored when the children return to play. The process is similar in 'The Star-Child', where the hero is transformed supernaturally from Narcissus-like beauty to toad-like ugliness, and only then becomes aware of his own cruelty to his mother:

I have been cruel to my mother, and as a punishment has this evil been sent to me. Wherefore I must go hence, and wander through the world till I find her, and she gives me forgiveness.[26]

For three years he wanders in search of his mother, until he is finally sold as a slave to a magician, who on three successive days sends him to look for three pieces of gold in a wood. He is helped in this task by a little hare, but each time, in spite of the fact that the magician will beat him, he gives the gold to a leper who would otherwise starve to death. When, after his last good deed, he walks through the city gate, his original beauty is restored, he finds his mother, and he is made king. The structure of the tale is similar to that of 'The Selfish Giant': selfish behaviour, of which the character is made aware by supernatural events, leads through different tests to insight and a new attitude. In 'The Happy Prince' and 'The Young King', the scenes of poverty and suffering indicate a disturbance in the social order, whereas in 'The Selfish Giant' and 'The Star-Child' there are strange and discomforting changes in nature – endless winter in the giant's garden, and the child's beauty transformed to ugliness – which function as external manifestations of a disturbed moral order. In all four tales, the relief of suffering and the restoration of the natural order are not ends in themselves, but serve to change the characters' moral values. The problems and their solutions are individual, though they have social implications.

In form and structure, Wilde's fairy-tales are very much in the tradition of European folk-tales.[27] The characters are one-dimensional, without psychological motivation, and generally they are simply the nameless bearers of particular qualities and functions: the happy prince, the selfish giant, the remarkable rocket. There is little or no description of their personal, social or historical background, and the story has no specific geographical or historical setting. On those occasions when Wilde does give some detailed description – for example in 'The Young King', 'The Birthday of the Infanta', and 'The Fisherman and his Soul' – the intention seems to be less a matter of directing the reader towards a precise setting than of the author indulging his predilection for lavish décor. The reduction of character to function and the general renunciation of any fixed time or place lead to a corresponding lack of complexity in the action itself. For the most part the problems and conflicts are limited to simple aesthetic, social or moral contrasts: beautiful/ugly, poor/rich, selfish/considerate. Changes of attitude or situation are not gradual, but, in nearly all cases, sudden and complete, often through the intervention of some supernatural agent. There are miraculous transformations rather than psychological developments.

In all the stories there is a single plot centred upon a single character, though the action may develop between two or even three figures whose relation to the hero is often contrastive or complementary. Little Hans' goodwill, extended to the point of self-sacrifice, stands in contrast to the miller's ruthless pragmatism; the happy prince and the star-child, on the other hand, are helped and befriended by the swallow and the hare. The active participation of talking animals and objects, incidentally, is as commonplace in Wilde as in so many folk-tales. There is also a tendency for the narrative to be divided up in patterns, as is most evident in the frequent use of triple themes: the young king's three dreams, the three good deeds of the swallow and the star-child, the soul's three journeys in 'The Fisherman and his Soul'. Unlike many folk-tales, however, Wilde's stories do not make use of any set formulae for the beginning or the end. According to Lutz Röhrich: 'Der Märchenausgang ist stereotyp: die Liebenden werden ein Paar; der Arme wird reich'[28] [the fairy-tale ending is stereotyped: the lovers become a pair; the poor man becomes rich], but this principle does not apply to Wilde's tales. Indeed some of them leave behind a rather bitter taste. Even the star-child who becomes king after passing all his tests, reigns for only three years: 'And he who came after him ruled evilly'.[29] The death of the fisherman and of the mermaid, and the broken heart of the dwarf in 'The Birthday of the Infanta', endow these tales with a note of gloom which is far from the conventional happy ending.

The style of the narrative is not always as simple as one might expect from such subjects, and the incorporation of archaic, even biblical turns of phrase, together with personifications and ornate descriptions are all indicative of a highly artistic use of language. This deliberate stiltedness of expression reinforces the sense of other-worldliness and, at the same time, uses its extra emotional values – derived from the reader's own recollection of the Authorized Version – to imbue the action with a sort of magic amounting in some cases to Christian exaltation. The manner in which the star-child addresses his mother after the long search shows no spontaneous joy of reunion, but sounds like the repentant sinner's plea for absolution:

'Mother, I denied thee in the hour of my pride. Accept me in the hour of my humility. Mother, I gave thee hatred. Do thou give me love. Mother, I rejected thee. Receive thy child now.'[30]

The archaic pronouns, and parallel sentences containing emotional contrasts such as pride/humility, hatred/love, are rhythmically reminiscent of biblical cadences, while their content is redolent of sin and forgiveness, guilt and expiation. Thus the situation is detached from the real world and set in an idealised Christian frame of reference. The use of allegory and personification reinforces the unrealistic tenor of the tales already effected by the nameless generality of the characters, the vagueness of space and time, and the simplicity of the plot. It is interesting to note how Wilde uses this particular artifice. In 'The Young King', for instance, the misery of the weavers and the ruby-seekers is at first described realistically, but then this description suddenly breaks off and is continued on an allegorical level: 'Death' and 'Avarice' look at the workers and quarrel over the booty. 'Ague', 'Fever' and Plague' appear as Death's mighty allies, and thus an all too realistic atmosphere is palliated by abstraction, and we are once more distanced from the ugliness of the everyday world.

The same escapist tendency is apparent in the descriptions of decorative settings, where the lure of the colourful, rare and costly is depicted 'mit verdichteter Sinnlichkeit'[31] [concentrated sensuality]. Assembled here is everything that has – in an industrialised, standardised and utilitarian world – become ever rarer and ever more expensive. For Wilde's *goût du précieux* does not confine itself to the stylised expression of an aesthetic philosophy of life, but it also mirrors his aristocratic predilection for the select, the exclusive, the elite. The young king, for instance, is in a room which sounds almost like the catalogue of a museum of arts and crafts listing the contents of some extraordinary interior:

The walls were hung with rich tapestries representing the Triumph of Beauty. A large press, inlaid with agate and lapis lazuli, filled one corner, and facing the window stood a curiously wrought cabinet with lacquer panels of powdered and mosaiced gold, on which were placed some delicate goblets of Venetian glass, and a cup of dark-veined onyx. Pale poppies were broidered on the silk coverlet of the bed, as though they had fallen from the tired hands of sleep, and tall reeds of fluted ivory bore up the velvet canopy, from which great tufts of ostrich plumes sprang, like white foam, to the pallid silver of the fretted ceiling. A laughing Narcissus in green bronze held a polished mirror above its head. On the table stood a flat bowl of amethyst.[32]

Frequently this *goût du précieux* is combined with a *nostalgie de l'étranger*, as in 'The Fisherman and his Soul', where the depiction of oriental splendour conveys an extra atmospheric charm. But the reader will search in vain for the intellectual edge, the wit and the paradox of the comedies, for these would not have fitted in at all with the predominantly moral tone of the tales. Nevertheless a different and perhaps disturbing discrepancy does arise between, on the one hand, the style with its mixture of simplicity, biblical and archaic expression, and decoratively aesthetic idiom, and on the other the content with its Christian and humanitarian sentiments. Even though Wilde did for the most part conform to the given conventions of the genre, he could not bring himself to renounce the formal trappings of his art and his well-known propensity for gems.

The literary conventions of the fairy-tale are not to be found in hand-books on poetics, but they manifest themselves variously in individual works. If a nineteenth-century English author had been asked for a classic representative of the genre, he would most certainly have come up with a single name: Hans Christian Andersen. The writings of Denmark's national poet, which had been available in numerous English translations since 1846, were widely read and immensely popular. Dickens had a very high regard for him, having first met him in 1847, and they became good friends, although their relations gradually cooled in later years.[33] Interest in Andersen was enhanced by the fact that England had no real tradition of her own in this genre, with the single exception of *Alice's Adventures in Wonderland* (1865). Dickens, Thackeray and Ruskin all failed to achieve a breakthrough with their tales, and so it was only natural that Wilde should follow the European tradition. One of the very first reviews of *House of Pomegranates* notes the impression that the stories are written 'somewhat after the manner of Hans Andersen'.[34] This vague feeling does not, however, become any more precise when one compares the work of the Irishman with the work of the Dane. The vanity of the remarkable rocket, and its adventures up until the unnoticed explosion, bear a certain similarity to Andersen's story of the proud darning-needle: 'who thought herself so fine that she fancied she must be fit for embroidery'.[35] After its flight, nothing of the rocket remains except its stick, which falls on the back of a goose, while the ambitious needle finishes up under a cart. Little Hans – could he be an allusion to Hans Christian Andersen? – in 'The Devoted Friend' reminds one of little Claus in 'Little Claus and Big Claus', but any initial similarity disappears entirely in the course of the story.

The clearest thematic links are to be found between 'The Fisherman and his Soul' and Andersen's 'The Little Mermaid'.[36] Both tales deal with the relationship between a human being and a mermaid. In Andersen's story the latter wishes to be rid of her tail so that she can become human and be close to the prince whom she loves and whose life – unbeknown to him – she once saved. Only if he marries her can she gain an immortal soul. If the prince gives his love to another – as happens towards the end of the story – then the mermaid must die. In 'Fisherman' Wilde takes up the same theme, but turns it the other way round: his fisherman falls in love with the mermaid. In order to win her love, he must rid himself of his soul, which eventually he does – following the instructions of a witch – by standing in the moonlight and cutting his shadow away from his body. Every year the wandering soul returns from distant lands to the sea where the fisherman lives, in order to tell him about its many adventures. Only in the third year, when the soul tells of a veiled dancer with feet like 'little white pigeons',[37] does the fisherman finally give way to the temptation and rejoin his spiritual companion. His soul, however, makes him commit wicked deeds because it had wandered the world for so long without a heart and had seen so much evil. The fisherman continues to love the mermaid, until one day he gives in to the soul's plea to enter his heart. Then the mermaid dies, and he himself, overcome by grief, dies as well.

The two main themes of this tale – the love between man and mermaid, and the separation of soul and body – are already to be found in Andersen's 'Little Mermaid' and also in 'Shadow', but both are of romantic origin. They are variations on the Undine theme in Friedrich de la Motte Fouqué's tale 'Undine' (1811) and the Schlemihl theme in Adelbert von Chamisso's novella *Peter Schlemihl's wundersame Geschichte* (1814). But the style, plot and outcome of Wilde's 'Fisherman' and Andersen's 'Little Mermaid' show how very differently these two authors regarded both their art and the world. Andersen tended towards a poetic transfiguration of the everyday world, lingering reflectively on homely, domestic realities to which he gave idyllic form in such narrative gems as 'The Brave Tin Soldier', 'The Darning-Needle', 'The Shirt-Collar', and 'The Ugly Duckling'. There is nothing like this in Wilde. And indeed how could one expect common ground between the shoemaker's son from Odense, whose parents owned just so much as 'to live from day to day',[38] and the snobbish Oxford graduate with his love of blue Chinese porcelain? The contrasting treatment of the Undine motif is certainly no coincidence. The little mermaid's longing to become human, to have an immortal soul and to share in human suffering springs directly from Andersen's love of the familiar and of that which is accessible to human experience. Wilde's 'Fisherman' is the direct opposite, for in his love there is none of the self-sacrifice that characterises Andersen's mermaid. His love is, rather, a mixture of aesthetic sensuality and the thrill of the abnormal, the unnatural inherent in this hybrid creature – it is far more the offshoot of her strange beauty than the outpouring of the fisherman's own emotions.

Her hair was a wet fleece of gold, and each separate hair as a thread of fine gold in a cup of glass. Her body was as white ivory, and her tail was of silver and pearl. Silver and pearl was her tail, and the green weeds of the sea coiled round it; and like seashells were her ears, and her lips were like sea-corals. The cold waves dashed over her cold breasts, and the salt glistened upon her eyelids.[39]

In two respects, this mermaid seems unnatural: the combination of woman and fish is a perversion of nature, giving rise to an extraordinary hybrid, whilst the aesthetic stylisation endows this monster with a seductive, almost mythical charm. While Andersen seeks familiar emotions and experiences in the trivia of his fairy-tale world, Wilde favours the exotic and the extraordinary. The journeys of the soul into distant lands, whose oriental splendours burst open the domestic confines of the reading public's predominantly insular imagination, reflect Wilde's own desire to penetrate into the unexplored regions of fantasy, to savour each new sensation to the full, and thus to escape from the worn-out world of the present. Wilde's mermaid does not symbolise a return to nature, but she represents total otherness, the anomaly that stands in absolute contrast to the normality and routine of everyday human relations – indeed she may even stand for what the psychologically orientated critics of Wilde have assumed to be the 'deviance' of the homosexual. What lures the fisherman away from the sprite is the feet of a woman – in other words: 'une femme complète . . . l'amour normal'.[40] But the search for such a woman, to whom his soul is supposed to lead him, is – as we learn from the tale itself – in vain.

'The Fisherman and his Soul' is strikingly different from the other tales in its scale, its complexity, and its decorative style. More than all the others it reveals motifs, thematic patterns and forms of expression that Wilde was to use again in subsequent works, particularly *The Picture of Dorian Gray*. The fisherman's separation from his soul anticipates Dorian's split identity, and the aesthetic attractions of the mermaid foreshadow Dorian's love for Sibyl Vane, whose acting talents fascinate him far more than her character. The relationship between a human being and a soulless hybrid opens up poetic possibilities that Wilde does not fully exploit in 'The Fisherman', but it is a theme to which he returns in his poem *The Sphinx*. The mixture of lust and fatal cruelty, which characterises the 'sensibilità erotica' of this composite creature and of Salomé, plays no part in 'Fisherman', but one can already sense the incipient form of the *femme fatale*, the symbol of female demonry. As for the elaborate depiction of precious objects and an exotic ambience, this too has its later echo in *Dorian Gray*, particularly Chapter 11, and in *Salomé* and the 'Sainte Courtisane'.

These thematic and stylistic links between the tales and Wilde's later works are not confined to 'The Fisherman and his Soul'. The dwarf gazing into the mirror at a deformed monster has its parallel in Dorian Gray's unveiling of the portrait which shows his bloodstained image, the painted likeness of his soul. Both are moments of revelation and self-knowledge which are shattering for the characters concerned. In 'The Birthday of the Infanta', the dwarf's illusion is destroyed by the reality of his appearance, while in *Dorian Gray* the beautiful and eternally youthful appearance of the protagonist cannot continue to mask the reality of his depraved soul. The structure of the two stories, however, is quite different. Dorian takes the opposite course from that of the dwarf, sacrificing his soul in order to preserve his youth and beauty. This contrary path also leads to a contrary end: instead of Christian transfiguration, the outcome is suicide – a psychological solution instead of a supernatural one.

In the tales, the simple plots are motivated by the basic contrasts between good and evil, beauty and ugliness, illusion and awareness, egotism and unselfishness; in Wilde's later fiction and drama, these contrasts are woven into more complex forms – for instance, the tension between aesthetic conduct and moral awareness in *Dorian Gray*, and the conflict between personal identity and social integration in the comedies. The thematic shifts of emphasis are unmistakable, and are only partly due to the fact that Wilde used different literary forms with different conventions. The blatant egotism of the rocket, for example: 'I am always thinking about myself, and I expect everybody else to do the same',[41] recurs later in the maxims of dandyism, but is charmingly refurbished: 'To love oneself is the beginning of a life-long romance.'[42]

The idealistic endings and the moral tone of many of the tales certainly suggest an underlying conformity to given conventions of the genre. At the same time, it is worth noting that despite his pose as the amoral *provocateur*, Wilde also remains true to conventional morality in his later works, with evil being punished and good rewarded: Dorian Gray stabs himself in front of his grotesque portrait, the 'good women' maintain the upper hand over the 'women with a past', Salomé is crushed between the shields of the soldiers, and the student in *The Sphinx* resists the charms of the seductive monster by looking at the crucifix. In the tales, Wilde was unburdened by the role the public expected him to play, and also by his own need to present himself as a wit and a clever but amoral outsider, and so he was quite free to tell his stories and to reveal another side of his character, that is, his conventional morality. The Basil Hallward in his personality had no need here of a Lord Henry at his side to counterbalance the moral norms with dazzling epigrams and smart philosophy.

The stories

In the fairy-tales, Wilde experimented with themes, structures and solutions within a comparatively simple framework; at about the same time he was writing a number of short stories which were published as a collection in 1891: 'Lord Arthur Savile's Crime. A Study of Duty', 'The Canterville Ghost. A Hylo-idealistic Romance', 'The Sphinx without a Secret. An Etching', and 'The Model Millionaire. A Note of Admiration'. In these stories, where he was not bound by the same rigid conventions of the fairy-tale genre, he begins to test out those literary techniques and strategies of presentation which in *Dorian Gray* and the comedies were to become his favourite forms of expression: irony, paradox, and the complete reversal of situations into their opposites. The title story begins

with a vivid description of a reception held by Lady Windermere in
Bentinck House for an illustrious assembly of aristocrats, clergy, artists
and politicians. One cannot help feeling that such an account of a *grande
soirée* could only be written by an author with first-hand experience:

> It was certainly a wonderful medley of people. Gorgeous peeresses chatted affably
> to violent Radicals, popular preachers brushed coat-tails with eminent sceptics, a
> perfect bevy of bishops kept following a stout primadonna from room to room, on
> the staircase stood several Royal Academicians, disguised as artists, and it was said
> that at one time the supper-room was absolutely crammed with geniuses. In fact, it
> was one of Lady Windermere's best nights.[43]

The hostess, who has developed an interest in palmistry, introduces
some of her guests to Mr Podgers, a 'chiromantist' – not a 'chiropodist',
as the Duchess of Paisley mistakenly calls him. His attention roused by
some remarkable proofs of the man's ability, Lord Arthur Savile asks
Mr Podgers to read his future for him. What the chiromantist sees in Lord
Arthur's palm and – after much hesitation, repeated refusals, and a
discreet discussion of the fee – is at last prepared to divulge, causes Savile
to rush away from the party: 'Murder! that is what the chiromantist had
seen there. Murder![44] Not that any shady characters were aiming to take
the life of this rich idler, but, on the contrary, he himself would one day be
driven by Fate to commit such a crime.

Tormented by fear, Lord Arthur rushes through the London night, in a
confusion of thoughts similar to those of Dorian Gray when he leaves
Sibyl Vane and hurries through the maze of streets. But despite this initial
agitation, Lord Arthur retains his commonsense and his awareness of the
immediate future. Is it not his duty to commit this deed and fulfil the
prophecy before he marries Sybil Merton, so that their marriage cannot be
tainted by such a crime? This situation demands courage and selfless
action, not a passive and cowardly attendance on Fate. After due
consideration, he chooses his victim: Lady Clementina Beauchamp, an
elderly lady with heart trouble, second cousin on his mother's side; his
method is to be a fast-working pill, which he selects after careful study of
toxicology. But all his efforts are in vain, because Lady Clem proceeds to
die a natural death. Lord Arthur does not give up, but tries again, this time
putting dynamite in a little French clock with a detonator installed by a
helpful German anarchist named Winckelkopf; this he sends as an
anonymous gift to the Dean of Chichester, a collector of antique clocks.
But this attempt also fails miserably: 'a little puff of smoke came from the
pedestal of the figure, and the goddess of Liberty fell off, and broke her
nose on the fender'.[45] Lord Arthur is in despair. Then one night, when he
is walking along the Thames Embankment, he sees a figure leaning over
the railing and, in the light of a street lantern, he recognizes him as
Mr Podgers, the palmist. On the spur of the moment he grasps the man's

legs and throws him into the river. Thus the prophecy is fulfilled, the long-postponed wedding can take place, and Lord Arthur Savile and his wife Sybil Merton can enter a clear future.

It is evident from this gem of black humour how far Wilde has moved away from the thematic structure, style and tone of the fairy-tales. The description of the *soirée*, the upper-class names of the ladies – Windermere, Jedburgh, Plymdale, all of which recur in the comedies – the pointed, epigrammatic dialogue of the characters, these all belong to the world of *Dorian Gray* and the social plays. Basically 'Lord Arthur Savile's Crime' is a parody on contemporary detective stories: instead of a search for the criminal, we have the character's search for the crime; his problem is to *become* a criminal, not to catch one. Ironically it is the prophet of the deed who unwittingly fulfils his own prophecy by becoming the victim. The narrative strategy aims at a kind of double snub to the readers. First, Lord Arthur makes himself the executor of a destiny which the reader might have expected him to suffer only passively; he takes the prophecy for an inevitable fate, when for all we know it might just as easily be a lot of hocus-pocus. Secondly, the prophecy does not relate to a happy event that one might look forward to, but to a murder, which Lord Arthur appears to regard – against all the expectations of common sense – as an act of duty, indeed of self-sacrifice, and which must be performed in order to leave the way clear for his marriage. His justification for this somewhat perverse interpretation runs along the following lines:

Many men in his position would have preferred the primrose path of dalliance to the steep heights of duty; but Lord Arthur was too conscientious to set pleasure above principle. There was more than mere passion in his love; and Sybil was to him a symbol of all that is good and noble. For a moment he had a natural repugnance against what he was asked to do, but it soon passed away. His heart told him that it was not a sin, but a sacrifice; his reason reminded him that there was no other course open. He had to choose between living for himself and living for others, and terrible though the task laid upon him undoubtedly was, yet he knew that he must not suffer selfishness to triumph over love.[46]

This paradoxical argument, in which concepts such as 'duty', 'sacrifice' and 'love' are used to justify a totally immoral deed, depends on the deed being beyond the scope of moral law. Once it is released from such conventional restrictions, it becomes in itself a morally neutral action, and thus only the performance of it is associated with values – it is then a task to be fulfilled as expeditiously as possible, without fear of recriminations from the conscience. By thus hollowing out the substance of the above-mentioned concepts, it becomes perfectly easy to use them in vindication of that which they should diametrically oppose: in actual fact, it is not his duty that Lord Arthur is fulfilling, but a flagrant violation of it; he is driven, not by the courage of self-sacrifice, but by the cold-blooded search for an unknown victim; and no reader will believe that this is a matter of love triumphing over selfishness. The ethical code of the fairy-tales is turned upside down in this story. But at the same time it is more than just a piece of farcical comedy. Just as in *The Importance of Being Earnest* Wilde ridicules the earnestness of Victorian life by playing with the name Ernest, so too in this 'study of duty', behind the mask of satire and black humour, he shows how the concept of duty can be misused if it is loosened from the bonds of what Kant called the 'categorical imperative'.

'Lord Arthur Savile's Crime' is a humorous treatment of a serious theme, but at times it becomes positively macabre, whereas 'The Canterville Ghost. A Hylo-idealistic Romance', despite an abundance of gruesome details, maintains its cheerful tone throughout and is much more in the vein of the fairy-tales. Mr Hiram B. Otis, an American minister, comes to England and buys Canterville Chase, a haunted castle, ignoring the dire admonitions of the previous owner, Lord Canterville. He tells Mr Otis about the ghost of Sir Simon de Canterville, who murdered his wife Eleonore in 1575. The down-to-earth American, however, has no time for ghosts, and he and his family soon move into their new residence. A mysterious bloodstain in the salon is energetically removed with 'Champion Stain Remover and Paragon Detergent', but inexplicably reappears every day. After a few days, the master of the house is rudely awakened by steps in the corridor and the rattle of chains, thereby losing for ever his doubts about the existence of the ghost. But Mr Otis does not in any way allow these events to disturb his peace of mind; he simply offers his unusual guest a bottle of 'Tammany Rising Sun Lubricator', with the remark that he should oil his chains.

This is the start of a tough time for Sir Simon. Despite his wonderful powers of transformation – sometimes he appears as 'Black Isaac, or the Huntsman of Hogley Woods', sometimes as 'Reckless Rupert, or the Headless Earl' – he simply cannot impress the Otis family, let alone scare them. On the contrary: during his nightly tours of the castle, he stumbles over cunningly hidden trip-wires, when he enters a room a jug of water falls on his head, and once he is struck rigid with terror as he is suddenly confronted by a ghost – not, of course, a colleague, but a figure cobbled together out of a bed-curtain, a sweeping-brush, a kitchen cleaver, and a turnip. Once again they have played a nasty trick on him. Broken by all these unnerving experiences, Sir Simon is one day sitting downcast and depressed in the 'Tapestry Chamber' when Virginia, the minister's daughter, comes in and apologises to him for the rude behaviour of her brothers. In the course of the conversation, the ghost tells her that he longs for a peaceful death, but this he can only have if she weeps for his past sins and prays for the salvation of his soul. She does as he asks, and after centuries of restless haunting, Sir Simon at last takes a well-earned rest.

'The Canterville Ghost'[47] is a delightful parody of the traditional ghost story. Instead of the spirit terrifying the occupants of the castle, he himself becomes the victim. The reversal of the conventional situation is accompanied by a reversal of the narrative perspective, because for most of the time the reader views events through the eyes of the tormented Sir Simon. What gives the story a special flavour is the fact that it also satirises the American way of life, which Wilde had experienced during his lecture tour in 1882. Among the features that seem to him typical of the American character are materialism, a predominantly pragmatic way of thinking, no sense of aesthetics, no sense of history, and generally no sense of culture. Everything can be bought, nearly everything can be made, and there is nothing that can resist the creative power of common sense. 'I reckon that if there was such a thing as a ghost in Europe, we'd have it at home in a very short time in one of our public museums, or on the road as a show.'[48] For mysterious bloodstains, there is the 'Champion Stain Remover' etc., ·rusted chains require lubricating oil, and the best medicine for indigestion is Dr Dobell's tincture. There could be no greater contrast than that between Mr Otis – the puritanically raised and republically minded representative of the New World, cherishing his 'republican simplicity'[49] and dismissing Sir Simon's family heirlooms as the 'appurtenances of idle luxury'[50] – and the discreet, conservative Lord Canterville, who can trace his family back to the sixteenth century and can even include a castle ghost among his ancestors. Wilde's delightful 'hylo-idealistic romance' in addition to parodying the ghost story, thus offers an additional and highly entertaining commentary on the different mentalities of two nations, although perhaps the difference is not always as great as it may appear. For he writes of Mrs Otis:

Indeed, in many respects, she was quite English, and was an excellent example of the fact that we have really everything in common with America nowadays, except, of course, language.[51]

Beside 'The Canterville Ghost' and 'Lord Arthur Savile's Crime', the remaining two stories in the collection of 1891 – 'The Sphinx without a Secret. An Etching' and 'The Model Millionaire. A Note of Admiration' – are of less interest. They are *feuilleton* anecdotes, once more structured on the principle of reversal, with a character finally turning out to be the opposite of what he or she had at first appeared to be. In 'The Sphinx without a Secret', the strange behaviour of the widowed Lady Alroy suggests to Lord Murchison that she has a secret to hide. During a party, for instance, she speaks on even the most banal topics with a hushed voice as if she is afraid of being overheard; letters must not be sent to her private address in Park Lane, but must be sent 'care of Whittaker's Library'. By chance, Lord Murchison one day sees her hurrying through an area of ill repute and entering a boarding-house to which she has the key. In answer to the question whom she met there, she replies abruptly: 'I went to meet no one.'[52] And strange as it may seem, this is the truth. As the landlady reports, the veiled lady simply sat in a room, read books, and had an occasional cup of tea. The narrator tells us at the end:

Lady Alroy was simply a woman with a mania for mystery. She took these rooms for the pleasure of going there with her veil down, and imagining she was a heroine. She had a passion for secrecy, but she herself was merely a Sphinx without a secret.[53]

A surprise, albeit a more pleasant one, also awaits Hughie Erskine in 'The Model Millionaire'. This good-looking but penniless young man needs exactly £10,000 to marry his beloved Laura Merton, 'the daughter of a retired Colonel who had lost his temper and his digestion in India, and had never found either of them again'.[54] One day Erskine is visiting his friend, the painter Alan Trevor, who is busy painting the portrait of an old, shabby beggar. Erskine is so touched by the sight of the beggar's sad face that he gives him a sovereign, even though this means that he won't be able to afford a carriage ride for the next fortnight. The reward for this noble deed follows immediately. The beggar is not a beggar: beneath the ragged clothes is concealed one of the richest men in Europe. Erskine promptly receives a cheque for £10,000, and so he can go ahead and marry Laura. Indeed millionaire models may be rare, but model millionaires are even rarer.

Adeline R. Tintner[55] has pointed out that this story may have been based on an anecdote that was going around concerning Baron James Mayer de Rothschild. The painter Delacroix suggested that the Baron should pose as a beggar, and in due course this eccentric financier, from the French side of the Rothschild family, arrived at the artist's studio where Delacroix's assistant, not knowing the real identity of the shabby-looking visitor, slipped him a one-franc piece. The following day the kind-hearted young man received a cheque for 10,000 francs, signed by James de Rothschild. This tale is told in two biographies of Rothschild, and the similarity between it and Wilde's story is surely too great to be mere coincidence.

Although in the fairy-tales and stories Wilde was still experimenting with existing forms, there is no doubt that here, for the first time, he was speaking with his own voice. He was now well on the way to establishing his own literary identity. The epigonic-style of the early poems and dramas had been overcome, even if he still had not found the perfect form to express his fantasy. After 1891 he wrote no more fairy-tales or short stories. Indeed, at this stage of his career, it was not clear whether his leanings were more towards literature or criticism. While his talent for story-telling had blossomed at social gatherings and had taken on permanent form in the tales and stories, at the same time his reviews were developing into critical essays. The late 1880s were a period of professional and artistic orientation, after he had set up house in Tite Street, following his marriage to Constance Lloyd in 1884 and the subsequent birth of his sons Cyril and Vyvyan. The family needed a regular income, and so Wilde took on the post of editor of *The Woman's World* – a strange job for a man who many biographers have suggested was already indulging in secret homosexual relationships as early as 1886. Certainly family life soon began to bore him as much as the daily routine of going to the office. His creative and critical spirit, and also his need to assume a prominent position in London's cultural scene, demanded new outlets which he sought beyond the confines of home and office. What, then, could be more natural than that his imagination should dream up stories where the extraordinary became possible, dreams could come true, and restrictions could magically be lifted. If the fairy-tales are still predominantly coloured by conventional Christian morality – 'Wilde is preaching not what he believes in, but what he feels he ought to believe in'[56] – a story like 'Lord Arthur Savile's Crime' shows that he is already exploring an alternative world. The moral defects that were taken seriously and expiated in the tales are here turned satirically on their heads. The ethic of 'Love thy neighbour' is given its ultimate twist in *The Soul of Man under Socialism*: 'One should sympathise with the entirety of life, not with life's sores and maladies merely, but with life's joy and beauty and energy and health and freedom.'[57] Selfless behaviour is no longer a form of social sympathy, but becomes an expression of aesthetic self-fulfilment. The tension between moral idealism and aesthetic individualism – which runs through Wilde's entire work – begins to take on recognisable form in the tales and stories, becomes personalised in the main characters of *Dorian Gray*, and determines the two poles of dandyism and respectability in the social comedies.

3   Personality and perfection. The lectures, *Reviews* and *Intentions*

Wilde's critical work has attracted increasing attention in the last twenty years. In 1969 Richard Ellmann edited a substantial selection of his critical writings under the title of *The Artist as Critic*,[1] while in the same year Stanley Weintraub published an anthology called *Literary Criticism of Oscar Wilde*.[2] A year later Carl Markgraf compiled an annotated edition of *Oscar Wilde's Anonymous Criticism* (1970),[3] while at the same time Karl Beckson was compiling for the Critical Heritage Series a comprehensive collection of criticism of Wilde's work by contemporaries and 'near-contemporaries'.[4] Then in 1973 Kevin H. F. O'Brien produced 'An Edition of Oscar Wilde's American Lectures',[5] the first critical edition of the hitherto badly neglected lectures that Wilde gave on his American tour of 1882. These various editors performed the valuable service of making accessible, and also partly revising, the less well-known texts among the *Reviews* and *Miscellanies* published in the first collected edition of 1908. The main body of Wilde's critical writings would seem thoroughly to justify all this editorial activity, for it is astonishingly varied and, despite certain debts to his predecessors, entitles him to pre-eminence amongst late-nineteenth-century critics, apart from Matthew Arnold and Walter Pater. As for the independence and originality of his work, this we shall be discussing in detail.

Wilde began his career as a critic with a discussion, the 'Grosvenor Gallery', in 1877 and a long essay 'The Rise of Historical Criticism'. This treatise was written for the 1879 Chancellor's English Essay Prize, which it failed to win. It was first published privately in 1905, but then only in part,[6] and deals mainly with the development of a critical, rational historiography in Ancient Greece and, in a short survey, its demise with Roman historiography. Wilde defines 'historical criticism' as 'part of that complex working towards freedom which may be described as the revolt against authority'[7] – in other words, a liberating, enlightening force which in politics paves the way towards democracy, and in the intellectual world constitutes the precondition for philosophy and science. The view of history as the workings of supernatural forces, avenging gods and Fate gradually gave way to a rational approach, based on general principles and the process of cause and effect; Wilde illustrates this development with reference to Herodotus, Thucydides and Polybios. He takes their positions as exemplifications of Comte's three stages of human history, as outlined in the fifth volume of his *Cours de philosophie positive* (1841): the 'état théologique', 'état métaphysique' and 'état positif'. From these we can derive the emergence of history from the darkness of mythological speculation into the light of scientific analysis. In contrast to the enlightened spirit of Greek historiography, however, Wilde regards Roman history as uncritical, and its authors as 'merely antiquarians, not historians'.[8]

Lothar Hönnighausen, in his article on 'Die englische Literatur 1870–1890' in volume 18 (Part 1) of the *Neuen Handbuches der Literaturwissenschaft* (1976),[9] stresses the fact that this essay – which in its serious, academic tone and its somewhat heavy, long-winded style is totally uncharacteristic of Wilde's later work – may be regarded as 'ein besonders instruktives Dokument' [a particularly instructive document] of 'der neuen Wissenschaftlichkeit' [the new scholarliness][10] of the nineteenth-century English intellect. Indeed, from the romantic concept of organic growth, through Comte's positivism, right up to Spencer's theory of evolution Wilde incorporates virtually every great thought system that had influenced the age. Perhaps the emergent eclecticism is one of the very few features that links this early work with Wilde's later writings. It was, however, to be his only excursion into history.

In addition to the lectures given in England and America in 1882 and 1883, the bulk of Wilde's theory of art and literature is contained in the essays 'The Truth of Masks' (original version 1885), 'The Decay of Lying' (1889), 'Pen, Pencil and Poison' (1889), and 'The Critic as Artist' (1890), which were published collectively in 1891 under the title *Intentions*. Also to be taken into account are the many Reviews edited by Robert Ross, with a few more that were printed later in *Miscellanies*; individual passages from the letters, *De Profundis*, the foreword to *The Picture of Dorian Gray*, 'The Portrait of Mr W. H.', and *The Soul of Man under Socialism* also reveal interesting aspects of Wilde's standpoint. The following study of Wilde's critical and aesthetic writings will mainly adhere to their chronological order, and will seek to set out their intellectual content, to establish thematic links, and to test their consistency. We shall also be asking to what extent Wilde was influenced by romantic and Victorian aesthetics as well as by French critics, and whether his views have had any effect on twentieth-century criticism of art and literature. A further consideration will be the originality of his work and its relation to the rest of his writings.

The American lectures

A great deal has already been written about Wilde's lecture tour of America in 1882, but considerably more attention has been paid to the journey than to the lectures. The anecdotes and witticisms abound: his statement at the customs that 'I have nothing to declare except my genius', his disappointment over the Atlantic, his drinking capacity, which wrung admiration even from the hardened silver-miners in Leadville. His journey took him as far as Louisiana in the south, Ontario in the north, California in the west, and New York in the east, and during the ten months he visited more than a hundred towns in America. More than 125 times he stood on the podium to address audiences who knew little about art but came more out of curiosity to see the original model of aestheticism so bitingly satirised by Gilbert and Sullivan in their opera *Patience* (1881), which had been the great success of the season. D'Oyly Carte, the American impresario, had been the driving-force behind this lecture tour, his aim being to stimulate interest in the opera and to increase his takings by exploiting current trends and using the real aesthete to publicise the satire. It was therefore scarcely surprising that from the very start the American public saw the young Wilde in the context predetermined by *Patience*: he was the ridiculous apostle of a modish cult of beauty, worshipping sunflowers and lilies, dressed in buckled shoes, silk stockings, knee-breeches, velvet jacket and huge cravat, and constantly reiterating words like 'intense', 'utter', 'consummate' and 'precious'. Headlines such as 'Oscar Wilde's Poetic Breathings',[11] 'The Gospel of Intensity',[12] or 'Utter Oscar',[13] showed how the local press viewed this visitor from the Old World, and clearly he was regarded as an extraordinary spectacle rather than as the purveyor of serious ideas about aesthetics. Furthermore, his thesis about the importance of the artist and the dignity of manual labour in a beautiful environment and with decorative tools was bound to arouse scepticism or total incomprehension among his listeners, since it stood in such stark contrast to the social and economic realities of the New World, where life consisted of agricultural and industrial trail-blazing through mechanical production. The contrast was vividly summed up by Lloyd Lewis and Henry J. Smith in their book of 1936, *Oscar Wilde Discovers America* [1882]:

In a nation where the businessman was dominant, Oscar Wilde's pleas for a Ruskinian Utopia were doomed to yawns, and his dreams of toilers happy in their labor certain to be regarded as ridiculous. The American industrialist, making money his goal and religion, could not or would not conceive that a laborer was interested in anything but the same objective. Didn't the worker get higher wages than his brothers in Europe? That was all that mattered.[14]

In his *[Personal] Impressions of America*,[15] with which Wilde began a lengthy lecture tour of England at the Prince's Hall, London on 9 July 1883, he drew a picture of America such as must have confronted many visitors from the Old World: an immeasurably broad and wealthy country, where everything seems gigantic and overdone, with the noisy hustle and bustle of the towns, the individual's emphasis on practical matters, the general indifference to art, and minds 'entirely given to business'.[16] Only American girls seem to stand outside this picture, for they appear to the speaker as 'little oases of pretty unreasonableness in a vast desert of practical common-sense'.[17]

Wilde's repertoire on the American tour consisted of just three lectures: 'The English Renaissance', 'The Decorative Arts', and 'The House Beautiful', of which the first two underwent considerable revision as the tour progressed. He began on 9 January 1882 at Chickering Hall, New York, with 'The English Renaissance'. In February he replaced this with 'The Decorative Arts', which he proceeded to use for the remaining nine months, reserving 'The House Beautiful' for those occasions on which he visited a town twice. The only time he dealt with a different topic was 5 April 1882 at Platt's Hall, San Francisco, when he talked about 'Irish Poets and Poetry of the Nineteenth Century'. Using the manuscript and contemporary newspaper reports, Robert D. Pepper reconstructed this talk and published it in 1972.[18]

It has already been pointed out that critics have generally paid very little attention to the lectures, and this neglect may be due in part to their lack of originality, which we shall be discussing in due course, but also to the unsatisfactory nature of the edited texts. For many years the only seemingly reliable edition was that contained in the volume entitled *Miscellanies*, which was published in 1908 as part of the first English collected works edited by Robert Ross. There the American lectures appeared under the following titles: 'The English Renaissance of Art', 'House Decoration' and 'Art and the Handicraftsman'. In 1973, however, Kevin H. F. O'Brien produced 'An Edition of Oscar Wilde's American Lectures' in the form of a dissertation in which he questioned the validity of Ross's texts. O'Brien based his edition on an inspection of all existing manuscripts together with a collection of over one hundred newspaper reports, which described and in some cases even reproduced Wilde's lectures in greater or lesser detail throughout the ten months of the tour. He came to the conclusion that Ross's edition in *Miscellanies* was incomplete and inaccurate.[19] According to O'Brien, even the titles are incorrect. As proof he quotes a letter from Wilde to Colonel Morse, D'Oyly Carte's agent in America, in which Wilde calls the first two lectures 'The English Renaissance' and 'The Decorative Arts'.[20] Under the title 'Art and the Handicraftsman' – apparently Ross's own invention – stands nothing more than 'a pastiche of manuscript fragments remaining after Ross put together ER 1 [The English Renaissance, First Version].'[21] The text which Ross called 'House Decoration' in fact comprises a mixture of the revised version of 'The Decorative Arts' and 'The House Beautiful'. In some instances, where Wilde was clearly guilty of plagiarism, the trustee of his literary estate either deleted the passages or discreetly provided a note to indicate the source of the material. One lecture, 'The House Beautiful', had escaped his attention altogether. It would seem that he had not gathered sufficient information about Wilde's tour and had not taken sufficient trouble over collating the various manuscripts.

As the texts of 'The English Renaissance' and 'The Decorative Arts' underwent several revisions in the course of time – only 'The House Beautiful' remained almost unaltered – O'Brien printed two versions of each, one early and one late, which he designated ER 1 and 2, and DA 1 and 2. ER 1 is identical to the lecture Wilde first gave on 9 January 1882 in New York, while ER 2 is the revised version which he read for the last time on 8 February in Buffalo. Similarly, DA 1 collates the first lecture given on 13 February in Chicago and all subsequent versions up until the writing of 'The House Beautiful' between 6 and 10 March. DA 2 reproduces the final talk on this subject, given on 14 October, together with additional material from preceding lectures. The texts of 'The House Beautiful' and DA 2 are almost exclusively reconstructions from newspaper reports, since there are no manuscripts.

In 'The English Renaissance' Wilde begins by insisting that it is not his intention to offer an abstract definition of art, but he wishes to follow the example of Goethe and represent art in its 'special manifestations'.[22] His main aim is to give a survey of the English Renaissance of Art, to investigate its origins, and to foretell its future development. What characterises this new movement is:

its desire for a more gracious and comely way of life, its passion for physical beauty, its exclusive attention to form, its seeking for new subjects for poetry, new forms of art, new intellectual and imaginative enjoyments.[23]

Its origin lies in the unification of classical and romantic concepts of art in a new aesthetic ideal which no longer clings to a representation of general and eternal truths, but seeks beauty in the transient, the relative, and the unusual. One of the main reasons for this change of perspective is to be found in a sphere outside that of aesthetic tradition: the French Revolution, with its demand that the individual be freed from the yoke of oppression. Without the spirit of political freedom, the individual cannot be emancipated. Keats marked the beginning of the art Renaissance in England, and the Pre-Raphaelites followed him. Fundamental to the emergence of this new artistic consciousness is recognition of the 'absolute' difference between the world of art and the 'world of real fact'.[24] Literature must never be confused with the direct expression of emotions and real experiences, but it forms itself out of the imaginative transformation of the empirical object into artistic form. The more distant this image is from reality, and the more alien and contradictory it is, the more perfect it will seem to the observer. Thus the poet, in choosing his subject-matter, is in no way bound by the problems of his time. Of course, not everything is uniformly suitable for subject-matter even if a 'poetical attitude'[25] is possible towards all things, but the poet will choose nothing 'that is harsh or disturbing or that gives pain . . . that is debatable . . . about which men argue'.[26] Wilde repeatedly stresses that the artistic quality of a piece of art or literature is not dependent on the subject-matter but on the perfect handling of form. What constitutes the actual social idea of art is manifested in 'the flawless beauty and perfect form of its expression'.[27] Since the merging of form and content is most pure in music, that must be seen as the artistic ideal *par excellence*. Next to the creative artist, the critic has nothing but a mediatory role:

The true critic addresses not the artist ever, but the public only; his work lies with it. Art can never have any other claim but her own perfection; it is for the critic to create for art the social aim too, by teaching the people the spirit in which they are to give it, the lesson they are to draw from it.[28]

What can the American addressees of this lecture learn from the English Renaissance? First and foremost, an enhanced sensitivity to everything beautiful, and the importance of beauty for the aesthetic structuring of the domestic and professional environment. Again he stresses that 'Art can never have any other claim but her own perfection',[29] and he goes on to celebrate its moral power, which sets the 'facts of common life'[30] in a new order:

let it be for you to create an art that is made by the hands of the people for the joy of the people too, an art that will be an expression of the loveliness and the joy of life and nature. There is nothing in common life too mean, in common things too trivial to be ennobled by your touch, nothing in life that art cannot sanctify.[31]

Furthermore, he claims that art is a force for peace, which by creating an atmosphere of spiritual community helps to strengthen brotherly ties between nations. 'We spend our days, each one of us, in looking for the secret of life. Well, the secret of life is in art.'[32]

Much of what Wilde said in his first lecture is repeated in his second, 'The Decorative Arts', the early and late versions of which differ in several areas. We shall refer to both in order to elucidate the subject-matter. Compared with 'The English Renaissance' the emphasis has shifted from the discussion of general aesthetic problems to the possibility of practical art and the importance of art in everyday life. More and more the 28-year-old Oxford graduate assumes the role of aesthetic judge and prophet, posing as the experienced connoisseur and in a tone of missionary zeal bombarding his audience with the gospel of beauty and its function in the lives of every one of them. With the same astonishing self-assurance and indeed impertinence as had accompanied his appointment of himself as 'Professor of Aesthetics and Art Critic' on the completion of his studies, Wilde now designated himself as founder of the Aesthetic Movement, even though nearly all his ideas stemmed from the men whose words he had heard or read just four years previously in Oxford. In American life he finds much that offends his personal taste. He is revolted by the flimsy, mass-produced furniture – 'not even honestly joined, but simply glued'[33] – the badly woven and dyed carpets, and the incomparably ugly cast-iron stoves that disfigured so many American homes. The cause of this poor quality and taste lies partly in the Americans' contempt for manual labour, and partly in the ever-increasing ugliness of the environment, which no longer inspires the craftsman with ideas for his work. Wilde's advice, though, is to seek themes, not in distant lands and times, but in the familiar world: 'find your subjects in everyday life'.[34] Can artistic inspiration be found in the desolation of the modern town, with its uniform, unimaginative architecture, its gaudy advertisements stretching out as far as the eye can see, its inhabitants in conventional, mainly dark-coloured clothes? There is only one way to alleviate this misery:

Give ... to your American workmen of today the bright and noble surroundings that you can yourself create. Stately and simple architecture for your city, bright and simple dress for your men and women – those are the conditions of a real artistic movement; for the artist is not concerned primarily with any theory of life but with life itself, with the joy and loveliness that should come daily on eye and ear for a beautiful external world.[35]

Of course the creation of a better environment is not the final solution to the problem. There must be schools of design, and museums where craftsmen can see models of 'what is simple and true and beautiful',[36] like the South Kensington Museum, for instance, in London (now the Victoria and Albert Museum). Even more important than the exhibition of priceless paintings in private galleries is the practical training of the younger generation. For this to come about, every school must contain a workshop where pupils can follow up their interests in the arts and crafts. Is not the finest basis of all education the practice of manual work together with the unfolding of artistic inclinations? By awakening the pupil to the charms of form and colour, one will sharpen his sensitivity to the beauty of nature. Thus aesthetic training is part of religious education, 'for all art is perfect praise of God, the duplication of His handiwork'.[37]

In his first lecture, Wilde set forth the origin and aims of the English Renaissance of art in a general way; in his second, he translated these aesthetic principles into artistic practice; in his third, 'The House Beautiful', which he first gave on 11 March in Chicago, and read for the last time on 14 October in Saint John (New Brunswick), he illustrated his thesis with a concrete example: the design of a house. In his role of the expert, he develops detailed plans relating to the building materials, the façade, interior décor, furniture and colours. For rich people he recommends marble, for the less well-off red brick or wood. As colours for the exterior, white and grey are to be avoided, and replaced by brown or olive-green. Particular attention must be paid to the colour harmony of the rooms. The best example of a successful colour composition is Whistler's famous 'Peacock Room'. Ceilings can be decorated with stucco or wood panelling, flower motifs or other 'pleasing designs'[38] are recommended for the walls, and parquet flooring with bridges of carpet is especially effective. Solid Queen Anne furniture and tasteful embroidery on cushions and curtains complete the pleasant décor of this House Beautiful, whose occupants will wear colourful clothes which follow the natural lines of the body. Taboo are artificial flowers, prints on the walls, doorknobs of lead in place of brass, and stuffed animals in the hall 'or anything else under glass cases'.[39]

Anyone familiar with the Victorian concept of art and with the Arts and Crafts movement will find little new in these ideas. Indeed they are not much more than a mixture of Pater, Ruskin and Morris, with an occasional dash of Swinburne and Matthew Arnold. One can frequently find turns of phrase, sentences or even whole paragraphs lifted straight from these writers. For instance, the opening two paragraphs of 'The English Renaissance', in which Wilde renounces any abstract definition of art and offers a brief survey of the aims of the movement, hark back to well-known passages in the preface to Walter Pater's *Studies in the History of the Renaissance* (1873). Other favourite Pater sources for Wilde to draw on are the 'Conclusion' to *Renaissance* and the essay, 'The School of Giorgione' (1877). More surprising than this uninhibited borrowing from his Oxford teacher, however, are the numerous debts to Ruskin and Morris. O'Brien points out in his introduction that one long passage in 'The English Renaissance', about two pages in all, is taken word for word from Ruskin's lecture, 'Modern Manufacture and Design' (1859).[40] 'The House Beautiful' (a title directly from Pater's *Appreciations*) is a distinctly audible echo of Morris's talk, 'Making the Best of it' (circa 1879) from *Hopes and Fears for Art*. However, it is not our task to delve into all the origins of Wilde's work; this must be left for a critical edition – for which indeed there is an urgent need. It must suffice to offer a single example of the way and the degree in which Wilde borrowed his material. There is a paragraph we have already quoted from 'The English Renaissance' where he has cobbled together ideas and phrases from at least three different sources: Ruskin's 'Modern Manufacture and Design' (1859), *Influence of Imagination in Architecture* (1857), and Morris's *The Beauty of Life* (1880):

Wilde	Ruskin/Morris
The steel of Toledo and the silk of Genoa did but give strength to oppression and add lustre to pride; let it be for you to create an art that is made by the hands of the people for the joy of the people too, an art that will be an expression of the loveliness and the joy of life and nature. There is nothing in common life too mean, in common things too trivial to be ennobled by your touch, nothing in life that art cannot sanctify.[41]	The steel of Toledo and the silk of Genoa did but give strength to oppression and lustre to pride ...[42] an art *made by the people for the people as a joy for the maker and the user*[43] ... Is there anything in common life too mean, – in common things too trivial, – to be ennobled by your touch?[44]

Even if one may presuppose that Wilde's purpose in giving these lectures was, apart from the financial side, to expound the programme of the Aesthetic Movement to the American public – and also to counteract the parody made of it in *Patience* (1881) – the extent of such 'borrowings' makes the omission of attributions inexcusable. Listeners could not possibly escape the impression that these ideas and fine expressions were the speaker's own. And indeed Wilde himself deliberately gave them to understand that he had founded this movement, whose programme he was now so eloquently propounding. This was not a matter of vague hints, for in all seriousness he begins one paragraph with the sentence: 'Let me tell you how it first came to me at all to create an artistic movement in England.'[45] He goes on to recount the well-known story of how he, Ruskin and others worked for two months building a road through marshland between Upper and Lower Hinksey: 'road making for the sake of a noble ideal of life'.[46] One reason for this fraudulent self-aggrandisement may lie in the conflicting roles forced on Wilde by the unexpected invitation to America. The public expected him to be an authority on matters of art and taste, 'Prophet and Pioneer',[47] the official representative of England's Aesthetic Movement, even though his literary activity up to that time could make him no more than its somewhat eccentric mouthpiece. After all, apart from one volume of poems, somewhat negatively received, and an unsuccessful play, he had published nothing that could remotely qualify him for the task now imposed on him by this tour. And as in the *Poems* and *Vera*, he is still unable to speak with a voice of his own but remains fully under the influence of his mentors. Once more it is this dependence of his early work on numerous literary predecessors that has resulted in the image of Wilde the Imitator – an image drawn by many critics and still not without its effect even today.

If one places Wilde's early aesthetics – in so far as this conglomerate of Pater, Ruskin, Morris and Swinburne can be called Wilde's – in the context of his later ideas, what is astonishing is the engagement with which he embraced the moral, social and even religious function of art, and the zeal with which he tried to win over the public. The task of art is not merely to make man's environment more beautiful, 'to make life more joyous',[48] but it is seen as a force to strengthen the brotherhood of man. One can scarcely believe one's eyes when reading that 'all art is perfect praise of God, the duplication of His handiwork'.[49] Can this really be Oscar Wilde? On the other hand, there are moments, particularly in 'The English Renaissance', when the outlines of the aesthetic programme underlying *Intentions* are clearly to be seen. For instance, he echoes Swinburne in designating 'the law of form or harmony'[50] as the only law, 'perfection'[51] is the sole aim of art, and we are called upon to 'Love art for its own sake'.[52] It is self-evident that such formalistic maxims are in direct contradiction to any concept that fuses art and life together. Wilde here falls victim to his own uncritical appropriation of heterogeneous ideas, culled from irreconcilable aesthetic systems and unthinkingly lumped together as if they were in unison. Indeed, how could one possibly combine Swinburne and Pater's ideas with those of Ruskin and Morris and not bring about a clash? Thus these epigonic lectures are full of inconsistencies and contradictions, and conformity triumphs over the qualities of originality and iconoclasm that are characteristic of Wilde's later critical thinking.

Departure from Ruskin in 'L'Envoi' and 'Lecture to Art Students'

There is reason to suppose that Wilde did not identify himself fully with all the ideas expressed in his American lectures. On 19 (?) February 1882, just over a month after his debut at Chickering Hall, New York, he sent a volume of poems by his Oxford friend James Rennell Rodd, with a lengthy introduction by himself, to the publisher J. M. Stoddart. The poems had already been published in England in 1881 under the title *Songs in the South*, and now with a few minor alterations, and some rather strange typography and design, they appeared as *Rose Leaf and Apple Leaf*. What is especially interesting is Wilde's introduction, 'L'Envoi', which he announced to Stoddart with the following statement: 'The preface you will see is most important, signifying my new departure from Mr. Ruskin and the Pre-Raphaelites, and marks an era in the aesthetic movement.'[53] If this pronouncement is to be taken seriously, it certainly had remarkably little effect on Wilde himself, as far as the appropriation of Ruskin's ideas for the lectures was concerned. But however one might interpret this discrepancy, it is clear where Wilde's real sympathies lay at this time. His championship of the moral, social and religious function of art is to be taken with a large pinch of salt. Set against the ideas so brilliantly and enthusiastically advocated in 'L'Envoi', the ideas put forward in the lectures are mere lip-service to other people's opinions.

What form does this departure from Ruskin take?

Now, this increased sense of the absolutely satisfying value of beautiful workmanship, this recognition of the primary importance of the sensuous element in art, this love of art for art's sake, is the point in which we of the younger school have made a departure from the teaching of Mr. Ruskin, – a departure definite and different and decisive.[54]

The two basic changes, then, to the Ruskin ideal of art lie in the absolute value of 'beautiful workmanship' and the 'primary importance of the sensuous element'. The former takes precedence over the subject-matter, and the latter takes precedence over the ideas. Such a view is indeed diametrically opposed to that of Ruskin, but to gain a full understanding of the differences between these two theories, which in themselves are representative of the two diverging approaches to art in the nineteenth century, we must first take a closer look at Ruskin's aesthetics.[55] A brief résumé is no easy task, if one bears in mind that his writings fill no less than thirty-nine thick volumes, each with its fair share of emotional, heterogeneous, dogmatic and inconsistent likes and dislikes. Ruskin stood in the philosophical tradition of Wordsworth and Carlyle. Unlike adherents of the Aesthetic Movement, he maintained an image of man and society that integrated the aesthetic into the moral and religious world order. This is the cardinal point of difference between him and Wilde, together with the other *décadents* of the late nineteenth century. For Ruskin, the artist was not an outsider seeking an elite status on the fringes of society by means of his autonomous art, but he was a responsible member of the community, making his contribution to it by means of his talent and the tools of his trade. Art must not be the privilege of a particular class, but is a social and national necessity.

The artist's first task is to teach people to see, to free them from the automatism of conventional perception, and to make them sensitive to the beauty of things. Since Ruskin interprets the universe as the physical manifestation of a divine presence, perception of beauty is akin to perception of God, and so visual sensitisation serves to heighten awareness of the moral and religious nature of man. Thus in the preface to the second edition of Volume I of his *Modern Painters* (1844) he defines his aim as:

to exhibit the moral function and end of art; to prove the share which it ought to have in the thoughts, and influence on the lives, of all of us; to attach to the artist the responsibility of a preacher, and to kindle in the general mind that regard which such an office must demand.[56]

The word 'moral', which vies with 'noble' as Ruskin's favourite epithet, requires definition. It is by no means to be identified simply with the ability to distinguish between good and bad, right and wrong, but denotes first and foremost man's emotional sensitivity. Following the lines laid down by Adam Smith's *Theory of the Moral Sentiments* (1759), Ruskin was convinced that moral attitudes and decisions were determined by feeling and not by intellect. 'All true and deep emotion',[57] however, contains an imaginative quality, and this is one of the reasons why imagination is the greatest cognitive and creative force:

Now, observe, while, as it penetrates into the nature of things, the imagination is pre-eminently a beholder of things, *as* they *are*, it is, in its creative function, an eminent beholder of things *when* and *where* they are N O T; a seer, that is, in the prophetic sense, calling 'the things that are not as though they were', and for ever delighting to dwell on that which is not tangibly present.[58]

Imagination enables the artist not only to penetrate to the truth of things, but also to create things which are not present, and to make them real. Shakespeare delivers the message even more succinctly:

And, as imagination bodies forth
The forms of things unknown, the poet's pen
Turns them to shapes, and gives to airy nothing
A local habitation and a name.[59]

Just as it is impossible to separate the imagination from the overall sensitivity of man, so too is it impossible to isolate man's perception of beauty as a single faculty. And so it cannot be called merely 'aesthetic', since this would confine the effect of beauty to a mere titillation of the senses. Hence Ruskin introduces the concept of a 'theoretic faculty', which concerns itself with the 'moral perception and appreciation of ideas of beauty'.[60] The impressions made by beauty on the observer are neither sensual nor intellectual, but 'moral'.

Art for Ruskin is the expression of man's moral sensitivity, and so on a political and social level it denotes the moral health of a nation. In *The Stones of Venice* (1851–53), the chapter entitled 'The Nature of Gothic' takes Venice and its decline as an example of the link between political and artistic decadence. When Venice was flourishing, its art was predominantly Gothic – which for Ruskin reflected the medieval cultural integration of faith, life and artistic form. The decline took place during the Renaissance, when art became aristocratic, that is to say un-Christian, alienated from the common people in its cold and luxurious élitism, and through its quest for formal perfection distancing itself from nature and life. If this idea of a link between art and social life is pursued to its logical conclusion, it is inevitable that eventually the art critic should himself become a social reformer, and indeed in *The Seven Lamps of Architecture* (1849), Ruskin had already shown his awareness of these implications of his theory. In his discussion of architectonic design he asked: 'Was it done with enjoyment – was the carver happy while he was about it?'[61] Later he was to tackle the problem even more directly in *The Political Economy of Art* (1857). It was not Ruskin, however, who pursued this particular path to its conclusion. That was the task of William Morris, who with enormous zeal applied to himself to investigating the social causes of the cultural crisis.

Morris was a socialist and a communist, while Ruskin was a moralist. Of course there are passages in Ruskin's work where he links the quality of a picture to the number of 'noble ideas' it contains. Thus Wilde's remark in 'L'Envoi' that: 'He [Ruskin] would judge of a picture by the amount of noble moral ideas it expresses'[62] could be supported, for instance, by a passage in the first volume of *Modern Painters* (1843):

The picture which has the nobler and more numerous ideas, however awkwardly expressed, is a greater and a better picture than that which has the less noble and less numerous ideas, however beautifully expressed. No weight, nor mass nor beauty of execution, can outweigh one grain or fragment of thought.[63]

But Wilde's account of Ruskin's position is an unfair foreshortening of his ideas. The Oxford Slade Professor of Fine Art was certainly not as narrow-minded as this one-sided, dogmatic insistence on noble subject-matter might imply. It is true that he never equated art with form but always demanded that it have an educational aim; however, he was at pains to point out that this aim was not necessarily conscious on the part of the artist. As he says of Homer's epics: 'they are not conceived didactically, but are didactic in their essence, as all good art is'.[64] The influence on the observer or reader occurs – for instance, with *The Iliad* – 'indirectly and occultly'.[65] His views on this question tend to fluctuate, and perhaps their clearest expression is to be found in a passage from *The Stones of Venice*, which is well worth quoting in full:

Now it is well, when we have strong moral or poetical feeling manifested in painting, to mark this as the best part of the work; but it is not well to consider as a thing of small account, the painter's language in which that feeling is conveyed; for if that language be not good and lovely, the man may indeed be a just moralist or a great poet, but he is not a *painter*, and it was wrong of him to paint. He had much better have put his morality into sermons, and his poetry into verse, than into a language of which he was not master . . . On the other hand, if the man be a painter indeed, and have the gift of colours and lines, what is in him will come from his hand freely and faithfully; and the language itself is so difficult and so vast, that the mere possession of it argues the man is great, and that his works are worth reading. So that I have never yet seen the case in which this true artistical excellence, visible by the eye-glance, was not the index of some true expressional worth in the work. Neither have I ever seen a good expressional work without high artistical merit: and that this is ever denied is only owing to the narrow view which men are apt to take both of expression and of art; a narrowness consequent on their own especial practice and habits of thought.[66]

Wilde's rejection of Ruskin's position takes no account of this passage, in which the problem of form and content is discussed in a far more balanced way than in the above-mentioned passage from *Modern Painters*, which certainly does devalue 'beauty of execution'. It is the earlier, already superseded ideas of Ruskin that Wilde attacks when he puts forward as a precondition for all art 'this increased sense of the absolutely satisfying value of beautiful workmanship'.[67] However, where he does depart fundamentally from Ruskin is in his interpretation of 'personality' and 'perfection', which for him denote the unmistakable individuality of art and its quest for perfection. In *The Nature of Gothic*, Ruskin stresses the very imperfection of Gothic art as a positive feature, putting forward the somewhat paradoxical claim that: 'no good work whatever can be perfect, and *the demand for perfection is always a sign of a misunderstanding of the ends of art*'.[68] This mistrust of perfection in art applies equally to the person of the artist himself:

in the higher or expressive part of the work, the whole virtue of it depends on his [the artist's] being able to quit his own personality, and enter successively into the hearts and thoughts of each person.[69]

It is clear from these two statements that the distance between Ruskin and Wilde could hardly have been greater.

Wilde's somewhat theatrical announcement to the world that he was making a 'departure from the teaching of Mr Ruskin' runs parallel to his adherence to Whistler at this time. The ideas of the controversial American painter, who spent most of his time in London and Paris, represent an extreme position in the Aesthetic Movement. They are in direct contrast to Ruskin's theories, and indeed in 1878 he actually filed a suit against Ruskin because the latter had dared to suggest in *Fors Clavigera* (1871–84), with reference to the exhibition of one of his pictures, that he demanded two hundred guineas 'for flinging a pot of paint in the public's face'.[70] Ruskin's irritation was caused by an ideal of art that Whistler later outlined in his *Ten O'Clock Lecture* (1885). This can be briefly summarised as follows: the artist is cut off from society as a 'monument of isolation';[71] art and reality are separate, for each aims only at its own perfection; finally, there is no connection between the subject-matter of a work of art and the harmony of its sound or colour, that is, its means of expression. Even Swinburne and Pater never went this far. Both regarded the unity of form and content as essential, even if they did not always attribute equal value to the two components.

It should not be thought that Whistler's influence on Wilde[72] was such that the latter suddenly adopted all the ideas and insights of a man twenty years his senior. But Whistler was a charismatic figure, and under the impact both of his personality and his artistic flair, Wilde veered away from Pater and Ruskin towards a more autonomous view of aesthetics. His writing was also influenced by the American's use of tone and colour combinations, as is evident from the impressionistic nature of some of the *Poems* (1881). Whistler, however, as egocentric as he was eccentric, and as hurtful as he was easily hurt, seemed to attach little importance to the spiritual affinity between himself and his rival in the art of 'épater le bourgeois' and later, in 1890, he was to write in the magazine *Truth* an article accusing Wilde of plagiarism, with reference to the latter's 'Lecture to Art Students' in 1883. He claimed that during Wilde's preparations, he had crammed him full of ideas 'that he might not add deplorable failure to foolish appearance, in his anomalous position as art expounder'.[73] This nadir in the relationship between two men who were so different in character and temperament, and yet so similar in their talent for wit and self-publicity, had been preceded by a prolonged clash that had enlivened the London cultural scene in the form of a correspondence, often in telegram style, publicly conducted in the columns of reputable journals.[74] What began as witty skirmishes soon took on a sharper personal tone, and Whistler's attacks in particular became increasingly vicious, just as the butterfly which he used to draw as a signature under his utterances gradually came to look more and more like arrows. The battle of wits soon sank to the level of mere insult-trading. Whistler called his former friend the 'fattest of offenders',[75] and Wilde poured scorn on the 'lucubrations of so ill-bred and ignorant a person as Mr Whistler'.[76] Perhaps one of the reasons for this inglorious end to their friendship lay in the fact that Whistler – whose friendships tended to be short-term anyway – found it easier to deal with pupils who called him 'Master' than to come to terms with rivals in the battle for the questionable favours of publicity. By the early 1890s, Wilde was certainly as witty a conversationalist and as charming a *provocateur* as the rather more abrasive painter, although Whistler had greater experience in the *The Gentle Art of Making Enemies*.

The influence of Whistler on Wilde, as evinced in 'L'Envoi' and in the 'Lecture to Art Students', did not, however, result in a consistent theory. The mixture of formal and content-orientated aesthetics leads to an on-going contradiction. In accordance with Whistler, the 'Lecture to Art Students' calls the artist 'an exquisite exception',[77] defines universality as the true quality of art, and seeks nothing more from a picture than 'a beautifully coloured surface';[78] and yet at the same time Wilde is proclaiming that: 'Without a beautiful national life, not sculpture merely, but all the arts will die'.[79] This is precisely the position of Ruskin. It is clear from such statements that at this time Wilde was still unable to bring together all the divergent ideas from different sources into a single, homogeneous theory of aesthetics. The concepts accumulate without sufficient thought as to their compatibility, and in particular Wilde seems to vacillate over the problem of the artist's relationship to his surroundings. To the students of the Royal Academy he announced that the artist had no need of 'beautiful surroundings'[80] because his concern was not with objects but with appearances, which were 'a matter of light and shade, of masses, of position, and of value'.[81] And yet in his discussion of Whistler's *Ten O'Clock Lecture*, he maintains:

An artist is not an isolated fact; he is the resultant of a certain *milieu* and a certain *entourage*, and can no more be born of a nation that is devoid of any sense of beauty than a fig can grow from a thorn or a rose blossom from a thistle.[82]

It is not until 'The Decay of Lying' (1889) and 'The Critic as Artist' (1890) that Wilde's aesthetics begins to take on a more consistent form, though even here – as we shall see – it is not possible to talk of a coherent system.

'The Decay of Lying' and the foundations of Wilde's aesthetics[83]

The essay is written in the form of a dialogue between Vivian and Cyril – the names, incidentally, of Wilde's two sons. Vivian has written an article about lying in art, and reads parts of it to Cyril, whose generally short interpolations are little more than indications of his own views, and cues for Vivian to set out his ideas in great detail. There is no question here of equal partners, and the dialogue form is a mere pretence at intellectual intercourse; in reality the speeches are monologues that expound the various topics. Nevertheless, the dialogue form does endow this essay, and also 'The Critic as Artist', with a certain dramatic dynamism. If one compares them both with the art criticism of Arnold or Ruskin, each of whom offers ready-made conclusions in a single 'reliable' voice, one must admit that Wilde avoids giving the impression of a narrow finality simply by showing how his insights develop; the rigidity of the theoretical tract is thereby softened, allowing a certain flexibility and openness to the positions represented. This was precisely Wilde's purpose, as he later explained in 'The Critic as Artist', for the dialogue enabled him to 'both reveal and conceal himself'.[84] Furthermore, it was a form that gratified his penchant for conversation and for paradox.

In analysing this essay, we shall be concerned not with following the sequence of the ideas, for this would simply entail repeating Wilde's ideas in their somewhat arbitrary order, but with examining the central theme – the relation between art and reality – with additional reference to other writings in so far as they shed light on the problem, illuminating areas which are not made sufficiently clear in the dialogue itself. This does not mean, however, that we shall finish up with a clear and coherent aesthetic system. The concept of a complete abstract philosophy of art would have been alien to Wilde's own artistic temperament, and it was not by chance that he entitled his collected aesthetic writings *Intentions*. Nor does it mean that we shall be confronted by a disconnected conglomerate of heterogeneous ideas and witty *aperçus*. Despite Wilde's love of the epigrammatic generalisation, the pithy witticism, the paradoxical reversal of current opinions, there are serious undertones that are as accessible to analysis as the apparently so unworldly farce of *The Importance of Being Earnest*, and while it is always difficult to separate the *poseur* from the critic, the latter must not be ignored because of the clowning of the former; to do so would be to assume that precise role of the philistine that Wilde was at such pains to attack.[85] Our task will be to extract the aesthetic substance, but not to impose a system on what Wilde never intended to systematise.

The provocation begins already with the title, which promises a treatise on the (highly desirable) disappearance of lies, whereas in fact the subsequent dialogue deals with the artist's relation to nature and life. A moral concept is given a totally new meaning in a totally new, aesthetic context, and what is morally obnoxious (lying) now constitutes the actual domain of art: 'the telling of beautiful untrue things'.[86] The title actually refers to the decline of the creative, non-mimetic imagination that forms the basis of artistic creation, and the increasing and undesirable emergence of naturalism, which was anathema to Wilde. For all the originality of this paradoxical title, though, the questions it raises have their roots deep in antiquity. In Book X of the *Republic*, Plato wrote that 'these poetical individuals, beginning with Homer, are only imitators, they copy images of virtue and the like, but the truth they never reach'.[87] Aristotle invoked Homer, who had 'taught the others the art of framing lies in the right way'.[88] Ovid spoke bluntly of the 'prodigiosa ... veterum mendacia vatum' [false tales of olden bards],[89] and in *Also Sprach Zarathustra* (1883–5) Nietzsche remarked that 'poets lie beyond measure'.[90] Down through the ages, poetic creation has been viewed as incompatible with truth, although there has never been a lack of effort to link beauty and truth and to stress the cognitive function of poetry.

Wilde's view of the artist as the 'creator of beautiful things'[91] and the task of art as 'the telling of beautiful untrue things'[92] shows clearly how far apart he was from Keats and many Victorians. It is not a view that eliminates the concept of truth, but one that radically subjectifies it, separating it from all objective references. Statement and object, idea and reality no longer correspond, no matter how complex and differentiated their relation might be in art. Truth has become 'a matter of style'[93] and exists independently of the factual world:

Truth in art is not any correspondence between the essential idea and the accidental existence; it is not the resemblance of shape to shadow, or of the form mirrored in the crystal to the form itself: it is no Echo coming from a hollow hill, any more than it is the well of silver water in the valley that shows the Moon to the Moon and Narcissus to Narcissus. Truth in Art is the unity of a thing with itself: the outward rendered expressive of the inward: the soul made incarnate: the body instinct with the spirit.[94]

This is a definition reminiscent of Pater's essay on style, in which poetry is described as 'the finer accommodation of speech to that vision within'.[95] Such a function relieves the concept of truth from any objective reference, and reduces it to being the expression of the individual's inner self. Without its obligation to maintain contact between word and reality, truth becomes 'partly a subjective attitude of mind'.[96]

The release of truth from reality, and its transformation into an autonomous entity bound only to the subjective self and its feelings, inevitably goes hand in hand with the attempt to separate art from nature and life. Vivian, Wilde's *alter ego* in 'The Decay of Lying', has long since lost the ability to enjoy nature, and he believes that the more concerned one is with art, the less interested one is in nature. The deficiencies of nature are all too obvious: – '[her] lack of design, her curious crudities, her extraordinary monotony, her absolutely unfinished condition'.[97] All of which is in stark contrast to art. Furthermore, nature is indifferent to man's need for communication – or even worse than indifferent: 'Nature hates Mind.'[98] If nature is seen as 'natural simple instinct'[99] in contrast to 'self-conscious culture',[100] the works resulting from such a view will always remain behind the times in which they are created. If nature is taken to be a 'collection of phenomena external to man',[101] one will only be able to extract so much from it as one has earlier put into it. What the individual sees, and how he sees it, will depend on the arts to whose influence he has been exposed. 'At present, people see fogs, not because there are fogs, but because poets and painters have taught them the mysterious loveliness of such effects.'[102] Thus Vivian can draw the paradoxical conclusion that nature imitates art.

It is evident that Vivian's ideas reflect Wilde's attempt once and for all to destroy the romantic concept of nature as the object and criterion for the truthfulness of art. However, his polemic foreshortening and distortion of the term 'nature' as meaning 'instinct' or 'collection of phenomena external to man' is far from the romantic concept. As was pointed out by J. W. Beach in his admirable *The Concept of Nature in the Nineteenth Century* (1936), this developed from a synthesis of scientific and religious ideas. The conformity, harmony, and functionalism of natural processes were seen as the universal workings of a benevolent divine providence, whose spiritual power guaranteed the unity and order of the cosmos. This concept of a harmonising, intelligible spirit unifying all parts of animate and inanimate nature led to the conviction that there must be an affinity between man, as a rational being, and the hidden spirit itself. Thus Wordsworth, in his Preface to the philosophical poem *The Excursion* (1814), spoke of the 'individual Mind' adjusting to the 'external World',[103] a formula to which Vivian's 'Nature hates Mind' seems to be a direct riposte. Like Wordsworth, Coleridge – following on from Schelling's equation of subject with object – identified the 'productive power' at work in nature with the 'intelligence, which is in the human mind above nature'.[104] This identification of man's spirit with that of nature presupposed a metaphysical, cosmological order linking God, man and nature. It was an order that was undermined and finally shattered by post-romantic generations, not least by way of Darwin's theory of evolution. In the history of aesthetic theory, Wilde was by no means the first to launch himself against nature. Baudelaire had called it 'laide' and replaced it with his 'paradis artificiels' preferring 'les monstres de ma fantaisie à la trivialité positive'.[105] The *fin de siècle* attitude towards nature was indeed summed up by Esseintes in Huysmans's *A rebours* (1884): 'la nature a fait son temps'.[106] With the fantastic, dreamlike images of the symbolists, and the androgynous figures created by Beardsley and Burne-Jones, art had finally established itself as a self-sufficient counter to nature.

Parallel to the destruction of nature is Wilde's rejection of the real world as a subject worthy of imitation by art.

VIVIAN (*reading*): 'Art begins with abstract decoration, with purely imaginative and pleasurable work dealing with what is unreal and non-existent. This is the first stage. Then Life becomes fascinated with this new wonder, and asks to be admitted into the charmed circle. Art takes life as part of her rough material, recreates it, and refashions it in fresh forms, is absolutely indifferent to fact, invents, imagines, dreams, and keeps between herself and reality the impenetrable barrier of beautiful style, of decorative or ideal treatment. The third stage is when Life gets the upper hand, and drives Art out into the wilderness. This is the true decadence, and it is from this that we are now suffering.'[107]

The three stages of art history described in this passage correspond to three different types of art measured by their varying proximity to life. Their sequence, which is by no means coincidental, contains a scale of values which Wilde the critic employed again and again. In the light of the above passage and pronouncements in other essays, the three types may be identified as 'decorative art', 'imaginative art' and 'realism'. Wilde's sympathies belong undoubtedly to decorative art, for that is the furthest removed from empirical reality. In 'The Critic as Artist' he states this preference explicitly and justifies it:

Still, the art that is frankly decorative is the art to live with. It is, of all our visible arts, the one art that creates in us both mood and temperament. Mere colour, unspoiled by meaning, and unallied with definite form, can speak to the soul in a thousand different ways ... By its deliberate rejection of Nature as the ideal of beauty, as well as of the imitative method of the ordinary painter, decorative art not merely prepares the soul for the reception of true imaginative work, but develops in it that sense of form which is the basis of creative no less than of critical achievement. For the real artist is he who proceeds, not from feeling to form, but from form to thought and passion ... A real passion would ruin him.[108]

Decorative art is indifferent to reality, whereas imaginative art transforms the raw material of real life into new forms and designs which again distance it from reality. This transformation of given material into 'artistic conventions'[109] is the task of the artist. Decadence sets in when reality takes over from the imagination, the resultant 'realism' constituting the third and despised stage of the historical process as Wilde sees it. He takes the history of the English drama as an illustration of his thesis: in its medieval beginnings, the drama was 'abstract, decorative and mythological',[110] with Shakespeare it developed into the perfect expression of an imaginative view of reality, and in the nineteenth-century melodrama it degenerated into a superficial reproduction of social life. The history of the novel also seems to him to reveal nothing but 'our monstrous worship of facts'.[111] He is particularly scathing about the work of Zola, which is 'entirely wrong from beginning to end'.[112] The difference between a book like Zola's *L'Assommoir* (1877) and Balzac's *Illusions perdues* (1837–44) is that between 'unimaginative realism' and 'imaginative reality'.[113]

In his polemic against artists who devote themselves neither to decorative nor to imaginative art, Wilde employs a grossly simplified concept of realism akin to what he calls in the *Reviews* 'literary photography'.[114] Could anyone seriously deny that even in the novels and stories of Zola and Maupassant, the 'slice of life' has been translated into the conventions of literary representation?

The preference for the imaginative artist rather than the realist brings to mind Baudelaire's distinction between the 'réaliste', whom he prefers to call 'positiviste', and 'l'imaginatif'. The former says of himself: 'Je veux représenter les choses telles qu'elles sont, ou bien qu'elles seraient, en supposant que je n'existe pas' [I want to represent things as they are, or rather as they would be, supposing that I did not exist], while the latter announces that: 'Je veux illuminer les choses avec mon esprit et en projeter le reflet sur les autres esprits' [I want to illuminate things with my spirit and project the reflection onto other spirits].[115] Wilde would also have been well aware of Pater's definition of 'imaginative literature' as 'this transcript, not of mere fact, but of fact in its infinite variety, as modified by human preference in all its infinitely varied forms'.[116]

In terms of literary history, the rejection of real life as the object of art makes a frontal attack on the concepts of romanticism and the Victorian age. In his preface to the second edition of the *Lyrical Ballads* (1800), Wordsworth indicated that the subject-matter of his poems was 'incidents and situations from common life'.[117] Matthew Arnold, in his essay on Wordsworth, considered the latter to be superior to Burns, Keats and Heine because: 'he deals more of *life* than they do'.[118] The term 'life' together with the question 'How to live?' was, of course, central to Arnold's critical writing: 'poetry is at bottom a criticism of life ... the greatness of a poet lies in his powerful and beautiful application of ideas to life'.[119] Poetry for him was a comforting interpretation of life, even to the extent that it could replace religion and philosophy. Poetry, as an alternative to the rational ideals of a scientific and technical view of the world, must act as a counter to these forces that were endangering and confining the imagination as well as destroying the feelings that were so vital an element of man's sensitivity. Hence the withdrawal into the private world, the path into Pater's 'narrow chamber of the individual mind'.[120] Wilde logically builds on his Oxford teacher's solipsism – 'each mind keeping as a solitary prisoner its own dream of a world'[121] – as a foundation for his aesthetic theory. Art, as he sees it, is a monad, a windowless edifice from which knowledge of life is neither accessible nor desirable. The world transforms itself into an aesthetic construct of our will and our imagination.

Things are because we see them, and what we see, and how we see it, depends on the Arts that have influenced us. To look at a thing is very different from seeing a thing. One does not see anything until one sees its beauty. Then, and then only, does it come into existence.[122]

In 'The Critic as Artist', Wilde goes into greater detail concerning the superiority of art over life, describing the relationship as follows:

GILBERT: ... Life! Life! Don't let us go to life for our fulfilment or our experience. It is a thing narrowed by circumstances, incoherent in its utterance, and without that fine correspondence of form and spirit which is the only thing that can satisfy the artistic and critical temperament. It makes us pay too high a price for its wares, and we purchase the meanest of its secrets at a cost that is monstrous and infinite.
ERNEST: Must we go, then, to Art for everything?
GILBERT: For everything. Because Art does not hurt us. The tears that we shed at a play are a type of exquisite sterile emotions that it is the function of Art to awaken. We weep, but we are not wounded ... It is through Art, and through Art

only, that we can realise our perfection; through Art, and through Art only, that we can shield ourselves from the sordid perils of actual existence.[123]

For the aesthete, life is 'narrowed by circumstances' and, as Gilbert says elsewhere, 'deficient in form'.[124] A past passion is like a dream, all that one once believed it seems incredible, and no emotion is exactly repeatable. Life means to act, but every action is guided by chance and is, in essence, incomplete, 'a blind thing dependent on external influences, and moved by an impulse of whose nature it is unconscious'.[125] Furthermore, action means decision, engagement, and to a degree loss of liberty. By contrast, art is the domain of freedom, since the emotions aroused are 'sterile'[126] and so require no subsequent action. Indeed, the reader or observer can actually choose the time at which he undergoes particular experiences or subjects himself to the moods of his choice: he may wander with Vergil through Purgatory, or live through the adventures of Manon Lescaut at will. He enjoys feelings that lead to no consequences. The aesthetic existence is an ersatz existence of unlimited freedom and potential. But of course this mode of being suffers from one fundamental drawback: it is not practicable. The practical end of such attempts to replace moral behaviour with aesthetic is nowhere more vividly depicted than in *The Picture of Dorian Gray*. And the biography of the poet, 'der ein Kunstwerk war',[127] ends with a tragic dénouement in which there is ironic confirmation of the paradoxical premise that life imitates art.

Anyone who regards life as superior to art will seek to stylise life into art, so that indeed the former will be nothing but an imitation of the latter. Thus Vivian argues in 'The Decay of Lying' that there is a particular type of feminine beauty – the woman with the long flowing hair, the ivory neck and the 'mystic eyes'[128] – who was only perceived after Rossetti had created her in his pictures. The Luciens de Rubempré and the Rastignacs of the world made their first appearance in the novels of Balzac, that is, on the stage of the *Comédie humaine*. People committed suicide because Rolla and Werther had shown them the way. This reversal of the traditional concept of art imitating life may seem paradoxical, but in the context of Wilde's aesthetic, solipsistic theory of cognition it is not illogical. If phenomena only exist because we see them, and if the object of our perception and the manner of our perceiving are dependent on the arts that have influenced us, then it follows that certain people and situations in life will seem like pure imitations of the artistic works we have experienced.

The loss of 'nature' and 'life' as criteria by which to judge works of art was bound to affect the manner in which the critic judged the work's internal relationship of form to content. The inseparability and interdependence of the two components had never been doubted by the

Victorians; the only differences of opinion concerned the balance between them and the degree to which each contributed to the quality of the work. Matthew Arnold's concept of 'criticism of life' as the main task of poetry was linked to the conditions of 'poetic truth' and 'poetic beauty', and these found expression in 'Truth and seriousness of substance and matter, felicity and perfection of diction and manner'.[129] Although Ruskin had no equal among Victorian critics in his condemnation of mere decoration, and stressed the vital importance of content, even he – as we have already seen in the passage quoted from *The Stones of Venice* (1851–3) – had 'never yet seen the case in which this true artistical excellence ... was not the index of some true expressional worth'.[130] Swinburne and Pater, whose concepts of art come nearest to pure aestheticism, were by no means in agreement on this question. It is true that Swinburne, in his book *William Blake* (1868), was still advocating unmodified formalism, but not long afterwards, no doubt under the influence of Victor Hugo and the Italian liberation movement led by Mazzini, he qualified this one-sided concept as follows: 'we refuse to admit that art of the highest kind may not ally itself with moral or religious passion, with the ethics or the politics of a nation or an age'.[131] Much clearer than this somewhat roundabout retraction of Swinburne's is Pater's later withdrawal of his defence of form in his early writings. In the Winckelmann essay of 1867 he calls poetry 'all literary production which attains the power of giving pleasure by its form, as distinct from its matter'.[132] And in 'The School of Giorgione' (1877), when he claims that all art seeks to emulate music because music achieves the perfect combination of form and content, he goes on to state 'that this form, this mode of handling should become an end in itself, should penetrate every part of the matter: this is what all art constantly strives after, and achieves in different degrees'.[133] Only in his later essay on style (1888), when distinguishing 'good art' from 'great art', does he modify this stance in a quite striking manner; he sets Thackeray's *Henry Esmond* above *Vanity Fair* on the grounds of its 'greater dignity of ... interests'.[134] By way of explanation, he then adds:

It is on the quality of the matter it informs or controls, its compass, its variety, its alliance to great ends, or the depth of the note of revolt, or the largeness of hope in it, that the greatness of literary art depends.[135]

There are no such statements to be found in Wilde. And yet his own presentation of this problem of form and content is marked by a similar vacillation between a formalistic approach, something along the lines of 'l'art pour l'art', and recognition of the need for the two components to be properly balanced. In *The Soul of Man under Socialism* he deals directly with this question:

All terms that one applies to a work of art, provided that one applies them rationally, have reference to either its style or its subject, or to both together. From the point of view of style, a healthy work of art is one whose style recognises the beauty of the material it employs, be that material one of words or of bronze, of colour or of ivory, and uses that beauty as a factor in producing the aesthetic effect. From the point of view of subject, a healthy work of art is one the choice of whose subject is conditioned by the temperament of the artist, and comes directly out of it. In fine, a healthy work of art is one that has both perfection and personality. Of course, form and substance cannot be separated in a work of art; they are always one.[136]

Even here, though, it is characteristic of Wilde that the function of style is made clear (to bring out the beauty and so produce the aesthetic effect), whereas that of the subject remains extremely vague. What may also be of incidental interest in this passage is his use of the word 'healthy'. Wilde was dealing here with 'art-abuse',[137] discussing terms which were fresh in his memory following the controversy over *Dorian Gray*. In addition to 'unhealthy', he also tackles such epithets as 'immoral', 'unintelligible', 'exotic' and 'morbid'.

The fact that Wilde recognises the inseparability of form and content does not, of course, mean that he regarded them as being of equal value. From his earliest writings onwards, he always gave precedence to form, sometimes to such a degree that his aesthetics verges on pure formalism. In his lecture on 'The English Renaissance', he follows Swinburne with the dogmatic assertion that 'art has only one sentence to utter, there is for her only one high law – the law of form or harmony'.[138] Gilbert, his mouthpiece in 'The Critic as Artist', indicates – as we have already seen – that form is the artist's starting-point and source of inspiration: 'For the real artist is he who proceeds, not from feeling to form, but from form to thought and passion'[139] – a claim which, in terms of literary history, may be said to trace the development of romantic aesthetics right up to Poe's 'Philosophy of Composition' (1846). A little later there follows a rapturous eulogy of form:

Form is everything. It is the secret of life ... it is Form that creates not merely the critical temperament, but also the aesthetic instinct, that unerring instinct that reveals to one all things under their conditions of beauty. Start with the worship of form, and there is no secret in art that will not be revealed to you.[140]

The passages quoted from *The Soul of Man under Socialism* and 'The Decay of Lying' show that Wilde frequently equated form with 'style', which was for him a *conditio sine qua non* of the work of art. Style – by which he means linguistic style – conditions both the origin and the credibility of art; it erects an 'impenetrable barrier'[141] to serve as a 'disjunction between the real world and the world of art'.[142] It is the concrete manifestation of the imaginative transformation wrought by the artist on his material, the linguistic seal of his individuality, the pre-condition for the sought-after 'perfection', and the signature of the 'personality'.

With his anti-realistic, formalistic aesthetics, what exactly was Wilde's attitude towards content in art? As is to be expected, this was the area in which the contradictions and deficiencies of his ideas – which we shall be examining later – were at their most apparent. In the context of the *Dorian Gray* debate, he understandably resists all attempts by critics to restrict the artist's subject-matter: 'To art belong all things that are and all things that are not.'[143] The necessity and indeed the justice of this demand were soon to be shown by the censor's ban on *Salomé*, on the grounds that it was forbidden to portray biblical characters on stage. Wilde's plea for his lifting of all restrictions was in keeping with the views of many Victorian critics, apart from one important aspect: he almost continually avoided giving any close definition of subject-matter, relying simply on vague generalisations. Only in his definition of the second category of art, as we have seen, does he talk of the 'rough material' of reality which art is to transform.

The majority of nineteenth-century critics were rather more precise. Macaulay, in his review of Moore's *Life of Lord Byron* (1830), says that: 'The heart of man is the province of poetry, and of poetry alone'.[144] Similarly, J. S. Mill defines this province as 'human nature, with all its enjoyments and sufferings'.[145] Matthew Arnold, in his preface to the *Poems* (1853) asks 'What are the eternal objects of poetry, among all nations, and at all times?' – to which he answers: 'They are actions; human actions.'[146] Swinburne, too, defines the subject-matter of poetry as 'the full life of man and the whole nature of things'.[147] And finally, for Ruskin the supreme task of art is '*to set before you the true image of the presence of a noble human being*'.[148]

Common to all these pronouncements is the reference to man: art and poetry are concerned with human beings – their thoughts, feelings and actions. Of course, the various critics and poets may not have realised this aim with the same intensity, but in Wilde's theoretical writing there is rarely any reference to 'human nature' or 'human interest'.[149] This does not mean that his tales and poems – for example, *The Ballad of Reading Gaol* – are devoid of human interest, but what is noticeable in his critical work is his indifference to, or positive dislike of anything that can be pinned down as subject-matter. The one exception – quite untypical of all his later work – is the American lectures he gave in his youth, while still under the influence of Ruskin. Here he does appeal to his listeners to 'make the subject of your art all that is noble in men and women'.[150] But this attitude had already changed by the time he was writing reviews for different London magazines. His discussion of the handbook *Dinners and*

Dishes, for instance, written for the *Pall Mall Gazette*, 7 March 1885, stresses the fact that 'The subject of a work of art has, of course, nothing to do with its beauty.'[151] In 'The Decay of Lying', Gilbert says: 'To art's subject-matter we should be more or less indifferent.'[152] Because of their lack of form, their monotony, and their chaotic condition, life and nature are always criticised and rejected as subjects for art.

In connection with this problem of content, a further problem arose which continually brought Wilde into conflict with his critics: the relationship between art and morality. There are two separate aspects here: one might begin by asking whether art should be forced to select and represent its subject-matter with the intention of improving morality and changing society. A more general question must then be whether art should have any didactic purpose whatsoever. Should it take sides in affairs of religion, morality, or politics? If so – and herein lies the second aspect of the problem – by what criteria should the critic evaluate the work of art: religious, moral, political, or aesthetic? Wilde tackled both aspects, most particularly during the public discussion of *Dorian Gray*[153] and in cross-examination during the Queensberry trial.

Just as he separated art from life, and strove to transform reality aesthetically, Wilde also believed 'that the sphere of Art and the sphere of Ethics are absolutely distinct and separate',[154] with the artistic experience – as might be expected – superior to moral conduct. His oft-quoted aphorism 'All art is immoral'[155] should not be regarded as a plea for boundless immorality, but is simply a somewhat provocative and melodramatic use of a term which, in the light of his critical writings, would more accurately have been 'amoral' or 'non-moral'. It was a position that he could not maintain consistently either in his theoretical or his literary work. For instance, in the preface to *Dorian Gray* there are some strangely incoherent ideas that do not seem to fit in comfortably with the separation of art from morality:

The moral life of man forms part of the subject-matter of the artist, but the morality of art consists in the perfect use of an imperfect medium. No artist desires to prove anything ... No artist has ethical sympathies. An ethical sympathy in an artist is an unpardonable mannerism of style.[156]

Here he seems to be caught between the decorative and the imaginative ideals of art, and indeed the contradictions continue in his own comments on *Dorian Gray*. For a man who claimed that all art was immoral, it seems astonishing that he should have confessed in a letter that *Dorian Gray* was 'a story with a moral'.[157] He did, however, remain adamant that books should not be judged according to their morality. During the Queensberry trial, when he was being cross-examined about *Dorian Gray* and another story wrongly attributed to him, called 'The Priest and the Acolyte', he maintained his earlier standpoint, regardless of the pressures of the situation he was in:

[CARSON]: This is in your introduction to *Dorian Gray*: 'There is no such thing as a moral or an immoral book. Books are well written, or badly written.' That expresses your view? –
My view on art, yes.
Then, I take it, that no matter how immoral a book may be, if it is well written, it is, in your opinion, a good book? –
Yes, if it were well written so as to produce a sense of beauty, which is the highest sense of which a human being can be capable. If it were badly written, it would produce a sense of disgust.
Then a well-written book putting forward perverted moral views may be a good book? –
No work of art ever puts forward views. Views belong to people who are not artists.[158]

In order to underline the incompatibility of art with any moral or political intention, Wilde frequently put forward the claim that 'All art is quite useless.'[159] This maxim might also be misunderstood if one were to interpret it in the sense of art having no consequences. In fact it takes up a concept that was central to Victorian middle-class ethics, namely that of 'utility', and renounces it in order to show that art has nothing to do with practical purposes. It does not set out to inspire actions, change opinions, or spread doctrines, but simply delights the observer with its beauty. In a letter to R. Clegg written in April (?) 1891, Wilde talks explicitly about the uselessness of art:

Art is useless because its aim is simply to create a mood. It is not meant to instruct, or to influence action in any way. It is superbly sterile, and the note of its pleasure is sterility. If the contemplation of a work of art is followed by an activity of any kind, the work is either of a very second-rate order, or the spectator has failed to realise the complete artistic impression. A work of art is useless as a flower is useless. A flower blossoms for its own joy. We gain a moment of joy by looking at it.[160]

This is a view much in accordance with that of Théophile Gautier, as expressed for instance in the Préface to his *Poésies complètes* (1845) and in the 'Préface' (1834) to his novel *Mademoiselle de Maupin* (1835). He, too, strongly resisted the usurpation of art by bourgeois concepts of utility: 'Il n'y a de vraiment beau que ce qui ne peut servir à rien; tout ce qui est utile est laid' [the only thing that is really beautiful is that which serves no purpose; everything that is useful is ugly].[161]

So far in this survey a great deal has been said about what art is not, but comparatively little about what it is. This is not due to a biased method of presentation, but to the generally negative nature of Wilde's aesthetic theory. Even when he seems to intend a positive statement about the nature of art, it comes out 'via negativa': 'Art never expresses anything but itself.'[162] It is open to question whether this charming but empty maxim really has the sense attributed to it by Ann R. Yaffe in her dissertation 'Oscar Wilde as Critic' (1972): 'Art expresses the imaginative response to life.'[163] Certainly his statement implies an important principle that underlies all his aesthetics: the idea that art is autonomous. Alien to reality, self-sufficient in every way, art develops irrespective of the forces of history, and therefore can never be taken for a reflection of nature or of life.

Remote from reality and with her eyes turned away from the shadows of the cave, Art reveals her own perfection, and the wondering crowd that watches the opening of the marvellous many-petalled rose fancies that it is its own history that is being told to it, its own spirit that is finding expression in a new form. But it is not so. The highest art rejects the burden of the human spirit, and gains more from a new medium or a fresh material than she does from any enthusiasm for art, or from any lofty passion, or from any great awakening of the human consciousness. She develops purely on her own lines. She is not symbolic of any age. It is the ages that are her symbols.[164]

The criterion by which art is to be measured cannot therefore have anything to do with 'recognition' or 'resemblance'[165] in relation to objective reality, but is based on the work's internal perfection, which is the artist's success in representing his idea of beauty with the tools of style and under the conditions laid down by his own sensitive temperament. Herein lies the essence of artistic expression. Wilde makes this even more explicit in a letter concerning a review of *A House of Pomegranates*. Annoyed by the critic's question whether he had written the fairy-tales in order to give pleasure to the English child, he gave as part of his answer the following pronouncement:

No artist recognises any standard of beauty but that which is suggested by his own temperament. The artist seeks to realise in a certain material his immaterial idea of beauty, and thus to transform an idea into an ideal. That is the way an artist makes things. That is why an artist makes things. The artist has no other object in making things.[166]

The concept of art as an autonomous form which, free from practical and moral intentions and from social and historical influences, fulfils its purpose by making beauty, was widespread in nineteenth-century aesthetics, called variously 'aestheticism' or — less comprehensively — 'l'art pour l'art'. From the first it was a European phenomenon, and not just a British aberration. Kant's definition of beauty as 'Form der *Zweckmässigkeit* eines Gegenstandes, sofern sie *ohne Vorstellung eines Zwecks* an ihm wahrgenommen wird'[167] [the form of the functionality of an object, in so far as the form is perceived through the object without any conception of a purpose] – defined in his *Kritik der Urteilskraft [Critique of Judgment]* (1790) – paved the way for this aesthetic development, as did Schiller's championship of aesthetic freedom in his letters *Über die ästhetische Erziehung des Menschen* [On the aesthetic education of man] (1795). Keats' love of beauty was to English literature what Gautier's cult of form was to French. Poe, Baudelaire, Flaubert, Swinburne, Pater, George Moore in the phase of his *Confessions of a Young Man* (1888), R. L. Stevenson with reservations, Whistler, Wilde and Stefan George are among the best known representatives of this aesthetic movement in art. It must be pointed out, however, that the common ground among all these literary figures lay not in a unified programme but in the similarity of their attitude towards art, which they regarded as a high, if not as the highest, value in life, an amoral game of the imagination, and a refuge from the utilitarian pressures of the middle-class social order.[168]

The relation between art and criticism in 'The Critic as Artist'

In 'The Decay of Lying' Wilde developed the basis of his aesthetics by dealing with the relationship between art and reality. In 'The Critic as Artist' he concentrates on criticism, and in particular on the interrelationship between critical and creative talent. The essay first appeared in the July and September editions of the magazine *The Nineteenth Century* (1890), under the title 'The True Function and Value of Criticism; with some Remarks on the Importance of Doing Nothing: A Dialogue'. The title is unmistakably reminiscent of Matthew Arnold's *The Function of Criticism at the Present Time* (1864).[169] When Wilde put the essay into his collection *Intentions*, he changed the title to 'The Critic as Artist', which was more apposite to his thesis, and also – like 'The Decay of Lying' – possessed a certain provocative attraction. This essay is also in dialogue form, with Gilbert representing the author and Ernest acting as a kind of devil's advocate.

In connection with the initial question of whether the Greeks were a nation of art critics, the problem arises as to the relation between critical and creative ability. Ernest makes the contentious remark that 'the creative faculty is higher than the critical',[170] to which Gilbert replies:

GILBERT: The antithesis between them is entirely arbitrary. Without the critical faculty, there is no artistic creation at all worthy of the name. You spoke a little while ago of that fine spirit of choice and delicate instinct of selection by which the artist realises life for us, and gives to it a momentary perfection. Well, that spirit of choice, that subtle tact of omission, is really the critical faculty in one of its most characteristic moods, and no one who does not possess this critical faculty can create anything at all in art. Arnold's definition of literature as a criticism of life was not very felicitous in form, but it showed how keenly he recognised the importance of the critical element in all creative work.[171]

It is because of this 'selection' and 'omission' that art is always 'self-conscious and deliberate',[172] resulting as it does from the constructive intelligence of the artist. While the creative impulse harbours the tendency merely to reproduce, the critical spirit is the guiding force behind innovation of forms and styles in art. But if the critical faculty is such an indispensable precondition for creative production, it follows that there can have been no 'creative age'[173] in history that was not at the same time a critical age.

In terms of the history of ideas, Wilde is by no means arguing in a vacuum here, for this was a theme that had already been discussed by Macaulay and Arnold. In his essay on John Dryden (1828), Macaulay expressed the view that 'the creative faculty, and the critical faculty, cannot exist together in their highest perfection',[174] his reason being that 'poetry requires not an examining but a believing frame of mind'.[175] Matthew Arnold was convinced that the free creative faculty was man's greatest gift, because therein lay the fulfilment of his happiness. Viewed in this light, 'the critical power is of lower rank than the creative'.[176] He does, however, concede in a broader context that the creative faculty is not confined exclusively to art and literature, but can also be found 'in criticising',[177] which would seem to indicate that for him the distinction between the two powers was not one of principle. The debate has gone on into the twentieth century. T. S. Eliot, in his introduction to *The Use of Poetry and the Use of Criticism* (1933) insists that there is a 'significant relation between the best poetry and the best criticism of the same period'.[178] Even earlier, in his essay 'The Perfect Critic' (1920), he rejected any separation of criticism from creativity, for: 'The two directions of sensibility are complementary.'[179]

Wilde had the same view, though not quite with the same balance. The creative faculty presupposes a critical faculty, and thus criticism is a creative activity, indeed an art:

ERNEST: But is Criticism really a creative art?

GILBERT: Why should it not be? It works with materials and puts them into a form that is at once new and delightful. What more can one say of poetry? Indeed, I would call criticism a creation within a creation. For just as the great artists, from Homer and Aeschylus, down to Shakespeare and Keats, did not go directly to life for their subject-matter, but sought for it in myth, and legend, and ancient tale, so the critic deals with materials that others have as it were, purified for him, and to which imaginative form and colour have already been added. Nay, more, I would say that the highest Criticism, being the purest form of personal impression, is in its way more creative than creation, as it has least reference to any standard external to itself, and is, in fact, its own reason for existing, and, as the Greeks would put it, in itself, and to itself, an end.[180]

Criticism is more creative than art itself because the object it deals with is already 'purified' of all traces of real life, so that criticism cannot be measured by any criterion outside itself. It stands in the same relation to art as art to objective reality. It has no obligation to describe, interpret or evaluate a poem, painting or sculpture by conventional standards, and formulates nothing but the personal impression of the critic; in this respect, it represents a kind of autobiography, 'the record of one's own soul'.[181] Wilde proceeds from the correct premise that aesthetic reality results from interaction between the producer and the receiver – 'the meaning of any beautiful created thing is, at least, as much in the soul of him who looks at it as it was in his soul who wrought it'[182] – but this leads him to extremes of subjective impressionism, with the work of art functioning as little more than an associative stimulus to the creative imagination of the critic. Thus the Arnold demand 'to see the object as in itself it really is'[183] is reversed by Wilde into the need 'to see the object as in itself it really is not'.[184] There is a similarly extreme subjectivism to be found in Anatole France, whose collected reviews and critical writings began to appear in 1888 under the title *La Vie littéraire*. He comes very close to Wilde's concept of the critic in the introduction to the *première série* of *La Vie littéraire*: 'Le bon critique est celui qui raconte les aventures de son âme au milieu des chefs-d'œuvre' [The good critic is the one who recounts the adventures of his soul in the midst of masterpieces].[185] There can be no doubt that Wilde was familiar with at least some of the Frenchman's work. He says in his letters that he has read *Le Puits de Sainte Claire* (1895), and he asks Ross to get him *Thaïs* (1890) and 'his [France's] latest works'[186] for when he is released from prison. The connections between Wilde and France, as yet scarcely noticed let alone researched, might make for an interesting study.

Part Two of the essay begins with Ernest asking whether the critic will not sometimes be a 'real interpreter'. In his reply, Gilbert says:

The critic will certainly be an interpreter, but he will not treat Art as a riddling Sphinx, whose shallow secret may be guessed and revealed by one whose feet are wounded and who knows not his name. Rather, he will look upon Art as a goddess whose mystery it is his province to intensify, and whose majesty his privilege to make more marvellous in the eyes of men.[187]

He rejects any form of criticism that seeks to describe, interpret and understand a work exclusively from the standpoint of its intentions. Analysis and exposition are banished to some 'lower sphere',[188] though this is not defined. The task is one of mystification, not enlightenment. But behind this apparently trivial paradox there is a very serious and important idea – namely that of subjective reception, which is creative in the sense that it helps to assemble meaning. The truthfulness and conviction of an interpretation will not depend on whether the interpreter has

managed, through analysis and exposition, to uncover the intention
behind a work, but it will derive from the degree to which his mature,
sensitive and discerning personality can reconstruct the work, thereby
performing an act of individual interpretation. If Rubinstein plays Beethoven's Sonata Appassionata, he does not simply reproduce Beethoven,
but 'Beethoven reinterpreted through a rich artistic nature, and made
vivid and wonderful to us by a new and intense personality'.[189] And
elsewhere Gilbert asks provocatively: 'Who cares whether Mr Ruskin's
views on Turner are sound or not?'[190] Wilde repeatedly points out how
vital it is for the personality to be trained to understand art and to be
sensitive to the delights of beauty. The dynamism of creative reception
depends upon such sensitivity and feeling for quality. The idea of
interpretation as an act of mystification is an indispensable component of
Wilde's provocative pose; but the underlying idea of a dynamic interrelationship between the processes of creation and reception is indisputable.

What qualities must the 'true critic' possess if he is to fulfil his task?
Wilde begins, typically, by stating what qualities he should *not* have: he
should not be 'fair', 'rational', or 'sincere' in the traditional sense.[191]
These, of course, were the very qualities that had always been regarded as
essential in the true critic. Alexander Pope, in his *Essay on Criticism*
(1711), describes the ideal man:

> But where's the Man, who Counsel *can* bestow,
> Still *pleas'd* to *teach*, and yet not *proud* to *know*?
> Unbiass'd, or by *Favour* or by *Spite*;
> Not *dully prepossest*, or *blindly right*;
> Tho' Learn'd, well-bred; and tho' well-bred, sincere;
> Modestly bold, and Humanly severe?
> Who to a *Friend* his Faults can freely show,
> And gladly praise the Merit of a *Foe*?
> Blest with a *Taste* exact, yet unconfin'd;
> A *Knowledge* both of *Books* and *Humankind*;
> Gen'rous *Converse*; a *Soul* exempt from *Pride*;
> And *Love to Praise*, with *Reason* on his Side?[192]

This is the neo-classical ideal, features of which recur frequently in the
nineteenth century. The criterion of 'sincerity' was particularly
esteemed.[193] It is the first quality mentioned by Matthew Arnold in his list
of attributes: 'criticism must be sincere, simple, flexible, ardent, ever
widening its knowledge'.[194] In his actual criticism he did not always
remain true to this theoretical basis, but at least in his Wordsworth essay
he laid great stress on the fact that the poetry derived its particular
strength from the 'profound sincereness with which Wordsworth feels his
subject, and also from the profoundly sincere and natural character of his

subject itself'.[195] Even earlier Carlyle, in his essay on Robert Burns (1828), saw 'sincerity' as the characteristic quality of the Scot's poetry.[196] It was a term that played a vital role in romantic poetics, and as M. H. Abrams pointed out in *The Mirror and the Lamp* (1953), it was indispensable to the poetic theories of the early nineteenth century and Victorian times. Until its reassessment by Wilde and the Symbolists, the concept had always retained traces of its ethical and religious origin. Romantics and Victorians such as Carlyle and Matthew Arnold used it to describe the concordance between the poet's subjective emotion and its external, objective, expression. If the two were in harmony, poetic truth was guaranteed.

Wilde took over this traditional concept, and injected it with a new meaning. He liberated it from all religious, moral and psychological implications, and related it solely to the critic's faithfulness to the ideal of beauty. Insincerity denoted an undogmatic approach and intellectual flexibility:

GILBERT: A little sincerity is a dangerous thing, and a great deal of it is absolutely fatal. The true critic will, indeed, always be sincere in his devotion to the principle of beauty, but he will seek for beauty in every age and in each school, and will never suffer himself to be limited to any settled custom of thought, or stereotyped mode of looking at things. He will realise himself in many forms, and by a thousand different ways, and will ever be curious of new sensations and fresh points of view. Through constant change, and through constant change alone, he will find his true unity. He will not consent to be the slave of his own opinions. For what is mind but motion in the intellectual sphere? The essence of thought, as the essence of life, is growth. You must not be frightened by words, Ernest. What people call insincerity is simply a method by which we can multiply our personalities.[197]

With Wilde's terminology, the link between subjective utterance and objective matter has been so loosened that in *Dorian Gray* Lord Henry can actually claim that 'the value of an idea has nothing whatsoever to do with the sincerity of him who expresses it'.[198]

What is essential in a critic, then, is not sincerity, fairness or reason, but 'a temperament exquisitely susceptible to beauty, and to the various impressions that beauty gives us'.[199] Wilde constantly reiterates that this quality, which he variously calls 'artistic temperament', 'temperament' or 'aesthetic sense', is the most important one for any critic. In his early lecture, 'The Decorative Arts', he stressed the vital role of the 'artistic temperament', 'without which there is no creation of art, there is no understanding of art, there is not even an understanding of life'.[200] Understanding literature is 'a question of temperament not of teaching',[201] as he writes on the subject 'To Read or not to Read'. Of course, this high esteem for a sense of beauty was a basic premise of all impressionistic criticism, for if the aesthetic reality of a work is to be gauged by its effect on the recipient, clearly the development of such a sense is of prime importance. Inevitably it was Pater who set out the classic formula:

What is important ... is not that the critic should possess a correct abstract definition of beauty for the intellect, but a certain kind of temperament, the power of being deeply moved by the presence of beautiful objects.[202]

If this temperament is so essential then it would seem that the artist must be the ideal critic – an idea that is taken up in the course of the essay. It is not a new idea. At the end of the 1870s, when he sued Ruskin for slander in respect of one of his pictures, Whistler stated explicitly during questioning: 'none but an artist can be a competent critic'.[203] Wilde, however, does not subscribe to this view:

GILBERT: The appeal of all art is simply to the artistic temperament. Art does not address herself to the specialist. Her claim is that she is universal, and that in all her manifestations she is one. Indeed, so far from its being true that the artist is the best judge of art, a really great artist can never judge of other people's work at all, and can hardly, in fact, judge of his own. That very concentration of vision that makes a man an artist, limits by its sheer intensity his faculty of fine appreciation. The energy of creation hurries him blindly on to his own goal. The wheels of his chariot raise the dust as a cloud around him. The gods are hidden from each other. They can recognise their worshippers. That is all.[204]

To illustrate his point, Gilbert alias Wilde cites Wordsworth, who regarded 'Endymion' as no more than a 'pretty piece of Paganism',[205] Shelley who found Wordsworth's poetry inaccessible, Milton who did not understand Shakespeare, and Reynolds who could not appreciate Gainsborough.

As becomes apparent towards the end of the essay, Wilde is aware that criticism cannot be viewed merely as a self-sufficient activity for private pleasure; it also has considerable social and cultural importance. This acknowledgment is perhaps a little surprising, as it scarcely conforms to the premise of total subjectivity in the business of criticism, but it is clear that Wilde, like Arnold before him in *The Function of Criticism at the Present Time*, regards the critic as an essential bearer of culture, familiar with all the elements of man's intellectual tradition, and selecting and handing down all that is worth preserving. The critic's influence lies in opening up new perspectives for his time, and imbuing it with historical consciousness. He is the purest example of the Arnoldian 'spirit of disinterested curiosity'[206] which underlies all cultural progress. In the sphere of literature, for instance the novel, it is the critical spirit that conditions all innovation both of form and content. 'He who would stir us now by fiction must give us an entirely new background, or reveal to us the soul of man in its innermost workings',[207] a demand subsequently fulfilled by such pioneers as Marcel Proust, James Joyce, and Virginia Woolf.

The cultural function of criticism carries with it political and social implications. By helping to create a particular intellectual climate that ignores and indeed breaks down national boundaries, it advances international understanding and eliminates prejudice. It can even – as Wilde optimistically visualises – bind Europe closer together and bring peace:

GILBERT: Criticism will annihilate race-prejudices, by insisting upon the unity of the human mind in the variety of its forms. If we are tempted to make war upon another nation, we shall remember that we are seeking to destroy an element of our own culture, and possibly its most important element. As long as war is regarded as wicked, it will always have its fascination. When it is looked upon as vulgar, it will cease to be popular. The change will, of course, be slow, and people will not be conscious of it. They will not say 'We will not war against France because her prose is perfect', but because the prose of France is perfect, they will not hate the land. Intellectual criticism will bind Europe together in bonds far closer than those that can be forged by shopman or sentimentalist. It will give us the peace that springs from understanding.[208]

There can be no doubting who were the two godfathers to these and many other ideas contained in Wilde's essay. The figures of Matthew Arnold and Walter Pater loom very large indeed. 'The Critic as Artist' can be seen as a response to Arnold's *The Function of Criticism at the Present Time* – a response given from the standpoint of a subjective 'aesthetic criticism' derived from Pater. If Wilde's position is marked by a certain eclecticism, this is because he had been unable to solve all the problems arising from his creative assimilation of two different theoretical lines of thought. A great deal has already been written about the influence of Arnold and Pater on Wilde,[209] but none of the meticulous philological research tracing the many verbal and philosophical parallels can disguise the fact that 'The Critic as Artist' is a highly original, brilliantly executed piece of criticism. And even if Wilde did take over individual ideas from the two sources named, he developed and extended them, changing their meaning by setting them in new contexts, and frequently – whether explicitly or implicitly – departing altogether from the lines laid down by his predecessors.

What links Wilde with Arnold is his belief in the social and cultural importance of criticism. Both are against a materialistic, utilitarian view of life, and stress the 'free play of the mind on all subjects'.[210] Arnold's idea of 'disinterestedness', the critic's independence of any political or practical ties, is echoed by Wilde:

GILBERT: It is Criticism that, recognising no position as final, and refusing to bind itself by the shallow shibboleths of any sect or school, creates that serene philosophic temper which loves truth for its own sake, and loves it not the less because it knows it to be unattainable.[211]

How did Wilde differ from Arnold? The main differences lay in their views on the relationship between the 'creative faculty' and the 'critical faculty', and also on the method according to which criticism should proceed. Arnold valued the creative faculty above the critical, and – as has already been indicated – he regarded the critic's task as being 'to see the object as in itself it really is'. This implies the philosophical possibility that an object *can* be known, and so literary criticism can be free from partiality and subjectivity. Wilde was totally opposed to this view. How could criticism be objective when cognition was a completely subjective act tending to emancipate itself from the object perceived rather than grasping it as itself? In this light Wilde saw it as essential that one should make a critical virtue out of a philosophical necessity and refine the 'artistic temperament', strengthening its creative impulses. The most reliable truth was that of one's own feelings.

In the 'Conclusion' to his *Studies in the History of the Renaissance* (1873),[212] Pater paved the philosophical way for Wilde's reversal of the Arnold thesis. In the Preface he says:

'To see the object as in itself it really is', has been justly said to be the aim of all true criticism whatever; and in aesthetic criticism the first step towards seeing one's object as it really is, is to know one's own impression as it really is.[213]

In this the critic is comparable to the artist, who is not concerned with reproducing reality as it is, but aims at a 'representation of such fact as connected with soul'.[214] Is it then the critic's task simply to enjoy his subjective impressions and then to communicate them to the public? Not for Wilde. In principle he accepts the subjective basis of Pater's concept of criticism, but he goes further. Pater regarded analysis of the 'virtue' of the object as an essential function of criticism,[215] thereby insisting on the continued link of critic to object. Wilde stresses the autonomy of the recipient: 'Criticism is the record of one's own soul.'[216]

In their historical continuity, the positions of Arnold, Pater and Wilde reflect changing phases in the Victorian philosophy of life.[217] In his influential essay on Arnold and Pater (1930), T. S. Eliot showed how Arnold's humanism could give rise to Pater's aestheticism. He argues that both concepts sprang from scepticism towards the Christian faith. Arnold reacted by trying to replace religion with culture, though without sacrificing the Christian moral basis. Pater developed the 'intellectual Epicureanism'[218] of the author of *Culture and Anarchy* (1869) and endowed art with the almost sacred status of religion. But Pater was still a moralist in so far as he remained deeply concerned about the 'true moral significance of art and poetry'.[219] We may extend these observations of

Eliot's by placing Wilde in this line of tradition, whereby he again takes up a position of his own because his theory of art and criticism is based on a radically subjectified view of cognition, and an insistence even greater than Pater's on the autonomy of the aesthetic. While Pater, in the final sentence of his 'Conclusion', still relates art to life, Wilde by contrast takes life to be a function of art.

'Shakespeare and Stage Costume' or 'The Truth of Masks'

In the 1880s Wilde's interests were by no means confined to aesthetic problems and the 'decorative arts', but were focused first and foremost on literature and the theatre. After his lengthy lecture tours of America and England, he began to work intensively as a critic in 1884–5, and from 1887–9 was, as has already been mentioned, chief editor of *The Woman's World*. Apart from reviewing new books and plays, he sometimes engaged in discussion of current literary problems, provided they interested him. His love of the theatre, and especially of Shakespeare, led him to respond to the challenge thrown down by Lord Lytton who, in December 1884, maintained in his review of *Miss Andersen's Juliet* that: 'The attempt to archaeologise the Shakespearean drama is one of the stupidest pedantries of this age of prigs.'[220] Wilde replied with the essay 'Shakespeare and Stage Costume', which he published in the May edition of *Nineteenth Century*, and later included in his collection of essays *Intentions*, having made a few rather revealing changes, including the title, which became 'The Truth of Masks'. It may at first sight seem surprising that he should have been concerned with the question of historical accuracy in the form of costume in the theatre, but in the past he had frequently tackled the theme of 'dress reform' in various lectures and articles for the *Pall Mall Gazette*.[221]

'Shakespeare and Stage Costume' had already been preceded by a shorter essay entitled 'Shakespeare on Scenery', published in the *Dramatic Review* of 14 March 1885,[222] in which he pointed out that Shakespeare had often complained about the limitations imposed on him by the meagre equipment of the Elizabethan theatre (e.g. in the Prologue to *Henry V*). If existing props were not enough to pinpoint the action or setting, he had to give the information by direct announcement or use 'locality boards', or incorporate it in the dialogue itself. Such exposition was of itself undramatic, and however vividly he might conjure up scenes in words, such an 'imaginative method'[223] could never match the visual presence of that scene in the process of creating illusions for the spectator:

Theatrical audiences are far more impressed by what they look at than by what they listen to; and the modern dramatist, in having the surroundings of his play visibly presented to the audience when the curtain rises, enjoys an advantage for which Shakespeare often expresses his desire ... the introduction of self-explanatory scenery enables the modern method to be far more direct, while the loveliness of form and colour which it gives us, seems to me often to create an artistic temperament in the audience, and to produce that joy in beauty for beauty's sake, without which the great masterpieces of art can never be understood, to which, and to which only, are they ever revealed.[224]

The actual nature of the scenery is of some importance for the overall effect of a production. Wilde prefers a painted décor to the large movable pieces of scenery that were quite common on the Elizabethan stage. For him, such sets are considerably more expensive and intrusive than 'scene-painting'.[225] 'A painted door is more like a real door than a real door is itself.'[226]

In 'Shakespeare and Stage Costume' Wilde concentrates on proving that Shakespeare was second to none in his awareness and utilisation of the decorative and dramatic possibilities offered by historically accurate costumes.[227] The many scenes with masks and disguises, as well as the sometimes detailed descriptions of characters' clothes, also prove that the Elizabethan theatre must have had a copious wardrobe at its disposal. A glance at Henslowe's *Diary* (1598) confirms how varied and colourful the costumes really were. Shakespeare himself constantly used 'dress metaphors' to express the gap between appearance and reality. And he also showed astonishing historical accuracy, according to Wilde, in the presentation of his characters and their actions:

Many of his [Shakespeare's] *dramatis personae* are people who had actually existed, and some of them might have been seen in real life by a portion of his audience ... And not merely did he select fact instead of fancy as the basis of his imaginative work, but he always gives to each play the general character, the social atmosphere in a word, of the age in question.[228]

These sentences were incorporated unchanged into 'The Truth of Masks', and one can scarcely believe that they stem from the same author as 'The Decay of Lying' and 'The Critic as Artist'.

But for Wilde the aesthetic value of Shakespeare's plays was certainly not dependent on their apparent truth to life, and 'archaeological accuracy' was only one of several conditions that contributed to the effect and quality of a production. Historically accurate costumes had to harmonise with the style and colours of the overall décor in order to create an artistic unity. This was not a matter of individual efficiency or democratic agreement, for only the 'cultured despot'[229] could guarantee the stylistic consistency of a production. Wilde concludes his remarks with an almost schoolmasterly résumé:

what I have tried to point out is that archaeology is not a pedantic method, but a method of realism, and that costume is a means of displaying character without description, and of producing dramatic situations and dramatic effects.[230]

The idea of an historically accurate production based on an authentic-seeming text, with costumes and props from the time represented, was by no means an innovation of the 1880s, but in fact was more in the conservative tradition. The Shakespeare productions of W. C. Macready at Covent Garden and Drury Lane (1837–43), Charles Kean at the Princess's (1850–9), and Henry Irving at the Lyceum (1878–1902) made their impact largely through their spectacular realism, with huge and expensive sets, lavish costumes and novel lighting effects. Some of these productions, such as Macready's *Coriolanus* (1838), are regarded as milestones of the nineteenth-century English theatre.

The inspiration for Wilde's essay would not, however, have come solely from contemporary theatre practice, but also from a man who, in his capacity as architect and designer, was responsible throughout the 1870s and 1880s for a number of historically accurate and highly decorative productions: E. W. Godwin. It was he who designed the furniture and, together with Whistler, the interior of Wilde's flat at 16 Tite Street.[231] What is less well known, however, is the fact that in addition to this kind of work, he was deeply immersed in the subject of historical costume. Between October 1874 and June 1875 he published a series of essays in *The Architect* on the theme of 'The Architecture and Costume of Shakespeare's Plays', which, according to Hilda Schiff, were 'full of suggestion for the material in "Shakespeare and Stage Costume"'.[232] In 1883 he actually founded a 'Costume Society' whose aims were the historical documentation and study of costume through the centuries. In 1884 he wrote a booklet on *Dress, and its Relation to Health and Climate* as his contribution to the 'International Health Exhibition'. In 1885 he assisted Lady Archibald Campbell with an open-air production of *As You Like It* at Coombe Wood near Kingston-on-Thames. Wilde said enthusiastically of this production that: '*As You Like It* has probably never been so well mounted, nor costumes worn with more ease and simplicity.'[233]

The author of 'Shakespeare and Stage Costume' must certainly have been aware that his plea for 'archaeological accuracy'[234] of costume, which evidently corresponded to current trends, was tantamount to accepting the realistic mode of presentation that was an integral part of the naturalists' case in the controversy of the 1880s. 1885–6 saw a peak of interest in the French realists and naturalists, with the first English editions of several novels by Zola and Flaubert, as well as the publication of George Moore's *A Mummer's Wife* (1885). In view of the protean changeability of Wilde's taste and of his aesthetic position, his conformity to the realistic tradition of theatre production, which in its turn reflected a current literary trend, might have passed without further comment if it had not been for the fact that he put his essay 'Shakespeare and Stage Costume' (newly entitled 'The Truth of Masks') in his collection *Inten-*

tions. Its conclusion alongside 'The Decay of Lying' and 'The Critic as Artist', in both of which he calls realism a 'failure'[235] and a method of yesterday, seems almost grotesque.

It is fascinating to observe how Wilde sought to fit this essay into its new surroundings. There are a few insignificant stylistic corrections, and a reference to Irving's production of *Much Ado About Nothing* on 11 October 1882 is replaced by Mrs Langtry's production of *Antony and Cleopatra* at the Princess's on 18 November 1890. But the first major change is the title, which puts the unmistakable imprint of Wilde's wit on the essay itself, as well as harmonising with the tone of the other titles in the collection. The dry, unoriginal 'Shakespeare and Stage Costume' becomes the paradoxical 'The Truth of Masks', with a new sub-title: 'A Note on Illusion'. The next problem was how to soften the pleas for historical realism without making any radical changes to the argument. The simplest and most economical method was to leave out the words 'realism' and 'realistic' altogether, or replace them by some other term, and in fact Wilde chose the latter course. Wherever he had spoken of the 'method of realism'[236] he now refers to 'a method of artistic illusion',[237] and the 'realistic dramatist'[238] is now rechristened an 'illusionist'.[239] Thus he was able to erase the offensive term so damaging to the aesthetics of *Intentions*, but of course the basic thesis still remained intact. What could he do? In face of such an apparently impossible task, some writers would have thrown in the towel. But here Wilde's ingenuity came into its own. Was it not one of the recognised principles of 'aesthetic criticism' that no critical standpoint could ever claim objective validity? In that case, it was essential for him to make it clear that his essay was merely the expression of a subjective attitude, open to revision at any time, and with no claim to any binding commitment. And so he appended to 'The Truth of Masks' a brand-new conclusion:

Not that I agree with everything that I have said in this essay. There is much with which I entirely disagree. The essay simply represents an artistic standpoint, and in aesthetic criticism attitude is everything. For in art there is no such thing as a universal truth. A Truth in art is that whose contradictory is also true. And just as it is only in art-criticism, and through it, that we can apprehend the Platonic theory of ideas, so it is only in art-criticism, and through it, we can realise Hegel's system of contraries. The truths of metaphysics are the truths of masks.[240]

And that would seem to be that. A change of title, a change of conclusion, 'realism' replaced by 'illusion', and the essay is ready for inclusion in *Intentions*. However, the operation can hardly be called an unqualified success, for the changes are merely cosmetic, and the basic argument remains exactly the same. In the circumstances it is extraordinary that Hilda Schiff, in her thesis 'A Critical Study of Oscar Wilde's "Intentions"', should conclude that the revisions constitute 'a definite change of tone'.[241] The appended conclusion in no way alters the earnest and polemic tone of the essay, but instead represents a dubious and artificial attempt to turn an unpretentious article on the importance of costume in Shakespeare's plays into a case study for applied 'aesthetic criticism'. The reader cannot help feeling that the above passage has simply been tacked onto the rest of the essay for no other purpose than to justify its inclusion in the collection. Wilde evidently wanted to pad *Intentions* out to a reasonable thickness, and so he was trying to tone down the contradictions to the aesthetic principles he had developed in the other essays. It might have been better if he had left the essay out altogether rather than manipulating it into its 1891 shape, and this suspicion seems to be confirmed by a letter he wrote to Jules Cantel in summer (?) 1891, authorising the translation of *Intentions* but adding:

Seulement je ne veux pas qu'il traduise le dernier essai 'La Vérité des Masques'; je ne l'aime plus. Au lieu de cela, on pourra mettre l'essai paru dans le *Fortnightly Review* le février dernier sur 'L'Ame de l'Homme', qui contient une partie de mon esthétique.[242]

[Only I do not want him to translate the last essay, 'The Truth of Masks'; I do not like it any more. Instead one can put the essay that appeared last February in the *Fortnightly Review*, 'The Soul of Man', which contains part of my aesthetics.]

Practical criticism in *Reviews*

Wilde's contribution to literary criticism was not confined to theory. For several years, and in particular from 1885 to 1890, he was critic for various magazines, including *Pall Mall Gazette, Dramatic Review, Saturday Review* and *The Speaker*. From 1887 onwards he also wrote a regular literary column entitled 'Literary and other Notes' (after 1889 it was called 'Some Literary Notes') in *The Woman's World*, of which he was editor. His output was so prolific that the volume of *Reviews*, which Robert Ross compiled for the collected works in 1908, contained well over five hundred pages. As Carl Markgraf's edition of Wilde's anonymous criticism adds very little to the Ross edition, as well as omitting all the signed reviews, we shall only be referring to the 1908 collection.

Most of the reviews concern literature, but there are also some discussions of works like *Dinners and Dishes*, a handbook on the evocative subject of 'How to be happy though married', and a history of embroidery and lacemaking. The length of the articles varies considerably: in multiple reviews he usually devoted just one paragraph to each book, whereas his discussion of Chuang Tzǔ's *Mystic, Moralist, and Social Reformer* (1889) covers ten pages. If one can judge by the colourful mixture of novels, poetry, essays, history etc. that Wilde dealt with, it would seem that he was not particularly selective in his choice of subject, but tended to review whatever was sent to him. In fact his increasingly precarious financial situation would hardly have allowed him to be selective.

In keeping with his basic theoretical premises, Wilde's critical eye dwelt mainly on form, and particularly on style. As he wrote in a letter to the *St James's Gazette* during the *Dorian Gray* debate, a lack of style was the one thing he could not forgive.[243] In an anonymous review of *Tuberose and Meadowsweet*, a book of poems by Marc-André Raffalovich, he complains that the poet evidently believes the word 'tuberose' to be trisyllabic, 'as if it were a potato blossom and not a flower shaped like a tiny trumpet of ivory'.[244] The offended Raffalovich replied with etymological justifications and a reference to Shelley, who had also used the word as a trisyllable. Whether the poet actually knew the identity of the critic is uncertain, but his derogatory remarks about Wilde in his article 'L'Affaire Oscar Wilde' (1895) – in which he implicitly labelled him a criminal – may perhaps be a pointer.[245] Wilde was particularly hard on George Saintsbury, who was already quite well-known in the 1880s even though most of his work on literary history was not published till later. Under the title 'Half-hours with the Worst Authors' Wilde tackles Saintsbury's essay on George Borrow, which appeared in *Macmillan's Magazine* in January 1886. After quoting fourteen examples of bad style, he concludes, 'These are merely a few examples of the style of Mr Saintsbury, a writer who seems quite ignorant of the commonest laws both of grammar and of literary expression.'[246] It may well be that here, too, the author managed to identify the critic, since the name of Wilde is conspicuous by its absence from Saintsbury's three-volume *History of Criticism and Literary Taste in Europe* (1900–4).

It is clear that Wilde was not prepared to pull his punches, even when his victims were well-known figures in the academic and literary fields. Even his respected former tutor in Ancient History at Trinity College, Dublin, John Pentland Mahaffy, was criticised by his former pupil because in his book *Greek Life and Thought* (1887) 'he has spoiled his account of Greek politics by a foolish partisan bias'.[247] W. M. Rossetti's biography of Keats is called 'a great failure',[248] Harry Quilter's *Sententiae Artis* is ruined by 'the extraordinary vulgarity of the style',[249] and Lord Henry Somerset's poetic talents are dismissed with devastating finality:

Lord Henry Somerset has too much heart and too little art to make a good poet, and such art as he does possess is devoid of almost every intellectual quality and entirely lacking in any intellectual strength. He has nothing to say and says it.[250]

Wilde was just as offended by inaccurate texts and bad design as he was by lack of style. The novel *From Heather Hills* annoyed him because the hero misquoted poetry, 'a privilege reserved for Mrs Malaprop',[251] and in a Rossetti biography he found the number of misquotations 'almost incredible'.[252] He could be equally scathing about the binding of a book: 'Dull as *Tiff* is – and its dullness is quite remarkable – it does not deserve so detestable a binding',[253] and he was especially vehement about the cover of a book of poems called *Women Must Weep* by Professor Harald Williams:

Women Must Weep, by Professor Harald Williams, has the most dreadful cover of any book that we have come across for some time past. It is possibly intended to symbolise the sorrow of the world, but it merely suggests the decorative tendencies of an undertaker and is as depressing as it is detestable.[254]

Wilde's criticism is not always so biting. He was just as adept at the more gentle, subtle kind of barb. On Walt Whitman's poems, for instance – a poet with whose concept of art he had virtually nothing in common – he remarks that 'the chief value of his work is in its prophecy, not in its performance'.[255] There is a certain finesse in the way in which he wraps his scorn for W. E. Henley's poetry in apparent esteem for the man himself. The charm of his *Book of Verses* lies not in the poems – where else might the reader find it? – but 'in the strong humane personality that stands behind both flawless and faulty work alike'.[256] There are even cautious digs at Swinburne and Pater. The former he does indeed praise as a great poet with a fine feeling for music and admirable technical skill, but there is, he suggests, a certain lack of artistic moderation: 'His song is nearly always too loud for his subject.'[257] This verdict on the author of *Poems and Ballads* (first series, 1866) was one that not even T. S. Eliot, in his essay 'Swinburne as Poet' (1920), could add to. As far as Pater was concerned, it was only natural that Wilde should treat his former tutor's writings with the greatest of respect, but he was far too honest a critic to ignore Pater's weaknesses totally:

Occasionally one may be inclined to think that there is, here and there, a sentence which is somewhat long, and possibly, if one may venture to say so, a little heavy and cumbersome in movement.[258]

It is the gentlest, most qualified of rebukes, but a rebuke it is all the same. On the positive side, there is Wilde's notably favourable judgment of the young Yeats. He was one of the first to recognise the exceptional talent of his Irish compatriot, noting in *The Wanderings of Oisin* (1889) 'nobility of treatment and nobility of subject-matter, delicacy of poetic instinct and richness of imaginative resource'.[259] These qualities enabled him to predict a great future for Yeats. Only rarely is his critical eye clouded by circumstances outside the work itself. It is merely to his contributions to *The Woman's World* that one can apply Robert Rhodes's observation that:

Much of this criticism seems to have been motivated less by an honest test of excellence than by the desire to avoid offence by catering to the presumed interests and predispositions of his clientele.[260]

What makes some of these reviews – even those of second- and third-rate authors – worth reading today is their brilliant style and ironic wit, which turns them into little gems of Wildean humour. His personality imprints itself so vividly on the material that one's attention is often drawn more to the critic than to the work under consideration. A collection of poems by the now forgotten H. E. Keene, for instance, was described to the readers of the *Pall Mall Gazette*, 12 April 1886, as follows:

We wish he would not write sonnets with fifteen lines. A fifteen-line sonnet is as bad a monstrosity as a sonnet in dialogue. The volume has the merit of being very small, and contains many stanzas quite suitable for valentines.[261]

He quite often plays with words: 'The aim of most of our modern novelists seems to be, not to write good novels, but to write novels that will do good.'[262] He characterises John Colliers, who wrote a *Manual of Oil Painting*, with the remark that 'his qualities are of a solid, indeed we may say of a stolid order'.[263] One of his most outrageous puns is to be found in the review of *The Chronicle of Mites*, a book of poems whose title and subject-matter were hardly likely to win the applause of this particular critic:

The Chronicle of Mites is a mock-heroic poem about the inhabitants of a decaying cheese who speculate about the origin of their species and hold learned discussions about the meaning of evolution and the Gospel according to Darwin. This cheese-epic is a rather unsavoury production and the style is at times so monstrous and so realistic that the author should be called the Gorgon-Zola of literature.[264]

Reviews of such major figures as Balzac, Ben Jonson, Swinburne, Pater and Yeats are still of interest to us today, for they are a convincing expression of Wilde's critical judgment. But if one compares some of his articles with the theories of art and criticism that he developed in 'The Decay of Lying' and 'The Critic as Artist', one cannot avoid noticing that, despite the many concordances, there are a number of inconsistencies. For example, he regards the realism of William Morris's translation of *The Odyssey* as a major quality: 'It is, in no sense of the word, literary; it seems to deal immediately with life itself, and to take from the reality of things its own form and colour.'[265] And frequently he failed to practise the extreme, subjective impressionism that he proclaimed to be the critic's ideal ('to see the object as in itself it really is not'). His practical criticism is far more along the lines of conventional journalism, despite the frequent and unmistakable seal of his epigrammatic wit. His articles always set out to convey to the reader the most vivid possible impression of the book under discussion, pointing out its faults and its qualities as well as its individual characteristics. They are certainly the personal and stylish judgments of a well-read and discerning mind, but he never gave totally free rein to his private feelings, any more than he hid behind uncommitted technical descriptions such as are often used to hide the critic's inability to distinguish good from bad. Perhaps what he wrote in a review of Roden Noel's *Essay on Poetry and Poets* (1886) comes closer to his own aims as a critic than do the striking ideas set forth in 'The Critic as Artist':

The fault of his book is that it tells us far more about his own personal feelings than it does about the qualities of the various works of art that are criticised. It is in fact a diary of the emotions suggested by literature, rather than any real addition to literary criticism, and we fancy that many of the poets about whom he writes so eloquently would be not a little surprised at the qualities he finds in their work.[266]

Applied 'aesthetic criticism': 'The Portrait of Mr W. H.'

Wilde's *Reviews* can scarcely be called 'creative' or 'aesthetic' criticism, but in his long essay 'The Portrait of Mr W. H.'[267] he comes very close to this ideal. The term 'essay' is a very loose one, bearing in mind the hybrid nature of the piece, which combines elements of a philological study with the narrative mode of a short story. In this highly original way, Wilde brought together his love of Shakespeare, his story-telling talents, and his sense of paradox, all of which make for a remarkable contribution to the 'art literature' of the late nineteenth century. The originality lies not in the thesis itself – even though Wilde announced to the publisher Blackwood in April 1889 'an entirely new view on the subject of the true identity of the young man to whom the sonnets are addressed'[268] – but in the ironic fictional parody of a classic problem of Shakespeare research: namely, the identity of Mr W. H.

The essay begins with Erskine and the narrator talking about literary forgeries. The conversation turns to Erskine's friend Cyril Graham, who believed that he had identified the addressee of Shakespeare's sonnets as Willie Hughes, a boy actor in Elizabethan times. The clue to the existence of such a person lay in the punning use of the words 'Will' and 'hew/hue' in Sonnets 20, 135 and 143. The theory in fact was not new.[269] Thomas Tyrwhitt in his *Observations and Conjectures upon some Passages of Shakespeare* (1766), and Edmond Malone in his supplement (1780) to the Samuel Johnson and George Steevens edition of Shakespeare (1780) had already mentioned it. And like Tyrwhitt and Malone, the fictitious Cyril is unable to find the name Hughes in the list of Shakespeare's actors, so that an important link in the chain is missing. But in order to convince the doubting Erskine of the truth of the theory, Cyril has a portrait of this supposed addressee forged in the style of the French painter Clouet, and pretends to have found the picture, quite by chance, 'nailed to the side of an old chest that he had bought at a farmhouse in Warwickshire'.[270]

Equally by chance Erskine discovers the forgery and challenges Cyril, who after a violent quarrel kills himself. In a farewell letter he tells Erskine:

> that the forgery of the picture had been done simply as a concession to me, and did not in the slightest degree invalidate the truth of the theory; and that in order to show me how firm and flawless his faith in the whole thing was, he was going to offer his life as a sacrifice to the secret of the Sonnets.[271]

The narrator is so impressed with Cyril's thesis that he resolves not to rest until he has convinced Erskine and all other doubters of its veracity. In the course of his research, he comes to the conclusion that the early procreation sonnets do not refer at all to the begetting of children, but are Shakespeare's invitation to Willie Hughes to a 'marriage with his Muse',[272] that is, to go on stage and be an actor. Unlike Cyril, who had believed George Chapman to be the 'rival poet', the narrator thinks this must refer to Marlowe. The identification with the author of *Dr Faustus* makes it necessary to date the sonnets earlier, and he attributes them to Shakespeare's first creative phase between 1590 and 1595. After he has spent some time developing Cyril's hypothesis, he sends the improved solution to Erskine with the appeal 'to do justice to the memory of Cyril Graham'.[273] Hardly has he sent off the letter when something quite remarkable happens. His firm and enthusiastic faith in his theory collapses, and it all seems to him a mere myth and idle dream.

Meanwhile, Erskine has been completely convinced by the letter, and when the narrator goes to see him, he refuses to be shaken by the argument that the Hughes hypothesis presupposes an existence of which there is absolutely no evidence. The fact that there is no trace of such an actor, Erskine argues, can be explained by his having assumed a *nom de plume*; after all, the acting profession had a bad reputation in Elizabethan times. Nothing can stop Erskine from devoting the rest of his days to proving that Willie Hughes was the addressee of the Sonnets. But in spite of all his efforts, he is as unsuccessful as Cyril Graham was before him. After two years, the narrator receives a letter from Erskine, who is in Cannes and is about to kill himself 'for Willie Hughes' sake'.[274] Very upset, the narrator hurries to Cannes, where he learns from Erskine's doctor that his friend did not commit suicide but in fact died of consumption.

The final version of the essay is in five parts, compared with three in the original. Part I of the magazine version is basically identical to the final Part I, Part II was extended into III and IV as well, while Part III forms the nucleus of the fifth section. The form is rather like that of a relay race, for the Hughes theory is first passed from Cyril Graham to the narrator via Erskine, is corrected by the narrator and passed on to Erskine again, and just before his death the latter returns the baton of responsibility to the narrator. It is clear from all this to-ing and fro-ing that the essay is less concerned with the objective proof of a theory than with its intersubjective communication. It is made clear by their own statements that Cyril Graham and Erskine do not perish because of any doubts they might have themselves about their theory, but because they find it impossible to make their subjective belief plausible and acceptable to others. Ironically, the only way they can prove the imagined truth of their idea is through lies: Cyril forges a picture and Erskine pretends suicide. In both instances, these are desperate and ultimately unsuccessful attempts to adapt awkward facts to fit in with a cherished idea, in other words to make reality a tool of the imagination. Without a doubt this adaptation of facts to a thesis, and Cyril's literary martyrdom as an extreme means of moral justification, are meant to parody the principles of scholarly research. Cyril's suicide and Erskine's pretended suicide, however, are both in accordance with the logical construction of the story; their fanatical efforts to endow a belief with the character of a verifiable fact clashes totally with Wilde's principles of criticism. All three men commit the same cardinal error by relying on scholarship to help them solve a problem of aesthetic belief – an unforgivable concession to the positivistic view of art and criticism. They want to prove the unprovable, and pass off an imaginative hypothesis as the result of textual analysis. Ignoring Keats's admonitory question: 'Do not all charms fly / At the mere touch of cold philosophy?'[275] they arrange their evidence in a 'dull catalogue of common things'.[276] The subjective vision, and the experience of art, are relative and personal and cannot be communicated by rational means. What first attracts the narrator to Cyril's theory is not its scholarly content, but its aesthetic charm: 'I had been touched by the story of Cyril Graham's death, fascinated by his artistic theory, enthralled by the wonder and novelty of the whole idea.'[277] But anyone who tries to spread his enthusiasm for an idea is liable to lose it, and when the narrator sends his letter to Erskine, his faith in the phantom disappears. Anyone who wishes to influence others loses his own identity: 'Influence is simply a transference of personality.'[278]

The romantic implications of the story are unmistakable,[279] for all the research done by Cyril Graham, Erskine and the narrator is based on the conviction that poetry expresses the feelings and passions of the poet. Like Wordsworth, they believe of the sonnets that – 'with this key / Shakespeare unlocked his heart'.[280] Cyril Graham knew that the plausibility of his theory could not depend on 'demonstrable proof or formal evidence',[281] but instead demanded 'a kind of spiritual and artistic sense'[282] on the part of the critic. This is the most important quality for the 'aesthetic critic' as described by Wilde in 'The Critic as Artist'. Even though many passages of the essay are crammed with quotations and show an intimate knowledge of the sonnets, to the extent that at times one might think it was a piece of text analysis, the whole thing can also be taken as a shining example of creative criticism at work. This relates not only to the philological problem being projected onto a fictional context, and an unprovable literary theory resulting in death, but also to the countless narrative interpolations in which the character of Willie Hughes takes on a strange kind of presence. Missing facts are replaced by cunningly devised fiction, the lack of proof is compensated by the fascination of Shakespeare's secret friend. What might be a classic test case for the biographical method of literary criticism here takes on the character of a vivid artistic experience in the life of the narrator. 'Art, as so often happens, had taken the place of personal experience.'[283] The extent to which speculative fantasy fills the gaps in the critic's knowledge can be gauged from the following passage:

I remember I used to wonder, at this time, what had been the social position and early life of Willie Hughes before Shakespeare had met him. My investigations into the history of the boy-actors had made me curious of every detail about him. Had he stood in the carved stall of some gilded choir, reading out of a great book painted with square scarlet notes and long black key lines? We know from the Sonnets how clear and pure his voice was, and what skill he had in the art of music ... I began to think of him not as the delicate chorister of a Royal Chapel, not as a petted minion trained to sing and dance in Leicester's stately masque, but as some fair-haired English lad whom in one of London's hurrying streets, or on Windsor's green silent meadows, Shakespeare had seen and followed, recognising the artistic possibilities that lay hidden in so comely and gracious a form, and divining by a quick and subtle instinct what an actor the lad would make could he be induced to go upon the stage.[284]

Frank Harris, in his Wilde biography, thought that the publication of 'The Portrait of Mr W. H.' did the author 'incalculable injury'.[285] He does not go on to give any details, but there can be little doubt that he was referring to the many homosexual allusions that run right through the story, giving it distinctly erotic undertones. This is already clear at the beginning, when Erskine describes his friend Cyril Graham in gushing terms similar to those with which Basil Hallward describes his model Dorian Gray. He stresses Cyril's unusual appearance, the grace of his movements, the charm of his manner. In a long section at the end of Part II of the extended version, mention is made that the relationship between Shakespeare and Willie Hughes was more than the practical association of dramatist and actor. References to Plato's *Symposium*, Montaigne and Winckelmann, and the second Eclogue of Vergil could leave the Victorian reader in no doubt as to the nature of this friendship. It is not least the homosexual element of the essay that would seem to confirm Wilde's description of creative criticism as 'the record of one's own soul.'[286]

116   Lectures, *Reviews* and *Intentions*

Art and crime: 'Pen, Pencil and Poison'

If one tries to apply the above maxim to 'Pen, Pencil and Poison', which
appeared in the same year as 'The Portrait of Mr W. H.', one cannot help
wondering what was the affinity between the soul of the author and that
of the man whom A. C. Swinburne, in his book on *William Blake* (1868),
once described as 'admirable alike as a painter, a writer, and a murderer':[287] Thomas Griffiths Wainewright. Who exactly was this man
whose life and work inspired Wilde to draw a biographical sketch of him?
It is evident from a glance at the *Dictionary of National Biography* that he
must have been a man of many parts. He was born in Chiswick in 1794,
lost both his parents at an early age, and was adopted by his grandfather,
who took responsibility for having him educated. When he left school, he
was first attracted to painting, and for a while frequented the circles of
Johann Heinrich Füssli and John Flaxman. He served an apprenticeship in
the studio of the portrait painter Thomas Phillips; evidently dissatisfied
with this, he next joined the army in 1814. This proved to be equally
uncongenial. During the years that followed he used various fantastic
pseudonyms, like Janus Weathercock and Egomet Bonmot, under which
he wrote art reviews and other articles for the famous *London Magazine*,
returned to painting – with moderate success – and made the acquaintance of several contemporary poets and authors, including Charles Lamb,
William Hazlitt and Thomas De Quincey. The latter considered him to be
an upstart *parvenu* living above his station, and commented that 'his
finery was but of a second-rate order'.[288]

In 1821 Wainewright married Frances Ward, daughter of the widowed
Mrs Abercrombie. A few years later, he and his wife moved into the house
of his uncle, George Edward Griffiths, who shortly afterwards died under
mysterious circumstances. Upon his death, the rather fine residence passed
to Wainewright, who then took in his mother-in-law as well as his wife's
two half-sisters Helen and Madeleine. Again it was not long before both
Mrs Abercrombie and Helen (whose life had previously been insured with
several companies for a total of £18,000) fell ill and died under similar
circumstances to those observed during the agonised death of Uncle
George. Although in all three cases doctors were unable to establish the
precise cause of death, there seems little doubt in the light of present-day
medical knowledge that Wainewright, who was heavily in debt, cold-
bloodedly poisoned his victims with strychnine, perhaps together with
other deadly but more gradual poisons.

As the insurance companies found the whole business very suspicious,
they refused to pay out the money, whereupon Wainewright deemed it
advisable to leave the country. In 1831 he fled to France. There he spent
the next few years of his life, including several months in prison for

carrying strychnine for which he could give no adequate explanation. In 1837 he returned to England, where he was soon identified, apprehended and put on trial. Ironically he was found guilty not of multiple murder but of forging cheques (which had happened many years before). He was sent for life to Van Diemens Land in Tasmania, and died in a Hobart hospital in 1852.

Wilde was not the first to be fascinated by Wainewright's shady character and adventurous life style. Thomas De Quincey recalled in his essay 'Charles Lamb and his Friends' (1848), which was in effect a review of Thomas Noon Talfourd's *Final Memorials of Charles Lamb ...* (1837–48), a dinner given by the publishers of the *London Magazine* in 1821, where Wainewright was present. Although he felt his colleague's showy clothes and behaviour to be 'commonplace',[289] he admired the sensitivity and good judgment with which 'Janus Weathercock' had written about the great painters of the Italian Renaissance. What fascinated him above all in Wainewright was – 'so much amiable puppyism on one side, so much deep feeling on the other'.[290] Thomas Noon Talfourd, a man of letters and for a while MP for Reading, drew a totally negative portrait of him:

The defect in his [Wainewright's] moral nature consisted perhaps chiefly in morbid self-esteem, so excessive as to overwhelm all countervailing feelings, and to render all the interests of others, all duties, all sympathies, all regards, subservient to the lightest efforts, or wishes, or enjoyments of the wretched idol. His tastes appreciated only the most superficial beauty; his vanities were the poorest and most empty; yet he fancied himself akin to greatness.[291]

The fact that Charles Lamb himself had taken a liking to such a vain and superficial egotist seemed to Talfourd explicable only in terms of Elia's 'sympathy in dissimilitude'.[292] The extremely negative tone of this description may perhaps have been influenced by the fact that Talfourd, who was also a judge, had never forgiven himself his boyhood friendship with someone who later turned to crime.

The impact of Wainewright's personality made itself felt not only in the memories of his contemporaries but also in the imaginations of writers. For instance, Bulwer-Lytton modelled the character of Gabriel Varney on him in *Lucretia or The Children of the Night* (1846), although the complexity of the real-life artist and murderer was simplified and rather flattened into that of a conventional criminal predisposed towards crime from the very start. In 1837 Dickens, on a tour of Newgate Prison, saw him very briefly, together with the actor Macready,[293] and is believed to have modelled Julius Slinkton on him in 'Hunted Down' (1859), though the similarities between Wainewright and Slinkton are somewhat tenuous.

In 1880 W. Carew Hazlitt published a collection of *Essays and*

Criticisms by Janus Weathercock which had appeared in various journals and were not easily obtainable. In his own essay, Wilde relied principally on information given in the biographical introduction that preceded the collection. He also knew De Quincey's essay and Swinburne's observations in *William Blake*. However, he always departs from the descriptions given by his predecessors when he wishes to stress Wainewright's aesthetic traits and to endow him with the qualities of a late romantic dandy. Hilda Schiff, whose 'Critical Study of Oscar Wilde's *Intentions*' examines Wilde's use of his sources, concludes that:

> Wilde's treatment of Wainewright is an up to date and diffused version of De Quincey's and Swinburne's; that is, it presents Wainewright solely in the light of his accomplishments in taste and his artistry and daring in conduct. Wilde knew that *not* to pass moral judgment in this way would be to shock his audience, an effect which he desired. This effect was reinforced by portraying Wainewright as something of a modern Baudelairean dandy, and by dwelling on implied similarities between his taste and conduct and those of the Symbolist writers in France.[294]

What was it about the character and work of Wainewright that fascinated Wilde? In the first instance, it must have been the double life of painter and murderer, writer and forger that attracted the attention of a man who also led two lives and had to pay for the destruction of the one with the loss of the other. Both came up against the law, both were put on trial, and both finished up in exile. In Wainewright, Wilde drew the portrait of a man who was, in many respects, his *alter ego*. Thus arose the romantically tinged picture of the young orphan, seduced by 'boyish dreams of the romance and chivalry of a soldier's life'[295] and becoming a Guard, then rediscovering his true vocation as a painter, living an artist's life, and finally seeing in crime the chance to unfold his personality to the full: aesthete, breaker of the fifth commandment, artist, rebel against the moral order. The writer who loved to surround himself with precious *objets d'art* appreciated the connoisseur and art-collector that he saw in Wainewright; the author of 'The Truth of Masks' found common ground with him in the 'necessity for archaeological accuracy in costume and scene-painting';[296] the author of 'The Critic as Artist' lauded him as a sensitive, impressionistic critic who had recognised very early that 'Art's first appeal is neither to the intellect nor to the emotions, but purely to the artistic temperament.'[297] In short, Wilde adopted Wainewright as a kindred spirit, a precursor of aestheticism, and a dandy. He had very little trouble converting the two-faced Janus Weathercock into a model individualist who extended the artist's freedom into the realm of middle-class morality and uninhibitedly broke the taboos in a manner that Wilde would never have dared. This literary appropriation of an historical character is similar to the manner in which the author of *De Profundis* took Christ and His Martyrdom as the historical paradigm of his own suffering as C.3.3. His attraction to Wainewright lay in what Baudelaire admired in Poe's literary art, *'l'exception dans l'ordre moral'*.[298]

The man who was equally at home with 'pen, pencil and poison' offered more, however, than mere starting-points for vicarious adventures; he could also be used as a mask behind which Wilde could provoke his readers through the thesis that crime had a positive influence on art: '[Wainewright's] crimes seem to have had an important effect upon his art'.[299] It is the potential challenge thrown down by this thesis that represents the real intention behind the essay. The idea of crime enriching the personality is one that comes up again soon afterwards in *Dorian Gray*, where it is said of the protagonist: 'There were moments when he looked on evil simply as a mode through which he could realise his conception of the beautiful.'[300] In the context of Wilde's literary development, the Wainewright sketch functions almost as a preliminary study for the novel. But what appears in 'Pen, Pencil and Poison' as an uncommitted variation on the theme, 'the fact of a man being a poisoner is nothing against his prose',[301] takes on concrete form with *Dorian Gray* as the dilemma of the *doppelgänger*, who is destroyed by the irreconcilability of the aesthetic existence with criminal action.

There must be some doubt as to whether the subject-matter of Wainewright and the form of the biographical essay were really suitable to express Wilde's ideas on the relation between art and crime. How could a reader truly sympathise with a cold-blooded poisoner – surely one of the basest of all criminals? In this particular case, there were not even the extenuating circumstances of poverty, extreme need or mental unbalance. Even if one were to abstain from making any moral judgment and simply take an aesthetic standpoint, the conclusion can only be that 'Wainewright n'est pas un artiste parfait'.[302] For there is nothing remotely disinterested in his actions, such as a purely scientific curiosity about dosage, application and effect of the poisons – 'murder considered as a fine art'; his motives are thoroughly base, as Jonathan Curling, his biographer, makes abundantly clear: 'Like his forgeries, Wainewright's murders were done merely to fill his spendthrift pocket.'[303]

What Wilde at first called 'A Study', and later more imaginatively sub-titled 'A Study in Green', is not the carefully documented life story of an historical figure, but is a subjectively coloured and selective Imaginary Portrait – it is applied aesthetic criticism. But his intentions might have been better served by a different structure: instead of choosing the conventional chronological order of events, he could more suitably have used a looser, essayistic technique to develop his ideas. As it is, the mode of presentation and the main points of Wilde's thesis are not in unison. There is a structural break between the formal account of a life and its subjective interpretation as illustrating a problem connected with philosophy of life in general, and this break is paralleled by the narrator's change of perspectives. The deliberately naive and amoral standpoint has to give way when the author drops the mask of neutrality with such provocative attempts at justification as 'the fact of a man being a poisoner is nothing against his prose'.[304]

Aesthetic individualism and perfection of form

If one analyses the aesthetic and critical writings that we have looked at so far, and searches them for consistency both in relation to one another and to Wilde's fiction, one cannot escape the fact that much of what he writes seems contradictory and eclectic. He was for ever reacting to existing ideas: he assimilated elements of romantic aesthetic theory, but rejected the romantic concept of nature, he vehemently opposed the common Victorian 'heresy of the Didactic',[305] joined Whistler in condemning the moral content of Ruskin's view of art, transformed Matthew Arnold's 'objective' criticism into subjective impressionism, and carried Pater's aesthetics to its formalist extremes. At no time does he ever argue with academic detachment or with the systematic classifications of the positivists, but he shocks, negates, and provokes. The one system he seems prepared to adopt is that of conforming to the public role he had created for himself. It is evident from his style alone that his aim is not to offer definite solutions, but he simply wishes to formulate revisable insights, new perspectives, and indeed 'intentions' rather than solid ideas. The conversational language and dialogic structure of the essays reflect the open-endedness of his art criticism, and in that respect they come closer to the nature of their subject-matter than many systematic treatises.

Indeed Wilde's 'réaction personelle violente'[306] in the form of radical rejection or productive assimilation could never have allowed the formation of a permanent and consistent theory. Contradictions abound between the early and late writings, and between the criticism and the fiction.[307] How, for instance, can one reconcile the message that art is a means of beautifying life and the world with Wilde's emphasis on its autonomy and its uselessness? How can the contemplative ideal of life be accompanied by a hedonistic philosophy of the moment? Where is the common ground between the historicity advocated in 'The Truth of Masks' and the ahistorical formalism of 'The Decay of Lying'? And how can criticism be 'the record of one's own soul'[308] if it is to retain its function as cultural history?

The many contradictions stem from a basic problem that underlies and pervades all Wilde's critical and fictional work: the relation between art and life. The reverence of art as the highest value could only lead either to an aesthetic life or to escapist isolation. Pater's conclusion to *Studies in the History of the Renaissance*, 'art comes to you proposing frankly to give nothing but the highest quality to your moments as they pass, and simply for those moments' sake',[309] and Whistler's definition of the artist as 'a monument of isolation'[310] sum up the two positions. On the other hand, Wilde was well aware that the work of art sprang from the individual, and for this reason if for no other must be linked in some way to empirical reality and historical change. Opposition to the Victorians' middle-class devotion to the useful and the edifying led to art breaking away from their moral and religious order, with the result that the sensual appearance and form of the work took on an absolute value. Perfection of form is the quality that endows the artist's creation with the seal of a self-sufficient counter-world, thus denoting his superiority to the crude and formless realities of life and nature. The extent of art's freedom is the extent to which it emancipates itself from all external pressure for didacticism. Furthermore, the aesthetic construct bears the signature of its creator's individual hand, for 'Art is Individualism, and Individualism is a disturbing and disintegrating force.'[311] The creation and the reception of art demand the sensitive temperament of an artistic individual – in short, 'personality'. 'Personality and perfection' represent the two poles of an approach to solving the problem of art versus life. In the reviews Wilde identified personality with the inimitable style of the artist, and perfection with learnable literary technique, but later he insisted on their unity: 'Technique is really personality.'[312]

Such a simple equation could not solve the problem, for it could not overcome the tensions between aesthetic individualism and decorative formalism. Not until T. S. Eliot's 'impersonal theory of poetry' was the logical conclusion drawn that 'Poetry ... is not the expression of personality, but an escape from personality.'[313] There could be no more radical formula for the banishment of the poet from his work. What began as a counter to individualistic aestheticism and impressionism at the turn of the century, aiming to rid literary criticism of its vague dependence on biography and psychology, and to pull the rug of subjectivity from under its feet, unexpectedly led to the elimination of the artistic subject. The disappearance of the poet, who until then had been the most important link between work and reality, resulted almost inevitably in form taking precedence over content. The dangers of this approach to literature did not become fully apparent until the poetics of New Criticism. This presupposed, amongst other things, the autonomy of art, interpretation based entirely on formal analysis to the exclusion of expression and effect – which were condemned as 'affective fallacy' and 'intentional fallacy' – and the use of a drastically reduced critical terminology, with constantly recurring key terms such as 'structure', 'texture', 'irony', 'paradox' and 'tension'. Instead of subjective interpretation, there was to be objective description based on 'close reading'. But New Criticism's exclusive concentration on the internal structure of a work, with its striving for neutrality, was bound by its very omissions to provoke the desire for a creative, hermeneutic approach, and so what began as a counter to the Wildean concept of criticism as art enjoyed a new lease of life[314] more than fifty years later in Staiger's *Kunst der Interpretation [The Art of Interpretation]* (1955).

This brief survey reveals just how dynamic were the problems that Wilde was grappling with. One may consider him to be a successor to the romantics, as did Lewis J. Poteet ('Romantic Aesthetics in Oscar Wilde's Prose', 1968) and Ann R. Yaffe ('Oscar Wilde as Critic', 1972), a representative of Victorianism 'at its most vital and self-questioning phase'[315] (Hilda Schiff, 'A Critical Study of Oscar Wilde's *Intentions*, 1960), or a 'significant fore-runner of the theory if not the practice of the "New Critics"'[316] (Robert E. Rhodes, 'The Literary Criticism of Oscar Wilde', 1964), but whichever view one subscribes to, there can be no denying that his position in late-nineteenth-century criticism, however eclectic, is original both in form and content, and is clearly distinct from that of his predecessors. René Wellek talked of his 'range and scope' and regarded him as 'the representative figure of the English aesthetic movement'.[317] Richard Ellmann, in the introduction to his edition of Wilde's critical writings, wrote that there were three and not two phases of criticism in the late nineteenth century, 'with Pater transitional between Arnold and Wilde'.[318] He did not, as we have seen, put together a consistent system, but along with Dorian Gray he could maintain of himself that 'he never fell into the error of arresting his intellectual development by any formal acceptance of creed or system'.[319] Yet despite all the individual contradictions, often resulting from exaggerations designed to shock the public, his critical work does reveal an undeniable coherence of themes and values. The aesthetic individualism and decorative formalism of his concept of art, and the subjective impressionism of his criticism, stem from his conviction that beauty is a value in itself, and that art is an irreplaceable and valuable experience of life, free from political intentions, moral obligations and utilitarian aims. In an age of materialism, spreading industrialisation and technology, Wilde insisted on the pre-eminence of art, and he succeeded more than any other critic in enhancing public awareness of its importance.

4   Authority and autonomy.
The Soul of Man under Socialism

George Bernard Shaw, in his 'Memories of Oscar Wilde', describes a
number of meetings with his Irish compatriot who had, like himself, left
Dublin to take up residence in London. These meetings did not exceed a
dozen in all, and Shaw has clear recollections of half of them. Towards the
end of the 1880s he was already a committed member of the Fabian
Society, and was giving numerous lectures in an effort to arouse interest in
his ideas. Wilde attended one of these talks, and indeed actually spoke at
the meeting:

At a meeting somewhere in Westminster at which I delivered an address on
Socialism, and at which Oscar turned up and spoke, Robert Ross surprised me
greatly by telling me, long after Oscar's death, that it was this address of mine that
moved Oscar to try his hand at a similar feat by writing 'The Soul of Man under
Socialism'.[1]

Unfortunately Shaw does not say which of his lectures it was. J. D.
Thomas, in his essay '"The Soul of Man under Socialism". An Essay in
Context',[2] believes it was his talk on Ibsen, which he gave to a large
audience on 18 July 1890 at St James's Restaurant and which, with its
substantial element of social criticism, formed the basis of his essay *The
Quintessence of Ibsenism* (1891). Bearing in mind the fact that the
Norwegian dramatist had become fashionable in the England of the
1880s, and that Wilde himself held him in high esteem, this theory may
not be too wide of the mark'. There is a certain parallel between Shaw's
'repudiation of duty by Man'[3] and Wilde's remark that 'Individualism
does not come to the man with any sickly cant about duty'.[4] Wilde's claim
that 'It is through disobedience that progress has been made'[5] is simply a
variation of Shaw's 'progress must involve the repudiation of an established duty at every step'.[6] Both speak critically of marriage and family
life, pleading for the abolition of legal constraints within the two institutions. These individual affinities cannot, however, be regarded as conclusive evidence that it was indeed Shaw's Ibsen lecture that Wilde attended.

Wilde's essay appeared in 1891, and has attracted little attention
among the critics – even such monographs as those of San Juan (1967) and
Nassaar (1974) barely mention it. By narrowing their perspective to that
of Wilde's sources, in this case a particularly unproductive line to follow,
critics have for instance overlooked the fact that *The Soul of Man under*

123

Socialism in part continues the debate in which Wilde had been engaged following the publication of Dorian Gray. If one compares the letters he wrote between June and August 1890 to the St James's Gazette, the Daily Chronicle and the Scots Observer, and his sharp condemnation of critics and readers who interfere with 'the individualism of imaginative art'[7] – as set forth in The Soul of Man under Socialism – then it is clear that he was continuing on a general level, that is, without direct reference to Dorian Gray, the discussion already begun on the autonomy of the artist, the self-sufficiency of art, and its relation to society. On the other hand, Wilde also sets out to make his contribution to a socialist transformation of society. Consequently, our analysis of this essay will be concerned with two problems: we shall begin with a survey of social conditions and socialist theories in the 1880s, so that we can define Wilde's own position all the more clearly. Then, on the basis of the above-mentioned cross-references to his aesthetics, we shall set forth the argument of the essay and interpret it in the context of Wilde's theory of art and philosophy of life. This will enable us to judge more accurately how far the essay covers the scope of its title, and whether it denotes a complete change in Wilde's position at the beginning of the 1890s, or merely a new formulation of the old position.

Social reality and socialist theory

The 1880s in England were a time of social and economic change.[8] The boom that took place between 1850 and 1870 was followed by a depression. Competition from continental industry, especially German, and from American agriculture transformed world markets, while improved sea transport led to the importation of cheap grain from America and the collapse of prices in England. Substantial imports of American meat, made possible by new techniques of freezing, had a similar effect, and at the same time the erection of customs barriers put a stop to free trade and cut heavily into British exports. With falling profits from agriculture, the number of farms dwindled and there was a mass exodus from the country. Between 1851 and 1881 the number of people working on the land decreased by half, while those in trade and industry doubled.[9] Slowly the consequences of this social–economic restructuring took on a more definitive shape, with England changing from an agricultural to an industrial state.

Despite rising wages and falling prices the distribution of income did not favour the worker. If the poverty line was somewhere in the region of 30s per week, over 30 per cent of the population of London were living in poverty.[10] The rapid increase in unemployment between 1885 and 1887 led to such a drastic deterioration in the already miserable conditions of the workers that there were ever more frequent demonstrations and riots. On 8 February 1886 around 20,000 people gathered in Trafalgar Square, mainly unemployed dockyard and building labourers, protesting against their appalling conditions. The crowd got out of control, and the ensuing riots went on for several days.[11] On 13 November 1887, 'Bloody Sunday', there were again violent confrontations between demonstrators and police. And the massive increase in social tension reached a climax with the London dock strike of 1889 which, perhaps partly through its disciplined conduct, aroused in large sections of the middle classes an unusual degree of sympathy for the workers and their justifiable demands.

This social and economic crisis had a direct effect on social consciousness. The gap between the prosperous privileged classes and the far more numerous poorer classes, eking out an existence at the very bottom of the scrap-heap, had become more blatant than ever before. In her autobiography *My Apprenticeship* (1926), Beatrice Webb mentions 'a new consciousness of sin among men of intellect and men of property'.[12] In addition to this uncomfortable awareness that the existing order was morally inadequate and had failed to provide a proper balance of welfare for all, there was a growing fear that the Trafalgar Square demonstrators might be merely the militant vanguard of a proletarian revolution that would sooner or later storm the citadels of the Establishment and take all power out of its hands. Another vital factor was that all confidence was shattered in the principle of individualism which had marked the *laissez-faire* capitalism of the Liberals as well as the progress ethic of the middle classes. The combination of guilt as regards the all-too-evident social injustice, fear of revolutionary upheaval, internal economic crises and restrictions on export trade, all amounted to a complex of problems which seemed beyond the capacity of any traditional form of solution.

Both right and left sides of the political spectrum were agreed on the fact that the crisis could not be overcome by traditional methods, and certainly not by those means at the disposal of the Charity Organisation Society. More and more credence was granted to the view that poverty was not God's just punishment of the person concerned, but was connected rather with unfair distribution of property, inadequate education, a lack of work, and bad living conditions. This change in the climate of opinion was part of a wider reorientation of social philosophy, described by Helen Lynd as follows:

The social philosophy of the 'eighties reduced the area of what was 'given' and could not be altered in society and enlarged the area of potentialities which human beings could do something about. It pushed further back the 'laws' of Nature and of God as confining men and began to push back the 'laws' of economic institutions. It restored human initiative in society and brought new expectations and new possibilities. Men became more sharply aware that institutions are man-made and, therefore, changeable.[13]

If the causes of poverty were social, then it could no longer be dismissed as a God-given fate or an economic law; man must recognise that it could be changed by appropriate measures. In his study *Life and Labour of the People of London* (1889–1903), which filled no less than seventeen volumes, Charles Booth had documented the misery of the poor with such a convincing array of facts and figures that no one could possibly plead ignorance on this subject. Previous economic and social politics had failed to solve the problem, and so now the urgent question arose as to whether the state did not have both the right and the duty to plan and structure the economy in such a way that it could bring about a change in the social pattern. This was the background against which there developed socialist ideas which led in the 1880s to the foundation of various bodies and which proved very attractive to intellectual circles as well as to the educated middle class of the time.[14] They were not thinking of authoritarian socialism, which would bring excessive restrictions on individual freedom, but of a socially organised state through which it was hoped that all members would be free to develop themselves. John Stuart Mill, in his *Autobiography* (1873), foresaw the most important social problem of the decades to follow:

The social problem of the future we considered to be, how to unite the greatest individual liberty of action, with a common ownership in the raw material of the globe, and an equal participation of all in the benefits of combined labour.[15]

Between the sixties and early eighties in England there had been no socialist movement worth mentioning,[16] with the possible exception of the Land and Labour League, which amongst other things demanded the nationalisation of land, shorter working hours, the abolition of the standing army, and universal suffrage. Small radical groups built up in Birmingham around Joseph Chamberlain and in London around Charles Dilke and, together with the Christian Socialists led by Stewart Headlam and the Republican Radical Secularists under Charles Bradlaugh, they helped to create a political atmosphere that was conducive to an extra-parliamentary movement towards socialism and anarchy.

Under the influence of Marx and the best-selling *Progress and Poverty* (1879) by the American Henry George, Henry M. Hyndman founded the Democratic Federation in 1881 (rechristened the Social Democratic Federation in 1884), with the aim of reviving Chartist ideas. He hoped to gain the support of radical groups that were dissatisfied with the Liberal policies of the government. But the political effectiveness of the Federation was blunted from the very start by internal tensions between the Marxist revolutionary activists and the anarchists, who found Hyndman's

Marxism too authoritarian and who were not disposed towards the founding of a political party anyway; there were also conflicts with the union side of the Federation, whose representatives were less interested in abstract ideas of revolution than in the acutely current problems of the working class. And so the Social Democratic Federation broke up just three years after its formation, when at the end of 1884 William Morris – who had only joined it the year before – took off with a splinter group of like-minded men and founded the Socialist League. Although the causes of this split are not fully known, it would seem that some members – particularly some of the anarchists – had major reservations concerning Hyndman's autocratic, centralist ideas. Around the mid 1880s there were altogether three serious, competing socialist groups: the SDF under Hyndman, the Socialist League under Morris, and the hitherto little-known Fabian Society, which was founded in 1884. There were also a number of anarchist groups whose membership revolved round the journal *Freedom*. A few smaller associations which demanded land reform and which operated partly on a regional level completed the left wing of extra-parliamentary opposition.

From the mid 1880s onwards, the Fabian Society[17] became increasingly important. Initially it was a little debating club in which a few middle-class moral idealists developed their visions of a more just society where happiness and prosperity could be assured for all. Among the most prominent members were G. B. Shaw and Beatrice and Sidney Webb; these were joined in 1885 and 1886 by Sydney Olivier, Graham Wallas, Annie Besant and William Clarke. Through public meetings and the Fabian tracts, which were an important organ of propaganda for the society, current social and political topics were discussed and made accessible to interested readers. Thanks to the high intellectual level on which these often explosive themes were handled, the various articles soon became widely known. Although the Fabians themselves often had different opinions, which made it difficult for them to put together a succinct programme, it can be said that from the social, political and economic points of view they steered a reformist course orientated by evolutionary change and not by any revolutionary overthrow of the status quo. Nevertheless, during the early phase of this movement, Shaw and Charlotte Wilson had in fact put forward revolutionary ideas. In 1889 the *Fabian Essays in Socialism* were published. These were in the nature of a manifesto, whose eight contributions from eight different authors conveyed a cross-section of Fabian thought. They were not based on any unified definition of socialism, but they did reveal a collectivist interpretation of the term. There was no unity on the question of whether the common goal could best be reached by nationalising all means of production, or by progressively taxing income and interest. In comparison with the quasi-religious moral idealism that characterised Fabian ideas during the earlier phase of the society's existence, social change as advocated in the *Fabian Essays* had become genuinely pragmatic, with far more emphasis on economic and political factors. But as Willard Wolfe stresses in his detailed study *From Radicalism to Socialism*, this new direction does not denote a total break with previous ideas:

Thus, despite the formal reorientation of Fabian theory, the traditional goal of social regeneration and the parallel tendency to identify Socialism with the triumph of social feelings and the building of a new moral world persisted in both the Fabian essays and in Fabian lectures of the 1890s; and the combination of such views (which were especially clear in the essays of Olivier, Wallas, and Besant) with the hard-nosed economic reasoning of Shaw and Clarke did much to give the essays their exceptionally wide-ranging appeal.[18]

A major influence on the Fabians and indeed on the whole socialist movement of the 1880s was the personality and work of William Morris.[19] In December 1884 he and some kindred spirits had separated from the SDF and formed the Socialist League, though this failed to develop substantially and finally dissolved in 1890. The anarchist wing of the League forced Morris out and later affiliated themselves to Kropotkin's Freedom Group, while their disappointed former leader gathered round him what was left of the faithful and founded the short-lived Hammersmith Socialist Society. At no time had he been able to identify with the radical activism of the anarchists in the Socialist League, but had always been more inclined towards working with information, propaganda and agitation: 'my business ... is to spread discontent'.[20]

Morris's demands for fundamental change were inspired by his dissatisfaction with an unjust, unbalanced distribution of wealth and property, capitalist exploitation, and the ugliness of industrial society. His social writings and his propaganda combine the humanitarian commitment of Ruskin, many of whose ideas he adopted, the revolutionary demands of Karl Marx, and his own lifelong appreciation of art as a particular form of aesthetic socialism. His programme pursued three basic aims: the abolition of the existing political and economic system, with its ruthless 'competitive Commerce'[21] and disproportionate division of society into the wealthy few and the many poor; a new evaluation of manual labour as a useful, creative and satisfying skill; emphasis on art in every citizen's life, with the concept being extended to 'the aspect of all the externals of our life'.[22] It is not least this extension of art that leads to the impression, in much of his writing, that Morris was a forerunner of today's ecology movement.

In his social and aesthetic writings – contained in *Hopes and Fears for Art*, 'Lectures on Art and Industry', 'Signs of Change', and 'Lectures on Socialism' – as well as in his Utopian novel *News from Nowhere* (1890),

Morris constantly invoked the vision of a society without central government or wasteful bureaucracy, whose members came together at local
level in communist federations; there is no private ownership, 'competition' has been replaced by 'association', and mechanical production –
apart from absolute necessities – gives way to manual labour. In this
simple and harmonious life, art is 'a help and solace to the daily life of all
men'.[23] Indeed art has become an integral element of work, which itself is·
seen as a satisfying creative activity. In Morris's vision of a future society,
art has been liberated from its elitist isolation, and the Utopian community is conceived as a kind of mammoth commune of artists.[24]

   Although there can be no doubting the sincerity of Morris's humanitarianism as evinced in his writings, his speeches and his work for the SDF
and later the Socialist League, many of his arguments are inconsistent and
naively Utopian. In fact his own firm produced luxury goods enjoying a
certain 'snob prestige' with the upper-middle classes – items such as
painted wallpaper and glasses, which were certainly not designed to be of
use to the workers whose problems lay so heavily on his heart. It is also
difficult to see how the practical, economic requirements of an industrial
society – even a communist society – could be met by the working
methods of the medieval guilds. Nevertheless, no praise is too high for
Morris's unceasing efforts to give art its due value in a materialistic
society. The artist was almost the linchpin of his ideal social order, and
indeed 'it was mainly because he was an artist that he became a
revolutionary'.[25] It was this aesthetic motivation that distinguished him
from all the other socialists of the 1880s, for they scarcely spared a
thought for the role of art in the society of the future. This is the point of
contact between Morris and Wilde and, in particular, *The Soul of Man
under Socialism*, although they each went in a totally different direction.
For Morris, Socialism marked a transitional stage on the way to a
communist 'Earthly Paradise', whereas Wilde saw it as a preliminary step
to the total fulfilment of the individual.

From socialism to individualism

To express his ideas on the ideal society, Wilde chose the form of the
essay. This allowed him to articulate his thoughts freely, without any of
the constraints imposed by formal structure or systematic analysis. He
deals mainly with two areas: initially he sketches the conditions which
necessitate an end to the current political and social order, and then he
outlines his plan for a future society characterised by a gradual transition
from socialism to individualism. Evolutionary changes in objective social
structures indicate changes in the subjective moral conduct of individuals.
The tension between the individual's struggle for autonomy and the

conformist pressures of authoritarian institutions, moral norms and public opinion, is illustrated by the artist's relation to society. The close link between the social and political subject-matter and Wilde's aesthetic theory makes it clear that this essay should not be construed exclusively as a design for Utopia.

Wilde begins with the somewhat abrupt remark that the chief advantage of socialism would lie in relieving men of the 'sordid necessity of living for others'.[26] The cure for social misery, above all poverty, lies neither in individual altruism nor organised charity, but in the attempt to change the basic social and economic order in such a way that poverty becomes impossible. The first step along this path is the abolition of private ownership:

Socialism, Communism, or whatever one chooses to call it, by converting private property into public wealth, and substituting cooperation for competition, will restore society to its proper condition of a thoroughly healthy organism, and ensure the material well-being of each member of the community. It will, in fact, give Life its proper basis and its proper environment.[27]

Among the poor, who have no private property, there is 'no grace of manner, or charm of speech, or civilisation or culture'.[28] In reality private property is a burden even for the rich, since it imposes countless unpleasant duties and economic burdens on them. Poverty, on the other hand, dulls awareness of its misery and paralyses the will to break free. This is why agitators are so necessary, since without them there could be no civilising progress. The poor man who can put up no opposition to his living conditions and is grateful for the crumbs that fall from the rich man's table must be regarded as a pitiful example of a perverted moral code. To recommend thrift to the poor man is like advising the hungry man to eat less. But the man who rises up against his poverty instead of passively subjecting himself to it is a 'real personality'.[29]

Disobedience, in the eyes of anyone who has read history, is man's original virtue. It is through disobedience that progress has been made, through disobedience and through rebellion.[30]

In striving for a socialist order, one must dispense with State interference, for 'no Authoritarian Socialism will do'.[31] All forms of government have proved false:

Despotism is unjust to everybody, including the despot, who was probably made for better things. Oligarchies are unjust to the many, and ochlocracies are unjust to the few. High hopes were once formed of democracy; but democracy means simply the bludgeoning of the people by the people for the people. It has been found out. I must say that it was high time, for all authority is quite degrading.[32]

In a socialist community, the state is nothing but an apparatus for the production and distribution of 'necessary commodities';[33] it looks after essentials, so that the individual can devote himself to beauty. In this future society there will be no cause for punishment, because the abolition of private property will do away with the main causes of crime – namely, hunger and poverty. Rising crime does not mean moral degeneration but is the consequence of blatant imbalance in the distribution of income; in other words, crime is conditioned by economic factors.

For all men to have greater opportunities of fulfilling themselves in an atmosphere of 'cultivated leisure',[34] the abolition of private property is not enough. It is also essential that all work which does not arise from intellectual or artistic concerns should be carried out by machines. Talk of the 'dignity of manual labour'[35] glosses over the incontestable fact that much manual labour is sheer misery: 'To sweep a slushy crossing for eight hours on a day when the east wind is blowing is a disgusting occupation.'[36] Together with reforms in the world of work, there must be changes in the family. Marriage in its present form will be abolished. Instead there will be a relationship without any legal obligations, and this will make love between man and wife 'more wonderful, more beautiful, and more ennobling'.[37]

Socialism, then, will deprive the State of its power, remove existing economic structures, and thus improve the social situation of all members of the community, but this does not represent the final goal of the evolutionary process. Political, economic and social reforms will lead, rather, to a state of individualism which will guarantee man's autonomy against any form of authority. The abolition of private property will favour this development, for wealth and property signify social recognition and material prosperity, and so in the past people have always striven to amass more and more money and goods until they finally have more than they need. This ceaseless quest for property hinders the individual from fulfilling his real task in life, which is the realisation of himself. This is caused by a misconception of individualism, for 'the true perfection of man lies, not in what man has, but in what man is'.[38] The individualistic philosophy of life will be put into practice automatically because its goal corresponds to man's effort to unfold his natural qualities. 'It [individualism] knows that people are good when they are let alone.'[39] In no way should individualism be confused with boundless egotism or personal affectation. On the contrary: 'When man has realised Individualism, he will also realise sympathy and exercise it freely and spontaneously.'[40] It is not individualism, but competition, conformity and the struggle for professional and social advancement that have led to 'sympathy' becoming such a rare commodity. But sympathy is not to be confined just to participation in one's neighbour's suffering, for this is ultimately an egotistic feeling, conditioned by fear of falling victim to the same circumstances. Wilde demands a different kind of 'sympathy':

One should sympathise with the entirety of life, not with life's sores and maladies merely, but with life's joy and beauty and energy and health and freedom. The wider sympathy is, of course, the more difficult. It requires more unselfishness. Anybody can sympathise with the sufferings of a friend, but it requires a very fine nature – it requires, in fact, that nature of a true Individualist – to sympathise with a friend's success.[41]

The 'true Individualist' will not find self-fulfilment in suffering, self-sacrifice or renunciation of the world, like the saints and martyrs of the Middle Ages, but in the ideals of the Renaissance: 'the beauty of life' and 'the joy of living'.[42]

The most intensive form of individualism is art, for art offers the most stubborn resistance to the pressures of conformity exercised by public opinion and its medium, the press. While philosophers and scientists are granted the right to develop their ideas independently of traditional norms, poets are expected to conform to a 'popular standard'.[43] The public greets any innovation of form or content with suspicion, because it does not correspond to what they are used to; such novelties are therefore dismissed as 'grossly unintelligible' or 'grossly immoral'.[44] Expressions such as 'exotic', 'unhealthy' and 'morbid' accompany the rejection of all attempts to extend the range of art and to find new ways of representing the changed subject. The grim relationship between the artist and society is caused by the authoritarian attitude of those who represent public opinion – the press and the critics, who are never prepared to appreciate a work of art as the individual expression of an autonomous personality. The public should not mould the artist, but the artist must be allowed to create in his reader a 'temperament of receptivity'.[45]

If we try to fit *The Soul of Man under Socialism* into the socialist movement of the 1880s as outlined earlier, the differences will be so apparent that one might almost take Wilde's essay as a tract against socialism. There is, for instance, a vast gulf between the Fabians' plans for reform – politically motivated, economically well thought out, and set forth in a series of socialist publications – and the romantic ideas of freedom and humanitarianism laid down in a one-off essay by a middle-class radical Liberal hiding behind the provocative mask of a classless anarchist. While the Fabians took great care to detail their ideas for a new economic order, Wilde simply talks in general terms of abolishing private property and replacing competition with cooperation. His restriction of the State's function to the production and distribution of essentials raises far more questions than it answers. Of course the social concepts of Hyndman, Shaw and Morris were not without their inconsistencies, but their criticism of society was based on a profound awareness of the social and economic situation and its historical development, sharp intellectual analysis, and total commitment to the possibility of a fairer, that is, a socialist, order in the future. With Wilde's essay one cannot escape the impression that his insights are based on a general and superficial knowledge of the problems of the East End – a knowledge gained not from direct experience of life in the lower classes, but from the passenger seat of a cab passing through the less reputable districts of London, or from the carefully scrutinised pages of a newspaper. Where Morris demands joy in work and profit for the general good, Wilde stresses the 'true pleasure and joy of living';[46] where Morris sees the main social function of art as making the environment more beautiful, Wilde insists on its aristocratic exclusiveness.

Clearly, then, it would be wrong to view Wilde's essay as a political answer to the concrete social problems of the East End, or as a constructive contribution to the development of socialist theory. He provides no link between the existing order and the ideal, but simply leaps from reality straight into Utopia. With fashionable slogans he articulates a very personal viewpoint which combines a radical longing for freedom, humanitarian commitment, and the aesthetic absolutism of his *Intentions*. This image of the individual free from all obligations and official pressures, able to devote himself exclusively to 'dreams of Art / And loftiest culture',[47] is already foreshadowed in the 'Eleutheria' section of the early *Poems*. Elsewhere, in addition to his abstract love of freedom, he adduces examples of political repression and social injustice, for instance the atrocities committed by the Turkish troops on Bulgarian freedom fighters in May 1876, to which he responds in his 'Sonnet. On the Massacre of the Christians in Bulgaria'. His first stage-play *Vera; or, The Nihilists* takes the side of the Nihilists against the Tsarist tyranny: 'Between the Nihilists and all men who wear crowns above their fellows, there is war to the death.'[48] And the fact that he was prepared to commit himself personally, and not merely to pay lip-service to such causes, may be illustrated by two examples. G. B. Shaw reports that Wilde was the only man he could find who was prepared to sign a petition on behalf of the eight Chicago anarchists,[49] seven of whom had been sentenced to death after the bloody demonstration in the Haymarket on 4 May 1886.[50] Not one of those whom Shaw had approached – 'all heroic rebels and skeptics on paper'[51] – had dared to commit himself publicly on this matter. 'It was a completely disinterested act on his [Wilde's] part; and it secured my distinguished consideration for him for the rest of his life.'[52] An equally unselfish act, recounted by Hesketh Pearson, was his standing bail for the anarchist poet John Barlas after the latter had fired some revolver shots at the House of Commons in 1891 to express his disapproval of existing conditions.[53] And the letters that Wilde wrote to the *Daily Chronicle* after he himself had been released from Reading Gaol, pleading for reform of the penal system, add a further dimension to this image of social engagement, which was always inspired by humanitarian far more than by political motives.[54]

As far as the content of the essay is concerned, it certainly does not answer the questions implied by its title; instead of being a contribution to the discussion of socialist theory, it is in fact a manifesto for aesthetic individualism. Its main statement can be summarised in a single sentence: after the abolition of private property and every type of authority, ideal social conditions will be established for individualism, which will make it possible for man to realise himself to the full extent of his personality, and which will find its loftiest manifestation in art. The frequency of such terms as 'individualism' – which occurs about fifty times in the twenty-five pages of the text – 'authority' (forty times) and 'personality' (some twenty-five times) is ample indication of the thematic focal points of Wilde's argument. With one tirade after another he attacks all forms of authority, whether it is man's political domination of man, the legalised exercise of power by institutions of the state or church, or the conformist pressure of public opinion, particularly the press, as evinced by the normative criticism of artists:

all authority is quite degrading. It degrades those who exercise it, and degrades those over whom it is exercised. When it is violently, grossly, and cruelly used, it produces a good effect, by creating, or at any rate bringing out, the spirit of revolt and Individualism that is to kill it. When it is used with a certain amount of kindness, and accompanied by prizes and rewards, it is dreadfully demoralising. People, in that case, are less conscious of the horrible pressure that is being put on them, and so go through their lives in a sort of coarse comfort, like petted animals, without ever realising that they are probably thinking other people's thoughts, living by other people's standards, wearing practically what one may call other people's second-hand clothes, and never being themselves for a single moment.[55]

To make such a radical, liberal negation of authority the basis of a future order is Utopian in the extreme, for 'auch eine spekulative Phantasie vermag sich eine Gesellschaft, im Grossen wie im Kleinen, ohne Autorität nicht vorzustellen'[56] [even a speculative fantasy cannot conceive of a society, large or small, without authority]. The relation between authority and freedom is not a complementary one in Wilde's eyes, but is antithetical, for he seems to identify authority solely with the exercise of power. In this respect he diverges almost as radically from the conservative concept of power, which was always bound up with legitimacy, as from the socialist interpretation. Marx and Engels never denied the principle of authority, for instance in the sense of a functionally limited authorisation to take charge of the production process. In his essay 'Von der Autorität' (1873), Engels felt obliged to inform the 'Antiautoritarier' that 'eine Revolution ... gewiss das autoritärste Ding [ist], das es gibt'[57] [a revolution [is] ... certainly the most authoritarian thing there is]. Even the collectivism of the Fabians, especially as conceived by Sidney Webb, has a thoroughly authoritarian character with its stress on state and economic control.

Wilde's profound mistrust of the principle of authority has its historical precedents in anarchism, whose best-known adherents from the late eighteenth to the early twentieth centuries were William Godwin, Pierre-Joseph Proudhon, Michail Bakunin, and Prince Peter Kropotkin.[58] Masolino d'Amico, in his study of 'Oscar Wilde between "Socialism" and Aestheticism',[59] has traced the intellectual affinity between Wilde's essay and the theories of the anarchists, among whom he includes William Morris. Such a detailed list of 'influences' is particularly tricky in this case, since the political ideas in *The Soul of Man* are so general that they are for the most part as socialist as they are anarchist. For example, the idea of abolishing marriage is to be found in Godwin,[60] Morris[61] and Shaw.[62]

By the beginning of the 1890s, Wilde's predilection for aesthetic individualism did not need any motivation from outside. Such critics as Edouard Roditi and George Woodcock have certainly overestimated the influence on *The Soul of Man* exerted by Chuang Tzǔ, a Taoist philosopher who lived in the fourth century BC. In 1889 the English version of *Chuang Tzǔ: Mystic, Moralist, and Social Reformer* was published, and on 8 February 1890 Wilde gave it a long and favourable review in the *Speaker*.[63] In fact many of the Chinese sage's beliefs coincided with those of Wilde, for example, faith in the value of 'inaction', the idea of self-fulfilment, the rejection of all forms of government, distrust of organised philanthropy, and the doctrine of the 'uselessness of all useful things'.[64] But the claim that these Taoist maxims were 'a decisive influence on Wilde's own philosophy',[65] or that they gave him the chance to 'transcend at last the political dilemmas of the dandy in a new creed of his own',[66] ignores the simple fact that the reviewer of the Chuang Tzǔ book was once a pupil of Pater in Oxford. Had not his teacher also proclaimed 'That the end of life is not action but contemplation – *being* as distinct from *doing*'?[67] Isobel Murray's conclusion is certainly correct: 'It would of course be absurd to see anything in the review as an instance of Chuang Tzǔ's influencing Wilde'.[68]

Anyone who develops himself along the lines laid down by Pater, devoting his life to the unfolding of his individuality, is a 'personality'. Wilde never tires of repeating this idea of intensive and perfect self-fulfilment, whose ideal is 'the beauty of life and the joy of living'[69] and whose goal is 'perfect harmony'[70] and 'peace'.[71] Free from egotism and the pursuit of selfish interests, man in this ideal state of individualism will adopt an attitude of brotherly sympathy towards all others. The vision of future co-existence, without any conflict, demands an optimistic view of man which has nothing in common with Hobbes's Leviathan. Wilde's premise 'that people are good when they are let alone'[72] is reminiscent of Rousseau's doctrine of man's original virtue in his natural state prior to civilisation. On the basis of this conviction, Wilde makes the development of individualism seem both natural and inevitable by brusquely adapting Darwin's principle of evolution. Herbert Spencer, Annie Besant and other social Darwinists had used the principle as scientific justification for their belief that society would advance 'from an incoherent homogeneity to a coherent heterogeneity'[73] or, in Annie Besant's words, 'from individual-istic anarchy to associated order'.[74] Wilde, however, turns Darwin's idea upside down by claiming that 'there is no evolution except towards individualism'.[75] The Utopian end-product of this process, the 'true personality of man', is a concept that he embraces with visionary fervour:

It will be a marvellous thing – the true personality of man – when we see it. It will grow naturally and simply, flowerlike, or as a tree grows. It will not be at discord. It will never argue or dispute. It will not prove things. It will know everything. And yet it will not busy itself about knowledge. It will have wisdom. Its value will not be measured by material things. It will have nothing. And yet it will have everything, and whatever one takes from it, it will still have; so rich will it be. It will not be always meddling with others, or asking them to be like itself. It will love them because they will be different. And yet while it will not meddle with others, it will help all, as a beautiful thing helps us, by being what it is. The personality of man will be very wonderful. It will be as wonderful as the personality of a child.[76]

This glorification of the personality is nothing new in Wilde's work. In 'Pen, Pencil and Poison' he played with the idea of 'an intense personality being created out of sin'.[77] In *Dorian Gray*, Basil Hallward on his first meeting with Dorian ascribes his fascination to the radiance of the latter's personality, which inspires him to 'an entirely new manner in art, an entirely new mode of style'.[78] Once again one has the feeling that in *The Soul of Man* Wilde is not directly concerned with current socialist theory or social reality, but is simply using the debate of the late 1880s as a vehicle for projecting into a social context his new philosophical and aesthetic ideas in the guise of a provocative anarchism. The negation of all external regulations and authority runs parallel to the rejection of reality as a starting-point for art; similarly the self-sufficiency and perfection of art are reflected in the autonomy and the search for perfection of the individual. The aesthetic absolutism of Wilde's theory of art demanded anarchic individualism as its social framework. It is perhaps inevitable that this excursion into new territory should lead to certain contradictions and obscurities. When one reads the essay, one cannot help wondering occasionally who is supposed to overthrow the existing system, and how the socialist process is actually to come about. We know from 'The Critic as Artist' that Wilde places a higher value on contemplation than on action, for:

Action is limited and relative. Unlimited and absolute is the vision of him who sits at ease and watches, who walks in loneliness and dreams.[79]

Under such conditions, changes beyond the realm of one's own subjectivity are impossible. It is therefore understandable that Wilde should have wished to leave the construction of his ideal society to the virtually automatic process of evolution, since this freed him from the necessity of personal action. The idea of art being superior to life, and of self-fulfilment as a subjective process of development, bears little relation to the goal of changing society. Here the argument becomes inconsistent, and it is clear that Wilde's transposition of his aesthetic theory into a social Utopia is not altogether a smooth one.

Wilde found his ideal of individualism by way of art, even if he does speak of socialism as a preparatory stage. He insists that his ideal concept of individualism is different from previous concepts, but the impression remains that basically he has simply taken over the liberal ideology of the Victorian middle classes. As we have already seen, however, the 1880s had witnessed a permanent shattering of faith in the blessings of a *laissez-faire* economy as well as in Liberalism: 'that it was not through Liberalism that a new order could come, was a crucial factor in the formulation of a new social philosophy'.[80] Wilde did not and could not associate himself with this progressive mode of thought, directly orientated as it was by social progress, because he was only converting his aesthetic theory into one of cultural and not social revolution. Thus for all its fashionably provocative façade, his essay remains politically embedded in the tradition of Victorian Liberalism, while philosophically it is indebted to Matthew Arnold's ideal of culture and Pater's aesthetic view of the world. Current revolutionary demands must be met by traditional evolutionary methods. Nevertheless, Wilde's provocation and conformity do not cancel each other out. Behind his rebellious posture there lies a serious humanitarian commitment to the freedom of the individual and to ending authoritarian oppression and injustice. The fact that Wilde could not express his convictions other than in the framework of his aesthetic individualism in no way detracts from the sincerity of those convictions.

5   Culture and corruption.
The Picture of Dorian Gray

On 6 December 1974 The Times Literary Supplement published the results of a questionnaire in which twenty-five eminent people were asked to name the books that had made the deepest impression on them during their childhood. John Sparrow named Ibsen's A Doll's House (1879) together with Wilde's The Picture of Dorian Gray, which he had read when he was five or six years old. If one also takes into account the fact that John Osborne read the novel when he was ten,[1] it might almost seem that this is a book for children rather than one which the Scots Observer critic described in 1890 as suitable material for the Criminal Investigation Department.[2] Quite apart from the literary precociousness of the above-mentioned readers, their statements are also indications of the remarkably wide appeal of the book. Walter Pater, despite certain reservations, admired 'the skill, the real subtlety of art, the ease and fluidity withal of one telling a story by word of mouth';[3] W. B. Yeats found it 'with all its faults ... a wonderful book',[4] and Lionel Johnson even devoted a prize-winning Latin poem to it under the title 'In Honorem Doriani Creatorisque Eius'.[5]

Most contemporary critics, however, were rather less sympathetic towards it, and judgment was for the most part negative.[6] The St James's Gazette called it 'stupid and vulgar',[7] and advised its readers to throw the book in the fire. The Daily Chronicle criticised its 'effeminate frivolity, its studied insincerity, its theatrical cynicism, its tawdry mysticism, its flippant philosophisings and the contaminating trail of garish vulgarity'.[8] Punch saw 'more of "poison" than of "perfection"'[9] in Wilde's work, while the Athenaeum concluded that 'the book is unmanly, sickening, vicious (though not exactly what is called "improper"), and tedious'.[10] The extent to which the public identified the hero's moral degradation with that of the author can be gauged from the fact that some years later Edward Carson, the public prosecutor, read out several lengthy passages in the course of Wilde's trial, suggesting that they represented Wilde's own 'perverted moral views'.[11] Carson's cross-examination of Wilde is in fact a classic example of the late Victorian controversy over the relation between art and morality.

In spite of, or perhaps even because of, these vehemently negative reviews, it was not long before the book had been translated into seven

138

languages: Dutch (1893), French (1895), German (1901), Italian (1905–6), Russian (1905), Swedish (1905) and Polish (1906). In Germany alone between 1901 and 1967 at least twenty different translations were published.[12] Countless reprints attest to its continued popularity in English-speaking countries, and would seem to confirm Alick West's claim that 'a mention of its title has meaning for millions all over the world'.[13]

Wilde's first and only full-length prose narrative is not only widely read, but is also one of those rare literary works that have inspired artists from other spheres: it has formed the basis for several operas, a ballet, and some half a dozen films, the first of which was directed by Axel Strøm in Denmark as long ago as 1910.[14] The dramatic content lends itself particularly well to stage adaptation, as evinced by G. Constant Lounsbery (1913), M. Nozière (1922), Constance Cox (1948), and most recently John Osborne (1973). While the *Scots Observer* of 5 July 1890 called the novel 'false to morality',[15] Osborne in the 1970s sub-titled his three-acter *A Moral Entertainment*.

How is one to account for this continued interest in and varied reception of *Dorian Gray*? The initial furore may have been mainly due to the fact that the novel violated the expectations of late-Victorian readers by renouncing the 'homely philosophy of life for the middle-class'[16] and laying full emphasis on the 'new Hedonism', which removed it from the moral framework to which those readers were accustomed. This, however, in no way explains the appeal that the book has had for subsequent generations. Perhaps the fascination lies in the original and highly dramatic mixture of supernatural fairy-tale – the magic portrait – and conventional moral issues. Or perhaps its source is the timeless fear of old age, with the dream of lasting youth and beauty. Or perhaps Dorian Gray's quest for unlimited and largely amoral enjoyment of all life's pleasures, together with the preservation of his good looks, makes him into a symbol that represents the repressed longings and hidden desires with which all readers can identify themselves: to defy the ravages of time without ever changing, to live without growing old, to enjoy without having to bear the marks of one's dissolution.

Origins. Magazine and book versions

The reasons for the novel's broad appeal and for its inspiring vitality, as evinced by the many adaptations, are as difficult to pinpoint as the various circumstances of its creation. In a letter to the *St James's Gazette* Wilde claims to have written it for his own pleasure,[17] but André Gide says that it was the result of a bet.[18] There is also the possibility that it arose from an actual incident. An anonymous account that appeared in the *St James's*

Gazette of 24 September 1890, and was reproduced by Stuart Mason in *Art and Morality* (1912), says that at Christmas 1887 Wilde sat for the Canadian painter Frances Richards. When she had finished his portrait:

'What a tragic thing it is,' he exclaimed. 'This portrait will never grow old, and I shall.' Then the passion of his soul sought refuge in prose composition, and the result was 'Dorian Gray'.[19]

There is no evidence to substantiate this story and, although it may conform nicely to Wilde's instinct for self-dramatisation, its authenticity has to be doubted.

Hesketh Pearson offers another version of the origins of the novel:

In the year 1884 Wilde used often to drop in at the studio of a painter, Basil Ward, one of whose sitters was a young man of exceptional beauty. Incidentally, Wilde must have been a god-send to many painters of the time, as his conversation kept their sitters perpetually entertained. When the portrait was done and the youth had gone, Wilde happened to say, 'What a pity that such a glorious creature should ever grow old!' The artist agreed, adding 'How delightful it would be if he could remain exactly as he is, while the portrait aged and withered in his stead!' Wilde expressed his obligations by naming the painter in his story 'Basil Hallward'.[20]

Pearson does not offer any evidence either, but this anecdote can be traced back to an unauthorised edition of *Dorian Gray* published by the Charterhouse Press in New York in 1904. In the 'Artist's Preface', which is signed by 'Basil Hallward', there is a similar account to Pearson's. Wilfried Edener's detailed introduction to his edition of the original version of the novel[21] shows how the preface to this pirate version, which Charles Nickerson calls an 'elaborate bit of publisher's puffery',[22] found its way into Wildean criticism. It was reproduced without comment in Mason's *Art and Morality*, after which Boris Brasol referred to it in *Oscar Wilde. The Man – the Artist* (1938):

the true genesis of *Dorian Gray* was revealed by Mr Basil Ward, the artist, in his preface to one of the later editions of the novel in book form.[23]

The 'Basil Hallward' of the 'Artist's Preface' thus became 'Basil Ward', and the authenticity of person and account was not questioned. Pearson evidently took over this version directly from Brasol, with his own addition that Wilde expressed his gratitude to the painter by naming his artist Basil Hallward. Thus cause and effect are turned upside down. There is no proof whatsoever that the 'Basil Hallward' of the 'Preface' ever existed. The development of this anecdote from an advertising stunt by an imaginative publisher to an accepted fact is a fine illustration of how literary legends may arise, but it also sheds a rather gloomy light on the state of Wildean research, which all too often has mixed truth and fiction inextricably together.[24]

Despite all the uncertainty surrounding the actual basis of the novel, what is certain is that it was written in response to an invitation from Joseph Marshall Stoddart, an acquaintance of Wilde's who worked for the American publisher Lippincott & Co. At a dinner party, Stoddart asked his two literary guests – Wilde and Arthur Conan Doyle – for a story to be published in *Lippincott's Monthly Magazine*. The creator of Sherlock Holmes recalls this memorable evening in his *Memories and Adventures* (1924), and says that Stoddart made them both promise to write something. The result was Wilde's *Dorian Gray* and his own *The Sign of Four* (1890).[25]

The party probably took place during 1889, as Wilde's correspondence with Stoddart shows that he was unable to meet the deadline for the manuscript, which was the beginning of October 1889. A letter written by Stoddart on 17 December of that year also reveals that he was not satisfied with the story that Wilde had offered – namely, 'The Fisherman and his Soul' – and was rejecting it. And so presumably it was not until late December 1889 or early January 1890 that Wilde began work on *Dorian Gray*, although this was also delayed by the fact that Wilde fell ill. The two manuscripts of the magazine version – the handwritten one in the Pierpont Morgan Library and the typewritten one in the William Andrews Clark Memorial Library – are full of deletions and corrections, which are clear testimony to the care Wilde took before committing himself to a final form. According to Donald L. Lawler, who has made a separate study of the two manuscripts, there are certain inconsistencies in the handwritten version – hitherto regarded as the original – which suggest that it may well be the revised version of an even earlier, unknown rough copy.[26]

Isobel Murray has pointed out that not all the revisions in the typescript are in the same handwriting, and it is clear that Stoddart edited the text and made changes that were not authorised by the author, although they were nearly all retained in the book version. Only in one instance did the author return to his original version: Basil's cry of 'Christ!'[27] on seeing the changed portrait of Dorian was altered by Stoddart to 'God!', but changed back again for the book. Murray attributes the censorship to 'an obscure sense of public decency which indicates a prurient and unliterary mind'.[28]

The novel finally appeared on 20 June 1890 on pages 3–100 of the July edition of *Lippincott's Monthly Magazine*. It consisted of thirteen chapters. After negotiations with the London publishing firm of Ward, Lock & Co., Wilde revised and extended the magazine version, wrote a new preface, and published it in book form in April 1891. The various changes and shifts of emphasis have been comprehensively dealt with by Wilfried Edener, in the above-mentioned introduction to his edition of the original version, and by Paul Goetsch, whose essay refers to the Edener edition,[29] and so there is no need for a detailed analysis here. It will suffice merely to summarise the most important changes and their effect. These consist above all in the addition of new elements of plot through Chapters III, V, and XV–XVIII, the expansion of existing passages through various insertions, and stylistic revisions ranging from the correction of misprints to the transposing of individual sections of the text. The main extensions are in the party scenes (chaps. III, XV, XVII–XVIII), the account of Dorian's parentage (chap. III), and the description of his double life (chap. XVI); the one major structural change is the addition of the James Vane episode.

On close inspection it will be seen that the effect of these changes on the narrative content generally goes beyond that of merely extending the magazine version for the sake of greater length. The frequent substitution of the word 'painter' for the proper name, and the omission of various details from Hallward's life, show that Wilde's concern was to accentuate his status as an artist. Parallel to this shift of emphasis from the private to the functional, there is a shift in the relationship between the painter and Dorian. In the original version, there was a passionate and erotic link between them, but now the stress falls on Basil's idealism, his sense of responsibility, and his good nature. Wilde accentuates the destructive side of Lord Henry – his irresponsibility and his cynicism – and so sharpens the contrast between the two characters, hereby bringing out all the more clearly the moral alternatives that they represent.

The insertion of the James Vane episode is the subject of much debate. Wilfried Edener sees it as damaging to the unity of the novel and leading to a 'Verflachung seines Stimmungsgehalts'[30] [flattening of its atmospheric content], while Edouard Roditi complains of 'the awkward lack of verisimilitude',[31] and Léon Lemonnier speaks of 'incidents lourdement machinés'[32] [heavily contrived incidents]. Robert Merle, however, maintains that the episode fulfils an important function in the structure of the novel. In the original version Dorian's suicide follows on too closely from the murder of Basil. During the latter Dorian seems cold-blooded and controlled, taking great care to eliminate all traces of the crime; and yet only a little later he appears frightened and insecure, and determined to reform. Merle argues that this change comes too quickly and is almost unmotivated. By separating these two critical sections of the plot, Wilde was able to make them more effective and more convincing. The James Vane episode also links up closely with the portrait motif as well as with the Sibyl Vane episode, and helps to 'traduire dans les faits l'évolution morale du héros'.[33] But however illuminating these arguments may be as regards the ideas behind the insertion, there still remains some doubt about its artistic quality, for it certainly smacks of melodrama: the avenging brother who eighteen years later is still obsessed with exacting punishment for the death of his sister, lying in wait for Dorian on the dark quayside, pistol in hand; the face of the avenger pressed against the conservatory window at Selby Royal; and finally the accidental death of the beater during the hunt – these are all elements of a somewhat outdated literary convention more akin to the penny dreadful than the serious novel. Wilde himself seems to have been aware of the problem, since he wrote in a letter:

Now, if I were criticising my book, which I have some thoughts of doing, I think I would consider it my duty to point out that it is far too crowded with sensational incident, and far too paradoxical in style, as far, at any rate, as the dialogue goes.[34]

Here he pinpoints the main weaknesses that characterise the novel's transference from magazine to book. But on the positive side, it is worth reminding ourselves of the newly shaped relationship between the three main characters, which as we have seen sharpens the contrast between Basil and Lord Henry. Critical consideration of the strengths and weaknesses will result in a judgment closer to Wilde's own than to the rather one-sided view of Isobel Murray, who suggests that 'he [Wilde] greatly improved the action, structure and balance of the novel, as well as minute details of style'.[35]

Structure and time-scheme

Dorian Gray, a handsome young man, is sitting for a portrait being painted by his friend Basil Hallward. He is drawn into conversation by Lord Henry, who outlines his philosophy of life which he summarises as 'new Hedonism'. The purpose of life is uninhibited 'self-development',[36] and beauty and youth are among the highest values. Dorian feels himself strongly attracted to these ideas, and fervently wishes that his portrait might age while he himself might keep his youthful appearance. He would willingly give his soul for this to come true.

Fascinated by the character and ideas of Lord Henry, he finds his influence increasingly irresistible, while at the same time there is a cooling in his relations with Basil. One day he goes to a small backstreet theatre, and sees an actress named Sibyl Vane. He is so enamoured of her talent that he confuses his passion for her art with true love, and eventually they become engaged. He proudly invites his friends Basil and Lord Henry to a performance, so that they can see her gifts for themselves. But on this particular evening her acting is appalling, and in his bitter disappointment and anger at such a let-down, he leaves her for ever. The pain of this parting is unbearable for Sibyl, who kills herself. Even before hearing the news of her death, Dorian has noticed a change in his portrait – there is a touch of cruelty in the mouth. Lord Henry dismisses Sibyl's death as a 'strange lurid fragment from some Jacobean tragedy',[37] and thereby succeeds in settling Dorian's nascent doubts about his own conduct and gives him a greater sense of detachment. The degree of Lord Henry's influence on his 'pupil' becomes evident from Dorian's pleasure at the changes in his portrait, which mirror the progressive corruption of his soul. But in order to conceal this from the eyes of others, he locks the picture up in what used to be the play-room at the top of the house.

Under the guidance of Lord Henry and of a secret 'Yellow Book', Dorian spends the next eighteen years enjoying all the opportunities open to a prosperous man of many interests, until finally vice and evil have become nothing but means of experiencing intense sensual and aesthetic pleasure. Rumours about his dissolute life style and his destructive influence on his friends and acquaintances prompt Basil into taking him to task. The sight of the portrait confirms Basil's worst fears. His horror at this moral depravity, and his biblical calls for repentance suddenly fill Dorian with an uncontrollable feeling of hatred, and in his rage he murders Basil. With the aid of the chemist Alan Campbell, Dorian is able to dispose of the corpse, but he cannot stop thinking of the portrait, which after the murder has a bloodstained hand, and his visits to parties and opium dens in London's docklands fail to drive his obsession away. He narrowly escapes assassination at the hands of James Vane, the brother of his former fiancée, who seeks vengeance on him, but when James is killed in a hunting accident on Dorian's country estate at Selby Royal, he feels safe for a while. His longing for a *vita nuova* finally makes him resolve to change his ways. But after his first good deed – forbearing to seduce Hetty Merton – the portrait, instead of registering the hoped-for sign of improvement, shows nothing but hypocrisy. In order to destroy the hideous face, emblem of his own conscience, he stabs the picture. A cry is heard, and when the servants enter the room, they find a beautiful portrait of their master as they know him, and next to it a dead man with a knife in his heart, his face withered and wrinkled. They can only identify him through the rings that he is wearing.

The novel is constructed in two parts which are separated by the very distinctive chapter XI. This condenses eighteen years of Dorian's life, contains no dialogue, and even differs stylistically from the other chapters. The first part of the novel (chaps. I–X) consists of two sections of narrative: the exposition (chaps. I–III) introduces the three main characters, the motif of the portrait, and Lord Henry's philosophy of life. This is followed by the Sibyl Vane story (chaps. IV–X). The basis of the plot is laid down by dialogues within the Vane family (chap. V) and between Dorian and his friends (chaps. IV and VI), and it reaches its climax with

Sibyl's death (chap. VII). The chapters that follow (VIII–X) narrate the effects of the new situation on Dorian and efforts to assuage these through conversations with Lord Henry and Basil. The first change in the portrait (chap. VII), however, and the subsequent decision to lock it away in an unused room, already indicates that Dorian is guilty of Sibyl's death, and this guilt cannot be erased even by the subtle arguments of his smooth-tongued and unscrupulous mentor.

The stigma permanently branded onto the portrait, denoting Dorian's cruel treatment of his fiancée and his responsibility for her suicide, stands in ironic contrast to his hasty efforts – under Lord Henry's tuition – to view these events impartially as a 'marvellous experience',[38] and thus his attempt to aestheticise his life is unmasked as a mechanism of suppression whose efficacy must remain dubious. From a structural point of view, this contrast between the superficial mastery of the situation, based on forgetting, and the changing portrait which preserves memory, creates a dynamic tension which focuses the reader's attention on future interaction between the portrait and the man portrayed. In this way, the moral development of the hero becomes the central theme.

The second half of the novel (chaps. XII–XX) can also be divided into two main sections that cover the murder of Basil (chaps. XII–XIV) and James Vane's pursuit of Dorian and his death (chaps. XVI–XVIII). There follows a long dialogue between Dorian and Lord Henry, in which both draw their conclusions, with the 'pupil' casting doubt on his mentor's principles and resolving to change his ways (chap. XIX). The novel ends with Dorian's suicide after his despairing recognition of the fact that a new beginning is not possible (chap. XX).

The structure of the novel depends on the selection and the chronology of the events. Sometimes whole sections, though integrated in the overall development of the story, seem almost self-contained both thematically and chronologically. The story begins one June afternoon (chaps. I–II) before Dorian's 21st birthday in Basil Hallward's studio. Chapter III begins at 12.30 the following day and ends with luncheon at Aunt Agatha's, which presumably finishes at some time in the late afternoon. It follows on closely from the two preceding chapters. There is a break after these three expository chapters, and the Sibyl Vane story begins a month later on a Tuesday in July,[39] continues the following Wednesday afternoon and evening (chaps. V–VII), and comes to a temporary halt early on Thursday morning with Dorian's return from the theatre (chap. VII). Chapters VIII–X, which deal mainly with the effects of Sibyl's death on Dorian, take place between Thursday afternoon[40] and Friday evening. The time covered by the first ten chapters is approximately five weeks, of which four have been left out between chapters III and IV, so that in fact only about one week is actually covered by the narrative.

After a summarised period of eighteen years, the story continues in chapter XII on 9 November, the eve of Dorian's thirty-eighth birthday,[41] and up until chapter XVIII covers about twelve days. The exact time of the end of the novel is difficult to pinpoint, but chaps. XIX and XX must take place approximately six months later, as Dorian mentions the month of May when referring to his affair with Hetty Merton.[42] This time-scheme, however, does not fit in with Lord Henry's remark in chapter XIX concerning the fact that people have been talking about Basil's disappearance for six weeks. Basil was murdered between 9 and 10 November, which would entail a remarkably long delay in public reaction if discussion did not begin until the following March.

Altogether the novel covers some nineteen years, of which just six days are dramatised in the first ten chapters, and twelve from chapter XII onwards. The manipulative skills of Wilde's imagination enable him frequently to break the chain of events, and by means of compression, expansion and omission weld it together again in a tight sequence of narrative phases, with detailed attention to the most important events of Dorian's life and the merest glance at the rest. This varied intensity of focus results in a kind of rhythmical structure which reveals a good deal about the author's intentions. He is clearly interested in a detailed presentation of the initial situation, races through the central phase prefigured by Lord Henry's hedonistic doctrine, and then dwells at length on the final phase, with the consequences of this doctrine for Dorian's life. The various climaxes of the story are reached in chapters II (exposition of 'new Hedonism'), VII (Sibyl's death), XIII (murder of Basil), and XX (Dorian's suicide). Time in this novel is not merely a matter of chronological order, but is also a vital element of the content, the concept of reality, and the characters' views of life, as we shall see later when we discuss Lord Henry's 'new Hedonism'.

Setting and society

Wilde's time-scheme is concerned with the chronology of fictitious events and not with their historical background. There are, for instance, no indications of the actual year or of actual events in the real world. As regards the locality, however, there are many precise details, with particular emphasis on the fact that much of the novel takes place in London. Only in chapters XVII–XVIII is the action moved to the vaguely situated country estate of Selby Royal.

Just as the time-scheme is not based on a continuous and monotonous sequence of events, so too does Wilde switch his settings. Sometimes these are simply indicated by name: 'the Albany',[43] 'the Park',[44] or 'Lady Narborough's drawing-room';[45] elsewhere there is the briefest of descriptions: 'the little Library of Lord Henry's house in Mayfair',[46] 'an absurd little theatre',[47] or 'dreadful places near Blue Gate Fields'.[48] A few more details are given in the descriptions of Basil's studio,[49] Dorian's playroom-cum-study where he hides his portrait,[50] the night walk through London to Covent Garden,[51] the drive to the quay,[52] and the opium den.[53]

The most frequently mentioned settings are Mayfair, which prior to the First World War used to be the most fashionable residential quarter in London, and some of the less refined areas, such as Euston Road, where the Vanes live, and Holborn, where Sibyl's theatre is situated. Others are further east, like the notorious docklands, and the slums of Whitechapel and Blue Gate Fields. The luxurious interiors of Dorian's West End house in Grosvenor Square and Lord Henry's in Curzon Street are in stark contrast to the 'shabby home'[54] of the Vanes, and the opium den near the docks, which looks as if it was once 'a third-rate dancing saloon',[55] with sawdust strewn over its floor. Mayfair and Whitechapel represent more than the geographical boundaries of the plot, for they denote the social extremes of the rich West End and the poor East End. Some of the characters are reluctant to venture into those areas that are not commensurate to their social status, and indeed this reluctance occasionally amounts to sheer hatred. When Dorian goes to Whitechapel at night and sees people's silhouettes behind the lighted windows, we are told that 'He hated them. A dull rage was in his heart'[56] – a reaction comparable to James Vane's unwillingness to go for a walk in Hyde Park ('only swell people go the Park'[57]) and also to his hatred for the aristocracy:

He [Dorian] was a gentleman, and he hated him for that, hated him through some curious race-instinct for which he could not account, and which for that reason was all the more dominant within him.[58]

The sharp contrasts between poverty and wealth, deprivation and surfeit, proletariat and aristocracy do not, however, inspire the narrator to any social criticism in the style, for instance, of a Mrs Gaskell, or Kingsley or Gissing. Lord Henry's maxim that 'The less said about life's sores the better'[59] is in no way modified by his casual remark that the East End is 'the problem of slavery, and we try to solve it by amusing the slaves'.[60] What fascinates Wilde is the glamour of noble names and the luxurious life style of a leisured class whose urbane ideals encompass exquisite manners, literary and artistic culture, witty conversation, and a sense of their élite position. This arrogant class-consciousness is nowhere more evident than in what is almost an aside of Lord Henry's, when he is invited by Dorian to a performance of *Romeo and Juliet*, and is so disgusted by the coarse behaviour of the audience that he replies to Dorian's comment that these people are also flesh and blood: 'The same flesh and blood as one's self! Oh, I hope not!'[61]

Wilde's sharply entertaining depiction of the cultural flair of the aristocracy and the upper middle class, with all the superficial gloss of their conversation, is not matched by his attempts to portray the lower social strata, 'the mean and squalid and socially disgraceful'[62] poor quarters of the East End, as described by Henry Mayhew, for instance, and so vividly drawn by Gavarni and Gustave Doré, and, above all, brought to life by the novels of Dickens. The author of *Dorian Gray* had the same experience of these areas as his hero – namely, through the windows of hansom cabs, or on foot at night, or from visiting shady taverns and other establishments of ill repute. Walter Bagehot once said of Dickens that he described London 'like a special correspondent for posterity';[63] he would go for frequent long walks, getting to know the maze of London's streets in such detail that he could then describe every step his characters took, even in the most out-of-the-way corners – one need only recall the route taken by Oliver Twist and the Artful Dodger from 'the Angel' (near Sadler's Wells Theatre) to a house near Field Lane. Wilde, however, had little interest in the precise whereabouts of his houses and characters. For Dorian, London east of Mayfair is 'a labyrinth of grimy streets and black, grassless squares'.[64] His walk from the Royal Theatre in Holborn to Covent Garden is described as follows:

Where he went to he hardly knew. He remembered wandering through dimly-lit streets, past gaunt black-shadowed archways and evil-looking houses. Women with hoarse voices and harsh laughter had called after him. Drunkards had reeled by cursing, and chattering to themselves like monstrous apes. He had seen grotesque children huddled upon doorsteps, and heard shrieks and oaths from gloomy courts.[65]

A naturalistic author would have used the opportunity for some social criticism, but here we have a fleeting and impressionistic tableau, with the reality of poverty somehow reduced to the level of alien fantasy. This tendency towards alien detachment is always to be felt when Dorian ventures into unfamiliar territory, as in his drive to the docklands. Behind lighted windows he sees 'fantastic shadows' which 'moved like monstrous marionettes, and made gestures like live things'.[66] Adjectives like 'fantastic', 'monstrous' and 'grotesque' show that Dorian only perceives these people as brief impressions which have a momentary aesthetic charm without ever imposing a lasting sense of their reality on him.

With all these different settings, London seems like a large stage – in the foreground the glamour of Mayfair, in the background the squalid vulgarity of the East End. There is no correspondence, however, between the social and geographical hierarchy and the scale of moral values. On the contrary, 'Culture and corruption'[67] go hand in hand. Dorian is set on his downward path by Lord Henry, and the decisive phases of the plot, revealing his increasing corruption, take place in the palaces of the West

End, not in the hovels of the East End. The representation of city life does not, however, consist only of the commonplace contrast between wealth and poverty or town and country[68] or sin and virtue – significantly, Dorian hopes to start his new life by forbearing to seduce the village girl Hetty Merton – but also of the idea of the labyrinth, the twisted mass of confusion. In his search for sensations, Dorian soon loses his way in a 'labyrinth of grimy streets',[69] or 'Where he went to he hardly knew.'[70] Even the experienced cab-driver who takes him to the quay loses his way in the maze of streets, which are compared to the 'black web of some sprawling spider'.[71] Instead of giving its inhabitants a sense of security, the inhospitable city creates an effect of disorientation,[72] which corresponds to man's difficult search for identity – a problem that is central for Dorian. In stressing this aspect of city life, Wilde is at one with other novelists who tackle the same theme: 'London obscures, annuls, or maims the identity of characters in search of their true self.'[73]

It is interesting to note that there are far more indoor settings than outdoor, which is a clear indication that the narrator is not interested in action and movement, such as one finds in the picaresque novel or other genres based on the motif of the journey, but is concerned with the inner nature and development of his characters and their relationships.[74] While the interior settings are mostly meeting-places for the aristocratic idlers, the outside areas are often places of refuge for Dorian, which he seeks out in moments of intellectual tension or emotional crisis. Examples of this are to be found in his wandering through London after leaving Sibyl alone in her unhappiness, stepping out onto the balcony after murdering Basil, the journey to dockland, where he hopes to find oblivion in the opium dens, and finally the ride to Home Farm, where he identifies the corpse of James Vane.

Dorian's house in Grosvenor Square is the setting for eight of the twenty chapters, and is undoubtedly the geographical focal point of the whole story. The luxury of its fittings – especially the collection of gems and *objets d'art* – is reminiscent of Jean des Esseintes's Fontenay-aux-Roses in Huysmans's *A Rebours* (1884). Within the house itself there is one room which is of particular interest to both the hero and the reader: Dorian's former playroom and study, where from chapter X onwards he hides his portrait. All the other settings form, as it were, concentric circles round this place – an impression that is reinforced by the fact that whenever Dorian leaves London for any length of time, he is drawn back as if by magic to this room. In succession he quits the house in Trouville that he had taken with Lord Henry, his winter residence in Algiers, and his country estate in Nottinghamshire, in order to rush back to London and see if the picture is still in place. As well as being the focal point, it is loaded with personal values which make it almost a shrine for 'the stainless purity of his boyish life'.[75] But what in the past was his refuge and a symbol of his purity, in the present becomes the scene of his crime and of his morbid delight in his growing depravity, and in the future is to be the setting for his suicide and the re-establishment of his identity in death. The room and the portrait form a kind of cross for the co-ordinates of time and space in this novel: the vertical axis – the portrait – symbolises the time-structure of Dorian's life story as a moral crisis, while the horizontal axis – the room – is the spatial refuge of the anti-hero, and so acts as a centre of orientation for the reader.

Structure, time and space in this story all confirm the vital significance of the portrait, which is already to be gauged from the title. We must now examine in greater detail its function in the plot, its relation to the characters – in particular Dorian – and its individual features.

The *doppelgänger* motif and the development of Dorian Gray

Dorian's personality is split into two parts which act and react independently and yet are linked together in a fantastic manner; the one is physical, the other spiritual, and the link is the changing portrait. This is a paradoxical variation of the theme of the *doppelgänger*, so beloved of the romantics and ever more frequent in nineteenth-century literature.[76] Wilde had already combined it with the 'pact with the Devil' theme in 'The Fisherman and his Soul', and it forms the basis of the plot of that tale. The origins of this dualistic concept of man are rooted far back in mythology and ultimately in man's belief in an after-life. In *The Golden Bough*, James George Frazer tells how many tribes – for example, the Eskimos on the islands of the Bering Strait – believe that a portrait is the seat of the soul.[77] Such dualistic concepts are not confined to ethnology and anthropology, but are also commonly found in religion and philosophy. The special place occupied by the motif in romantic literature is due to the increased philosophical and critical awareness of the individual and his multifariousness.

Dorian's fatal desire for his youth and beauty to be preserved arises from a latent narcissism which is stimulated by Lord Henry's ideas and takes on concrete form at the sight of the portrait. According to Freud, the phenomenon of narcissism constitutes a phase in the history of the libido characterised by the fact that first of all it is the self that is the object of love, and only later is this place occupied by another person.[78] Indeed from the very beginning there is a distinctly autoerotic relationship between Dorian and his portrait, linked with his fear of growing old and the complementary longing to remain young, which 'den Zusammenhang der Todesangst mit der narzissistischen Einstellung verrät[79] [betrays the connection between fear of death and the narcissistic attitude]. 'Youth is the only thing worth having. When I find that I am growing old, I shall kill myself.'[80] When Basil wishes to destroy the portrait, Dorian is shocked and stops him: 'It would be murder! . . . I am in love with it, Basil. It is part of myself.'[81] His narcissism simply transfers itself to this idealised self. Out of the contrast between the ideal and actual self, bound as it is to reality, there emerges a feeling of pain in face of the transience of beauty, and this gives rise to the intense desire to resist the destructive force of *tempus edax*.

The Sibyl Vane episode[82] dramatises the new principles that Dorian has taken over in chapter II from his mentor Lord Henry, and it brings about the first inner conflict in his development. The clash is between his aesthetic sensitivity to her theatrical art and his moral responsibility towards her as his fiancée. He is drawn to her physical beauty, her protean versatility which enables her to play so many different roles, and the sheer magnetism of her artistry. One night she is Imogen, and the next Juliet. To Lord Henry's question as to when she is Sibyl Vane, he answers: 'Never.'[83] It is not the woman herself that fascinates him, but the aesthetic attraction of her art. Hence, it is not reality but the game of possibilities, reflecting his own existence, that has him in its thrall.

In complete contrast, Sibyl sees in Dorian the embodiment of 'what Love himself should be'.[84] She cannot perceive that her different roles and swift changes, which have no intrinsic reality for her, are precisely the attraction for him, with his sensitivity to art and his insatiable desire for variety. Her blossoming love overshadows her histrionic gifts, because the passion she feels as a woman is beyond what can be captured on the stage, and so there opens up a huge gap between the theatrical pretence, of which she is all too aware, and the genuineness of her love for Dorian; but for him there is no such gap, because he sees Sibyl's character only in terms of her function as an artist. For Sibyl the reality of art changes to illusion without credibility the moment she is confronted with real life in the form of her love. But while at the beginning of the episode Dorian could inform Lord Henry that 'She is everything to me in life',[85] by the end he can tell her to her face, 'You are nothing to me now.'[86] Their false view of each other has disastrous consequences for them both: Sibyl commits suicide, and Dorian's brutal treatment of her leaves 'lines of cruelty'[87] round the mouth of the portrait – the first of many changes that are ultimately to lead him to the same fate as Sibyl. He has to recognise that even though art and reality can be kept apart during aesthetic contemplation, the separation becomes illusory when art leads to real-life action, as it does with his engagement to Sibyl.

If in chapter II the portrait was still a reflection of Dorian's extreme narcissism, now it changes into a 'visible emblem of conscience',[88] registering his reprehensible conduct and demanding recognition of his selfishness and cruelty to such an extent that he resolves to put things right. He writes Sibyl a letter in which he begs forgiveness and reproaches himself for his 'madness'.[89] His repentance and desire for improvement show that during this phase of his development, his moral sense is still intact. Shortly before the discussion with Lord Henry that is to change his view of the situation, he declares:

I know what conscience is, to begin with. It is not what you told me it was. It is the divinest thing in us. Don't sneer at it, Harry, any more – at least not before me. I want to be good. I can't bear the idea of my soul being hideous.[90]

It is at this point in the action that Lord Henry's mephistophelean function becomes particularly clear. Instead of taking his friend's scruples seriously, he is all the more insistent on stylising Sibyl's death to a sort of aesthetic spectacle, so that he can relieve Dorian of his responsibility for it. The fact that Dorian adopts Lord Henry's principles is evident not only from his argument with Basil in chapter IX, when he uses them in defence against the painter's reproaches, but also earlier, towards the end of chapter VIII:

He felt that the time had really come for making his choice. Or had his choice already been made? Yes, life had decided that for him – life, and his infinite curiosity about life. Eternal youth, infinite passion, pleasures subtle and secret, wild joys and wilder sins – he was to have all these things. The portrait was to bear the burden of his shame: that was all.[91]

There is also a change in his attitude towards the portrait. Initially it had reflected his narcissism, then it symbolised his incipient moral depravity, and now increasingly it becomes the source of morbid enjoyment: 'there would be a real pleasure in watching it. He would be able to follow his mind into its secret places. This portrait would be to him the most magical of mirrors.'[92]

With the murder of Basil, through which he finally gives up the role of the mere spectator, Dorian's perverse flirtation with his own moral decline now sinks into common criminality. After the painter's death, art is no longer the prime orientation of Dorian's life, for it is no longer possible for him to aestheticise evil. Vileness cannot now be regarded as beautiful: 'Ugliness was the one reality.'[93] Reality viewed as ugliness, a projection of his own entanglement in vice, must become the opiate for his piercing sense of guilt. This acknowledgment of ugliness as the one reality is a complete reversal of his previous ideas. The divergent lines of his development and the changes in the portrait seem for one moment to coincide, as the depravity in the painting is paralleled by the apotheosis of ugliness; this is the negative counterpart to the beginning of the novel, where the external beauty of the portrait corresponded to the moral integrity of the man portrayed. The new convergence, however, offers an illusory harmony, because the moral sense proves to be the more durable and the more valid reality, as evinced early on after the suicide of Sibyl Vane, with great clarity in chapter XI, and finally – most tellingly of all – with Dorian's own death:

Once it had given him pleasure to watch it [the portrait] changing and growing old. Of late he had felt no such pleasure. It had kept him awake at night . . . It had been like conscience to him. Yes, it had been conscience. He would destroy it.[94]

Dorian's suicide is a logical outcome. It unmasks his salving of conscience by aesthetic philosophy as mere self-deception, and by removing the fantastic symbolism of the portrait, it restores the unity and totality of the individual. The fact that this unification can only come about through death represents a deeply pessimistic view of the problem of human identity – a view that has been of profound significance for the twentieth-century novel.

Dorian's failure has been attributed by some critics to his falsifying Lord Henry's doctrine, and proving to be 'inférieur à sa destinée'.[95] Albert J. Farmer presents this view as follows:

Doué d'une jeunesse éternelle et d'une beauté invulnérable, il n'aboutit à rien de mieux qu'à se laisser envahir par des scrupules de conscience. La conscience . . . Cet esthète ne comprend donc pas qu'il s'agit là d'un contresens esthétique? Ce prétendu disciple du culte de la beauté n'est, au fond, qu'un philistin.[96]

[Blessed with eternal youth and an invulnerable beauty, he ends up doing nothing better than allowing himself to be invaded by scruples of conscience. Conscience . . . Does not this aesthete understand that this is a matter of an aesthetic perversion? This would-be disciple of the cult of beauty is basically nothing but a philistine.]

Such an interpretation would seem to miss the point of the problem: it is not that a young 'philistin' is too feeble to satisfy the demands of an aesthetic, hedonistic doctrine, but that above all this philosophy offers inadequate orientation for human conduct. Ultimately it is unable to relieve the tediousness of life, and its unlimited quest for pleasure and its stylisation of life into a work of art prove to be incapable of suppressing thoughts of death as well as moral awareness.

Basil Hallward

Dorian tends to blame the painter of his portrait for the misery he has to endure: 'Basil had painted the portrait that had marred his life. He could not forgive him that.'[97] Some modern critics seem to have adopted the same line, and place Basil Hallward at the centre of the story. Houston A. Baker, Jr, interprets the novel in the light of Wilde's aesthetic theories, and regards it as the 'tragedy of the artist'.[98] Basil is guilty because he has put too much of himself into the painting, thereby betraying his own idealistic concept of art and, ultimately, playing a decisive role in Dorian's decline and fall: 'Hallward's excessive self-consciousness, his selfish desires, and his jealous zeal in keeping Dorian from others have corrupted the simple, natural, and affectionate model who sat for the portrait.'[99] Like Baker, Robert Keefe in his essay 'Artist and Model in "The Picture of Dorian Gray"'[100] makes the painter a central figure, and closely investigates 'the nature of Basil's crime and the mechanism of its effect on Dorian'.[101] He calls Lord Henry's influence 'dramatic', whereas the portrait's effect on Dorian is 'overwhelming',[102] and he regards it as the prime cause of the changes in Dorian's life.

Such attempts to blame Basil for the failure of his model's hedonistic experiments are based either on a reduction of the importance of Dorian's relationship with Lord Henry, or on a possible confusion of cause with starting-point. There can be no doubt that the sight of the portrait awakens Dorian's latent narcissism by confronting him with his own beauty. But it is Lord Henry's philosophy that imposes upon this sharpened awareness a growing desire which is finally to split the self in two:

The sense of his own beauty came on him like a revelation. He had never felt it before. Basil Hallward's compliments had seemed to him to be merely the charming exaggerations of friendship. He had listened to them, laughed at them, forgotten them. They had not influenced his nature. Then had come Lord Henry Wotton with his strange panegyric on youth, his terrible warning of its brevity. That had stirred him at the time, and now, as he stood gazing at the shadow of his own loveliness, the full reality of the description flashed across him. Yes, there would be a day when his face would be wrinkled and wizened, his eyes dim and colourless, the grace of his figure broken and deformed. The scarlet would pass away from his lips, and the gold steal from his hair. The life that was to make his soul would mar his body. He would become dreadful, hideous, and uncouth.[103]

The device of a kind of narrated monologue, beginning with 'Yes', shows clearly the extent to which Dorian has already identified himself with Lord Henry's ideas and has internalised the basic longing for eternal youth and beauty.

In his view of life and art, Basil Hallward is a moralist and an idealist, whose values are essentially middle class,[104] consisting as they do of such criteria as 'honour' ... 'goodness' ... 'purity' ... 'a clean name' ... 'a fair record'.[105] This man, who wears a Waterbury watch and turns down a lucrative commission for a portrait because the man concerned leads a 'dreadful' life,[106] regards his artistic talent not as the status symbol of a cultural elite, but rather as a fatal stigma that threatens to isolate him from his fellow men; fear of social ostracism causes him to embrace a certain degree of conformity: 'It is better not to be different from one's fellows.'[107] Always suspicious of Lord Henry's cynicism, he is from the very start drawn towards Dorian with a 'love that dare not speak its name'. The personality of his model inspires him to a new style of art which fuses classical and romantic elements and harmonises body and soul. This inspiration through Dorian leads to a conflict between reality and his idealistic concept of art, for the portrait – 'a wonderful work of art, and a wonderful likeness as well'[108] – shows that the aesthetic ideal has been replaced by idolatry of the handsome youth. Basil and Sibyl Vane are both destroyed by the fact that they cannot reconcile their art with the real world. The actress fails because she loses faith in the reality of her art when she feels the genuineness of her love for her 'Prince Charming'. The painter tries to make his model into a lasting ideal that will resist the transformations of time, and learns the painful lesson that this is impossible. 'I want the Dorian Gray I used to paint'[109] is a sad attempt to hold on to the moral perfection of the old Dorian; Basil is struggling against the inescapable fact that everything earthly is transient, and his words reflect his dependence on illusion, which prevents him from accepting the reality of Dorian's life.

Hallward's entanglement in the fiction of a good Dorian Gray is often pointed up ironically, particularly in chapter IX. He misunderstands Dorian's refusal to exhibit the painting in Paris as confirmation of his (Basil's) belief that the portrait reveals his own innermost feelings and therefore cannot be made accessible to the public. For different reasons they both try to keep their own secrets, and they are both unable to master the difficulty of life as art. Such a view of life, like Dorian's desire to replace conscience with aesthetic conduct, proves to be as illusory as the attempt to make a work of art into a moral criterion for judging reality.

Basil Hallward's death results from the failure of his concept of life and art.[110] His murder marks the climax of Dorian's corruption, and it is presented with great psychological sensitivity. Hallward, with his integrity and his good nature, is almost a father-figure for Dorian, and has become a sort of 'latent double'.[111] There is a particularly revealing passage in which Dorian resolves to show the painter the long-hidden portrait:

There was the madness of pride in every word he uttered. He stamped his foot upon the ground in his boyish insolent manner. He felt a terrible joy at the thought that someone else was to share his secret, and that the man who had painted the portrait that was the origin of all his shame was to be burdened for the rest of his life with the hideous memory of what he had done.[112]

His joy at the prospect of revealing his secret is due to his unconscious hope that he will now be freed from the heavy burden of his guilt – a burden his soul has been unable to accept. At the same time, he would like to place this guilt on the creator of the portrait – 'the origin of all his shame' – by making him responsible not only for the changes in the picture, but also for his own moral decline. When Basil, however, calls him to account and tells him to repent and pray, Dorian realises that he cannot impose a sense of guilt on Basil. Tormented by the reproaches, he feels like a 'hunted animal',[113] and instinctively wishes to rid himself of his tormentor, that is, of the man who in fact represents his own super-ego. And this is why Dorian kills Basil.

Lord Henry Wotton

Dorian's paranoid behaviour towards Basil cannot disguise the fact that, apart from himself, the man most responsible for his misguided exist-ential experiment is his mentor, Lord Henry Wotton. This dandy, irre-sponsible intellectual, moral anarchist and smooth-tongued, cynical man of the world represents a counter-position to that of the well-adjusted Basil Hallward, and he is 'peculiarly Oscar's mouthpiece'.[114] Observa-tion, analysis and experiment are the scientific methods he uses in his psychological study of men's behaviour: 'Human life – that appeared to him the one thing worth investigating.'[115] The results of this 'experimen-tal method'[116] form the basis of his many theories, for it is the findings of the psychologist that provide the thinker with material for his phil-osophy. In principle he remains true to the contemplative attitude, leaving it to Dorian to put his ideas into practice, but this is not always so – there are moments in the novel when he actively interferes in the development of his pupil and guides him in a certain direction. His theories are bound neither to his personality nor to any personal set of values, for 'the value of an idea has nothing whatsoever to do with the sincerity of the man who expresses it'.[117] This aphoristic distinction between 'sincerity' and 'authenticity' – the subject of an historical study by Lionel Trilling[118] – explains the gap between his practical deeds and his theoretical specu-lations, for although he rejects the idea of influencing others as immoral, nevertheless he closely observes the effect of his hedonistic philosophy on Dorian and revels in its success. Cynically, he recommends to Dorian a life of sensual pleasure, while he himself enjoys looking on from a safe intellectual distance. Herein lies the mephistophelean aspect of his char-acter.[119]

Dorian's fatal error is to take Lord Henry's theories as practical guides for life; he does not realise that in reality they represent the cynicism of a rich, bored and irresponsible idler, who finds that talking to Dorian is 'like playing upon an exquisite violin. He answered to every touch and thrill of the bow.'[120] There is one point at which Dorian is on the verge of exposing the falsity of his mentor's precepts – namely, when he feels the devotion of Sibyl's love: 'the mere touch of Sibyl Vane's hand makes me forget you and all your wrong, fascinating, poisonous, delightful theories'.[121] But he has already lost the strength of will to free himself from these *fleurs du mal*.

The destructive intellectual is a figure very much in the tradition of Victorian anti-intellectualism,[122] and indeed this mistrust of science and concern with the scientist's social responsibilities has continued to play its part in twentieth-century literature, for instance with Bertolt Brecht's *Leben des Galilei* (1938/39), first performed in 1943; Friedrich Dürrenmatt's *Die Physiker* (1962); and Heinar Kipphardt's *In der Sache J. Robert Oppenheimer* (1964). Lord Henry's scientific references are predominantly to psychology, which had undergone a rapid and stormy development during the second half of the nineteenth century. This new area of study had been raised to the status of an 'exact' science by such pioneers as Gustav Fechner with his psychophysics, Hermann Helmholtz (together with Johannes Müller) and his principle of specific sensual energy, and Wilhelm Wundt, who founded the first institute for experimental psychology in Leipzig in 1879. When Lord Henry wonders 'whether we could ever make psychology so absolute a science that each little spring of life would be revealed to us',[123] he is merely echoing a question that had been asked many times in the world of science. The special emphasis laid on 'sensations' in the doctrine of 'new Hedonism' corresponds to the importance attached to the study of the organs of the senses, psychophysical interaction, and the problem of perception as basic components of experimental psychology.

'New hedonism'

The hedonistic programme that Lord Henry sets out for his protégé may be nothing more than a psychological experiment for him, but for Dorian it contains a vital and complex problem of ethics. What, though, are Lord Henry's main precepts? He regards the aim of life as being the self-fulfilment of the individual. Self-denial makes the soul sick,[124] and obligations to others do not exist: 'One's own Life – that is the important thing.'[125] Between the body and the soul there are secret and intimate connections, a kind of psychophysical interaction. The separation of these two components of the character – which Christianity especially has fostered – must be overcome by Dorian making of the senses 'elements of a new spirituality'.[126] However, the exterior – all that can be seen and touched – plays a greater role in Lord Henry's philosophy than the interior, the realm of the spirit: 'The true mystery of the world is the visible, not the invisible.'[127] Thus, bodily beauty is 'the wonder of wonders'.[128] As this beauty and the receptiveness of the senses are above all the privileges of fleeting youth, this is a time of life that must be savoured to the full. In chapter XI Lord Henry's 'new hedonism'[129] is briefly summarised in a manner that places it in an historical tradition:

Yes, there was to be, as Lord Henry had prophesied, a new Hedonism that was to recreate life, and to save it from that harsh, uncomely puritanism that is having, in our own day, its curious revival. It was to have its service of the intellect, certainly; yet, it was never to accept any theory or system that would involve the sacrifice of any mode of passionate experience. Its aim, indeed, was to be experience itself, and not the fruits of experience, sweet or bitter as they might be. Of the asceticism that deadens the senses, as of the vulgar profligacy that dulls them, it was to know nothing. But it was to teach man to concentrate himself upon the moments of a life that is in itself but a moment.[130]

The new hedonism, then, is to be an ethical alternative to puritanism. It is based on the Epicurean and Cyrenaic schools of philosophy, in which pleasure (ἡδονή) is the only good in life. In the moral and philosophical debate of the 1870s and 1880s in Oxford, led by F. H. Bradley (*Ethical Studies*, 1876) and T. H. Green (*Prolegomena to Ethics*, 1883), hedonism played an important part, but only as a negative counterpart to the neo-Hegelian, idealistic teachings of 'school' philosophy. Lord Henry's concept of 'self-development' is substantially identical to Bradley's central idea of 'self-realization', which he sees as 'the most general expression for the end in itself'.[131] But Bradley's answer to the question of whether self-realization can consist in 'pleasure for pleasure's sake' is an emphatic no, because pleasures are 'a perishing series'[132] and hedonism is ultimately 'illusory and impalpable'.[133] He develops these ideas in the framework of a general polemic against the code of utilitarian ethics promulgated during the nineteenth century by Jeremy Bentham and John Stuart Mill and including the hedonistic motive among its principles.[134] The concept of utilitarianism embraced both Mill's 'Greatest Happiness Principle' and Bentham's 'happiness of the party whose interest is in question'.[135] In addition to Bradley, there are other critics of utilitarianism – for example, John Grote (*An Examination of the Utilitarian Philosophy*, 1870), Henry Sidgwick (*The Methods of Ethics*, 1874), and G. E. Moore (*Principia Ethica*, chapter 3, 1903) – who cast doubts on the philosophical soundness of some of Mill's arguments, but never deny the social importance of the hedonistic motive.

One can gain an altogether different impression from Pater's 'Conclusion' to his *Studies into the History of the Renaissance* (1873). In this short but highly significant philosophical manifesto, Pater combines the epistemological scepticism and the hedonistic ethics of the Cyrenaic school with a sensual aestheticism that has its roots in romantic idealism (Kant, Schiller, Keats) and continues through Poe, Gautier, Baudelaire and Swinburne right up to the *fin de siècle*. The passage quoted from chapter XI of *Dorian Gray* simply summarises the most important ideas of Pater's 'Conclusion', which together with *Marius the Epicurean* (1885) had an extraordinary influence on the writers and critics of the next few decades – in particular, George Moore, Arthur Symons and Lionel Johnson.

The reduction of experience to the actuality of the moment, and the concept of life as an inconsequential and discontinuous sequence of intense moments 'ästhetisiert Wirklichkeit zu einem Stimmungsträger und "anästhetisiert" damit zugleich ihre soziale Problematik'[136] [aestheticises reality into being a bearer of mood, and at the same time 'anaesthetises' its social problems]. Such a philosophy has far-reaching consequences. It can produce no lasting commitment beyond the momentary acceptance of an idea, a theory or a system, and as far as the moral sphere is concerned, the effects of an action are not considered and therefore provide no guide as to whether the action is permissible or not. Man's life is little more than 'a question of nerves, and fibres, and slowly built-up cells',[137] and man himself is driven by an insatiable 'curiosity about life'[138] to hunt continually for 'sensations', for *nouveaux frissons*. This hectic pursuit of intense moments, which will be not only 'new and delightful'[139] but also strange, must ultimately lead to evil becoming the object of aesthetic emotions. It is a logical consequence of the new hedonism developed in Pater's 'Conclusion' that at the end of chapter XI it is said of Dorian that 'There were moments when he looked on evil simply as a mode through which he could realise his conception of the beautiful'.[140]

As John Pick has argued convincingly in his essay 'Divergent Disciples of Walter Pater',[141] Wilde ceased to follow his Oxford tutor's philosophical path, which led him from the ambiguity of the 'Conclusion' to the clarification of his ideas in *Marius*. It may be assumed that either Wilde had misunderstood Pater's intentions in *Marius*, or he had viewed it through his own aesthetically coloured spectacles. In *De Profundis* he writes of Pater's protagonist:

Marius is little more than a spectator: an ideal spectator indeed, and one to whom it is given 'to contemplate the spectacle of life with appropriate emotions', which Wordsworth defines as the poet's true aim: yet a spectator merely, and perhaps a little too much occupied with the comeliness of the vessels of the Sanctuary to notice that it is the Sanctuary of Sorrow that he is gazing at.[142]

This interpretation ignores the profound seriousness with which Marius seeks a valid philosophy of life, approaching different positions, then abandoning them, until finally his longing for an ideal world that will transcend the material one leads him (though not unequivocally) towards a Christian view of life. He is in no way satisfied with a purely aesthetic philosophy: 'The moral attitude developed in his childhood makes a purely aesthetic appreciation of life impossible for him.'[143]

The new hedonism of *Dorian Gray* is not to be confused with the new Cyrenaicism contained in chapter IX of *Marius*. Forewarned by the attacks directed against him by critics of the 'Conclusion', Pater explicitly rejects the concept of hedonism as a description of the phase Marius is going through:

the charge of 'hedonism', whatever its true weight might be, was not properly applicable at all. Not pleasure, but fullness of life, and 'insight' as conducing to that fullness – energy, variety, and choice of experience, including noble pain and sorrow even, loves, such as those in the exquisite old story of Apuleius, sincere and strenuous forms of moral life, such as Seneca and Epictetus – whatever form of human life, in short, might be heroic, impassioned, ideal: from these the 'new Cyrenaicism' of Marius took its criterion of values.[144]

In Marius's 'aesthetic education', then, pleasure is not the only criterion. He never loses himself in 'a kind of idolatry of mere life',[145] but is at pains to integrate all his different experiences of life into a synthesis. It is this breadth of receptivity that is lacking in Dorian's concept of self-fulfilment, for his interests are confined to the uninhibited development of his own personality and gratification of his desires. There is an inner restlessness in Marius that drives him through a variety of situations on his way to an ideal that lies beyond the material world; earnestly he searches for the 'equivalent of that Ideal, among so-called actual things'.[146] Dorian's development cannot be called a search – one only searches if one hopes to find something – but is, rather, simple 'curiosity about life'.[147] The harsh reproach that Wilde directed at his friend Douglas may apply equally to Dorian: 'you had no motives in life. You had appetites merely.'[148] As Dorian has no overall concept of moral order, and his view of the world does not even contain the hope of finding one, nothing remains for him but to try to intensify his life both quantitatively, through a maximum of 'pleasurable emotions', and qualitatively, through transforming each moment into an experience of passion or aesthetic satisfaction. The division of the self is inevitable, and is manifested not only in the dualism of portrait and portrayed, but also in the disintegration of the individual into 'a being with myriad lives and myriad sensations, a complex multiform creature'.[149] Unlike *Marius the Epicurean*, Wilde's novel describes 'nicht die Suche nach Einheit des Ichs mit sich selbst, sondern dessen Aufspaltung'[150] [not the unity of the self with itself, but its decomposition].

Formal and thematic tradition

In *Dorian Gray*, Wilde broke with a basic thematic tradition of the Victorian novel, described by the critic John Halperin as:

the moral and psychological expansion of protagonists who begin in self-absorption and move, through the course of a tortuous ordeal of education, to more complete self-knowledge.[151]

One need only glance at some of the most significant novels of the nineteenth century to verify this thesis. Elizabeth Bennet (*Pride and Prejudice*, 1813) and Emma Woodhouse (*Emma*, 1816) both make their way from blind prejudice and misconceptions of the world to a more realistic view. In Dickens's *Great Expectations* (1860–1) the very structure of the story is the process of Pip's maturity. The hero of George Eliot's *Adam Bede* (1859) begins by showing little sympathy for the weaknesses of his fellow-men, but ends up as a man of compassion. In *Middlemarch* (1871–2) the naive enthusiasm and unrealistic idealism of Dorothea Brooke are transformed by her marriages to Casaubon and Will Ladislaw into 'beneficent activity',[152] enabling her to contribute to the 'growing good of the world'.[153] In Meredith's *The Ordeal of Richard Feverel* (1859) and *The Egoist* (1879), the egotism of Sir Austin Feverel and Sir Willoughby Patterne is laid bare by their conflicts with reality, while for Henry James's Isobel Archer (*The Portrait of a Lady*, 1881) it is only the unhappy marriage with Gilbert Osmond that makes her consciously question her 'unquenchable desire to think well of herself'.[154] Not all these novels are 'Entwicklungsromane' [novels of development], but in all of them the main characters undergo a process of initiation which leads them to greater self-awareness and helps them to establish a new personal and social identity. There are still remnants of this pattern even in *Dorian Gray* – for instance, in the Hetty Merton episode (chapter XIX), where Dorian describes his vain attempt to break free from his inner isolation and egotism.

This narrative dramatisation of the loss of identity is a kind of parody on the classic *Bildungsroman* and its ilk, in which the hero's personality develops from selfish egotism to compassionate maturity. It is paralleled by a perceptible isolation from reality, which is conveyed particularly vividly by the technique of the narrated monologue.[155] This device, like the interior monologue, conveys the subjectivity of the character's view of reality, both in its content – with the extreme egocentricity of the 'new hedonism' – and its form, which is an impressionistic mode of description. The narrated monologue occurs most frequently in those passages where Dorian becomes aware of his beauty and appropriates Lord Henry's ideas as his own, and where Lord Henry reflects on his influence over Dorian. The increasing use of the device mirrors the increasing internalisation of reality, and anticipates the 'stream of consciousness' technique used later by James Joyce and Virginia Woolf. Loss of identity and isolation from reality are, of course, among the most common themes of modern literature.[156]

The modern subject-matter and narrative technique are nevertheless counterbalanced by a firm adherence to certain conventions of the genre – for instance, the omniscient narrator, whose authorial comments frequently punctuate the narrative, and also the link between the themes themselves and nineteenth-century literary tradition.[157] Dorian's desire to preserve his youthful beauty, while his portrait bears the alterations of age, and his fatal willingness even to sacrifice his soul to this end, may be seen simply as a variation on the theme of the devil's pact to be found in the legends of Faust and Theophilus. Close inspection reveals, perhaps somewhat surprisingly, that the *pactum cum diabolo* is not the only similarity between the novel and Goethe's play, for there are more links to be found both in characters and in plot. The relationship between Lord Henry and Dorian resembles that between Mephisto and Faust, while Dorian's love for Sibyl Vane, and her tragic end, may be said to echo the Gretchen tragedy; even Sibyl's brother, James Vane, who wants to avenge his dishonoured sister and dies in the cause, has his counterpart in Valentin. And the divided self of Dorian corresponds to Faust's cry of: 'Zwei Seelen wohnen, ach! in meiner Brust'[158] [Two souls, alas, dwell in my breast].

Do these parallels really mean that *Dorian Gray* is simply a 'revamping of the Faust legend'?[159] Even if it is not a Faust story in the strict sense of the term, it cannot be denied that elements of the legend (e.g. Faust's thirst for experience and knowledge of the world, his quest for the unattainable, and his tragic guilt) are presented in the novel from a quite new perspective; the universality of the theme, however, is reduced to the simple polarity of aesthetic and hedonistic pleasure versus morality. Of the metaphysical breadth of Goethe's *Faust* little remains except the basic conflict between good and evil. And the parallels between characters do nothing to alter this fact. It is therefore difficult to accept wholeheartedly Hans-Peter Gerhardt's view, seizing on a comment by Achim von Arnim, that 'Oscar Wilde in *The Picture of Dorian Gray* seinen "ihm gemässen" *Faust* geschrieben hat'[160] [In *The Picture of Dorian Gray* Oscar Wilde wrote the *Faust* that 'suited' him].

The link between the devil's pact motif and the idea of eternal youth had already been used, less directly, by Charles M. Maturin in his novel *Melmoth the Wanderer* (1820).[161] Wilde was actually distantly related to the author of this classic Gothic novel – Maturin was his great-uncle – knew the book, and on his release from prison adopted the pseudonym 'Melmoth' in order to 'prevent postmen having fits'.[162] In Book I of this horror story, Biddy Brannigan says of old Melmoth: 'though ... considerably advanced in life, to the astonishment of his family, he did not betray the slightest trace of being a year older than when they last beheld him'.[163]

But when he is nearing his end, his features suddenly take on all the signs of advanced age, just as Dorian's body does after his suicide:

now the lines of extreme age were visible in every feature. His hairs were as white as snow, his mouth had fallen in, the muscles of his face were relaxed and withered – he was the very image of hoary decrepid debility.[164]

It is also possible that Wilde got the idea of the magic portrait from Maturin. There is a portrait of the wanderer which, like Dorian's, is kept in an unused, junk-filled room. Young John Melmoth, when he first sees this picture, feels drawn above all to its eyes, and even has the impression that they move. Later, when he learns from a codicil in his dead uncle's will that he is to destroy this strange portrait, he thinks he sees a smile on the canvas face, and feels a 'horror indescribable at this transient and imaginary resuscitation of the figure'.[165]

Other precedents of the portrait motif are to be found in E. A. Poe's 'The Oval Portrait' (1842)[166] and an episode in Disraeli's *Vivian Grey* (1826).[167] In Poe's short story, a painter devotes himself to the immense task of painting an absolutely true-to-life portrait of his wife, never noticing that the strain of sitting for hours on end, week after week, is exhausting her and destroying her health. When he at last puts in the final stroke of his brush and cries: 'This is indeed *Life* itself!'[168] he realises that his model is dead. The basic idea of art as opposed to life is certainly common ground between Poe's story and Wilde's, but otherwise there is little similarity between the two tales.

Richard Aldington, in his introduction to a selection of Wilde's works, was the first to point out a passage in Disraeli's *Vivian Grey* (1826) where there is an even more vivid description of a living portrait than in *Melmoth*.[169] Mrs Felix Lorraine tells the story of Max Rodenstein, 'a being so beautiful in body, and in soul, you cannot imagine',[170] and she lays special emphasis on the fact that one day she was horrified to see how the eyes of a portrait of Rodenstein moved, with the lids trembling and finally closing. This event took place at the same moment, so it transpired, as Rodenstein himself was killed at the battle of Leipzig.

Here, as in Maturin's novel, the portraits take on a horrible fascination by way of their supernatural animation, which terrifies the observer. The peculiarity of the Dorian portrait, however, lies not in the animation of the features but in the continual changes that symbolise the protagonist's moral decline. The idea of a portrait exposing hidden guilt can be found in a short story of Nathaniel Hawthorne's, which has hitherto been overlooked by Wildean research: 'Edward Randolph's Portrait'. This is one of the four 'Legends of the Province House', which appeared in the collection of *Twice-Told Tales* (1837, extended in 1842). At the centre of this story is a mysterious portrait, which has been so badly damaged by 'age, damp, and smoke'[171] that its features are totally unrecognisable. After some time, the present governor of the province, in whose room the picture is hanging, makes a decision that is contrary to the wishes of the people, whereupon the features suddenly become visible on the dark canvas: the portrait is that of the first and universally hated governor:

> The expression of the face, if any words can convey an idea of it, was that of a wretch detected in some hideous guilt, and exposed to the bitter hatred and laughter and withering scorn of a vast surrounding multitude. There was the struggle of defiance, beaten down and overwhelmed by the crushing weight of ignominy. The torture of the soul had come forth upon the countenance.[172]

If one also takes into account the fact that this tale contains a character named Alice Vane, it is perhaps not too far-fetched to assume that Wilde was acquainted with 'Edward Randolph's Portrait'.

Another possible influence on Wilde, as regards the portrait motif as a structural element, has been suggested by Edouard Roditi in his monograph on Wilde. The reference is to Balzac's *La Peau de chagrin* (1831), which incidentally was itself written under the influence of *Melmoth the Wanderer*.[173] The basic idea of this novel, which was the French author's first major success, concerns a piece of shagreen (in this case leather from the skin of a wild ass) which has magic qualities: it can fulfil its owner's every wish, but shrinks a little with every wish it grants. Complete disappearance means the death of the owner. It is self-evident that as regards content there is little similarity between the two books – Dorian's pursuit of pleasure leads only indirectly to the shortening of his life, and its prime effect is on the conscience. As regards form, however, there are definite links: in both there is a magical, symbolic object which reflects and to some degree determines the fate of the protagonist as well as moulding the structure of the work itself. It can also be assumed fairly conclusively that Wilde knew Balzac's novel, as he held the great Frenchman in the highest esteem and throughout 1882/83 never travelled without having his works for company.[174] Robert H. Sherard says that his veneration for Balzac was so great that during his stay in Paris in 1883 he used to work in a white hooded dressing-gown, and had also acquired an ivory walking-stick with a turquoise-studded knob.[175] It must be added, however, that these Balzacian requisites did not inspire the author to any great literary or epic achievements, and indeed with hindsight the whole charade seems rather pathetic when one realises that at the time Wilde was struggling to write the blank verse of his far from triumphant *Duchess of Padua*.

As we have seen, the interaction between portrait and protagonist in *Dorian Gray* is a variation on the theme of the *doppelgänger* so common in romantic literature. Typical examples are E. T. A. Hoffmann's *Die*

Elixiere des Teufels (1815–16), E. A. Poe's 'William Wilson' (1839), Dostoievsky's *The Doppelgänger* (1846), Maupassant's *Le Horla* (1887), and R. S. Stevenson's *The Strange Case of Dr Jekyll and Mr Hyde* (1886). Wilson's double and Dorian's portrait have in common the fact that they each represent the hero's conscience. There are also similarities in their endings: when the double tries to stop Wilson from seducing a duchess at the Roman Carnival, Wilson stabs him. This murder also means the end of Wilson himself, for his double says, '*In me didst thou exist – and, in my death, see by this image, which is thine own, how utterly thou hast murdered thyself.*'[176] Wilde may well have been influenced, too, by Stevenson's representation of man's duality, in which the psychological components may be separated and, indeed, with the help of science, actually controlled.

Isobel Murray, editor of *Dorian Gray* in the series of Oxford English Novels, has drawn attention to another possible source that has hitherto been overlooked. This is the novel *Ashes of the Future (A Study of Mere Human Nature): The Suicide of Sylvester Gray* by Edward Heron-Allen, an acquaintance of Wilde's. It was published in 1888. Like Dorian, Sylvester is young and good-looking, and his aim in life is 'to amuse himself';[177] the occasional pangs of conscience brought about by this life style are dispelled by the narrator with words that are reminiscent of Lord Henry's: 'Your own history, viewed and criticised merely as a work of art, will lose its importance, its horrors, for you.'[178] Isobel Murray quotes several other similarities between the two books which would seem to strengthen the impression that Wilde owed some of his ideas to Heron-Allen.

One particularly interesting fact is that Sylvester Gray, like the hero of the 'Yellow Book' in chapter XI of *Dorian Gray*, is afraid of mirrors. This is a feature that was not to be found in Huysmans's *A Rebours*, which Wilde drew on as a model for the book that was to corrupt Dorian.[179] It may well be that this was a detail that Wilde had confused with his memories of *A Rebours*, thereby also confusing those critics who expect complete congruence between a work and its sources. In fact, chapter XI offers source-hunters a rich field[180] with its many descriptive and also historical details, such as the enumeration and description of various perfumes, strange musical instruments, precious stones, embroidery, tapestry, liturgical robes and different textiles. Bernhard Fehr, Walter Fischer and Isobel Murray have all shown what reference books and South Kensington Museum Art Handbooks Wilde used in order to learn about these various objects. He was particularly indebted to Ernest Lefébure's *Broderie et dentelles* (1887), a handbook of embroidery and lace-making, which was translated into English by Alan S. Cole and published in England the following year, meriting a lengthy review by

Wilde himself. Virtually the whole paragraph describing Dorian's liking for embroidery and tapestry, beginning with the sentence 'Then he turned his attention to embroideries',[181] is lifted bodily from his review of Lefébure's book as published in November 1888 in *The Woman's World*.[182] It is clear that Wilde not only used and re-used his successful epigrams, but also had no scruples about transplanting whole passages from one text to another in order to simplify the painstaking business of writing. More than most authors, he tended to follow the motto: 'Je prends mon bien où je le trouve.' More than once this led to his being accused of plagiarism, as well as casting doubt on his seriousness as an artist.

Theory of the novel and narrative practice

Dorian Gray holds a special place in the Victorian narrative tradition because of its departure from realism and its movement towards a more aesthetic and psychological form of literature. In the controversy over naturalism during the 1880s and 1890s, Wilde was emphatically against Zola, condemning his work as 'entirely wrong from beginning to end'.[183] But he was equally opposed to the violent, moralistic campaign which regarded the reception of this French novelist, and of others with similar aims, as presaging an approaching era of moral decay, and which insisted on trotting out the old clichés about French libertinage. Wilde saw the indignation of the Victorian middle classes as equivalent to Tartuffe's hypocrisy at the moment of his exposure, and instead he put forward purely aesthetic arguments. He objected to the fact that such work dealt only with the everyday lives of the 'lower orders',[184] and also to the technique of presentation by which Zola sought to describe the 'dreary vices' and the 'drearier virtues'[185] of his characters with documentary precision. He demanded that literature should have 'distinction, charm, beauty and imaginative power',[186] and distinguished between the novels of Zola and Balzac as being 'unimaginative realism' on the one hand, and 'imaginative reality' on the other.[187]

Wilde regards the current state of the narrative art as being lamentable – most novels are 'quite unreadable'[188] – and this can only be changed in two ways:

He who would stir us now by fiction must either give us an entirely new background, or reveal to us the soul of man in its innermost workings. The first is for the moment being done for us by Mr Rudyard Kipling. As one turns over the pages of his *Plain Tales from the Hills*, one feels as if one were seated under a palm-tree reading life by superb flashes of vulgarity ... As for the second condition, we have had Browning, and Meredith is with us. But there is still much to be done in the sphere of introspection. People sometimes say that fiction is getting too morbid. As far as psychology is concerned, it has never been morbid enough. We have merely touched the surface of the soul, that is all.[189]

It is clear that for *Dorian Gray*, Wilde chose the second course, relegating external action to the background and concentrating on the spiritual development of his characters. But it is difficult to justify his description of the novel as 'an essay on decorative art'[190] – a comment that could only apply at most to chapter XI. It is a description, however, that should not be taken too literally, for it is meant mainly as an attack on the truth-to-life of the naturalists and their 'scientific' view of reality. There is a contradiction between Wilde's demand that fiction should extend the 'sphere of introspection'[191] – as indeed twentieth-century novelists have preferred to do – and his classification of *Dorian Gray* as 'an essay on decorative art', but the contrast is reflected by the imbalance in the book between psychology and aestheticism. In this respect Wilde's position is rather like that of Lord Henry, who would like to write a novel 'as lovely as a Persian carpet, and as unreal',[192] but in fact is far more fascinated by 'scientific analysis of the passions'[193] and the mysterious link between body and soul.

During the controversy that followed the publication of the novel, Wilde admitted that he had not succeeded in subordinating the moral effect to the aesthetic, explaining his views in the *St James's Gazette* as follows:

All excess, as well as all renunciation, brings its own punishment. The painter, Basil Hallward, worshipping physical beauty far too much, as most painters do, dies by the hand of one in whose soul he has created a monstrous and absurd vanity. Dorian Gray, having led a life of mere sensation and pleasure, tries to kill conscience, and at that moment kills himself. Lord Henry Wotton seeks to be merely the spectator of life. He finds that those who reject the battle are more deeply wounded than those who take part in it. Yes; there is a terrible moral in *Dorian Gray* – a moral which the prurient will not be able to find in it, but which will be revealed to all whose minds are healthy. Is this an artistic error? I fear it is. It is the only error in the book.[194]

In the book version of the novel, Wilde included a preface which contains an epigrammatic formulation of his aesthetic ideas.[195] His intention was to make his position clearer to future critics by inculcating them with the 'right' set of artistic values in the hope of influencing their reviews. But he also took the precaution of putting in the preface a response to unfavourable reactions: 'When critics disagree the artist is in accord with himself.' If one takes this accord seriously and compares Wilde's theoretical precepts with the novel itself, one cannot help being struck by certain inconsistencies. How, for instance, is one to reconcile the thesis that 'There is no such thing as a moral or an immoral book', as claimed in the preface, with the description of the yellow book in chapter X as 'a poisonous book'?[196] The closing sentence of the preface reads: 'All art is quite useless', and yet Basil's painting, Sibyl's acting and the 'poisonous book' itself are far from being 'useless' in Dorian's life. On the contrary, the course of the story lays great stress on the effect of art on life, as well as the effects of life on art.

Dorian Gray as an autobiographical confession

The interaction between art and life is not only an important element in the novel, but also offers an illuminating starting-point for a study of the links between the subject-matter and Wilde's own life. Although Wilde clearly had affinities with 'decadent' literature and the poetics of Gautier, Baudelaire and Huysmans, the main cause of his fascination with the *doppelgänger* motif is certainly to be found in his own personality and in the social conditions in which he lived and worked. The moral and legal taboo on homosexuality played a considerable part in his double life – a duplicity to which in the long run he was not psychologically suited. He reacted to the conflict of roles imposed on him from outside with feelings of guilt, and sought to free himself from these by means of the trial and an unconsciously longed-for atonement. The repetition of such words as 'secret', 'sin', 'crime', 'shame' and 'vice' is all too revealing, and although they contribute towards 'an atmosphere of moral corruption',[197] they may also be seen as literary reflections of Wilde's own guilt. Within this framework, the *doppelgänger* motif becomes the fictional objectification of the author's own uncontrolled double life: 'It is the confession, not the priest that gives us absolution.'[198]

Autobiographical interpretations of *Dorian Gray*, such as those of Philipp Aronstein,[199] Léon Lemonnier,[200] Arthur H. Nethercot[201] and Aatos Ojala,[202] are reinforced by a noteworthy passage in a letter, where Wilde identifies himself with the main characters:

it [*The Picture of Dorian Gray*] contains much of me in it. Basil Hallward is what I think I am: Lord Henry what the world thinks me: Dorian what I would like to be ... in other ages, perhaps.[203]

This testimony need not be taken to mean that the novel *is* to be interpreted along biographical lines, but it is certainly a key passage for any understanding of Wilde himself. His identification of himself with Basil Hallward may at first seem astonishing, but it confirms the thesis that Wilde's pose as the intellectual, provocative dandy, avant-garde and anti-middle class, was nothing more than – a means of effectively and publicly negating the Victorian values which – in secret – had a far greater influence on him (as is shown by his actual life) than his mockery would suggest. The three main characters are the separate components of his split personality:[204] Basil Hallward represents his moral 'super-ego': Dorian Gray is his driving-force, his 'id', with its attendant feelings of guilt manifested in the portrait; and Lord Henry wears his public mask as well as anticipating his own attempt and ultimate failure to solve his problem through hedonism.

If in fact one does read the novel as a personal confession, one cannot avoid a feeling almost of horror, because the fiction is strangely prophetic of Wilde's real-life fate. The relation between Basil and Dorian, with its fatal outcome, bears certain resemblances to Wilde's friendship with Lord Alfred Douglas, which began in 1891. In both cases the older artist feels an intense emotional attachment to the rich young aristocrat, who is the dominant partner. At the very beginning of the novel Basil confesses: 'As long as I live, the personality of Dorian Gray will dominate me',[205] just as Wilde's attitude towards Douglas is summed up by his confession that 'my will-power became absolutely subject to yours'.[206] Dorian murders the now burdensome Basil, just as Wilde was ruined artistically and socially by a trial that only came about because of the interference of his peevish and vengeful friend. Wilde's thesis that nature imitates art seems to have been confirmed by his own life.

Dorian Gray as decadent art

The autobiographical line is not the only approach to this novel. Nor can it be reduced to a mere reworking of the *doppelgänger* motif. As has already been mentioned, its form parodies that of the *Entwicklungsroman* in so far as it describes the inevitable fall of an anti-hero.[207] In this respect it is an important example of literary decadence.[208] It contains almost all the elements ascribed to decadence: narcissistic egotism, a provocative scorn for moral and social conventions, preference for the artificial as opposed to the natural, pleasure-seeking, experience for the sake of experience, an atmosphere of decay, the death-wish, a retreat from the everyday present into the luxurious *paradis artificiels* of distant times and exotic places, 'style ingénieux, compliqué, savant, plein de nuances et de recherches'.[209]

In addition there are many more details that are typical of decadent literature, such as the figure of Wagner and his music – particularly the opera *Tannhäuser*, which after its scandalous Parisian première in 1861 became a symbol of avant-garde art in Europe. Dorian listens to the overture and finds in it an expression of the 'tragedy of his own soul'.[210] Without doubt the conflict between earthly and heavenly love, between Venusberg Bacchanalia and religious longing, which underlies the overture, is a musical encapsulation of his own divided self. But as Wilde's knowledge of music was extremely limited, it may well be that the *Tannhäuser* reference and its link with the hero's spiritual situation sprang from literary rather than musical sources. One is reminded of

Baudelaire's interpretation of *Tannhäuser*, in his essay *Richard Wagner et Tannhäuser à Paris* (1861), in which he stresses the dualism of body and soul:

Tannhäuser représente la lutte des deux principes qui ont choisi le cœur humain pour principal champ de bataille, c'est-à-dire de la chair avec l'esprit, de l'enfer avec le ciel, de Satan avec Dieu. Et cette dualité est représentée tout de suite, par l'ouverture, avec une incomparable habileté.[211]

[*Tannhäuser* represents the struggle between the two principles that have chosen the human heart as their principal battlefield, that is the flesh against the spirit, hell against heaven, Satan against God. And this duality is represented at once, by the overture, with incomparable skill.]

In addition to the decadent Wagnerism placed by Erwin Koppen at the centre of his detailed study, proving that Wagner may be seen as 'signifikantes Element des Erscheinungsbildes der Décadence-Literatur',[212] there is also mention of Venice, a town which in nineteenth-century literature ranked alongside Rome as a classic paradigm of civilisation in decline and of death. Byron's 'Ode on Venice' (1819) and *Childe Harold* (1812), Platen's *Sonette aus Venedig* (1825), Thomas Mann's *Tod in Venedig* (1912), Maurice Barrès's *La Mort de Venise* (1920) are all examples of how the vision of this dying city inspired the imagination of the writer.[213] While leafing through Gautier's *Emaux et Camées* (1852; final edition 1872), Dorian comes upon 'Variations sur le carnaval de Venise', and is enchanted by the lines 'Devant une façade rose / Sur le marbre d'un escalier' from the poem 'Sur les lagunes',[214] which he feels contain 'the whole of Venice'.[215] The special fascination this town has for Dorian does not, therefore, lie in the melancholy of its decay, but rather in the picturesque charm of its gondolas, archways, marble steps and palaces.

One may extrapolate from the above observation that Wilde did not by any means import all the clichés of French decadence in their original form. Dorian's development is attributed neither to a particular neurotic disposition, as with Des Esseintes in *A Rebours*, nor to hereditary disease combined with a bad environment, as with Zola's Rougon-Macquart family. Nor was Wilde the first to bring French literary trends across to England. Two years earlier George Moore had turned away from naturalism with his novel *Confessions of a Young Man* (1888), putting forward ideas of *décadence* very similar to those of the 'new hedonism'. The Moore persona also feels drawn to the concept of a 'new aestheticism'[216] and is 'intensely alive to all impulses, and unsupported by any moral convictions'.[217] The description of his double life in Paris, where he spends one evening in the company of thieves and burglars, and the next dining with a duchess or a princess, has certain parallels with Dorian's various activities, particularly in chapter XI. In a revealing dialogue

between the first-person narrator and his conscience, the ruthless development of self is taken to be 'the rescue and the individualization of the
ego',[218] but there are already hints of the consequences that are to bring
about the downfall of Wilde's hero: when the self-satisfied narrator claims
that 'I have torn you [conscience] all to pieces long ago', conscience replies
– in a sententious aphorism anticipating the dénouement of *Dorian Gray*
– 'destroying me you have destroyed yourself'.[219]

Moore's self-portrait, in which – as Paul Goetsch rightly points out – he
'den jugendlichen Bohemien, der er wohl in Wirklichkeit war, in einen
dekadenten Ästheten um[deutet]'[220] [re-interprets the young Bohemian
that he probably was in reality, as a decadent aesthete], is certainly drawn
in more vivid colours than was Wilde's dandy. Thus his fictitious *alter ego*
can go to such extremes as maintaining that he would behead all the
Japanese in Japan and elsewhere if thereby a single drawing of Hokusai
might be preserved from destruction.[221] His cynical Epicureanism is
particularly striking in his attitude towards women:

I'm not a Casanova. I love women as I love champagne – I drink it and enjoy it; but
an exact account of every bottle drunk would prove flat narrative.[222]

When this superficial, man-of-the-world attitude is allied to a crude and
lordly detachment, the resultant view of women is such as may be found in
German Impressionism, for instance. One recalls Liliencron's remark
about women: 'Was die Weiber betrifft: geniessen, fortschmeissen. Je
m'en fiche!!!'[223] [As far as women are concerned – enjoy, chuck out. I
couldn't care less!!!]

If one compares Wilde's treatment of the *sensibilità erotica* with the
work of the continental *décadents*, it is obvious that he refrains from any
risqué details of erotic conduct as well as from the description of sexual
perversions and anomalies such as androgyny, sadism, incest, flagellation,
necrophilia etc. Even homosexuality, which for the Victorians was still a
taboo vice, is only hinted at in the name of Dorian and in Basil's
passionate attachment to his model. In order to show just how different
the French *décadents* were from Wilde, it will suffice to quote a scene from
A Rebours, where Des Esseintes tries to overcome his impotence by
having his partner, a female ventriloquist, imitate during intercourse the
voice of a man coming home unexpectedly, hammering on the door and
demanding entrance. This perverse 'aphrodisiac' is meant to stimulate the
flagging sexuality of the hero:

il [Des Esseintes] éprouvait des allégresses inouïes, dans cette bousculade, dans
cette panique, de l'homme courant un danger interrompu, pressé dans son
ordure.[224]

[he [Des Esseintes] experienced unheard-of joys in this feverishness, in this panic,
of the man in danger, interrupted, hurried in his lasciviousness.]

Such a scene would be unthinkable in Wilde's work. By comparison with French literary sexuality as in Catulle Mendès's *Zo'har* (1886), Rachilde's *Monsieur Vénus* (1889), Joséphin Péladans's *L'Androgyne* (1891), Octave Mirbeau's *Jardin des supplices* (1899), or, to name an English example, Aubrey Beardsley's *Venus and Tannhäuser* – which could only be published after radical revision with the title 'Under the Hill' (1896) – *Dorian Gray* seems quite anodyne, and makes one really question whether Wilde and his work can truly be said to contain 'l'âme de la "décadence"'.[225] Consideration for the prudishness of his Victorian readers, and his own moral sensibility – for in his writings he never showed much sympathy for libertinage – led to this insular version of continental literary decadence being extremely restrained as far as the treatment of sexuality was concerned. Instead the emphasis is shifted to the protagonist's entanglement in all the contradictions of his aesthetic and hedonistic view of the world. The literary figure of the French *décadent* and that of the Wildean dandy combine to form a new character for the English novel, and so the decadent subject-matter of *Dorian Gray* is set in a new frame of reference – that of the late Victorian conflict between art and morality.

Dorian Gray and the crisis of Victorian identity

Art, like science, is a means of getting to know reality, and so the importance of a novel is not confined to its subject-matter, its place in literary tradition and literary history, or its autobiographical references, but it also consists in the way in which the work reacts to the historical situation from which it emerges. In this respect, *Dorian Gray* is the expression of a fin-de-siècle crisis both of culture and of society. The symptoms of this crisis are the replacement of social obligations by sociable relations, together with the individual's withdrawal from society into a position of egocentric self-fulfilment, the parasitic element of which is unmistakable. In addition there is the link between aesthetic education and moral corruption in the aristocracy, whose claims to social leadership in the state are thereby invalidated. Signs of breakdown in the Victorians' view of themselves at the beginning of the industrial age, with the attendant loss of a complete and enclosed picture of man and world, had already been noted by Ruskin:

We have much studied and much perfected, of late, the great civilized invention of the division of labour; only we give it a false name. It is not, truly speaking, the labour that is divided; but the men: – Divided into mere segments of men – broken into small fragments and crumbs of life.[226]

The weakening of religious faith, scepticism towards an increasingly scientific cosmology, rapid changes in the environment due to technology and industrialisation – all these contributed to an intellectual climate in which the old orders began to crumble, while new ones had not yet established themselves. The 'new Hedonism' was a response to this upheaval in terms not of attack or of constructiveness, but simply of escapism: the individual was to adopt a position counter to society, renouncing any active role in its reshaping, and simply occupied with the intense satisfaction of his own needs. 'To be good is to be in harmony with one's self ... Discord is to be forced to be in harmony with others.'[227] There could scarcely be a clearer expression of the change from man's social responsibility to individual anarchism.

Matthew Arnold, in his critical study of English social and political life, *Culture and Anarchy* (1869), had already warned against the dangers of irresponsibly 'Doing as one likes'. He regarded the goal of cultural development as being 'a fuller harmonious development of our humanity'.[228] In the 1860s Arnold's response to the decline of Christianity, the worship of material progress, the absolutism of liberal ideas, and disdain for reason, was to construct a new ideal for a culture which relied on the unity of 'sweetness and light', beauty and reason. In the 1890s Wilde could do nothing more than narrate the break-up of all moral and aesthetic concepts. The reformist impulse, which Arnold saw as being inspired by the force of the 'Hellenistic' ideal with its *'spontaneity of consciousness'*[229] having to triumph over the Hebrew *'strictness of conscience'*,[230] was something that Wilde would also have approved of, but it was an idea that took on a completely different slant and value through being radically subjectified and detached from all social obligations. Optimistic belief in an objective ideal of cultural development thus degenerated into pessimistic resignation to a narrow culture of 'pleasure'.

This negation of social ties and scorn for moral conventions has the inevitable result, 'dass man das eigene Ich zur Welt erweitern muss'[231] [that one has to expand one's own self to being the world].

> There were times when it appeared to Dorian Gray that the whole of history was merely the record of his own life, not as he had lived it in act and circumstance, but as his imagination had created it for him, as it had been in his brain and in his passions.[232]

The central position of the individual, who confines the world to his own framework of experience, is confirmed by frequent use of the word 'personality',[233] which is reminiscent of Nietzsche's cult of the personality.[234] Basil is so deeply impressed by Dorian's personality that he ascribes 'an entirely new mode of style'[235] to its influence, and Lord Henry sums up his 'pupil's' development as follows:

> He had made him [Dorian] premature. That was something. Ordinary people waited till life disclosed to them its secrets, but to the few, to the elect, the

mysteries of life were revealed before the veil was drawn away. Sometimes this was the effect of art, and chiefly of the art of literature, which dealt immediately with the passions and the intellect. But now and then a complex personality took the place and assumed the office of art; was indeed, in its way, a real work of art, Life having its elaborate masterpieces, just as poetry has, or sculpture, or painting.[236]

If a complex personality can be a 'real work of art', then art and life become one, but this aesthetic mixture and evaluation of moral factors cannot work, for aesthetic conduct and awareness of good and evil belong to two different codes which cannot be set at the same level, despite Lord Henry's mephistophelean sophistry. The fascination of evil, which for him is essentially something positive – he talks of 'beautiful sins',[237] and calls sin 'the only colour-element left in modern life'[238] – is never more than an element of his theory, which when put into practice brings about the downfall of Dorian. The novel's dénouement disproves his thesis that 'Art had a soul, but that man had not',[239] and discredits Wilde's provocative claim that 'Sin is an essential element of progress.'[240] Real life shows this to be no more than a defiant, almost propagandist attack on middle-class values, whose surface glitter can scarcely conceal the super-ficiality of its content.

Much of the book's morbid enjoyment of vice and sin stems from 'pride of individualism'[241] at violating middle-class norms and Christian pre-cepts; this anti-philistinism cannot, however, prevent the ultimate con-firmation of the very moral sense which it appears to attack. The moral question of how to live, which preoccupied people in the 1890s,[242] becomes all the more pressing in *Dorian Gray* as the attempted solutions become all the more immoral. The novel is typical of the transition between Victorianism and the Modern Age in that on the one hand it represents a powerful challenge to Victorian orthodoxy, and on the other never really breaks free from its ideological premises. To counter utili-tarian ideas, Wilde proclaims the uselessness of art and the charm of idleness; to replace evangelical fervour and moral righteousness, through which earthly life is regarded merely as preparation for life on the other side, he advocates consistent hedonism here and now; and against middle-class respectability he prefers the uninhibited self-fulfilment of the individual, whose only limitations are imposed not by any *consensus omnium*, but simply by the range of his own potential. Undoubtedly all this reflects the split in the Victorian identity, which was the inevitable result of the conflict between the Victorians' severe public morality and their private need to satisfy their natural desires. Hypocrisy was rife. In *The Importance of Being Earnest* Wilde exposed the pomposity of his contemporaries by reducing it to absurdity; in *Dorian Gray* he uses the *doppelgänger* motif to present the 'scholar' and 'citizen of the world'[243] together with the 'other Victorian'.[244]

As far as the problem of a *modus vivendi* is concerned, the novel can only offer a pessimistic solution. It depicts a hedonistic attempt to compensate for the lack of universal guidelines across the Victorian 'darkling plain' by substituting life itself, that is, an intensive perception of and pleasure in all experiences open to the senses and the imagination; the attempt is doomed to failure. Theory is contradicted by practice, life overwhelms art, and the voice of conscience will not be hushed by aesthetics. Basil fails to translate his idealistic concept of art into reality, Lord Henry's destructive activity runs counter to his demand for 'philosophic contemplation',[245] Sibyl's acting talent is ruined by the reality of her love, and Dorian's idea of life as art cannot be reconciled with his moral consciousness. The hoped-for synthesis fails to materialise. Spiritual isolation and man's alienation from society are followed by loss of identity. Life is stylised into art, and there is no aim other than unlimited pleasure, but the final effect of this is meaninglessness, disillusionment and *ennui* – the very enemies that the characters had set out to conquer: 'Life is a great disappointment.'[246] The artist has betrayed his ideals, the intellectual has sacrificed his moral responsibility, the scientist becomes accomplice to the criminal, and aesthetic sensitivity degenerates into commonplace hedonism and criminality. Individual and society, art and life, aesthetic conduct and moral awareness are irreconcilable, and the tensions between them destroy all hope of a new life. All that remains for Dorian at the end is a resigned awareness of the nature of his failure:

Culture and corruption ... I have known something of both. It seems terrible to me now that they should ever be found together.[247]

6 Sensuality and suggestion. *Salomé* and *The Sphinx*

Salomé

The characters and themes of the biblical story of Herod Antipas, the dance of Herodias's daughter – later to be named Salome – and the beheading of John the Baptist are amongst the most popular subjects in art, music and literature. Hugo Daffner's detailed and richly illustrated history of the Salome story[1] reproduces over 200 paintings, miniatures, murals, drawings and sculptures, as well as illustrations from the applied arts such as weaving and embroidery, and all these bear ample witness to the artistic inspiration offered by this tiny episode. What was painted by Botticelli, Dürer, Rubens, Gustave Moreau and Lovis Corinth was turned into an oratorio by Alessandro Stradella, and an opera by Richard Strauss; in literature the subject was tackled by the authors of *Heliand*, of *Ysengrimus*, of various late medieval mysteries, and in the nineteenth century by such writers as Heine, Mallarmé, Flaubert, Laforgue, Wilde and Yeats. From early days the tragedy of the Baptist was developed and extended, with new characters and new interpretations embellishing the short, factual account given in the gospels (Matthew 14:1–12; Mark 6:14–29).

Composition, first performance, and Beardsley's illustrations
There are almost as many legends surrounding the composition of Wilde's tragedy as there are around the original tale itself. The anonymous critic who reviewed the first French edition of the play, expressing his 'unfavourable opinion'[2] of it, thought it had been written for Sarah Bernhardt – a suggestion adhered to by Ingleby and others.[3] This, however, is a misconception probably due to the fact that the great French actress accepted the part of Salome and in June 1892 actually started rehearsals at the Palace Theatre in London. A week after the *Times* review, Wilde wrote to the paper to set the record straight: 'my play was in no sense of the words written for this great actress'.[4] This is confirmed by Robert Ross in his introductory comments on *Salomé* in the first and second collected editions of 1908 and 1909.

Many critics have doubted whether Wilde could have written the play in French without a good deal of help, but there is also considerable

176

disagreement as to the quality of his French.[5] Hesketh Pearson considers the question to be undecided, but tends to the view that Wilde probably wrote the first draft in English, 'because of the obvious influence of the Song of Solomon on some of the longer passages and because in the first flush of inspiration he would naturally write in English'.[6] This romantic idea of composition is contradicted not only by the elaborate and artificial style in which the play is written, but also by the different manuscripts that have survived, all of which are in French, as well as by the author's own statements:

> My idea of writing the play was simply this: I have one instrument that I know I can command, and that is the English language. There was another instrument to which I had listened all my life, and I wanted once to touch this new instrument to see whether I could make any beautiful thing out of it.[7]

Such statements must, of course, be viewed with a certain amount of caution bearing in mind Wilde's predilection for exaggeration and self-advertisement, not to mention the desire to shine the most impressive light upon his own genius. Perhaps he really did wish to touch the 'new instrument', or perhaps he was influenced by the fact that in the nineteenth century the most important literary treatments of the Salome theme had, apart from the episode in Heine's 'Atta Troll', come from the pens of French authors. It is also worth pointing out that a theatrical success could give Wilde easier access to the best literary circles in Paris – which during the 1890s he was particularly anxious to achieve – and attract the attention of the French public. But the reasons for his writing in French can only remain for the most part speculative, and we remain dependent on his own utterances.

There is one further legend about the writing of this play. Frances Winwar and Hesketh Pearson offer a version which suggests that Wilde told the story to some French friends over lunch, went back to his room at the Grand Hotel, 29 Boulevard des Capucines, Paris, happened to see a 'blank book' lying on the table, and there and then wrote down the story.[8] This is also a somewhat romantic account of the genesis of a work, and attributes to Wilde a creative spontaneity and intensity which he certainly never showed on any other occasion. Clyde de Ryals has compared an early manuscript with the 'final fair copy' in the Rosenbach Foundation Museum, and finds the above account extremely unlikely.[9] Innumerable revisions and corrections – mainly grammatical – by Pierre Louÿs, to whom the play is dedicated, point to a fairly prolonged period of composition.

If one keeps in mind certain statements in Wilde's letters, together with the known biographical facts, then the following is the most likely course of events: from late October or early November until early December

1891, Wilde was living in Paris, where he met Edmond de Goncourt, renewed his contact with Stéphane Mallarmé, and got to know Pierre Louÿs and André Gide. For most of this period he stayed at the Grand Hotel already mentioned. The paper of the two early manuscripts – the Texas one, dated 'Paris, November 1891' and the Bodmer Library one, Cologny, Geneva – bears the trademark of a stationer's in the same street, Boulevard des Capucines. In December 1891, Wilde sent a manuscript of *Salomé* together with a letter to his new friend Pierre Louÿs, expressly stating that the play was still unfinished and uncorrected but that 'l'idée de la construction'[10] was clear; this indicates for certain that the play was written between late October and early December 1891 in Paris. Further evidence lies in the fact that the manuscript corrected by Louÿs is almost identical with the text of the first edition. There is no contradiction in Wilfrid S. Blunt's diary entry of 27 October 1891:

I breakfasted with him [George Curzon], Oscar Wilde, and Willy Peel, on which occasion Oscar told us he was writing a play in French to be acted in the Français. He is ambitious of being a French Academician.[11]

If Blunt's recollection is correct, and he is not confusing the *plan* for a French play with work actually in progress, and if Wilde was not taking the will for the deed, then we can say the work was begun in London in October and was continued and finished in Paris in November.

Pierre Louÿs was not the first or the only person to see the manuscript of *Salomé*. There were other French-speaking friends who helped correct Wilde's language. Stuart Merrill and Adolphe Retté both confirm that Merrill, an American poet who lived in Paris and wrote in French, was the first to receive a manuscript with a request for corrections. Wilde, however, was not entirely confident in the American's knowledge of French and so sent the draft to Retté, who says that he simply crossed out 'des anglicismes trop formels'[12] and suggested a few other changes. Only then did a new version go to Pierre Louÿs.

It is not known when Wilde got the corrected version back from Louÿs. In any case, he was far too preoccupied with the forthcoming world première to worry about the publication of *Salomé*. And so the work was abandoned for a while. In June 1893 he informed Pierre Louÿs of the surprising news that Sarah Bernhardt was going to play the part of Salome. He said he had met the actress at Henry Irving's home and read her extracts from the play. 'La Divine' had then apparently stated on the spot that she wished to play Salome.[13] Rehearsals began that same month at the Palace Theatre in London, but the Examiner of Plays for the Lord Chamberlain forbade the performance because of the biblical origin of the characters. Wilde was naturally furious at this ban, and his initial reaction was to renounce his British citizenship and become a Frenchman, thereby inspiring a cartoon in *Punch* which showed the renegade as a *poilu*. At least, however, he had the satisfaction of enlisting the support of William Archer, who also protested vehemently against the censorship. It may well be that the famous critic's friendly advice that it would not be wise 'to turn tail and run away from a petty tyranny'[14] influenced Wilde to reverse his rather hasty decision.

Disappointment over his failure to get *Salomé* staged in England, and the fact that he started work on *A Woman of No Importance* that August, led to the play being left once more on the shelf. After the London débâcle, Sarah Bernhardt did try to have the play produced in Paris at the theatre of Porte-Saint-Martin, but this enterprise also came to nothing. Wilde's correspondence with the French publisher E. Bailly, director of the Librairie de l'Art Indépendant, reveals that it was not until December 1892 that preparations began for printing. Wilde asked Bailly to send proofs to Marcel Schwob and Pierre Louÿs, though Bailly appears to have sent them only to the former.[15] Schwob, to whom Wilde dedicated his poem *The Sphinx* two years later, made only 'two or three slight alterations',[16] according to Robert Ross, and made little effort to adapt the language to the demands of the Académie Française. Thus despite its formal correctness, the text does not always sound idiomatic to the ears of a Frenchman, but has a certain exotic tinge which is by no means out of place, given the style and setting of the piece.[17]

On 22 February 1893, more than a year after its completion, the play was finally published in Paris by the Librairie de l'Art Indépendant and in London by John Lane. In August of the same year, Lord Alfred Douglas finished his English translation, which the author, however, did not like; it had to undergo so many revisions that it seemed inappropriate to allow the translator's name to be given on the title page; the name Douglas is only to be found in the dedication, in which he is named as translator.[18] The translation was published on 9 February 1894 and was accompanied by a series of illustrations by Aubrey Beardsley which were later to become famous.[19]

The attraction of Beardsley's drawings lies in the originality of their black-and-white composition and the seductive grace of their lines. Little monsters with big heads and bulging eyes, and faun-like bodies half hidden in the foliage of scaly rosebushes alternate with billowing robes and subtly varied peacock feathers. They conjure up an imaginary world which is a fantastic projection of erotic prurience and lascivious dreams. Wilde showed little enthusiasm for Beardsley's pictures because he found them too 'Japanese' and so out of keeping with the 'Byzantine' spirit of his play.[20] In any case relations between author and illustrator – perhaps the two outstanding representatives of pure aestheticism and decadence at the end of the nineteenth century – were already somewhat strained, as Wilde had rejected Beardsley's offer to translate *Salomé* into English. Beardsley may well have been deeply hurt by this rejection, especially as he took his own literary talents very seriously. Characteristically he took revenge by caricaturing the author in some of the *Salomé* illustrations – notably *The Woman in the Moon*, *Enter Herodias* and *The Eyes of Herod*. The drawings have been criticised for being irrelevant to the text, or for distorting it rather than illuminating it.[21] The criticism of irrelevance may be true of such pictures as *The Black Cape*, but it does not apply to *The Dancer's Reward*, for instance, where Salome grasps the severed and bleeding head of the Baptist which is being held up from the depths by 'un grand bras noir'[22] according to the text. There are many such points of contact between Beardsley's erotically suggestive, boldly stylised pictures and Wilde's artificial and essentially sensuous text.

On 11 February 1896 *Salomé* at last had its first performance at the Théâtre de l'Œuvre in Paris. Lugné-Poë was the director, and Lina Munte played Salome. In 1901 there were several productions in Germany, for example, in Berlin, Munich and Breslau. Max Reinhardt directed the production, which opened on 15 November 1902 at the Kleines Theater in Berlin. The English première did not take place until 10 May 1905, being presented by the New Stage Club at the Bijou Theatre.[23] There was another production in 1906 by the Literary Theatre Society. The year before, Richard Strauss had used Hedwig Lachmann's German translation as the basis of his opera, which was immensely successful and has lost none of its power even today. By 1909 Wilde's version of the Salome story was so popular that Walter Ledger's bibliography in the second edition of the collected works lists over forty translations and reprints.

Construction, main themes and the symbol of the moon

The scene of the play is a great terrace in the Palace of Herod Antipas, Tetrarch of Judaea, set above a banqueting-hall in which a feast is just taking place. Narraboth, the Syrian Captain of the Guard, is watching the young Princess Salome and is entranced by her beauty. While the soldiers comment on the Jews who are down in the hall arguing about religion, and while the Nubian and the Cappadocian talk about religion in their own countries, the voice of Jokanaan suddenly rings out from the cistern in which he is being held prisoner. He prophesies the coming of the Redeemer.

Salome comes on to the terrace, to escape from the lustful gaze of her stepfather. She is fascinated by the voice of Jokanaan and wants to see him. Narraboth says it has been forbidden by the Tetrarch. His resistance, however, soon crumbles in the face of Salome's charms, and he opens the cistern, from which Jokanaan emerges. He launches into a vehement condemnation of Herodias, Herod's wife, who has committed many sins, and although at first Salome seems shocked by his maledictions, she is soon entranced by him. She describes his eyes, is enamoured of his voice, and finally exclaims: 'Jokanaan! Je suis amoureuse de ton corps!'[24] His brusque rejection of her only serves to increase her passion, which expresses itself in the desire to kiss his mouth. Narraboth, in despair at these words, kills himself, but even then Salome continues to ignore him totally. Jokanaan curses the seductive Princess as 'fille d'adultère' and 'fille d'une mère incestueuse'[25] and goes back into his cistern.

Herod, accompanied by Herodias, the Roman envoy Tigellinus and other guests, comes onto the terrace in search of his stepdaughter. He is full of gloomy premonitions and is depressed by the Nazarenes' report that 'Messias' has come, who raises the dead. For diversion he tells Salome to dance for him. She refuses at first, but then agrees to dance after he has promised to give her whatever she wants – 'fût-ce la moitié de mon royaume'.[26] She performs the dance of the seven veils, and for her reward demands the head of Jokanaan. Herod is shocked at this monstrous request and tries to make her change her mind, but finally has to accede because of the oath that he had sworn. The black arm of the Executioner reaches forth from the cistern, bearing the head of Jokanaan on a silver shield. Salome can now fulfil her desire: 'Je baiserai ta bouche, Jokanaan.'[27] Herod is appalled, and in the final words of the play commands 'Tuez cette femme!'[28]

The unity of time, place and action effects an impression of compression and intensity, with the action centring on Salome's wooing of Jokanaan, her dance, the beheading of the Baptist, and Salome's death. Unlike Flaubert, Wilde is careful not to separate the scenes into banqueting-hall and prison, but combines them with the adjacent terrace.

The set consists of a terrace above a banqueting-hall, a gigantic staircase to the right, a cistern surrounded by a wall of green bronze to the left, and moonlight. From the very beginning Wilde makes skilful use of the horizontal and vertical structures of his set, his exposition – in some ways reminiscent of *Hamlet* and also of Maeterlinck's *La Princesse Maleine* – employing the classical device of teichoskopia. The characters on the terrace – the soldiers, the young Syrian Captain, Herodias's page and others – describe the hall and the people in it from an external perspective, thereby achieving two things: they introduce the main characters, and they sow the seeds for later developments. Salome's entrance marks the end of the exposition, and her dialogue with Jokanaan forms the central section of the plot, leading finally to her demand that he be beheaded (peripeteia) and her death (catastrophe). The structure of the play is in three distinct sections: exposition, up to Salome's entrance; centre, culminating in the death of Narraboth; final scene, beginning with the entrance of Herod, and ending with Salome's death. Although the play is in one continuous act, this structure contains in compressed form all the elements of the classical five-act tragedy. The tension is enhanced by the use at certain key moments of a tripling technique that Wilde had already used in the fairy-tales: for instance, Salome is attracted by Jokanaan's body, then his hair, and finally his mouth; Herod invites Salome three times – to drink wine, to eat fruit, and then to sit with him; towards the end he tries to divert her from her gruesome aim with three different offers: 'une grande émeraude ronde',[29] his 'beaux paons blancs',[30] and 'des bijoux'.[31]

The central position of Salome is brought out on the level of the sub-plot by her relations with Herod on the one hand and Narraboth on the other. The lasciviousness of Herod makes him a willing tool in the hands of Herodias's daughter, and thus gives tragic impetus to the development of the story, whereas the Syrian's hopeless love has a quite different function: Salome is as unmoved by his adoration as Jokanaan is by her sensuous passion. At the same time her indifference even after the young Captain's suicide points the way towards the cruelty she is later to show in her dealings with the Baptist. The calculating manner in which she uses Narraboth's love in order to make him disobey the Tetrarch's orders anticipates the way she is later to exploit her attractions in bending Herod to her will.

Sex is the motivating force behind all the main characters but one: Herod is driven by lust, Salome by sensual passion, and Narraboth is obsessed with Salome's beauty. The erotic motif contains subtle tensions between the virginity of Salome and her violent sensuality, and between the lust of her ageing stepfather, whom Jokanaan accuses of incestuous relations with Herodias, and the sterility of which his wife accuses him. The lasciviousness of the virgin lusting after the chaste prophet, and the desires of the sterile old man lusting after his stepdaughter – this certainly represents a decadent variation on the old romantic theme of love. Rafael Cansinos-Assens, in his long and detailed introduction to a Spanish anthology of Salome texts by such authors as Flaubert, Wilde, Mallarmé, Eugenio de Castro and Apollinaire, points out that the erotic relations of the characters are generally linked to social or ethical taboos:

Todos los amores que insinúan en el poema su anhelo de consumación ... se manifiestan la forma de congojas eróticas, como aspiraciones sexuales cohibidas en su desarrollo por un veto ético ó social.[32]

[All those forms of love that in the text indicate desire for consummation ... are manifested as erotic anxieties that might be compared to sexual desires whose development is inhibited by an ethical or social taboo.]

At the centre of this web of relationships, which to a large extent constitutes what there is of plot, stand Salome, the beautiful and sensuous daughter of Herodias, and Jokanaan, the religious fanatic. The clash between their interests, together with their monomanic or narcissistic obsessions, makes true communication impossible. With the other characters, too, any hopes of an emotional response remain unfulfilled, and all erotic expectations are frustrated. They all react to this disappointment with aggression: Salome demands the head of the man she loves, Herod has Salome executed, and Narraboth kills himself. Jokanaan is at first the object of Salome's sensual desire, and then falls victim to her scorned love and wounded pride, while Salome herself is regarded by the Baptist as a profane 'fille de Sodome',[33] the embodiment of evil and seductive womanhood. The extremities of this relationship are marked by sensuality and spirituality, erotic passion and religious fanaticism, body and soul – a vital theme in *Dorian Gray* and in the dramatic fragment 'La Sainte Courtisane'. There is no meeting-point between Salome's eroticism and the prophet's asceticism. The latter may be said to contain a certain amount of ambivalence, if one is to judge by the different interpretations of different critics. In 1913 Friedrich Karl Brass described Jokanaan with the somewhat simple epithets of purity and openness[34] – a view flatly contradicted by the psychoanalytical school as represented, for instance, by Christopher S. Nassaar in 1974, who interprets the prophet's death as follows:

A sword is an explicit phallic symbol, moreover, and Iokanaan's desire to see Salome pierced with swords – swords controlled and directed by him – suggests his repressed lust for her. At the same time, he wants to see her destroyed and hidden from view by shields. The prophet's end – a severed head, eyes closed, in a position of sexual 'intercourse' with Salome – sums up the essence and horror of Iokanaan. He possesses the object of his desire, but is, and will forever remain, unconscious of the fact.[35]

Even if one can accept that the phallic symbol of swords may indicate repressed lust, the suggestion that the prophet's death is combined with 'a position of sexual intercourse with Salome' is surely rather far-fetched.

In the character of Salome, whose sensual thirst can only be satisfied by the death of Jokanaan – a decadent variation on the paradoxical theme of 'each man kills the thing he loves', as expressed in *The Ballad of Reading Gaol* – the motifs of sex, death and fate serve to build up the figure of the *femme fatale*. This late romantic descendant of the *belle dame sans merci* marks the decadent phase of nineteenth-century eroticism charted in great detail by Mario Praz in *La carne, la morte e il diavolo nella letteratura romantica* (1930) (*The Romantic Agony*, trans. by Angus Davidson, London 1933). The beautiful but demonically cruel woman, who in Praz's terms alternates with the demonic, Byronic hero, is to be found in such characters as Matilda (M. G. Lewis, *The Monk*, 1796), Carmen (P. Mérimée, *Carmen*, 1845), Cléopâtre (Th. Gautier, *Une Nuit de Cléo-*

pâtre, 1838), Salammbô (G. Flaubert, *Salammbô*, 1862) and Anactoria (A. C. Swinburne, 'Anactoria', 1866). It is worth pointing out, however, that unlike all these other sirens that lure men to their destruction, Salome does not succeed in conquering Jokanaan. And although she undoubtedly has certain sadistic traits, almost vampire-like towards the end, when she bites the dead lips 'comme on mord un fruit mûr',[36] she is not presented throughout as a sadist or 'lustful vampire'.[37] She does not have the cold-blooded desire to cause pain to others and to revel in their suffering, but is drawn rather as one possessed of a passion, losing sight of reality through her manic eroticism, and in her blindness actually resembling Jokanaan, of whom she says: 'Tu as mis sur tes yeux le bandeau de celui qui veut voir son Dieu.'[38]

A similar fatal blindness is to be observed in Herod. Superstitious and full of scruples about the arrest of his man 'qui a vu Dieu',[39] vacillating in mood and emotion, he keeps struggling to avoid confrontation with reality and to suppress all conflict. He does not want to talk about his wife's separation from her first husband, his brother, or about the prophet's accusation that he has committed incest. He interprets Salome's request for the Baptist's head as a desire for vengeance, and he knows he has been looking too much at his stepdaughter, but resolves not to look at her any more:

Il ne faut regarder ni les choses ni les personnes. Il ne faut regarder que dans les miroirs. Car les miroirs ne nous montrent que des masques.[40]

[Neither at things nor at people should one look. Only in mirrors should one look, for mirrors do but show us masks]

He does not realise that it is in fact a mask that has sealed his fate. He plunges into guilt because he has been seduced by Salome's 'mask' into swearing the fatal oath which binds him to the very decision that he had constantly avoided making.

A mysterious force seems to govern all these characters, creating an ominous atmosphere of doom that permeates the play right from the start. The young Syrian is enchanted by Salome's beauty, but is warned by the page not to look at her. Herod has 'l'air sombre',[41] and slips in the blood of the dead Narraboth, which he takes as an 'ill omen'. Jokanaan, like Herod later on, hears the 'battement des ailes de l'ange de la mort'.[42] Premonitions of disaster and vague feelings of fear suggest that supernatural forces are interfering with events on earth, and that the characters are powerless against the workings of fate.

The central symbol for this atmosphere of fatality and also for the characters' changing moods and visions of Salome is the moon.[43] As an image and as a theme it links together all the main motifs of sex, death and fate. At the beginning of the play, the page compares it to a 'femme morte',[44] and later to the hand of a dead woman 'qui cherche à se couvrir avec un linceul'.[45] And when his friend Narraboth kills himself, he even accuses the moon of interfering in man's destiny: 'Je savais bien que la lune cherchait un mort.'[46] For the young Syrian and for Herod the moon crystallises all their dreams and erotic desires directed towards Salome. Narraboth compares it to a 'petite princesse qui porte un voile jaune',[47] and sees her smile through 'nuages de mousseline'.[48] Herod projects his libidinous desires on the moon, which appears to him to be 'toute nue', like a 'femme hystérique qui va cherchant des amants partout'.[49]

Whether the moon symbolism of this play can be linked with the Cybele myth, which in biblical times was widespread in Rome and throughout Asia Minor, is very questionable. Christopher S. Nassaar clearly regards the link as definite, because in mythology Cybele is a symbol of the aggressive, sexually perverse woman 'whose sterile sex impulse is directed towards the subjugation and castration of the male'.[50] The idea that Salome should have wanted the Baptist to be castrated seems a little unlikely in the light of her sensual longings. As for the remainder of the argument, in folklore the various phases of the moon have always been associated with coming and going, and life and death in the sublunar world, and so the reference to Cybele seems if anything a little gratuitous. Even in Shakespeare there is frequent mention of the moon's influence on man's fate, and anyone who controls it possesses supernatural powers.[51] A more likely assumption than Nassaar's is that which suggests that Wilde was inspired by two literary works which he knew well: Maeterlinck's *Princesse Maleine* and Flaubert's *Salammbô*. Friedrich Karl Brass, whose dissertation gives a detailed account of source material, offers convincing evidence of the Belgian Symbolist's strong influence on Wilde's *Salomé*, but he does not establish any such influence on the part of Flaubert in relation to the moon motif; this may well be due to the fact that he only considers *Hérodias*, whereas *Salammbô*, daughter of the Punic king, is as closely linked to the moon goddess Tanit as Salome is to the fateful moon itself.[52]

Evocative style and variations on a traditional theme

The compressed effect that Wilde achieves by adhering to the classical unities and by concentrating the action on his main character, as well as through an atmosphere consistently linked to the themes of sex, death and fate, is strengthened by a number of linguistic and stylistic devices. These consist mainly of repetitions – often functioning as leitmotivs – aesthetic imagery with decorative comparisons and exotic names, evocative words such as 'étrange', 'sombre', 'pâle', and colourful effects created by combining different fields of imagery and sensation through synaesthesia. Salome's last speech is a vivid example of the iterative and associative tenor of the style:

LA VOIX DE SALOME: Ah! j'ai baisé ta bouche, Iokanaan, j'ai baisé ta bouche. Il y avait une âcre saveur sur tes lèvres. Etait-ce la saveur du sang? ... Mais, peut-être est-ce la saveur de l'amour. On dit que l'amour a une âcre saveur ... Mais, qu'importe? Qu'importe? J'ai baisé ta bouche, Iokanaan, j'ai baisé ta bouche.[53]

[Ah! I have kissed thy mouth, Jokanaan, I have kissed thy mouth. There was a bitter taste on thy lips. Was it the taste of blood? ... But perchance it is the taste of love ... They say that love hath a bitter taste ... But what of that? What of that? I have kissed thy mouth, Jokanaan, I have kissed thy mouth.]

This closing monologue, framed by the repetition of 'j'ai baisé ta bouche', centres upon the words, 'saveur', repeated three times, and 'l'amour', repeated once. Syntactically and semantically the central section moves from statement ('Il y avait' ...) to questions and speculations ('Etait-ce' ... 'Mais peut-être' ... 'On dit que' ...), and finally to apparent indifference as regards the 'saveur' ('Mais, qu'importe?'). Even verbally Salome never leaves the confines of her voluptuous eroticism, which is underlined by all the insistent repetitions, and indeed like Jokanaan himself she remains imprisoned throughout the play in her own ideas, and incapable of taking part in any true dialogue. The repetitions also play an important part in building up an atmosphere of fatality, for they endow events with an aura of inevitability. In structural terms, they act as connecting links that bind the one-act play together. Wilde was very conscious of this function, as is evident from a letter to Alfred Douglas:

The recurring phrases of *Salome*, that bind it together like a piece of music with recurring *motifs*, are, and were to me, the artistic equivalent of the refrains of old ballads.[54]

The repetitions are particularly effective when the motifs are linked to premonitions of doom, for example, 'Il peut arriver un malheur',[55] 'mauvais présage',[56] 'un battement d'ailes gigantesques'.[57] Merely looking at someone is enough to evoke an atmosphere of doom and to entangle the character in a fatal web. Looking at Salome means yielding to her sexual charms, and only Jokanaan remains immune to her art. Of him she says: 'Si tu m'avais regardée, tu m'aurais aimée'.[58]

The importance for Wilde of the visual impact of his play is evident from the colourful effects and from the vivid sensuality of the language. Emotions are always aroused by way of visual perception, and are never separated from their associations with the senses: 'le monde moral semble n'être perçu qu'indirectement à travers ses manifestations sensibles'.[59] Narraboth's love for Salome, and her own sexual longing for Jokanaan, are both expressed by rich similes and metaphors. She compares the

Baptist's eyes to 'des trous noirs laissés par les flambeaux sur une tapisserie de Tyr',[60] and his white body is like 'le lis d'un pré que le faucheur n'a jamais fauché'.[61] Her passion is at its most intense when she talks of his mouth:

SALOME: C'est de ta bouche que je suis amoureuse, Iokanaan. Ta bouche est comme une bande d'écarlate sur une tour d'ivoire. Elle est comme une pomme de grenade coupée par un couteau d'ivoire. Les fleurs de grenade qui fleurissent dans les jardins de Tyr et sont plus rouges que les roses, ne sont pas aussi rouges. Les cris rouges des trompettes qui annoncent l'arrivée des rois, et font peur à l'ennemi ne sont pas aussi rouges. Ta bouche est plus rouge que les pieds de ceux qui foulent le vin dans les pressoirs. Elle est plus rouge que les pieds des colombes qui demeurent dans les temples et sont nourries par les prêtres. Elle est plus rouge que les pieds de celui qui revient d'une forêt où il a tué un lion et vu des tigres dorés. Ta bouche est comme une branche de corail que des pêcheurs ont trouvée dans le crépuscule da [de] la mer et qu'ils réservent pour les rois . . .! Elle est comme le vermillon que les Moabites trouvent dans les mines de Moab et que les rois leur prennent. Elle est comme l'arc du roi des Perses qui est peint avec du vermillon et qui a des cornes de corail. Il n'y a rien au monde d'aussi rouge que ta bouche . . . laisse-moi baiser ta bouche.[62]

[It is thy mouth that I desire, Jokanaan. Thy mouth is like a band of scarlet on a tower of ivory. It is like a pomegranate cut with a knife of ivory. The pomegranate-flowers that blossom in the gardens of Tyre, and are redder than roses, are not so red. The red blasts of trumpets, that herald the approach of kings, and make afraid the enemy, are not so red. Thy mouth is redder than the feet of those who tread the wine in the wine-press. Thy mouth is redder than the feet of the doves who haunt the temples and are fed by the priests. It is redder than the feet of him who cometh from a forest where he hath slain a lion, and seen gilded tigers. Thy mouth is like a branch of coral that fishers have found in the twilight of the sea, the coral that they keep for the kings . . .! It is like the vermilion that the Moabites find in the mines of Moab, the vermilion that the kings take from them. It is like the bow of the King of the Persians, that is painted with vermilion, and is tipped with coral. There is nothing in the world so red as thy mouth . . . Let me kiss thy mouth.]

The profusion of images, comparisons, intensifications and synaes-thesia ('les cris rouges') all serve to conjure up an astonishing vision of redness. Wilde combines images from various exotic fields ('les jardins de Tyr', 'les mines de Moab', 'l'arc du roi des Perses') to broaden the scope of his effect, and often extends his comparisons with descriptive relative clauses – the branch of coral has been found by fishers in the twilight of the sea, for instance, and it is the coral 'qu'ils réservent pour les rois'. Such extensions are not meant to make the images more precise; they provide, as it were, luxurious decorations – a feature characteristic of Wilde's style – but at the same time they prevent the monotony that might set in through a sequence of images in short sentences. This evocative and vividly decorative style takes on a lyrical quality which, to some extent, replaces the action typical of traditional drama; the senses and the emotions are continually being stimulated by the aesthetic evocation of moods, by the tension between unbridled eroticism and ascetic renunciation, and by the suggested presence of an irresistible fate. Wilde was very conscious of the fact that his play transcended traditional borders:

> If I were asked of myself as a dramatist, I would say that my unique position was that I had taken the Drama, the most objective form known to art, and made it as personal a mode of expression as the Lyric or the Sonnet, while enriching the characterisation of the stage, and enlarging – at any rate in the case of *Salome* – its artistic horizon.[63]

In this self-assured estimation of his position as a dramatist, Wilde is no doubt thinking of the tradition of English drama, but his achievement is by no means 'unique' in the context of European theatre. The techniques he uses in *Salomé* belong to a literary movement that had considerable influence on French literature during the 1880s and 1890s: namely, Symbolism. This arose as an idealistic reaction to positivist philosophy, which underlay realistic and naturalistic aesthetics; it developed through the work of Poe, Schopenhauer, Swedenborg and Wagner, and although as a movement it was quite heterogeneous, its main object was to re-establish the endangered autonomy of art and to validate subjective views of reality:

> L'artiste, le vrai poète, ne doit peindre que selon qu'il voit et qu'il sent. Il doit être *réellement* fidèle à sa propre nature. Il doit éviter comme la mort d'emprunter les yeux et les sentiments d'un autre homme, si grand qu'il soit; car alors les productions qu'il nous donnerait seraient, relativement à lui, des mensonges, et non des *réalités*.[64]

> [The artist, the true poet, must paint only according to what he sees and what he feels. He must be *really* faithful to his own nature. He must avoid like death any borrowing from the eyes and emotions of another man, no matter how great he may be; for if he does not, the productions he would give us would be, in relation to himself, lies and not *realities*.]

The radical subjectifying of reality, and the consequent aim of the Symbolists 'to communicate unique feelings',[65] was accompanied by particular regard for creative fantasy. This led to a revaluation of language in the literary process. In his programmatic poem 'Art poétique', Verlaine replaced the plastic poetic ideal of the *parnassiens* with music; in his *Correspondances,* Baudelaire talked of the connection between sensual, synaesthetic experience and the spiritual dimension; Mallarmé distorted, alienated and even destroyed reality in order to construct his own hermetic objectivity out of linguistic signs – a *poésie pure*, beyond the reaches of *hasard*. With Mallarmé above all the breakdown of the denotative elements of language led to deliberate ambiguity and obscurity, which renders the language almost incomprehensible at first, though it can be painstakingly deciphered or absorbed by way of its evocative effects. One way in which the evocative power of the word could be increased was by reducing its surface connections with reality and using it as a bearer of mood, a symbol charged with associations; in this manner it could evoke the mysterious, the unsayable, without actually having to name it. Thus describable reality was transformed into a spiritual condition – an *état d'âme*. It was a Belgian writer who, in the early 1890s, translated this mystical concept of reality into drama: Maurice Maeterlinck. In plays like *La Princesse Maleine* (1889), *Les Sept Princesses* (1891), and *Pelléas et Mélisande* (1892), which Debussy made into an opera, he sought to penetrate the world of appearances and familiar surfaces in order to convey through them an atmosphere of mystery, fear and doom. Maeterlinck explains his transmutation of Symbolist aesthetics into drama as follows:

il faut qu'il y ait autre chose que le dialogue extérieurement nécessaire. Il n'y a guère que les paroles qui semblent d'abord inutiles qui comptent dans une œuvre. C'est en elles que se trouve son âme. A côté du dialogue indispensable, il y a presque toujours un autre dialogue qui semble superflu. Examinez attentivement et vous verrez que c'est le seul que l'âme écoute profondément, parce que c'est en cet endroit seulement qu'on lui parle. Vous reconnaîtrez aussi que c'est la qualité et l'étendue de ce dialogue inutile qui détermine la qualité et la portée ineffable de l'œuvre. Il est certain que, dans les drames ordinaires, le dialogue indispensable ne répond pas du tout à la réalité; et ce qui fait la beauté mystérieuse des plus belles tragédies se trouve tout juste dans les paroles qui se disent à côté de la vérité stricte et apparente.[66]

[there must be something other than the externally necessary dialogue. There is scarcely anything that counts in a work except the words which at first seem useless. It is in them that its soul resides. Next to the indispensable dialogue there is almost always another dialogue that seems superfluous. Look closely and you will see that that is the only one the soul listens to profoundly, because it is only in this place that the soul is spoken to. You will also recognise that it is the quality and the extent of this useless dialogue that determines the quality and the inexpressible significance of the work. It is certain that, in ordinary plays, the indispensable dialogue does not correspond at all to reality; and what makes the mysterious beauty of the finest tragedies is situated precisely in the words that speak beside the strict and apparent truth.]

The basis of this account also illuminates the ideas that underlie *Salomé*. Wilde was in fact familiar with the work of this Flemish author, and actually met him after his release from prison.[67] Robert Ross was one of the first to name Maeterlinck, together with Flaubert and the Bible, as 'obvious sources'[68] of the play, and the studies by Brass and Ernst Bendz show in detail the extent to which Wilde imitated the Symbolist technique of *Maleine* and *Sept Princesses*. Brass concludes that in fact there was a considerable degree of influence by Maeterlinck on

Wilde,[69] and Bendz says that the two writers were identical in their 'intention artistique'.[70]

Echoes of the Bible are frequent, and a comparison between the English version of *Salomé* and the Song of Solomon in particular will show that Wilde had not only the cadences of biblical language in his ears but also various images:

SALOME: ... Thy mouth is like a band of scarlet.[71]

The Song of Solomon: Thy lips *are* like a thread of scarlet.   (4:3)

SALOME: Thy body was a column of ivory set on a silver socket.[72] ... Thy hair is like the cedars of Lebanon.[73]

The Song of Solomon: His legs *are as* pillars of marble, set upon sockets of fine gold: his countenance *is* as Lebanon, excellent as the cedars.   (5:15)

SALOME: Thy hair is like clusters of grapes.[74]

The Song of Solomon: This thy stature is like to a palm tree, and thy breasts to clusters *of grapes.* (7:7)

SALOME: Neither the floods nor the great waters can quench my passion.[75]

The Song of Solomon: Many waters cannot quench love, neither can the floods drown it.   (8:7)

The two biblical accounts[76] of the beheading of the Baptist have the following elements in common: Salome has no name, but is referred to as Herodias's daughter; she asks for John's head at her mother's bidding, and has no sexual leanings towards him; Herod Antipas's motive for arresting the prophet lies in the latter's public condemnation of his marriage to his brother Philip's former wife. They differ in their view of the Tetrarch – whom St Mark erroneously calls King – and his attitude towards John: St Mark, whose account is more concise and concrete, says that Herod saw John as being 'a just man and an holy',[77] respected him because of his sound advice, and only had him beheaded because of his oath; according to St Matthew, the people honoured John and it was they who held Herod back from executing him. St Mark explicitly mentions an executioner, whereas St Matthew does not.[78]

It will be immediately obvious that Wilde has completely restructured the story, with his central figure being Salome, who no longer acts on behalf of her mother but follows her own inclinations, motivated by her desire for John. It should be pointed out, however, that even this change is not original, for it is to be found in the animal epic *Ysengrimus* (I, 1139ff) written in Latin around the middle of the twelfth century by the Flanders master Nivardus. It is virtually certain that Wilde would not have known this work, but there is a distinct possibility that he would have been familiar with Heine's reworking of the material in *Atta Troll* (1843). In this literary and political satire, which Heine himself translated into French in 1847 for the magazine *Revue des deux mondes*, and which was available in T. S. Egan's English translation from at least 1876 onwards, there is a quite new relationship between Herodias and the Baptist. The hate-filled, vengeful wife of the Tetrarch is turned into a beautiful princess who is in love with John – following folklore tradition – and since her love is unrequited, she wants to have his head, and finally dies crazed with passion.[79] Clearly there is a good deal in common between Wilde's Salome and Heine's cruel and beautiful but somewhat morbid Herodias, who kisses the severed head passionately,[80] and throws it up in the air and catches it laughing childishly.[81]

Heine romanticised the biblical tale by introducing the love motive, which took on a sensual and morbid tone also to be felt in the Salome sonnet by William Wilde, Oscar's brother.[82] In contrast, Flaubert's story *Hérodias*, whose importance as a model for *Salomé* was quickly recognised and perhaps somewhat exaggerated, tackles the theme realistically; Flaubert is at pains to recreate the historical background as vividly as possible, though he does not hesitate to depart from historical accuracy when this does not fit in with his aesthetic requirements. No writer before or after Flaubert has conjured up the oriental atmosphere of Herod's court with such narrative power: the opulent feast with the Roman envoys Vitellius and Aulus, the hundred white horses hidden in the casemates of the fortress of Machaerous, the religious fanaticism of the Jews, the Tetrarch's political quarrels with the Arabs. Although there can be no doubt that Wilde borrowed some material from the great French novelist – particularly descriptive details relating to the background – it is equally undeniable that his version of the tale can in no way be regarded as merely a compressed, dramatic imitation of Flaubert. This is already clear from the fact that in *Hérodias* Salome, 'en zézayant',[83] speaks only fifteen words; Wilde has vastly extended her role and changed her motivation, with the dance and the demand for the Baptist's head both resulting from her own will. This is indeed Wilde's 'trouvaille essentielle'[84] or, as Ernst Bendz puts it, his 'coup de maître'.[85]

Enrique Gómez Carrillo recalls in his memoirs the time when Wilde was preoccupied with his play, and describes how every painting and every literary portrait of Salome inspired him to new visions of his eponymous heroine. One picture above all appears to have come closest to his vision of the princess: 'Seul le tableau de Gustave Moreau incarnait, pour lui, translucide, l'âme de la princesse-ballérine légendaire, de la divine Hérodiade de ses rêves'.[86] No less familiar to Wilde than Moreau's *L'Apparition*, in which Salome is decked out with oriental jewellery and gazing enraptured at the radiant and bleeding head of the Baptist, was Huys-

mans's description of the picture in *A Rebours*. Just as Pater's literary
evocation of the Mona Lisa in his Leonardo essay typifies his impressionistic art criticism, so too does Huysmans use language to create out of
one picture a *fin de siècle* symbol of a *beauté fatale*. Pater used the Mona
Lisa to stimulate his associative fantasy into visions of metamorphoses
that transformed the subject into timeless, placeless myth; it encompassed
all modes of thought and life, was formed by Greece, by Rome, by the
mysticism of the Middle Ages and by the sins of the Borgias, changing into
the point of crystallisation for 'strange thoughts and fantastic reveries and
exquisite passions'.[87] In similar fashion Des Esseintes, the main character
in Huysmans's novel, finds that Salome loses the vague individuality she
possesses in the Bible, and instead becomes a

déité symbolique de l'indestructible Luxure, la déesse de l'immortelle Hystérie, la
Beauté maudite ... la Bête monstrueuse, indifférente, irresponsable, insensible,
empoisonnant, de même que l'Hélène antique, tout ce qui l'approche, tout ce qui
la voit, tout ce qu'elle touche.[88]

[deity symbolic of indestructible Luxury, the goddess of immortal Hysteria,
accursed Beauty ... the monstrous Beast, indifferent, irresponsible, insensible,
poisoning like the Helen of Antiquity all that approaches her, all that sees her, all
that she touches.]

Salome as *fin-de-siècle femme fatale*

Wilde combined Maeterlinck's symbolism with the rich imagery of the
Song of Solomon, the exoticism of Flaubert, and the sensuality of Moreau
as interpreted by Huysmans, and out of all these elements he created a
fin-de-siècle femme fatale. There is little similarity between his Salome and
Mallarmé's esoteric dream creature Hérodiade or Flaubert's tractable
virgin. The morbid charm of Wilde's eponymous heroine lies in the
exciting mixture of chastity and desire, erotic heat and the cold indifference with which she views the death of two men. At times she seems
almost to be in a trance, possessed by her passion. She has no moral
awareness or sense of responsibility. Her courtship of Jokanaan totally
reverses the traditional, nineteenth-century concept of the submissive
woman, and indeed she assumes many of the androgynous features which
at the end of the nineteenth century were often associated with virginity.[89]

   Wilde's fascination with this material, and the changes he made to it,
were not unconnected with his personal life at the time. By emphasising
the cruelty of woman, Wilde may well have been consoling himself for and
justifying his homosexuality. Edmund Bergler, interpreting the play
psychologically, goes even further:

Having proved to his own satisfaction that woman is cruel, Wilde's homosexual
role changes from that of an 'experimenter' to that of a devotee. Chronologically,

the story fits: Wilde wrote 'Salome' in 1891, four years before his trial. One can justifiably claim that 'Salome' marks the turning point in Wilde's life.[90]

But even if we accept the connection between demonic female sensuality and the author's homosexuality – with the figure of Jokanaan obviously standing for Wilde himself – such a view of the play as a 'drama of homosexual guilt and rejection'[91] seems far too one-sided. And so does the thesis that the play is the 'Darstellung der Wirkungen, die durch eine abnorme Veranlagung, oder sagen wir, Disposition des weiblichen Geschlechtsorganismus hervorgebracht werden – Wirkungen, die zugleich die deutlichsten Symptome einer Geisteskrankheit aufweisen'[92] [representation of effects brought about by an abnormal nature or, let us say, disposition of the female sex organism – effects which at the same time demonstrate the clearest symptoms of a mental illness]. Salome is certainly not a nymphomaniac or a pathological case.

In terms of theatrical and literary tradition, the originality of *Salomé* lies in the manner in which Wilde has changed the nature of what constitutes drama. Just as later in his comedies he replaces the tensions of plot with stimulation of the intellect, so too in *Salomé* does he dispense with the traditional tensions and in their place supply stimuli for the sensual and aesthetic instincts of his audience. The effect of the play depends less on its immediate impact than on its powers of suggestion and evocation. Aesthetic impressions carry with them intimations of psychic states, in keeping with Wilde's maxim that 'All art is at once surface and symbol.'[93] One may, for instance, perceive the changes in the colour of the moon, but one's deeper concern is with the symbolic significance of these changes. The components of this decadent classic are atmosphere, puppet-like characters each with their one fixation – whether sexual or religious – the rich imagery and iterative exoticism of the language, and the evocative motifs of sex, death, fate, incest and sterility. It was Joyce who summed up the effect most tellingly: 'a polyphonic variation on the rapport of art and nature'.[94]

The Sphinx

Seen against the background of the social comedies, *Salomé* may at first sight seem like a piece of literary driftwood that has made its way across from decadent France to the shores of Victorian England, but in fact its position in the Wildean canon is by no means isolated. Even if Wilde was never again to create such a fascinating mixture of unbridled sexual passion and savage vengeance as in this tale of the Judaean princess who became a decadent *femme fatale*, nevertheless the theme of perverse eroticism in an exotic setting occurs again in the long poem *The Sphinx*, which was published a year after *Salomé*. Conjectures regarding the time of its composition range from Wilde's student days in Oxford through his Parisian stay in 1883 right up to the early 1890s. The editor of the letters, Rupert Hart-Davis, relying on information provided by Robert H. Sherard, suggests 'that Wilde began his long poem *The Sphinx* when he was still at Oxford and finished it now in Paris, though it was not published till 1894'.[95] This statement, dependent purely on the memory of a none too reliable biographer, is somewhat surprising coming from such a circumspect scholar as Hart-Davis, for in terms of style, the poem undoubtedly comes closer to *Salomé* than to any of the earlier writings. This does not mean, however, that the various claims made by Stuart Mason,[96] Robert H. Sherard and Albert J. Farmer[97] are mutually exclusive, since we may assume that the idea of the poem originated in Oxford, an early draft was written in 1883 – probably just a fragment – and finally in the early 1890s this was revised and rewritten in its final form.[98] The manuscript of *The Sphinx*, which was thought to have disappeared, was discovered by Charles Ricketts and given in 1904 to Robert Ross, who bequeathed it to the British Museum in 1909.[99]

Construction and poetic technique

The poem consists of eighty-seven couplets whose long lines if divided in half give a rhyme-scheme of abba. W. E. Henley, in his review 'The Sphinx up to Date' in the *Pall Mall Gazette* of 9 July 1894,[100] pointed out that this in fact is the verse form of Tennyson's *In Memoriam* slightly disguised. But by reshaping the quatrain into a couplet of sixteen-syllable lines, Wilde was not merely indulging in a typographical trick but was creating a form that suited his descriptive intentions. As regards its length, the poem is comparable to 'Panthea', but much shorter than *The Ballad of Reading Gaol* and some of the *Poems* – notably, 'The Garden of Eros', 'The Burden of Itys', 'Humanitad', and 'Charmides'.

Within the structure of eighty-seven verses there is a clear division into three, while these three sections are also sub-divided. Verses 1–10 describe the statue of the Sphinx, which stands in a dim corner of the writer's room. The idea of all the centuries lived through by this mythological woman–beast makes the writer curious about its past experiences. Verses 11–74 depict the predominantly erotic adventures of the Sphinx, culminating in the lengthy Ammon episode. The penetrating gaze and the animal sensuality of this hybrid creature fill the writer with insecurity and disgust, and at the end of the poem (verses 75–87) he turns away from it to seek his salvation in the crucifix. The 'lovely languorous Sphinx' of verse 7 has turned into a 'False Sphinx' (verse 86) and a 'Hideous animal' (verse 84).

This structural link between the first ten and the last thirteen verses, with the writer being initially attracted but finally repelled, has its parallel in the central Ammon episode (verses 37–64). Initially the god is portrayed in all his splendour, with marble limbs, azure eyes and milk-white throat (verses 37–54), living in a a house with a thousand lamps, and attended by a thousand priests; then suddenly, after the abrupt caesura in verse 54 ('– and now') the time changes from past to present, and of the former glories of the god, nothing remains but fragments 'scattered here and there'.

The contrast between past magnificence and present decay is also paralleled in the transformation of the Sphinx from a 'lovely seneschal' (verse 6) to a repulsive demon. The main turning-point, then, comes in verse 54, since this is where the speaker's attitude begins to change: at first he only tells her to go back to Egypt and search for the remains of the god; then he comforts her with the assurance that her lovers are not all dead (verses 65–74) – a passage that slows the action down – but the various imperatives, 'Away to Egypt!' (verse 65) and 'Back to your Nile!' (verse 70), clearly denote a growing alienation between speaker and Sphinx that leads to a final break, with a cry of 'Away!' (verse 79) and the reiterated injunction to 'Get hence!' (verses 75 and 84), which corresponds effectively to the reiterated call of 'Come forth' in verses 6 and 7.

The large central section of the poem can itself be split up into several recognisable parts. At first the speaker addresses the Sphinx with questions and imperatives (verses 11–22), wishing to be told about her memories in general. Verses 23–26 narrow the perspective to her lovers, and there follows a long series of questions about these, mostly introduced with the conjunction 'or'. After the speaker has ascertained that Ammon was her lover, there is a detailed description of the god in his former glory and then in his present state of ruin (verses 37–64). The speaker tells the Sphinx to search for these ruins (verses 61–64) and 'wake mad passions in the senseless stone!' (verse 62). In verses 11–36 the dominant mode is the question and request; in the Ammon episode this is replaced by decorative description, but from verse 61 onwards it is the imperative form that takes over. Thus the first and last sections are set in contrast to each other, with questions replaced by imperatives.

In Egyptian mythology, the Sphinx was a fabulous creature that was worshipped as a royal symbol; later in Greek antiquity prophetic powers were ascribed to it.[101] It could be either male or female and was originally a hybrid with a human head and a lion's body, though there were also sphinxes with the head of a ram or a hawk. As well as being unnatural monsters, they are steeped in mystery, reaching back as they do into the unfathomable past. The very first lines evoke something of this mystery:

> In a dim corner of my room for longer than my fancy thinks
> A beautiful and silent Sphinx has watched me through the shifting
>   gloom.

Inviolate and immobile she does not rise she does not stir
For silver moons are naught to her and naught to her the suns that
reel.

The narrator's restricted time perspective is contrasted to the immemorial history of the Sphinx – a contrast reinforced by the latter's indifference to the natural sequence of night and day. The contrast between the timelessness of the Sphinx and the presence of the narrator is subtly enhanced by the 'shifting gloom' which seems to blur all contours. The interplay of light and dark is underlined by the contrasting sounds of palatal and velar vowels, as in the rhymes of 'room/gloom – thinks/ Sphinx' and the combinations of 'shifting gloom' and 'dim corner'. Thus the figure of the Sphinx is placed and fixed, and yet at the same time set in a fascinating twilight area that reinforces the impression of dark mystery evoked by the title. The contrast is further strengthened by the syntactic and metric lay-out of the first line, where time and place are put together without even a conjunction, separated only by the caesura.

In the second line of the first verse the syntactical unit extends beyond the first half line, so that the two halves run together. There is also a shift of tenses, from the present in line one to the perfect in line two, indicating the indeterminate duration of the watching. These lines also establish the relationship between speaker and statue, for the Sphinx watches him ceaselessly, and the rigidity of the statue and its gaze is conveyed by the massive polysyllabic adjectives with which the second verse begins: 'inviolate' and 'immobile'. The speed of time flowing is then captured by the sequence of single syllable words (apart from 'silver'), with parallel syntactic structures in the first line and chiasmus in the second.

These first two verses exemplify the prosodic virtuosity and subtle orchestration that characterise Wilde's enhanced sensitivity to language. In the course of the poem he uses the full range of poetic devices, such as alliteration, assonance, internal rhyme, chiasmus, parallelism, anaphora etc., and, in creating an atmosphere of oriental sensuality and splendour, he uses an immensely rich and colourful array of exotic words and names, especially allusions to myth, to ancient places, events and characters, and to precious objects. Initially the colours are confined to different shades of gold ('yellow', 'tawny', verses 5 and 8), but such restriction would run contrary to Wilde's eclectic taste as well as to his artistic intentions, and so the whites and greys and golds that were Whistler's predilection are combined with Pre-Raphaelite blues, golds, reds and greens in a veritable kaleidoscope of colours that correspond to the colourfulness of the various episodes he depicts. In this respect he does not always remain true to the precepts laid down in his early lecture on 'Art and the Handicraftsman': 'all beautiful colours are graduated colours, the colours that seem about to pass into one another's realm'.[102]

Wilde's love of impressionistic ornamentation – as evinced in his 'Fantaisies décoratives' and 'Symphony in Yellow' – is by no means an isolated personal style but in fact is typical of the 'Yellow Nineties' and the Pre-Raphaelite movement.[103] Richard Le Gallienne, in his review of John Gray's book of poems *Silverpoints*, regards the one-sided devotion to 'colour sense' as the very nucleus of decadence:

In what does decadence consist? In a self-conscious arrangement of 'coloured' vowels, in a fastidious distribution of accents, resulting in new and subtler harmonies of verse – say some. In the choice for themes of disease and forbidden things generally – . . . The real core of decadence is to be found in its isolated interests . . . Its recent development almost entirely confines its outlook on life to the colour-sense. It puts men and dead game on the same basis – of colour.[104]

Behind these utterances lies the idea of the close relationship between the arts which played such an important part in poetological discussion during the nineteenth century, and which gave experimental inspiration to poets ranging from Gautier and his *Symphonie en Blanc Majeur* (1849), through Baudelaire's *Correspondances* (1857) and Verlaine's 'Art poétique' (1884), right up to T. S. Eliot's *Four Quartets* (1943) and Paul Celan's 'Todesfuge' (1952) (in Celan, *Poems*, ed., intro. and trans. by Michael Hamburger, New York 1980). Wilde's debts to painting are completely in keeping with his rejection of nature and the real world as material for art, as well as with his mistrust of all content-orientated aesthetics. This recourse to other arts has two advantages: first, the non-verbal media make it possible for disturbing elements of reality to be reduced and so for the ideal of 'decorative art' to be at least approached; secondly, the existing piece of art will already have attained a degree of aesthetic refinement and formal perfection which could not be achieved by the actual subjects in their raw state of reality. This is why Wilde maintains that

The conception of making a prose poem out of paint is excellent. Much of the best modern literature springs from the same aim. In a very ugly and sensible age, the arts borrow, not from life, but from each other.[105]

With his love of intensified effects, Wilde sometimes puts his colour adjectives into compounds, such as 'blue-faced' (verse 57) or 'yellow-striped' (verse 60). Such *epitheta ornantia* are typical of his effectively stylised use of language, especially when the compounds are further linked by assonance ('brick-built', verse 26) or alliteration ('subtle-secret', verse 37). The colourfulness is reinforced by the frequent references to precious stones and metals, rare woods and fine cloths. These add to the impression of unheard-of opulence and luxury.

On pearl and porphyry pedestalled he was too bright to look upon:
For on his ivory breast there shone the wondrous ocean-emerald.
(verse 48)

Quite apart from enhancing the impressionistic charm of the scene, these precious objects form the basis of an exotic world of dreams whose ornate luxury betrays the imaginative longings of the poet fleeing from an age of repellent utilitarianism and materialism. There are few poems of the late nineteenth century in which the romantic scenery of Nature is so consistently replaced by the visionary landscape of art.

As has already been mentioned, Wilde uses many strange words and names to convey the exoticism of his oriental subject-matter.[106] Biblical monsters such as Behemoth and Leviathan stand side by side with gods from Egyptian and Greek mythology, for example, Ammon, Anubis, Isis and Osiris. There are also fabulous beasts like the hippogryph, tragelaph and basilisk. Frequently such archaic names and words are linked together to increase their effect in this extraordinary, Parnassian world of art. Verse 10 offers a good example:

> But you can read the Hieroglyphs on the great sandstone obelisks,
> And you have talked with Basilisks, and you have looked on
> Hippogriffs.

Such rhymes as 'catafalque'/'Amenalk' (verse 13), 'sarcophagus'/ 'Tragelaphos' (verse 32), 'splashed'/'Pasht' (verse 33) and 'Talc'/'Orei-chalch' (verse 35) show how little this poem owes to the romantic concept of a 'spontaneous overflow of powerful feelings';[107] instead it is based on an aesthetic creed of unemotional artistry and deliberate manipulation of language.

The exotic vocabulary coincides with strange imagery which is strikingly similar to that of *Salomé*. The tongue of the Sphinx is compared to a 'scarlet snake that dances to fantastic tunes' (verse 77). The two main elements of this image – snake and dance – are particular favourites of the late romantics.[108] The throat of the Sphinx is like 'the hole / Left by some torch or burning coal on Saracenic tapestries' (verse 78). Verse 15 offers a particularly vivid image:

> Lift up your large black satin eyes which are like cushions where one sinks!
> Fawn at my feet, fantastic Sphinx! and sing me all your memories!

Both colourful and tactile it is strongly reminiscent of Baudelaire's lines in *Le Chat*:

> Et laisse-moi plonger dans tes beaux yeux,
> Mêlés de métal et d'agate.[109]

If anything, Wilde's image surpasses that of the great French poet in its expressive and evocative power, and such mastery of language surely gives the lie to those critics who dismiss him as an unoriginal imitator. All too often these critics, orientated as they are by the hunt for sources, fail to distinguish between Wilde's absorption of influences and his ability to create something new out of them. The same two-stage process must apply to all artists, and the only difference lies in how conscious they and we are of those influences. In Wilde's case, the level of consciousness is simply higher than usual.

Wilde's flight from the grey industrial reality of Victorian England into an exotic dream world of rich colours, strange images and precious objects also takes him into a realm where both time and space expand indefinitely. The age of the Sphinx is 'A thousand weary centuries' (verse 9), in contrast to the speaker's 'twenty summers' (verse 9), while huge lizards, monstrous hippos, and the giant god Anubis roam an almost surreal landscape which cannot be encompassed within normal dimensions. Ammon is like a 'galley argent-sailed' (verse 39), he has a 'giant granite hand' (verse 58) and 'Titan thews' (verse 60). The fantastic breadth of space takes in the old Phoenician trade-centre of Sidon (verse 52), Abana and Pharphar, the rivers of Damascus (verse 83), and such places in Asia Minor as Colchis (verse 49), Lycia (verse 26) and Kurdistan (verse 45). This is a world that cannot be fixed in space or in time, and its unity lies only in its evocative exoticism.

Exotic atmosphere and erotic fantasy

The bizarre artificiality of the poem's style corresponds precisely to the unnaturalness of its subject-matter. The exotic atmosphere and sexual perversity are linked together – and indeed for a Victorian reader would be virtually identical – in a dream world that promises unlimited freedom for sensual and sexual experience. The shocking behaviour of the Sphinx, whose choice of partners owes nothing whatsoever to middle-class concepts of morality, seems to confirm the commonplace western concept of eastern promiscuity. This 'half woman and half animal' (verse 6) makes 'gilt-scaled dragons writhe and twist with passion' (verse 25), and gryphons 'with metal flanks' leap on her in her 'trampled couch' (verse 24); she lures the 'ivory-horned Tragelaphos' to her bed (verse 32), and even couples with the legendary chimera, that fire-breathing monster that once laid waste to Lycia and was seen in Flaubert's 'Tentation de Saint-Antoine' as a symbol of 'fantaisie' and 'caprice indomptable'.[110] It is true that all these erotic adventures are presented through the speaker's questions, but the interrogative presentation has an affirmative and evocative effect. The questions suggest dialogue rather than monologue, counteracting what might otherwise be the flatness of a merely factual account, so that the narrative takes on a more dynamic tone which helps to excite the reader's imagination.

In the lion-and-tiger episode, the 'sensibilità erotica' takes on a distinctly decadent tone:

Follow some roving lion's spoor across the copper-coloured plain,
Reach out and hale him by the mane and bid him be your paramour!
Couch by his side upon the grass and set your white teeth in his
    throat
And when you hear his dying note lash your long flanks of polished
    brass
And take a tiger for your mate, whose amber sides are flecked with
    black,
And ride upon his gilded back in triumph through the Theban gate,
And toy with him in amorous jests, and when he turns, and snarls, and
    gnaws,
O smite him with your jasper claws! and bruise him with your agate
    breasts   (verses 71–4)

The mixture of lust and deadly cruelty is a clear link with the literary
tradition of the *femme fatale*. Her 'curved archaic smile' (verse 43)
elsewhere called 'subtle-secret' (verse 37), is like that of the Gioconda as
described by Pater in his essay on Leonardo da Vinci. Mario Praz, in *La
carne, la morte e il diavolo nella letteratura romantica* (1930), traces the
different forms of this character from dark romanticism through to the *fin
de siècle*, with detailed analyses. Of course the ancestors go even further
back, to Lilith, Delilah, Helen, Cleopatra, and all the other legendary
sirens of yore. As can be seen from the lines quoted above, Wilde's Sphinx
is even more vampire-like and androgynous than his Salome, and the
emphasis laid on her extraordinary lovelife makes her female sensuality
far more demonic than that portrayed in the play.

Indeed by the end of the poem, the statue of the Sphinx has become a
wicked demon brought from hell by a 'snake-tressed fury' (verse 81) and
admitted to the speaker's room ('a student's cell', verse 82) by a 'songless
tongueless ghost of sin' (verse 82). This violent aversion to the Sphinx is
an indication of the fascination which her dangerous charms hold for the
speaker, and to which in secret he no doubt longs to succumb. By now she
had already become a symbol that crystallises all the suppressed erotic
desires that torment the observer, for the preceding visions are nothing
other than projections of his own sensuality given concrete form by the
imagery and the experiences recounted. The weary, somewhat half-
hearted mention of the crucifix at the end offers a moral alternative that
seems pallid and scarcely credible after this orgy of pagan passion. It is
almost as if Wilde has taken fright at his own daring and has run back at
the last moment to the safety of Victorian moral convention.

The none too convincing conclusion to this poem once again raises the
possibility of biographical interpretation. This would apply not only to
the conflict between Wilde's Hellenistic inclinations and his vague but
never completely extinct longings for faith, but also and above all to the
subject of his homosexuality. Arthur Ransome said *The Sphinx* was 'more

personal to Wilde than anything in *Poems*,[111] and Léon Lemonnier
regarded the monster as Wilde's homosexual *alter ego*:

A Oxford, le monstre est apparu dans la vie de Wilde; plus tard, à la veille de son
mariage, il le caresse une fois encore; mais c'est seulement au faîte de sa puissance
temporelle qu'il ose enfin le regarder en face et le montrer à tous.[112]

[At Oxford the monster made its appearance in Wilde's life; later, on the eve of
his marriage, he caressed it once more; but it is only at the height of his temporal
power that at last he dares to look at it directly and to show it to all.]

This interpretation, suggesting the poet's guilt at his homosexuality and a
desire to express it in poetic code, may perhaps find support in the fact
that various other works – especially *Dorian Gray* – abound in words like
'sin' and 'guilt' that evince an acute moral awareness. Undoubtedly a
writer who was so concerned about his public image and reputation as
Wilde would have suffered a great deal more from the social taboo on his
sexual inclinations than might be gauged from his mere confession of a
'love that dare not speak its name'.[113]

But the biographical interpretation should not make us lose sight of the
poem's formal and thematic dependence on the tradition of literary
exoticism.[114] Wilde's *nostalgie de l'étranger* is part of a movement which
awakened in him, as in other *décadents*, the desire to find not the 'blue
flower' of the romantics, but the artificial paradises sought by Baudelaire.
Discontent with everyday reality aroused in him and in many other poets
and artists a boundless sense of *ennui*. A passion for foreign lands,
especially the Orient, and for past times, above all antiquity and the
Renaissance, points not only to the frustrations of a sensitive soul trapped
in space and time, but also to the problems of the extreme individualist
whose lack of moral and social ties forces him to seek compensation in
fantastic visions of distant worlds. This impressionistic and decadent
mentality finds expression in enjoyment of the unnatural, for example, the
androgynous ideal, a melancholy veneration of beauty and transience,
love of emotional extremes, perversion, excess and luxury. The romantic
medievalism of the Pre-Raphaelites develops into the nostalgic exoticism
of the *fin de siècle* generation.

Friedrich Brie calls this longing for distant lands and times a 'Sonder-
strömung innerhalb der Romantik'.[115] In English literature such exotic
trends are to be observed above all in such romantic authors as William
Beckford (*Vathek*, 1786), S. T. Coleridge (*Kubla Khan*, 1798), Thomas
De Quincey (*Confessions of an English Opium Eater*, 1821), and also in
the essays of Thomas G. Wainewright, the subject of Wilde's 'Pen, Pencil
and Poison'. A special case is the work of Edgar Allan Poe, which had
great influence on Baudelaire; the latter was one of the main representatives of the French exotic movement, which was to have longer-lasting

literary effects than the Anglo-Saxon movement. Other major French exoticists were Théophile Gautier (*Mademoiselle de Maupin*, 1835; 'Fortunio', 1838; *Une Nuit de Cléopâtre*, 1838), Gustave Flaubert (*Novembre*, 1842; *Salammbô*, 1862; *La Tentation de Saint-Antoine*, 1874), Gérard de Nerval (*Voyage en Orient*, 1869), and the *parnassiens*, particularly Leconte de Lisle (*Poèmes antiques*, 1852). Various early studies of Wilde's sources have shown that he was especially influenced by Gautier's *Emaux et Camées* (1852; final version 1872), Flaubert's *Tentation de Saint-Antoine* (1874), Baudelaire's cat sonnets, and the Sphinx and Chimera episode in Huysmans's *A Rebours* (1884).[116] There is also an unmistakable similarity between Wilde's *Sphinx* and Poe's 'The Raven' (1845),[117] which towards the end of the poem also appears to be a 'thing of evil'[118] whose eyes have 'all the seeming of a demon'.[119] Just as Wilde's speaker orders the creature to leave his room ('Get hence', verse 84), the raven is told: 'Get thee back into the tempest and the Night's Plutonian shore!'[120] But significantly Poe's speaker does not finally turn to the crucifix, for the remorseless 'nevermore' of the raven leaves no hope for the solution of life's problems.

The art world as a counter-world

Quite apart from the tradition of exotic literature in which the poem's theme is firmly rooted, Pater's method of 'creative criticism', as practised in his Mona Lisa interpretation, is a clear influence on the formal design of *The Sphinx*. Pater, too, uses verbal pictures to stimulate the associative imagination of his reader. Just as the figure of Gioconda undergoes a series of fantastic metamorphoses to become an 'epiphany of eternal life'[121] constantly being renewed without ever losing its content, so the many episodes of Wilde's poem seek to replace poetic imitation of reality by symbolist suggestion. From an attitude of quiet contemplation, the speaker gradually evokes a bizarre 'world as will and idea' within which the individual components take on a new inner consistency by means of an act of artistic permutation. Replacing active experience of reality by imaginative visions while adopting an attitude of outer passivity is a favourite pose of the *décadents*, particularly fostered by Des Esseintes. For instance, instead of going to England as planned, he contents himself with visiting English-style pubs in Paris, which give him the illusion of being in England. This illusion is completed by his reading the description of London museums in *Baedeker*. Aversion to factual reality makes him take refuge in a multiplicity of possibilities which break down the natural barriers of space and time. Only in this way can one's thirst for *nouveaux frissons* be satisfied.

The Sphinx motif fuses aesthetic attraction, erotic liberty, and the *fin-de-siècle* spiritual crisis into a single highly expressive symbol that is both biographical and historical. Instead of the romantic view from the window, the observer now finds that his room is opened up to an unlimited vista through the visions conjured up by the Sphinx's experiences. What begins in the *parnassien* style as *transposition d'art* continues with bizarre concepts of pagan sensuality, finally to fade out in a conventional gesture towards Christianity. But even the contrast between demonic sensuality and Christian guilt is left implicit – there are no moral polemics in this poem. And undoubtedly the lust for 'madder music' and 'stronger wine'[122] makes a far deeper and more lasting impression than any vague prophecy of redemption. The weary resignation of the conclusion is in fact deeply pessimistic, since the man on the cross 'weeps for every soul that dies, and weeps for every soul in vain' (verse 87).

The poem keeps leaping from one scene to the next, and the strange juxtaposition of the various episodes is in some ways reminiscent of the ornamental style of *art nouveau*, which is characterised by the 'arabeskenhafte Rhythmisierung der Bildfläche'.[123] A close relationship can be discerned between Wilde's stylistic technique in *The Spinx* and the techniques of the symbolist painters. There is no longer a naturalistic view of space, colour becomes an autonomous means of expression, there is a predilection for cyclic sequences, and suggestion takes precedence over imitation. The Sphinx figure itself is a popular motif to be found, for instance, in D. G. Rossetti's 'The Question or The Sphinx', Gustave Moreau's 'Ödipus und die Sphinx', and several paintings by Franz von Stuck. As Lothar Hönnighausen's detailed and thorough study *Präraphaeliten und Fin de Siècle* has shown, it ranks alongside the snake, the dance and the rose as one of the basic Symbolist images, which can be seen as 'Ausdruck der spätromantischen Spiritualität'.[124]

The Sphinx is certainly a typical piece of decadent aesthetic poetry. Nevertheless, the view that it is 'Wilde's fullest expression of his most extreme idolisation of art over life',[125] and 'the quintessence of art for art's sake',[126] requires some modification. Despite all its artifices and its unreality, it remains tightly bound both to the poet's own world and to that of the society in which he lived. In its atmosphere of exotic promiscuity it represents an attack on the repressive morality of the Victorians. The individual's ultimate feelings of guilt in relation to such promiscuity may well be traced to Wilde's own life-story, as has been pointed out already, but these in themselves are a reflection of the normative pressure exerted by the real world.

Even within the poem itself, the separation of art and life is by no means as complete as it may appear. It is not simply an 'experiment at playing with words'[127] or as meaningless as a 'cross-word puzzle'.[128] The narrator is unable to maintain his detachment from the statue. Just as Dorian Gray's portrait intrudes into the life of the protagonist, so too does the

Sphinx break out of its aesthetic confines to enter into the sphere of morality. If at first the motivating force is a flight from reality into a dreamlike counter-world, by the end the poem has become an expression of a very real spiritual crisis, reacting if only indirectly to a very determinate phase in the history of social attitudes towards sex. By communicating an experience of other worlds, the *nostalgie de l'étranger* provides a framework within which the real-life situation becomes all the clearer. Thus the departure from contemporary reality leads unexpectedly to enhanced awareness of the acute problems with which the poet was faced.

7 Pathos and paradox.
Lady Windermere's Fan, A Woman of No Importance and An Ideal Husband

After the failure of his two dramas *Vera; or, The Nihilists* and *The Duchess of Padua* in the early 1880s, Wilde rediscovered the theatre at the beginning of the 1890s. More than any other medium it offered him the chance to bask in the limelight of public attention. Nowhere else could his brilliant gift for conversation be so profitably marketed, and the combined promise of possible financial reward, recognition as a dramatist, and satisfaction of personal ambition proved to be irresistible. His increased need for money at this time was caused by his friendship with Lord Alfred Douglas, whom he had got to know in 1891 through Lionel Johnson, and with whom he formed a very close relationship from 1892 onwards; this resulted in a very expensive life style, with lunch at the Café Royal, dinner at the Savoy, snacks at Willis's, and weekly outgoings of between £80 and £130.[1] Wilde's extravagance, his inability to keep expenses level with income, and his vanity in trying to emulate and impress his aristocratic friend through his generosity were to land him in deep trouble, as we know from *De Profundis*.[2] In order to continue his good life with Bosie, he needed a substantial boost to his income, and this was highly unlikely to come about through more volumes of poetry, fairy-tales or novels. The theatre was where the rich pickings lay, and this was the lure that shaped Wilde's future career as a dramatist; aesthetic considerations were minimal – as is clear from the fact that he himself had a low opinion of the aesthetic value of his plays. He is said to have told André Gide: 'mes pièces ne sont pas du tout bonnes; et je n'y tiens pas du tout ... Mais si vous saviez comme elles amusent!'[3]

It would seem that at least up until the 1950s Wilde critics have tended to adopt the author's own judgment. Apart from generally brief mentions in theatre histories, chapters in monographs, and various dissertations, mainly American, there are very few essays that treat these plays in any depth,[4] although renewed interest in Wilde is reflected by the comparatively recent monographs of Alan Bird, *The Plays of Oscar Wilde* (1977) and Katharine Worth, *Oscar Wilde* (1983). *The Importance of Being Earnest* is of course, the most popular subject of study – nine out of twelve essays listed by Dietrich Peinert in his 1968 research report[5] are devoted to it. On *Lady Windermere's Fan* there is a detailed structural analysis by Cleanth Brooks and Robert B. Heilman,[6] and an interpretation by Armin Geraths;[7] the author of the present volume has written an interpretation of *An Ideal Husband*,[8] but apart from the various monographs, no attention at all has been paid to *A Woman of No Importance*. There are very few studies from a purely theatrical point of view, along the lines of 'Drama als Sonderform theatralischer Aktivität',[9] an aspect that has long been sadly neglected.

The main criticism levelled at the comedies is that there tends to be a certain imbalance between dialogue and plot, 'thèmes' and 'thèses', aesthetic world view and philistine morality. 'The light dialogue of the satirical comedy of manners was not yet properly fitted to the heavier plot of the problem-play'[10] claims Edouard Roditi. Robert Merle attributes the diffuseness to a disproportion between the 'thèse suggérée par l'intrigue, et la thèse suggérée par l'auteur'.[11] Arthur Ganz's instructive essay following on from his dissertation 'The Dandiacal Drama'[12] emphasises the idea that the individuality of these social comedies stems from the clash between 'sentimental plots' and 'the dandiacal world':[13]

Each of these plays contains two worlds, not only contrasting but conflicting. One is the world of the sentimental plots, where ladies with mysterious pasts make passionate speeches and the fates of empires hang on intercepted letters and stolen bracelets. This is the world I will call Philistine. Opposed to it is the dandiacal world, where witty elegants lounge about tossing off Wildean epigrams and rarely condescend to notice, much less take part in, the impassioned actions going on about them. The tension between these two worlds gives to the society comedies their peculiar flavor, their strength, and unfortunately their weakness.[14]

Developing this same argument, Ian Gregor[15] regards the essence of the plays as consisting in the conflict 'between manners and morals, between style and content, between the author and his characters'.[16] Wilde's main dramaturgical problem was to find 'a world fit for the dandy to live in'.[17] He did not succeed in doing so until *The Importance of Being Earnest*.

There can be little denying the truth of all these observations, even if one should perhaps qualify Arthur Ganz's argument by pointing out that the clash is not only between the 'dandiacal' world and the 'Philistine', but is also within the figure of the dandy himself, between his characterisation and his function in the plot. These interpretations, however, are only aspects of something more complex and more profound. The clash between dandies and Philistines, or between orthodox dénouements and non-conformist subject-matter, is certainly built into the dialogue of all the plays, but it is not the decisive influence on the plot, the characters or their attempts at communication. The real problem of the plays is the tension between the individual and society, between public and private life, between established social and moral norms and their deliberate violation. The direct result of this conflict is the continual efforts of the characters to redefine their identity within the framework of their need for personal expression and the parts they play in society. The rigorous codes and conventions, and the pressure to conform, produce in some characters illusory expectations by which they then judge others; but they also produce outsiders who will use any means – including immorality – to integrate themselves into society, because otherwise they will be socially left out in the cold. It will now be our task to examine how this problem is dealt with on the level of the drama as a literary text and as a mediator between author and audience, and to analyse the techniques by which the social and moral perspectives are set out; finally, we shall discuss the place of these comedies in the history of the theatre.

Plot: subject-matter

The similarity between the basic situations and motifs of the comedies shows that variety was not Wilde's concern.[18] In all the plays, A's life contains a secret that is known to B and is useful for him or her to achieve certain aims. Lord Windermere knows the secret of his wife's origins, which he wishes to keep from her, and which Mrs Erlynne can exploit for purposes of blackmail. Similarly, the corrupt politician Robert Chiltern tries to hide an earlier indiscretion from his wife, and thus puts himself at the mercy of the scheming Mrs Cheveley, who knows about this black spot in his past. Mrs Arbuthnot does not want her illegitimate son Gerald to know that Lord Illingworth is his father.

In all cases there is a secret that either sets the plot in motion or at least has a decisive influence on its course. Furthermore, this secret always concerns something in conflict with social or moral conventions, that is, the indiscretions of Mrs Erlynne and Mrs Arbuthnot, and the corruption of Chiltern. Apart from in *Lady Windermere's Fan*, where the lady herself never learns the identity of Mrs Erlynne, the past fault is always revealed or confessed by the guilty party, who then asks for forgiveness or, at least, understanding. The pattern of secret and revelation, guilt and forgiveness, is obviously applicable to Wilde's own situation in the 1890s, and one can easily see the comedies as a reflection of his inner isolation in view of the social taboo on homosexuality. Thus the trauma of his life becomes the *idée fixe* of his work.

Robert Merle rightly points out the 'plaidoyer personnel'[19] expressed by the motif of forgiveness in the dénouement. The unconscious desire to punish himself, resulting from the continual tension between a '*besoin d'aveu*' and a '*besoin de sécurité*'[20] – a desire that may be seen as the sign of an overwhelming guilt complex – may well explain Wilde's otherwise incomprehensible decision to set in motion the wheels of the law that was to destroy him. This seems a far more likely interpretation than any 'keen sense of the dramatic'[21] or a 'masochistic attraction to danger'.[22] If, however, we merely regard these plots as Wilde's sublimated confession and plea for forgiveness, we shall ourselves be guilty of making the psychological and biographical interpretation the be-all and end-all. In fact, Wilde's concern was not with the guilt of Sir Robert Chiltern or of Mrs Arbuthnot, or with its origins or its effects on their consciences; the comedies deal with the revelation or threatened revelation of a past lapse, together with the consequences or possible consequences. Guilt and sin are never viewed as psychological phenomena but only as social problems. The central conflict is between the individual and society.

The society presented in the comedies is basically that of the aristocracy and the upper middle classes in London – 'our little parish of St James's'.[23] It is a relatively closed community, distinguished by its status, possessions and class conventions of language and behaviour. These collective characteristics ensure homogeneity and also act as barriers against intruders from outside. Membership of this circle is achieved either by birth or by social climbing. The most common method of permanent entry is marriage, and the most common means of contact is through invitation to one of the 'in' houses. The very fact that Mrs Erlynne is invited to Lady Windermere's birthday party makes her acceptable in the eyes of the Duchess of Berwick: 'Of course, she must be all right if *you* [Lady Windermere] invite her.'[24] Violation of the norms leads to sanctions, mainly indicated by the person concerned departing from the London scene. Mrs Erlynne turns her back on England, Lord Darlington announces a similar course ('I shall be away for many years'),[25] Mrs Arbuthnot intends to go away with her son Gerald when Lord Illingworth has come on the scene, and Sir Robert Chiltern considers – if somewhat half-heartedly – retiring from public life and 'living somewhere alone ... abroad perhaps, or in the country away from London, away from public life'.[26] Exile abroad, or life in the country far from the capital – these are the courses of action open to those who are guilty of breaking the rules. The consequences of such exile are vividly described by Mrs Erlynne in conversation with her daughter, Lady Windermere:

You don't know what it is to fall into the pit, to be despised, mocked, abandoned, sneered at – to be an outcast! to find the door shut against one, to have to creep in by hideous byways, afraid every moment lest the mask should be stripped from one's face, and all the while to hear the laughter, the horrible laughter of the world, a thing more tragic than all the tears the world has ever shed. You don't know what it is. One pays for one's sin, and then one pays again, and all one's life one pays. You must never know that.[27]

It is evident that the pressure of conformity, which applies equally to insiders and to outsiders trying to enter the circle, must lead to conflict between, on the one hand, their view of themselves and of the world, and on the other the roles they are forced to adopt on pain of publicly inflicted sanctions. The subject-matter and the conflict in each of Wilde's comedies consists in the struggle of the insiders to maintain their position or of the outsiders to break in, and of the individual's need to fulfil himself independently of this pressure to conform. If one were to draw a diagram depicting the interactions of the conflicting characters, it would be made up of lines leading into the circle from outside, and other lines running from the centre towards (and out of) the circumference. Attempted integration and disintegration are the two prevailing processes, and the identity of the characters emerges from the clash between their private actions and their public roles.

If one defines identity as a 'dauerndes inneres Sich-Selbst-Gleichsein sowie ein dauerndes Teilhaben an bestimmten gruppenspezifischen Charakterzügen'[28] [permanent, inner equality with oneself as well as a permanent participation in specific group characteristics], then evidently it consists both of personal and of social elements. Thus social integration means the establishment of social identity. The self-sacrifice and tactical cold-bloodedness of Mrs Erlynne, the declaration of love and the uncommitted dandyism of Lord Darlington, the spontaneous evasiveness and social preoccupations of Lady Windermere – these may all be viewed as forms of conflict in the realisation of personal and social identity. Of all the main characters, it is Lady Windermere who is least successful in experiencing continuity of the self – 'I am afraid of being myself'[29] – because she subjects herself most completely to the exigencies of her role. Mrs Erlynne longs for social identity, but she partially regains her personal identity because she is capable of maternal feelings towards her daughter and of acting responsibly for her sake, whereas Lady Windermere herself is trapped in her role as the admired and respected wife of a rich aristocrat, incapable of establishing a personal identity in the face of her social constrictions.

Unlike Mrs Erlynne – whose attempt to break into the circle is doomed to failure, except for the partial compensation of her marriage to Lord Augustus Lorton – Mrs Arbuthnot in *A Woman of No Importance* does not even attempt to acquire social recognition, but stays within her role as an outsider, though this is qualified by her image as a 'good woman'. When Lord Illingworth, prompted by Gerald's letter, offers to marry her, she declines. This offer by the cynical aristocrat – equally surprising for both audience and other characters – does not stem from any sudden reawakening of passion for his former mistress, but is based purely on the idea that the marriage would ensure his son's place in society and would thus advance his career. This is simply a variation on the theme of Wilde's first successful play, *Lady Windermere's Fan*, in which Lady Windermere is revealed as the daughter of Mrs Erlynne, who had left her husband for a lover who, in turn, had abandoned her. In *A Woman of No Importance*

Gerald is the son of Mrs Arbuthnot, who left her lover because he refused to marry her. In both comedies the situation is based on the fact that a woman with a past now has problems in the present resulting from her previous unconventional behaviour. Much of the dramatic tension derives from initial concealment of the link between past and present. In the first play, Mrs Erlynne's identity is in fact never revealed to her daughter, whereas in the second the relationship between Gerald and his father is disclosed in Act 3 at a moment of high melodrama. The main structural difference between the two plays, however, is that in the first the situation is developed from the relationship between mother and daughter (Mrs Erlynne – Lady Windermere), whereas in the second the focal point is the relationship between mother and former lover. In terms of the structure, Mrs Arbuthnot corresponds to Mrs Erlynne, Gerald to Lady Windermere, and – with a few divergences – Lord Illingworth to Lord Darlington, although in terms of themes and motivation there are, of course, differences.

The clash between public and private life is particularly vehement in *An Ideal Husband*. Mrs Cheveley, a scheming woman from Vienna, demands that Sir Robert Chiltern, in his capacity as Under-Secretary for Foreign Affairs, should give political support to what he knows to be a fraudulent canal project in Argentina in which the lady has invested a considerable sum of money. In order to add the necessary weight to her demands, she threatens to publish a compromising letter that Chiltern wrote eighteen years before, when secretary to Lord Radley, to Baron Arnheim, a speculator, advising him to buy shares in the Suez Canal – a letter written just three days before the British government closed the market in these shares. For this act of betrayal he was paid £110,000, a sum which he trebled within five years. Now he is faced with a choice between risking his social and political career and burdening his conscience for a second time. As he did eighteen years before, he opts for the second course. It needs a discussion with his wife – who knows from what he has told her that the canal project is fraudulent – to make him change his mind.

The conflict set in motion by Mrs Cheveley's attempted blackmail is complicated by the motif of political corruption being interwoven with one of love. In the development of the plot, this becomes clear through Chiltern's decision not to support the project after all. Once again the clash is between public and private life, with Chiltern the politician having to grapple with Chiltern the husband in an almost schizophrenic division of identities. In his public, political life he can dismiss his support of a Stock Exchange swindle as 'a question of rational compromise'[30] dictated by circumstances, but in his private, married life he must accept that a precondition for his wife's love is his own moral integrity. This critical dichotomy between his political and his moral understanding of himself is yet another variation on the basic theme of all Wilde's comedies: the individual's search for a personal and social identity within a social world that is split by the conflict between a puritan moral order and a pragmatic ethic of success.

Plot: construction

The conflict between conformity and rebellion as regards social and moral conventions gives Wilde's plots a direct relation to contemporary, late Victorian reality, but their construction often leaves something to be desired. St John Hankin complains that 'in the age of Ibsen and of Hauptmann, of Strindberg and Brieux, he [Wilde] was content to construct like Sardou and think like Dumas *fils*'.[31]

All too frequently chance and improbability replace logical com-position. Thus, for instance, in Act 3 of *An Ideal Husband* the plot progresses through all kinds of artificialities that arise neither from the individual characters nor from the preceding events, but are simply crude threads drawn from the repertoire of the French *pièce bien faite* and clichés drawn from comic tradition. These include the chair falling over and betraying the presence of Mrs Cheveley, the stolen bracelet as part of the counter-plot, the stolen letter, the concealment scene, and the motifs of mistaken identity and deceiver deceived. The dramatic tensions of the first two acts degenerate into melodrama just when one would have expected a psychological deepening of the conflict. The mechanics of plot-manipulation take the place of organically motivated composition, with chance taking over from inevitability, and the constellation of characters diverting attention from the central conflict which was concen-trated in the first two acts on the character of Sir Robert Chiltern.[32]

The strengths and weaknesses of Wilde's technique are best seen by analysing the construction of *Lady Windermere's Fan*. The early stages of the plot are distinguished by the skilful exposition, which is built up through a network of subtle allusions to earlier events, and which, combined with techniques of delay and compression, makes for very effective theatrical composition. Right at the start Lord Darlington admires his hostess's fan, so that the reader or spectator is informed quite naturally about her birthday and the party that is to take place that evening. In the ensuing conversation Darlington's request for her friend-ship – 'You may want a friend some day'[33] – prepares the way for his declaration of love in Act 2. When he confronts her with the hypothetical case of an unfaithful husband, in order to find out her reactions, he is as it were playfully anticipating the supposed breach of faith by Windermere. The scene with the Duchess of Berwick which follows this dialogue has a twofold function: first, the Duchess's account of Windermere's visits to

Mrs Erlynne sets the main plot in motion, and secondly the mention of Mr Hopper and his attraction to Agatha, her daughter, looks forward to the sub-plot which is to be developed and concluded in the next act. The exposition, in fact, prepares us for all aspects of the plot: the relationships between Lady Windermere and Mrs Erlynne, Lady and Lord Windermere, Lady Windermere and Lord Darlington, Lord Windermere and Mrs Erlynne; also the sub-plots revolving round the Duchess of Berwick, her daughter Agatha and Mr Hopper, the rich Australian, and Lord Augustus Lorton and Mrs Erlynne.

The main plot is dominated by the relationship between Lady Windermere and Mrs Erlynne, and this is already made clear by the thematic progression of the exposition. The most powerful 'Detailspannung'[34] is achieved by the delayed appearance of Mrs Erlynne together with Lady Windermere's declared intention of striking her in the face with her fan.[35] Expectations aroused by the pattern of plan and fulfilment, or mention of a person and his or her subsequent appearance, direct all attention to the birthday party, the arrival of Mrs Erlynne, and Lady Windermere's reaction. The first crisis, then, is to be reached in Act 2. This technique of delaying the appearance of the main character is comparable to that used by Goethe in *Egmont* and Molière in *Tartuffe*, where the eponymous heroes are not seen until Act 2 and Act 3 respectively.

Parallel to the compression of the action is the compression of time, which runs from 5.0 p.m. on a Tuesday to 1.30 p.m. on the following day. Cleanth Brooks and Robert B. Heilman[36] have rightly pointed out the dangers of condensing so many events into such a short period, and their detailed analysis draws attention to the attendant improbabilities. Is it, for instance, likely that Darlington and the Duchess would visit the Windermeres just a few hours before the official birthday party, to which they have both been invited, and furthermore would they really choose such a time to undermine the birthday girl's relations with her husband? Why does Windermere's invitation to Mrs Erlynne come so late? We shall see presently that in such matters of detail, Wilde did not always pay sufficient attention either to construction or to motivation.

At the centre of Act 2, in which the characters have gathered for the birthday ball and which somewhat resembles Act 1 of *An Ideal Husband* in its dramatic development, there stands Lady Windermere's confrontation with her supposed rival Mrs Erlynne. The grand climax is initially delayed by Mr Hopper's wooing of Agatha and by Lord Lorton's interest in Mrs Erlynne, but when Mrs Erlynne does finally appear – 'one of the most brilliant delayed entrances in English drama since that of Mrs Millamant in *The Way of the World*'[37] – it is almost an anticlimax, for instead of hitting her with the fan, Lady Windermere simply drops it. Various conversations between Cecil Graham, Mrs Erlynne, Lady Jedburgh, Dumby, Lady Plymdale and Lord Augustus Lorton defuse the situation, and lead into Darlington's declaration of love which Lady Windermere at first rejects but later decides to accept, leaving the house to go and join Darlington. Thus in Act 2 the previously separate relations between Lady Windermere and Darlington and Lady Windermere and Mrs Erlynne are linked in such a way that Lady Windermere's bitterness at the presence of her 'rival' and at her husband's behaviour motivates her seeking refuge with Darlington. The fact that three times in this act she is called upon to make decisions shows clearly that her attitude is of prime importance here – 'In other words, the act is essentially hers, dramatizing her psychological development.'[38] Towards the end of the act, however, there is a change of perspective, and the initiative passes over to Mrs Erlynne.

The plot undergoes a strategic development in Act 3, with a change in the relationship between Lady Windermere and Mrs Erlynne, without the latter ever revealing her identity and thus risking a slide into sentimental melodrama. By compromising herself socially through an act of selflessness, she enables her daughter to escape unnoticed from an awkward situation in Darlington's flat. The plot now pushes the two women in opposite directions: while Lady Windermere is saved from social ostracism and is forced to revise her hitherto totally negative attitude towards Mrs Erlynne, the latter sabotages her own attempts to gain acceptance in society. The almost tragic irony of this change lies in the fact that the daughter's position in society can only be preserved through the renewed social exile of the mother.

In this act, however, there are several weaknesses as regards motivation. In order to get Mrs Erlynne to visit Darlington's house, Wilde had to resort at the end of Act 2 to the hackneyed trick of the letter discovered by chance. Equally coincidental and melodramatic is the unexpected return of the gentlemen at the very moment when the two ladies are about to leave Darlington's residence. It is also highly unlikely that two ladies could get into Darlington's house in the middle of the night without a servant knowing about it and informing Darlington on his return. Nor is it altogether plausible that Lady Windermere could slip out of a room unnoticed by the five men who are in it. One might also ask why these five men should have left the club and returned to Darlington's house anyway. Windermere's remark, 'It is very good of you, Lord Darlington, allowing Augustus to force our company on you'[39] is hardly a justification. And would a woman who is in the process of leaving her husband really take his birthday present – the fan – with her to the home of his rival?[40]

In their analysis of Act 3 Brooks and Heilman maintain that it is perfectly legitimate for Wilde to use the device of a concealment scene, with the two women overhearing the conversation of the men, but they feel that the scene lacks conviction:

since the concealed women can actually l e a r n nothing from what they overhear, the conversation on the stage can have no effect on them. Hence the scene depends for its effect entirely upon the possibility of discovery of the concealed persons.[41]

If, however, one considers the actual subject-matter of the conversation, one will note that the first part concerns relations between Lord Augustus Lorton and Mrs Erlynne, and the second is about Darlington's feelings towards a 'good woman'.[42] Since the two women being discussed are actually listening in to the conversation, it is unlikely that they will 'learn nothing' or that there will be 'no effect'. Furthermore, the whole discussion on good women and women with a past is highly relevant to the themes of the play and to the contrast between the two women listening in.

In Act 3 the relationships between Lady Windermere and Mrs Erlynne, and Lord Windermere and Mrs Erlynne, have begun to change, and in Act 4 the reversal of the initial attitudes is completed. In Act 1 Lady Windermere referred to Mrs Erlynne as 'this infamous woman',[43] whereas in Act 4 she says: 'I don't think Mrs Erlynne a bad woman – I know she's not.'[44] In Act 1 Lord Windermere pleaded eloquently for her reinstatement in society, but in Act 4 he calls her 'a bad woman preying upon life'.[45] This structural and thematic link between Act 1 and Act 4, between exposition and dénouement, is certainly at the core of the ironic effect of the play,[46] which is reinforced by the fact that the new attitudes towards Mrs Erlynne are as inaccurate as the old. Her actions show her to be neither 'a very good woman'[47] (Lady Windermere) nor 'as bad as a woman can be'[48] (Lord Windermere). In this context, the titular fan plays an important role in preparing the ironic effect: in Act 2 Lady Windermere intends to use it as a weapon against her supposed rival in order to prevent her social rehabilitation, while in Act 3 its discovery in Darlington's house gives Mrs Erlynne the opportunity to save her daughter from social disgrace.

Characters

//The main characters in the comedies consist of Wildean dandies (Lord Darlington, Lord Illingworth, Lord Goring), 'good women' (Lady Windermere, Hester Worsley, Lady Chiltern), and women with a past (Mrs Erlynne, Mrs Arbuthnot, Mrs Cheveley). The minor characters include aristocratic grandes dames (Duchess of Berwick, Lady Hunstanton, Lady Markby), marriageable young ladies (Lady Agatha Carlisle, Mabel Chiltern), and more-or-less serious gentlemen (Lord Windermere, Gerald Arbuthnot, Sir Robert Chiltern). There are also countless peripheral figures, such as assorted aristocrats, church dignitaries, politicians and servants.

Undoubtedly the dandies are amongst the most attractive of Wilde's characters. They are distinguished externally by their exquisite sense of dress and manners, and psychologically by their blasé detachment from and aesthetic opposition to bourgeois utilitarianism. These qualities denote the ideal of cultured individualism, manifested personally through narcissistic self-fulfilment, and socially through aristocratic elitism. With his aura of personal distinction, combining egotism with urbane sociability and witty charm, the dandy cultivates a view of life and the world that is totally alien to the course of history since the French Revolution. Baudelaire regarded dandyism as a transitional phenomenon between aristocracy and democracy:

Le dandysme apparaît surtout aux époques transitoires où la démocratie n'est pas encore toute-puissante, où l'aristocratie n'est que partiellement chancelante et avilie. Dans le trouble de ces époques quelques hommes déclassés, dégoûtés, désœuvrés, mais tous riches de force native, peuvent concevoir le projet de fonder une espèce nouvelle d'aristocratie, d'autant plus difficile à rompre qu'elle sera basée sur les facultés les plus précieuses, les plus indestructibles, et sur les dons célestes que le travail et l'argent ne peuvent conférer.[49]

[Dandyism appears especially during periods of transition when democracy is not yet all-powerful, and when the aristocracy is only partially tottering, and debased. In these troubled times, some men who have lost their social position, their illusions and their occupations – but all rich in natural strength – are able to conceive the project of founding a new type of aristocracy, all the more difficult to break up because it will be based on those most precious, most indestructible faculties and those celestial gifts that work and money cannot provide.]

From a social and economic point of view, the emergence of these Wildean dandies is influenced by the growth of the leisured classes, above all the aristocracy and the *jeunesse dorée* of the rich upper-middle class – principally from the circles of high finance and commerce. They avoid all useful work, and their social prestige is measured according to their 'conspicuous leisure'.[50] This idle, unproductive wasting of time comes out clearly at the beginning of *An Ideal Husband* with Mabel Chiltern's description of Lord Goring's normal day. The fact that Lord Caversham disapproves of his son's idle life shows the difference between the generation of active pioneers, for whom idleness was something shameful, and the new generation which lives on the capital of its elders and has moved so far away from the work ethic that idleness is regarded as a sign of prestige, and pleasure may be postulated as the aim of life. For social climbers emanating from the *nouveaux riches*, dandyism offered the aristocratic attitude as a compensation for non-aristocratic birth; it also enabled middle-class origins to be concealed behind the façade of the *arbiter elegantiarum*. On the other hand, some of the old nobility could use this dandyism as a means of distinguishing between themselves and the middle-class upstarts.[51]

The typical showplace for the dandy is the salon, and his favourite mode of self-presentation is conversation. From practical life he flees into a *bios theoretikos*, where he can theorise instead of having to act. In this detached position, he is free from all involvement and responsibility, and his resultant relation to society is thoroughly ambivalent: he despises it and negates its norms and conventions, but he cannot abandon it completely because this would mean losing the audience which he needs in order to achieve his personal effect. This simultaneous scorn for and dependence on society gives rise to cynicism, to 'negative Erhebung über die Werte, denen die Gesellschaft sklavisch anhängt'[52] [negative elevation above the values to which society slavishly adheres].

This ambivalent attitude towards life and society, preferring being to doing and aesthetic freedom to ethical commitment, is the reason why the dandy is so difficult to integrate into the plot of the play. The incongruence between dialogue and action, often criticised as an artistic weakness in Wilde's work, is due fundamentally to this problem, that is, to the impossibility of filling the dandy's ethical vacuum with mere aesthetic contemplation. Reality does not allow life to be aestheticised through absolute form; nor does it permit the moral alternative of the hedonistic philosophy of the moment, as set out in Pater's 'Conclusion' and as already negated by the dénouement of *Dorian Gray*. Mrs Allonby's aphorism that 'Life ... is simply a *mauvais quart d'heure* made up of exquisite moments'[53] cannot alter the fact that life is much more than this.

Of all the dandy figures, Lord Goring is certainly the most striking. When he first enters, he is described as a 'flawless dandy'[54] and is branded by his father as a 'good-for-nothing'[55] who leads an idle life which, as we learn from Mabel Chiltern, consists of riding at 10.00 a.m., going to the opera three times a week, changing his clothes five times a day, and dining out every night of the season. The care he lavishes on his clothes – a main feature of the dandy according to Carlyle[56] – is made apparent at the beginning of Act 3:

Enter LORD GORING *in evening dress with a buttonhole. He is wearing a silk hat and Inverness cape. White-gloved, he carries a Louis Seize cane. His are all the delicate fopperies of Fashion. One sees that he stands in immediate relation to modern life, makes it indeed, and so masters it. He is the first well-dressed philosopher in the history of thought.*[57]

The desire for perfection in the outer appearance not only demonstrates the dandy's formal distinction and exquisite taste, but also symbolises what Baudelaire calls the aristocratic superiority of his spirit,[58] which is manifested in his pronounced individualism if not egotism. This vanity and narcissistic cultivation of one's own originality entails flight from any painful confrontation with social reality, whose values cannot be accepted; this, however, does not mean that such aesthetic and hedonistic opposition to philistine morality and non-artistic, utilitarian thought presages social revolution. Nothing could be further from the dandy's mind than changing the society that conditions his existence and provides an indispensable sounding-board for his personal effectiveness.

The 'negative Freiheit'[59] from the environment which springs from the irreconcilable difference between the norms of the individual and those of society, and which in extreme cases may lead to self-destruction (Dorian Gray) or the destruction of others (Wainewright), is expressed through a cynical rejection of moral conventions and a paradoxical distortion of spiritual values. The desire for effect is achieved on the intellectual level by dominating the partner in conversation. To achieve this end, the dandy uses paradox, giving an extraordinary twist to some current idea or opinion and thereby shattering his partner's habitual expectations. By bewildering others, the dandy is assured of his superiority, while at the same time the playful character of his paradoxical language enables him to withdraw from any philosophical commitment. A good example of this is the conversation between Lord Goring and Mabel Chiltern in Act 1.

MABEL CHILTERN: You are very late!
LORD GORING: Have you missed me?
MABEL CHILTERN: Awfully!
LORD GORING: Then I am sorry I did not stay away longer. I like being missed.
MABEL CHILTERN: How very selfish of you!
LORD GORING: I am very selfish.
MABEL CHILTERN: You are always telling me of your bad qualities, Lord Goring.
LORD GORING: I have only told you half of them as yet, Miss Mabel![60]

Lord Goring's narcissistic flirtation with his own depravity – also to be seen in Wilde's other dandies[61] – shows what little importance he attaches to conventional morality, and at the same time it is a provocation to his partner. But the cynical pose of the intellectual mocker, so evident in the conversations between Goring and Mabel Chiltern, should not be mistaken for a total lack of moral responsibility. In the scenes with Sir Robert Chiltern and Mrs Cheveley in Act 2, as well as in his planned marriage to Mabel, it becomes clear that behind the mask of the *immoraliste* there is in fact a serious moral involvement which he seeks in vain to cover up with his paradoxical language. It must, however, be noted that the change from intellectual detachment, so typical of the aesthetic attitude, to the earnest adviser of Acts 2 and 4 as well as to the committed protagonist in Act 3, reveals a certain incongruity between the demands of the plot and the feasibility of the dandy figure.

The other dandies reveal this same vacillation between intellectual detachment and emotional involvement. Lord Darlington changes from uncommitted dalliance to stormy passion, and Lord Illingworth's provocative immorality changes to serious courtship of the mother of his illegitimate son. These switches from distant aestheticism to engaged action create major difficulties as regards characterisation. The values which the dandy publicly denigrates or ridicules eventually turn out to be at least partial guidelines for his behaviour towards the 'good women'. The most blatant example is Lord Illingworth's offer of marriage to Mrs Arbuthnot, a fallen woman, which completely shatters one's previous conception of his character. This dramatic inconsistency may well have been conditioned by Wilde's own duality – the combination of Lord Henry and Basil Hallward – which he transferred to his dandy characters who all bear the hallmark of the conformist rebel. Only when he was able to place his dandy in a world of pure play, namely in *The Importance of Being Earnest*, could he surmount these problems and thus put together his most convincing and most successful play.

Counterbalancing the anti-morality of the dandies is the virtue of the 'good women', for example, Lady Windermere, Hester Worsley, and Lady Chiltern. They are strictly and puritanically moral, severely critical of those who have sinned, and intellectually somewhat narrow-minded. This character, recurrent in various forms throughout nineteenth-century literature, represents the popular ideal of the obedient and virtuous wife who knows her place, is 'watched over by Household Gods',[62] brings up her host of children in the true Christian spirit, and provides a refuge for her husband from the pressures of his work. This highly conservative image acknowledges the superiority of the male which Lord Goring, for instance, attributes to man's life proceeding 'upon lines of intellect', whereas woman's follows 'curves of emotions'.[63] It is a concept that fits in well with the doctrine which Lancelot Smith wishes to inculcate into the heroine Argemon in Kingsley's *Yeast*, namely 'that the heart, and not the brain, enshrines the priceless pearl of womanhood'.[64]

Wilde treats all his variations on this character with a degree of irony by casting doubt on the self-righteous morality that underlies all their actions. Lady Windermere is forced to recognise that people cannot be so readily divided into the good and the bad, Hester Worsley finally realises that it is not God's law that children must atone for the sins of their parents, and Lady Chiltern quickly sacrifices her motto that 'Circumstances should never alter principles'[65] when circumstances offer ministerial office to her husband, though his corrupt past should, according to her principles, disqualify him from such a post. With Lady Windermere and Lady Chiltern Wilde brings out the contrast between ethical theory and practice by placing them both in compromising situations that make their oft-proclaimed immunity to the temptations of life seem highly questionable.

Lady Windermere's change of attitude towards Mrs Erlynne is the result of a learning process that has been differently assessed by different critics. Brooks and Heilman believe she has learnt 'that good and evil are not easily determined by simple rules, that they do not often exist in pure form, so to speak';[66] Morse Peckham, however, objects that she has merely questioned her own judgments and not the codes that underlie them.[67] Her ideals remain the same. As we have already seen in our analysis of the dénouement, Lady Windermere's new awareness that the good and the bad are not 'two separate races or creations'[68] does not in fact enable her to question the validity of her moral criteria. These led to her initial rejection of Mrs Erlynne, and even the latter's noble deed of self-sacrifice – which ought at least to blur the boundaries between her moral categories – results only in a switch of judgment and not of code. Her final remark to Lord Lorton, 'Ah, you're marrying a very good woman!'[69] is just as undifferentiated as her negative comments in Act 1.

There is a similar gap between the puritanical norms and the pragmatic requirements of reality as experienced by Lady Chiltern. Her former classmate Mrs Cheveley reports that Lady Chiltern always won 'the good conduct prize'[70] at school – an observation later reinforced by her ironic comment on the letters addressed to Lord Goring: 'The ten commandments in every stroke of the pen, and the moral law all over the page.'[71] Her own husband says she is free from all weaknesses and all temptations, and is 'pitiless in her perfection'.[72] The reader or spectator will therefore be in suspense as to her reaction when she learns of her husband's guilt, but in Act 4 we see that these rigid principles are not put into practice as far as Sir Robert is concerned. It is true that at the end of Act 2 she is appalled that her husband should have sold out to the highest bidder, and deceived the world. He is no better than a common thief in her eyes, and yet there is no more drastic consequence than her letter to Goring, in which this so perfect lady writes: 'I want you. I trust you. I am coming to you.'[73] If we bear in mind her declaration in Act 1 that a person's past life is the only criterion by which he or she is to be judged, and money from a 'tainted' source is a 'degradation', then her later conduct seems all too inconsistent, as does the entire characterisation – especially as she is not allowed a single entrance throughout Act 3, where Wilde could at least have inserted some motivation for the change. In Act 4 she suddenly adopts the arguments of Lord Goring, who had pleaded on behalf of Chiltern's continuance of his political career. And yet at first she had spontaneously agreed to her husband's half-hearted suggestion that he should reject the cabinet post. Now she actually echoes Goring's very words:

LADY CHILTERN: A man's life is of more value than a woman's. It has larger issues, wider scope, greater ambitions. Our lives revolve in curves of emotions. It is upon lines of intellect that a man's life progresses. I have just learnt this, and much else with it, from Lord Goring. And I will not spoil your life for you, nor see you spoil it as a sacrifice to me, a useless sacrifice![74]

This argument is quite remarkable coming from an active member of the Women's Liberal Association and an advocate of higher education for women, but what is doubly shocking is the speed with which such a lady of principle can switch allegiance to the success ethic of her opportunistic husband. Hitherto her naive idealisation of him, coupled with her ignorance of his past, results in a situation of unconscious irony, but now her acceptance of his corruption as a basis for the furtherance of his political career gives rise to a totally different sort of irony, relating not to the situation but to her strict moral principles. The Act 1 precept that 'Circumstances should never alter principles'[75] has been turned completely on its head.

We might mention in passing that while Lady Chiltern embodies many elements of the contemporary view of women, her character and her marital relations have a good deal in common with those of Wilde's wife Constance. Just like Sir Robert, Wilde had a secret to conceal from his wife (his homosexuality), and just like Lady Chiltern, Constance was inclined to balance her intellectual inferiority with a high degree of emotion and admiration.[76] Chiltern's passionate appeal for forgiveness at the end of Act 2 could be read almost word for word as a plea to Constance, who – as we learn from the letters of C.3.3. – did indeed forgive him.[77]

Beside the unworldly moral rigidity of the 'good women', the women with a past seem to have a far more realistic view of life. Mrs Erlynne, Mrs Arbuthnot and Mrs Cheveley have in common certain irregularities of conduct which the Victorians especially would have regarded as scandalous: Mrs Erlynne abandoned her child and her marriage for a lover, Mrs Arbuthnot is an unmarried mother, and Mrs Cheveley – 'A work of art ... but showing the influence of too many schools'[78] – has been married twice and is now using underhand methods to make Lord Goring her third husband. The overriding aim of two of them – Mrs Arbuthnot is the exception – is to be reintegrated in society. The scheming and indeed criminal side of Mrs Cheveley's character is emphasised, while Mrs Erlynne and Mrs Arbuthnot are presented rather more sentimentally through their maternal roles. Both are actually designated as 'good women'.[79] But the basic distinction between good women and those with a past undoubtedly corresponds to the two extremes of the historical Victorian view of woman: virgin and whore, mother and *demi-mondaine*, idealised domestic angel and despised fallen woman.

Mrs Erlynne is a divorcée said by Dumby to look like an '*édition de luxe*' of a wicked French novel, meant specially for the English market'.[80] Very early in her marriage, when her child was still in its cradle, she left her husband for a lover, who in turn deserted her. According to the Duchess of Berwick, she has taken a house in Curzon Street, Mayfair, six months ago, goes riding in the park every afternoon, and generally imitates the social behaviour of London's aristocratic and upper-middle-class circles. She is also trying to bring about her social re-integration by getting herself invited to balls in distinguished houses, and wants to improve her status by marrying Lord Augustus Lorton – in similar vein to Paula Tanqueray in Pinero's *The Second Mrs Tanqueray*. In pursuit of her ambitions she does not hesitate to blackmail Lord Windermere, who gives her an invitation to the evening ball and also pays her large sums of money in order to preserve his wife's illusions about the identity of her mother. The significance of the invitation to the Windermeres' birthday ball can be gauged from the Duchess of Berwick's changed attitude towards Mrs Erlynne. In Act 1 she describes her as:

that horrid woman. She dresses so well, too, which makes it much worse, sets such a dreadful example. Augustus – you know my disreputable brother – such a trial to us all – well, Augustus is completely infatuated about her. It is quite scandalous, for she is absolutely inadmissible into society. Many a woman has a past, but I am told that she has at least a dozen, and that they all fit.[81]

But after the invitation, in Act 2 she says:

Of course, she must be all right if *you* [Lady Windermere] invite her. A most attractive woman, and has such sensible views on life. Told me she entirely disapproved of people marrying more than once ... Can't imagine why people speak against her.[82]

How will such an attractive, but calculating and pragmatic woman, who knows how to manipulate others for her own purposes, act when she sees her own daughter in a situation exactly like her own of twenty years before? Will maternal instinct triumph over social ambition? And how will such a new experience affect the rest of her life? A letter of 23 February 1893 from Wilde to an unknown addressee sheds interesting light on these considerations:

The psychological idea that suggested to me the play is this. A woman who has had a child, but never known the passion of maternity (there are such women), suddenly sees the child she has abandoned falling over a precipice. There wakes in her the maternal feeling – the most terrible of all emotions – a thing that weak

animals and little birds possess. She rushes to rescue, sacrifices herself, does follies
– and the next day she feels 'This passion is too terrible. It wrecks my life . . . I don't
want to be a mother any more.' And so the fourth act is to me the psychological
act, the act that is newest, most true. For which reason, I suppose, the critics say
'There is no necessity for Act IV'.[83]

The clash between Mrs Erlynne's spontaneous emotions as a mother
and her intellectual, almost aesthetic view of life is resolved by a cynically
pragmatic mode of conduct. She contemplates emotional ('heart'[84]) and
moral values ('repentance'[85]) from the standpoint of fashion, and so seeks
to endow them with an aesthetic lack of commitment, in accordance with
her maxim of 'manners before morals'.[86] She keeps an intellectual
distance in order to cover up her emotional involvement, because loss of
social identity would be too high a price to pay for continued experience
of the self. There can be no compromise between social ambitions
('career'[87]) and truth to herself, for she is in a social situation where the
divorced woman cannot discharge her maternal role without damaging
herself and indeed her daughter, too.

This change of attitude, in which with hindsight she reduces her
spontaneous action to the level of a calculated pose, becomes evident
during a long speech she makes in conversation with Lord Windermere:

MRS ERLYNNE (*with a note of irony in her voice*): ... Besides, my dear
Windermere, how on earth could I pose as a mother with a grown-up daughter?
Margaret is twenty-one, and I have never admitted that I am more than
twenty-nine ... Why should I interfere with her illusions? I find it hard enough to
keep my own. I lost one illusion last night. I thought I had no heart. I find I have,
and a heart doesn't suit me, Windermere. Somehow it doesn't go with modern
dress ...it spoils one's career at critical moments.[88]

Mrs Erlynne's change of role – from conventional mother to dandified
detachment – is brought about by a clash between committed emotion
and uncommitted intellect, very similar to the conflict within Lord
Darlington, although his development moves in the opposite direction.
Mrs Erlynne flees from earnest involvement to critical observation,
whereas Darlington switches from the *immoraliste* to the passionate
lover.

If Mrs Erlynne is the sentimental woman with a past, Mrs Cheveley in
An Ideal Husband is the criminal variant. She is the schemer who sets the
whole plot in motion, and her demand that Chiltern support the fraudulent Canal project in exchange for the incriminating letter to Arnheim is
no more to her than a purely commercial matter. Any moral considerations are masked by her cynical pragmatism:

SIR ROBERT CHILTERN: It is infamous, what you propose – infamous!
MRS CHEVELEY: Oh, no! This is the game of life as we all have to play it, Sir
Robert, sooner or later![89]

It is not without irony that the corrupt political climber should be accusing the no less corrupt speculator of infamous conduct. Mrs Cheveley, however, is not too impressed by such a reproach, especially as she had already seen through Chiltern's hypocrisy when he thought he could get away with his pose as an 'English gentleman'.[90] In any case she is highly suspicious of all morality, for she regards it as an 'attitude we adopt towards people whom we personally dislike'[91] – it is a mania which forces everyone 'to pose as a paragon of purity, incorruptibility, and all the other seven deadly virtues'.[92]

Her attitude towards Lady Chiltern is one of complete aversion, but towards Sir Robert she is pitilessly frank – treatment which contrasts ironically with Chiltern's continued efforts to play the role of the ever-honourable politician:

SIR ROBERT CHILTERN: A political life is a noble career!
MRS CHEVELEY: Sometimes. And sometimes it is a clever game, Sir Robert.[93]

The depraved blackmailer and the corrupt politician, being both on the same level of the pragmatic ethic of success, are much closer to each other than Chiltern and his wife. Mrs Cheveley herself points this out:

In this world like meets with like. It is because your husband is himself fraudulent and dishonest that we pair so well together. Between you and him there are chasms. He and I are closer than friends. We are enemies linked together. The same sin binds us.[94]

Mrs Cheveley, however, just like Paula Tanqueray, is trying to break out of her social position as a *déclassée* by marrying into the upper crust of London society. But after her appeal to the emotions of her former fiancé has been rejected, because he now believes that she was only after his money, she once more falls back on the technique of blackmail: 'on the morning of the day you marry me, I will give you Robert Chiltern's letter'.[95] The commercial basis of her conduct – already evident in the attempt to blackmail Chiltern – is all the more repugnant here, since she is trying to exploit the friendship between Goring and Chiltern in order to obtain a promise of marriage. Goring, however, succeeds in fastening the stolen brooch – which can also be used as a bracelet – in such a way that it cannot be unfastened, and thus by threatening to call the police he is able to extract the letter from her. The surprise, rage and despair of the blackmailed blackmailer result in a completely changed appearance. In previous stage directions she has been described as *'looking radiant and much amused'*[96] or *'smiling'*,[97] but now

A curse breaks from her ... she tries again to unclasp the bracelet, but fails ... a paroxysm of rage, with inarticulate sounds ... trembling ... in an agony of

physical terror. Her face is distorted. Her mouth awry. A mask has fallen from her.[98]

In all this there is more than a touch of Victorian melodrama.[99] Such a transformation would be a clear indication to the audience that the character was guilty, while at the same time the twisted, unmasked face would contrast most vividly with the 'white image of all good things'[100] which Chiltern believes to be personified by his wife.

Of these women with a past, Rachel Arbuthnot in *A Woman of No Importance* occupies a special place. She, too, is a woman who has sinned and indeed is always aware of her fault – 'I am a tainted thing.'[101] But in the eyes of the other characters she is 'a thoroughly good woman'.[102] She actively helps the sick and the needy, as well as doing a good deal of church work. Her painful, almost masochistic guilt complex about her dishonourable past drives her into social isolation. She compensates for her lack of outside contact through her intense emotional attachment to her son. The morbid and unrelieved suffering of her way of life, however, is not altogether consistent with the fact that she has never regretted the sin that caused it. She confesses to Gerald:

You are more to me than innocence. I would rather be your mother – oh! much rather! – than have been always pure . . . Oh, don't you see? don't you understand! It is my dishonour that has made you so dear to me. It is my disgrace that has bound you so closely to me. It is the price I paid for you – the price of soul and body – that makes me love you as I do. Oh, don't ask me to do this horrible thing [to marry Illingworth]. Child of my shame, be still the child of my shame!'[103]

This outspoken justification of her situation as an unmarried mother must have seemed to the patrons of the Haymarket Theatre like a very progressive plea for a liberal attitude towards such problems. But the apparent attack on ideal Victorian morality in the form of 'innocence' is somewhat neutralised by its final sentence, as is any emancipative effect. If Wilde had intended to give special emphasis to the unmarried mother's feeling of guilt, what in fact he achieved was an impression of almost sickly sentimentality. Hesketh Pearson in his biography of Wilde recalls that even several years after the first production of the play, this final sentence remained a 'humorous gag'[104] among the actors.

Wilde was simply unable to give convincing expression to the powerful emotions of his serious characters. The originality of his epigrammatic wit stands in stark contrast to the sentimental clichés of his would-be serious dialogue. Mrs Arbuthnot's fear of losing her son to her former seducer Lord Illingworth, and her attempt to make him withdraw his offer to Gerald, yields the following collection of unintended gems:

Don't come now, and rob me of – of all I have in the whole world. You are so rich in other things. Leave me the little vineyard of my life; leave me the walled-in garden and the well of water; the ewe-lamb God sent me, in pity or in wrath, oh! leave me that. George, don't take Gerald from me.[105]

One might expect such bombast from a melodrama, but not from a Wilde comedy.

Mrs Arbuthnot, like Mrs Erlynne, endures a conflict between her social and her personal identity. She has so accepted her role as the unmarried mother – socially stigmatised with such terms as 'disgrace', 'dishonour'[106] and 'sorrow'[107] – that she regards her permanent feeling of guilt as a natural consequence of her lapse. But this conformity to the expectations of the social system in which she lives clashes with her attempt to maintain continuity between her past and her present. She is aware of the paradox of her situation, for she says: '... in the mire of my life I found the pearl of price'[108] (imagery which is once again embarrassingly trite).

Unfortunately, Wilde could only resolve this conflict by resorting to sentimentality. The pathetic cry 'Child of my shame, be still the child of my shame!'[109] is meant to be a defiant assertion of the self and a protest against society's intrusion into the private sphere, but it also implies acceptance of her discredited social position, even though just a few lines earlier it had seemed as if she was questioning the validity of those ethics underlying Victorian disapproval of illegitimacy. Although she vehemently rejects her son's suggestion that she should marry Lord Illingworth, and thus opposes convention, there is a wide gap between her self-assertive refusal to marry this aristocratic *libertin* and her sentimental, masochistic lamentations over the misery of her existence, which may simply be Wilde's concession to the questionable public taste of his time, and can most certainly be regarded as artistically unconvincing. William Archer's judgment of this character offers an apt summary:

In short, the play would have been a much more accomplished work of art if the character of Mrs Arbuthnot had been pitched in another key.[110]

Alongside the dandies, good women, and women with a past there are various minor characters who are not drawn with any great distinction. As we have already seen, these consist mainly of marriageable young ladies, husbands or men trying not to become husbands, and *grandes dames*. While Mrs Erlynne and Mrs Cheveley see marriage as a chance to break into desirable social circles, Lady Agatha Carlisle and Mabel Chiltern regard it as the natural goal of all their up-bringing and, especially, of the so-called season. In all the plays there are examples of vigorous encouragement or – in the case of an unwanted liaison – interference by the parents. These young ladies are either totally subservient to the will of the mother (Lady Agatha in *Lady Windermere's Fan*) or have to overcome the resistance of the brother (Mabel in *An Ideal Husband*). There are certain distinctions, though, in characterisation.

Lady Agatha's stereotype 'Yes, mamma' makes her into a caricature of the mother-dominated daughter, whereas Gwendolen and Cecily in *The Importance of Being Earnest* (which is to be discussed in detail in the next chapter) are far more wilful and thus much more akin to the 'new woman' of the late 1890s. One reason for the daughter's subservience to the mother was the fact that since parents were able to keep their emotional distance from the wooer, they could judge more accurately the commercial and social prospects of the candidate. Gillian Avery describes the Victorian marriage process as follows:

The disposing of a daughter in marriage was one of the important reasons for the yearly move to London, and one of the factors to be taken into consideration when a financially embarrassed landowner wondered if he could afford the expense of keeping on his London house ... The more regular alliances were usually negotiated by the mothers ... Ideally, he should be the wealthy heir of a landed family: a younger son, however well-connected, was undesirable because of his poor prospects and lack of income.[111]

Of the aristocratic *grandes dames* husband-hunting for their daughters, the Duchess of Berwick (*Lady Windermere's Fan*) and Lady Bracknell (*The Importance of Being Earnest*) are amongst Wilde's most successful characters. They combine an imperious temperament and rigid conservatism with the playful posing of the dandy, both of them dominating the stage with their entertaining, superficial but always witty barrage of conversation. Beside them the leading male characters, such as Lord Windermere, Gerald Arbuthnot and Sir Robert Chiltern seem like pale ciphers, so colourless is their dialogue.

As we have already noted, all the comedies are built on the conflict between the public and the private spheres, with the pressure of the former and its demand for conformity tending to dominate the latter with its struggle for personal identity. Accordingly the characterisation tends to lay greater emphasis on social motivation at the expense of psychological. Characters on the whole are not developed by way of their particular inner conflicts and do not act primarily from the need to make personal decisions. When they do act, it is in order to mediate between conventional pressure to conform to the role imposed by their social group, and their own private desire for self-fulfilment, but there is scarcely any individualisation in the tradition of the realistic drama. Instead of emphasising the unmistakable uniqueness of each of his figures, Wilde stresses their linguistic and behavioural adaptation to their social role and hence to each other. His tools are irony, parody and caricature. And when characters do act from personal motives, and protest – consciously or unconsciously – against the powers-that-be (Mrs Erlynne and Mr Arbuthnot are outstanding examples), the presentation degenerates into pathetic sentimentalism.

This lack of individualisation and psychological motivation makes many of the characters seem like interchangeable puppets, with none of the complex and unpredictable vitality of real human beings. Instead we are presented with the mask, but not with the truth behind the mask, and indeed this is one of the ideas that fascinated Wilde. André Gide was one of the first to recognise and document the importance of the mask both for Wilde himself and for his works. He says that the need for some kind of screen stemmed from Wilde's acute awareness of the influence of social proprieties as well as his struggle for 'protection personnelle'.[112] This view is confirmed by a letter Wilde himself wrote to Philip Houghton, probably towards the end of February 1894:

To the world I seem, by intention on my part, a dilettante and dandy merely – it is not wise to show one's heart to the world – and as seriousness of manner is the disguise of the fool, folly in its exquisite modes of triviality and indifference and lack of care is the robe of the wise man. In so vulgar an age as this we all need masks.[113]

It is difficult to determine whether the lack of psychological depth in his characters resulted from his fear of showing his heart (or theirs) to the world – in other words a defence mechanism against society's intrusion into the sensitive privacy of the psyche – or whether the predilection for masks was itself a disguise for a certain creative shallowness – in other words, the mask covered another mask.

Language and dialogue

It is neither characterisation nor plot construction that endows Wildean comedy with its unique flavour, which is derived above all from the language and the dialogue. This is what distinguishes Wilde from all other dramatists, and it constitutes the originality of his contribution to the history of English comedy. The dialogue is mainly in the form of conversations, of which 'das möglichst kluge, geschickte, beziehungs-reiche Setzen der Worte den Hauptzweck ... bildet'[114] [the main aim is the most clever, skilful and evocative composition of the words]. This observation applies first and foremost to the conversations conducted by the dandies. Instead of communicating ideas by elucidating viewpoints, exchanging opinions or discussing problems, they formulate for the sake of formulating. Their reluctance to be pinned to content or to any sort of commitment is both result and evidence of their use of language as an intellectual game. Everything they say can be revoked, or changed at will, for it is all hypothetical. Out of their arbitrary fancies and subjective associations, their partners try to make something general or absolute, and since the utterances are often supremely trivial, the effect is one of total 'Unernst', which makes all argument seem like carping pedantry, but on the other hand conveys a sort of conciliatoriness which could easily collapse in the face of opposition from any firmly held view.

The device most commonly used by the dandies is paradox. Their style of epigrammatic compression gives striking form to their ostentatious dismissal of established current views of reality, and by this means they demonstrate their intellectual superiority, conceal their own opinions, and leave themselves sufficient latitude to escape all commitment. Their systematic deviation from the norm gives linguistic expression to their special social position, and their momentary thwarting of expectations by their reversal of orthodox opinions is the 'démarche fondamentale'[115] of Wilde's thought. He once indicated that he regarded his penchant for this process as the intellectual equivalent to his 'perversity ... in the sphere of passion'.[116]

Wilde's paradoxes contain a wide range of aesthetic qualities, reaching from the mechanical, rhetorical specimen – merely inverting some current phrase – to the critical *aperçu*, uncovering the contrast between appearance and reality and confirming Wilde's statement in *Dorian Gray* that 'the way of paradoxes is the way of truth. To test Reality we must see it on the tight-rope.'[117] But one can have too much of a good thing, and it must be said that the profusion of paradoxes lessens their effect, while the repetition of the same mechanical process of construction leads inevitably to a degree of monotony bemoaned by the critics of all the premières. This may explain why John Drinkwater felt that Wilde's weakness as an artist lay in his 'want of taste',[118] while Mary McCarthy found 'something *outré* in all of Wilde's work':[119]

the trouble with Wilde's wit is that he does not recognize when the party is over. The effect of this effrontery is provoking in both senses; the outrageous has its own monotony, and insolence can only strike once.[120]

One reason for this barrage of wit may be a hedonistic passion for multiplving effects, based on the dubious premise that quantity will increase ɪuality; another is perhaps the idea of gaining success by sheer weight of numbers. There is certainly a marked lack of literary tact and aesthetic economy, and the constant repetition of the same device seems to confirm the limitations already noted in relation to plot and character – namely, a distinct lack of breadth and variety.

The point of the dandy's dialogue is the witty aphorism, and so there is never any real communication with the partner; instead the dialogue is virtual monologue, expressing the narcissism and extreme subjectivism of the dandy. As has already been mentioned, society is his sounding-board, giving him a feeling of superiority but not of community, and his lack of commitment to anything makes all the dialogue seem strangely inconsequential – a mere string of *bons mots* that serve no other purpose than to shine for an instant. 'Weil die Konversation unverbindlich ist, kann sie nicht in Handlung übergehen'[121] [because the conversation carries no obligation, it cannot turn into action]. And this does not apply only to the dandies. When, for instance, Algernon describes the sick Bunbury, one might expect sympathy from Lady Bracknell, whereas instead she responds indignantly: 'I think it is high time that Mr Bunbury made up his mind whether he was going to live or to die.'[122]

The predominant paradox must also be seen in the context of the clash between aesthetic philosophy and the intellectual tradition of Victorianism. The paradox is a manifest attack on tradition, whether it be state institutions or social conventions, and it stresses the role of the dandy or artist as an outsider. It is not, however, merely an aggressive gesture on the part of a non-conformist minority, but it is also a verbal mask which protects the individual from social pressures to conform. The apparently aggressive intention to *épater le bourgeois* in fact conceals the fear of a sensitive individualist whose growing feeling of resignation makes him far less interested in changing other people than in stopping other people from changing him. He appears to be satisfied with the morbid pleasure he gains from the effect of his contradictory existence upon a materialistic and philistine society.

The paradoxical principle underlying Wildean dialogue might best be illustrated by an example from Act 3 of *An Ideal Husband*, in which Lord Goring has a chat with Phipps his butler:

LORD GORING: Got my second buttonhole for me, Phipps?
PHIPPS: Yes, my lord. (*Takes his hat, cane, and cape, and presents new buttonhole on salver.*)
LORD GORING: Rather distinguished thing, Phipps. I am the only person of the smallest importance in London at present who wears a buttonhole.
PHIPPS: Yes, my lord, I have observed that.
LORD GORING: (*taking out old buttonhole*): You see, Phipps, Fashion is what one wears oneself. What is unfashionable is what other people wear.
PHIPPS: Yes, my lord.
LORD GORING: Just as vulgarity is simply the conduct of other people.
PHIPPS: Yes, my lord.
LORD GORING (*putting in new buttonhole*): And falsehoods the truths of other people.
PHIPPS: Yes, my lord.
LORD GORING: Other people are quite dreadful. The only possible society is oneself.
PHIPPS: Yes, my lord.
LORD GORING: To love oneself is the beginning of a lifelong romance, Phipps.[123]

It is all too obvious here that Lord Goring is not conducting a conversation with his servant, but is merely using the presence of the latter as a means of making an impact on the audience. An immediate comic effect is produced by the contrast between the mechanical repetition of 'Yes, my lord' and the varied observations made by Goring. What is basically a monologue is characterised by its sudden changes of direction, as it jumps from the buttonhole at the beginning to self-love at the end. The only continuity is that of association, as one idea leads Goring spontaneously to the next, with each one momentarily appearing to assume some sort of validity. Each statement is an absolute generalisation, with the one concrete detail (the buttonhole) leading to a succession of abstract epigrams. These aphorisms should in no way be taken as evidence of a critical, analytical use of language as it searches for definition or differentiation, for in fact it represents the solo effort of the dandy (subtly orchestrated by the servant's gentle refrain) to establish the profile of his own special existence. In leaping from one standpoint to another, he is illuminating himself rather than any given topic.

The fact that these words are not directed towards the partner, that their content is of no particular relevance to anything, and that they are spoken for the effect of their wit rather than for any other purpose, should not be taken to mean that they have no function in the drama. On the contrary, these very features manifest the dandy's lack of commitment and his gigantic narcissism: 'The only possible society is oneself.' The individual formulates his own world, and sets it off against the world outside, for other people are 'quite dreadful'.

Clearly, then, the dandy dialogues are not meant to develop or exchange ideas, but are designed to disguise and to shock. Effect is everything. The dislocation between language and character is also an indication of the discrepancy between personal identity and social role. Since content is generally irrelevant, what matters is the form in which the statement is designed to meet the demands of the situation. A typical example of the meaninglessness of content as opposed to the efficacy of form is the reception for Lady Windermere's birthday guests:

DUMBY: Good evening, Lady Stutfield. I suppose this will be the last ball of the season?
LADY STUTFIELD: I suppose so, Mr Dumby. It's been a delightful season, hasn't it?
DUMBY: Quite delightful! Good evening, Duchess. I suppose this will be the last ball of the season?
DUCHESS OF BERWICK: I suppose so, Mr Dumby. It has been a very dull season, hasn't it?
DUMBY: Dreadfully dull! Dreadfully dull!
MRS COWPER-COWPER: Good evening, Mr Dumby. I suppose this will be the last ball of the season?
DUMBY: Oh, I think not. There'll probably be two more.[124]

The single stereotype question, the various contradictory answers, and the questioner's adaptation of his own reaction to the direction of the answer guarantees that there will be no social communication here; gaps are maintained and not bridged, so that they themselves become an expression of the lack of communication. There is something very akin here to the dialogue of absurd drama. Wilde also uses the mechanical questions and the protean reactions of Dumby as a means of criticism, implicitly denouncing the predominance of manners over content, and the sheer hollowness of all these set formulae. For parody is by its nature implied criticism. Wilde entertains society by mocking it, although he never explicitly denigrates its norms by way of his characters' actions. Language as a means of reproducing reality reproduces nothing here but the superficial façade of a society that uses intellectual in-breeding to acquire its exclusivity. This artificial, almost ritualised conversation is the exaggerated expression of an urbane culture whose refinement is at one and the same time the mask and the symbol of its decadence.

The witty dialogue of the snobbish leisure class is the hallmark of the Wildean comedy, but its originality is counter-balanced by the cliché-ridden speeches in which his characters reveal their genuine emotions. Lord Darlington's passionate declaration of love in Act 2 of *Lady Windermere's Fan*, when he melodramatically offers her his life, or Mrs Arbuthnot's fear of losing her son to Lord Illingworth – these are passages that positively creak with worn-out phrases and images that seem all the more incongruous against the background of the dandies' wit. Wilde's inability to find convincing language that would convey genuine emotion allies itself somewhat unhappily with his apparent adherence to the tradition of the nineteenth-century medodrama. And yet from a critical standpoint there is a strange sort of consistency to be discerned between these two different facets of the Wildean comedy: just as the dandy's lack of commitment leads to cynical insincerity, so too does the sentimentality of the serious characters emerge as a pose – sentiment as a substitute for emotion. The split between emotion and intellect is typical of Wilde himself. It is as if the intellect had been fostered at the expense of the heart, and yet underneath the heart still struggles to make its presence felt: the intellectual *provocateur* and *immoraliste* is little more than a mask for the middle-class moralist.

There are many examples of these serious dialogues which, unlike those of the dandies, are directly relevant to the plot. They include conversations between Lord and Lady Windermere at the beginning of Act 4, Mrs Arbuthnot and her son Gerald towards the end of Act 3, Sir Robert Chiltern and Mrs Cheveley in Act 1, Sir Robert and Lord Goring, Mrs Cheveley and Lady Chiltern, and Sir Robert and Lady Chiltern in Act 2 of *An Ideal Husband*. These dialogues comprise open confrontation, and what Armin Geraths, in an interpretation of *Lady Windermere's Fan*, describes as 'Dissoziierung von Sprache und Charakter' [dissociation of language and character] as 'zentrales Prinzip in [der] Komödiendichtung Wildes'[125] [central principle in Wilde's comic writing] does not apply here. That which Sir Robert calls nebulously 'affair' and 'speculation' is a straightforward 'swindle' in Mrs Cheveley's language, to which she adds: 'Let us call things by their proper names.'[126] And when Sir Robert speaks of the Stock Exchange speculator Arnheim as 'A man of culture, charm, and distinction', thus seeking to give an aesthetic gloss to the latter's dubious business dealings, the dandy Goring responds with a somewhat unexpected moral tone: 'Damned scoundrel!'[127]

So far we have looked at two forms of dialogue: the cheerful, uncommitted witticisms of the dandies, ranging from pure *étalage de l'esprit* to aphoristic social parody, and the serious conversations aimed at direct communication or confrontation of a problem. Between these two there is another, special form of 'hidden' dialogue, in which one partner, under cover of a hypothetical situation or a general question, seeks to find out the other's attitude to a situation of which the audience is aware though the other character is not. An example is the following piece of dialogue between Mrs Cheveley and Lady Chiltern:

MRS CHEVELEY: I see that after all these years you have not changed a bit, Gertrude.
LADY CHILTERN: I never change.
MRS CHEVELEY (*elevating her eyebrows*): Then life has taught you nothing?
LADY CHILTERN: It has taught me that a person who has once been guilty of a dishonest and dishonourable action may be guilty of it a second time, and should be shunned.
MRS CHEVELEY: Would you apply that rule to every one?
LADY CHILTERN: Yes, to every one, without exception.[128]

The irony of this conversation lies in the fact that Lady Chiltern commits herself to a generalised moral precept which, if applied to her own husband, would have to result in her leaving him. The irony is compounded by her intending these utterances as a dig at Mrs Cheveley herself.

This hidden dialogue, which is particularly prevalent in conversations between the dandies and the good women, serves primarily as a hypothetical cover under which the speaker tests his or her partner's reaction without any personal commitment to the viewpoint represented. Such tactics are particularly evident in the passage in which Lord Darlington offers Lady Windermere his friendship. This innocent word camouflages a far from innocent purpose:

LORD DARLINGTON (*after a slight hesitation*): ... I think we might be great friends. Let us be great friends.[129]

His real intentions are revealed explicitly in Act 2:

LORD DARLINGTON: Between men and women there is no friendship possible. There is passion, enmity, worship, love but no friendship. I love you.[130]

In Act 1, however, it is left to the partner to speculate on whether or not the words refer to extra-marital relations. Darlington is not committed, though his intentions are sufficiently open for him to have to withdraw rather swiftly when challenged. Lady Windermere appears to see through his words, and asks: 'Why do you say that?' in order to solidify the link between language and meaning, whereupon Darlington skilfully parries the blow with a generalisation: 'Oh! – we all want friends at times.'[131] In this way he defuses the situation by retreating once more into non-commitment.

The experimental nature of Darlington's dialogue is also revealed in the second section of this conversation, which he introduces with a fictitious example:

LORD DARLINGTON (*still seated*): Do you think – of course I am only putting an imaginary instance – do you think that in the case of a young married couple, say about two years married, if the husband suddenly becomes the intimate friend of a woman of – well, more than doubtful character – is always calling upon her, lunching with her, and probably paying her bills – do you think that the wife should not console herself?
LADY WINDERMERE (*frowning*): Console herself?
LORD DARLINGTON: Yes, I think she should – I think she has the right.
LADY WINDERMERE: Because the husband is vile – should the wife be vile also?
LORD DARLINGTON: Vileness is a terrible word, Lady Windermere.
LADY WINDERMERE: It is a terrible thing, Lord Darlington.[132]

With his 'imaginary instance', which in fact is directly relevant to Lady Windermere and is later to take on urgent reality, Lord Darlington is trying to pin Lady Windermere down to a firm decision on which he can rely. Technically the casual remark concerning a couple 'about two years married' is a skilful anticipation of the supposed infidelity of Lord Windermere. But when Lady Windermere tries to steer the conversation into the deeper waters of tit-for-tat morality, Darlington again wriggles away from commitment by switching to a comparatively harmless level: he attacks the terms she uses on aesthetic grounds: 'Vileness is a terrible word.'

This technique of concealment, mainly designed to serve the tactical purposes of the dandy, of whose linguistic arsenal it is a characteristic weapon, also shows the efficacy of certain social norms which make it impossible to speak directly of private, intimate matters. When eventually Lord Darlington does violate the conventions in Act 2, with his explicit declaration of his love for Lady Windermere, he is rejected with the very revealing statement: 'I am afraid of being myself.'[133] A little later, as a consequence of this rejection, he resolves to leave the country for a few years. It is a situation somewhat reminiscent of *The Second Mrs Tanqueray* (1893): Aubrey Tanqueray's bold but, as it turns out, misguided liaison with the fallen woman Paula leads to a similar outcome: he withdraws to his country estate, where he lives as a social recluse.

It is typical of the language of Lord Darlington and various other Wildean characters that there is a 'Dominanz des öffentlichen Sprachcodes über das individuelle Ausdrucksverlangen'[134] [dominance of the public language code over the individual desire for expression]. This observation of Paul Goetsch applies to the dialogue conventions of the realistic drama, but with certain reservations it is equally true of Wilde's comedies. Conformity to the public code, and suppression of personal expression, are not total, however, as is shown by the example of the Darlington scenes quoted; in fact the alternation of techniques – non-commitment, hidden dialogue, witty aphorisms, and direct expression – is in itself a manifestation of the continual search for compromise, as the characters find themselves caught between the pressure to conform to the demands of a particular section of society and the need to consolidate their own individuality. The language, like the plots, arises from the conflict between public and private life.

Social and moral criticism

The dominance of the dialogue and the paucity of the action in these plays make for largely undramatic drama, a fact that is linked closely to a change of function as regards the dialogues that are purely conversational. Instead of advancing the plot, they thematise it, focusing upon topics that are only of general relevance to the tale being told, for example, the relationship between individual and society, the battle of the sexes, marriage and family, religion and upbringing, etc. With a few exceptions there is no detailed discussion of these topics; for the most part they are simply glanced at by way of the odd trenchant remark, but the accumulation of such remarks certainly results in a coherent overall picture. Eric Bentley is right to claim that 'What begins as a prank ends as a criticism of life. What begins as intellectual high-kicking ends as intellectual sharp-shooting.'[135]

The attitude of the characters towards the society they live in – basically London's leisure class, consisting of aristocrats and the rich bourgeoisie – is ambivalent. Lord Illingworth regards it as 'a necessary thing',[136] whereas the aged Lord Caversham sees London society as 'a lot of damned nobodies talking about nothing',[137] a view confirmed with equal vigour by Mabel Chiltern: 'It is entirely composed now of beautiful idiots and brilliant lunatics.'[138] Lady Markby's enquiry after the Duke of Marlborough's health, 'Brain still weak, I suppose?'[139] and her observation that 'the season as it goes on produces a kind of softening of the brain'[140] help to conjure up a very clear picture of the decadence of the 'barbarians', whose downfall had already been prophesied many years before by Matthew Arnold.

The sharpest protest against contemporary society is delivered by Hester Worsley in Act 2 of *A Woman of No Importance*:

You rich people in England, you don't know how you are living. How could you know? You shut out from your society the gentle and the good. You laugh at the simple and the pure. Living, as you all do, on others and by them, you sneer at self-sacrifice, and if you throw bread to the poor, it is merely to keep them quiet for a season. With all your pomp and wealth and art you don't know how to live – you don't even know that. You love the beauty that you can see and touch and handle, the beauty that you can destroy, and do destroy, but of the unseen beauty of life, of the unseen beauty of a higher life, you know nothing. You have lost life's secret. Oh, your English society seems to me shallow, selfish, foolish. It has blinded its eyes, and stopped its ears. It lies like a leper in purple. It sits like a dead thing smeared with gold. It is all wrong, all wrong.[141]

This vehement tirade by the idealistic Hester, condemning the exploitative and parasitic nature of society, offers a vivid portrait of the idle, self-centred and ultimately sterile upper classes. But it does not end with a call for change. The climax is a moral judgment. Hester does not view society from the perspective of social contrasts which must be reduced or eradicated, but from that of morality which revolts against the decadence of the leisure class. This typifies the social criticism in all the plays – first and foremost it is moral, and its prime concern is with the question 'how to live?'

The importance of wealth and property, together with the increasing commercialisation of life and the subservience of morality to business form a central motif in the plot of *An Ideal Husband* and a significant theme in *Lady Windermere's Fan*. Lord Windermere uses his financial resources to preserve his wife's social standing and her personal illusions about the moral integrity of her supposedly dead mother, while Mrs Erlynne uses his money to buy her way into London society. She even tries to increase her chances in the marriage market by extortionate demands for a yearly pension of £2,500, disguised as an inheritance from fictitious relatives. Lady Windermere is therefore quite right to characterise Mrs Erlynne as one of those women who is 'bought and sold'.[142]

The commercial nature of human relations is also brought out by

various puns connected with the verb 'to pay', which in addition to its
financial associations is used socially in the expression 'paying a compliment'. This is made very clear by Lord Darlington's word-juggling in
conversation with Lady Windermere:

LADY WINDERMERE: Well, you kept paying me elaborate compliments the
whole evening.
LORD DARLINGTON (*smiling*): Ah, nowadays we are all of us so hard up, that
the only pleasant things to pay *are* compliments. They're the only things we *can*
pay.[143]

Mrs Erlynne's appeal to her daughter to keep quiet about the visit to
Darlington's rooms is also phrased in commercial terms:

MRS ERLYNNE: ... You say you owe me something?
LADY WINDERMERE: I owe you everything.
MRS ERLYNNE: Then pay your debt by silence. That is the only way in which it
can be paid.[144]

Lord Darlington and Dumby both allude to the mercenary nature of
women,[145] while Lady Berwick does not consider 'younger sons'[146] to be
suitable candidates for the hand of her somewhat simple daughter Agatha,
who seems incapable of any response other than 'Yes, mamma.' Lady
Berwick's success in marrying Agatha off to the rich Australian Mr
Hopper seems to confirm Lady Windermere's disillusioned tirade in Act 1
against modern pragmatism: 'Nowadays people seem to look on life as a
speculation.'[147]

   Particular areas for moral criticism are the relations between the sexes,
marriage, and the family. The paradoxical reversal of conventional
attitudes draws the audience's attention to the private realities behind the
public façades. Lady Plymdale, for instance, regards public harmony
between marriage partners as a possible indication of private friction:

LADY PLYMDALE: ... It's most dangerous nowadays for a husband to pay any
attention to his wife in public. It always makes people think that he beats her when
they're alone.[148]

In *A Woman of No Importance* Mrs Allonby defines the ideal husband as
follows:

He [the ideal husband] should persistently compromise us in public, and treat us
with absolute respect when we are alone. And yet he should be always ready to
have a perfectly terrible scene, whenever we want one, and to become miserable,
absolutely miserable, at a moment's notice, and to overwhelm us with just
reproaches in less than twenty minutes, and to be positively violent at the end of
half an hour, and to leave us for ever at a quarter to eight, when we have to go and
dress for dinner. And when, after that, one has seen him for really the last time,
and he has refused to take back the little things he has given one, and promised
never to communicate with one again, or to write one any foolish letters, he should

be perfectly broken-hearted, and telegraph to one all day long, and send one little notes every half-hour by a private hansom, and dine quite alone at the club, so that every one should know how unhappy he was.[149]

The basic comic situation that makes this speech so effective is the reversal of the traditional Victorian roles of man and woman. The 'ideal husband' is caricatured as a sort of plaything at the mercy of his wife's every whim. This runs contrary to all nineteenth-century expectations, and the comic effect is enhanced by the exaggeration implicit in such adverbs as 'persistently', 'always', 'perfectly' and 'absolutely'.

This caricature of the 'ideal husband' as a puppet – paralleled by Lady Caroline's attitude towards her husband, Sir John – illustrates the fact that relations between dialogue and plot are not strictly functional but, as we have pointed out, also thematic. The conversation circles round a variety of topics which are closely connected with the plot. The thematic framework of this particular play is formed by the relationship between the sexes, and the focal point is double standards of morality. When Gerald urges his mother to marry Lord Illingworth in order to comply with convention, Mrs Arbuthnot bitterly rejects the demand:

MRS ARBUTHNOT: I will not. You talk of atonement for a wrong done. What atonement can be made to me? There is no atonement possible. I am disgraced; he is not. That is all. It is the usual history of a man and a woman as it usually happens, as it always happens. And the ending is the ordinary ending. The woman suffers. The man goes free.[150]

This last lament is fully confirmed by the social history of women in the nineteenth century.

The social inequality of men and women was evident not only from the limited number of professions open to women – that of domestic servant was by far the most popular – but also from their different status within marriage. Furthermore, women were supposedly inferior intellectually: 'You women live by your emotions and for them'[151] says Lord Illingworth, whereas men are possessed of 'gigantic intellects'.[152] It was a German, Paul Julius Möbius, who towards the end of the nineteenth century actually tried to explain this intellectual inferiority physiologically:

[Es] ist ... nachgewiesen, daß für das geistige Leben ausserordentlich wichtige Gehirntheile, die Windungen des Stirn- und Schläfenlappens, beim Weibe schlechter entwickelt sind als beim Manne und daß dieser Unterschied schon bei der Geburt besteht.[153]

[[It] has been ... proved that parts of the brain which are extraordinarily important for the intellectual life, the convolutions of the frontal and temporal lobes, are less developed in women than in men, and that this difference is already in existence at birth].

Women were brought up in complete ignorance of sex and to believe in the superiority of men, the object of the whole exercise being future marriage, with the character of the husband often far less relevant than his social status or the institution of marriage itself. Blanche, a character in Augier's *Les Fourchambault*, puts the situation in a nutshell: 'Le mariage étant la seule carrière des demoiselles, la personne du mari importe moins que son état dans le monde'[154] [marriage being the only career for single women, the person of the husband is less important than his status in the world]. The idealisation of marriage and of pre-marital chastity was counterbalanced by scorn for the fallen woman, who was rejected by society and often could escape only through prostitution or suicide. Mrs Arbuthnot accuses Lord Illingworth of having had 'a life of joy, and pleasure, and success'[155] while she has had to endure nothing but sorrow. Hester Worsley expresses her bitterness at these same double standards:

HESTER: Lord Henry Weston! I remember him, Lady Hunstanton. A man with a hideous smile and a hideous past. He is asked everywhere. No dinner-party is complete without him. What of those whose ruin is due to him? They are outcasts. They are nameless. If you met them in the street you would turn your head away. I don't complain of their punishment. Let all women who have sinned be punished.[156]

Audiences, theatres and premières

Hester Worsley's tirade is the exception rather than the rule, and for the most part Wilde's social criticism remains mild in tone. This fact must be viewed in conjunction with the type of audience he was writing for. This was no longer a 'côterie [sic] of courtiers and courtesans'[157] as in the time of the Restoration, but the St James's audience would still have contained many aristocrats as well as well-known politicians, artists, literati and 'innumerable notables in every walk of life'.[158] The same applied to other theatres. The audience at an Irving première in the Lyceum, for instance, included the Prince and Princess of Wales, the Right Hon. W. E. Gladstone, Lord Rosebery, the Duke of Beaufort, A. C. Swinburne, James Whistler, Wilkie Collins etc.[159] In an appreciation of George Alexander, Hesketh Pearson described the London theatre and its audiences as follows:

For the most part, his [George Alexander's] theatre mirrored to absolute perfection the people who patronized its stalls. He knew, none better, that the stalls enjoyed the gilded pill of romance about themselves, and that the gallery loved to see the stalls swallow it. No real medicine was possible, for his audiences wouldn't pay to be choked or for the privilege of having a nasty taste in the mouth. The light parts had to be charmingly playful, the serious parts had to be pleasantly sentimental, and the plot had to savour of scandal without being in any way truthfully objectionable... The working classes were seldom, if ever, introduced. Significant social problems were carefully avoided. It was the drama of the genteel – the Apotheosis of the Butterfly.[160]

In his choice and production of plays, Alexander adhered to a principle which Pearson describes as 'correct riskiness',[161] and the expression applies equally well to Wilde's dramatic writing. It simply means that the audience would only accept a certain degree of moral and social criticism within tightly drawn boundaries; if these were exceeded, the audience would cease to enjoy the theatre and would lose interest in it.

The characters and plots of Wilde's plays are drawn to conform to this situation. In the elegant, witty, épater-le-bourgeois dandy, the equally idle though far less witty men about town that sat in Wilde's audience would see themselves reflected. Similarly, those pillars of female respectability, the 'good women', confirmed the codes with which a broad, property-orientated section of the audience would identify – an audience which 'was still to a large degree woman-dominated – if not in actual numbers, at least in the matter of manners'.[162] Thus Wilde was able to satisfy the requirements of his audiences on two levels: the smart set enjoyed the elegance and luxury, as did the snobbish middle classes who were always partial to the glamour of great names, while characters such as Lord Illingworth confirmed their prejudices about the decadence of the aristocracy and about their own moral superiority. At the same time the aristocratic Establishment enjoyed the dismissal of norms adhered to by the middle class, which towards the end of the nineteenth century was bidding to take the place of the nobility. Even when the plays do launch attacks on the 'rich people in England', as in Hester Worsley's tirade, the basis of the contemporary social order is never seriously questioned, for it is only the way of life of these rich people that is criticised. Wilde clearly had a sure instinct as to the proportions of propriety and provocation that would satisfy his respectable public, both by confirming their values and also by shocking them with non-conformist attitudes that would keep the good women, ideal husbands and well-behaved daughters from getting bored. The somewhat arrogant comment he made on *A Woman of No Importance* shows that he was not altogether happy about the effect of his play on London audiences:

People love a wicked aristocrat who seduces a virtuous maiden, and they love a virtuous maiden for being seduced by a wicked aristocrat. I have given them what they like, so that they may learn to appreciate what I like to give them.[163]

Of course, not every London theatre boasted audiences drawn from the upper middle class and the aristocracy, along with the Prince of Wales and his retinue of 'first-nighters'.[164] The social east–west divide was also reflected in the theatres. Anyone, for instance, who enjoyed productions at the Britannia Public House in Wapping, whose licence was withdrawn in 1872 'for harbouring questionable characters',[165] or at the Mile End Empire in Stepney, would almost certainly never have set foot in Covent Garden or the Theatre Royal, Drury Lane. An Act for Regulating Theatres, passed in 1843, gave performing rights to smaller theatres as well, and although this certainly livened up the theatre scene in London, the tone-setting social and cultural section of society still concentrated its attention on a few famous West End establishments. In the 1890s these included the two theatres where Wilde's plays were first produced: the St James's Theatre (*Lady Windermere's Fan* and *The Importance of Being Earnest*) and the Haymarket, Theatre Royal (*A Woman of No Importance* and *An Ideal Husband*). At the time they were both run by notable actor-managers: George Alexander and Herbert Beerbohm Tree.

The St James's 'theatre of distinction'[166] was opened in 1835 (and torn down in 1957) in King Street, Piccadilly, and it was taken over in February 1891 by George Alexander, who in a very short time had raised it 'from comparative obscurity to as fashionable a theatre as could be found anywhere'.[167] Milestones along this road to success included, apart from Wilde's plays, Haddon Chambers's *The Idler* (1891), Pinero's *The Second Mrs Tanqueray* (1893), and H. A. Jones's *The Masqueraders* (1894), while Henry James's *Guy Domville* (1895) proved to be a failure. W. Macqueen-Pope in his history of the theatre describes its atmosphere as follows:

In truth, the St James's became an aristocrat among theatres, and reflected in its heyday – the late Victorian and Edwardian epoch – all that was best in the life of this country. Elegant and rich people filled its stalls, its dress circle and its two boxes. People of substance but less social standing booked for the upper circle, and the rest of the playgoers made for the pit and the gallery.[168]

This, then, was the setting for Wilde's comeback after his failures with *Vera* and *The Duchess of Padua*. It is scarcely surprising that there was a degree of friction between Alexander, the experienced practitioner, and Wilde, the equally self-assured but far less experienced author. During rehearsals of *Lady Windermere's Fan* they disagreed on the question of when Mrs Erlynne's true identity should be revealed. Wilde wanted it to take place in Act 4, but in a letter written in mid February 1892 Alexander pleaded for an earlier revelation at the end of Act 2. Initially Wilde refused to make the change. The première took place on 20 February 1892, and one year later, on 6 February 1893, the first American performance was given at Palmer's Theatre, New York. It was published on 9 November 1893 by Elkin Mathews & John Lane, with a cover design by C. H. Shannon, in a print of 500 copies at 7s 6d and 50 large-format copies at 15s.

The play was a huge success.[169] The ovation from the first-night audience brought Wilde on stage, and with a smile on his face and a cigarette in his hand he proceeded to make a little speech, the text of which was written down by a member of the theatre staff and was later to arouse the displeasure of the critics:

'Ladies and Gentlemen: I have enjoyed this evening *immensely*. The actors have given us a *charming* rendering of a *delightful* play, and your appreciation has been *most* intelligent. I congratulate you on the *great* success of your performance, which persuades me that you think *almost* as highly of the play as I do myself.'[170]

The play ran continuously from 20 February 1892 till 29 July, then went on tour until 31 October, after which it returned to London until 3 December. It was replaced by R. C. Carton's *Liberty Hall*. A week after the première, on 27 February 1892, a letter appeared in the *St James's Gazette* in which Wilde rejected the insinuation that he had acted upon suggestions and criticisms from various newspapers and had made changes in his play, including an earlier revelation of Mrs Erlynne's identity.[171] Wilde said that he had taken his decision as a result of recommendations made by friends whom he had invited to a little first-night party. Clearly Wilde decided very soon after the première to make the change which George Alexander had suggested but which just a few days previously he had vehemently rejected in a letter. Then he had expressed the view that an earlier revelation would reduce the dramatic effectiveness of Act 3, especially as the audience would thus know that the self-sacrifice was being made by Lady Windermere's mother. This would destroy an important element of surprise, since such a sacrifice would not be unexpected on the part of a mother. He also thought that a premature identification would ruin the last act:

the chief merit of my last act is to me the fact that it does not contain, as most plays do, the explanation of what the audience knows already, but that it is the sudden explanation of what the audience desires to know, followed immediately by the revelation of a character as yet untouched by literature.[172]

This dispute over the single detail of an earlier or later disclosure of Mrs Erlynne's identity put a strain on relations between the author and the director. These were not improved by an article in *The Daily Telegraph* which appeared on the day of the première under the title 'Puppets and Actors', in which Wilde discussed the relationship between text, performance and production as follows:

the actable value of a play has nothing whatsoever to do with its value as a work of art ... the personality of the actor is often a source of danger in the perfect presentation of a work of art. It may distort. It may lead astray. It may be a discord in the tone or symphony. For anybody can act ... There are many advantages in puppets. They never argue. They have no crude views about art ... They recognise the presiding intellect of the dramatist.[173]

In the context of his dispute with George Alexander, Wilde appears to have forced himself into the virtually untenable position of separating the two major components of theatrical presentation: text and performance, with all his weight thrown on the side of text. This would seem to be borne out by the final sentences of the passage quoted.

The critics greeted the play as 'clever and entertaining',[174] 'a pleasure',[175] and a 'good play',[176] although there were also doubts about the author's artistic talents.[177] There was general criticism of the plot, from accusations of 'staleness',[178] and 'weatherworn'[179] to the laconic statement that 'the plot does not matter'.[180] There were even some critics who questioned whether this really was a theatre play at all.[181] The anonymous critic in The Westminster Review considered it very unlikely that a woman like Lady Windermere could possibly leave her husband simply because of the chatter of an old gossip (the Duchess of Berwick). It was also extremely improbable that Lord Windermere would have allowed relations with his wife to reach such a critical stage without taking her into his confidence much sooner. But much praise was heaped on the quality of the dialogue – 'exquisitely funny' – with particular emphasis on its epigrammatic style and on the pointed social criticism.[182] Some critics, however, noted that in fact all the characters talked like Wilde himself: 'in this Cloud-Cuckoo-Town of Mr Wilde's, all its inhabitants [are] equally cynical, equally paradoxical, equally epigrammatic'.[183]

Despite the reservations, Wilde's first drawing-room comedy was a resounding success, not least financially, since after deducting all costs George Alexander was able to claim a clear profit of £5,570 0s 11d.[184] Wilde needed the royalties[185] urgently to finance his expensive life style, and it was essential for him to retain the public's interest by means of further plays. And so in quick succession there followed A Woman of No Importance and An Ideal Husband, which were both performed at the famous Haymarket, Theatre Royal (founded in 1720), which alongside Drury Lane was one of the oldest theatres in London and has survived, after several renovations, right up to the present day.[186] Like George Alexander at the St James's, Herbert Beerbohm Tree, half-brother of the incomparable Max, had made the theatre immensely successful during the 1890s. He had taken it over from the Bancrofts in 1887. The history of the Haymarket reflects all the changes in stage technique and production styles that took place between the middle and the end of the century: the proscenium gave way to the picture-frame stage, there were improvements in off-stage technology, productions became more realistic, the director gained in importance, and the repertoire system combined with that of the long run. In addition to Shakespeare – such as the famous production of The Merry Wives of Windsor (1889) in historically authentic costumes and with lavish sets – Beerbohm Tree produced contemporary plays by Haddon Chambers, H. A. Jones and Sidney

Grundy. His greatest success was undoubtedly *Trilby* (1895), a dramatisation of the Du Maurier novel, with the then virtually unknown
Dorothea Baird in the main part and himself playing the role of Svengali.
The audience, coming through the imposing Corinthian portico and
entering this 'theatre of perfection',[187] was much the same as that which
frequented the St James's, though it was if anything a touch more
exclusive. W. Macqueen-Pope describes this noble temple of the muses as
follows:

Under Tree, the Haymarket became the smartest theatre in London in every sense
of the word. It was not only the so-called 'Smart Set' who went there, for the
theatre became the centre of the social world of London, in so far as any theatre
can, and remained so until Tree opened His Majesty's. His audiences were as
brilliant as his plays ... Great people came to see a great man in a great
production. The theatre was an aristocrat, and the audiences of the Haymarket,
under Tree, were aristocratic playgoers from the gallery downwards. It is
something which will never again be seen.[188]

There could scarcely have been a more appropriate theatre for the plays
of an author who was portraying and satirising so perfectly the social life
of the 'smart set'. When Beerbohm Tree suggested to Wilde that he should
write something for the Haymarket, he jumped at the opportunity, and in
the summer of 1892 began work on a play which bore the provisional title
of *Mrs Arbuthnot*. It received its première on 19 April 1893, and apart
from a break of three nights ran until 16 August.[189] The audience's
enthusiastic response was accompanied by shouts for the author, from
whom no doubt they were expecting an original speech such as he had
delivered after the première of *Lady Windermere's Fan*. The author,
however, merely replied laconically from his box: 'Ladies and Gentlemen,
I regret to inform you that Mr Oscar Wilde is not in the house.'[190] The
main characters were played by Beerbohm Tree as Lord Illingworth, Mrs
Bernard Beere as Mrs Arbuthnot, and Fred Terry as Gerald Arbuthnot, a
part which Wilde had originally wanted to be played by his friend Sydney
Barraclough. Rose Coghlan arranged the American première at the Fifth
Avenue Theatre in New York, and it took place on 11 December 1893;[191]
the first German production was on 4 September 1903 at the Neues
Theater in Berlin.

Reviews were similar to those of *Lady Windermere's Fan*, along the
lines used by the anonymous critic of the *Saturday Review*: 'deficient ... in
action ... redundant in idle talk'.[192] There was universal praise for the
wit, the brilliant dialogue, and Wilde's intellectual glitter, but the critics
found his repetitive use of the same devices – paradox and epigram –
ultimately wearisome and monotonous. The lack of artistic variety led to
a 'monotony of cleverness',[193] as an anonymous critic wrote in an open
letter to Wilde, signed 'The Candid Friend'.

A few months after the première of *A Woman of No Importance*, Wilde began work on *An Ideal Husband*. The long letter which Wilde wrote in 1897 from Reading Gaol to Lord Alfred Douglas, and which was later to be given the title *De Profundis*, reveals that in September 1893 he had already finished Act 1 within a week.[194] At this time he used to work in a flat that he had rented in St James's Place in order to concentrate fully on the play. His lack of success in this respect is clear from the reproaches he levels against Douglas for constantly distracting him from his work. Wilde finally succeeded in getting Bosie's mother to persuade her son to leave England early in December on a protracted trip abroad. Only then could Wilde get down to writing the remaining three acts.[195]

The work must have dragged on until late January 1894, since a letter Wilde wrote to Lewis Waller in mid January indicates that he had finished the first three acts and had started on the fourth. He wanted the script to be ready by mid March, but a typescript from 'Mrs Marshall's typing agency' bears the date of 19 February 1894,[196] which clearly denotes that he finished ahead of his own schedule. In fact he sent a copy of the play to the artist Philip Houghton at the end of February.[197]

John Hare, another London actor-manager who had already rejected Pinero's *The Second Mrs Tanqueray*, turned the play down, and it was finally given its première on 3 January 1895 at the Haymarket Theatre, with Lewis Waller as Sir Robert Chiltern, Julia Neilson as Lady Chiltern, Florence West as Mrs Cheveley, and Charles Hawtrey as Lord Goring. It ran continuously for 111 performances, and was taken off on 6 April, the day after Wilde's arrest and subsequent imprisonment in Holloway. There was, however, no immediate connection between the two events, since Beerbohm Tree needed the theatre for his presentation of *John A'Dreams*.[198] Wilde's play was transferred to the Criterion, where it ran from 13 April to 27 April before it was finally taken off. This coincided with the beginning of Wilde's trial, which opened on 26 April in accordance with Paragraph 11 of the Criminal Amendment Act of 1885.

Two years after the première, on 30 October 1897, Wilde wrote to his friend Robert Ross that he had asked Lewis Waller to give a copy of the play to the publisher Smithers, as the original had been lost during the auction of Wilde's property.[199] Smithers, who also published the *Ballad of Reading Gaol*, took out copyright on 27 April 1899.[200] The play was published in the same year with a cover designed by Charles H. Shannon. On 10 May 1914 George Alexander risked a new production of *An Ideal Husband*, but it was less successful and had to be taken off on 27 July, having lost nearly £2,000.[201]

This failure fulfilled a forecast made by Arthur B. Walkley in his review of the première: 'the brilliant success is infinitely outweighed by the ostensible failure, not merely in actual achievement, but in significance, in promise for the future'.[202] Nine of the remaining reviews, however, indicate that a full house greeted the première with every sign of success.[203] The critics all agreed that the play was 'highly entertaining',[204] 'diverting',[205] and 'unapproachably playful'.[206] This effect was attributed above all to the device of the paradox, which both Arthur B. Walkley and Clement Scott called a 'trick'.[207]

Nearly all the critics, however, point to certain weaknesses in the play. Archer criticises the characterisation of Sir Robert Chiltern, the epigrammatic overloading of the dialogue, and the disproportionate amount of 'inferior chatter'.[208] Shaw finds it incomprehensible that Mrs Cheveley knocks over a chair when she is in Lord Goring's rooms,[209] and the *Athenaeum* critic bemoans the fact that a treacherous rogue like Sir Robert ends up with a post in the Cabinet.[210] Even though most of them confirm that the première was a success, their final judgment is predominantly negative: 'unquestionably poor' (Wells), 'poor, sterile, vulgar' (Walkley), 'helpless, crude, clumsy, feeble, vulgar' (Henry James). The American novelist and critic William Dean Howells seems to be the only one whose praise is totally unqualified; he calls the play 'not only an excellent piece of art, but all [*sic*] excellent piece of sense'.[211]

Generally speaking, the critics found themselves in a position not dissimilar to that of neo-classical Shakespeare critics, who could not deny the success of Shakespeare's plays but felt obliged to apply their own criteria, according to which certain artistic elements had to be designated as 'faults'. George Bernard Shaw, in his discussion of the première, pinpoints this dilemma of the critic from his own standpoint as a sort of sympathiser *malgré lui*:

They [the critics] laugh angrily at his [Wilde's] epigrams, like a child who is coaxed into being amused in the very act of setting up a yell of rage and agony.[212]

Traditions of form and content

Many critics complained not only about the conveyer-belt production methods of 'Oscar Wilde Epigram and Paradox Company, Limited',[213] but also about the fact that the author obviously had no scruples as regards re-using passages from his own earlier works. The extent of his 'self-plagiarism' has never been fully recognised. A textual comparison between *The Picture of Dorian Gray* and *A Woman of No Importance*, and particularly between Lord Henry and Lord Illingworth, shows that Wilde took over a large number of paradoxes and epigrams word for word and even transplanted whole dialogues from the novel into the play. This somewhat questionable rationalisation of the artist's work is particularly noticeable in Act 1, with the conversations between Lady Hunstanton and the MP Kelvil, and in the Act 3 dialogue between Illingworth and Gerald, where the older man introduces the younger to the art of living. Both passages make substantial use of material from Chapters III, IV, and V of the novel, where Lord Henry develops his views of life. As an example, we might compare the following:[214]

A Woman of No Importance	The Picture of Dorian Gray
LADY STUTFIELD: The world says that Lord Illingworth is very, very wicked. LORD ILLINGWORTH: But what world says that, Lady Stutfield? It must be the next world. This world and I are on excellent terms. (*Sits down beside* MRS ALLONBY.) LADY STUTFIELD: Every one *I* know says you are very, very wicked. LORD ILLINGWORTH: It is perfectly monstrous the way people go about, nowadays, saying things against one behind one's back that are absolutely and entirely true.[215]	Lady Narborough hit him [Lord Henry] with her fan. 'Lord Henry, I am not at all surprised that the world says that you are extremely wicked.' 'But what world says that?' asked Lord Henry, elevating his eyebrows. 'It can only be the next world. This world and I are on excellent terms.' 'Everybody I know says you are very wicked', cried the old lady, shaking her head. Lord Henry looked serious for some moments. 'It is perfectly monstrous,' he said at last, 'the way people go about nowadays saying things against one behind one's back that are absolutely and entirely true.'[216]

The fact that complete sections of dialogue can be transplanted in this way vividly illustrates the narrow range of Wilde's characterisation as well as a certain artistic narcissism that is perhaps rather less than admirable.

The epigrammatic language of the dandies was something new in nineteenth-century drama, whereas the plot and characterisation contain traditional elements of the well-made play, the melodrama, and – in its early stages – the problem play. It was already obvious to contemporary critics that Wilde's plots and characters had a good deal in common with those of French plays. Arthur B. Walkley[217] pointed out in his review of *Lady Windermere's Fan* that Jules Lemaître's *Révoltée*, which was first produced on 9 April 1889 at the Théâtre de l'Odéon in Paris, also contained a divorcée – Mme de Voves, who intervened in order to stop her daughter, Hélène Rousseau, 'cette enfant de ma folie et de mes larmes',[218] from entering into an affair with the notorious *roué* Jacques de Bretigny. Thus she seeks to spare her married daughter from the fate that she herself has suffered. Even if Wilde was inspired by the basic situation in this play, it must be pointed out that he changed it considerably. Hélène Rousseau's attempt to break out of her marriage is not motivated by wounded pride – as with Lady Windermere – but by *ennui*; furthermore, there is no relationship between her husband and Mme de Voves comparable to that between Lord Windermere and Mrs Erlynne. Mme de Voves also reveals that she is Hélène's mother as early as Act 3, whereas Mrs Erlynne never gives away her secret to her daughter.

There are more striking similarities between Act 2 of *Lady Winder-*

mere's Fan and *L'Etrangère* by Alexandre Dumas *fils*. In both plays an outsider – Mrs Clarkson in *L'Etrangère* – gets herself invited to a ball in a noble house. The grouping of Duc de Septmonts, Cathérine de Septmonts and Mrs Clarkson is very like that of Lord and Lady Windermere and Mrs Erlynne, especially as the *aventurière* Mrs Clarkson gives the host's wife cause for jealousy.

Mrs Erlynne's blackmail of Lord Windermere is a motif found both in Augier's *Le Mariage d'Olympe* (2.9) and T. W. Robertson's *Ours*. In the former, Irma blackmails her son-in-law Henri, who offers her a large sum to go away, and in the latter Sir Alexander Shendryn pays out a substantial amount in order to prevent his wife from finding out about her brother's misdeeds.

As with *Lady Windermere's Fan*, Wilde was clearly influenced by certain French plays in the writing of *A Woman of No Importance*. His favourite authors were once again Dumas *fils* and Augier. Kelver Hartley, in his study of French influences on Wilde, compares Dumas's *Le Fils naturel* with Wilde's play, and declares: 'Il n'y a rien dans tout ceci [*A Woman of No Importance*] qui n'est pas contenu presque textuellement dans *Le fils naturel*'[219] [There is nothing in all this which is not contained almost word for word in *Le fils naturel*]. But a careful reading will show that this claim is grossly exaggerated and quite untenable as it stands. At the centre of Dumas's play is Jacques Vignot, illegitimate child of a working woman, Clara Vignot, and the socially superior Charles Sternay, who has seduced her but refuses to acknowledge the child. The son later falls in love with a niece of Sternay's, but his father refuses to allow the marriage. Only after Jacques has had a glittering career in the foreign service is Sternay, for selfish reasons, prepared to allow the marriage to his niece, to recognise his son, and to give him his name. Jacques refuses, and prefers to keep his mother's name.

It is clear even from a superficial glance that the subject-matter and the characters of the two plays have a lot in common. Both deal with the problem of the unmarried mother and the illegitimate child in a society that imposes grave sanctions on such people. The constellation of characters Clara Vignot – Charles Sternay – Jacques – Hermine is much like that of Mrs Arbuthnot – Lord Illingworth – Gerald – Hester. All that is missing from Wilde's play is the kinship between the seducer and the future wife of the illegitimate child. But despite these similarities, there are substantial differences in treatment. For instance, in *A Woman of No Importance* the father wishes to set his illegitimate son on a professional career, whereas in Dumas the situation is reversed, with the father's political career being made dependent on the goodwill of his son, who has now advanced ahead of him. In *Le Fils naturel* the problem of the illegitimate son is very much the focal point of the action, so that Jacques is the central character, but in *A Woman of No Importance* it is the relationship between the former seducer and the fallen woman that dominates.

The situation of Mrs Arbuthnot and her illegitimate son Gerald also has a parallel in Augier's comedy *Les Fourchambault*, which was first produced in Paris on 8 April 1878. Like Mrs Arbuthnot, Mme Bernard leads a 'vie claustrale'[220] and is anxious to conceal her past. But in contrast to Mrs Arbuthnot, the mother has no hesitation in answering her son's question about the identity of his father, and so there is nothing melodramatic about this situation. The father, M. Fourchambault, however, does not learn the identity of his son Bernard, though the latter tells Fourchambault's son Léopold that he is his brother. The similarities between Augier and Wilde do not, therefore, reach beyond the parallel situation of unmarried mother and illegitimate child.

There are thematic traces of French theatre in *An Ideal Husband* as well. In an interview with Gilbert Burgess, Wilde denied that he had borrowed certain elements of the plot from Sardou's *Dora*, the English translation of which was published in New York in 1877 and again, in a revised version, in 1884. Clement Scott, however, in reviewing the première, wrote:

> The similarity between Mr Oscar Wilde's 'Ideal Husband' and Sardou's 'Dora' is too marked not to be noticed. The hero, instead of being accused of stealing an important dispatch, is charged with selling a State secret. A new Zicka is introduced who blackmails the hero, instigated by another Baron Stein, who is an Austrian speculator; and instead of detection by a peculiar secret, we have a wonderful diamond bracelet, which has been stolen by the adventuress, who does not know it is a patent bracelet that cannot be unlocked except by some mysterious formula known only to one individual.[221]

There are also several striking similarities to some of Dumas *fils*'s plays other than *Le Fils naturel*. The name of the French attaché, Vicomte de Nanjac, occurs as Raymond de Nanjac in *Le Demi-Monde*. The misunderstanding over Lady Chiltern's letter to Lord Goring, which is stolen by Mrs Cheveley and sent to Sir Robert, has its parallel in *L'Ami des femmes*, where de Montègre passes Jane de Simerose's letter on to her husband, from whom she is separated, in order to compromise her. In both cases, however, the husbands think that the letters are gestures of reconciliation from their wives. But Robert Merle rightly points out that Wilde made certain changes in this incident:[222] Lord Goring is not presented as Lady Chiltern's lover, unlike de Montègre's relationship with Jane de Simerose, and he himself does not send the letter off in order to cause unpleasantness between Lady Chiltern and her husband.

The many ideas that Wilde took over from Dumas *fils* and other nineteenth-century French dramatists are a clear indication of Wilde's indebtedness and adherence to a tradition that was already established in comic drama. These French dramatists, however, were not the only influence on him. He was well acquainted with the plays of his English contemporaries, such as A. W. Pinero's *The Cabinet Minister* (1890). In this play the unscrupulous financier Joseph Lebanon blackmails the wife of the cabinet minister Julian Twombley, who is heavily in debt, into giving him secret information about the government's decision on the Rajputana canal project, so that he can use his inside knowledge in order to make a fortune on the London Stock Exchange. This situation is very similar to Mrs Cheveley's attempt to blackmail Sir Robert Chiltern into supporting the Argentine canal project in which she has invested heavily.

Wilde's ideas were drawn not only from contemporary literature but also from current events. Chiltern's past guilt and Mrs Cheveley's financial speculations are both connected with canal projects. Chiltern's crime took place against a real background – namely, Disraeli's purchase of shares in the Suez Canal – and although the Argentine canal project in which Mrs Cheveley has invested has no counterpart in reality, Chiltern's remark that this project is 'a second Panama'[223] shows Wilde's interest in events that were going on right up to the time of the play's first production. In Paris on 10 January 1893 a suit was brought against the directors of the Compagnie du Canal Interocéanique, who were accused of deception and wasting shareholders' money.[224] In the course of this trial, there arose increasing suspicions of political corruption:

When the mud was stirred up, one began to find politicians mixed up with the request for parliamentary authority to issue the lottery loan. Insinuations about parliamentary corruption were made, and although obviously exaggerated they became more and more aggressive ... After the autumn of 1892, parliamentary corruption became the talk of the town.[225]

This current 'talk of the town' may well have provided the historical frame of reference for Wilde's 'Argentine Canal'.[226]

Wilde's familiarity with post-romantic French drama is reflected not only in his ideas but also in his dramatic skill, learned from the rich intrigue and tightly constructed plots of the *pièces bien faites*[227] of Augier, Dumas *fils* and Sardou. The plot of the so-called well-made play propels the play along 'in Form unerwarteter Ereignisse unmotiviert'[228] [in the form of unexpected events, unmotivated]. Changes in the dramatic situation are not staged through the dialogue but are, as it were, derived from outside.[229] Such artificial linking techniques are to be found in all Wilde's plays. Typical examples are letters either found or stolen or mistaken in *Lady Windermere's Fan* and *An Ideal Husband*, properties such as a forgotten fan or a stolen brooch, and sheer coincidences such as the chair being knocked over and thus revealing Mrs Cheveley's presence to Chiltern. Unlike the experienced practitioner A. W. Pinero, who began his career as an actor, Wilde had no direct links with the theatre, and so he had to acquire his knowledge another way. He was interested not only in matters of technique, but also in the themes used by his predecessors, and in this respect he was particularly drawn to Dumas *fils*. The figure of the *raisonneur*, used by the Frenchman as a mouthpiece for his ideas on social reform, clearly influenced Wilde's dandy figures. Themes frequently dealt with by Dumas included those of the idealised fallen woman sacrificing her private hopes of love to the demands of society (*La Dame aux camélias*, 1852), the beautiful adventuress expecting social advancement through marriage (*Le Demi-Monde*, 1855), and the illegitimate child (*Le Fils naturel*, 1858). All of these recur in Wilde's plays, albeit in different forms.

As well as adopting themes and techniques from the well-made play, Wilde also took up elements of a popular genre that had great influence on the English theatre from the end of the eighteenth century right through to the 1880s: the melodrama.[230] This form of play undoubtedly owed its popularity to the fact that it satisfied the public's desire for entertainment and illusion. '*Melodrama is the Naturalism of the dream life*'[231] wrote Eric Bentley. Good is always rewarded, evil always punished, social life is ultimately regulated by right, order and justice, and the hero's exciting adventures, the heroine's terror, and the villain's wicked machinations always lead finally to the defeat of the villain and the idyllic union of hero and heroine. Here we have a pseudo-reality, whose sweet and simple morality offers a comforting counter-balance to the harsh and unjust realities of the new industrial age. From M. G. Lewis's *The Castle Spectre* (1797) and Thomas Holcroft's adaptation of *Coelina* entitled *A Tale of Mystery* (1802), to Dion Boucicault's *The Colleen Bawn* (1860) and Tom Taylor's *The Ticket-of-Leave Man* (1863), right up to Henry Arthur Jones's *The Silver King* (1882), the genre always contains the same basic elements: an abundance of incidents and settings, intense emotion, episodic action with surprising and fateful changes of situation, the curtain falling at moments of high suspense, stock characters, absolute polarisation of good and bad, characters grouped in tableaux, atmospheric musical background, and a happy ending.

Most of the items on this list can be found to a greater or lesser extent in Wilde's comedies. A typical example might be the end of Act 3 in *A Woman of No Importance*, which is an almost classic piece of melodrama:

MRS ARBUTHNOT: Stop, Gerald, stop! He is your own father! GERALD *clutches his mother's hands and looks into her face. She sinks slowly on the ground in shame.* HESTER *steals towards the door.* LORD ILLINGWORTH *frowns and bites his lip. After a time* GERALD *raises his mother up, puts his arm*

round her, and leads her from the room.[232]
                    Act drop

The shock revelation that Illingworth is Gerald's father, the intense
emotion right at the end of an act, the mother sinking to the ground 'in
shame' – these are all very much in the melodramatic tradition. So too are
the sudden return of the gentlemen in Act 3 of *Lady Windermere's Fan*,
the following concealment scene, Lady Windermere's spectacular flight,
and the discovery of Mrs Erlynne. The idealised good women are also
somewhat similar to the typical heroines of the melodrama – beautiful,
naive and virtuous. On the other hand, however, Wilde never indulges in
sensation for its own sake, in hectic action, lavish spectacle or extremism.
Language and dialogue nearly always take precedence over action, and
there is an underlying critical attitude towards relations between the
individual and society which certainly distinguishes Wilde's plays from
the melodrama.

Despite the fact that Wilde continually touches on the conflict between
public and private life, one certainly cannot assign the comedies to the
genre of the problem play.[233] One never has the impression that any one
of them is 'a play in which action, characters, and dialogue are subordinated to a study of an idea or a problem'.[234] The beginnings of the
problem play, which dominated the English theatre from Shaw through to
the First World War, are to be found in the work of T. W. Robertson,
H. A. Jones and A. W. Pinero, though for the most part these dramatists
tended to confirm the social status quo. This was a tradition, however,
that did not suit Wilde at all, for it ran contrary to his anti-realistic
concept of art, and in any case he was not really interested in social
problems. He lacked the involvement necessary to plead for social reform.
As a conservatively liberal aesthete, it suited him both politically and
artistically to adopt the lofty detachment of the observer poking fun at the
weaknesses and deficiencies of social man and his institutions, ridiculing
the rigidity of social conventions without ever actually departing from
them.

Conversation between criticism and conformity

Our glance at the traditions of form and content in which Wilde's plays
are situated might lead to the false conclusion that his achievement lay
merely in putting together melodramatic situations, using techniques
from the well-made play, and projecting them onto a background of social
criticism as current in the problem play. If this were indeed the case, it
would be difficult to understand why the works of T. W. Robertson,
S. Grundy, H. A. Jones and countless other nineteenth-century play-

wrights have been more or less forgotten, whereas Wilde's plays keep reappearing in the repertoire, and indeed reaching an even wider public through the medium of television. If we are to do full justice to Wilde's individuality and originality, we should perhaps look at his work against the background of the English comic tradition.

Wilde was as incapable of the harsh satirical realism of a Ben Jonson as he was of the latter's moral and didactic engagement. He was even more distant from the comedies of Shakespeare, whose variety of plots and characters, and mixture of cheerful romance, pastoral idyll, farce, verbal and situational humour, fantasy and black comedy were far beyond his range, although his masterpiece *The Importance of Being Earnest* remains one of the most popular landmarks of the English comic theatre. Even in the sphere of language, where the two dramatists might perhaps come closest, Shakespeare's style is infinitely more varied, and is never confined – as Wilde's so often is – to 'Taffeta phrases, silken terms precise'.[235]

There is, however, a certain affinity to the comedies of Congreve and Sheridan, in the seventeenth and eighteenth centuries, though less to those of the early Restoration, such as Etherege's *The Man of Mode* (1676) and Wycherley's *The Country Wife* (1673), whose obscenities and loose sexual morality are nowhere to be found in Wilde's plays. If one compares the latter with Congreve's *The Way of the World* (1700)[236] or Sheridan's *The School for Scandal* (1777), one cannot help being struck by the similar wit and satire permeating the dialogue. There is no question of Wilde having imitated their style, for his own conversational gift was the only resource he needed to draw on, but clearly this was the line of his descent. It is worth noting that the line continued well into the twentieth century. The comedy of manners was taken up as a genre by St John Hankin and J. M. Barrie, William Somerset Maugham and, above all, Noel Coward. The versatile and productive Coward, who dominated the theatre of the 1920s, was as adept and as trenchant as Wilde in his portrayal of the smooth, urbane surface of the idle, sophisticated set. He, too, used sharply pointed dialogue as his main weapon in plays such as *Hay Fever* (1925) and *Private Lives* (1930). This is not the case with Maugham, though, who gained his effects more through his formal gifts for well-observed characterisation and theatrically effective plotting. His *Lady Frederick*, in the play of the same name, is somewhat reminiscent of Wilde's women with a past, and what is arguably his best play, *The Circle* (1921), has a variation on the elopement theme used in *Lady Windermere's Fan*. The tradition of plays that are carried by the sheer brilliance of their wit might even be said to have continued through to the present day in the person of Tom Stoppard, whose dialogue is rich with precisely those unexpected twists and turns of phrase that characterise Wilde at his best.

In comparison to the plays of his predecessors and indeed his successors in the history of English drama, Wilde's comedies evince a kind of aesthetic suppression: with some of the characters, emotion is either throttled back or dispensed with altogether, while others go over the top in their sentimentality, so that the emotion seems to consist of hollow rhetoric emanating from the author's intellect rather than from his heart. The epigrammatic stylisation of language, leading to conversation without commitment, the reduction of character to soulless stereotype, and the restriction of plot to somewhat half-hearted conflicts between private interests and the need to conform to given conventions – all these features combine to make the comedies seem like portraits of the leisured classes, which react with cynicism to all intellectual and emotional commitment, and which see their main aim in life as being to preserve the status quo. The dominance of talk over action, and of aesthetics over morality, and the commercialisation of life reflect the social reality of this class, whose material prosperity made them both unable and unwilling to undertake any idealistic steps towards change, and indeed encouraged them to devote their energies if anything to maintaining the social order which had endowed them with their privileges. Life and culture for them are primarily a matter of verbal facility and formal perfection. For this reason the plays may be called 'drawing-room comedies', since their humour resides largely in their imitation of behaviour in London's salons; they are also conversation-pieces, since dialogue is the principal method whereby this social class confirms itself. The conduct of the characters is regulated by manners, which also dictate the paradoxical style of their language. The plays indeed document the glamorous decadence of the idlers, whose only reaction to a changing world is witty conversation and intellectual narcissism. Society exists merely to be their sounding-board – they talk, therefore they are. Hence Lord Illingworth's illuminating remark: 'To be in [society] is merely a bore. But to be out of it simply a tragedy. Society is a necessary thing.'[237]

As far as the development of British drama was concerned, Wilde made two vital contributions: a new style of language, and a new critical perspective. His dazzling use of epigram and paradox, and the incorporation of witty conversation for its own sake, were original features that emanated directly from his own peculiar gifts as a conversationalist. The new critical perspective consisted in his scepticism as regards the efficiency of linguistic communication at a time when social consensus was becoming increasingly difficult, his focus on the dilemma of the individual seeking meaningful identity in the clash between public and private life, and his undermining of traditional conventions. All of these loom large in the modern view of reality, and in the modern dramas of playwrights such as Beckett, Osborne and Pinter. But for all that, one cannot call Wilde an 'angry young man' of the 1890s. His critical attitude did not spring from any violent dissatisfaction with social conditions, as expressed by Osborne's Jimmy Porter, for instance, but from the desire to amuse his audience with paradoxical shock effects. The problems which he set on his stage may well have demanded 'modern' solutions, but instead he glossed them over with convention. His liberal intellect and flair for language remained tightly bound to a conservative temperament that was deeply rooted in the existing order. While Ibsen tackled the problems realistically, Wilde came down on the side of the illusionists.[238] It is true that Lady Windermere learns that life is too complex to be reduced to hard and fast rules, and ultimately she no longer believes 'that people can be divided into the good and the bad as though they were two separate races or creations'.[239] But she never learns the true identity of Mrs Erlynne, just as her husband never learns of her late-night visit to the rooms of Lord Darlington. It is as if Wilde took one step towards reality, but then stopped because he lacked the courage to commit himself. Illusion remains preferable to reality. This extraordinary mixture of Victorian orthodoxy and anti-Victorian provocation, theatrical cliché and verbal originality, is typical of an author who in his writings as in his life remained consistently a conformist rebel.

8 Propriety and parody.
The Importance of Being Earnest

On Valentine's day, the 14th February 1895, there was a snow-storm more severe than had been remembered in London for years. A black, bitter, threatening wind blew the drifting snow. On that dark sinister winter's night, when the first representation of '*The Importance of Being Earnest*' was produced at the St James's Theatre, it was with difficulty that one drove there at all, one had to go very slowly on account of the horses. Crowds of hansoms, broughams, carriages of all kinds blocked little King Street.[1]

Despite the appalling weather, recalled so vividly by Ada Leverson, fashionable London streamed into the West End in order to see Wilde's latest play *The Importance of Being Earnest* at the St James's. Everyone knew that the plot and dialogue would offer the very opposite of what was promised by the stolid-sounding title, but there was great suspense as to how the famous author would now move on from *The Ideal Husband* (running concurrently at the Haymarket), and as to what new paradoxes he would come up with this time. The first-night audience had no cause to regret their journey, for the play and the production soon made them forget completely the bitterly cold weather outside. The main parts were played by George Alexander as John Worthing, Allan Aynesworth as Algernon Moncrieff, Irene Vanbrugh as Gwendolen Fairfax, Evelyn Millard as Cecily Cardew, and Rose Leclercq as Lady Bracknell. The première was a triumphant success, and the play ran for eighty-six performances from 14 February till 8 May 1895.

Many new productions followed. The founder of the Independent Theatre, Jacob T. Grein, reports of one on 2 December 1901 in which Wilde's name was omitted from the handbills and replaced with 'by the author of *Lady Windermere's Fan*'.[2] During the 1909/10 season Hesketh Pearson actually saw the play seven or eight times.[3] A production at the Globe Theatre on 31 January 1939 saw John Gielgud play the role of John Worthing with great success.[4] Today it ranks as one of the classics of English comedy, and even inspired Jean Anouilh in 1954 to write a two-act adaptation.[5]

As usual, Wilde was amongst the first to praise his own play: 'the first act is ingenious, the second beautiful, the third abominably clever'.[6] Even if other critics were somewhat less enthusiastic, there could be no doubt that the première was a great success. However, there is also no doubt that the reviews generally were not as positive as for his previous plays. Some dismissed the play as a farce that was not worthy of serious consideration, and many failed to see any level below that of sheer foolery. There was also a certain amount of confusion caused by the theatrical and artistic originality of the play, which simply defied comprehension and evaluation by the normal criteria of dramatic theory.[7] Nevertheless, the humour was recognised by all, with comments such as 'very good nonsense' (H. G. Wells),[8] 'extraordinarily funny' (H. Fyfe),[9] and 'undoubtedly amusing' (*Truth*).[10] Only George Bernard Shaw had scruples about his own enjoyment, for he called the play 'really heartless' and 'essentially hateful'.[11] It seemed to him to lack emotion, so that the laughter was destructive. His review was basically negative:

I cannot say that I greatly cared for *The Importance of Being Earnest*. It amused me, of course; but unless comedy touches me as well as amuses me, it leaves me with a sense of having wasted my evening.[12]

Perhaps the play left him untouched because it never develops the social and moral problems at which it hints – unlike the detailed criticism that he developed in his own plays.

History and composition

The history of the play's composition is a complex one, and indeed research is still far from complete, but it may be summarised as follows:[13] From the original manuscript to the first published edition there were at least seven different stages:

1   The first draft was written in August and September 1894 at The Haven, 5 Esplanade, Worthing, where Wilde was staying with his family.[14] Vyvyan Holland, one of Wilde's sons, remembers the time well, and recalls that his father used to work on the play in the mornings, and devote the afternoons to his children, demonstrating his remarkable imagination 'in the all-important architectural matter of building sand-castles'.[15]
    This handwritten first draft consists of four notebooks, quarto size, which somehow got separated. Wilde's executor Robert Ross gave the manuscripts of Acts 3 and 4 to the British Museum (Add. Ms. 37948), but the other books disappeared for many years. They did not surface again until after the death of the wife of Arthur Clifton, a friend of Wilde's, and they were then auctioned in London in 1950, and became the property of the American collector George Arents. Today the manuscripts of Acts 1 and 2 are in the Arents Tobacco Collection of the New York Public Library.
2   Wilde corrected this draft version and had it typed, but this script was

also extensively revised, and the originals of Acts 1, 3 and 4 are also to be found in the New York Public Library.

3   This corrected version was newly typed, but according to Vyvyan Holland this, too, was revised and retyped, although there does not appear to be any evidence of such a later script. All that is known is that at least one script was typed by Mrs Marshall's typewriting agency between 3 October and 25 October 1894.[16] Wilde sent a copy of the provisional four-act version, which at this stage was entitled *Lady Lancing* (to prevent the real title from being leaked prematurely), to George Alexander around 25 October. His letter includes the following remark: 'Of course, the play is not suitable to you at all: you are a romantic actor: the people it wants are actors like Wyndham and Hawtrey.'[17]

It is difficult to decide whether this was a subtle move designed to provoke actor and producer Alexander, as Vyvyan Holland supposes,[18] or whether Wilde really did think that the two actors he named were better qualified. What is certain, however, is that Alexander followed Wilde's directive and passed the play on to Charles Wyndham, who took his time deciding on whether to produce it or not. It may well be that Alexander himself was not interested at first because he was busy producing Henry James's *Guy Domville* which was unsuccessfully premiered on 5 January 1895. Only then did Alexander ask Wyndham to return the play to him, which Wyndham did on condition that he should be given an option on Wilde's next play.

4   On the director's insistence, Wilde had to make cuts in his text, and these were completed by 20 January, since by that date rehearsals were already underway and Wilde had left for Algeria with Alfred Douglas. In order to obtain a licence, a copy of the play had to be submitted to the Lord Chamberlain's Office. The copy was dated 30 January, and had been shortened to three acts. .

5   The various changes in the text can be seen from a comparison between the licensing copy, George Alexander's rehearsal copy – which is now in the Harvard Theatre Collection – and the first published edition. From the differences, Joseph W. Donohue, Jr, concludes that Alexander's copy was a newly revised version which comes closest to the play as it was first performed.[19]

6   In a letter dated 4 May 1898, Wilde asked his publisher Smithers to have a typescript made of Alexander's copy of the three-act version.[20] This typescript of 1898 is also part of the Arents Tobacco Collection in the New York Public Library, and contains a large number of handwritten changes. It is different in many places from the performance text.

7   The text of the first edition, published by Smithers in 1899 – probably
    in February – was based on this revised typescript, but there a few
    further changes which show that Wilde was correcting his text even at
    the proof stage.

The three-act version of 1899 was also used in the collected works of 1908
and in later editions,[21] and the general public knew nothing of the original
version. The four-act edition was translated into German by Freiherr
Hermann von Teschenberg in Leipzig in 1903 under the title *Ernst sein!* –
but this was initially ignored by Wilde scholars. The German translation
was probably based on the script that was sent to Alexander and the
whereabouts of which is unknown. In 1954 H. Montgomery Hyde
published in the *Listener* one of the scenes cut from the first version, and in
1956 Sarah A. Dickson edited the original version. This two-volume
edition, of great interest to bibliophiles, contains a transcription of the
manuscript, a facsimile of the typescript of Acts 1, 3 and 4, and a
manuscript version of Act 2. In 1957 Vyvyan Holland brought out an
edition of the original four-act version. This he reconstructed by comparing the German translation of 1903 with all existing manuscripts and
typescripts, as well as with the first edition of 1899. Holland was
convinced that his reconstruction must have been almost identical to the
original work.

What, then, are the main differences between the final three-act text and
the four-act versions? The most radical changes are to be found in Acts 2
and 3, which were drastically cut and compressed to form the central
section of the play, while the original Act 4 became the new Act 3. Among
the cuts was one complete scene in which a new character – Lawyer
Gribsby – appeared with a view to imprisoning Algernon for debt.
Another character to disappear was the gardener, Moulton, though he
only had a few lines anyway. Some of the names were changed – notably
Lady Brancaster became Lady Bracknell, and Montford was rechristened
Algernon Moncrieff. Altogether the reductions amount to some 20 per
cent of the text, and the cuts certainly result in a tighter construction and a
greater density of comic effect.

In his first three comedies, Wilde had been directly influenced by French
theatre, but there seem to be no immediate sources for *The Importance of
Being Earnest*.[22] An extensive essay by two American scholars, Charles
B. Paul and Robert D. Pepper, seeks to prove that the raw material was
provided by Alfred de Musset's comedy *Il ne faut jurer de rien* (1836),[23]
and elsewhere they claim: 'Almost the entire play, in plan and detail, is (we
think) an adaptation, cleverly disguised, of "*Il ne faut jurer de rien*".'[24] In
order for this thesis to be properly tested, we must first outline the plot of
Musset's play. To prevent his uncle, Van Buck, from disinheriting him,

Valentin promises to marry Cécile de Mantes, but only on condition that it proves to be impossible for her to be seduced within a week.[25] He goes incognito with his uncle Van Buck to Baronesse de Mantes's castle in order to test Cécile. After a few setbacks, he succeeds in arranging a rendezvous with her. She spontaneously declares her love for him, together with a disarming assumption that they will be married at once, and so Valentin renounces his 'alter ego', the seducer Lovelace, and takes Cécile as his wife.

Plot, motivation and characters have virtually nothing in common that would justify calling Wilde's play an adaptation of Musset's. The latter dramatises the story of a would-be seducer who finally succumbs to the naive charm of his intended victim. Such elements of the tale as the rendezvous in the moonlit forest, the tear-stained *billet doux*, and the flight of the imprisoned Cécile belong far more to romantic drama than to Wilde's urbane theatre. The superficiality of the Paul–Pepper thesis is evident from such statements as: 'The wager that Valentin makes with his uncle, Wilde turned into the Bunburying of Algy'.[26] It remains a mystery as to how a bet relating to the seduction of a girl within a week, or marriage to her, can be equated with Algernon's invention of a sick friend living in the country.

There seems to be more substance in the suggestion contained in some reviews of the première that the play echoes the farcical comedies of William Schwenck Gilbert. There are indeed similarities between Gilbert's *Engaged* (1877) and Wilde's play, as indicated by Erika Meier in the Wilde chapter of 'Realism and Reality'.[27] In Gilbert's play, Symperson takes so seriously the intended suicide of Cheviot Hill, a 'young man of property', that he even takes the precaution of wearing mourning-dress. The stage direction is:

Enter S Y M P E R S O N, *in deep black; he walks pensively, with a white handkerchief to his mouth.*[28]

In *The Importance of Being Earnest* Jack's grief at the death of his fictitious brother is described as follows:

Enter J A C K *slowly from the back of the garden. He is dressed in the deepest mourning, with crape hatband and black gloves.*[29]

After Cheviot Hill has made it clear that he has no intention of dying, the disappointed Symperson – who would have benefited from his death to the tune of £1,000 – flies into a rage:

S Y M P E R S O N: Consented to live? Why, sir, this is confounded trifling. I don't understand this line of conduct at all; you threaten to commit suicide; your friends are dreadfully shocked at first, but eventually their minds become reconciled to the prospect of losing you, they become resigned, even cheerful; and when they have brought themselves to this Christian state of mind, you coolly inform them that you have changed your mind and mean to live.[30]

This passage may call to mind Lady Bracknell's reproach to Algernon over his sick friend's indecisiveness:

LADY BRACKNELL: Well, I must say, Algernon, that I think it is high time that Mr Bunbury made up his mind whether he was going to live or die. This shilly-shallying with the question is absurd.[31]

The scene in which Algernon eats up the cucumber sandwiches made for Lady Bracknell also has a parallel in *Engaged*, where in Act 2 Belinda develops a passion for the cakes that have been set aside for Minnie's wedding.[32] Clearly in matters of plot, style, and humour Wilde is much closer to Gilbert's farcical comedy than to Musset's *Il ne faut jurer de rien*, but even the above examples could be attributed as much to coincidence as to influence.

Plot and techniques

'What is the plot? He would be daring and audacious who set out to describe it.'[33] Despite St John Ervine's warning, we shall try to summarise the main strands so that the reader may gain some idea of the often confusing interplay of situations:

At the centre of the plot are two young men, John Worthing and Algernon Moncrieff, who have both invented fictitious acquaintances in order to have an alibi for their occasional sorties. John lives in the country, calls himself Jack, and plays the role of the morally upright guardian of his adoptive father's grand-daughter, Cecily Cardew; he justifies his journeys to London through the worrying escapades of his fictitious younger brother Ernest. Algernon, on the other hand, escapes from his unpleasant social obligations in London by pretending to visit a sick friend called Bunbury who lives in the country. Jack is courting Gwendolen Fairfax, a cousin of Algernon's, but she is only interested in men whose first name is Ernest, and so he is considering having himself rechristened. He also has to overcome the opposition of Gwendolen's mother, the class-conscious Lady Bracknell, who disapproves of Jack's dubious origins – he was found in a handbag on Victoria Station – and cannot regard it as 'an assured basis for a recognized position in good society'.[34]

Algernon, who has seen through his friend's double life, is interested in Jack's pretty ward Cecily, and assuming the name of Ernest – that is pretending to be Jack's younger brother – goes to the Worthings' country estate, where he woos her. This subterfuge is particularly appropriate as Cecily, like Gwendolen, has a predilection for the name

Ernest. The complications come to a head when Jack returns unexpectedly from London and – dressed in black – announces the death of his brother Ernest. Meanwhile, Gwendolen has also arrived, and in conversation with Cecily discovers that they both appear to be engaged to the same man. Called to account, Algernon and Jack are forced meekly to disclose their true identities, but this leads to new problems because both girls refuse to accept that they are engaged to men whose names are not Ernest. Jack and Algernon therefore make arrangements with Dr Chasuble, the vicar, to rechristen them.

The baptism, however, proves to be unnecessary, at least for Jack. Lady Bracknell recognises Miss Prism, Cecily's present governess, as a maid who had formerly been in the service of Lord Bracknell. As we now learn, twenty-eight years ago – 'in a moment of mental abstraction'[35] – instead of the manuscript of a three-volume novel, she had accidentally placed a baby in her hand-bag, which she had left in the cloakroom at Victoria Station. Thus the identity of Jack is revealed: he is the son of Lady Bracknell's sister, Mrs Moncrieff, and is therefore Algernon's elder brother; furthermore, he was baptised Ernest John. As Cecily accepts Algernon's declaration that only one of the two brothers could possibly be called Ernest, and in the meantime Dr Chasuble and the spinster Miss Prism have formed a tender attachment, the play ends with three couples locked in embrace.

It is understandable that theatre critics who were used to the plays of H. A. Jones, Pinero, Ibsen and Shaw should have found themselves somewhat disorientated by such a work, and inclined to throw up their hands in helpless protest rather than accept the challenge of something quite new in the history of English comedy. The anonymous critic of *Truth*, for instance, thought that any serious review of the play would be like investigating the ingredients of a soufflé after dinner.[36] Even the famous critic William Archer regarded this 'absolutely wilful expression of an irrepressibly witty personality' – as he called the play – as being only the product of a fantasy that 'imitates nothing, represents nothing, means nothing, is nothing'. Following a dictum of Pater's, he set it in the context of music, calling it a '*rondo capriccioso*, in which the artist's fingers run with crisp irresponsibility up and down the keyboard of life'.[37]

How Wilde runs up and down the 'keyboard of life' may already be seen from closer inspection of the title, which is perhaps the best starting-point for any interpretation. The obvious homonymic word-play between 'Ernest' and 'Earnest' is underlined by the sub-title, which is, 'A trivial comedy for serious people'. The earnest folk to whom the play is addressed are, of course, the Victorians, for whom the epithet is highly apposite. Devotion to duty, a strict work ethic, hatred of idleness – these were characteristic of the puritanical and evangelical traditions that marked the Victorian attitude to life. Taking life seriously meant taking God seriously (even if God was sometimes hard to distinguish from Mammon): it meant facing up to fundamental problems of metaphysics and morality, as well as to the practical demands of growing industrialisation and technology. The earnestness of life had two dimensions: one moral and intellectual, the other practical and existential. While Carlyle, Newman, Dr Thomas Arnold, Matthew Arnold and George Eliot wrestled with crises of faith and the search for new moral criteria, the vast majority of the people fought for their daily bread. Carlyle described the *Zeitgeist* of early Victorianism as follows:

The time for levity, insincerity, and idle babble and play-acting, in all kinds, is gone by; it is a serious, grave time.[38]

Public seriousness at the time is perhaps encapsulated by Theobald Pontifex, in Butler's *The Way of All Flesh* (posthum. 1903), who had his son baptised Ernest, on grounds elaborated by the author:

The word 'earnest' was just beginning to come into fashion, and he [Mr Pontifex] thought the possession of such a name might, like his having been baptised in water from the Jordan, have a permanent effect upon his character, and influence him for good during the more critical periods of his life.[39]

The irony of Wilde's title consists in the fact that the only earnest item in the play is the name Ernest – there is little sign of seriousness in the situations or the characters. The verbal irony of the title continues logically and consistently throughout the action, with earnestness being trivialised and the name Ernest being taken seriously.[40] Cecily and Gwendolen set so much store by the name that they make their choice of marriage partner dependent upon it. On the other hand, Lady Bracknell considers Jack's being found in a hand-bag as nothing but a cause for reproach that he should have shown such contempt for the 'ordinary decencies of family life';[41] she is not in the least interested in the extraordinary fate of such a foundling. By focusing on this violation of the 'decencies', she reduces a potentially pathetic situation to a mere breach of social etiquette, and life to a question of style. Gwendolen sums up the priorities that apply to this whole play: 'In matters of grave importance, style, not sincerity, is the vital thing'.[42]

Wilde opposes Victorian earnestness with a philosophy of the surface, which his sub-title denotes with the word 'trivial'. This is his conceptual counter to 'serious' and 'earnest', and carries connotations of intellectual and moral detachment from reality, concentrating on the inessential and insignificant surface of things. His view of the trivial is expressed in *De Profundis*:

The trivial in thought and action is charming. I had made it the keystone of a very brilliant philosophy expressed in plays and paradoxes.[43]

The contrast between the trivial and the serious, as expressed in the sub-title, and the punning irony of the name Ernest coupled with the quality of earnestness, prefigure the comic effect of the play. The irony and the comedy arise primarily from the continual interplay between, on the one hand, an intellectual and trivialising perspective of events and situations that seem to demand an earnest, emotional response or conformity to social propriety, and on the other hand an earnest and ponderous way of looking at things that are trivial and external. This constant clash of opposing perspectives results in the reader's or spectator's habitual expectations for ever being punctured. The method governing this continual alienation of reality by way of the artistic imagination at play is the principle of inversion. This becomes the behavioural norm, while paradox is its verbal expression. The role of the sexes, for instance, is reversed in the matter of courtship: when Jack wishes to propose to Gwendolen, he stutters to a halt, and she has to take the initiative; similarly, Algernon – so experienced in 'Bunburying' – learns that for three months, as can be proved by her diary, Cecily has already cast him as her fiancé. The comedy of this scene, however, does not reside solely in the fact that the action springs from Cecily, but also in the parody of 'love at first sight', an ever-popular romantic theme. Imagination does not follow reality, but anticipates it, in accordance with the paradoxical thesis of Vivian in 'The Decay of Lying': 'Life imitates art far more than Art imitates life.'[44]

In this apparently weightless, light-hearted world of fantasy, where Jack wears mourning because of the death of a non-existent brother, while his friend Algernon is simultaneously pretending to be the brother as he declares his love to Cecily, the laws of Nature are flouted as blatantly as those of everyday life. Nothing is safe from the playfulness of the intellect – the emotions of love and grief, and the objective extremes of birth and death. Even these are deprived of their factualness and become subject to the whims of the subjective viewpoint, being unexpectedly transformed into malleable phenomena. When she hears from Algernon that Bunbury is dead, after the doctors had discovered that he could no longer be alive, Lady Bracknell responds:

LADY BRACKNELL: He seems to have had no great confidence in the opinion of his physicians. I am glad, however, that he made up his mind at the last to some definite course of action, and acted under proper medical advice.[45]

What matters to Lady Bracknell is not the fact of Bunbury's death but the fact that he 'acted under proper medical advice'. Conventional expectations are thereby stood on their head, since Bunbury apparently did not benefit from this advice but simply died. It is even conceivable here that this paradox represents a satirical jibe at the deficiencies of medical practice in Wilde's day. But what matters above all to Lady Bracknell is social propriety. In a form of cross-examination satirising the conventional Victorian approach to marriage, she questions Jack about his age, income, property in town and country, political beliefs and origin. After learning, to her consternation, that he has lost both parents – which she regards as a sign of 'carelessness'[46] – and appears to have no relations at all, as he was found in a hand-bag, she urges him 'to make a definite effort to produce at any rate one parent, of either sex, before the season is quite over'.[47]

Lady Bracknell's worship of rank and title, respectability and social prestige makes her the classic figure of social snobbery and narrow-mindedness. She shakes her head to hear that Jack lives on the 'unfashionable side' of Belgrave Square, and in her arrogance she embodies that stratum of society which Wilde himself could never reach, however much he loved to bask in its glamour. This was the meeting-place of rigid conservatism, philistinism, and dandified aestheticism.[48] In no other character is the separation of emotion from intellect, already a feature of characterisation in the earlier comedies, so consistent and so dominant as in Lady Bracknell. She regards sympathy with invalids as 'morbid',[49] and tells Algernon to ask the sick Bunbury to avoid a relapse on Saturday if possible, as she has arranged the last dinner-party of the season for that day and would like Algernon to attend. There is a fine example of this mixture of Victorian conventionality and aesthetic alienation in the scene where Jack kneels in order to propose, and Lady Bracknell enters unexpectedly:

LADY BRACKNELL: Mr Worthing. Rise, sir, from this semi-recumbent posture. It is most indecorous.
GWENDOLEN: Mamma! [*He tries to rise; she restrains him.*] I must beg you to retire. This is no place for you. Besides, Mr Worthing has not quite finished yet.
LADY BRACKNELL: Finished what, may I ask?
GWENDOLEN: I am engaged to Mr Worthing, mamma.
[*They rise together*].
LADY BRACKNELL: Pardon me, you are not engaged to anyone. When you do become engaged to someone, I, or your father, should his health permit him, will inform you of the fact. An engagement should come on a girl as a surprise, pleasant or unpleasant, as the case may be. It is hardly a matter that she could be allowed to arrange for herself ...[50]

Lady Bracknell does not ask why Jack is kneeling, and she is not concerned with her daughter's feelings towards him. All that matters to her is the visitor's extraordinary posture, and her sole purpose is to restore social decorum. What is basically a serious situation is rendered ridiculous by the formal perspective through which she views it, and the visual comedy of the tableau is underlined by the rigid formality of the language.

The dignified stiltedness of Lady Bracknell's dialogue effectively shatters one's expectations of a spontaneous emotional reaction. Jack's kneeling position is viewed neither as the unbearable servility of a potential marriage candidate, nor as a symbolic, pre-marital exchange of roles, but it simply arouses her repugnance because it clashes with her idea of what is 'decorous'. The absurdity of this perspective, which concentrates on the surface and not on the essence, serves to throw a satirical light on the Victorian convention of parents deciding on their children's choice of partner. All too often the daughter's emotions counted for less than the financial situation of the wooer, and here as elsewhere in the play Lady Bracknell becomes the mouthpiece for such conventions. When later on, for instance, Jack reveals that his ward Cecily has a fortune of about £130,000, Lady Bracknell suddenly finds Cecily a 'most attractive lady'.[51]

A character like Lady Bracknell, whose urbanity barely disguises her relationship to the matchmaker of classical comedy, stands out as a comic figure primarily because she combines Victorian conventions with aesthetic attitudes. The latter throw into relief the deficiencies of the former, so that in laughing at her, the predominantly middle-class Victorian audience could scarcely avoid also laughing at themselves. There is a similar incongruity of perspective to be observed in Miss Prism, Cecily's governess and the authoress of a lost three-volume novel 'of more than usually revolting sentimentality'.[52] Unlike Lady Bracknell she brings a more moral tone to her insistence on propriety. Her Christian name, Laetitia, stands in ironic contrast to the stiff conformity of her conduct and the sententious nature of her somewhat affected language – already hinted at by her surname, which suggests a combination of 'prim' and 'prissy'.[53] The superficiality of her ostentatious respectability is evidenced by her response to the news of Ernest's death: 'What a lesson for him! I trust he will profit by it.'[54] The paradox of this reaction lies in the fact that she regards Ernest's dissolute life style as being responsible for his death, and so death should now inspire him to a greater insight into his own wrong-doing. Just how a dead man is supposed to see his own death as a punishment, and profit from the insight, is left unclear. The triviality of her attitude lies in the grotesque clash between her moral severity and the actual situation.

There is a similar reaction when Jack asks her to identify the hand-bag in which he was found:

MISS PRISM [*calmly*]: It seems to be mine. Yes, here is the injury it received through the upsetting of a Gower Street omnibus in younger and happier days. Here is the stain on the lining caused by the explosion of a temperance beverage, an incident that occurred at Leamington. And here, on the lock, are my initials. I had forgotten that in an extravagant mood I had had them placed there. The bag is undoubtedly mine. I am delighted to have it so unexpectedly restored to me. It has been a great inconvenience being without it all these years.[55]

While Jack waits in great suspense for her answer, she proceeds to go into all the minute details when, in the context, one would simply have expected her to say whether or not this really is the bag she lost twenty-eight years ago in Victoria Station. And even after she has at last confirmed that the bag is hers, she does not say a single word about the all-important fact that this clears up the mystery of Jack's origins. The 'injury', the stain and the initials are not regarded as clues to the existential significance of the bag, but merely evoke memories of the past. Jack's agony of suspense is in stark contrast to Miss Prism's total disinterest in the fate of the baby she once deposited in the bag. Just as Ernest's death served only to inspire her to moral sententiousness, so too does this hand-bag episode leave her emotionally quite untouched – she seems to have completely shut out any sense of personal responsibility for what happened. Thus she trivialises a serious situation, ignoring both the fate of the child and her own part in that fate, and concentrating all her attention on one superficial aspect of the affair, which is the identity of the bag.[56] This alone is worthy of 'earnestness'.

Not all the characters succeed in replacing emotional involvement with intellectual detachment as completely as does Miss Prism; nor do they all conform to the social conventions of propriety as perfectly as Lady Bracknell. The long dialogue between Cecily and Gwendolen in Act 2, when they both realise that they appear to be engaged to the same man, is one instance where the protective coating of perfect manners is seen merely to be a cover for 'that dreadful universal thing called human nature':[57]

CECILY [*Advancing to meet her.*]: Pray let me introduce myself to you. My name is Cecily Cardew.
GWENDOLEN: Cecily Cardew? [*Moving to her and shaking hands.*] What a very sweet name! Something tells me that we are going to be great friends. I like you already more than I can say. My first impressions of people are never wrong.
CECILY: How nice of you to like me so much after we have known each other a comparatively short time. Pray sit down.
GWENDOLEN [*Still standing up.*]: I may call you Cecily, may I not?
CECILY: With pleasure!
GWENDOLEN: And you will always call me Gwendolen, won't you?
CECILY: If you wish.
GWENDOLEN: Then that is all quite settled, is it not?
CECILY: I hope so [*A pause. They both sit down together.*]

Then they discover that they are apparently engaged to the same man:

CECILY: Do you suggest, Miss Fairfax, that I entrapped Ernest into an engagement? How dare you? This is no time for wearing the shallow mask of manners. When I see a spade I call it a spade.
GWENDOLEN: [*Satirically.*]: I am glad to say that I have never seen a spade. It is obvious that our social spheres have been widely different.[58]

The excessive affection of the first dialogue is already rather suspect as it is so unmotivated. One would in fact have expected Gwendolen to be rather more reserved and indeed surprised to find such a pretty young girl in her fiancé's house. And shortly before meeting Gwendolen, Cecily had presumed that she must be 'one of the many good elderly women who are associated with Uncle Jack in some of his philanthropic work in London'.[59] Both have good cause to be suspicious, but they mask their feelings with exaggerated politeness.

The exchange of elaborate courtesies is like a ritual whose ceremonial character is underlined by the symmetry of the movements. Cecily and Gwendolen move towards each other, shake hands, stand for a moment or two, and then sit down together. Once they have sat, both the physical and the verbal ceremonies of introduction are completed. In these symmetrical movements, which are also to be observed elsewhere in the play, Otto Reinert detects 'a kind of dance, slow and elaborate, a visual image of the artifice of sophisticated courtship and a major device in the play's esthetic distancing'.[60] Gradually, ineradicable differences emerge, but at first the two young ladies retain their polite tone. Their adherence to the formalities laboriously holds up a façade which threatens at any moment to collapse. The stage directions reveal a formal parallel between their actions and their words. After Cecily has revealed that she is engaged to Ernest Worthing, they both rise 'quite politely' (Gwendolen) and 'very politely' (Cecily), and produce their diaries in order to prove their engagements. The tempo of the dialogue slows down: Gwendolen speaks 'meditatively', Cecily 'thoughtfully and sadly', but then it accelerates through such key words as 'entanglement' and 'entrapped', until it reaches a climax with the passage quoted. The ritual of manners is now denounced as a masquerade, though the masks are only laid aside for a brief moment. Gwendolen's barbed comment on their different social spheres wounds through satire and not through crude insults or ranting complaints. The entrance of servants immediately exercises a 'restraining influence'[61] on the two girls, who then proceed to talk in the most formal terms about town and country life, while nevertheless firing little arrows at each other through the formality.

The symmetrical gestures and movements express an artificiality that permeates the whole play and indeed links it together. It becomes an artistic mode of alienating reality, with the characters at times appearing almost mechanical, like puppets rather than people. As well as shaping the dramatic situation, as in the rivalry and reconciliation of Acts 2 and 3, for instance, or in the final tableau of the three couples embracing, the symmetry and parallelism also shape the dialogue, which abounds in repetitions and inversions. When the two young ladies realize that the supposed Ernest is actually Algernon, and Ernest alias Jack is really John, they react so uniformly that they no longer seem to be individuals:

GWENDOLEN: My poor wounded Cecily!
CECILY: My sweet wronged Gwendolen![62]

This reduction of individuality, and hence of possible variation, is conveyed by the syntactic parallel which has a comic effect as described by Bergson: 'du mécanique plaqué sur du vivant'.[63] The process is taken one step further in the chorus at the beginning of Act 3:

[*Gwendolen beats time with uplifted finger.*]
GWENDOLEN AND CECILY [*Speaking together.*]: Your Christian names are still an insuperable barrier. That is all!
JACK AND ALGERNON [*Speaking together.*]: Our Christian names! Is that all? But we are going to be christened this afternoon.[64]

Of all the formal techniques, however, the most potent in this play is the paradox. As the stylistic pendant to the constructional principle of inversion, it systematises the counter to orthodox opinion. It arises from the desire to disconcert the partner by way of the unexpected formulation. Effect is all, and at times one has the impression of being confronted by perfect rhetorical specimens, each little gem exquisitely prepared and mounted. But the paradoxes cannot simply be dismissed as cheap effects, for in many instances they serve to explode established conventions, thereby exposing to view those aspects of reality that had hitherto been cloaked by existing norms. In Act 1, for instance, Lady Bracknell and Algernon are talking about the widowed Lady Harbury, whose husband died fairly recently:

LADY BRACKNELL: I'm sorry if we are a little late, Algernon, but I was obliged to call on dear Lady Harbury. I hadn't been there since her poor husband's death. I never saw a woman so altered; she looks quite twenty years younger

. . .

ALGERNON: I hear her hair has turned quite gold from grief.[65]

The reader or spectator is not surprised that Lady Harbury has been altered by her husband's death, but he certainly does not expect her to have become younger or to have hair that has turned 'quite gold from grief'.[66] The conventional cliché of the grieving widow, ageing and with even more grey hair than before, is quite shattered by Wilde, who depicts a rejuvenated woman 'who seems ... to be living entirely for pleasure now'.[67] The substitution of 'gold' for the expected 'grey' is particularly effective, for the unconventional and unnatural change of hair colour may also allude to the inheritance which the pleasure-loving widow is now enjoying. Such paradoxes illustrate vividly how social decorum is to be seen merely as a mask of conformity, and they also bring out the true motives that lurk behind the mask. Lady Harbury's inability to mourn, thanks to the golden days that now lie ahead of her, may be seen as a parallel to Lady Bracknell's evaluation of Jack and Algernon as candidates for the hands of Gwendolen and Cecily – their suitability being judged in accordance with their incomes. Emotions such as grief and love have no place in either case. Materialistic considerations are all-important, and morality is reduced to a matter of business.

'Bunburying'

Paradox and inversion, parallelism and symmetry are formal and structural techniques which transform the premises of the title into a theatrical spectacle: what is earnest is to be trivialised, and what is trivial is to be taken seriously. Victorian earnestness, as manifested in political, moral and religious orthodoxy, produced through all its suppressions one special form of conduct which enabled individual needs to be fulfilled without violating the social codes it imposed: this was hypocrisy, 'the most characteristic vice of the age'.[68] Propriety replaced personal integrity, pretentious moralism covered up suppressed sensuality, and religious conformity masked growing scepticism. Hypocrisy, prudery, bigotry and phariseeism were the commonplace consequences, as illustrated in Victorian literature by such characters as Bulstrode, Brocklehurst and Pecksniff.

One form of this hypocrisy is depicted in a story told by Taine in his *Notes sur l'Angleterre*.[69] A respectable Englishman, who eschews all pleasure on a Sunday when he is at home, and who conforms to all the proprieties of the middle class, occasionally goes to Paris on business, and there he avails himself of all the facilities which the French capital has to offer on a Sunday. Taine was an expert on English literature and society, and his little anecdote recalls a major theme in *The Importance of Being Earnest*: namely Jack and Algernon's 'Bunburying'.[70] They both invent purely fictitious characters in order to supply themselves with alibis: Bunbury is always sick, and brother Ernest is always getting into the 'most dreadful scrapes'.[71] Algernon needs a means of escaping his social obligations, while Jack wants to escape the moral pressure brought to bear on him by his position as Cecily's guardian:

When one is placed in the position of guardian, one has to adopt a very high moral tone on all subjects. It's one's duty to do so. And as a high moral tone can hardly be said to conduce very much to either one's health or one's happiness, in order to get up to town I have always pretended to have a younger brother of the name of Ernest, who lives in the Albany, and gets into the most dreadful scrapes.[72]

The only way Jack can surmount the barriers of hypocrisy demanded by society is to lead a double life. The conformist Jack pretends to obey the conventions, while the Bunburying (or 'Ernesting') Jack sees through them, recognises their damaging effect on health and happiness, and so merely uses them as a means to satisfy his own needs. For him the conventions are the fiction, and 'Ernest' provides him with the reality. Algernon follows a similar line when he declares:

Well, one must be serious about something, if one wants to have any amusement in life. I happen to be serious about Bunburying.[73]

Earlier Algernon has remarked, 'My duty as a gentleman has never interfered with my pleasure in the smallest degree',[74] and in this clash between ethical and social demands (duty) and individual desires (pleasure) we may see a striking parallel to the situation of Wilde himself. At the time when he wrote the play, he, too, was leading a double life, which the trials were to depict in all its intimate details before a sensation-seeking public. His public life consisted of living with wife and children in Tite Street, socialising with famous artists, scholars and literary figures, attending glamorous dinner parties and enthusiastically applauded theatre premières; his private life was 'feasting with panthers' in male brothels, rented flats and hotel rooms, consorting with homosexuals most of whom were far below his social and intellectual level, and calling every now and then on the procurer Alfred Taylor in Little College Street.[75]

Against this background, Franz Zaic's biographical interpretation of the play, drawing on an essay of Arthur Nethercot's, has a degree of justification.[76] He is undoubtedly right to claim that in this work Wilde was playing with things that were serious and weighty, and which were of vital importance to him at the time of writing: 'mit dem Problem der Identität und mit der Frage nach der Wahrheit'[77] [with the problem of identity and with the question of truth]. The desire to split the self – already to be seen in the *doppelgänger* motif of *Dorian Gray* – and the invention of fictitious alibi-characters can certainly be interpreted as projections of the author's secret wishes. The danger of such a biographical approach – a danger which Zaic does not entirely avoid – is that 'Bunburying' may be too narrowly equated with the single problem of identity. Zaic actually speaks of 'Verwirrung der Identitäten'[78] [confusion of identities], whereas in fact the most striking aspect of the whole theme, stressed again and again, is the social one, since both Algernon and Jack are striving to break out of the restrictions imposed on them by their social obligations. It would seem to be a more fruitful approach to view 'Bunburying' more in terms of the polarity of personal identity and social role-playing than in terms of the split self. What is abundantly clear, though, is that with his Ernest and Bunbury motifs Wilde has recognized and unmasked Victorian earnestness and Victorian hypocrisy as interdependent attitudes.

There is one final paradox: Jack does in fact turn out to be called Ernest, and furthermore he does have a younger brother. What had appeared to be fiction is in fact reality, whereas the reality of 'Bunburying' now becomes a fiction. Jack insists that he has no brother, but this is untrue. Algernon's warning in Act 1 that 'The truth is rarely pure and never simple'[79] is confirmed by the dénouement. Lies therefore prove to anticipate the truth, and claims of truthfulness are not fulfilled by reality. One can no longer rely on one's preconceptions of truth, and indeed truth itself is only relative. But Wilde never allows his paradoxes and provocations to deepen into a genuine problem – they remain embedded in the themes of his play, and the reader or spectator is left to make what he will of his own laughter.

While on the subect of themes, there is one final ironic application of the title theme that we might glance at in passing. The importance of being earnest applies no less to the actors than to the characters, for it is a commonplace in the theatre that for comedy to be funny, it must be acted seriously. Writing of Wilde's play, Sir John Gielgud describes the delicate balance required: 'to act with a deadly seriousness, yet to keep an inner consciousness of fun, the fun with which one plays seriously a very elaborate practical joke'.[80] The actor must take the trivialities of the situation just as seriously as the character he is playing if the comedy is to exert its full effect. Thus he will fulfil the avowed intention of the author himself:

That we should treat all the trivial things of life seriously, and all the serious things of life with sincere and studied triviality.[81]

Nonsense or satire?

The difficulty of classifying this confusing picture-puzzle of a play is clear from the different reactions of different critics. Few would deny that *The Importance of Being Earnest* ranks among the best of Wilde's works and indeed among the best of English comedies;[82] but opinions vary considerably as to the intentions of the play and its categorisation. Some have been so dazzled by the paradoxes that they see nothing but 'a trifle' (Ingleby),[83] 'delirious nonsense' (Symons),[84] 'sheer fun and hilarity, the apotheosis of Tomfoolery' (Pearson),[85] and the expression of a 'spirit of delicate fun'

(Ransome).[86] Others, however, see it as a fantasy (Lemonnier, Jordan),[87] parody (Foster),[88] burlesque (Partridge),[89] 'a kind of dandiacal Utopia' (Ganz),[90] or a play on the problems of identity and truth (Zaic).[91] Harold E. Toliver stresses the balance between 'sport and seriousness'[92] as characterising the play. Geoffrey Stone talks of it in linguistic terms as a 'meta-play'.[93] Most critics call it a farce (Sherard, Brasol, Perry, St John Ervine, N. James, D. Parker),[94] or a kind of farce with satirical intentions (Bentley, Reinert).[95] The author himself classified it as a 'farcical comedy',[96] for the basic idea is reminiscent of the farce, while the dialogue is that of the traditional comedy of manners.

But such pigeon-holing and labelling tells us little about the intentions and effects of the play itself. We have already noted that the world Wilde created was more than just an unrealistic and weightless fantasy, or 'dandiacal Utopia', to use Ganz's term. Even though it is certainly a consistent expression of his aestheticism and a theatrical exposition of his philosophy of triviality, the play is also – from the individual paradox to the whole style and texture, from the isolated incident to the overall structure of the plot, from the punning title to the final curtain – a massive social satire on the Victorian mentality, and above all on the attitudes of the aristocracy and the middle classes. Under attack are the absurd veneration of rank, name and birth, social and moral hypocrisy, and the commercialisation of life as exemplified by the marriage market. The play draws its life from its spirit of negation, and herein lies its liberating effect. By constantly snapping the chains of the reader's or spectator's expectations, it forces him off the well-worn tracks of his habitual manner of thinking, which becomes an object of ridicule, and so makes him adopt the unaccustomed and seemingly nonsensical counter-position of the aesthetic observer. He is made to laugh at the hollow superficiality hidden behind the mask of earnestness, and to mock the rich façade of conventional role-playing which likewise covers up an empty space. If the play appears to be an unrealistic, or even anti-realistic fantasy, where everything is seen *sub specie ludi*, there is still no escaping the realism behind its critique of society's pressure on the individual. This critique is achieved by reducing the importance of being earnest to the level of a name – all that seems to matter is outward form, which might collectively be called propriety. Even language to a large extent loses its communicative function, and as a series of inconsequential aphorisms aims at external effect rather than internal substance. In this respect language, too, is a façade with nothing behind it. It is the expression of an intellectual detachment by means of which any emotional involvement is made to lead nowhere, while the conventions which it appears to uphold are made to seem absurdly unreal. Life is reduced to a game, but the rules of the game are the very norms which the Victorian spectator would have followed in all earnestness during his everyday life.

When the characters do take something seriously, the something is trivial, and there are no intellectual convictions or values to support the earnestness. The ridiculous name-fetish, the eccentricity of the characters, the absurdity of the situations all combine to form a protest against middle-class insistence on normality, on conformity to existing conventions and traditions. But Wilde offers nothing to fill the empty space behind the façades, and so ultimately one might well extrapolate from this play the melancholy message of a world that has lost its means of orientation, can no longer cling unconditionally to any faith, and sees truth as a relative and malleable dimension. While other writers, however, devoted themselves earnestly to the task of confronting and mastering such doubts, Wilde reacted with 'iconoclastical gaiety'.[97] Earnestness for him degenerated into mere outward form, because he was not concerned with solving existential problems. In this respect his play uses farcical comedy to give an ironic picture of the reverse side of the Victorian upper classes while at the same time depicting both critically and realistically the face they presented to the real world.

While on 4 February 1895 Wilde was enjoying the greatest success of his theatrical career, personal tragedy was lurking close at hand. The Marquess of Queensberry, Bosie's father, described by Bosie himself in one book as an 'inhuman brute' and a 'madman',[98] was prowling round St James's accompanied by two musclemen and armed with a bunch of carrots and turnips which he intended to hand over to Wilde at the end of the play or, as Pearson suggests, to throw at Wilde's head.[99] George Alexander got to know of the Scottish lord's intentions and succeeded in getting him barred from the theatre. But Queensberry did not give up, and instead devised a new challenge. Four days after the première, on 8 February at 4.30 p.m., he handed to the porter of the Albemarle Club, of which Wilde was a member, an envelope containing a card with the message: 'Oscar Wilde posing as a somdomite' (*sic*). The challenge worked, and fate took its course. Wilde brought a suit against the Marquess, seeking legal protection from a society whose faults and weaknesses he had so often criticised. To his own detriment he mistook the laughter and applause of his theatre audience for Victorian middle-class acceptance and approval of his eccentric and provocative way of life. In the original version of the play there is a scene which uncannily anticipates his arrest and detention in Holloway Prison, thus confirming his own paradox that Nature imitates Art:

GRIBSBY [*Pulls out watch*]: I am sorry to disturb this pleasant family meeting, but time presses. We have to be at Holloway not later than four o' clock; otherwise it is difficult to obtain admission. The rules are very strict.

ALGY: Holloway!

GRIBSBY: It is at Holloway that detentions of this character take place always.

ALGY: Well, I really am not going to be imprisoned in the suburbs for having dined in the west end. It is perfectly ridiculous.

...

GRIBSBY: The surroundings I admit are middle class; but the gaol itself is fashionable and well-aired ...[100]

9 Apologies and accusations. *De Profundis* and *The Ballad of Reading Gaol*

Wilde's arrest on 5 April 1895, following the failure of his libel action against Queensberry, and the subsequent trial in which he was found guilty of violating the Criminal Law Amendment Act of 1885, meant the loss of his social position and also ultimately of his art. When found guilty, he stammered: 'And I? May I say nothing, my lord?'[1] to which the judge made no reply, but merely gestured to the two warders to take Wilde away to his cell. The famous and successful author became overnight 'the figure and letter of a little cell in a long gallery, one of a thousand lifeless numbers':[2] C.3.3. His name was struck from posters and handbills, his books withdrawn from the shops, and his person became either the target of holier-than-thou moralists or simply a taboo subject. His family went abroad, and all his property at 16 Tite Street was auctioned off or in part actually looted. Social degradation was accompanied by estrangement from his friend Alfred Douglas.

The new situation demanded new attitudes. How could his public role, which until now he had always played as the celebrated aesthete and hedonist, be adapted to fit in with his present position as convict C.3.3.? What new identity could he assume? What had really caused the catastrophe, and what possible shape could his future have? To what extent was the disaster due to external circumstance, intrigue and the influence of others, and to what extent was it all his own fault? On the ruins of his career and indeed his life, he now had to build a new view of himself in accordance with the new situation. The paradox is all too evident, for how could his personal identity – which could only be formed through continuity of experience – be related to the transformation in his public life, which was now denied all continuity and instead could suffer only disintegration in what was soon to become pseudonymous exile? *De Profundis* represents the first major, direct response to all these questions, while *The Ballad of Reading Gaol* offers a poetically foreshortened, symbolically coded answer.

De Profundis: text and edited versions

A major factor in the many misunderstandings of the text is the fact that the manuscript of *De Profundis* has only been available since 1960 in the

275

British Museum, and was not published in its complete, original form until 1962 (by Rupert Hart-Davis). Earlier critics had access only to versions that were bedevilled by cuts, omissions, transpositions and other defects. It is impossible to say exactly when *De Profundis* was begun, but a letter that Wilde wrote to More Adey on 18 February 1897[3] suggests that he had already started it at the beginning of the year. It was finished by the end of March. On the day after his release from prison on 19 May 1897, he gave the letter in a sealed envelope to his friend Robert Ross,[4] to whom it should originally have been posted on 1 April, but the Prison Commission had refused to allow it. Together with the letter, Wilde gave to Ross, who was to be his literary executor, detailed instructions which strengthen the suspicion that he had never intended the letter to Douglas to be a purely personal communication, but had written it with a view to at least partial publication. Ross was to have two typed copies made of the manuscript, one for himself and one for Wilde, and the original was to be sent to Douglas; a few precisely indicated sections were also to be copied and sent to the 'Lady of Wimbledon' (Adela Schuster) and Frank Forbes-Robertson, both friends of Wilde's. According to Ross, he sent a copy to Alfred Douglas on 9 August 1897, who acknowledged receipt of it.[5] The fact that a copy was sent, however, seems to contradict Wilde's instructions that Douglas was to have the original. Perhaps Wilde changed his mind, or perhaps Ross made the decision himself with a view to preserving the original for posterity, and to countering any possible charge of forgery. Existing sources do not provide us with any conclusive evidence either way.

Until the day he died, Lord Alfred Douglas maintained that he never received this letter. From his first public statements on the matter, in *Oscar Wilde and Myself*, right through to his last book *Oscar Wilde. A Summing-up*, in which he did revise some of his earlier views, Douglas insisted that he knew nothing about the unpublished parts of the letter until he heard about them during the Arthur Ransome trial.[6] The parts he was referring to were those relating to himself, which Ross had omitted from the first edition of the letter. Ransome's 1912 monograph on Wilde had made it clear that *De Profundis* had not been addressed to Ross – as many had previously thought – but to 'a man to whom Wilde felt that he owed some, at least, of the circumstances of his public disgrace'.[7] As this man was frequently referred to as Wilde's friend, whom he had met again in Naples after his release, there was scarcely any need for him to be named directly – it was evident that the reference was to Alfred Douglas. Douglas, however, felt that some passages of Ransome's book were libellous, and so he sued him. Ransome, in his defence, alluded to the unpublished sections of *De Profundis*, large extracts of which were read out to the court. The textual evidence was provided by a copy of the original, which Ross had left to the British Museum in 1909. Convinced by the passages referring to Douglas, the court dismissed the suit and acquitted Ransome.

This, however, still does not tell us whether Douglas received the letter or not. Ross is undoubtedly the more reliable witness in this matter, but there is at least one substantial piece of support for Douglas's version. In 1905 he wrote a review of *De Profundis* for the magazine *Motorist and Traveller*,[8] and this shows clearly that he had no idea of the identity of the addressee or of the fragmentary character of the text he was discussing. He speaks of an 'interesting posthumous book ... written in passionate sincerity at the time',[9] whereas after getting to know the letter in its entirety, he commented: 'I had great difficulty in finding a single statement which could not be demonstrated to be utterly, deliberately and ridiculously false.'[10] A hint as to a possible solution to the controversy is offered by Douglas himself in his *Autobiography*. There he mentions receiving a letter from Ross containing some of Wilde's comments about him. But it was not clear to him whether Wilde had written these comments himself, or Ross had collected them from various conversations. After glancing through the letter, 'a very long one of many pages',[11] he had torn it up and thrown it in the Marne. H. Montgomery Hyde uses this passage to support his hypothesis that this letter might have contained extracts from *De Profundis*. Douglas had perhaps not read as far as the start of the published sections, so that when he came to write his review, he could not actually recognise the text.[12] One would have thought, however, that after hearing the unpublished sections in the trial of 1913, he would have recalled the letter.

The publication of *De Profundis* is a no less complicated story. Under pressure from Max Meyerfeld, who did a great deal to promote Wilde's work in Germany, Ross consented to allow a shortened version of the manuscript to be translated. The German text appeared in January and February 1905 in the *Neue Rundschau*, under the title 'De Profundis. Aufzeichnungen und Briefe aus dem Zuchthaus in Reading' [Notes and Letters from Reading Gaol]. The main title was Ross's idea, probably following a suggestion made by E. V. Lucas, the well-known critic and publisher's reader. Wilde had once called the letter 'Epistola: In Carcere et Vinculis'.[13] Shortly after the publication in Germany, Methuen and Co. published a version which had been shortened even more than the German text. Up until 1908 no less than twelve editions were published in England before the text, together with some additional material, was incorporated into the first collected edition of Wilde's work.[14]

Ross was anxious to prevent Douglas from annotating and publishing in America the sections of *De Profundis* that had remained unknown until the Ransome trial, for the text would not have been protected by British copyright in America, and so at great speed he had fifteen copies printed by the publisher Paul R. Reynolds; two of these were presented to the Library of Congress, Ross kept twelve, and in order to comply with existing regulations, one copy was offered for sale.[15] The typescript from which the others were printed went by way of Robert Ross to Max Meyerfeld, who translated it into German, this version being published in 1925 by S. Fischer Verlag in Berlin, under the title *Epistola in Carcere et Vinculis*. Vyvyan Holland erroneously assumed that this typescript was identical to the original, and published the text in England in 1949 with the sub-title *The First Complete and Accurate Version of 'Epistola: in Carcere et Vinculis' the Last Prose Work in English of Oscar Wilde*. When Rupert Hart-Davis was preparing his edition of Wilde's letters, he compared Holland's edition with the original and came to the conclusion that it was neither complete nor accurate, as it contained 'several hundred errors'.[16] These were caused mainly by misreadings of Wilde's handwriting, mistakes made in dictation, 'corrections' of the grammar, and inexplicable juggling with individual passages and even whole paragraphs. Ross had also left out about 1,000 words which Douglas and his family must have found particularly obnoxious. And so it was not until *Letters* was published in 1962 that the first reliable version appeared of the famous letter that had been written in 1897.

Alfred Douglas as evil genius and inspiration

The fact that Wilde in his desperate situation should have sought a scapegoat for his misery is psychologically all too easy to understand. Alfred Douglas was the chosen victim. His conduct towards Wilde once the latter had disappeared behind bars made him especially suitable for the role. His total silence must have been as painful to C.3.3. as his tactless efforts to publish his friend's letters in *Mercure de France* without first asking Wilde's permission.[17] Outlawed by society, shunned by those who had been his friends, abandoned by the man who had stood closest to him during his years of success, and punished for actions that so many others had committed without penalty, Wilde became increasingly embittered by emotions that he needed to purge by writing. And so this becomes 'the most important letter of my life',[18] beginning with 'Dear Bosie' and ending, eighty-four pages[19] later, with 'Your affectionate friend'. It is as much a course of therapy to heal his battered soul as an attempt to communicate with someone outside himself. The importance of expressing his personal thoughts and feelings through this familiar medium is confirmed by a letter which Wilde wrote to Robert Ross and which was originally meant to accompany the manuscript of *De Profundis*:

Whether or not the letter does good to his [Douglas's] narrow nature and hectic brain, to me it has done great good. I have 'cleansed my bosom of much perilous stuff' . . . I need not remind you that mere expression is to an artist the supreme and only mode of life. It is by utterance that we live. Of the many, many things for which I have to thank the Governor there is none for which I am more grateful than for his permission to write fully to A. D. and at as great length as I desired. For nearly two years I had within me a growing burden of bitterness, much of which I have now got rid of.[20]

Wilde's sharp criticisms of Douglas are concentrated in the first section of the letter and in a few pages towards the end. He views the effects of their 'ill-fated and most lamentable'[21] friendship as having been utterly negative on both his life and his art. Intellectual and moral humiliation, artistic and financial ruin, the loss of his social position – these were the consequences of a relationship which from the very start was un-balanced.[22] Incapable of any concentrated mental effort, devoted to interests that failed to extend beyond 'meals and moods',[23] Douglas was never at any time able to bring ideas or inspiration that would enrich the intellectual atmosphere so essential for Wilde. He was never one of those 'who could play gracefully with ideas but had arrived at violence of opinion merely'.[24]

Bosie's closed mind and lack of flexibility, linked to his irritable temperament and vain obstinacy, and their paucity of common interests made their relationship seem to Wilde 'intellectually degrading'.[25] What was more, this mentality and character, together with other factors, had led finally to the ruination of Wilde's art:

You had been idle at your school, worse than idle at your university. You did not realise that an artist, and especially such an artist as I am, one, that is to say, the quality of whose work depends on the intensification of personality, requires for the development of his art the companionship of ideas, and intellectual atmo-sphere, quiet, peace, and solitude. You admired my work when it was finished . . . but you could not understand the conditions requisite for the production of artistic work. I am not speaking in phrases of rhetorical exaggeration but in terms of absolute truth to actual fact when I remind you that during the whole time we were together I never wrote one single line . . . my life, as long as you were by my side, was entirely sterile and uncreative.[26]

Wilde illustrates this last criticism with a detailed description of a typical day in September 1893 (though he must in fact mean October), when he had rented rooms in St James's Place in order to work un-disturbed on his play *An Ideal Husband*. Douglas used to turn up at around 12 noon, they would talk for a while, and then go for lunch at around 1.30 p.m. This usually lasted until about 3.30 p.m., when Douglas would go to his club for an hour before presenting himself again at tea-time. He would stay on until it was time for their evening meal, which they took either in Tite Street or at the Savoy. Then a late supper at Willis's rounded off the day: 'That was my life for those three months, every single day, except during the four days when you went abroad.'[27]

Naturally this life style demanded not only time but also money, which according to Wilde invariably came from his own purse. In this context, too, he goes into almost pedantic detail over the money he wasted on Douglas that year:

When I tell you that between the autumn of 1892 and the date of my imprisonment I spent with you and on you more than £5,000 in actual money, irrespective of the bills I incurred, you will have some idea of the sort of life on which you insisted. Do you think I exaggerate? My ordinary expenses with you for an ordinary day in London – for luncheon, dinner, supper, amusements, hansoms and the rest of it – ranged from £12 to £20, and the week's expenses were naturally in proportion and ranged from £80 to £130.[28]

Wilde's sources of income were in no way rich enough to allow such expenses over a period of time. Very soon he was in considerable difficulty. This continual financial drain certainly contributed to his later insolvency, but he was less upset by the loss of the money than by the fact that Douglas simply took it for granted that his friend would carry on paying for his pleasures – without moderation, without thanks and 'without grace'.[29]

But even more painful than the financial ruin, ingratitude, artistic sterility and intellectual disproportion that characterised his relationship with Douglas was the 'ethical degradation'[30] that led ultimately to his trial and imprisonment. He does not doubt that Douglas loved him. But 'In you Hate was always stronger than Love.'[31] Hate made him blind to his worsening relations with his father and his friend, while 'the prospect of a battle in which you would be safe delighted you'.[32] Hate produced that 'terrible lack of imagination'[33] which Wilde regarded as Bosie's real weakness. If one accepts Wilde's description, it was always Douglas who imposed his will, followed his own fancy, and had not the slightest consideration for his partner. Wilde's explanation for this is as follows:

Through deep if misplaced affection for you: through great pity for your defects of temper and temperament: through my own proverbial good-nature and Celtic laziness: through an artistic aversion to coarse scenes and ugly words: through that incapacity to bear resentment of any kind which at that time characterised me: through my dislike of seeing life made bitter and uncomely by what to me, with my eyes really fixed on other things, seemed to be mere trifles too petty for more than a moment's thought or interest – through these reasons, simple as they may sound, I gave up to you always ... Your meanest motive, your lowest appetite, your most common passion, became to you laws by which the lives of others were to be guided always, and to which, if necessary, they were to be without scruple sacrificed.[34]

Of the many examples he gives to illustrate Bosie's behaviour, we may take a single scene that took place between 10 and 13 October 1894 in the Grand Hotel, Brighton. Douglas was in bed with 'flu, and Wilde helped him to pass the time as agreeably as possible by bringing him fruit, flowers and books and keeping him company. When, a few days later, Wilde fell ill himself, Bosie took no care of him at all but, in fact, reproached and even threatened him, writing him a thoroughly nasty, callous letter: '*When you are not on your pedestal you are not interesting. The next time you are ill I will go away at once.*'[35]

Further evidence of this destructive relationship, as viewed retro-spectively by C.3.3., lay in Bosie's reaction to his father's aggressive conduct, which became outright provocation in the form of an insulting card left at Wilde's club. Instead of using every means in his power to prevent his friend from destroying himself in a trial that could only end in artistic and social ruin, he had done all he could to encourage Wilde to take this step. Driven by hatred for Bosie's father, and obsessed with the desire to 'see him "in the dock" ',[36] Wilde had ignored the advice of those who had warned him against suing Queensberry:

Between you both [Douglas and Queensberry] I lost my head. My judgment forsook me. Terror took its place. I saw no possible escape, I may say frankly from either of you. Blindly I staggered as an ox into the shambles. I had made a gigantic psychological error. I had always thought that my giving up to you in small things meant nothing: that when a great moment arrived I could reassert my will-power in its natural superiority. It was not so. At the great moment my will-power completely failed me.[37]

On reading all these pages of reproaches and criticisms, the impartial reader can scarcely avoid asking why Wilde should have remained friends for four years with a man who apparently possessed almost nothing but negative qualities: an intellectual parasite, a financial exploiter, and a bad-tempered, vain and unimaginative egoist. What does the picture drawn by the author of *De Profundis* have in common with the addressee of the ardent love-letters written just two years earlier from Holloway Prison, calling Bosie 'my sweet rose, my delicate flower, my lily of lilies',[38] and assuring him of 'immortal ... eternal love'?[39] Perhaps Wilde's isolation during his long imprisonment and his detachment from the past may have made him see the unpleasant aspects of this relationship more clearly, now that the illusion had been broken. But on the other hand his embitterment at Bosie's lack of emotional support made his fall from lofty social heights even harder to bear, and it led to certain distortions and even falsehoods in his account of their relationship. For instance, the claim that his life with Douglas was 'entirely sterile and uncreative'[40] is a gross exaggeration, for we have already seen how much Wilde wrote between 1891 and 1895. But to call *De Profundis* 'the ravings of a lunatic'[41] and to say that its author was not 'mentally responsible'[42] for it, as Douglas did in his books, is an equally exaggerated and polemic reaction. The truth may well lie between biographical facts and autobiographical interpretation as something highly complex and ambivalent: for Wilde, Douglas was, at one and the same time, the evil genius and the source of inspiration, the dreaded tormentor and the beloved friend, the *homme fatal.*

Wilde does not by any means ignore his own part in the breakdown of their relationship, but one does sometimes wonder how self-critical he really is. He often precedes his worst criticisms of Bosie with such expressions as 'I blame myself' or 'I blame myself for having allowed'.[43] Later he even confesses that neither Bosie nor his father 'multiplied a thousand times over'[44] have ruined him, but that he and he alone is responsible. But against the long list of his friend's faults and weaknesses, illustrated by countless examples, he can identify only one major fault on his own account that might have had any adverse influence, and that is his weak will. And where the will is weak, can one really be held totally responsible for one's moral behaviour? Behind the mask of the reasonable man, magnanimously confessing his own responsibility for his downfall, could Wilde not hope·for a degree of sympathy and forgiveness from his reader as he attributed the disaster to his own fatal weakness of will – so much more forgivable than financial exploitation and intellectual sponging? Could any reader fail to be moved by the tale of a great artist, but alas a weak-willed man, brought to ruin by a tyrannical parasite? Wilde's willingness to forgive his tormentor at the end of this long series of accusations was not merely an attempt to cleanse his soul of bitterness; it was also a basic element in the apologetic defence strategy of the letter. The role of the martyr forgiving his executioner guarantees sympathy, and indirectly the reader finds himself called upon to exercise precisely this Christian virtue as he considers the case of C.3.3.

Portrait of the artist as martyr

The attack on Alfred Douglas that constitutes the first part of the letter also constitutes the first stage of Wilde's search for a new identity. His description of the relationship is followed by an attempt to draw from his past, present and foreseeable future the basis for a different view of himself and of his social situation. He needs to know how much of his old philosophy can be used to shore up the construction of his new life. Can his art continue once his social life has been shattered? If he were to re-establish himself as an artist, would he then be able to re-establish himself in society? Or is he doomed now to remain a social outcast?

Wilde begins his stock-taking by considering the past. The retrospective picture he draws of himself is in glowing, if not quite realistic colours, whereas his portrait of the present is far darker, no doubt with a view to stressing the contrast between earlier greatness and current misery. Once 'a man of world-wide reputation',[45] a king in the realm of art, and indeed for many its 'supreme arbiter',[46] he now finds himself situated between the child murderer Gilles de Retz and the Marquis de Sade 'in the lowest mire of Malebolge'.[47] His account of his past social and artistic position suddenly soars off into superlatives:

I was a man who stood in symbolic relations to the art and culture of my age ... The gods had given me almost everything. I had genius, a distinguished name, high social position, brilliancy, intellectual daring: I made art a philosophy, and philosophy an art: I altered the minds of men and the colour of things: there was nothing I said or did that did not make people wonder: I took the drama, the most objective form known to art, and made it as personal a mode of expression as the lyric or the sonnet, at the same time I widened its range and enriched its characterisation: drama, novel, poem in rhyme, poem in prose, subtle or fantastic dialogue, whatever I touched I made beautiful in a new mode of beauty: to truth itself I gave what is false no less than what is true as its rightful province, and showed that the false and the true are merely forms of intellectual existence. I treated Art as the supreme reality, and life as a mere mode of fiction: I awoke the imagination of my century so that it created myth and legend around me: I summed up all systems in a phrase, and all existence in an epigram.[48]

This stylisation of Wilde's glorious *alter ego* is undoubtedly more a matter of wishful thinking and rose-coloured spectacles than of the plain and simple facts. But on the other hand, he does not spare himself in his description of his own less glorious self. He has been a *flâneur*, a dandy, a 'man of fashion',[49] who all too often let himself be 'lured into long spells of senseless and sensual ease',[50] surrounding himself with inferior beings and wasting his own genius. He confesses to having lived a life 'full of perverse pleasures and strange passions',[51] and in the hunt for 'new sensations' – as advocated in Lord Henry's 'new hedonism' – he had lost his self-discipline and had made himself a slave to his desires. He even admits: 'I grew careless of the lives of others.'[52]

One waits in suspense to see what conclusions he will draw from this two-sided account. Will he acknowledge the contradiction between his emphatic avowal that art is his greatest passion, and his uninhibited devotion to pleasure as the most enjoyable way of life? On the contrary: 'I don't regret for a single moment having lived for pleasure.'[53] His one mistake was to have lain only on 'the sungilt side of the garden',[54] for after all, the other side also had its secrets, and these too must be explored. The validity of the pleasure principle is not questioned, it merely needs to be supplemented. 'Humility' and 'sorrow' are the two most important additions to his experience, and these serve to correct his aesthetic, hedonistic philosophy. Morality is no help to him – 'I am a born antinomian'[55] – and religion is equally useless, for he cannot believe in that which eludes sight and touch; reason does not help either, because it only tells him that the laws justifying his condemnation are false. It is the privilege of the suffering man – and so of Wilde himself – 'to have become a *deeper* man'.[56] And so suffering now seems to him 'the supreme emotion of which man is capable',[57] while at the same time it is 'the type and test of all great Art'.[58]

Identification with suffering as the mode of future self-realisation is not seen as a break with his past life and opinions, but, as we have seen, it is a necessary and long overdue extension. He does not wish in any way to deny or suppress his past experiences, and so this is the only way in which he can fully accept himself in his new situation as a 'common prisoner of a common gaol'.[59] But for moral support he needs the example of a great historical figure, whom he interprets as being the prototype of the suffering artist: Jesus Christ.[60] According to Wilde, there is a close link between the life of Christ and that of the artist, for both possess an 'intense and flamelike imagination'.[61] The carpenter's son from Galilee was 'the most supreme of Individualists'[62] for whom there were no laws but only exceptions. He therefore embodied the essence of romanticism. This is particularly evident in His attitude towards sin and suffering, which seemed to Him 'beautiful, holy things, and modes of perfection'.[63] His life is 'the most wonderful of poems',[64] and the gospels are 'four prose-poems about Christ'.[65]

The portrait which C.3.3. draws of Christ clearly contains less of the son of God than of a somewhat idealised Wilde. The dominant personality, the romantic artist, and the great individualist are all descriptions that Wilde was in the habit of applying to himself. He sees Jesus as a charismatic figure whose life and work, especially the last Stations of the Cross, are like an heroic epic of unheard-of tragic proportions, such as not even Aeschylus or Sophocles, Dante or Shakespeare, had ever conceived. The miracles can be attributed quite naturally to the 'charm of his personality'.[66] The aestheticising of Christ,[67] who is said to have spread his teachings not in Aramaic but in Greek, Wilde's favourite language, must be seen in the context of growing nineteenth-century atheism, which deprived the biblical figure of His divine status. The foundations of this development were laid by the transformation of Hegel's dialectics into materialistic and nihilistic interpretations of culture and history – as practised especially by such left-wing philosophers as Feuerbach, Marx and Engels – as well as by Nietzsche's writings, Schopenhauer's pessimism, and the anti-metaphysical, scientific positivism of Comte. Furthermore, ever since romanticism the tendency had been to focus more upon Jesus's life, so that he became the rebellious 'Jésus sans-culotte' of the French Revolution, and later appeared on the barricades of 1848[68] as the victorious liberator, resurrected after the Crucifixion and now triumphing over his persecutors. It was this tradition that had paved the way for Wilde's *fin-de-siècle* portrait of Christ, the aesthetic individualist.

A significant contribution to the changes in Christology during the nineteenth century was made by the different attempts to describe the life of Jesus. David Friedrich Strauss (*Das Leben Jesu*, 1835) wrote a radical critique of the Bible, declaring most of the gospels to be myth; Ernest Renan (*Vie de Jésus*, 1863) created a glorified, romantic and extremely popular vision of 'l'individu qui a fait faire à son espèce le plus grand pas vers le divin'.[69] Wilde knew Renan, for he mentions him twice in *De Profundis*, and actually quotes a passage from *Vie de Jésus* which had stuck in his memory.[70] It was also one of the titles he named on a list of books which he requested and which, on 29 July 1896, were allowed – with a few exceptions – by the then governor of Reading Gaol. It is quite likely that Renan's book gave him several ideas. Renan lays special emphasis on Jesus's extraordinary personality, 'un homme de proportions colossales',[71] whose main concern was 'l'intérêt de l'humanité'.[72] Wilde speaks in similar vein of his 'Titan personality'[73] and his morality as a form of 'sympathy'.[74] According to Renan, Jesus proclaimed 'la royauté de l'esprit',[75] and Wilde declares that for Jesus 'the spirit alone was of value'.[76] Clearly the two conceptions of Christ had a good deal in common.

The link between Wilde's picture of Christ and the tradition of Renan and nineteenth-century theology, however, is of only secondary importance to our understanding of this section of the letter. Far more significant is the question why Wilde should have unfolded such a detailed portrait of Christ, bearing so many features of his own situation and idealised self. One cannot help surmising that in drawing such a parallel between himself and this Messianic figure, he was trying to endow his personal degradation with a certain historical dignity. He saw C.3.3. standing beside Christ – two prophets of an individualistic aesthetic gospel, personifications of the romantic artist *par excellence*, united in their struggle against the Pharisees of yesteryear and the Philistines of today, despised and rejected, punished and finally martyred for their cause. For a man to whom style meant so much, there must have been deep satisfaction in sharing a destiny with Jesus Christ. He says that Verlaine and Kropotkin had led 'two of the most perfect lives',[77] and does not forget to mention that both spent some years in prison, as if somehow this had been indispensable to the perfection of their artistry.

If Wilde proclaims that 'There is only one thing for me now, absolute Humility',[78] there seems little sign of it in these images of a Wildean Christ. Even if one ignores Martin Luther's admonition that true humility never knows that it is humble,[79] there are many other grounds for presuming that neither humility nor suffering played much of a part in Wilde's coming to terms with his new existence. What continually emerges is his determination to lose as little as possible of his old identity and only to accept as much as necessary of his new isolation. What he does accept is in any case beyond his control – the fact of his imprisonment and the resultant destruction of his social life. While the bourgeois Wilde laments the gracelessness of his fall – 'Everything about my tragedy has been hideous, mean, repellent, lacking in style'[80] – the artist can at least appreciate the heroic proportions of that tragedy. By identifying C.3.3. indirectly with Christ, and by building an analogy between his own life and that of Verlaine and Kropotkin, he is erecting a monument to a self which, even if it is different from before, is at least as imposing and impressive: instead of the dandy fallen from his pedestal, we now have the portrait of the artist as martyr. No humble, uncomplaining resignation to his fate, but instead its aesthetic elevation to the scale of an historic drama – this was how Wilde was able to adapt himself to his new situation. He becomes the spectator of a play in which he himself is the tragic hero, perishing in the battle for art against the petty plotting of the villains Douglas and Queensberry. He seems to revel in the spectacle of his fall, which is a unique and wonderful piece of theatre. His suffering becomes a new and extraordinary emotional adventure, which at times he can enjoy almost with detachment. When, in the second trial, prosecuting counsel Lockwood accused him of appalling misdemeanours – 'like a thing out of Tacitus'[81] – he was less perturbed by the content of the attack than by the perspective from which it was delivered, and he thought: '*How splendid* it would be, if I was saying all this about myself!'[82] When he was being transferred from Wandsworth to Reading, he had to wait in prison uniform and handcuffs for half an hour at Clapham Junction, exposed to the gaze of a gaping crowd. Even in this humiliating situation, he saw himself and especially his fellow convicts from a distance: 'We are the zanies of sorrow. We are clowns whose hearts are broken.'[83]

It would, however, be wrong to claim that Wilde did not at times genuinely suffer from prison life. But this suffering was never so intense or so lasting that it made any basic difference to his aesthetic hedonism. The situation did not, of course, permit any further indulgence in dandyism, and gestures of humility and avowals of suffering were far more suited to the new role, which was meant to convince the Victorian public that the justly punished sinner was now in sackcloth, had abjured his shallow 'Wardour Street aestheticism',[84] had seen the error of his ways and was now duly bearing his cross. Wilde no doubt hoped that by conforming to such Victorian expectations, he would prepare the way for society to forgive him, for it is clear from his peace-offering that he had not entirely lost hope of ultimate rehabilitation and reintegration:

I claim on my side that if I realise what I have suffered, Society should realise what it has inflicted on me: and that there should be no bitterness or hate on either side.[85]

A '*cri de cœur*', or a literary conceit? This mixture of role-playing and self-disclosure, with one eye on the reaction of the public, written in a clear, rich and sometimes even decorative style, has aroused different responses from the critics. The main discussion centres on the question of 'sincerity'.[86] Those who take the suffering and the Christ analogy seriously interpret *De Profundis* as 'The Birth of a Soul',[87] or 'le sanglot d'un blessé qui se débat'.[88] Those who, in the light of later developments, doubt the sincerity of the new insights call the letter 'emotionally unconvincing'[89] and insist on its 'transparent insincerity'.[90] And finally the meticulousness of the style and the construction – both in relation to the organisation of the individual sections and the recurrence of certain leitmotivs – strongly suggest that Wilde was concerned less with private self-expression than with 'the triumph of the literary temperament over the most disadvantageous conditions'.[91] What, then, is the intention of this letter? Is it a cry from the heart or a literary essay, a confession in the tradition of Saint Augustine and Rousseau, or a stylistic exercise on themes drawn from life? In short, which is more important, the aesthetic motive or the autobiographical?

No one can deny that any comparison between the statements in the letter and Wilde's behaviour in exile will lead to the conclusion that the letter was insincere. How could he have begun his letter with the sharpest criticisms of his friend Douglas – including total moral and intellectual bankruptcy – and yet have ended by suggesting that they should meet again, and indeed just a few months later have actually moved into a flat with him? In his artistically sterile and restless exile, are there any signs at all that pleasure, in so far as it was still available to him, was not the leading priority? How seriously can one take the claim that 'The external things of life seem to me now of no importance at all',[92] when one knows very well that without the applause of the public and the stimulus of a particular life style, he was incapable of creating? Did he not himself proclaim that '*la joie de vivre* is gone, and that, with will-power, is the basis of art'.[93]

There are certain statements in the letter that can only seem insincere in the light of his actual behaviour when he was in exile, but the comparison is perhaps unfair. Views change when circumstances change, and a man in prison may sincerely turn away from things and people that he will sincerely embrace when he is free. A charge of inconstancy may seem more apt than one of insincerity. This, however, is not a defence of Wilde's sincerity, but a rejection of one line of attack. At the time of writing it may well be that Wilde was giving expression to his moods, thoughts and longings of the moment, but one's judgment of his sincerity will have to depend on one's interpretation of his style rather than of his life.

One vivid illustration of the difference between the feelings of the moment and later behaviour can be seen in a passage on nature:

I have a strange longing for the great primeval things, such as the Sea, to me no less of a mother than the Earth ... Society, as we have constituted it, will have no place for me, has none to offer; but Nature, whose sweet rains fall on unjust and just alike, will have clefts in the rocks where I may hide, and secret valleys in whose silence I may weep undisturbed. She will hang the night with stars so that I may walk abroad in the darkness without stumbling, and send the wind over my footprints so that none may track me to my hurt: she will cleanse me in great waters, and with bitter herbs make me whole.[94]

There can be little doubt that with his awareness of his isolation and of society's rejection of him, Wilde would have longed for the haven that nature could offer him. And yet his very efforts to bring this longing to life lead to an elegiac idyll that arouses our suspicions. One can feel the literary fantasy of the author grasping the momentary, but genuine, emotion, and expanding it into a Rousseau-like vision of a way of life which, even after the shock of Reading, could scarcely come naturally to such a totally urbane being as Wilde. Later on, when he was in fact living in the country, in Berneval-sur-Mer, a few months were as much as he could take: 'I simply cannot stand Berneval. I nearly committed suicide there last Thursday – I was so bored.'[95] Whenever a spark of feeling leads the imagination towards a mode of living – the longing for security leading to a life in nature, or suffering leading to the pose of the martyr – there is a transition from original to aesthetically fashioned emotion, and a link is established between the mechanism of conforming to the role expected by the public and Wilde's insight into his own identity.

The strange inconsistency of the letter need not, as we have seen, be evidence of insincerity. Max Beerbohm's very revealing discussion of *De Profundis*, however, suggests that artistic expression did not follow emotion, but preceded it: 'emotion came through its own expression. The artist spoke, and the man obeyed. The attitude was struck, and the heart pulsated to it.'[96] If this was indeed so, one might ask why Wilde should have wanted humility and suffering to play such a vital part in his new life. The answer may perhaps be that whenever he was revealing emotions and attitudes that seemed foreign to him – and hence insincere to us – he was in fact guided by what he regarded as other people's expectations. The role of the martyr was to prepare the way for social reintegration, which would not have been possible for the prophet of pleasure.

As already mentioned, the structural care and the eye for stylistic effect have both been regarded as indications of insincerity. But literary expression for Wilde could not possibly take on the form of factual documentation. He was incapable of *not* stylising his expression, and it made no difference whether the material was fictional or autobiographical. His contact with reality had always been imbued with a conscious detachment, and so why should his emotional involvement, 'recollected in tranquillity', have made it impossible for him to transmute reality in his own imaginative style? Indeed, was it not precisely his art that now gave him the chance to understand his own situation and, by writing, analysing, and even glorifying it, actually to master it? Even when he is most intimately caught up in a situation, he seeks detachment in order to remain in control. The inseparable bond between his sincerity and his eloquence may be illustrated by the passage describing the death of his mother:

Her death was so terrible to me that I, once a lord of language, have no words in which to express my anguish and my shame. Never, even in the most perfect days of my development as an artist, could I have had words fit to bear so august a burden, or to move with sufficient stateliness of music through the purple pageant of my incommunicable woe. She and my father had bequeathed me a name they had made noble and honoured not merely in Literature, Art, Archaeology and Science, but in the public history of my own country in its evolution as a nation. I had disgraced that name eternally. I had made it a low byword among low people. I had dragged it through the very mire. I had given it to brutes that they might make it brutal, and to fools that they might turn it into a synonym for folly. What I suffered then, and still suffer, is not for pen to write or paper to record.[97]

Scarcely has the 'lord of language' announced that he has no words, when he is aestheticising his grief into the 'purple pageant of my incommunicable woe', and launching himself into an equally purple passage of eloquent self-pity.

Are we then to conclude that *De Profundis* is less a *cri de cœur* than 'the artistic essay of an artist'?[98] Given the nature of the man, there is no reason why it should not have been both in equal measure, since he could only express his emotions by stylising them. But the question must remain open to each individual reader's own judgment.

What *can* be said with a good degree of certainty is that the letter fulfilled a double function for Wilde. First, it enabled him to express such oppressive feelings as bitterness and disappointment, caused by Douglas's behaviour, and wounded pride at the injustices of the law. These he attempts to master by writing, fashioning, and aestheticising. Herein lies the therapeutic function of the letter. The length, style and intellectual strategy of the letter, however, together with Wilde's own instructions concerning the making of copies, indicate that at least some passages were meant for publication. And so the letter cannot be viewed merely as the private outpourings of the heart. It is, rather, a comprehensive *apologia pro vita sua*,[99] in which at a critical point in his development Wilde draws up a statement of account both for himself and for the public, concerning his relationship with Douglas, the reasons for his downfall, and his past, present and future position in art and in life. The new situation of the artist and citizen, of the private self and the public figure demanded definition. The portrait that he draws of himself is perhaps dictated by deliberate tactics, or perhaps by unconscious conformity to public expectations, but it is a picture that society will be able to accept and for which it might even reward him with rehabilitation: the weak-willed artist, betrayed in his art by an aristocratic parasite, a *mauvais génie*, and driven into a suicidal lawsuit, thence to languish in prison, atoning for his one-sided philosophy of pleasure, learning to appreciate the value of humility and suffering, and finally leaving his place of purification, a mature man, made perfect by this necessary experience of life, without bitterness, willingly fitting into his role of the outcast, seeking only to heal his wounds amid the elemental forces of nature. Herein lies the pragmatic function of the letter. Yet again, Wilde the rebel comes to terms with Wilde the timid conformist, and provocation and conformity join together in an attitude that is less redolent of the individualism so frequently invoked than of something that smacks almost of opportunism.

The content, then, is a mixture of defence and attack, and the intention one of therapy through self-expression and public justification and rehabilitation; as a whole, it presents no basic change in Wilde's view of art or of life. But one cannot and should not ignore the fact that the bitter experience of Reading Gaol did lead to a new awareness and a sharpened social conscience. The two letters to the *Daily Chronicle* and Wilde's last poem *The Ballad of Reading Gaol*, all of which reveal a hitherto unexpected zeal for a social cause – that of prison reform – indicate that imprisonment did at least leave some mark on him. But the new awareness did not lead to any new creative impulse, and this in itself is evidence of how little long-term effect it had on him. In reading *De Profundis* one is continually aware, despite the destruction of Wilde's social existence, that his pride in his extraordinary personality remains unbroken, and one senses the presence of the artist symbolically marking out his position in the art and culture of his time. He does indeed write *de profundis*, but he himself remains *in excelsis*, standing next to Christ, his place assured in the pantheon of all those writers who share his fate.

The Ballad of Reading Gaol

In the *Pall Mall Gazette* of 3 January 1889, under the title 'Poetry and Prison', Wilde reviewed a collection of poems by Wilfred Scawen Blunt.[100] He begins by saying that prison life has had 'an admirable effect'[101] on Blunt's qualities as a poet, and ends with the words:

it must be admitted that by sending Mr Blunt to gaol he [Mr Balfour] has converted a clever rhymer into an earnest and deep-thinking poet.[102]

In writing these lines, Wilde could never have dreamt that just a few years later they would be directly applicable both to his life and to his development as a poet from the early *Poems*, and the later *Sphinx*, to *The Ballad of Reading Gaol*. The radical change from these poetic experiments – more epigonic than original – to a simple style, realistic subject, and at times propagandist tone, came about not from any revision of his aesthetic theory, but from the shock of his imprisonment. The sensitive aesthete, accustomed to luxury and all the graces of social life, must have been appalled by life in Reading Gaol, with its inhumanity and degradation, forced labour, bad food, unhygienic sanitary arrangements, and its system of petty punishments for even the smallest offences against prison regulations. The reduction of human existence to the satisfaction of basic needs, together with almost total isolation from the outside world – four letters could be written in a year, and four twenty-minute visits received – threatened both the physical and the spiritual man, and even led to thoughts of suicide.[103]

This extreme situation had its effect on Wilde both as a person and as an artist. Indeed the interdependence of life and art is clear from a letter he wrote to Carlos Blacker: '*la joie de vivre* is gone, and that, with will-power, is the basis of art'.[104] As we have already seen, it would be wrong to assume that the trauma of Reading caused any basic change in his philosophy, but there *were* changes, and these went deeper than Wilde himself would have admitted when he proudly announced: 'I am far more of an individualist than I ever was.'[105] His individualism was no longer that of the supreme 'lord of language', deliberately flaunting his mask of the *provocateur*, but that of the outsider, with no choice but to lead the life of a pariah. His bitter and humiliating experiences in prison sharpened his moral awareness and his capacity for suffering and sympathy, for human solidarity and justice. Late in life, indeed too late, he had to learn that his philosophy of the moment, directed towards pleasure and enjoyment, was – for all its attractions – a superficial and ultimately inadequate basis for life. Being forced to live so close together with other convicts, the elitist individualist woke up to a social reality he had never known before, and this expressed itself not only in his personal intervention on behalf of the warder Martin, against whose dismissal he protested publicly in a letter to the *Daily Chronicle*, but also in his sharp criticisms of prison practices.

Wilde was, however, reluctant to apply the effects of his new experiences to the practice of his art. This was because he never fundamentally altered the aesthetic premises he had laid down in *Intentions*, and never adapted them to his changed view of reality. He was forced by circumstances and not by his new insights into adopting solutions that ran counter to his previous aesthetic codes. Everything he wrote about the composition of the *Ballad* reflects this conflict. In a letter to Frank Harris, written in February 1898, he says:

> I, of course, feel that the poem is too autobiographical and that *real* experiences are alien things that should never influence one, but it was wrung out of me, a cry of pain, the cry of Marsyas, not the song of Apollo. Still, there are some good things in it. I feel as if I had made a sonnet out of skilly.[106]

Even in *Dorian Gray* there had been a striking contrast between the theses of the Preface and the dénouement of the novel itself. But nowhere is the concept of autonomous art more clearly refuted than in Wilde's last poem.

In analysing the *Ballad*, it is impossible to confine oneself to its aesthetic problems, with 'a romantic artist ... working on realistic material'.[107] What is far more to the point is the effects of the author's personal involvement and changed social circumstances on the ideas and strategies of the poem, for the conditions that gave rise to the *Ballad* are as vital to its understanding as was the relationship between Wilde and Lord Alfred Douglas to the understanding of *De Profundis*. Both texts represent Wilde's attempts to get over the moral shock of Reading and of his social downfall. In *De Profundis*, the effort takes the form of a letter in which, by recounting the story of his relations with Douglas, he tries to come to terms with his past life, his fall, and a possible new life in the future. In *The Ballad of Reading Gaol* his subjective experiences become objectified in a poem that addresses itself to the public. At its centre is the execution of a guilty man – a single, concrete case, but at the same time an abstract problem relating to human guilt in general. It is not difficult to discern the autobiographical context, or the close bond between the criminal's fate and that of the poet. The strategy Wilde uses both in *De Profundis* and in the *Ballad* imposes an impressive pattern on what would otherwise be an amorphous collection of personal experiences – this is the pattern of apology and accusation, with a realistic appraisal of the status quo on the one hand, and a confirmation of his previous concepts of art and life on the other. As for the aesthetic problem mentioned above, in relation to the composition of the *Ballad*, it is simply the result of the *l'art pour l'art* exponent, the successful author, and the witty but notorious *enfant terrible* attempting to combine his past identity with the new one of the outsider.

Composition, literary tradition, and effect

The starting-point of the poem's composition was an actual event – which is in itself a contradiction of Wilde's theory of art.[108] On 7 July 1896 Charles Thomas Wooldridge, a soldier in the Royal Horse Guards (Blue), was hanged at Reading Gaol for murdering his wife, Laura Ellen –

apparently out of jealousy. Convict C.3.3. did not witness the execution himself, but the event was a topic of conversation among the prisoners and made a deep impression on him. Just a few days after his release, he told his friend Robert Ross, 'I have begun something that I think will be very good.'[109] From the letters he wrote to various people in July and August, it is clear that he was working continuously on the *Ballad*. On 24 August he sent the incomplete manuscript to the publisher Leonard Smithers to have it copied. Owing to his move from Berneval-sur-Mer to Naples, where he and Lord Alfred Douglas were to share a flat in the Villa Giudice in Posilipo, the completion of the poem was again postponed. To the version written in Berneval he added Parts V and VI, as well as several extra verses which strengthened the propaganda element and the romantic, aesthetic style. Not until October did the poem take on its final form. As Wilde did not consider publication just before Christmas to be particularly apt – 'I am hardly a Christmas present'[110] – publication was put off until 13 February 1898. Sales were good, no doubt partly because the public had guessed the identity of C.3.3. In 1898 alone Leonard Smithers issued six impressions, amounting to over 5,000 copies. A year later there was a seventh printing, this time with the name of the author in square brackets after the pseudonym. After Wilde's death there were pirate editions bearing the date 1899, the number of copies being unknown.

An indication of the poem's wide popularity is the fact that it was translated into nearly all European languages. In the year of its first publication, a French prose translation by Henry-D. Davray in collaboration with the author appeared in the May edition of *Mercure de France*.[111] At least six different German translations were made in the ten years following Wilde's death, the first of them published by the Insel Verlag in 1903. In his bibliographical study, Abraham Horodisch[112] lists thirty-two different illustrated editions in a period of forty-five years,[113] including seven Spanish translations, five Italian, eight Dutch and eight Flemish. Even in Eastern Europe the *Ballad* attracted a good deal of attention. The first Czech translation, by Jiři Almar (1901), was soon followed by Russian (1903), Hungarian (1908), and Polish (1911) versions.

The poem lends itself to illustration. The publisher Smithers had tried right from the start to get Beardsley to do some drawings, but nothing came of the project. Wilde's own attitude in this regard was ambivalent. In a letter to Smithers he opposes illustration, arguing that this would detract from the beauty of the poem and would contribute nothing to its 'psychological revelations';[114] but in conversations with the French translator Davray, he expressed interest in the idea of illustrations. In fact, nine years went by before the first illustrated edition appeared in 1907 in

New York, with pen-and-ink drawings by Latimer J. Wilson. The same
year saw the impressionistic woodcuts of Erich Heckel, an artist of the
'Brücke'.[115] Artistically outstanding were the woodcuts of Frans Masereel
for the 1923 edition published by the Drei-Masken-Verlag in Munich, and
also Alfred Kubin's frontispiece for the 1918 translation by Felix Grafe,
published by the Hyperion Verlag in Berlin. Critical applause for the
poem has not diminished even to this day. It is the only text of Wilde's to
be recommended by Denys Thompson:[116] 'it is one of the major poems
of the era, with more drive behind it than any other Victorian poem of
its length'.[117]

Its importance may also be gauged from the fact that in 1936
W. B. Yeats included a version shortened by himself in his *Oxford Book of
Modern Verse*.[118] This version consists of only 38 of the original 109
verses. Although Yeats's use of the preposition 'from' indicates clearly
that this is only a selection, certain statements he makes in his introduction to the anthology suggest that he had a somewhat more radical
intention:

Now that I have plucked from the *Ballad of Reading Gaol* its foreign feathers it
shows a stark realism akin to that of Thomas Hardy, the contrary to all its author
deliberately sought. I plucked out even famous lines because, effective in themselves, put into the Ballad they become artificial, trivial, arbitrary; a work of art
can have but one subject ... I have stood in judgement upon Wilde, bringing
into the light a great, or almost great poem, as he himself would have done had
he lived; my work gave me that privilege.[119]

Clearly Yeats considered his version to be superior to Wilde's, but the
assumption that Wilde would have done the same is speculative to say the
least.

In view of Yeats's stature as poet and critic, and bearing in mind the fact
that his shortened version became so well known, it is worth taking a brief
look at what he made of Wilde's poem. Evidently the two criteria for the
cuts were the maintenance of 'stark realism' and the preservation of
artistic unity – 'one subject'. The most striking omissions are of Parts V
and VI and the final verses 81–9 of Part IV (approximately one quarter of
the whole). Yeats's version ends at verse 80 of Part IV, precisely where
narration gives way to propaganda:

> They think a murderer's heart would taint
>   Each simple seed they sow.
> It is not true! God's kindly earth
>   Is kindlier than men know,
> And the red rose would but blow more red,
>   The white rose whiter blow.[120]

Yeats also cuts verses 5–16 of Part I, leaving only the beginning (verses
1–4), from which the reader knows that the accused must hang. Thus the

leitmotif of the whole ballad is omitted: 'Yet each man kills the thing he loves.'[121] Presumably Yeats felt that by making the fate of the individual into a general symbol of guilt, Wilde had destroyed the unity of his subject-matter. The same criterion led to the removal of the many sections that together form an *apologia*, arousing the reader's sympathy and understanding. Together with this condensation of the action, Yeats strips the realistic style of all romantic appendages. Thus the dance of the evil sprites in Part III has to go, as well as the prisoners' visions of terror during the night before the execution.

There are in fact certain similarities between Yeats's version and the original Wilde poem written in Berneval. This was published in 1911 by Robert Ross in the *Selected Poems of Oscar Wilde, including 'The Ballad of Reading Gaol'*, omitting the sections Wilde added when he was in Italy. The omissions comprise verse 11 of Part I, verses 2, 3, 6–9 of Part II, verses 3, 6, 11, 18–25, 31, 32 of Part III, verses 12, 18, 20, 21 of Part IV, and the whole of Parts V and VI. Certainly the omission of the last two parts and the dance of the sprites brings the Yeats version in line with that written in Berneval, though the other cuts make it seem highly unlikely that Yeats actually used the Ross text as his model. In any case, we cannot even be sure that Yeats was familiar with this edition.

At least one critic was convinced that Yeats's version was an improvement over the original. Rudolf Stamm wrote:

Hat er [Yeats] nicht mehr getan als mit dem Mittel der Auslassung ein spätviktorianisches in ein modernes Gedicht umzustilisieren? Er hat mehr getan. Indem er die Ballade von ihren Schlacken reinigte, hat er ein besseres Gedicht aus ihr gemacht.[122]

[Has he [Yeats] not done more than use the means of omission to restyle a late Victorian poem into a modern one? He has indeed done more. By ridding the ballad of its dross, he has made a better poem out of it.]

This, of course, is a judgment that is open to question. But what *is* clear is that Wilde's intentions were altered so radically that the result was a *different* poem. One might also add that 'dross' was not all that Yeats removed.

From the very start, critics have noted similarities between the *Ballad* and earlier poems in the genre, such as Coleridge's *The Rime of the Ancient Mariner* (1797), Thomas Hood's *The Dream of Eugene Aram, the Murderer* (1819), and A. E. Housman's *A Shropshire Lad* (1887). Alfred Douglas states categorically in *Oscar Wilde and Myself* that 'his actual model was "The Dream of Eugene Aram", with "The Ancient Mariner" thrown in on technical grounds'.[123] There are indeed similarities between Wilde's ballad and Hood's: they both use the comparatively unusual six-line stanza, with alternating lines of four and three beats, and both have a murder as their central subject. But the presentation is totally different. Aram, tortured by his conscience, tells a schoolchild the story of his deed, in the form of a dream which is a barely disguised confession; the murderer in Wilde's poem is to a large extent exonerated from his crime and shown as an outwardly calm personality who is resigned to his fate. In keeping with the totally different direction of the ideas, the sufferings of the prisoner in Wilde's poem are not viewed from his perspective, and are not described as the effects of a guilty conscience; they are seen from the viewpoint of the prisoners as a whole, and experienced as an internalisation of the approach of death. It is therefore very difficult to see any justification for Douglas's claim that Hood's poem was the 'actual model' for Wilde's.

At most it may be said that Hood influenced Wilde's prosodic technique, and the same may be said of Coleridge's *The Rime of the Ancient Mariner*, with its frequent use of internal rhymes. There are, however, occasional similarities of phrasing and imagery,[124] such as the dance of the evil sprites in Part III of the *Ballad*, which certainly recalls lines from *The Ancient Mariner*:

> About, about in ghostly rout
> They trod a saraband.[125]

Coleridge's lines are:

> About, about, in reel and rout
> The death-fires danced at night.[126]

The dice-throwing scene in verse 52 of Part III also has a counterpart in Coleridge, when 'Life-in-Death' plays dice with 'Death' for the ship's crew.[127] But such echoes are few and far between, and certainly do not justify Ifor Evans's sweeping statement that 'Wilde adapted phrase, mood, and rhythm from *The Ancient Mariner*'.[128]

There is, however, a certain affinity both in subject-matter and in atmosphere between *The Ballad of Reading Gaol* and poem no. IX in A. E. Housman's *A Shropshire Lad*.[129] This tells of an execution in Shrewsbury prison and of the nightwatch by the speaker, who wants his friend to sleep well. Both poems take the part of the condemned man, of whom Housman writes:

> A better lad, if things went right,
> Than most that sleep outside.[130]

But again it would be going much too far to say that this poem was a source or even a definable influence on Wilde, even though the latter was known to have been particularly impressed by it.[131] No doubt all the above-mentioned poems by Hood, Coleridge and Housman provided ideas both for the technique and the atmosphere of Wilde's ballad, but no artist can ever escape some influence, whether conscious or unconscious, through preceding works, and in the present case it seems most unlikely that convict C.3.3. would have needed any literary model to inspire a poem that was based on his own first-hand experience.

Apology and accusation

The poem comprises 109 stanzas divided into six sections of different length. Part I, with 16 stanzas, tells of a prisoner who murdered the woman he loved, and was condemned to death for the crime. In the 13 verses of Part II, the condemned man becomes more and more the focal point of the life-and-death fears that oppress the speaker and his fellow prisoners. The fate hanging over him seems a personal threat to all of them:

> We watched him day by day,
> And wondered if each one of us
> Would end the self-same way.[132]

Part III, the longest with 37 verses, describes how the prisoners see the condemned man for the last time, flanked by two warders, note the freshly dug grave – 'the yellow hole / Gaped for a living thing'[133] – and have terrible dreams the night before the execution, as if they themselves had been condemned to death. Part III closes with a vision of the execution. The remaining sections presented an awkward problem of composition, since such a dramatic crescendo could all too easily have descended to an abrupt loss of tension. Part IV, however, with its 23 verses, shows in detail how the dead man's punishment is extended even after death, for he is buried hurriedly, hidden in a hole beneath 'a stretch of mud and sand'[134] without even a cross or flowers to mark it. The chaplain refuses to give him a Christian burial and does not even say a final prayer.

The author's intention is clear: the persecution and destruction of the prisoner, continuing even beyond his death, show the inhumanity of man to man. Thus Wilde brings about a smooth transition from the narrative account of one man's fate in Parts I–III to his more general attack on the legitimacy of such punishments, as well as the laws underlying them, in Part V. The very first lines of this 17-verse section show that we are no longer concerned with the guilt of the individual but with the abstract problem of collective human and social guilt:

> I know not whether Laws be right,
> Or whether Laws be wrong.[135]

What he does know, however, is that men's laws lead to evil, in contrast to those of God:

> But God's eternal Laws are kind
> And break the heart of stone.[136]

Part VI contains just three verses, which conclude the *Ballad* by once more taking up the theme that 'each man kills the thing he loves', repeating almost word for word the relevant verse in Part I.

It is clear from this brief account of the poem's construction that the execution of the prisoner constitutes its narrative base, whereas its philosophical centre is the problem of guilt and the responsibility of those who pass judgment. The skill with which the two movements have been linked together has already been mentioned. The massive attack on the penal system and the appalling conditions created by 'Humanity's machine'[137] is part of a consistent strategy throughout the poem, whereby the guilty are exonerated, and their guilt refashioned into a collective sign of the human condition or of social injustice. This defensive, apologetic trend is apparent right from the beginning:

> He did not wear his scarlet coat,
>   For blood and wine are red,
> And blood and wine were on his hands
>   When they found him with the dead,
> The poor dead woman whom he loved,
>   And murdered in her bed.

In addition to the fact that he loved her, we learn at the end of the second verse that

> I never saw a man who looked
> So wistfully at the day.

Clearly our sympathies are meant to lie with the murderer.

It must be noted that Wilde made certain changes *vis-à-vis* the actual event on which his poem is based. These changes shed some light on the intentions underlying the poem. The *Reading Mercury* report of 10 July 1896, and Stuart Mason's comments accompanying his reproduction of it, reveal that Wooldridge was a soldier who killed his wife out of jealousy, cutting her throat 'in a very determined manner'.[138] The murder took place on the road between Windsor Station and the village of Clewer. Nowhere in the report is there any mention of the man being under the influence of alcohol at the time of the murder. In Wilde's poem the victim is no longer the wife, but the 'woman whom he loved', the murder takes place in her bed, and not on a road, and the motive is not jealousy but the influence of alcohol, since 'blood and wine were on his hands'. The picture is therefore completely different. According to the newspaper report, Wooldridge was a cold-blooded murderer who killed his wife in a quite vicious manner, whereas in the poem he becomes a pitiful man who was scarcely responsible for his actions. The paradoxical link between love and death, already alluded to in the first verse, becomes generalised a few verses later:

> Yet each man kills the thing he loves,
> By each let this be heard,
> Some do it with a bitter look,
> Some with a flattering word.
> The coward does it with a kiss,
> The brave man with a sword![139]

Implicit is the fact that not every man must pay for this killing with his own life.

Wilde's changes are clearly meant to evoke sympathy for and interest in the condemned man, creating a degree of moral and emotional involvement, but verse 7 brings out the deeper-lying intention of the author. If each man kills the thing he loves, but only one individual has to pay the penalty, then individual guilt becomes relativised and the punishment therefore seems unjust. Not only does Wilde thus exonerate the murderer, but he also appears to place the 'brave man' who kills with the sword above the 'coward' who does so with a kiss. Are the crimes indeed identical? Can one, for instance, claim that Judas was as much a murderer as Brutus? The theme is one that pervades the whole poem, being prepared in verses 1–6, stated explicitly in verse 7, and taken up again in the last two verses (108–9), but one cannot help detecting a degree of sophistry in the argument, which deliberately blurs all distinctions between physical destruction and psychological circumstance.[140] Wilde's strategy is to attribute guilt to everyone, so that inevitably the punishment of the individual appears like an arbitrary and monstrous injustice on the part of the law.

In this process of exoneration, through relativising guilt and spreading it collectively, lies Wilde's defensive intention. As the poem moves from an individual fate to broad social criticism, its strategic aim becomes clear: the individual case is to symbolise social injustice.

From here it is not difficult to take one step further and assume that this poetic transformation of an actual event is impregnated with the personal experience and attitude of the author in relation to his own situation. Robert Merle interprets the poem from a mainly psychological standpoint, and regards the choice of subject-matter and the manner of its implementation as a substitution for Wilde's own guilt. He supports this thesis by pointing out that Wilde never acknowledged the justice of his punishment, even though it was right according to the letter of the law. If he had appealed to the public directly, and under his own name, in protest against his conviction, he would have been accused of trying to defend homosexuality. There can be no doubt that he would have found little sympathy among a public which in any case was generally against him if not actually hostile to him. In such circumstances, the only way in which he could protest publicly was to '*prendre la défense d'un criminel qui ne fut pas lui-même, et d'un crime qui ne fut pas le sien*'.[141] The emphasis placed on the idea that every man is guilty but not everyone has to pay the penalty, that is, die for his crime, fits in with this autobiographical interpretation. It must have seemed bitterly unjust to convict C.3.3. that he was having to pay for an offence that so many others were equally 'guilty' of, but were not being punished for. Indeed why had Lord Alfred Douglas himself not been put on trial?

There are many passages in the poem where his personal experiences have clearly led to his condemnation of the penal system. His criticism is directed against the physical conditions and effects of imprisonment, and also against the behaviour of officialdom in such institutions. The prisoners suffer from hunger and thirst, and the 'brackish water'[142] they are made to drink is as vile as the 'bitter bread'[143] they must eat. The narrow cell is like a 'foul and dark latrine',[144] and it is impossible to sleep on the small, hard, 'three-plank bed'.[145] Children weep with hunger, simpletons are whipped, old people are mocked, and imprisonment generally is a barbaric torture that can only lead to mental and physical injury:

> It is only what is good in Man
> That wastes and withers there.[146]

The denunciation of such conditions, especially in verses 95–7, coincides almost word for word at times with the criticism Wilde expressed in his two letters to the *Daily Chronicle*. In the first, published on 24 March 1898 under the heading 'Prison Reform', he forcefully advocates a number of reforms for the prison system. He claims that the food, mainly 'weak gruel, suet, and water',[147] is so bad and inadequate that prisoners are always hungry and frequently suffer from diarrhoea. Sanitary conditions in the cells are appalling: after 5.0 p.m. toilets must not be used or pots emptied. The wooden beds cause permanent insomnia. But even worse than the effects of these terrible conditions on the prisoners' physical state are the psychological consequences of imprisonment:

The present prison system seems almost to have for its aim the wrecking and the destruction of the mental faculties. The production of insanity is, if not its object, certainly its result. That is a well-ascertained fact. Its causes are obvious. Deprived of books, of all human intercourse, isolated from every humane and humanising influence, condemned to eternal silence, robbed of all intercourse with the external world, treated like an unintelligent animal, brutalised below the level of any of the brute creation, the wretched man who is confined in an English prison can hardly escape becoming insane.[148]

The second letter to the *Daily Chronicle*, published on 28 May 1898 under the heading 'The Case of Warder Martin. Some Cruelties of Prison Life', is Wilde's protest against the dismissal of Warder Martin from Reading Gaol for having broken regulations by giving cakes to some of the children in the prison. Wilde knew Martin to be a kind and helpful man, whose humane manner helped to make the ordeal of prison life a little more bearable – for 'a pleasant "Good-morning" or "Good-evening" will make one as happy as one can be in prison'.[149] In this letter he takes the opportunity to be more precise in his criticisms of the prison system. In particular he attacks the treatment of children, for whom the harsh, impersonal atmosphere of a prison cell was doubly cruel. He also describes the case of a feeble-minded prisoner who had broken prison regulations and been whipped with a 'cat-of-nine-tails',[150] although in view of his mental condition – made worse still by all the beatings – he should never have been held responsible.

A comparison with the letters shows clearly that Part V of the poem, especially verses 95–7, corresponds to the personal experiences of C.3.3. His criticisms do not stop at the dreadful material conditions of prison life, but also apply to the officials and administrators of the system, such as the governor, warders, doctor, chaplain, and everyone and everything else connected with 'officialism'.[151] Verse 32 reads:

> The Governor was strong upon
> The Regulations Act:
> The Doctor said that Death was but
> A scientific fact:
> And twice a day the Chaplain called,
> And left a little tract.[152]

The impersonality of these officials is conveyed not only by the definite articles and capital letters – stressing function rather than individuality – but also by the prosodic pattern of the verse. The regular iambic alternation of unstressed and stressed syllables, and the equally regular alternation of four-beat and three-beat lines, allow not the slightest rhythmic variation. The uniformity of the metre is a formal expression corresponding exactly to the uniformity of prison life, in which the individual is degraded to the status of a number to be dealt with anonymously by a machine. Differences are eliminated by, among other things, the same clothes, and the same haircut. With the official obliteration of all external differences goes the danger that the fate of the individual will also be swallowed up in the collective mass, and the individual's problems will be met, not with individual treatment, but by the blanket solutions laid down by universal regulations. Such phrases as 'Fools' Parade', 'Devil's Own Brigade' and 'merry masquerade'[153] – momentarily depicting the prisoners from an outside perspective – reflect the painful contrast between the mask imposed and the inner self fighting for its own dignity; indeed the word 'merry' here is clearly an ironic attempt to give an aesthetic gloss to a desperate situation, or at least to avoid viewing it emotionally. By making themselves the objects of their own perception, they may briefly escape from their suffering subjectivity.

The portraits of the governor, doctor and chaplain generally correspond to Wilde's description of them in various letters, particularly those to the *Daily Chronicle*. At the time of Wooldridge's execution, Henry B. Isaacson was governor of Reading Gaol. With an allusion to the Roman dictator Sulla, Wilde describes him as a

'mulberry-faced Dictator': a great red-faced, bloated Jew who always looked as if he drank, and did so ... Brandy was the flaming message of his pulpy face.[154]

The harshness of his regime can be gauged from the fact that when he was replaced by Major J. O. Nelson – whom Wilde called 'a man of gentle and humane character'[155] – the number of punishments for breaking prison regulations sank by more than half.[156]

The original doctor for whom death was a 'scientific fact' was one Oliver Maurice, who was in charge of medical matters at Reading Gaol. He seems to have taken very little care of C.3.3. He did nothing to help Wilde with the earache from which he suffered after a fall at Wandsworth Prison Chapel, and he paid no attention to Wilde's complaints of eye trouble. It may well be that Wilde's early death – due to a purulent middle-ear infection which penetrated through to the midbrain – was caused by inadequate medical treatment during his imprisonment. His own explanation for the poor standard of medical treatment goes straight to the heart of the matter: most prison doctors had flourishing private practices, and often took on additional duties in other institutions, so that they had little time to devote to their incarcerated patients. But it must remain open to question whether they were all 'brutal in manner, coarse in temperament, and utterly indifferent to the health of the prisoners',[157] as Wilde, perhaps understandably, maintained.

No less negative is his impression of the prison chaplains with whom he came into contact. His second letter to the *Daily Chronicle* describes them as follows:

The prison chaplains are entirely useless. They are, as a class, well-meaning, but foolish, indeed silly men. They are of no help to any prisoner. Once every six weeks or so a key turns in the lock of one's cell door, and the chaplain enters. One stands, of course, at attention. He asks whether one has been reading the Bible. One answers 'Yes' or 'No', as the case may be. He then quotes a few texts, and goes out and locks the door. Sometimes he leaves a tract.[158]

Wilde seems to have sympathy only for the situation of the warders:

... he to whom a watcher's doom
Is given as his task,

Must set a lock upon his lips,
And make his face a mask.[159]

These lines suggest that the general unwillingness to talk was due to the
warders' function rather than to any innate cruelty. Wilde's pleasant
experiences with Thomas Martin, who was entrusted with supervising
C.3.3. a few months before his release, would certainly have influenced
and justified such a positive description, especially as the two became
quite friendly. The warder supplied Wilde with the *Daily Chronicle*, and
sometimes also with weekly magazines like the *Saturday Review* or the
Spectator, thus deliberately ignoring regulations. But too positive an
attitude towards the warders in general would have run counter to
Wilde's propagandist intentions in the poem and, as we have seen, if it
came to a choice between artistic considerations and truth to life, art
always came first.

'A romantic artist is working on realistic material'

With these words the critic Arthur Symons, in a detailed review of the
Ballad, summed up one of the major difficulties that confronted Wilde
when the poem was first conceived.[160] His bitter personal experiences of
the inhumane prison system would have tempted him to launch an
unbridled attack on that system, subordinating poetry to propaganda. But
how could such an attack square with the hitherto sacrosanct aesthetic
creed he had always preached? How could the definition of the artist as
the 'creator of beautiful things'[161] be reconciled to the real-life situation of
convict C.3.3. in 1897–8? From the very beginning the conflict between
the subject-matter, which demanded a realistic and psychological style,
and the author's concept of autonomous art threatened to split his style
irreconcilably. It was a problem of which Wilde was fully aware, and in a
letter to Ross he regrets the fact that he did not succeed in fully solving it:

The poem suffers under the difficulty of a divided aim in style. Some is realistic,
some is romantic: some poetry, some propaganda. I feel it kèenly, but as a whole I
think the production interesting: that it is interesting from more points of view
than one is artistically to be regretted.[162]

One might note in passing that this statement contains the almost perfect
reply to Yeats. Wilde had clearly anticipated (and accepted) the Yeats
criteria, but had nevertheless chosen to retain the mixture since that alone
fulfilled his intention.

Wilde goes on to say that from an artistic point of view, a prison as the
subject of poetry presented the same difficulties as a latrine. For him a cell
had neither form nor colour, and so could only be depicted by way of its
effect on the psyche of the prisoner. The problem summed up so neatly by
Symons entails the further complication that the author had to adapt his
style to the simplicity and earnestness of the subject. This was a com-

pletely new challenge to Wilde. Realistic presentation was essential if the dramatic events and the grim environment were to appear authentic. For the most part, Wilde solved these problems convincingly. With just a few exceptions, which we shall consider later, his diction is simple and unpretentious, and the prosody is free from forced effects. At one point, in verse 4, there is even a prison slang word which endows the dialogue with complete authenticity: '*That fellow's got to swing*'. There is detailed observation without any rhetorical tricks:

> The warders strutted up and down,
>   And watched their herd of brutes,
> Their uniforms were spick and span,
>   And they wore their Sunday suits,
> But we knew the work they had been at,
>   By the quicklime on their boots.[163]

Both stylistically and structurally the poem relies a good deal on repetition, a technique typical of the ballad in general. Alliteration, assonance and consonance all play their part in the effective instrumentation of sound, as in the line 'We banged the tins, and bawled the hymns'.[164] Individual word repetitions frequently extend beyond lines and verses, establishing overarching links, as with 'souls in pain' in verses 4, 5 and 21, or 'wistful', which is continually associated adjectivally or adverbially with the appearance of the condemned man.

There are also individual lines that are repeated elsewhere as refrains or reprises.[165] And most striking of all is the repetition of verse 7, slightly varied, at the very end of the poem – a verse that contains the main theme of the whole poem. Repetition as a means of instrumentation, combined with an overall thematic coherence, helps to create a closely knit texture of interlinking references whose basic patterns – particularly through the repetition – endow the poem with an atmosphere of constraint and immutability. Thus the form itself expresses the monotony of prison life and the irrevocable fate that awaits the condemned man. The technique of repetition had also played a part in *The Sphinx*, but the change in its function is radical. In the earlier poem repetition had served to link episodes together in a colourful, decorative panorama, whereas in the *Ballad* it helps to structure the story and to imbue it with its dramatic character.

Although realistic diction is dominant throughout the poem, Wilde could not divorce himself totally from the aesthetic impressionism of his earlier poetry. This is particularly evident in the dance of the evil sprites in Part III:

> With mop and mow, we saw them go,
>   Slim shadows hand in hand;
> About, about, in ghostly rout

> They trod a saraband:
> And the damned grotesques made arabesques,
> Like the wind upon the sand!

> With the pirouettes of marionettes,
> They tripped on pointed tread:
> But with flutes of Fear they filled the ear,
> As their grisly masques they led,
> And loud they sang, and long they sang.
> For they sang to wake the dead.[166]

Such polysyllabic words as 'saraband', 'arabesques', 'pirouettes' and 'marionettes', all of which occur in the earlier poem 'The Harlot's House', belong more to the exotic vocabulary of *The Sphinx* than to the austere diction of the *Ballad*. Critics differ as to whether and how far this interpolation disturbs the artistic unity of the poem. Bernhard Fehr regarded this transplant from 'The Harlot's House' as a mistake,[167] as such an 'Echo einer dekadenten Note'[168] did not fit in with the atmosphere of its new surroundings. Merle also acknowledged the dissonance between this passage and its context, but in contrast to the German critic he stressed the 'harmonie profonde' with the 'atmosphère morale'[169] of the poem, for 'Réalisme et romantisme forment dans *la Ballade* une alliance nécessaire'.[170] Merle was following up an explanation given by Wilde in a letter to Ross, in which he justifies the interpolation of these romantically inspired verses. He regarded them as 'a balance'[171] to the realism. Even if one might question the necessity of this balance and change of style, and even if the interpolation does affect the artistic homogeneity of the poem, it can scarcely be said to have reduced the overall power of expression. Indeed one might argue that only through such grotesque fantasy could Wilde capture the nightmare quality of the period before the execution – rather like Shakespeare's Richard III enduring his nightmares before the battle of Bosworth.

The power of the poem derives first and foremost from the speaker's sympathy with the condemned man. This human involvement in a matter of life and death may appear at first sight only to concern the fate of one individual, but the design of the poem shows a much deeper intention. It dramatises the situation of the outsider who is being destroyed by an unjust society, and since guilt lies not with the criminal but with the laws that have condemned him and the society that has made and imposed those laws, the poem raises the whole problem of social justice.

This basic theme of the poem, sophistic as it may be, combines apology and accusation. The attitude of the speaker seems to be identical to that of Wilde towards his own conviction. The fate of the murderer Wooldridge is transmuted into that of the suffering outcast, languishing in Reading Gaol. No doubt this is why Wilde himself thought the poem 'too autobiographical'. Like *De Profundis* it is an attempt through writing to cope with the new and appalling reality of his downfall, Both works are the literary expression of an *apologia pro vita sua*. This, then, is the defence. The attack is on the society that casts out the guiltless and torments them with such inhumanity.

If the *Ballad* is seen in the context of Wilde's work generally, the autobiographical component provides a degree of continuity. Otherwise it may seem to have little in common with the rest of the canon. There is nothing left of the flowery, epigonic rhetoric of the *Poems*, or – apart from the dance of the sprites – the exotic imagery of the *Sphinx*. On the surface there may seem to be points in common with Dorian Gray, who saw evil as a means of expressing beauty, or the narrator in 'Pen, Pencil, and Poison', who concluded from his account of the poisoner Wainewright's career that there was no 'essential incongruity between crime and culture'.[172] But for Dorian and Wainewright, crime as the most extreme deviation from social norms offered the attraction of hedonistic self-realisation. The aim was to extend the individual's freedom to its furthest and most pleasurable limits. In *The Ballad of Reading Gaol* the individual remains bound to the community through suffering, sympathy and solidarity. The very perspective from which the criminal's fate is viewed – namely, that of the other prisoners – is totally different from the individualistic presentation of the earlier works. Even if the fate of the individual may still lie at the heart of the poem, it is now a paradigm of suffering and social injustice, instead of self-indulgence and pleasure-seeking.

In this critical view of injustice may perhaps be seen another hint of continuity linking Wilde's swan-song with his essay *The Soul of Man under Socialism*, but the nature of the criticism is quite different. In the essay, social injustice was a phenomenon perceived through the intellect, and thanks to the activities of Shaw and the Fabian Society it had taken on a certain fashionable actuality. *Reading Gaol* deals with personal experience of reality, which affected the author right through to his innermost being and called forth an emotional and moral reaction. It is the authenticity and sincerity of these emotions that gives rise to the criticism and endows it with its authority. The reader feels that Wilde's prime concern is to lend expression to his experience, not to please a particular audience. It is, perhaps, one of the paradoxes of his literary career that what was arguably his most convincing work of art should have been created when he had lost his audience and when he departed most radically, if also reluctantly, from his own aesthetic theory.

Thus the trivial, provocative, never-too-earnest scourge of moral orthodoxy turned into a personally committed moral and social critic. But however radical and unexpected this transformation may seem, the break with the past is not total. As we have already seen many times in the earlier works, the moral component was always present, even if it was only implicit and even if critics have generally tended to overlook it. The main hope and consolation for the prisoners lies in Christ and divine justice:

> ... God's eternal Laws are kind
> And break the heart of stone.[173]

This embrace of the Christian idea of redemption seems like a retreat to a haven no longer taken seriously by many Victorian intellectuals. A concrete social problem of the present is answered by questionable mysteries from the past. In this Wilde is once more clinging to established traditions of faith such as are always invoked when questions cannot be answered intellectually but require moral solutions. No matter how penetrating and provocative his criticism may be, his ultimate response is naive and conformist. At the end of his literary career, he remains what he always was – the conformist rebel.

10   Plans, sketches and fragments

Wilde's fatal decision to take up the Marquess of Queensberry's challenge
and sue, even though it should have been all too obvious that the suit
would go against him, had disastrous consequences not only for his family
and his own life, but also for his writing. (The family emigrated shortly
after his arrest, changing their name to Holland. His wife Constance died
in Genoa in 1898, and his elder son Cyril was killed in the First World
War. Vyvyan, the younger son, later wrote several books about his
father.) Labelled by sections of the press as an amoral monster, hypocriti-
cally shunned by the public as *res tacenda*, kicked out of hotels by
narrow-minded owners, even on the Continent, Wilde could find none of
the peace of mind necessary for creative work, and he could no longer
hope to win back the public that had applauded him so enthusiastically at
productions of *An Ideal Husband* and *The Importance of Being Earnest*,
prior to his arrest. Perhaps others in a similar situation might have exerted
more will-power and taken up the struggle against injustice, but Wilde
was not made of such material. His resistance was brief and abortive: two
letters to the *Daily Chronicle*, protesting vehemently about the miserable
conditions pertaining in English prisons, and *The Ballad of Reading Gaol*,
a mixture of apology and accusation, a poetically disguised plea for
forgiveness, and an open critique of 'Humanity's machine'. Previously his
opposition to Victorian social and aesthetic norms had always been
tailored to the expectations and susceptibilities of his bourgeois audiences, and had been more of an intellectual challenge than a fundamental
questioning of established conventions. But when this subtle game of
provocation and conformity no longer functioned, because Wilde had
gone too far in his violation of the rules, he was left with only two possible
courses of action: either he must break totally with society and wage open
war, or he must passively accept the outsider's role imposed on him.
Should he become the revolutionary or the martyr? In fact, there was no
choice. He had to be the martyr, because he could never acknowledge the
finality of the break and so live without the hope – however tenuous – that
one day, after a due period of atonement, he would be taken back into the
social fold again. But his journey into exile was rather different from that
of the *persona non grata* temporarily going away with his return ticket
safely tucked into his pocket. This journey was a last goodbye to his art.

308

For in his heady days of success Wilde's Parnassus had towered not over Delphi but over Belgrave Square – the fashionable side, of course.

In what direction might his literary career have turned had it not foundered on this débâcle? The answer to this question is not as speculative as it might seem, for it can be based on various sketches, fragments and plans for future projects. There can be no doubt that his interest lay almost exclusively in the theatre, which is scarcely surprising in view of his successes in the 1890s. But what *is* surprising is that neither of the surviving fragments – namely, 'La Sainte Courtisane or The Woman Covered with Jewels' and 'A Florentine Tragedy' – had anything in common with the subject-matter or style of the social comedies. In the former play, he returns to groups of characters, themes and the exotic setting of *Salomé*, while the latter is an attempt at blank verse tragedy in the manner of the unfortunate *Duchess of Padua*.

The plot of 'La Sainte Courtisane'[1] centres on the successful efforts of the beautiful courtesan Myrrhina, from Alexandria – whose name is reminiscent of one of the Athenian women (Μυρρίνη) in Aristophanes' *Lysistrata* – to make the hermit Honorius, who lives in the Egyptian desert near Thebes, adopt her way of life:

Come with me, Honorius, and I will clothe you in a tunic of silk. I will smear your body with myrrh and pour spikenard on your hair. I will clothe you in hyacinth and put honey in your mouth.[2]

Honorius finally gives way to her, and decides to renounce his ascetic isolation in favour of the pleasures of the town. But at the same time Myrrhina loses faith in her own previous way of life, repents her sins, and longs for a new start in the Christian spirit, 'so that my soul may become worthy to see God'.[3]

One is struck immediately by the similarity between the Myrrhina/ Honorius motivation and that of Salomé/Jokanaan. Both pairs embody the contrast between sensuality and the spirit, earthly pleasure and religious asceticism. This theme and the common motif of the *femme fatale* who brings about the Baptist's death and the hermit's loss of faith, are combined with another idea that had already appeared in the prose poem 'The Teacher of Wisdom' and the essay 'The Portrait of Mr W.H.' In the latter, the narrator loses confidence in the accuracy of Cyril Graham's thesis (that the young actor Willie Hughes was the addressee of Shakespeare's sonnets) at the very moment when he succeeds in convincing Erskine of its validity. There is an interesting comment here on the nature of influence:

Influence is simply a transference of personality, a mode of giving away what is most precious to one's self, and its exercise produces a sense, and, it may be, a reality of loss.[4]

'La Sainte Courtisane' is virtually an illustration of this thesis. Wilde's own openness to such a 'transference of personality' in the literary sphere may be seen from the similarities between his play and Anatole France's *Thaïs* (1890).[5] This *conte philosophique* – based on medieval sources such as the *Legenda aurea* by Jacobus de Voragine and *Pafnutius* by Hrotsvit von Gandersheim – tells how the beautiful Thaïs, dancer, actress and *fille de joie* from Alexandria, is converted by the religious anchorite Paphnuce, who like Honorius comes from the monastery at Thebes. Although he succeeds in converting the courtesan and getting her to enter a convent, he himself falls prey to erotic dreams and visions, attracted as he is by the sensuous Thaïs, and finally his soul is eternally damned.

The novel is written very much in the bitingly ironic style of Voltaire's *Candide*; it delivers a violent attack on religion, and in particular on the ascetic demands of Christianity. The subtlety of this irony, which permeates the whole work, lies in the fact that Paphnuce always sheds the most doubt on his own religious premises when he appears to be acting fully in accordance with them, for in reality – without even knowing it himself – he has long since fallen victim to his sensual desires. With his biblical diction and imagery the zealous anchorite indignantly rejects that which in secret he craves for. He sits at the top of a column in the middle of a ruined temple, having withdrawn there from fear of earthly temptations – an ironic jibe at the idea that worldly temptations may be escaped by means of cloistered isolation – and from there he cries:

Encore des tentations! Encore des pensées immondes! Encore de monstrueux désirs! Seigneur, fais passer en moi toute la luxure des hommes, afin que j'expie toute![6]

[More temptations! More unclean thoughts! More monstrous desires! Lord, make all the lasciviousness of men pass within me, so that I may expiate it all!]

He revels in sensuous fantasies and erotic daydreams, together with a suppressed *nostalgie de la boue* which he has to conceal behind the mask of the self-sacrificial and penitent sinner, pretending that this is simply a test imposed by God, so that he may enjoy the experience all the more intensively, untroubled by his conscience.

Although Paphnuce never has the self-awareness of a Tartuffe, deliberately acting out the piety of false devotion, the conflict between natural desires and ascetic repression does lead to a form of hypocrisy which is shown to be inherent and indeed inevitable in religious faith. This is the polemic target of the book, and the words spoken by Hilarion to Saint Antony in Flaubert's *La Tentation de Saint-Antoine* might be equally applied to Paphnuce:

HILARION: Hypocrite qui s'enfonce dans la solitude pour se livrer mieux au débordement de ses convoitises! Tu te prives de viandes, de vin, d'étuves, d'esclaves et d'honneurs; mais comme tu laisses ton imagination t'offrir des banquets, des parfums, des femmes nues et des foules applaudissantes! Ta chasteté n'est qu'une corruption plus subtile, et ce mépris du monde l'impuissance de ta haine contre lui![7]

[Hypocrite plunging into solitude in order to revel all the more freely in the excesses of his desires! You deprive yourself of meats, wine, hot baths, slaves and honours, but how you allow your imagination to offer you banquets, perfumes, naked women and applauding crowds! Your chastity is nothing but a subtler form of corruption, and this scorn for the world is the impotence of your hatred of it!]

The openly anti-religious feeling of *Thaïs* is completely absent from 'La Sainte Courtisane', and indeed such feeling would have been unusual in Wilde. The subject-matter of his dramatic fragment is, rather, the polarity of ascetic Christian piety and sensual heathen hedonism, the conflict being finally resolved by reciprocal conversion. It was a conflict that Wilde himself had continually faced since his Oxford days, and it runs like a leitmotif through all his work, from the early poems right through to *De Profundis* – the clash between an Epicurean philosophy of the moment, and the spirit of Christianity. At three critical points of his life – namely, during his student days, on the day of his release from prison, and shortly before his death – this clash gave rise to a fleeting embrace of faith. It never went as far as true conversion, but it gave evidence of and expression to a spiritual thirst that was never quenched.

In 1893 and 1894, while he was working on 'La Sainte Courtisane', Wilde was also writing a play whose language, subject-matter and setting were very akin to *The Duchess of Padua*. This was 'A Florentine Tragedy'.[8] A fragmentary one-acter – first performed in English in 1906[9] with the missing exposition having been written by T. Sturge Moore – it takes place in the house of the Florentine merchant Simone, who returns from a business trip to find his wife Bianca in the company of Guido Bardi, a son of the Prince of Florence. Simone treats his noble guest with all due reverence, and after the initial courtesies tries to woo him as a potential customer, but at the same time various casual allusions to 'husbands that wear horns'[10] show his real appraisal of the situation. Behind the mask of the naive, subservient host, whose only interest seems to be making use of the opportunity to talk the rich and generous nobleman into buying his wares, there hides a cool-headed and deeply dishonoured husband, who is only waiting for confirmation of his suspicions – a confirmation that is not long in coming. Bianca feels disgusted by her husband's uncouth behaviour, while Guido finds this 'windy brawler in a world of words'[11] getting on his nerves, and so the two of them announce their love quite openly. When at last the guest wishes to leave, Simone provokes him into a fight, in the course of which

he disarms the nobleman and finally strangles him with his bare hands.
Immediately afterwards the play ends with the memorable lines:

BIANCA: Why
Did you not tell me you were so strong?
SIMONE: Why
Did you not tell me you were beautiful?
(*He kisses her on the mouth.*) CURTAIN[12]

Wilde's second attempt to write a blank-verse tragedy would surely, even
if he had finished it, have been as great a failure as *The Duchess of Padua*,
with which it has a great deal in common. The name of the merchant,
Simone, is like that of the Duke of Padua, Simone Gesso, and Guido Bardi
is a combination of Guido Ferranti, the young man who wishes to avenge
his father, and Taddeo Bardi, a nobleman in the Duke's entourage.
Nevertheless, a certain originality cannot be denied to Wilde's variation
on the traditional theme of cuckoldry – a subject particularly common in
the Italian novella from the fourteenth to the sixteenth centuries, for
example, in the work of Boccaccio, Bandello and Straparola, as well as in
countless mediaeval farces, carnival plays and Renaissance comedies. The
cuckold was a traditional figure of fun, either stupidly ignorant of the
activities of his wife and her lover, or else aware of the betrayal and
merely looking on helplessly. Wilde removed the comic element by
putting the deceived husband in the superior position of knowing the
truth and merely playing the fool for tactical reasons. The reader or
spectator is very soon aware of this, and is therefore able to enjoy the
ironic tension between the merchant's feigned naiveté and actual superiority. The spectator is almost in the role of a detective as he watches the
unravelling of the true relationship between Bianca and Guido. But the
cuckold motif is really only the background to another theme, which is
recognition of other people's identity – a theme that played a major part
in Wilde's social comedies. The end of the play, with its very abrupt
reversal of attitudes as Simone and Bianca come together again after the
fight, is singularly lacking in finesse. Apart from the crudely sensational
ending, the play also irritates with its uncomfortable echoes of Shakespeare. The lines with which Bianca invites her lover to a nocturnal tryst
are particularly grating, with their all too obvious derivation from *Romeo
and Juliet*:

BIANCA: But come before the lark with its shrill song
Has waked a world of dreamers. I will stand
Upon the balcony.
GUIDO: And by a ladder
Wrought out of scarlet silk and sewn with pearls
Will come to meet me. White foot after foot,
Like snow upon a rose-tree.[13]

Unfortunately, 'La Sainte Courtisane' and 'A Florentine Tragedy' remained merely as fragments, but a whole series of other plays never went beyond the planning or sketching stage. These include 'The Cardinal of Avignon', 'Ahab and Isabel', 'Pharaoh', and A Wife's Tragedy. In his Wilde bibliography, Mason included a scenario of 'The Cardinal of Avignon',[14] which must have been written in April 1894. At the centre of the play is an ambitious cardinal who hopes to be elected Pope, but who is also in danger of succumbing to the earthly charms of his pretty ward. She is engaged to a young man, but the cardinal destroys their relationship by pretending that the girl's suitor, who never knew his father, is the brother of the girl, although in actual fact he is the son of the future Pope himself, who had an illicit love affair in his youth. The fiancé is shocked at having come so near to an incestuous relationship, and at the behest of the cunning cardinal – who is, of course, protecting his own interests – he tries to convince the girl that they must break off their engagement because he does not love her enough. The girl is plunged into despair, and kills herself. In a long final scene, the cardinal confesses all his wicked machinations, reveals himself to be the young man's father – a scene clearly analogous to that in Act 3 of A Woman of No Importance – and also confesses his love for his ward. The young man, who at first was quite prepared to kill his father – now elected Pope – in revenge for his fiancée's death, is so overcome by the situation that he turns his weapon against himself and dies on the bier of his beloved.

In depicting the conflict between love and ambition in the character of the cardinal, Wilde takes up elements from Salomé and 'La Sainte Courtisane', combining them in a typically decadent mixture of the sacred and the profane. Both the subject-matter and the plot construction as Wilde sketched them are reminiscent of Elizabethan plays (one thinks in particular of Angelo's perfidy in Measure for Measure) and perhaps also of Racine's tragedies, with their depiction of guilty passion and the destruction of young love. Of course the final form of the play might well have differed from this initial sketch, but whether the intrigues of the unworthy cardinal would have earned the applause of audiences expecting witty conversational pieces from the Wilde they knew is a matter that must remain open to speculation.

Nothing remains of the drama 'Pharaoh' apart from its title and a brief mention in a letter of 1 October 1897, in which Wilde expresses his intention to start work on it when he has completed 'A Florentine Tragedy'.[15] But for the plot of 'Ahab and Isabel' a few indications do remain. In all probability the basis of the story is to be found in a prose poem entitled 'Jezebel', an oral version of which is said to have been heard by the anglophile French journalist Henry-D. Davray – a personal acquaintance of Wilde's – along with various other stories 'au moment des liqueurs, dans un restaurant des Champs-Elysées, en plein air par une chaude soirée'.[16] In his book *Son of Oscar Wilde*, Vyvyan Holland published an English version as remembered by Gabrielle Enthoven. The story runs as follows: Queen Isabel, a particularly deadly version of the *femme fatale* in the Salomé mould, covets the vineyard which lies before her palace and belongs to Naboth, a young standard-bearer of the Royal Guard and a close friend of King Ahab's. In order to please his wife, the King wishes to buy the land for whatever price Naboth wants, but the latter refuses to sell. Isabel appears to accept this refusal, but the following day summons the young man to her. She stages a love scene and, at the crucial moment, calls out to her husband, who promptly rushes to the scene and 'mad with blind rage'[17] stabs his friend. When his passion has subsided, he regrets his deed and breaks into loud lament. Faced with this tragic situation, the heartless Isabel says nothing but:

Nay, King, thy lamentations are foolish and thy tears are vain; rather shouldst thou laugh, for now the vineyard where the grass is green and where the doves fly is mine own.[18]

It is interesting to note that Wilde has changed the original Old Testament story. The episode on which the prose poem is based is to be found in Book I of Kings. There the Israelite King Ahab offers Naboth either another vineyard or money, but Naboth refuses. In order to console her husband, Jezebel intrigues against the luckless Naboth by hiring two men to swear that he blasphemed against God and the King. Although the accusations are totally unfounded, Naboth is taken out of the city and stoned to death. Wilde changes this story in two important details: it is not Ahab but Jezebel (or Isabel) who desires the vineyard, and it is she who plots on her own behalf by making it seem as if Naboth is lusting after her. Just as with the Salome story, Wilde places the female in the very centre of the action, so that her fatal role is given full emphasis, and so that the plot is given an erotic tone.

Scholars have tended to ignore the sketch of a play with the (presumably temporary) title 'A Wife's Tragedy', which was auctioned in 1928 under the title 'A Woman's Tragedy', as listed in Dulau's sales catalogue of Wilde manuscripts and Wildeana.[19] In *Theatre Research International* (1982), Rodney Shewan published a transcribed reconstruction of the unpaginated manuscript which is to be found in the William Andrews Clark Memorial Library (University of California, Los Angeles).[20] The script contains no dramatis personae, and there are hardly any stage directions; nor are there any names next to the dialogue, and there is no indication of the order of scenes within the acts. The play takes place in Venice, but no time is specified. The fragmentary nature of the script allows only vague speculations as to the plot. There is no mention of such a play in any of Wilde's letters, and in trying to date it, Rodney Shewan has to rely mainly on textual 'evidence'. He concludes that the sketch may have been written between 1887 and 1889; the recognisable elements of plot and character would seem to indicate that it was a mixture of melodrama and social play – perhaps a 'trial run for Lady Windermere's Fan'.[21]

Apart from this none-too-promising sketch and the other plans and fragments already mentioned, Wilde also came up with the idea for a play which eventually was written not by himself but by Frank Harris. This was *Mr and Mrs Daventry*.[22] The circumstances under which Wilde sold options to different people – for example, George Alexander, Horace Sedger, Louis Nethersole, Leonard Smithers, Herbert Beerbohm Tree, Cora Brown-Potter,[23] and Ada Rehan – shed a good deal of light on his situation during the last years of his life in exile.[24] Constantly in need of money, and incapable of any more creative work, he used his reputation as a once successful dramatist to indulge in dubious business affairs. Harris, who learned from Smithers about Wilde's supposed intention to write a new play, indicated his interest but soon learned that the intention had never been serious. Finally he offered to buy the idea, after Wilde had promised to write the first act himself – a promise which, however, he never kept.

When in autumn 1900 the enterprising former editor of the *Fortnightly Review* and the *Saturday Review* was ready to make his debut as a dramatist, he found himself confronted with an unpleasant surprise in the form of a 'horde of people'[25] all with valid rights to the play and all demanding satisfaction. Not until these matters had been resolved was it possible for *Mr and Mrs Daventry* to be given its première on 25 October 1900 at the Royalty Theatre in London, with Mrs Patrick Campbell and Fred Kerr in the main roles. Despite many unfavourable reviews, the play ran till 23 February, and made quite a handsome profit for Harris. The reviews did contain a few positive points – particularly those by J. T. Grein[26] and Max Beerbohm,[27] who had replaced George Bernard Shaw as drama critic of the *Saturday Review*. Grein wrote:

If Mr Harris had been an experienced playwright, this theme might have led him to write an epoch-making drama. The material is all there, but the method is immature.[28]

When one realises that the material stemmed from Wilde, one can well imagine what a success the play might have been if the 'method' had also been his.

At the centre of the play is Mrs Daventry, who inwardly has grown apart from her husband. She describes their desolate marriage as follows: 'We get on like other people it seems to me; now worse, now better – with no tastes, no ideas, no feelings in common.'[29] Relations between the couple reach breaking-point when, despite his wife's vehement opposition, Mr Daventry insists on inviting Mr and Mrs Langham, with the latter of whom he evidently enjoys intimate relations. A climax is reached when Mrs Daventry secretly witnesses a tender tête-à-tête between her husband and Mrs Langham, and when Mr Langham is on the verge of discovering the pair together, she coolly saves the situation by inventing a good reason for the two of them to be alone in a locked room. Shortly afterwards, however, she leaves her husband and considers the offer of an old friend, Mr Ashurst, a rich member of the leisured class who assured her of his help 'if ever you were in a fix'.[30] But Mr Daventry also turns to this old family friend for help in the matter of his broken marriage. Ashurst is selfless enough to accede to Daventry's request, but Mrs Daventry emphatically rejects the suggestion that she should return to her husband. Thereupon Ashurst invites her to stay with him, and she accepts. They live together happily for a few months, and then the deserted husband arrives and tries to persuade his wife to come back – at first with pleas and promises of a better future, but then with threats that he will kill Ashurst in a duel. Only when Mrs Daventry begs him on her knees to 'spare the father of my child'[31] does he realise the hopelessness of his quest, and then he kills himself.

If in reading the play one keeps Wilde's comedies in mind, one cannot help viewing *Mr and Mrs Daventry* as a sort of variation on *Lady Windermere's Fan*, with a serious ending. Instead of Lord Windermere's ostensible mistress, Mrs Erlynne, there is a real mistress, Mrs Langham. In the first act of each play there is an invitation from the husband to the mistress or supposed mistress, and in both plays the wife must decide whether to accept the offer of an admirer – Lady Windermere finally rejects Lord Darlington's offer to take her abroad, whereas Mrs Daventry accepts Ashurst's invitation to live with him. Where the plays differ, however, is in the very positive depiction of Mrs Daventry's desertion of her husband, which in formal terms is a breach of the marriage contract, and also in the emphasis laid on a woman's right to love outside the legalised but humanly discredited marriage conventions. Here, undoubtedly, is a new and provocative view of social reality that marks the transition from the nineteenth to the twentieth century. The novelty becomes even clearer if one compares Mrs Daventry with Paula Tanqueray: the latter has to give way to the pressures of outside circumstances, whereas the former pursues the path of personal happiness, and succeeds against all opposition.

Harris in fact stuck very close to Wilde's original idea, but the dialogue and some of the curtain lines show that the play was written by an author of little experience and without the epigrammatic wit of the author of *The*

Importance of Being Earnest. Nevertheless, some of the scenes are very true to life – a quality sometimes missing from Wilde – and this no doubt can be attributed to the very eventful career, not always restricted to journalism, which Harris enjoyed and which we may also enjoy through his four-volume autobiography vividly entitled *My Life and Loves* (1925–30). H. Montgomery Hyde's judgment of the play, given in the detailed introduction to his edition of it, seems eminently fair:

> *Mr and Mrs Daventry* can hardly be described as a great play. But it is full of interest, and in its day was regarded as powerful if unconventional 'theatre'.[32]

What is perhaps astonishing is that this play, plus the various sketches and fragments we have discussed, would seem to indicate that Wilde had no further plans for any comedies. They indicate three different directions in which his theatrical writing might have gone, but none are comic: 'La Sainte Courtisane' and 'Ahab and Isabel' would have continued the Symbolist line established by *Salomé*, with an exotic, biblical setting, stylised language, a lyrical drama of words rather than action, dominated by the cruel but desirable *femme fatale*. With 'A Florentine Tragedy' Wilde would have continued along the lines of *The Duchess of Padua*, in the tradition of the Elizabethan tragedy of love and revenge, though without the large cast, the hectic action, and the dramatic *élan*. The abrupt, set-piece ending clearly shows the influence of symbolist drama. And finally the plans for *A Wife's Tragedy* and *Mr and Mrs Daventry* indicate that Wilde would have returned to the themes and structures of his social comedies, but would have used them for serious ends and with serious endings. The question of whether this tragic mode was the best form of literary expression for him, and whether his poetic diction and decorative, Symbolist style would have taken him further than his gift for conversational dialogue, is unfortunately one that can never be answered, although the honest critic is bound to admit that he has his doubts.

Conclusion

Our study of Wilde's works has shown clearly that there is far more to the Wilde phenomenon than the fascination of a legend. Behind the wide range of forms that he used – poetry, prose and drama – and of real-life roles that he played, there is an unmistakably original artistic talent. This lies partly in the productive appropriation of literary traditions, but also in the provocative yet conformist attitude he adopted towards Victorian society, and in his attempt to preserve the autonomy of art against bourgeois interference. His literary *œuvre* is as two-headed as Janus: it looks backwards to Victorian and late romantic traditions, with its nineteenth-century exoticism, and its good or fallen women, dandies and *doppelgänger*; and it looks forwards as it sows the seeds of modernism with its growing gulf between individual and society, its scepticism towards linguistic communication, its crises of identity and its artistic autonomy. It is true that one never senses any deep-seated *malaise* or any tormented soul fighting against the status quo, and yet one is always aware that this is an artist speaking as critic, a homosexual 'outsider' who was himself drawn into the clash between public and private life; even his brilliant and witty conversation manipulates language into paradox. While acting as a precursor of the modern age, he remained at heart – perhaps *malgré lui* – a true Victorian. It is worth reminding ourselves of his comment on the characters of *Dorian Gray*:

Basil Hallward is what I think I am: Lord Henry what the world thinks me: Dorian what I would like to be – in other ages perhaps.[1]

This fascinating self-assessment is a clear indication of Wilde's awareness that in one person he combined a variety of different roles. And yet his life and work – for all the changes they may both have seemed to undergo – were consistently stamped with a pattern of form and expression that remained relatively unaltered. Both were a continual personal compromise between Basil Hallward and Lord Henry, a mediation between provocation and conformity, symbolising the transition from the Victorian age to modern times. More than anyone else Wilde embodied the glamorous decadence of the *belle époque* – the poet who was a work of art[2] – the Narcissus gazing at the reflection of his countenance from all angles, and yet also revealing the physiognomy of his time, a victim of his own hubris but also of the double standards of an era in transition.

How else is one to view the drama of his life other than as the paradox of the conformist rebel? What other explanation could there be for the conduct of a man who appealed to the justice of a society whose values he had consistently mocked? When Lord Queensberry left the fateful card at the Albemarle Club with the message 'Oscar Wilde posing as a somdomite [sic]', he may well have stepped beyond the bounds of gentlemanly behaviour, but in reality he was understating his case. The provocation brought forth in Wilde all those characteristics of which he himself had probably been the least aware, for he reacted as a 'champion of Respectability in conduct, of Puritanism in life, and of Morality in Art'.[3] He committed himself to a senseless and suicidal law-suit in which from the very start he had nothing to gain and everything to lose. He wantonly transgressed the limits of social tolerance by summoning an aristocrat to court in the name of a morality which, in his public role, he had challenged and ridiculed again and again. He alone was unable to see that he was overplaying his hand. Somehow he believed – perhaps unconsciously – that the magic charm of his conversation would win the applause of the court just as his wit had won over his theatre audiences, and only in retrospect was he able to realise the 'absolute idiocy' and 'vulgar bravado'[4] of his actions. And yet even in retrospect the blame was far from being his alone. His last works clearly support Alfred Kerr's thesis that the fault lay with society: '[Wildes'] langsame Hinrichtung bleibt der letzte greifbare Akt des Mittelalters'[5] [[Wilde's] slow execution remains the final tangible act of the Middle Ages].

This was a life whose individual phases unfolded like the acts of a drama, combining all elements of the classical tragedy: exposition in Dublin and Oxford, rise and high point in London, fall in the dock at the Old Bailey, and catastrophe in Reading Gaol. The tragic turning-point came with the decision to sue Lord Queensberry. The death of the tragic hero did not in fact follow on directly from the catastrophe, but the source of his inspiration had dried up, and the loss of his artistic creativity was a kind of death in itself. The changes of the plot were accompanied by almost symbolic changes of name: Oscar Fingal O'Flahertie Wills Wilde rose to the heights of the universally acclaimed 'Oscar', then fell to the anonymity of C.3.3., and finally in exile hid away under the pseudonym of 'Sebastian Melmoth'. These last two names were not even his own, but were borrowed – significantly – from a Christian martyr and the hero of Charles R. Maturin's novel *Melmoth the Wanderer* (1820). Thus the loss of name, the loss of social position and the loss of creativity all went hand in hand, for without an audience Wilde had lost his incentive, without the incentive he lost his art, and without his art he was no longer Oscar.

'Life imitates art far more than Art imitates life.'[6] Thus did Wilde stand the traditional theory of art on its head, and there can indeed have been few authors who combined life and art, aesthetic theory and literary practice so closely and yet at the same time so paradoxically. In his early critical work he proclaimed that art should beautify the world and the things of everyday life, and yet later he was for ever extolling its autonomy and its absolute uselessness. In theory 'the sphere of Art and the sphere of Ethics [were] ... absolutely distinct and separate',[7] and yet this principle is shattered by the fate of Dorian Gray. Wilde believed in individualism as a principle of life and in the autonomy of art, and so both in art and in criticism he laid the accent on personality, while at the same time he strove for perfection of form, since form alone could raise art above the amorphousness of life and nature. But the public individualist was for ever being held back by the hidden conformist – 'my ruin came, not from too great individualism of life, but from too little'[8] – and the formal perfectionist lacked the industry, earnestness and obsessiveness of a Flaubert ever to achieve his goal. In terms of literary history, he linked the expressive art of the romantics with the aestheticism of the *l'art pour l'art* movement to create an anti-Victorian, decorative formalism which directly opposed Ruskin's moral basis for art, and which with its critical subjectivity opposed Matthew Arnold's ideal 'to see the object as in itself it really is'.[9] And so his art and his criticism oscillate between the cult of the personality and the search for formal perfection, integrating past traditions and yet pointing into the future, and centring upon the one concept that seemed almost obsessively to link his life and art together – the all-importance of style.

If the loss of Wilde's life style also destroyed his creative art, this is only consistent with the fact that he was always more of a life-artist than a desk-artist – 'a man of the ivory megaphone rather than of the Ivory Tower'.[10] His Muse lived in Mayfair and St James's, not in Berneval-sur-Mer. Was he, then, a man of action who, in W. B. Yeats's words, 'could not endure the sedentary toil of creative art?'.[11] Certainly he did not devote his life to his art, even if he did proclaim that such a life would be the ideal form of cultivated idleness. The champagne at Willis's was far too good, the glamour of dinner-parties far too seductive, the homosexual adventures – 'feasting with panthers'[12] – far too exciting. Self-realisation was the goal of his life, and his preferred means were art and pleasure. But to what extent could such a hedonistic philosophy be put into practice? Given the combination of aesthetic conduct and moral awareness, was it not inevitable that this way of life should lead to a split identity? *The Picture of Dorian Gray* gives a vivid answer to the question. Self-realisation for Dorian does not entail the harmonious development and ripening of the individual, as in the classic *Bildungsroman*, but on the contrary means breaking away from the moral order, with a general 'Enthemmung der Persönlichkeit'[13] [disinhibiting of the personality]. When the individual's actions are no longer guided by moral responsibility, the *doppelgänger* existence of a Dorian becomes merely the outer sign of a far more fundamental division of the self into myriad realms of experience linked only by their part in the endless search for new impressions and pleasures. The restless extension of experience, regardless of value, and the hedonistic savouring of the moment are accompanied by aestheticised emotions and intellectual detachment from all moral consequences, and in due course these factors destroy Dorian's soul and bring him to his downfall. What begins as self-realisation of the personality through the cultivation of youth and eternal beauty ends in self-deception and crime – culture and corruption are the two poles that represent the charm and the danger of this new hedonism.

In social terms, this philosophy is equivalent to anarchic liberalism, with the interests of the individual no longer being curtailed for the good of the community, but with social requirements subordinated to those of the individual. This in fact is the quintessence of Wilde's essay *The Soul of Man under Socialism*, whose fashionable title may well awaken false expectations. It is far from being a practicable, carefully thought out plan of social reform based on first-hand knowledge of life in the East End; it is, on the contrary, a radically liberal, anti-socialist piece of personal propaganda. While Morris, Shaw and the Fabians saw socialism as a way to a more just social order, or as a stepping-stone on the road to a communist paradise on earth, Wilde regarded it merely as a prelude to the full expansion of individualism, with state authority being replaced by the autonomous (artistic) personality. Basically he used the socialist debate of the 1880s as a pretext to disguise himself as an anti-bourgeois anarchist while in fact pursuing bourgeois liberalism to its extremes and blending it with his own theory of aesthetic individualism. The negation of state authority and the emphasis on free self-realisation are the social and political sides of his concept of autonomous art, with the artist being free from all moral obligations. In this respect, the essay presents a social–theoretical framework for *Dorian Gray* and for Wilde's aesthetic theory.

The Soul of Man under Socialism offers a Utopian vision of society, but it is no revolutionary call-to-arms, and it has little to do with the urgent problems of East End poverty. It allowed an essentially non-political author to simulate social commitment, while at the same time leaving him plenty of room for manoeuvre should he be taken to task for the dangerous implications of his ideas. In this way Wilde could act the bold *provocateur*, marching at the forefront of the struggle for social progress, but never completely burning his bridges back to the salons of the rich and powerful whom he was attacking. His criticism is a challenge partially muted by its form, in much the same way as his comedies sugar the pills with epigrams and paradoxes.

Wilde's social criticism was never so radical or so humourless as to endanger his role as entertainer to a fairly well-disposed nation. The themes of his first three comedies show just how conscious he was of the different roles required in private and in public life and reinforced by the threat of sanctions against those who refused to play them. The conflicts arise from the attempts of outsiders to regain their place in society while the insiders endeavour to consolidate their own positions, and from the desire of the individual to realise himself in opposition to the pressure imposed upon him to conform. There is continual and unresolved tension between personal identity and social integration, and this is most strikingly reflected by the duality of the dandy figure, who oscillates between intellectual detachment and emotional involvement, between public role and private need for self-expression. The dialogue itself alternates between the uncommitted conversation-piece and the direct communication of personal truths, again demonstrating the conflict between public and private life that determines the course of each of the plots.

Only in *The Importance of Being Earnest* do the social and moral problems of the first three comedies give way completely to aesthetic play in accordance with the rule that 'In matters of grave importance, style, not sincerity, is the vital thing.'[14] Wilde reduces earnest Victorian morality to the proportions of a name, making an ethical attitude into a formal aesthetic category, and by means of this parody he shows just how far he has distanced himself from the earnestness of his contemporaries. In fact the social and economic crisis of the 1880s had already discredited Victorian codes of ethics, and so it is scarcely surprising that Wilde depicts them as mere façades of public propriety.

There is, however, more to Wilde's comedies than the conflict between public and private life and, latterly, the parody on Victorian earnestness. The struggle between individual and society, between provocation and conformity, is also autobiographical. The plays are transmuted self-portraits, incorporating various of Wilde's own identities, from the character with the 'guilty secret' to the middle-class moralist who was only too aware of the conflict between the hidden sin and the public confession, between guilt and the desire for absolution. For all his insistence on the autonomy of art, his own was highly dependent on his own life and on the social atmosphere of his time. Since the romantics first emancipated the artist, none flaunted his individuality more universally than Wilde, and none was more harshly punished for his temerity. He himself came from a middle-class family, but he scorned the philistinism of the bourgeoisie with such passion that one suspects he had never fully detached himself from them. His sympathy lay with the aristocracy. There

was in his individualistic philosophy and aesthetic formalism an eminently elite and exclusive tenor: fine-sounding titles were irresistible for
him, as is evident from a mere glance at the cast list of his characters. The
aristocracy were possessed of all the means whereby his ideals could be
realised – a life of cultivated idleness, high society, financial security. In
fact he was often at his wit's end to pay his debts and feed his family,
sometimes having to rush away from London for a few weeks to escape
from his creditors – though not always successfully. To compensate for
his middle-class background, he would assume the airs of an aristocrat,
and this was his downfall. He came from the middle class, rebelled against
their norms, and so could scarcely expect sympathy from them; he aspired
to the ideals of the aristocracy, but was never rewarded with their
acceptance. And so he remained an outsider, passing himself off as
anti-bourgeois, and for ever pandering to the nobility, thereby over-
reaching himself. As in his art – 'strong adjectives followed by weak
nouns'[15] – so in his life: one of his last witticisms is said to have been 'I am
dying, as I have lived, beyond my means.'[16]

Wilde's political inactivity, and his instinct for the degree of latitude the
mighty would allow their jesters, never deserted him until the moment
when he decided to sue Lord Queensberry. And yet even this crisis made
no radical changes in the make-up of the conformist rebel. Undoubtedly
his experiences in Reading added a new dimension to his vision of reality:
inedible food, squalor, isolation, humiliation, the suffering of hungry
children, the beating of weak-minded simpletons. And the shared pain
made him sensitive to the warmth of solidarity, and to the comfort of a
few words of sympathy from his fellows. But these two years of hardship
and forced labour failed to change the individualistic hedonist into a
social fighter; the anti-bourgeois protester was still without revolutionary
earnestness. His journey into exile did not lead him to passionate
opposition against the injustices of society, but only to resignation, a
passive acceptance of a futureless existence behind the mask of an
assumed name, with nothing to relish except the scraps of a few bright
memories.

His last works purge his soul from the trauma of Reading, the one
directly and the other poetically seeking to present his new role, both to
himself and to the public, as an almost natural rounding-off of a life that
had hitherto been lived only on the 'sungilt side of the garden'.[17]
Humility, modesty and suffering are now the correctives to a still
unquestioned philosophy of pleasure. But even this new virtue of humility
does not prevent him from seeing himself, the artist, as martyr standing
side by side in suffering with Christ – a comparison that allows him to
endow his pathetic situation with an aura of historical greatness and
hence with that quality that was otherwise so sorely missed: the quality of

style. In reconstructing a new identity on the ruins of the old, he was still tentatively hoping for forgiveness and rehabilitation. He appealed to the sympathy and sense of justice of his contemporaries, depicting his fall as that of a great but fatally weak-willed man and artist, brought down by a *mauvais génie* from the heights of fortune, where the century had woven 'myth and legend'[18] around him, to the depths of misery, where now he languished in gaol between Gilles de Retz and the Marquis de Sade. Who could be so hard-hearted that they would fail to be moved by such a tragedy?

The pattern of attack (on Douglas) and defence (of his own behaviour) that underlies *De Profundis* clearly reveals its strategy for arousing public sympathy, whereas in *The Ballad of Reading Gaol* the strategy is only indirect, since it is woven into the story of the condemned prisoner. But just as in the letter Wilde's attack on Douglas relieves him of his own responsibility, so too in the poem does his attack on the penal system – at times so direct as to make the *Ballad* seem almost like a propagandist pamphlet – indicate that the real guilt lies beyond himself. No one could deny that C.3.3.'s experiences and insights determined the artistic perspective of the *Ballad*, and in this respect his last two works are a unique *apologia pro vita sua*, as he seeks not only justification but also reconciliation. To a degree he was successful with Douglas, since their break was not final, but Victorian society never did forgive him.

The interplay between provocation and conformity enables us to understand the ambivalent attitude of the homosexual Wilde and the bourgeois Wilde towards society; it also typifies his attitude towards the literary traditions which he inherited and proceeded to use in his own way. The element of conformity ranges from unabashed plagiarism – as we saw in some of his American lectures – through the creative adaptation of unusual rhythms and forms of expression, to the subtle exploitation of symbolist imagery and dramatic technique in *Salomé*. But it would be wrong to confirm the old prejudice that Wilde was merely an unoriginal, insincere imitator who could only reproduce the *déjà lu*. In much of what he wrote, he was very much his own man, and brought a new style into the literature of his time. On what models of English Literature are the tales of *The Happy Prince* and *A House of Pomegranates* based? What nineteenth-century drama can measure up to the wit and brilliance of *The Importance of Being Earnest*? Who else made the general public so aware of such topics as autonomous art, autonomous artists, or the importance of the critical mind? Certainly no one more than the 'apostle in the high aesthetic band',[19] the author of *Intentions*.

But at the same time one must acknowledge that a philosophy of hedonistic self-realisation, withdrawing from the demands of the real world on the grounds of its formlessness, seems essentially narrow and inhumane. And a theory of art that rejects unity of form and content in favour of form alone seems critically superficial. Art without social and humanitarian commitment, based only on the satisfaction of individual desires, seems ultimately shallow and barren. It must also be acknowledged that intercourse with ideas and literary forms of the past did not always lead to artistic fertility. Perhaps this was because, in Max Beerbohm's words, 'Mr Wilde was not ... a born writer',[20] or perhaps he simply lacked the devotion and industry to endure Yeats's 'sedentary toil'. Indeed one of the difficulties in assessing the value of Wilde's work is the fact that the artist and charlatan, poet and poser, originator and imitator all worked so closely together. At first sight it is almost impossible to understand how a mind of such rich and critical originality could so often remain trapped in the circles drawn by his predecessors. And even his drastic reversal of the beliefs and codes of his time is less a matter of independence than of amusing contrariness. Perhaps the basic cause of this phenomenon lies in the fact that Wilde had no direct access of his own to reality. To him, reality meant the spectacle of self-presentation, it was a kind of jolly masked ball with himself the only participant, while others stood admiringly in the wings to watch him. At no time was his stage bigger than the dimensions of the shadow cast by his own ego. With this highly selective concept of reality, beneath an aesthetic gloss (apart from his two last works), his many roles and the many genres in which his fantasy expressed itself were simply natural modes of self-portrayal. Thus the provocative cult of personality and the eclectic absorption of literary traditions do not contradict each other but instead come together as complementary forms of his concept of reality. They did, however, prevent him from confronting the intellectual and material problems of his time with any of the commitment or artistic subtlety of the great writers before and after him.

How, then, is one to evaluate his achievement? And where does he stand in the literary context of his own age? In terms of literary history, is he an epigonic romantic, a Victorian in disguise, or – in the flattering company of Baudelaire and Nietzsche – a member of the nineteenth-century European avant-garde in the movement against the bourgeoisie? What artistic label is to be attached to a man who worked as poet, critic, dramatist, essayist, novelist, story-teller, aphorist, and editor of a women's magazine? Thomas Mann set him beside Nietzsche, because he saw them as both standing together in a 'Zeit des ersten Anrennens der europäischen Intelligenz gegen die verheuchelte Moral des viktoriani-schen, des bürgerlichen Zeitalters'[21] [time of the first assault by European intelligence against the sham morality of the Victorian, the bourgeois age]. Hans Mayer saw him as the outsider, the citizen of Sodom, lamentably betrayed by the Enlightenment.[22] Simone de Beauvoir feels 'des affinités intellectuelles avec lui',[23] while Richard Ellmann says he is 'the one writer of the nineties whom everyone reads or, more precisely, has read'.[24] It is an observation confirmed by the countless reprints, new editions, film, television, stage and radio versions by which his work is still being presented to the public today, and which prove beyond doubt that Oscar still lives. In England perhaps he is undervalued, in Germany – at least initially – perhaps overvalued; he has often been scorned or ignored by the literary establishment, but his fame has in no way diminished through the years. Certainly one reason for this is the modernity of his critical, provocative intellect, whose spirit of contradiction was for ever manifesting itself in its attacks on fossilised conventions and entrenched authority in all its forms. He was the artist as critic, though never the passionate poet, with eye 'in a fine frenzy rolling',[25] and his criticism was laced with wit which, by flashing against the grain of the familiar, could open up new perspectives on old ideas. His epigrams and aphorisms and the intellectual charm of his language – creating gems that are still quoted with relish – admirably fulfil one of the oldest and most cherished of all the functions of literature, which is to entertain. Such a gift should not be scorned, for without doubt it is one of the main reasons for Wilde's survival.

For all the faults both of his life and his art, and for all his contradictions, vanities and artificialities, the personality and the work continue to exercise fascination on each new generation. The conformist rebel continues to conform and to rebel, but he is never too earnest in the role, and even if one might look back and exclaim 'Alas, poor Oscar', there can be no denying that he was 'a fellow of infinite jest, of most excellent fancy'.[26]

Abbreviations

Letters refers throughout to *The Letters of Oscar Wilde*, ed. by Rupert Hart-Davis, London 1962.

ABC	*American Book Collector*	BC	*Book Collector*
AJES	*The Aligarh Journal of English Studies*	BHPSO	*Bulletin of the Historical and Philosophical Society of Ohio*
AKG	*Archiv für Kulturgeschichte*	BJA	*British Journal of Aesthetics*
AL	*American Literature*		
AM	*American Mercury*	BNI	*Book Notes Illustrated*
Anglia Bbl	*Anglia Beiblatt*	BNYPL	*Bulletin of the New York Public Library*
Annpl	*Annales politiques et littéraires*	BooksB	*Books and Bookmen*
AN & Q	*American Notes and Queries*	BPAP	*Bulletin of the Philadelphia Association for Psychoanalysis*
Antab	*Antike und Abendland*		
AntigR	*Antigonish Review*	BuR	*Bucknell Review*
AO	*Annals of Otology ...*	BUSE	*Boston University Studies in English*
ar	*american review*		
Archiv	*Archiv für das Studium der Neueren Sprachen und Literaturen*	BuW	*Bühne und Welt*
		CanF	*Canadian Forum*
Archives	*Archives d'anthropologie criminelle, de médecine légale et de psychologie normale et pathologique*	CathW	*Catholic World*
		CE	*College English*
		CentR	*The Centennial Review*
		ChL	*Children's Literature*
ARev	*Architectural Review*	CJIS	*Canadian Journal of Irish Studies*
ArL	*Archivum linguisticum*		
ArQ	*Arizona Quarterly*	CL	*Comparative Literature*
Asch	*American Scholar*	CLAJ	*College Language Association Journal (Morgan State College, Baltimore)*
AtM	*Atlantic Monthly*		
Ausw.	*Auswahl*		
AZ	*Allgemeine Zeitung (München)*	CM	*Cornhill Magazine*
		CompD	*Comparative Drama*
		ContempR	*Contemporary Review*
BA	*Books Abroad*	ConvL	*Convorbiri literare* (Iasi)
BB	*Books and Book-Plates*	CountryL	*Country Life*
BBz	*Berliner Börsenzeitung*	CQ	*Cambridge Quarterly*

327

CRCL/RCLC Canadian Review of
            Comparative
            Literature/Revue
            canadienne de littérature
            comparée
Currl   Current Literature
CurrO   Current Opinion
CVE   Cahiers Victoriens et
            Edouardiens du Centre
            d'Etude et de recherches
            victoriennes ...
            (Montpellier)

DA   Dissertation Abstracts
            (International)
DM   Dublin Magazine
DNS   Die Neueren Sprachen
DR   Dalhousie Review
DRev   Dublin Review
DRs   Deutsche Rundschau
DUJ   Durham University
            Journal
DUM   Dublin University
            Magazine

EA   Etudes anglaises
EdR   Edinburgh Review
EIC   Essays in Criticism
            (Oxford)
EL   Everyman's Library
ELH   Journal of English
            Literary History
ELN   English Language Notes
            (Univ. of Colorado)
ELT   English Literature in
            Transition (1880–1920)
EM   English Miscellany
EngRev   English Review
Epl   Entretiens politiques et
            littéraires
E & S   Essays and Studies
ES   English Studies
ESA   English Studies in Africa
            (Johannesburg)
ESC   English Studies in
            Canada
ESt   Englische Studien
ETJ   Educational Theatre
            Journal

EWN   Evelyn Waugh
            Newsletter
FAZ   Frankfurter Allgemeine
            Zeitung
FBl   Faust-Blätter
FL   Le Figaro littéraire
FortR   The Fortnightly
            Review
FR   French Review
FreeR   Free Review
FS   French Studies
FZ   Frankfurter Zeitung
GraphM   Graphologische
            Monatshefte
GRev   La Grande Revue
GRM   Germanisch-romanische
            Monatsschrift
GuW   Glauben und Wissen

HarpM   Harper's Magazine
HarpNMM   Harper's New Monthly
            Magazine
HarpW   Harper's Weekly
HarvM   Harvard Monthly
HibbJ   Hibbert Journal
HJM   Haldeman-Julius
            Monthly
HSL   Hartford Studies in
            Literature
HudR   Hudson Review

IB   Irish Book
IHS   Irish Historical Studies
IIL   Izvestija na Instituta za
            Literatura
IJS   International Journal of
            Sexology
IllZ   Illustrierte Zeitung
ILN   Illustrated London
            News
IMWK   Internationale
            Monatsschrift für
            Wissenschaft und Kunst
it   insel taschenbuch

JA   Judy's Annual
JAAC   Journal of Aesthetics
            and Art Criticism

JbsZ	*Jahrbuch für sexuelle Zwischenstufen* (Leipzig)	MacM	*Macmillan's Magazine*
		Maga.	*Blackwood's Magazine*
JEGP	*Journal of English and Germanic Philology*	MD	*Modern Drama*
		MedAHS	*Medical Aspects of Human Sexuality*
JGE	*Journal of General Education*	MedH	*Medical History*
		MedlJ	*Medico-legal Journal*
JIL	*Journal of Irish Literature*	Mercure	*Mercure de France*
		MEW	Karl Marx und Friedrich Engels, *Werke*, vol. 1 seqq., Berlin 1956 seqq.
JML	*Journal of Modern Literature*	
JOSA	*Journal of the Oriental Society of Australia*	
		MFS	*Modern Fiction Studies*
K & C	*Kunst en Cultuur* (Brussels)	MHRev	*Malahat Review*
		MidQ	*The Mid-West Quarterly*
KCHG	*King's College Hospital Gazette*	MinnH	*Minnesota History*
		MKS	*Monatsschrift für Kriminalpsychologie und Strafrechtsreform*
KoK	*Kirke og kultur* (Oslo)	
KR	*Kenyon Review*	
KSJ	*Keats-Shelley Journal*	MLA	*Modern Language Association of America*
LetN	*Lettres Nouvelles*	
LFQ	*Literature/Film Quarterly*	MLN	*Modern Language Notes*
LGRP	*Literaturblatt für germanische und romanische Philologie*	MLQ	*Modern Language Quarterly*
		MLR	*Modern Language Review*
LH	*Literarischer Handweiser*	
		MMWH	*Montana Magazine of Western History*
LibR	*Library Review*	
LiLi	*Zeitschrift für Literaturwissenschaft und Linguistik*	MP	*Modern Philology*
		MuK	*Maske und Kothurn*
		MunsM	*Munsey's Magazine*
Listy	*Listy pro uměni a kritiku*	
		NA	*Nuova Antologia*
LitE	*Das literarische Echo*	NAR	*North American Review*
LivA	*The Living Age*	
LJ	*Library Journal*	Nat(E)R	*National (and English) Review*
LLLM	*Life and Letters and The London Mercury*	
		NB	*Die neue Bücherschau*
LMag	*London Magazine*	NBR	*North British Review*
LoM(B)	*London Mercury (and Bookman)*	NC	*Nineteenth Century*
		NCA	*Nineteenth Century and After*
L & P	*Literature and Psychology*	
		NCBEL	*The New Cambridge Bibliography of English Literature*
LudM	*Ludgate Monthly*	
LWU	*Literatur in Wissenschaft und Unterricht*	NCF	*Nineteenth-Century Fiction*

NCTR	*Nineteenth Century Theatre Research*	PEGS	*Publications of the English Goethe Society*
NEQ	*New England Quarterly*	Piz	*Prawo i zycie*
NewR	*New Review*	PJb	*Preußische Jahrbücher*
NewRep	*New Republic*	PLL	*Papers on Language and Literature*
NewS(Nat)	*New Statesman (and Nation)*		
		Pméd	*Presse médicale*
NewW	*New World*	PMLA	*Publications of the Modern Language Association of America*
NFP	*Neue Freie Presse (Vienna)*		
NL	*Les Nouvelles littéraires*	PMLC	*Papers of the Manchester Literary Club*
NM	*Neuphilologische Mitteilungen*		
NMQ(R)	*New Mexico Quarterly (Review)*	PPNCFL	*Proceedings of the Pacific Northwest Conference on Foreign Languages*
NovR	*Novel Review*		
Nph	*Neophilologus*		
N & Q	*Notes & Queries*	PQ	*Philological Quarterly*
NRddm	*Nouvelle Revue des deux mondes*	PR	*Partisan Review*
		PrS	*Prairie Schooner*
NRev	*Nouvelle Revue*	PRSM	*Proceedings of the Royal Society of Medicine*
NRF	*Nouvelle Revue Française*		
NRs	*Neue (Deutsche) Rundschau*	PsyR	*Psychoanalytic Review*
		PublW	*Publisher's Weekly*
NsM	*Neusprachliche Mitteilungen aus Wissenschaft und Praxis*	PULC	*Princeton University Library Chronicle*
		PURBA	*Panjab University Research Bulletin* (Arts)
NTP	*Nederlands Tijdschrift voor Psychologie*		
NVT	*Nieuw Vlaams Tijdschrift*	QJS	*Quarterly Journal of Speech*
NY	*The New Yorker*	QR	*Quarterly Review*
NYHTB(R)	*New York Herald Tribune Book(s) Review*	QRL	*Quarterly Review of Literature*
NYRB	*New York Review of Books*	RAA	*Revue anglo-américaine*
		RB	*Revista do Brasil*
NYTBR	*New York Times Book Review*	RBelg	*Revue de Belgique*
		Rbl	*Revue blanche*
NZ	*Die Neue Zeit (Stuttgart)*	Rbph	*Revue belge de philologie et d'histoire*
ÖstR	*Österreichische Rundschau*	RColl	*Reading and Collecting*
		Rddm	*Revue des deux mondes*
		RealN	*Realtà Nuova*
OL	*Orbis Litterarum*	Reur	*Revue européenne*
OR	*Occult Review*	Revbl	*Revue bleue*
PBSA	*Papers of the Bibliographical Society of America*	RevP	*Revue de Paris*
		Revpl	*Revue politique et littéraire*

RevRev	*Review of Reviews*	SNNTS	*Studies in the Novel* (North Texas State University)
ReyN	*Reynolds's Newspaper*		
Rheb	*Revue hebdomadaire*		
RHL	*Revue d'histoire littéraire de la France*	SOED	*Shorter Oxford English Dictionary*
Rhr	*Revue de l'histoire des religions*	SoRA	*Southern Review* (Adelaide, Australia)
RIP	*Rice Institute Pamphlet*	SP	*Studies in Philology*
		SpirL	*Spirit Lamp*
RivI	*Rivista d'Italia*	SSF	*Studies in Short Fiction* (Newberry College, S.C.)
RLC	*Revue de Littérature Comparée*		
RLM	*Revue des Lettres Modernes*	StML	*Stimmen aus Maria-Laach*
RLV	*Revue des Langues Vivantes*	Studies	*Studies. An Irish quarterly review*
Rmond	*Revue mondiale*	SZ	*Stimmen der Zeit*
Rmus	*Revue musicale*		
RoLit	*România Literară*	TA	*Theatre Annual*
RoR	*Romanian Review*	TC	*Twentieth Century*
Rpsic	*Revista de psicoanalisis*	ThA	*Theatre Arts*
RR	*Romanic Review*	ThR	*Theatre Research International*
RS	*Research Studies* (Washington State University)	ThS (Ohio)	*Theatre Studies. The journal of the Ohio State University Theatre Research Institute*
RUS	*Rice University Studies*		
RUSEng	*Rajasthan University Studies in English*	TLS	*The Times Literary Supplement*
SAQ	*South Atlantic Quarterly*	TM	*Temps modernes*
		TQ	*Texas Quarterly*
SatR(Lit)	*Saturday Review (of Literature)*	Ts.	Taunus
		TSL	*Tennessee Studies in Literature*
SB	*Studies in Bibliography. Papers of the Bibliographical Society of the University of Virginia*	TSLL	*Texas Studies in Literature and Language*
SCSML	*Smith College Studies in Modern Languages*	UCC	*University of California Chronicle*
SEL	*Studies in English Literature, 1500–1900*	UES	*Unisa Studies in English*
		UKR	*University of Kansas Review*
SeR	*Sewanee Review*		
SGG	*Studia Germanica Gandensia*	UMSE	*University of Mississippi Studies in English*
ShawR	*Shaw Review*	UPB	*Universidad Pontificia Bolivariana* (Medellín)
ShS	*Shakespeare Survey*		
SLT	*Svensk Litteraturtidskrift*	UR	*University Review* (Kansas City)

URev	*University Review* (Dublin)	WHR	*Western Humanities Review*
UTB	*Uni-Taschenbücher*	WRev	*Waterloo Review*
UTQ	*University of Toronto Quarterly*	WTW	*Writers and their Work*
UZMOPI	*Učenye Zapiski. Moskovskij oblastnoj pedagogičeskij institut imeni N.K. Krupskoj* (Moscow)	WWR	*Walt Whitman Review*
		YCGL	*Yearbook of Comparative and General Literature*
VIJ	*Victorians Institute Journal*	YES	*Yearbook of English Studies*
VKM	*Velhagen & Klasings Monatshefte*	YR	*Yale Review*
VN	*Victorian Newsletter*	YULG	*The Yale University Library Gazette*
VossZ	*Vossische Zeitung*	ZAA	*Zeitschrift für Anglistik und Amerikanistik*
VP	*Victorian Poetry*	ZFEU	*Zeitschrift für französischen und englischen Unterricht*
VQU	*Virginia Quarterly Review*		
VS	*Victorian Studies*	ZPsych	*Zentralblatt für Psychoanalyse*
WB	*Wissenschaftliche Buchgesellschaft*	ZRG	*Zeitschrift für Religions- und Geistesgeschichte*
WBEP	*Wiener Beiträge zur Englischen Philologie*	ZRPh	*Zeitschrift für Romanische Philologie*
WC	World's Classics	ZSex	*Zeitschrift für Sexualwissenschaft*
WestmB	*Westminster Budget*		
WestmR	*Westminster Review*		
WetB	*Wetenschappelijke Bladen*		

Notes

Introduction

1 *De Profundis*, in *Complete Works of Oscar Wilde*. With an introduction by Vyvyan Holland, London and Glasgow 1966 [1948], p. 912. This edition will subsequently be referred to as *Complete Works*.

2 André Gide, 'Oscar Wilde', *L'Ermitage* (June 1902), 415.

3 An excellent survey is given by Ian Fletcher and John Stokes, 'Oscar Wilde', in *Anglo-Irish Literature. A Review of Research*, ed. by Richard J. Finneran, New York 1976, pp. 48–137. *Suppl.* 1983, pp. 21–47.

4 'The Critic as Artist', in *Complete Works*, p. 1010.

5 *Oscar Wilde. The Story of an Unhappy Friendship*, London 1905 [1902], p. 14. Sherard's other publications include *The Real Oscar Wilde*, London 1916, and *Bernard Shaw, Frank Harris and Oscar Wilde*, London 1937. On the relationship between Wilde and Sherard, see Kevin H. F. O'Brien's essay, 'Robert Sherard: Friend of Oscar Wilde', ELT 28 (1985), 3–29.

6 See also *The Autobiography*, London 1929; *Without Apology*, London 1938; *Oscar Wilde. A Summing-up*, London 1940, 1950.

7 See the reviews by Ernst Bendz, ESt 52 (1918), 342–66; Bernhard Fehr, Anglia Bbl 36 (1925), 361–4; E. M. Forster, *Spectator* 141 (29 July 1938), 194–5; Raymond Mortimer, NewS 16 (30 July 1938), 189; Arnold Palmer, LoM(B) 38 (1938), 368–9; Léon Lemonnier, EA 3 (1939), 61–2. On the history of this biography and its revisions, see 'Correspondence. The Harris–Wilde Memoir', NewS 16 (6 Aug. 1938), 215; (13 Aug. 1938), 247; (20 Aug. 1938), 280.

8 *A Study of Oscar Wilde*, New York 1912, p. 12.

9 *Oscar Wilde. A Critical Study*, London 1912, p. 16. Repr. New York 1971.

10 *Oscar Wilde. The Man – the Artist*, London, 1938, p. 25.

11 Johann Wolfgang Goethe, *Aus meinem Leben. Dichtung und Wahrheit*, Book 7, in *Sämtliche Werke*, vol. 10, Zürich and Munich 1977 [1948], p. 312. (Artemis-Gedenkausgabe).

12 Arthur Symons, *A Study of Oscar Wilde*, London 1930, p. 88.

13 Ibid., p. 47.

14 Ibid., p. 48.

15 Ibid.

16 Lemonnier, *Oscar Wilde*, Paris 1938, p. 31.

17 Ibid., p. 65.

18 Ibid., p. 100.

19 Ibid., p. 201

20 *Oscar Wilde*, Paris 1948. Repr. with slight changes, Paris 1984. Page numbers in these notes always refer to the 1948 edition. Also entitled *Oscar Wilde. Appréciation d'une œuvre et d'une destinée*, Rennes 1948.

21 *Oscar Wilde*, Paris 1948, p. 478. This is the edition from which subsequent quotations are taken.

22 Ibid.

23 Ibid., p. 480.

24 Ibid., p. 245.

25 Ibid., p. 487.

26 Ibid., p. 490.

27 Ibid., pp. 489–90.

28 *The Paradox of Oscar Wilde*, New York 1949, p. 4. On this book see the reviews by Raymond Mortimer, *Sunday Times*, 3 July 1949, 3; W. H. Auden, PR 17 (1950), 390–4; DeLancey Ferguson, NYHTB(R), 19 Feb. 1950, 5; George Freedley, LJ 75 (15 Jan. 1950), 108; Paul Goodman, *Furioso* 5 (1950), 80–2; *Nation* (13 May 1950), 456; William P. Sears, *Churchman* (Hartford, Conn.) (15 April 1950), 18; W. Y. Tindall, SatR(Lit) 33 (4 March 1950), 20; UTQ 20 (1950), 301; Frances Winwar, NYTBR, 16 Feb. 1950, 12; Alan S. Downer, MLN 66 (1951), 282–3; W. D. T[empleman], *Personalist* 32 (1951), 290–1.

29 Woodcock, *The Paradox of Oscar Wilde*, p. 250.

30 Ibid., p. 236.

31 Bernhard Fehr, *Studien zu Oscar Wilde's Gedichten*, Berlin 1918, p. ix.

32 Ibid., p. 125.

33 *Walter Pater's Einfluss auf Oscar Wilde*, Bonn 1913. (Bonner Studien zur englischen Philologie. 8).

34 *The Influence of Pater and Matthew Arnold in the Prose-Writings of Oscar Wilde*, Gothenburg and London 1914.

35 'Die persönlichen und literarischen Beziehungen zwischen Oscar Wilde und James MacNeill Whistler', ESt 65 (1931), 217–52.

36 Charles B. Paul and Robert D. Pepper, 'The Importance of Reading Alfred. Oscar Wilde's Debt to Alfred de Musset', BNYPL 75, no. 10 (1971), 506–42.

37 *Oscar Wilde*, Norfolk, Conn. 1947, p. 7. On this monograph see the reviews by Stanley Hyman, QRL 4 (1947–9), 320–2; Carlos Baker, NYTBR, 23 May 1948, 26; CE 9 (Feb. 1948), 290; J. C. Garrett, CanF 27 (Feb. 1948), 259–60; John Gassner, ThA 32 (1948), 99; Paul Goodman, KR 10 (1948), 340–6; see also the author's response and Paul Goodman's reply in KR 10 (1948), 699–700. David Sachs, *Furioso* 3 (1948), 78–80; C. V. Wicker, NMQ(R) 18 (1948), 244; Vernon A. Young, *Accent* 8 (1948), 235–7; John M. Raines, BA 23 (1949), 79.

38 Roditi, *Oscar Wilde*, p. 123.

39 Ibid., p. 124.

40 Ibid.

41 See Albert J. Farmer, *Le Mouvement esthétique et 'décadent' en Angleterre (1873–1900)*, Paris 1931. (Bibliothèque de la Revue de littérature comparée. 75); Louise Rosenblatt, *L'Idée de l'art pour l'art dans la littérature anglaise pendant la période victorienne*, Paris 1931. (Bibliothèque de la Revue de littérature comparée. 70).

42 Aatos Ojala, *Aestheticism and Oscar Wilde*, pt I. Helsinki 1954, p. 12. See also the reviews in DM 31 (Apr.–June 1955), 43–4; Marjorie Thompson, MLR 50 (1955) 570–1; Hermann Heuer, Archiv 193 (1956/57), 207–8; Herbert Huscher, *Anglia* 74 (1956), pp. 382–5; Robert L. Schneider, JEGP 55

(1956) 348–9; Hans-Joachim Lang, *Euphorion* 51 (1957), 97–100; A. J.
Farmer, EA 11 (1958), 170; Robert L. Peters, JAAC 17 (1958), 135–6;
Marjorie Thompson, MLR 53 (1958), 626; J. Weisgerber, Rbph 36 (1958),
993–4; A. Norman Jeffares, ArL 11 (1959), 72–4; Gerhard Müller-Schwefe,
Anglia BbL 78 (1960), 386–9.
43 Ojala, *Aestheticism and Oscar Wilde*, pt. 1, p. 222.
44 An exception is St John Ervine's *Oscar Wilde. A Present Time Appraisal*
(1951), which is riddled with errors, polemic distortions and a consistent tone
of denigration. For instance, at one point he says: 'Oscar ... was damned on
the day he was born, and would have done better to have died in his childhood
as his sister, Isola, who followed him, did.' Ibid., p. 9.
45 'Die Technik der Dramen Oscar Wildes', unpublished diss., Vienna 1923.
46 'Oscar Wilde as Playwright. A Centenary Review', *Adelphi* 30 (1954),
212–40. First appeared as Introduction to Oscar Wilde, *Five Famous Plays*,
London and New York 1952; pp. 7–31.
47 'The Divided Self in the Society Comedies of Oscar Wilde', MD 3 (1960),
16–23.
48 'Comedy and Oscar Wilde', SeR 74 (1966), 501–21.
49 'Ironie et paradoxes dans les comédies d'Oscar Wilde. Une interprétation',
Thalia 1 (1978), 35–53.
50 'Stages of Desire. Oscar Wilde's Comedies and the Consumer', *Genre* 15
(1982), 315–36.
51 'Oscar Wilde, "Lady Windermere's Fan"', in Cleanth Brooks and Robert B.
Heilman, *Understanding Drama*, New York 1948, pp. 34–82.
52 'Wilde as Parodist. A Second Look at "The Importance of Being Earnest"',
CE 18 (1956), 18–23.
53 'The Importance of Being Earnest', BuR 9 (1958), 143–58.
54 'The Meaning of "The Importance of Being Earnest"', MD 6 (1963), 42–52.
55 'Wilde and the Importance of "Sincere and Studied Triviality"', MD 5 (1963),
389–99.
56 'Oscar Wilde's Great Farce "The Importance of Being Earnest"', MLQ 35
(1974), 173–86.
57 *The Artist as Critic. Critical Writings of Oscar Wilde*, ed. by Richard Ellmann,
New York and London 1968.
58 *Literary Criticism of Oscar Wilde*, ed. by Stanley Weintraub, Lincoln Nebr.
1968.
59 'Kunstlehre und Kunstanschauung des Georgekreises und die Ästhetik Oscar
Wildes', unpublished diss., Bern 1957.
60 'A Critical Study of Oscar Wilde's "Intentions"', M.A. thesis, University of
London, 1960.
61 'The Literary Criticism of Oscar Wilde', unpublished Ph.D. thesis, University
of Michigan, 1964.
62 'The Critic as Artist', in *Wilde and the Nineties. An Essay and an Exhibition*,
ed. by Charles Ryskamp, Princeton, N.J., 1966, pp. 1–21. Repr. with some
alterations in *Encounter* 29, no. 1 (1967), 29–37; *The Artist as Critic. Critical
Writings of Oscar Wilde*, ed. by Richard Ellmann, New York 1968, pp. ix–
xxviii; Richard Ellmann, *Golden Codgers. Biographical Speculations*,
London and New York, 1973, pp. 60–80.

336   Notes to pages 9–11

63 'Arnold, Pater, Wilde, and the Object as in Themselves They See It', SEL 11 (1971), 733–47.
64 'Criticism as Art. Form in Oscar Wilde's Critical Writings', SP 70 (1973), 108–22.
65 'Anarchy and Culture. The Evolutionary Turn of Cultural Criticism in the Work of Oscar Wilde', TSLL 20 (1978), 199–215.
66 Epifanio San Juan, Jr, *The Art of Oscar Wilde*, Princeton, N.J. 1967, p. 17. On this book see the reviews by Thomas Flanagan, VS 11 (1967), 254–5; Billy J. Harbin, QJS 53 (1967), 305–6; E. H. Mikhail, MD 10 (1967/68), 439–40; TLS 17 Aug. 1967, 741; Norman W. Alford, MHRev 5 (Jan. 1968), 123–4; Harry W. Rudman, BA 42 (1968), 279; Richard Tobias, VP 6 (1968), 196–9; Frederick T. Wood, ES 49 (1968), 377; Seamus Beane, Studies 58 (1969), 214–16.
67 San Juan, Jr, *The Art of Oscar Wilde*, p. 48.
68 Ibid., p. 62.
69 Ibid., p. 68.
70 Ibid., p. 197.
71 Ibid.
72 Ibid., p. 157.
73 Ibid., p. 205.
74 Christopher S. Nassaar, *Into the Demon Universe. A Literary Exploration of Oscar Wilde*, New Haven and London 1974, p. xii. On this study see the reviews by Karl Beckson, NCF 29 (1974), 360–3; Ronald Bryden, NewS (22 Mar. 1974), 409–10; *Choice* 11 (May 1974), 439; Stuart Curran, SEL 14 (1974), 667–8; René Elvin, Rddm (May 1974), 476; John J. Pappas, VS 18 (1974), 244; Suzanne Sutton, LJ 99 (15 Feb. 1974), 488; Russell Jackson, YES 5 (1975), 324–5; Chris Snodgrass, *Criticism* 17 (1975), 102–9; J. B. Bullen, N & Q 23 (n.s.) (Feb. 1976), 95–6; Gabriel Merle, EA 24 (1976), 623–4; Nicholas A. Salerno, ELT 19 (1976), 64–5.
75 Karl Beckson, review of Nassaar, *Into the Demon Universe*, NCF 29 (1974) 361.
76 See Donald H. Ericksen, *Oscar Wilde*, Boston 1977. (TEAS. 211); John Stokes, *Oscar Wilde*, London 1978; Robert K. Miller, *Oscar Wilde*, New York 1982. (Modern Literature Ser.).
77 Rodney Shewan, *Oscar Wilde. Art and Egotism*, London 1977, p. 1.
78 Ibid., p. 6.
79 See Elizabeth Cullingford, review of Shewan, *Oscar Wilde*, SNNTS 10 (1978), 476: 'a work of criticism, no less than a work of art, should have a satisfactory shape, and this book has none: it is all out of proportion'; Nicholas Grene, review of Shewan, *Oscar Wilde*, N&Q 26 (Aug. 1979), 363: 'With Shewan we sometimes find ourselves unable to see the trees for the undergrowth.' In contrast to these negative verdicts, Ian Fletcher calls Shewan's book 'the most distinguished general study that has as yet appeared' (VS 22 (1978), 490), and the no less competent Wilde specialist Karl Beckson says it is 'one of the best studies of Wilde to appear in many years' (WHR 33 (1979), 76–7).
80 J. E. Chamberlin, *Ripe Was the Drowsy Hour. The Age of Oscar Wilde*, New York 1977, p. xii.
81 Ibid., p. 170.

82 Philip K. Cohen, *The Moral Vision of Oscar Wilde*, Rutherford, N.J. and London 1978, p. 11.
83 Ibid., p. 13.
84 Ibid., pp. 13–14.
85 *Oscar Wilde, The Picture of Dorian Gray*, Munich 1986 (UTB 1388).
86 Alan Bird, *The Plays of Oscar Wilde*, London 1977, p. 7.
87 See, for instance, Rupert Croft-Cooke, *The Unrecorded Life of Oscar Wilde*, New York 1972; Martin Fido, *Oscar Wilde*, London 1973, 1976 (paperback edn); H. Montgomery Hyde, *Oscar Wilde. A Biography*, London 1976: Also issued as Magnum edn, London 1977; Louis Kronenberger, *Oscar Wilde*, Boston and Toronto 1976; Sheridan Morley, *Oscar Wilde*, London 1976; *Oscar Wilde. Leben und Werk in Daten und Bildern*, ed. by Norbert Kohl, Frankfurt/M. 1976. (it 158). Repr. with slight alterations Frankfurt/M. 1986; Richard Pine, *Oscar Wilde*, Dublin 1983. (Gill's Irish Lives).
88 *Kunst und Gesellschaft*, Munich 1973, p. 28.
89 Ibid.

1 Epigonic experiments. The early poems and plays

1 *The Letters of Oscar Wilde*, ed. by Rupert Hart-Davis, London 1962, p. 77. Hereafter cited as *Letters*.
2 *Athenaeum*, 23 July 1881, in *Oscar Wilde. The Critical Heritage*, ed. by Karl Beckson, London 1970, p. 34.
3 *Spectator*, 13 Aug. 1881, in ibid., p. 45.
4 *Athenaeum*, 23 July 1881, in ibid., p. 36.
5 *Saturday Review*, 23 July 1881, in ibid., p. 37.
6 Hesketh Pearson, *The Life of Oscar Wilde*, London 1960 [1946], p. 59.
7 *Punch*, 10 Nov. 1866. Quoted from *Swinburne. The Critical Heritage*, ed. by Clyde K. Hyder, London 1970, p. xxii.
8 A typically negative reaction is that of Arthur Ransome: 'The most obvious quality of this work, and that which is most easily and most often emphasized, is its richness in imitations.' *Oscar Wilde. A Critical Study*, London 1912, p. 40. See also Averil Gardner, '"Literary Petty Larceny". Plagiarism in Oscar Wilde's early poetry', ESC 8 (1982), 49–61.
9 Bernhard Fehr, *Studien zu Oscar Wilde's Gedichten*, Berlin 1918, p. 132. Cf. also H. Mutschmann's critique of this book, 'Zu Oscar Wildes Gedichten', Anglia Bbl 30 (1919), 294–309, and Fehr's reply, 'Über Oscar Wildes Gedichte und anständige Kritik', Anglia Bbl 31 (1920), 138–43.
10 Epifanio San Juan, Jr, *The Art of Oscar Wilde*, Princeton, N.J. 1967, p. 20.
11 Fehr, *Studien zu Oscar Wilde's Gedichten*, p. 1. Fehr translates this title as 'Bewegung' (motion) instead of 'Satz' (movement of a symphony).
12 Detailed bibliographical information about the individual poems is given by Stuart Mason [Christopher S. Millard] in *A Bibliography of the Poems of Oscar Wilde*. Giving particulars as to the original publication of each poem, with variations of readings and a complete list of all editions, reprints, translations, etc. With portraits, illustrations, facsimiles of title-pages, manuscripts, etc., London 1907. See also the notes in both critical editions of the poems: Bobby Fong, 'The Poetry of Oscar Wilde. A Critical Edition', unpublished Ph.D. thesis, University of California at Los Angeles, 1978: DA

39, no. 9, 1979, p. 5523-A; and Nanci J. White, 'An Annotated Edition of the Poems of Oscar Wilde', unpublished Ph.D. thesis, York University (Canada), 1980: DA 41, no. 10, 1981, pp. 4396–4397-A.

13 'Sonnet to Liberty', lines 4–7, in *Complete Works of Oscar Wilde*. With an introduction by Vyvyan Holland, London and Glasgow 1966 [1948], p. 709.

14 Ibid., line 9.

15 Ibid., line 10.

16 Ibid., lines 13–14.

17 See R. C. K. Ensor, *England 1870–1914*, Oxford 1949 [1936], pp. 44–5.

18 'Sonnet on the Massacre of the Christians in Bulgaria', line 14, in *Complete Works*, p. 714.

19 Hoxie N. Fairchild, *Religious Trends in English Poetry*, vol. V, *1880–1920*, New York and London 1962, p. 142.

20 'Theoretikos', lines 7–14, in *Complete Works*, p. 716.

21 Ibid., lines 12–13, in ibid., p. 716.

22 'The Garden of Eros', verse 37, line 6, in ibid., p. 722.

23 Ibid., verses 38–9, in ibid., p. 722.

24 *Lamia*, pt. II, lines 229–37, in *The Poetical Works of John Keats*, ed. by H. W. Garrod, London 1962 [1908], pp. 176–7.

25 'Milton', Aug. 1825, in *Works*, ed. by Lady Trevelyan, vol. V, London 1866, p. 4.

26 *Complete Works*, p. 1089.

27 'Rome Unvisited', verses 12–13, in ibid., pp. 729–30.

28 *The Rice Institute Pamphlet* 42, Oct. 1954, pp. 32–52.

29 Ibid., p. 42.

30 Ibid. See also J. Charbonnier, 'L'Intellectualisme d'Oscar Wilde', RAA 12 (1935), 514; Vincent O'Sullivan, *Aspects of Wilde*, New York 1936, p. 56; Frank Brennand, *Oscar Wilde*, London 1960, p. 37.

31 *Complete Works*, p. 915.

32 *Letters*, p. 31. David Hunter-Blair, a fellow student of Wilde's, confirms these leanings towards Catholicism: 'Wilde made no secret in his intercourse·with his many college friends of his Catholic proclivities and leanings'. 'Oscar Wilde as I Knew Him', DRev 203 (1938), 97.

33 'San Miniato', verse 4, lines 3–4, in *Complete Works*, p. 725.

34 Ibid., verse 2, line 2.

35 Cf. the motif of sin in 'Charmides', verse 19, line 1, in *Complete Works*, p. 755, and verse 109, line 2, in ibid., p. 770; also in 'Taedium Vitae', line 14, in ibid., p. 788; and 'The New Remorse', line 1, in ibid., p. 806.

36 'Panthea', verse 14, lines 5–6, in *Complete Works*, p. 782.

37 Ibid., verse 29, line 6, in ibid., p. 784.

38 Ibid., verse 24, lines 2–3, in ibid., p. 783.

39 *Studien zu Oscar Wilde's Gedichten*, p. 125.

40 'Panthea', verse 16, in *Complete Works*, p. 782.

41 Ibid., verse 18, lines 1–2, in ibid., p. 782.

42 Ibid., verse 17, lines 3–4, in ibid., p. 782.

43 'Humanitad', verse 73, line 6, in ibid., p. 801.

44 *Letters*, p. 34.

45 Ibid., p. 35.

46 'Easter Day', line 11, in *Complete Works*, p. 731.

47 Lines 12–14, in ibid., p. 728.
48 André Gide, 'Oscar Wilde', *L'Ermitage* (June 1902), 408.
49 '"Charmides" is the most successful of the five poems, chiefly because the poet has a definite story to tell, and hence is less inclined to wander off into the misty cloudland of his own sensations.' Homer E. Woodbridge, 'Oscar Wilde as a Poet', *Poet Lore* 19 (1908), 443; Léon Lemonnier, *Oscar Wilde*, Paris [1938], p. 29, considers the poem 'le plus significatif' of all the *Poems*, and Robert Merle, *Oscar Wilde*, Paris 1948, p. 176, calls it 'le plus long, le plus significatif, le plus beau poème du recueil'.
50 'Charmides', verse 45, line 5, in *Complete Works*, p. 759.
51 Ibid., verse 61, line 2, in ibid., p. 762.
52 Ibid., verses 109–10, in ibid., p. 770.
53 Ibid., verse 61, line 4, in ibid., p. 762.
54 Ibid., verse 110, line 2, in ibid., p. 770.
55 Ibid., verse 109, in ibid., p. 770.
56 *The Picture of Dorian Gray.* The Preface, in ibid., p. 17.
57 Pearson, *The Life of Oscar Wilde*, p. 56.
58 'Apologia', verse 8, lines 1–2, in *Complete Works*, p. 785.
59 'Quia Multum Amavi', verse 3, line 3, in ibid., p. 786.
60 'Silentium Amoris', verse 3, lines 5–6, in ibid., p. 786.
61 'Glykyprikos Eros', verse 15, lines 3–4, in ibid., p. 803.
62 Wilde regarded these two poems as untypical of his work. See *Letters*, p. 325.
63 *Saturday Review*, 23 July 1881, p. 118, in *Oscar Wilde. The Critical Heritage*, p. 37.
64 Fehr, *Studien zu Oscar Wilde's Gedichten*, p. 115.
65 W. B. Yeats thought so highly of this poem that he included it in the anthology *A Book of Irish Verse*, London 1895. Cf. also Stuart Mason [Christopher S. Millard], *A Bibliography of the Poems of Oscar Wilde*, pp. 21–3. But see also the critical interpretation of the poem by David R. Clark, *Lyric Resonance*, Amherst, Mass. 1972, pp. 57–65.
66 Wilde considered this poem to be 'one of the best sonnets I have written'. *Letters*, p. 325. See the essay by Brooks Wright, 'On the Sale by Auction of Keats' Love Letters. A Footnote to Wilde's Sonnet', KSJ 7 (1958), 9–11.
67 On Wilde's impressionistic poems and his connections with Whistler, see the essays by Gerda Eichbaum on 'Die persönlichen und literarischen Beziehungen zwischen Oscar Wilde und James MacNeill Whistler', ESt 65 (1931), 217–52, and 'Die impressionistischen Frühgedichte Oscar Wildes unter besonderer Berücksichtigung des Einflusses von James MacNeill Whistler', DNS 40 (1932), 398–407; and Birgit Borelius, *Oscar Wilde, Whistler and Colours*, Lund 1968. (Scripta Minora Regae Societatis Humaniorum Litterarum Lundensis, 1966–7. 3).
68 On this poem see Bernhard Fehr, 'Oscar Wildes "The Harlot's House"'. Eine kritisch-ästhetische Untersuchung', Archiv 134, n.s. 34 (1916), 59–75, and J. D. Thomas, 'The Composition of Wilde's "The Harlot's House"', MLN 65 (1950), 485–8.
69 J. D. Thomas, 'Oscar Wilde's Pose and Poetry', *Rice Institute Pamphlet*, 42, p. 47. The author is referring here to the five long poems.
70 Boris Brasol, *Oscar Wilde. The Man – the Artist*, London 1938, p. 97.
71 Edouard Roditi, *Oscar Wilde*, Norfolk, Conn. 1947, p. 31.

72　Ibid., p. 38.
73　Cf. 'wasted days' and similar phrases in 'The New Helen', verse 10, line 8, in *Complete Works*, p. 735; 'Apologia', verse 1, line 4, in ibid., p. 785; 'Glyky-prikos Eros', verse 15, line 2, in ibid., p. 803; 'To L.L.', verse 14, line 1, in ibid., p. 810.
74　'Humanitad', verse 18, lines 1–2, in ibid., p. 793.
75　'The Burden of Itys', verse 56, lines 3–6, in ibid., p. 744.
76　Joseph Foster, *Alumni Oxonienses: the Members of the University of Oxford, 1715–1886* ..., vol. 3, Oxford 1891. Repr. Nendeln (Liechtenstein) 1968, p. 1553.
77　As evidence, one can point to a passage in *The Soul of Man under Socialism*, in which Wilde wilfully set the nihilists' anti-authoritarian ideas in the same context as the 'Christian ideal': 'A Russian who lives happily under the present system of government in Russia must either believe that man has no soul, or that, if he has, it is not worth developing. A Nihilist who rejects all authority because he knows authority to be evil, and welcomes all pain, because through that he realises his personality, is a real Christian. To him the Christian ideal is a true thing.' *Complete Works*, pp. 578–82.
78　For the details of the assassination and the trial, see Günther Stökl, *Russische Geschichte. Von den Anfängen bis zur Gegenwart*, Stuttgart 1973 [1961], pp. 578–82.
79　While he was writing the play – i.e. between 1878 and 1880 – a number of articles appeared on the political and cultural development of Russia. Examples are Herbert Cowell, 'England and Russia', Maga. 123 (Mar. 1878), 374–90; William C. Keppel, 'The Aggression of Russia and the Duty of Great Britain', QR 145 (Apr. 1878), 534–70; Herbert Cowell, 'Eastern Prospects', Maga. 124 (Oct. 1878), 499–510; C. E. Trevelyan, 'England and Russia', MacM 42 (June 1880), 152–60. Between 1878 and 1880 the *Contemporary Review* also published a series of articles by T. S. Elizaveta D. Bezobrazova covering contemporary life and thought in Russia. See, for instance, vol. 31 (Feb. 1878), 620–32; vol. 32 (June 1878), 599–624; vol. 33 (Aug. 1878), 165–79; (Oct. 1878), 599–614; vol. 34 (Dec. 1878), 175–87; (Feb. 1879), 594–604; vol. 35 (Apr. 1879), 157–72; (June 1879), 571–80.
80　*ContempR* 36 (June 1879), 422–57; (Aug. 1879), 875–902; (Sept. 1879), 120–47.
81　DUM 91 (1878), 652–64.
82　*The World*, 30 Nov. 1881, p. 12; quoted by Stuart Mason, *Bibliography of Oscar Wilde*, p. 254.
83　See the correspondence between Wilde and Marie Prescott in Mason, *Bibliography of Oscar Wilde*, pp. 257–70. Frances M. Reed's edition, 'Oscar Wilde's "Vera; or, the Nihilists". A Critical Edition', unpublished Ph.D. thesis, University of California at Los Angeles, 1980: DA 41, no. 4, 1981, p. 1617-A incorporates the changes Wilde made (partly at the suggestion of Marie Prescott) for the production of 1883.
84　*Oscar Wilde. The Critical Heritage*, p. 56.
85　Ibid., p. 57.
86　Mason, *Bibliography of Oscar Wilde*, p. 273.
87　E.g. the following: Ransome, *Oscar Wilde*, London 1912, p. 64: 'worthless melodrama'; Symons, *A Study of Oscar Wilde*, London 1930, p. 67: 'The plot

is melodramatic, and the whole action altogether futile'; Brasol, *Oscar Wilde*, p. 100: 'a mediocre, if not altogether flimsy, specimen of modern dramaturgy'; St John Ervine, *Oscar Wilde*, London 1951, p. 90: 'a mindless melodrama'.

88 *Vera; or, The Nihilists*, in *Complete Works*, p. 688.
89 Ibid., pp. 675–7.
90 Ibid., p. 681.
91 Ibid.
92 Ibid., p. 688.
93 Ibid., p. 686.
94 Ibid.
95 *Letters*, p. 148.
96 *Vera*, in *Complete Works*, p. 651.
97 Ibid., p. 648.
98 Ibid., p. 669.
99 Ibid., p. 684.
100 See J. N. Westwood, *Endurance and Endeavour. Russian History, 1812–1971*, London 1973, p. 85.
101 *Vera*, in *Complete Works*, p. 670.
102 *The Golden Labyrinth. A Study of British Drama*, London 1962, p. 306.
103 *Vera*, in *Complete Works*, p. 656.
104 *The Merchant of Venice*, III.i.52–6. Shakespeare quotations from the Arden edition.
105 *Vera*, in *Complete Works*, p. 680.
106 *Macbeth*, I.v.40–1 and 47–8.
107 *Vera*, in *Complete Works*, p. 686.
108 Ibid., p. 665.
109 DUMBY: Experience is the name everyone gives to their mistakes. *Complete Works*, p. 418.
110 Pearson, *Life of Oscar Wilde*, p. 62. Similarly Harris, *Oscar Wilde* (1959), p. 47.
111 See the letter to Marie Prescott written in March/April (?) 1883.
112 *Letters*, p. 128.
113 Ibid., p. 130 and p. 132.
114 Robert H. Sherard, *The Real Oscar Wilde*, London 1916, p. 236.
115 Mason, *Bibliography of Oscar Wilde*, p. 327. See also other reviews of the première in *Oscar Wilde. The Critical Heritage*, pp. 87–9.
116 *Letters*, p. 757.
117 *The Duchess of Padua*, in *Complete Works*, p. 587.
118 Ibid., p. 608.
119 Ibid., p. 613.
120 Ibid., p. 609.
121 See also Brenda M. Livingstone, 'Oscar Wilde and the Tragic Mode', unpublished Ph.D. thesis, University of California at Riverside, 1972, p. 73: 'That she [Beatrice] actively seeks revenge as a way of denying her love rather than passively substituting contempt, indifference, or self-pity, for example, may be accepted, but the ease with which she carries out her revenge is more consistent with a person less conscious of injustice than the Duchess.'
122 *The Duchess of Padua*, in *Complete Works*, p. 592.

123 Ibid., p. 625.
124 Ibid., p. 627.
125 *Letters*, p. 137.
126 *The Duchess of Padua*, in *Complete Works*, p. 586.
127 Ibid., p. 596.
128 Ibid., p. 587.
129 Ibid., p. 619.
130 *Letters*, p. 141.
131 *The Duchess of Padua*, in *Complete Works*, pp. 645–6.
132 Ibid., p. 621.
133 *Lucrèce Borgia*, in Victor Hugo, *Œuvres complètes*. Chronological edition published under the direction of Jean Massin, vol. 4, Paris 1967, p. 660.
134 See *The Trial of Oscar Wilde. From the Shorthand Reports*, Paris 1906, p. x; Arthur Symons, *A Study of Oscar Wilde*, p. 69; Farmer, *Le Mouvement esthétique et 'décadent' en Angleterre*, p. 129; Woodcock, *The Paradox of Oscar Wilde*, p. 36; Alfred Douglas, *Oscar Wilde and Myself*, London 1914, p. 224, describes Wilde's evaluation of Webster as follows: 'He [Wilde] would have it that Webster's "Duchess of Malfi" was a much better play and much better poetry than any of Shakespeare's and, as he admired little that he did not sooner or later try to imitate, it is possible that we owe his "Duchess of Padua" to this view.'
135 See also the following judgments: Philipp Aronstein, *Oscar Wilde. Sein Leben und Lebenswerk*, in *Oscar Wilde, Werke in fünf Bänden*, vol. I, Berlin 1922, p. 79: 'Schwulst, Rhetorik und unechtes Pathos überwuchern die Handlung. Das Stück ist ohne jede Originalität (Bombast, rhetoric and insincere pathos stifle the plot. The play is devoid of originality); Choisy, *Oscar Wilde*, p. 56: 'Cette pièce est la plus faible du théâtre Wildien' (this play is the weakest in the theatre of Wilde); Brasol, *Oscar Wilde*, p. 153: '*The Duchess of Padua*, on the whole, is but a weak paraphrase of various Shakespearean texts'; Lemonnier, *Oscar Wilde*, p. 47: 'peut-être la moins originale de toutes ses œuvres de longue haleine' (perhaps the least original of all his full-length works); Merle, *Oscar Wilde*, p. 322: 'C'est une histoire plus sombre encore que *Vera*, où ce qu'il y a de moins bon dans Shakespeare, et de pire dans Hugo, s'étonnent de se trouver réunis' (It is an even more sombre tale than *Vera*, where what is least good in Shakespeare and what is worse in Hugo are amazed to find themselves united); St John Ervine, *Oscar Wilde*, p. 110: 'It is dreadful rubbish, almost as bad as *Vera*'; Ojala, *Aestheticism and Oscar Wilde*, pt 1, p. 186: 'Wilde's most ambitious and most unfortunate attempt at drama'.
136 Winwar, *Oscar Wilde and the Yellow Nineties*, New York and London [1940], 1958, p. 107.
137 *The Duchess of Padua*, in *Complete Works*, p. 583.

2   The selfish and the selfless. The fairy-tales and stories

1 *Athenaeum* (1 Sept. 1888), 286. Quotations taken from *Oscar Wilde. The Critical Heritage*, p. 60.
2 *Oscar Wilde. The Critical Heritage*, p. 61.
3 Ibid., p. 59.

4 For details of German translations of the fairy-tales, see 'Oscar Wilde-Bibliographie' in the German edition of this book: *Oscar Wilde. Das literarische Werk zwischen Provokation und Anpassung*, Heidelberg 1980, pp. 563–9.

5 Anselm Schlösser, *Die englische Literatur in Deutschland von 1895 bis 1934 mit einer vollständigen Bibliographie der deutschen Übersetzungen und der im deutschen Sprachgebiet erschienenen englischen Ausgaben*, Jena 1937, p. 82.

6 *The Life of Oscar Wilde*, London 1946, p. 141.

7 Merle, *Oscar Wilde*, Paris [1948], p. 261.

8 Ibid., p. 273.

9 Ibid., p. 274.

10 See the collection of essays entitled *Märchenforschung und Tiefenpsychologie*, ed. by Wilhelm Laiblin, Darmstadt 1969. (Wege der Forschung. 102).

11 Theodor W. Adorno, *Ästhetische Theorie*, Frankfurt/M. 1970, p. 20.

12 *Morphologie des Märchens*, ed. by Karl Eimermacher, Munich 1972, p. 26.

13 'The Decay of Lying', in *Complete Works*, p. 992.

14 Ibid., p. 978.

15 *Letters*, p. 219.

16 Ibid., p. 221.

17 Ibid., p. 259.

18 'The Devoted Friend', in *Complete Works*, p. 309.

19 Ibid.

20 *Into the Demon Universe. A Literary Exploration of Oscar Wilde*, New Haven and London 1974, p. 20.

21 See Jerome Griswold, 'Sacrifice and Mercy in Wilde's "The Happy Prince"', ChL 3 (1974), 103–6.

22 'The Young King', in *Complete Works*, p. 233.

23 Woodcock, *The Paradox of Oscar Wilde*, New York 1949, pp. 148–9.

24 David M. Monaghan, 'The Literary Fairy-Tale. A Study of Oscar Wilde's "The Happy Prince" and "The Star-Child"', CRCL/RCLC 1, no. 2 (1974), 156. Robert K. Martin, 'Oscar Wilde and the Fairy Tale. "The Happy Prince" as self-dramatization', SSF 16 (1979), 76, offers an autobiographical interpretation of the fairy tale: 'In the fairy tale Wilde dramatizes himself as the Happy Prince, a man who renounces the Palace of Sans-Souci, who gives up his worldly wealth, in order to share his goods with the poor and to share his happiness with his beloved Swallow.'

25 Lothar Hönnighausen, *Die englische Literatur 1870–1890*, in *Jahrhundertende-Jahrhundertwende* (pt I), ed. by Helmut Kreuzer, Wiesbaden 1976, p. 386. (Neues Handbuch der Literaturwissenschaft. 18).

26 'The Star-Child', in *Complete Works*, p. 278.

27 On the theory and history of the fairy-tale, see Stith Thompson, *The Folktale*, New York 1951 [1946]; Hedwig von Beit, *Symbolik des Märchens. Versuch einer Deutung*, 3 vols., Bern 1960–5 [1952–7]; *Märchenforschung und Tiefenpsychologie*, ed. by Wilhelm Laiblin, Darmstadt 1969. (Wege der Forschung. 102); André Jolles, *Märchen*, in *Einfache Formen*, Tübingen 1972 [1930], pp. 218–46; Vladimir Propp, *Morphologie des Märchens*, ed. by Karl Eimermacher, Munich 1972 [1969]; Max Lüthi, *Das europäische Volksmärchen. Form und Wesen*, Munich 1974 [1947]; Lutz Röhrich, *Märchen und Wirklichkeit*, Wiesbaden 1974 [1956]; Max Lüthi, *Das Volksmärchen.*

Ästhetik und Anthropologie, Düsseldorf 1975; Lüthi, *Märchen*, Stuttgart 1976 [1962] (Sammlung Metzler. 16); Bruno Bettelheim, *The Uses of Enchantment. The Meaning and Importance of Fairy Tales*, New York 1976; Jens Tismar, *Kunstmärchen*, Stuttgart 1977 (Sammlung Metzler. 155); Friedmar Apel, *Die Zaubergärten der Phantasie. Zur Theorie und Geschichte des Kunstmärchens*, Heidelberg 1978; Dieter Petzold, *Das englische Kunstmärchen im neunzehnten Jahrhundert*, Tübingen 1981; Volker Klotz, *Das europäische Kunstmärchen. Fünfundzwanzig Kapitel seiner Geschichte von der Renaissance bis zur Moderne*, Stuttgart 1985.

28 *Märchen und Wirklichkeit*, p. 233.

29 'The Star-Child', in *Complete Works*, p. 284.

30 Ibid., pp. 283–4.

31 Volker Klotz, 'Märchen und Wirklichkeit. Über Kunstmärchen von der Spätromantik bis Kafka. 3. Zwischen Kleinkram und Geschmeide: Hans Christian Andersen und Oscar Wilde'. Talk given on German radio (Deutschlandfunk), 28 December 1976. Manuscript, p. 13.

32 'The Young King', in *Complete Works*, p. 226.

33 See Elias Bredsdorff, *Hans Andersen and Charles Dickens. A Friendship and its Dissolution*, Copenhagen 1956.

34 *Pall Mall Gazette* (30 Nov. 1891), 3. Quotation taken from *Oscar Wilde. The Critical Heritage*. p. 113. See also Alice Herzog's study of sources, 'Die Märchen Oscar Wildes', unpublished diss., Mulhouse 1930.

35 'The Darning Needle', in Hans Christian Andersen, *Fairy Tales*. Transl. by Mrs H. B. Paull, London [1882], p. 245.

36 See also Volker Klotz, 'Märchen und Wirklichkeit ...'. German radio, 1976.

37 'The Fisherman and his Soul', in *Complete Works*, p. 265.

38 Hans Christian Andersen, *The True Story of my Life*, transl. by Mary Howitt, London 1926.

39 'The Fisherman and his Soul', in *Complete Works*, p. 248.

40 Merle, *Oscar Wilde* [1948], p. 272.

41 'The Remarkable Rocket', in *Complete Works*, p. 313.

42 'Phrases and Philosophies for the Use of the Young' (1894), in *Complete Works*, p. 1206.

43 'Lord Arthur Savile's Crime', in *Complete Works*, p. 168. See Alfons Klein, 'Motive und Themen in Oscar Wildes "Lord Arthur Savile's Crime"', in *Motive und Themen in Erzählungen des späten 19. Jahrhunderts. Bericht über Kolloquien der Kommission für literaturwissenschaftliche Motiv- und Themenforschung 1978–1979*, pt 1, ed. by Theodor Wolpers, Göttingen 1982, pp. 66–87.

44 'Lord Arthur Savile's Crime', in *Complete Works*, p. 175.

45 Ibid., p. 188.

46 Ibid., p. 178.

47 Alfred Douglas's claim in *Oscar Wilde and Myself*, London 1914, p. 234, that Wilde's story was a copy of Lane Falconer's *Cecilia de Noël*, London 1891, was disproved by W. Fischer, 'Über eine angebliche Quelle von Oscar Wildes Erzählung "The Canterville Ghost"', Nph 10 (1924), 42–9, on the grounds that Wilde's story appeared four years earlier than *Cecilia de Noël*. Isobel Murray points out a striking similarity between 'The Canterville Ghost' and Edward Heron-Allen's 'Autobiography of a Disembodied Spirit', in *A Fatal*

Fiddle, Chicago 1889. Murray, *The Picture of Dorian Gray*. Introduction, London 1974, p. xxiii (Oxford English Novels).
48 'The Canterville Ghost', *Complete Works*, p. 193.
49 Ibid., p. 213.
50 Ibid., p. 212.
51 Ibid., p. 194.
52 'The Sphinx without a Secret', in *Complete Works*, p. 218.
53 Ibid.
54 'The Model Millionaire', in *Complete Works*, p. 219.
55 'A Rothschild Anecdote as a Source for Oscar Wilde's "The Model Millionaire"', N&Q 24 (n.s.), no. 1 (Jan.–Feb. 1977), 45–6. Similar versions of the anecdote are to be found in Frederic Morton, *The Rothschilds. A Family Portrait*, New York 1962, p. 72 and Virginia Cowles, *The Rothschilds. A Family of Fortune*, London 1973, p. 97.
56 Edward Lucie-Smith, 'For Herod', NewS (18 May 1962), 728.
57 *The Soul of Man under Socialism*, in *Complete Works*, p. 1101.

3 Personality and perfection. The lectures, *Reviews* and *Intentions*

1 *The Artist as Critic. Critical Writings of Oscar Wilde*, ed. by Richard Ellmann, New York 1969.
2 *Literary Criticism of Oscar Wilde*, ed. by Stanley Weintraub, Lincoln, Nebr., 1969. (Regents Critics Series).
3 Carl Markgraf, 'Oscar Wilde's Anonymous Criticism. An Annotated Edition', unpublished Ph.D. thesis, University of California, Riverside, 1970: DA 32, no. 2, p. 975-A.
4 *Oscar Wilde. The Critical Heritage*, ed. by Karl Beckson, London 1970.
5 Kevin H. F. O'Brien, 'An Edition of Oscar Wilde's American Lectures', unpublished Ph.D. thesis, University of Notre Dame, 1973: DA 34, no. 5, 1973, p. 2647-A
6 *The Rise of Historical Criticism*, Hartford, Conn. 1905. (Privately printed?) Reprinted 1969. This edition contains only the first part of the manuscript, which was lost after the auction of the Wilde estate in April 1895 and turned up again after some time in America. Ross later discovered parts 2 and 3, which he published together with the known text in the first collected edition of Wilde's works in 1908, not 1909 as stated by H. Montgomery Hyde, *Oscar Wilde. A Biography*, London 1976, p. 39. Chapters 1–3 of the full text appeared in this edition as part of the volume containing 'Lord Arthur Savile's Crime and other Prose Pieces', pp. 223–66, while the rest was published later in *Miscellanies*, pp. 181–228.
7 'Rise of Historical Criticism', in *Complete Works*, p. 1105.
8 Ibid., p. 1146.
9 *Jahrhundertende – Jahrhundertwende* (pt 1), ed. by Helmut Kreuzer, Wiesbaden 1976, pp. 359–400. Hönnighausen gives 1876 as the date for 'The Rise of Historical Criticism'. As this essay was written for the Chancellor's English Essay Prize of 1879, it is more likely to stem from 1878–9. In any case it would be more logical to name the first year of publication, as Hönnighausen normally does elsewhere.

10 Hönnighausen, 'Die englische Literatur 1870–1890', in *Jahrhundertende – Jahrhundertwende*, p. 364.
11 *Boston Evening Journal*, 10 Jan. 1882, in O'Brien, 'An Edition of Oscar Wilde's American Lectures', p. 208.
12 *Boston Evening Transcript*, 10 Jan. 1882, in ibid., p. 205.
13 *Buffalo Morning Express*, 9 Feb. 1882, in ibid., p. 208.
14 Lloyd Lewis and Henry J. Smith, *Oscar Wilde Discovers America*, New York 1936, p. 70.
15 The lecture was first published by Stuart Mason [Christopher S. Millard] in 1906 (Sunderland, Keystone Press), together with an introduction. Mason printed the version Wilde had given under the title 'Impressions of America' on 24 September 1883 in Wandsworth Town Hall.
16 Ibid., p. 35.
17 Ibid., p. 34
18 'Irish Poets and Poetry of the Nineteenth Century'. A lecture delivered in Platt's Hall, San Francisco on Wednesday 5 April 1882, edited from Wilde's manuscript and reconstructed, in part, from contemporary newspaper accounts with an introduction and biographical notes by Robert D. Pepper, San Francisco 1972. See also Michael J. O'Neill, 'Irish Poets of the Nineteenth Century. Unpublished Lecture Notes of Oscar Wilde', URev (Dublin) 1 (1955), pp. 29–32.
19 O'Brien, 'An Edition of Oscar Wilde's American Lectures', p. 1.
20 Ibid., p. 30.
21 Ibid., p. 31.
22 Ibid., p. 51
23 Ibid., p. 52.
24 Ibid., p. 66.
25 Ibid., p. 68.
26 Ibid.
27 Ibid., p. 71.
28 Ibid., p. 75.
29 Ibid.
30 Ibid., p. 91.
31 Ibid., p. 96.
32 Ibid., p. 98.
33 Ibid., p. 139.
34 Ibid., p. 151.
35 Ibid., p. 146.
36 Ibid.
37 Ibid., p. 159.
38 Ibid., p. 177.
39 Ibid., p. 173.
40 See ibid., pp. 77–8, and John Ruskin, 'Modern Manufacture and Design' (*The Two Paths*, III), in *The Works of John Ruskin*, ed. by E. T. Cook and Alexander Wedderburn, vol. XVI, London 1905, pp. 339–40.
41 O'Brien, 'An Edition of Oscar Wilde's American Lectures', p. 96.
42 Ruskin, 'Modern Manufacture and Design', in *Works*, vol. XVI, p. 345.
43 William Morris, 'The Beauty of Life', in *The Collected Works of William Morris*. With an introduction by May Morris, vol. XXII, London 1914, p. 58.

44 Ruskin, 'Influence of Imagination in Architecture' (*The Two Paths*, IV), in *Works*, vol. XVI, p. 366.
45 O'Brien, 'An Edition of Oscar Wilde's American Lectures', p. 126.
46 Ibid., p. 127.
47 'The Prophet and Pioneer', Boston Daily Globe, 1 Feb. 1882, in O'Brien, ibid., p. 208.
48 O'Brien, ibid., p. 176.
49 Ibid., p. 159.
50 Ibid., p. 53. Swinburne wrote: 'I ... revere form or harmony as the high one law of all art.' 'Matthew Arnold's New Poems' (1867), in *The Complete Works of Algernon Charles Swinburne*, ed. by Edmund Gosse and Thomas J. Wise, vol. XV, London and New York 1926, p. 115 (Bonchurch edition).
51 O'Brien, 'An Edition of Oscar Wilde's American Lectures', p. 75.
52 Ibid., p. 84.
53 *Letters*, p. 96.
54 'L'Envoi', in *Miscellanies*, p. 31.
55 On Ruskin's aesthetics, see Henry Ladd, *The Victorian Morality of Art. An Analysis of Ruskin's Esthetic*, New York 1932; Graham Hough, 'Ruskin', in *The Last Romantics*, London and New York 1961 [1947], pp. 1–39; John D. Rosenberg, *The Darkening Glass. A Portrait of Ruskin's Genius*, New York 1961; René Wellek, 'John Ruskin', in Wellek, *A History of Modern Criticism: 1750–1950*, vol. 3, *The Age of Transition*, London 1970 [1966], pp. 136–49; George Landow, *The Aesthetic and Critical Theories of John Ruskin*, Princeton 1971; Billie A. Inman, 'Ruskin's Reasoned Criticism of Art', PLL 13 (1977), 372–82; Elizabeth K. Helsinger, *Ruskin and the Art of the Beholder*, Cambridge 1982.
56 *Modern Painters*, vol. I. Preface to the second edition (1844), in *Works*, vol. III, p. 48.
57 Ibid., vol. II, in *Works*, vol. IV, p. 287.
58 Ibid., vol. III, in *Works*, vol. V, p. 181.
59 *A Midsummer Night's Dream*, V.i.14–17, in William Shakespeare, *The Complete Works*, ed. by Peter Alexander, London and Glasgow 1960 [1951], p. 218.
60 *Modern Painters*, vol. II, in *Works*, vol. IV, p. 35.
61 *The Seven Lamps of Architecture*, in *Works*, vol. VIII, p. 218.
62 *Miscellanies*, p. 32.
63 *Modern Painters*, vol. I, in *Works*, vol. III, p. 91.
64 *The Queen of the Air*, in *Works*, vol. XIX, p. 307.
65 Ibid., p. 308.
66 *The Stones of Venice*, vol. I, Appendix 15, in *Works*, vol. IX, pp. 448–9.
67 *Miscellanies*, p. 31.
68 *The Stones of Venice*, vol. II, in *Works*, vol. X, p. 202.
69 *Modern Painters*, vol. III, in *Works*, vol. V, pp. 124–5.
70 James McNeill Whistler, *The Gentle Art of Making Enemies*, London 1953 [1890], p. [1].
71 'Mr Whistler's "Ten O'Clock"', in Whistler, *The Gentle Art of Making Enemies*, p. 155.
72 See Gerda Eichbaum, 'Die persönlichen und literarischen Beziehungen zwischen Oscar Wilde und James McNeill Whistler', ESt 65 (1931), 217–52;

Hesketh Pearson, *The Man Whistler*, London 1952, pp. 118–21; Birgit Borelius, *Oscar Wilde, Whistler and Colours*, Lund 1968. (Scripta Minora Regiae Societatis Humaniorum Litterarum Lundensis. 67, 3.)

73 *Letters*, p. 253, note 1.
74 This correspondence was collected and printed in *Wilde v Whistler. Being an Acrimonious Correspondence on Art between Oscar Wilde and James A. McNeill Whistler*, London 1906. (Privately printed.)
75 *Letters*, p. 253, note 1.
76 Ibid., p. 254.
77 *Miscellanies*, p. 313.
78 Ibid., p. 320.
79 Ibid., p. 318.
80 Ibid.
81 Ibid.
82 'Mr Whistler's Ten O'Clock', in *Miscellanies*, pp. 65–6.
83 On Oscar Wilde's aesthetic and and critical writings, apart from the relevant sections of the various monographs, see the following: Alice I. Perry Wood, 'Oscar Wilde as a Critic', NAR 202 (1915), 899–909; Fritz K. Baumann, 'Oscar Wilde als Kritiker der Literatur', unpublished diss., Zürich 1933; Ursula Risse, 'Kunstanschauung und Kunstschaffen bei Oscar Wilde', unpublished diss., Freiburg im Breisgau 1951; Liselotte Grabig, 'Gesellschaftsschilderung und Gesellschaftskritik bei Oscar Wilde', unpublished diss., Halle 1954; Guido Glur, 'Kunstlehre und Kunstanschauung des George-Kreises und die Ästhetik Oscar Wildes', unpublished diss., Bern 1957; Hilda Schiff, 'A Critical Study of Oscar Wilde's "Intentions"', M.A. thesis, University of London, 1960; Robert E. Rhodes, 'The Literary Criticism of Oscar Wilde, unpublished Ph.D. thesis, University of Michigan, 1964: DA 25, no. 6, 1964, p. 3582; Hilda Schiff, 'Nature and Art in Oscar Wilde's "The Decay of Lying"', E&S 18 (n.s.) (1965), 83–102; René Wellek, 'Oscar Wilde', in Wellek, *A History of Modern Criticism: 1750–1950*, vol. 4, *The Later Nineteenth Century*, London 1970 [1966], pp. 407–16; Richard Ellmann, *The Critic as Artist as Wilde*, Encounter 29 (1967), 29–37. Repr. in *The Artist as Critic. Critical Writings of Oscar Wilde*, ed. by Richard Ellmann, New York 1969, pp. ix–xxviii; Seymour Migdal, 'The Poseur and the Critic in some Essays of Oscar Wilde', DR 47 (1967), 65–70; Lewis J. Poteet, 'Romantic Aesthetics in Oscar Wilde's Prose', unpublished Ph.D. thesis, University of Minnesota, 1968: DA 29, no. 3, 1968, p. 907-A; J. D. Thomas, 'The Intentional Strategy in Oscar Wilde's Dialogues', ELT 12 (1969), 11–20; Stanley Weintraub, 'The Critic in Spite of Himself', in *Literary Criticism of Oscar Wilde*, pp. ix–xxxvi; Markgraf, Introduction, in 'Oscar Wilde's Anonymous Criticism', pp. xiii–xcviii; Lewis J. Poteet, 'Romantic Aesthetics in Oscar Wilde's "Mr W. H."', SSF 7 (1970), 458–64; Wendell V. Harris, 'Arnold, Pater, Wilde and the Object as in Themselves They See It', SEL 11 (1971), 733–47; J. E. Chamberlin, 'Oscar Wilde and the Importance of Doing Nothing', HudR 25 (1972), 194–218; Barbara Currier, 'The Gift of Personality. An Appraisal of "Impressionist Criticism"', unpublished Ph.D. thesis, Columbia University, 1972: DA 33, no. 10, 1972/73, p. 5673-A: Wilde chapter, pp. 168–82; Steven J. Fox, 'Art and Personality. Browning, Rossetti,

Pater, Wilde and Yeats', unpublished Ph.D. thesis, Yale University, 1972: DA 33, no. 2, 1972, p. 751-A: Wilde chapter, pp. 189–229; John E. Hill, 'Dialectical Criticism. Essays on the Criticism of Swinburne, Pater, Wilde, James, Shaw and Yeats', unpublished Ph.D. thesis, University of Virginia, 1972: DA 33, no. 7, 1972/73, p. 3648-A: Wilde chapter, pp. 70–81; Marvel Shmiefsky, 'Oscar Wilde: "The Critic as Artist" (1891)', in Shmiefsky, *Sense at War with Soul. English Poetics (1865–1900)*, The Hague 1972, pp. 106–77; George Stavros, 'Pater, Wilde, and the Victorian Critics of the Romantics', unpublished Ph.D. thesis, University of Wisconsin, 1972: DA 33, no. 5, 1972, p. 2344-A: Wilde chapter, pp. 139–214; Ann R. Yaffe, 'Oscar Wilde as Critic', unpublished Ph.D. thesis, University of London, 1972; Herbert Sussman, 'Criticism as Art. Form in Oscar Wilde's Critical Writings', SP 70 (1973), 108–22; R. J. Green, 'Oscar Wilde's "Intentions". An Early Modernist Manifesto', BJA 13 (1973), 397–404; Bruce Bashford, 'Oscar Wilde, his Criticism and his Critics', ELT 20 (1977), 181–7; George Stavros, 'Oscar Wilde on the Romantics', ELT 10 (1977), 35–45; Bruce Bashford, 'Oscar Wilde and Subjectivist Criticism', ELT 21 (1978), 218–34; Michael S. Helfand and Philip E. Smith II, 'Anarchy and Culture. The Evolutionary Turn of Cultural Criticism in the Work of Oscar Wilde', TSLL 20 (1978), 199–215.

84 'The Critic as Artist', in *Complete Works*, p. 1046.
85 Seymour Migdal is of the opinion that 'what Wilde, as a serious critic, has to say obviates the necessity for the continual self-posturing that we find in his essays'. 'The Poseur and the Critic', 70.
86 'The Decay of Lying', in *Complete Works*, p. 992.
87 *Republic*, 600 e., in *The Dialogues of Plato*, vol. 1, translated by B. Jowett, New York 1920 [1892].
88 *Poetics*, in *The Complete Works of Aristotle*, ed. by Jonathan Barnes, revised Oxford translation, Princeton University Press 1984, p. 2336.
89 Ovid, *Amores*, III.VI.17. in Ovid, *Heroides and Amores*. With an English translation by Grant Showerman, 2nd edn, revised by G. P. Goold, Cambridge, Mass., and London 1977 [1914], p. 469.
90 Friedrich Nietzsche, *Thus Spake Zarathustra*, translated by A. Tille, revised by M. M. Bozman, London 1933, p. 116. See also Maria Bindschedler, *Nietzsche und die poetische Lüge*, Basel 1954.
91 *The Picture of Dorian Gray*. The Preface in *Complete Works*, p. 17.
92 'The Decay of Lying' in *Complete Works*, p. 992.
93 Ibid., p. 981.
94 *De Profundis*, in *Complete Works*, p. 920.
95 'Style', in *Appreciations*, London 1915 [1889], p. 10. (Library edition.)
96 Walter Pater, *Plato and Platonism. A Series of Lectures*, London 1910 [1893], p. 187. (Library edition).
97 'The Decay of Lying', in *Complete Works*, p. 970.
98 Ibid., p. 971.
99 Ibid., p. 977.
100 Ibid.
101 Ibid.
102 Ibid., p. 986.

103 Preface to the edition of 1814, in *The Poetical Works of Wordsworth*, ed. by Thomas Hutchinson. A new edition, revised by Ernest de Selincourt, London 1961 [1936], p. 590.
104 S. T. Coleridge, *The Friend* (1818), vol. III, Sec. 2, Essay X, in *The Collected Works of Samuel Taylor Coleridge*. Vol. IV, *The Friend*, ed. by Barbara E. Rooke, vol. I, London 1969, pp. 497–8.
105 *La Reine des facultés*, in *Salon de 1859*. *Œuvres complètes*. Preface, presentation and notes by Marcel A. Ruff, Paris 1968, p. 396.
106 *A Rebours. Avec une préface de l'auteur écrite vingt ans après le roman*, n.p. [Fasquelle éditeurs], 1974, p. 51. See also Whistler's statement in his *Ten O'Clock Lecture*: 'That Nature is always right, is an assertion, artistically, as untrue, as it is one whose truth is universally taken for granted. Nature is very rarely right, to such an extent even, that it might almost be said that Nature is usually wrong: that is to say the condition of things that shall bring about the perfection of harmony worthy a picture is rare, and not common at all.' *The Gentle Art of Making Enemies*, p. 143.
107 'The Decay of Lying', in *Complete Works*, p. 978.
108 'The Critic as Artist', in ibid., pp. 1051–2.
109 'The Decay of Lying', in ibid., p. 991.
110 Ibid., p. 978.
111 Ibid., p. 973.
112 Ibid., p. 974.
113 Ibid., p. 976.
114 *Reviews*, p. 283.
115 Baudelaire, in *Salon de 1859*: 4, 'Le Gouvernement de l'imagination', in *Œuvres complètes*, p. 400.
116 'Style', in *Appreciations*, pp. 10–11.
117 *The Poetical Works of Wordsworth*, ed. by Thomas Hutchinson, p. 734.
118 'Wordsworth', in *Poetry and Criticism of Matthew Arnold*, ed. by A. Dwight Culler, Boston 1961, p. 340.
119 Ibid., p. 339.
120 'Conclusion', in *The Renaissance. Studies in Art and Poetry*, London 1910, p. 235 (Library edition).
121 Ibid.
122 'The Decay of Lying', in *Complete Works*, p. 986.
123 'The Critic as Artist', in ibid., p. 1038.
124 Ibid., p. 1034.
125 Ibid., p. 1023.
126 Ibid., p. 1038.
127 Wolfgang Koeppen, 'Der Dichter, der ein Kunstwerk war', FAZ, no. 121 (5 June 1976), Supplement.
128 'The Decay of Lying', in *Complete Works*, p. 982.
129 'Byron', in *Poetry and Criticism of Matthew Arnold*, p. 356.
130 *The Stones of Venice*, vol. I, Appendix 15, in *Works*, vol. IX, p. 449.
131 *A Study of Victor Hugo. L'Année terrible* (1872), in Bonchurch edition, vol. XIII, p. 243. On Swinburne's concept of art and poetry, see T. S. Eliot, 'Swinburne as Critic', in *The Sacred Wood. Essays on Poetry and Criticism*, London 1967 [1920], pp. 17–24; Ruth C. Child, 'Swinburne's Mature Standards of Criticism', PMLA 52 (1937), 870–9; John A. Cassidy, *Alger-*

non C. Swinburne, New York 1964; Thomas E. Connolly, *Swinburne's Theory of Poetry*, New York 1964; Robert L. Peters, *The Crowns of Apollo. A Study of Victorian Criticism and Aesthetics*, Detroit 1965; René Wellek, 'Algernon Swinburne', in Wellek, *A History of Modern Criticism*, vol. 4, pp. 371–81; Meredith B. Raymond, *Swinburne's Poetics. Theory and Practice*, The Hague 1971. (De proprietatibus litterarum. Series practica. 17); Marvel Shmiefsky, 'Swinburne's Anti-Establishment Poetics', VP 9 (1971), pp. 261–76.

132 'Winckelmann', in *The Renaissance*, p. 230. On Pater's concept of art and poetry see T. S. Eliot, 'Arnold and Pater', in Eliot, *Selected Essays*, London 1966 [1932], pp. 431–43; Ruth C. Child, *The Aesthetic of Walter Pater*, New York 1940, reprinted New York 1969; Graham Hough, 'Pater', in Hough, *The Last Romantics*, pp. 134–74; René Wellek, 'Walter Pater's Literary Theory and Criticism', VS 1 (1956), 29–46; Wolfgang Iser, *Walter Pater. Die Autonomie des Ästhetischen*, Tübingen 1960 (English translation by David Wilson: *Walter Pater. The Aesthetic Moment*, Cambridge 1987); Germain d'Hangest, *Walter Pater. L'homme et l'œuvre*, 2 vols., Paris 1961; Robert V. Johnson, *Walter Pater. A Study of his Critical Outlook and Achievement*, Melbourne University Press 1961; Solomon Fishman, 'Walter Pater', in Fishman, *The Interpretation of Art. Essays on the Art Criticism of John Ruskin, Walter Pater, Clive Bell, Roger Fry and Herbert Read*, Berkeley, Calif./Los Angeles 1963, pp. 43–72; Marvel Shmiefsky, 'A Study in Aesthetic Relativism. Pater's Poetics', VP 6 (1969), 105–24; Claus Uhlig, 'Walter Pater und die Poetik der Reminiszenz. Zur literarischen Methode einer Spätzeit', *Poetica* 6 (1974), 205–27.

133 'The School of Giorgione', in *The Renaissance*, p. 135.
134 'Style', in *Appreciations*, p. 38.
135 Ibid.
136 *The Soul of Man under Socialism*, in *Complete Works*, p. 1093.
137 Ibid.
138 O'Brien, 'An Edition of Oscar Wilde's American Lectures', p. 53.
139 'The Critic as Artist', in *Complete Works*, p. 1052.
140 Ibid.
141 'The Decay of Lying', in *Complete Works*, p. 978.
142 Rhodes, 'The Literary Criticism of Oscar Wilde', p. 84.
143 *Letters*, p. 261.
144 *Critical and Historical Essays*, in *Works*, ed. by Lady Trevelyan, vol. 5, London 1866, p. 404. On Macaulay's concept of poetry in general, see Stanley T. Williams, 'Macaulay's Reading and Literary Criticism', PQ 3 (1924), 119–31; René Wellek, 'Thomas Babington Macaulay', in Wellek, *A History of Modern Criticism*, vol. 3, pp. 125–31; Terry Otten, 'Macaulay's Critical Theory of Imagination and Reason', JAAC 28 (1969), 33–43; Terry Otten, 'Macaulay's Secondhand Theory of Poetry', SAQ 72 (1973), 280–94; Norbert Kinne, *Die Literaturkritik Thomas Babington Macaulays und ihre Rezeption*, Frankfurt/M. 1979; S. Nagarajan, 'Macaulay's Literary Theory and Shakespeare Criticism', AJES 4 (1979), 142–55.
145 'Tennyson's Poems', WestmR 30 (July 1835), 423. On Mill's concept of poetry in general, see Alba H. Warren, Jr, 'John Stuart Mill, thoughts on Poetry and its Varieties, 1833', in Warren, *English Poetic Theory, 1825–*

1865, Princeton, N.J., 1950, pp. 66–78; John M. Robson, 'J. S. Mill's Theory of Poetry', UTQ 29 (1960), 420–38; René Wellek, 'John Stuart Mill', in Wellek, *A History of Modern Criticism*, vol. 3, pp. 132–6; Francis P. Sharpless, *The Literary Criticism of J. S. Mill*, The Hague 1967; W. David Shaw, 'Mill on Poetic Truth. Are Intuitive Inferences Valid'? TSLL 23 (1981), 27–51.

146 *The Complete Prose Works of Matthew Arnold*, ed. by R. H. Super, vol. I, *On the Classical Tradition*, Ann Arbor, Mich., 1960, p. 3.

147 *Notes on Poems and Reviews* (1866), in Bonchurch edition, vol. XVI, p. 370.

148 *Lectures on Art II* (1870), in *Works*, vol. XX, p. 46.

149 See Rudolf Beck, *Poetry and Human Nature. Studien zum Vokabular der viktorianischen Literaturkritik*, Nuremberg 1974. (Erlanger Beiträge zur Sprach- und Kunstwissenschaft. 52).

150 'The Decorative Arts', in O'Brien, 'An Edition of Oscar Wilde's American Lectures', p. 120.

151 *Reviews*, p. 1.

152 'The Decay of Lying', in *Complete Works*, p. 976.

153 The texts are to be found in *Art and Morality. A Defence of 'The Picture of Dorian Gray'*, ed, by Stuart Mason, London 1908. Revised and extended under the title *Art and Morality. A Record of the Discussion which followed the publication of 'Dorian Gray'*, London 1912; *Letters*, pp. 257–72; *Oscar Wilde. The Critical Heritage*, pp. 67–86.

154 'The Critic as Artist', in *Complete Works*, p. 1048.

155 Ibid., p. 1039.

156 *The Picture of Dorian Gray*, Preface, in *Complete Works*, p. 17.

157 *Letters*, p. 259.

158 *The Trials of Oscar Wilde*, ed. by H. Montgomery Hyde, London 1949 [1948], p. 124. (Notable British Trials Series).

159 *The Picture of Dorian Gray*, Preface, in *Complete Works*, p. 17.

160 *Letters*, p. 292.

161 *Mademoiselle de Maupin*, chronology and introduction by Geneviève van den Bogaert, Paris 1966, p. 45.

162 'The Decay of Lying', in *Complete Works*, p. 991.

163 Yaffe, 'Oscar Wilde as Critic', p. 167.

164 'The Decay of Lying', in *Complete Works*, p. 987.

165 *Letters*, p. 301.

166 Ibid., p. 302.

167 *Kritik der Urteilskraft*, ed. by Karl Vorländer, Hamburg 1968 [1790], p. 77. (Philosophische Bibliothek. 39a.).

168 On the development of the 'l'art pour l'art' movement in general, and English aestheticism in particular, see Walter Hamilton, *The Aesthetic Movement in England*, London 1882; Albert Cassagne, *La Théorie de l'art pour l'art en France, chez les derniers romantiques et les premiers réalistes*, Paris 1906, reprinted 1959; Friedrich Brie, *Ästhetische Weltanschauung in der Literatur des XIX. Jahrhunderts*, Freiburg im Breisgau 1921; Rose F. Egan, 'The Genesis of the Theory of 'Art for Art's Sake' in Germany and in England', SCSML pt. 1, vols. 2, 4 (July 1921), 5–61; pt 2, vols. 5, 3 (April 1924), 1–33; Joseph Mainsard, 'L'Esthétisme de Pater et de Wilde', *Etudes* 194

(1928), 525–52; Albert J. Farmer, *Le Mouvement esthétique et 'décadent' en Angleterre (1873–1900)*, Paris 1931 (Bibliothèque de la Revue de littérature comparée. 75); Albert L. Guérard, *Art for Art's Sake*, New York 1936, reprinted 1963; John Wilcox, 'The Beginnings of l'Art pour l'Art', JAAC 11 (1952/53), 360–77; Aatos Ojala, *Aestheticism and Oscar Wilde*, 2 parts, Helsinki 1954–5. (Annales Academiae Scientiarum Fennicae. Ser. B, 90, 2; 93, 2); Irving Singer, 'The Aesthetics of "Art for Art's Sake"', JAAC 12 (1954), 343–59; Lorentz Eckhoff, *The Aesthetic Movement in English Literature*, Oslo 1959; Karl Heisig, 'L'Art pour l'Art. Über den Ursprung dieser Kunstauffassung', ZRG 14 (1962), 201–29 and 334–52; Houston A. Baker, 'The Idea in Aestheticism 1866–1899', unpublished Ph.D. thesis, University of California, Los Angeles 1968: DA 29, no. 6, 1968, p. 1862-A; Elizabeth Aslin, *The Aesthetic Movement. Prelude to Art Nouveau*, London 1969; Robert V. Johnson, *Aestheticism*, London 1969. (The Critical Idiom. 3); Robin Spencer, *The Aesthetic Movement. Theory and Practice*, London 1972; Norbert Kohl, '"L'Art pour l'Art" in der Ästhetik des 19. Jahrhunderts', Lili 8, H.30/31 (1978), 159–74; Ralph-Rainer Wuthenow, *Muse, Maske, Meduse. Europäischer Ästhetizismus*, Frankfurt/M 1978 (edition suhrkamp. 897); *The Aesthetes. A Source Book*, ed. by Ian Small, London 1979; Ulrich Horstmann, *Ästhetizismus und Dekadenz. Zum Paradigmakonflikt in der englischen Literaturtheorie des späten 19. Jahrhunderts*, Munich 1983; *Die 'Nineties'. Das englische Fin de siècle*, ed. by Manfred Pfister and Bernd Schulte-Middelich, Munich 1983. (UTB. 1233).

169 The correct title of the essay when first published in the *National Review* of November 1864 was 'The Functions of Criticism at the Present Time'. This was changed in 1865, when Arnold put together a collection of essays in criticism, to *The Function of Criticism at the Present Time*.

170 'The Critic as Artist', in *Complete Works*, p. 1020.

171 Ibid.

172 Ibid.

173 Ibid., p. 1021.

174 *Works*, vol. V, p. 86.

175 Ibid., p. 87.

176 *The Function of Criticism at the Present Time*, in *The Complete Prose Works of Matthew Arnold*, vol. III, p. 260.

177 Ibid.

178 'there is a significant relation between the best poetry and the best criticism of the same period. The age of criticism is also the age of critical poetry.' *The Use of Poetry and the Use of Criticism. Studies in the Relation of Criticism to Poetry in England*, London 1964 [1933], p. 30.

179 'The Perfect Critic', in *The Sacred Wood. Essays on Poetry and Criticism*, London 1967 [1920], p. 16.

180 'The Critic as Artist', in *Complete Works*, p. 1027. This idea of 'creative criticism' resembles romantic art criticism. Incorporating an observation of Friedrich Schlegel's, Walter Benjamin writes: 'Es ist klar: für die Romantiker ist Kritik viel weniger die Beurteilung eines Werks als die Methode seiner Vollendung. In diesem Sinne haben sie poetische Kritik gefordert, den Unterschied zwischen Kritik und Poesie aufgehoben und behauptet: "Poesie kann nur durch Poesie kritisiert werden. Ein Kunsturteil, welches nicht selbst

ein Kunstwerk ist, ... als Darstellung des notwendigen Eindrucks in seinem
Werden ... hat gar kein Bürgerrecht im Reiche der Kunst. Jene poetische
Kritik ... wird die Darstellung von Neuem darstellen, das schon Gebildete
noch einmal bilden wollen ... wird das Werk ergänzen, verjüngen, neu
gestalten.'" [It is clear: for the romantics, criticism is much less the judgment
of a work than the method of its completion. In this sense they demanded
poetic criticism, removed the distinction between criticism and poetry, and
maintained that: 'Poetry can only be criticised through poetry. A judgment of
art which is not itself a work of art ... as a representation of the essential
impression while it comes into being ... has no civic rights in the realm of art.
That poetic criticism ... will represent the representation anew, will seek to
reformulate what has already been formulated ... will complete, rejuvenate
and reshape the work.'] *Der Begriff der Kunstkritik in der deutschen
Romantik*, ed. by Hermann Schweppenhäuser, Frankfurt/M. 1973 [1920],
pp. 63–4. (suhrkamp taschenbuch wissenschaft. 4).

181 'The Critic as Artist', in *Complete Works*, p. 1027. Criticism is 'the only
civilised form of autobiography', and the critic's task is 'to chronicle his own
impressions'. Ibid., pp. 1027–8.
182 Ibid., p. 1029.
183 'On Translating Homer', in *The Complete Prose Works of Matthew Arnold*,
vol. I, p. 140.
184 'The Critic as Artist', in *Complete Works*, p. 1030.
185 *La Vie littéraire I*, in: *Œuvres complètes*. New edition edited by Jacques
Suffel, vol. 15, Paris n.d., p. 11.
186 *Letters*, p. 522 and p. 645.
187 'The Critic as Artist', in *Complete Works*, p. 1033.
188 Ibid., p. 1032.
189 Ibid., p. 1034.
190 Ibid., p. 1028.
191 Ibid., pp. 1047–8.
192 *An Essay on Criticism*, lines 631–42, in Scolar Press facsimile, Menston
(Yorkshire) 1970, pp. 36–7.
193 On 'sincerity' as a critical term, see M. H. Abrams, 'Poetic Truth and
Sincerity', in Abrams, *The Mirror and the Lamp. Romantic Theory and the
Critical Tradition*, New York 1953, 1958, pp. 312–20; Herbert Read, *The
True Voice of Feeling. Studies in English Romantic Poetry*, London 1953;
Henri Peyre, *Literature and Sincerity*, New Haven and London 1963;
Donald Davie, 'On Sincerity. From Wordsworth to Ginsberg', *Encounter* 31,
no. 4 (1968), 61–6; Lionel Trilling, *Sincerity and Authenticity*, Cambridge,
Mass., 1972.
194 *The Function of Criticism at the Present Time*, in *The Complete Prose Works
of Matthew Arnold*, vol. III, p. 285.
195 'Wordsworth', in *Poetry and Criticism of Matthew Arnold*, p. 345.
196 *Works*, ed. by H. D. Traill, vol. 26, London 1899, p. 267. (Centenary
edition.) On Carlyle's concept of poetry in general see Frederick W. Roe,
Thomas Carlyle as a Critic of Literature, New York 1910; Alba H. Warren,
Jr, 'Thomas Carlyle, "The Hero as Poet. Dante: Shakespeare" 1840', in
English Poetic Theory, 1825–1865, pp. 79–92; René Wellek, 'Thomas
Carlyle', in Wellek, *A History of Modern Criticism*, vol. 3, pp. 92–100;

A. Abbott Ikeler, *Puritan Temper and Transcendental Faith. Carlyle's Literary Vision*, Columbus, Ohio 1972; Jobst-Christian Rojahn, 'Der romantische Dichter als viktorianischer Held. Zur Dichtungstheorie Thomas Carlyles', in *Englische und amerikanische Literaturtheorie. Studien zu ihrer historischen Entwicklung*, ed. by Rüdiger Ahrens and Erwin Wolff, vol. 2, Heidelberg 1979, pp. 57–81; Matthew P. McDiarmid, 'Carlyle on the Intuitive Nature of Poetical Thinking', in *Thomas Carlyle 1981. Papers given at the International Thomas Carlyle Centenary Symposium*, ed. by Horst W. Drescher, Frankfurt/M. 1983, pp. 125–39.

197 'The Critic as Artist', in *Complete Works*, p. 1048.
198 *The Picture of Dorian Gray*, in ibid., p. 23.
199 'The Critic as Artist', in ibid., p. 1049.
200 O'Brien, 'An Edition of Oscar Wilde's American Lectures', 102–3.
201 *Reviews*, p. 43.
202 *The Renaissance*, Preface, p. x.
203 *The Gentle Art of Making Enemies*, p. 6.
204 'The Critic as Artist', in *Complete Works*, p. 103.
205 Ibid.
206 Ibid., p. 1041.
207 Ibid., p. 1054.
208 Ibid., p. 1057.
209 See Ernst Bendz, 'Notes on the Literary Relationship between Walter Pater and Oscar Wilde', NM 14, nos. 5/6 (1912), 91–127; Eduard J. Bock, *Walter Pater's Einfluss auf Oscar Wilde*, Bonn 1913. (Bonner Studien zur englischen Philologie. 8); Ernst Bendz, *The Influence of Pater and Matthew Arnold in the Prose-Writings of Oscar Wilde*, Gothenburg and London 1914; John Pick, 'Divergent Disciples of Walter Pater', *Thought* 23 (1948), 114–28; Wendell V. Harris, 'Arnold, Pater, Wilde and the Object as in Themselves They See It', SEL 11 (1971), 733–47.
210 *The Function of Criticism at the Present Time*, in *The Complete Prose Works of Matthew Arnold*, vol. III, p. 268.
211 'The Critic as Artist', in *Complete Works*, p. 1057.
212 On the philosophical content of the 'Conclusion' and its place in the history of ideas, see Norbert Kohl, 'Memento Vivere. Walter Paters Philosophie des Augenblicks in der "Conclusion", eine Interpretation', AntAb 20 (1974), 135–50.
213 *The Renaissance*, Preface, p. viii.
214 Pater, 'Style', in *Appreciations*, p. 10.
215 *The Renaissance*. Preface, pp. ix–x: 'And the function of the aesthetic critic is to distinguish, to analyse, and separate from its adjuncts, the virtue by which a picture, a landscape, a fair personality in life or in a book, produces this special impression of beauty, or pleasure, to indicate what the source of that impression is, and under what conditions it is experienced. His end is reached when he has disengaged that virtue, and noted it, as a chemist notes some natural element, for himself and others.'
216 'The Critic as Artist', in *Complete Works*, p. 1027.
217 'The aesthetic doctrines of each [Arnold, Pater, Wilde], grounded in various conscious degrees of denial of a transcendent world, generate philosophies of life which define the ideal relation of the individual to the world. The total

views of Pater and Wilde modify those of Arnold, but the three clarify and in a sense justify each other. Arnold's position, carried far enough, implies Wilde's, and does so in a much more fundamental way than T. S. Eliot has suggested.' Wendell V. Harris, 'Arnold, Pater, Wilde, and the Object as in Themselves They See It', SEL 11 (1971), 747.

218 Eliot, 'Arnold and Pater' (1930), in Eliot, *Selected Essays*, London 1966 [1932], p. 437.
219 'Wordsworth', in *Appreciations*, p. 62.
220 *The Nineteenth Century* (16 Dec. 1884), 886.
221 See for example 'Women's Dress', in *Miscellanies*, pp. 47–51; 'More Radical Ideas upon Dress Reform', in ibid., pp. 52–62; 'The Relation of Dress to Art. A Note in Black and White on Mr Whistler's Lecture', in ibid., pp. 68–72. See also Stella M. Newton, *Health, Art and Reason. Dress Reformers of the 19th Century*, London 1974.
222 Reprinted in *Reviews*, pp. 6–10.
223 Ibid., p. 9.
224 Ibid., pp. 8–9.
225 Ibid., p. 10.
226 Ibid.
227 On Shakespearian costume and stage equipment generally, see M. Channing Linthicum's study, *Costume in the Drama of Shakespeare and his Contemporaries*, New York 1936, reprinted 1963; F. M. Kelly, *Shakespearian Costume for Stage and Screen*, completely revised by Alan Mansfield, London 1970 [1938]; Andrew Gurr, *The Shakespearean Stage, 1574–1642*, Cambridge 1970, esp. pp. 128ff; T. J. King, *Shakespearean Staging, 1599–1642*, Cambridge, Mass., 1971.
228 'Shakespeare and Stage Costume', NC 17 (May 1885), 810.
229 Ibid., 817.
230 See the chapters on W. C. Macready, Charles Kean and Henry Irving in George C. D. Odell, *Shakespeare – From Betterton to Irving*, vol. II, London 1920, reprinted 1963; M. St Clare Byrne, 'Fifty Years of Shakespearian Production: 1898–1948', ShS 2 (1949), 1–20.
231 See H. Montgomery Hyde, 'Oscar Wilde and his Architect', ARev 109–10 (1951), 175–6.
232 Hilda Schiff, 'A Critical Study of Oscar Wilde's "Intentions"', p. 221. With reference to Godwin's influence on Wilde, see also John Stokes, *Resistible Theatres. Enterprise and Experiment in the Late Nineteenth Century*, London 1972, pp. 61–4.
233 *Reviews*, p. 35.
234 'Shakespeare and Stage Costume', 814.
235 'The Decay of Lying', in *Complete Works*, p. 979.
236 'Shakespeare and Stage Costume', 818.
237 'The Truth of Masks', in *Complete Works*, p. 1078.
238 'Shakespeare and Stage Costume', 805.
239 'The Truth of Masks', in *Complete Works*, p. 1065.
240 Ibid., p. 1078.
241 Schiff, 'Critical Study', p. 203.
242 *Letters*, p. 295.

243 'the only thing that ever prejudices me against a book is the lack of literary style'. *Letters*, p. 262.

244 *Reviews*, p. 13.

245 'Quand je l'accuse [Wilde] de criminalité je ne m'occupe plus des actes sexuels qu'on lui a reprochés, mais du rôle qu'il a joué, de l'influence qu'il a prise et si mal employée, des jeunes vanités qu'il a faussées, des vices qu'il a tant encouragés.' [When I accuse him (Wilde) of criminality, I am no longer concerned with the sexual acts he has been blamed for, but with the role that he has played, the influence he has exerted and used so badly, the youthful dandies he has led astray, and the vices that he has encouraged so much]. 'L'Affaire Oscar Wilde', *Archives* 10, no. 58 (1895), 445.

246 *Reviews*, p. 39.

247 Ibid., p. 214.

248 Ibid., p. 182.

249 Ibid., p. 115.

250 Ibid., p. 462.

251 Ibid., p. 164.

252 Ibid., p. 150.

253 Ibid., p. 181.

254 Ibid., p. 271.

255 Ibid., p. 401.

256 Ibid., p. 352.

257 Ibid., p. 520.

258 Ibid., p. 541.

259 Ibid., p. 524.

260 Rhodes, 'The Literary Criticism of Oscar Wilde', p. 162.

261 *Reviews*, p. 53.

262 Ibid., p. 440.

263 Ibid., p. 120.

264 Ibid., p. 295.

265 Ibid., p. 155.

266 Ibid., p. 117.

267 The piece first appeared in the July 1889 edition of *Blackwood's Magazine*. Further plans to publish the essay separately, or to extend it and put it in a collection with 'The Decay of Lying', and 'Pen, Pencil and Poison', came to nothing. Nevertheless, after its publication in *Blackwood's*, Wilde altered the original to such a degree that the final version is more than double the length. In 1893 the longer version was supposed to be published by Elkin Mathews & John Lane. However, the partnership broke up and the two publishers could not agree on who was to take over what, as a result of which the plan fell through. The arrest of the author then brought any further plans for publication to an abrupt end. For some time it was believed that the manuscript had been returned to the author by the publishers and was then lost after the auction of his possessions in Tite Street. However, according to H. Montgomery Hyde, 'The Portrait of Mr W. H.', TLS, 5 Dec. 1958, p. 705, and Rupert Hart-Davis (ed.), *Letters*, p. 365–6, note 4, it was discovered many years later among the belongings of a deceased employee of Lane's, one Frederick Chapman, whose widow sold it through the American

publishing firm of Mitchell Kennerly to the collector A. S. W. Rosenbach. In 1921 Kennerly published a very limited edition of the complete text. It was not until 1958 that Vyvyan Holland edited *The Portrait of Mr W. H. The greatly enlarged version prepared by the author after the appearance of the story in 1889 but not published.* See also Horst Schroeder, *Oscar Wilde, 'The Portrait of Mr W. H.' – Its Composition, Publication and Reception*, Braunschweig 1984. (Braunschweiger anglistische Arbeiten. 9), and Horst Schroeder, *Annotations to Oscar Wilde, 'The Portrait of Mr W. H.'*, Braunschweig 1986. Privately printed.

268 *Letters*, p. 243.
269 With reference to the countless attempts to identify the mysterious Master W. H., see *A New Variorum Edition of Shakespeare. The Sonnets*, ed. by Hyder E. Rollins, vol. II, Philadelphia and London 1944, Appendix 8, pp. 177–241.
270 'The Portrait of Mr W. H.', in *Complete Works*, p. 1158.
271 Ibid., p. 1160.
272 Ibid., p. 1165.
273 Ibid., p. 1196.
274 Ibid., p. 1199.
275 *Lamia*, Part II, verses 229–30. *The Poetical Works of John Keats*, ed. by H. W. Garrod, London 1962 [1956], p. 176.
276 Ibid., p. 177.
277 'The Portrait of Mr W. H.', in *Complete Works*, p. 1197.
278 Ibid., p. 1196.
279 See Lewis J. Poteet, 'Romantic Aesthetics in Oscar Wilde's "Mr W. H."' SSF 7 (1970), 458–64.
280 From *Miscellaneous Sonnets*, pt. II, in *The Poetical Works of Wordsworth*, p. 206.
281 'The Portrait of Mr W. H.', in *Complete Works*, p. 1156.
282 Ibid.
283 Ibid., p. 1194.
284 Ibid., p. 1182.
285 *Oscar Wilde*. Including 'My Memories of Oscar Wilde' by George Bernard Shaw and Introductory Note by Lyle Blair, East Lansing, Mich., 1959 [1916], p. 69.
286 'The Critic as Artist', in *Complete Works*, p. 1027.
287 *The Complete Works of Algernon Charles Swinburne*, ed. by Edmund Gosse and Thomas J. Wise, vol. 16, London 1926, p. 116.
288 Thomas De Quincey, 'Charles Lamb and his Friends', NBR 10 (Nov. 1848), 204.
289 Ibid.
290 Ibid., 205.
291 *Final Memorials of Charles Lamb* ..., vol. 2, London 1848, pp. 22–3. Equally negative is the view of Brian W. Proctor, *Autobiographical Fragment and Biographical Notes* ..., London 1877, p. 188, where he describes Wainewright as 'a man who was absolutely a fop, finikin in dress, with mincing steps, and tremulous words, with his hair curled and full of unguents, and his cheeks painted like those of a frivolous demirep'.
292 Talfourd, *Final Memorials of Charles Lamb*, vol. 2, p. 8.

293 See *Macready's Reminiscences* and *Selections from his Diaries and Letters*, ed. by Frederick Pollock, vol. 1, London 1875, pp. 225–6.

294 'A Critical Study of Oscar Wilde's "Intentions"', p. 278.

295 'Pen, Pencil and Poison', in *Complete Works*, p. 994.

296 Ibid., p. 1001.

297 Ibid., p. 997.

298 'Edgar Poe, sa vie et ses œuvres' (1856), in Baudelaire, *Œuvres complètes*, p. 345.

299 'Pen, Pencil and Poison', in *Complete Works*, p. 115.

300 *The Picture of Dorian Gray*, in ibid., p. 115.

301 'Pen, Pencil and Poison', in ibid., p. 1007.

302 Lemonnier, *Oscar Wilde*, p. 97.

303 *Janus Weathercock. The Life of Thomas Griffiths Wainewright 1794–1847*, London 1938, p. 275.

304 'Pen, Pencil and Poison', in *Complete Works*, p. 1007.

305 Edgar Allan Poe, 'The Poetic Principle' (1849), in *Tales, Poems, Essays*. With an introduction by Laurence Maynell, London and Glasgow 1966 [1952], p. 488.

306 Lemonnier, *Oscar Wilde*, p. 91.

307 Robert Merle, *Oscar Wilde*, Paris 1948, attributes this vacillation between different standpoints to Wilde's '*complexe de fuite*' (p. 253), and goes on: On s'étonne, en lisant *Intentions*, qu'un ensemble de formules aussi nettes puisse laisser une impression confuse. C'est que Wilde ne s'arrête jamais aux positions qu'il vient de conquérir. A peine conquises, il les abandonne ... De la vie, il se réfugie dans l'art, de l'art, il se réfugie dans la critique. De la critique, il se réfugie dans la contemplation et de la contemplation, dans la vie esthétique.

[One is amazed, on reading *Intentions*, that a collection of such precise formulae could leave an impression of confusion. It is because Wilde never stops at the positions he has just mastered. No sooner has he mastered them than he abandons them ... From life he takes refuge in art, from art he takes refuge in criticism. From criticism he takes refuge in contemplation, and from contemplation, in the aesthetic life.] p. 244.

308 'The Critic as Artist', in *Complete Works*, p. 1027.

309 'Conclusion', in *The Renaissance*, p. 239.

310 *The Gentle Art of Making Enemies*, p. 155.

311 *The Soul of Man under Socialism*, in *Complete Works*, p. 1091.

312 'The Critic as Artist', in ibid., p. 1054.

313 'Tradition and the Individual Talent' (1919), in *Selected Essays*, p. 21.

314 Robert Weimann, '*New Criticism' und die Entwicklung bürgerlicher Literaturwissenschaft. Geschichte und Kritik autonomer Interpretationsmethoden*. Second revised and extended edition, Munich 1974 [1962], p. 102.

315 Schiff, 'Critical Study', p. ii.

316 Rhodes, 'Literary Criticism', with references to the interpretation of the literary criticism of Wilde and the Aesthetic Movement as a forerunner to modernism, see also Ruth Z. Temple, 'The Ivory Tower as Lighthouse', in *Edwardians and Late Victorians*, English Institute Essays 1959, ed. by Richard Ellmann, New York 1960, pp. 28–49, and R. J. Green, 'Oscar Wilde's "Intentions". An Early Modernist Manifesto', BJA 13 (1973), 397–404.

317 'Oscar Wilde' in *A History of Modern Criticism*, vol. 4, pp. 415–16.

318 Introduction, 'The Critic as Artist as Wilde', in *The Artist as Critic*, p. xi.
319 *The Picture of Dorian Gray*, in *Complete Works*, p. 106.

4 Authority and Autonomy. *The Soul of Man under Socialism*

1 George Bernard Shaw, 'My Memories of Oscar Wilde', in Harris, *Oscar Wilde* (1959), p. 331.
2 RUS 51 (1965), 83–95.
3 *The Quintessence of Ibsenism*, London 1926 [1891], p. 17.
4 *The Soul of Man under Socialism*, in *Complete Works*, p. 1100.
5 Ibid., p. 1081.
6 *The Quintessence of Ibsenism*, p. 7.
7 *The Soul of Man under Socialism*, in *Complete Works*, p. 1091.
8 With reference to the economic and social history of the 1880s, see Helen M. Lynd, *England in the Eighteen-Eighties. Toward a Social Basis for Freedom*, New York 1945; Herman Ausubel, *In Hard Times. Reformers among the Late Victorians*, New York 1960; Sydney G. Checkland, *The Rise of Industrial Society in England, 1815–1885*, London 1964; William H. B. Court, *British Economic History, 1870–1914. Commentary and Documents*, Cambridge 1965; Richard S. Sayers, *A History of Economic Change in England, 1880–1939*, London 1965; G. Kitson Clark, *An Expanding Society: Britain, 1830–1900*, Cambridge 1967; Eric Hobsbawm, *Industry and Empire. An Economic History of Britain since 1750*, London 1968; Peter Mathias, *The First Industrial Nation. An Economic History of Britain, 1700–1914*, London 1969; Gareth S. Jones, *Outcast London. A Study in the Relationship between Classes in Victorian Society*, Oxford 1971; Judith Ryder and Harold Silver, *Modern English Society. History and Structure, 1850–1970*, London 1970; Richard Tames, *Economy and Society in Nineteenth-Century Britain*, London 1972; Janet Roebuck, *The Making of Modern English Society from 1850*, London 1973; Neil Tonge and Michael Quincey, *British Social and Economic History, 1800–1900*, London 1980, chap. 9.
9 Lynd, *England in the Eighteen-Eighties*, p. 28.
10 Ibid., p. 53. See also Checkland, *The Rise of Industrial Society in England*, pp. 225–32.
11 Jones, *Outcast London*, pp. 291ff.
12 *My Apprenticeship*, London 1950 [1926], p. 154.
13 Lynd, *England in the Eighteen-Eighties*, pp. 424–5.
14 'Der Sozialismus konnte von Anfang an weite Kreise des gebildeten, wohlhabenden Bürgertums auf seine Seite ziehen, er wurde zeitweise in der guten Gesellschaft und an den alten Universitäten geradezu Mode.' [Socialism was from the very start able to get large sections of the educated, prosperous middle class on its side; for a time it was actually fashionable in high society and at the old universities.] Edgar Reichel, *Der Sozialismus der Fabier. Ein Beitrag zur Ideengeschichte des modernen Sozialismus in England*, Heidelberg 1947, p. 27.
15 Mill, *Autobiography*, London 1873, p. 232.
16 On the history of socialist thought in the 1880s, see G. D. H. Cole, *A History of Social Thought*, 5 vols., London 1953–1960, esp. vol. II, *Marxism and*

Anarchism, 1850–1890, and vol. III, pt 1, *The Second International, 1889–1914;* George Lichtheim, *A Short History of Socialism,* London 1970; Thomas L. Jarman, *Socialism in Britain. From the Industrial Revolution to the Present Day,* London 1972; Stanley Pierson, *Marxism and the Origins of British Socialism. The Struggle for a New Consciousness,* Ithaca 1973; Stanley Pierson, *British Socialists. The Journey from Fantasy to Politics,* Cambridge, Mass., and London 1979.

17 On the Fabian Society, see Edward R. Pease, *The History of the Fabian Society,* London 1918, 1963; Reichel, *Der Sozialismus der Fabier;* Alan M. McBriar, *Fabian Socialism and English Politics, 1884–1914,* Cambridge 1962; Willard Wolfe, *From Radicalism to Socialism. Men and Ideas in the Formation of Fabian Socialist Doctrines, 1881–1889,* New Haven and London 1975; Peter Wittig, *Der englische Weg zum Sozialismus. Die Fabier und ihre Bedeutung für die Labour Party und die englische Politik,* Berlin 1982.

18 Wolfe, *From Radicalism to Socialism,* pp. 296–7.

19 On William Morris's socialism, see Gustav Fritzsche, *William Morris' Sozialismus und anarchistischer Kommunismus. Darstellung des Systems und Untersuchung der Quellen,* Leipzig 1927 (Kölner anglistische Arbeiten. 3); Graham Hough, 'William Morris', in *The Last Romantics,* London and New York 1961 [1947], pp. 83–133, esp. pp. 102ff; G. D. H. Cole, *Socialist Thought: Marxism and Anarchism, 1850–1890,* esp. pp. 415ff; Edward P. Thompson, *William Morris. Romantic to Revolutionary,* London 1955; R. Page Arnot, *William Morris. The Man and the Myth,* London 1964; James W. Hulse, *Revolutionists in London. A Study of Five Unorthodox Socialists,* Oxford 1970, pp. 77–110; Paul Meier, *La Pensée utopique de William Morris,* Paris 1972; Paul Thompson, *The Work of William Morris,* London 1977, esp. chaps. 11–13; Jack Lindsay, *William Morris. His Life and Work,* New York 1979, esp. chaps. 12–14.

20 'Art, Wealth, and Riches' [1883], in *The Collected Works of William Morris,* vol. XXIII, London 1915, p. 159.

21 'Art and Socialism' [1884], in *Collected Works,* p. 205.

22 'Art under Plutocracy' [1883], in *Collected Works,* p. 165.

23 Ibid., p. 164.

24 Karl Honnef, *Dichterische Illusion und gesellschaftliche Wirklichkeit. Zur ästhetischen Struktur und historischen Funktion der Vers- und Prosaromanzen im Werk von William Morris,* Munich 1978, p. 82. See also the following passage from *News from Nowhere:*
'The art or work-pleasure, as one ought to call it, of which I am now speaking, sprung up almost spontaneously, it seems, from a kind of instinct amongst people, no longer driven desperately to painful and terrible overwork, to do the best they could with the work in hand – to make it excellent of its kind, and when that had gone on for a little, a craving for beauty seemed to awaken in men's minds, and they began rudely and awkwardly to ornament the wares which they had made; and when they had once set to work at that, it soon began to grow ... Thus at last and by slow degrees we got pleasure into our work; then we became conscious of that pleasure, and cultivated it, and took care that we had our fill of it; and then all was gained, and we were happy. So may it be for ages and ages.'
News from Nowhere, or an Epoch of Rest. Being some Chapters from a Utopian Romance, ed. by James Redmond, London and Boston 1973, pp. 114–15.

25 Hough, *The Last Romantics,* p. 102.

26 *The Soul of Man under Socialism*, in *Complete Works*, p. 1079.
27 Ibid., p. 1080.
28 Ibid.
29 Ibid., p. 1081.
30 Ibid.
31 Ibid., p. 1082.
32 Ibid., p. 1087.
33 Ibid., p. 1088.
34 Ibid., p. 1089.
35 Ibid., p. 1088.
36 Ibid.
37 Ibid., p. 1086.
38 Ibid., p. 1083.
39 Ibid., p. 1100.
40 Ibid., p. 1101.
41 Ibid., pp. 1101–2.
42 Ibid., p. 1102.
43 Ibid., p. 1091.
44 Ibid., p. 1092.
45 Ibid., p. 1096.
46 Ibid., p. 1083.
47 'Theoretikos', in *Complete Works*, p. 716.
48 *Vera*, in *Complete Works*, p. 677.
49 'My Memories of Oscar Wilde', in Harris, *Oscar Wilde*, p. 334.
50 See *1886, Haymarket. Die deutschen Anarchisten von Chicago. Reden und
    Lebensläufe*, ed. by Horst Karasek, Berlin 1975.
51 'My Memories of Oscar Wilde', in Harris, *Oscar Wilde*, p. 334.
52 Ibid.
53 Pearson, *The Life of Oscar Wilde*, p. 97.
54 A. E. Dyson, 'The Socialist Aesthete', *The Listener*, 24 Aug. 1961, p.
    274, stresses the humanitarian aspect of the essay: 'The warmth and humanity of
    The Soul of Man under Socialism must be apparent to anyone who reads it
    with an unbiased mind, whether he agrees with the viewpoint, and is familiar
    with the background or not.'
55 *The Soul of Man under Socialism*, in *Complete Works*, p. 1087.
56 Theodor Eschenburg, *Über Autorität*, Frankfurt/M. 1976 [1965], p. 257. On
    the concept of authority, see also Theodor W. Adorno, *The Authoritarian
    Personality*, New York 1950; Hannah Arendt, 'Was ist Autorität?' in *Frag-
    würdige Traditionsbestände im politischen Denken der Gegenwart*,
    Frankfurt/M. 1957, pp. 117–68; *Autorität*, ed. by Hans Joachim Türk, Mainz
    1973; Carl J. Friedrich, *Tradition und Autorität*, Munich 1974.
57 MEW, vol. 18, Berlin 1962, p. 308.
58 On the theory and history of anarchism, see Max Nettlau, *Der Anarchismus
    von Proudhon zu Kropotkin. Seine historische Entwicklung in den Jahren
    1859–1880*, Berlin 1927, reprinted Glashütten (Ts.) 1972; Nettlau,
    *Anarchisten und Sozialrevolutionäre. Die historische Entwicklung des Anar-
    chismus in den Jahren 1880–1886*, Berlin 1931, reprinted Glashütten (Ts.)
    1972; G. D. H. Cole, *Socialist Thought: Marxism and Anarchism, 1850–
    1890*, London 1954; James Joll, *The Anarchists*, London 1964; *Anarchismus.*

Theorie, Kritik, Utopie. Texte und Kommentare, ed. by Achim von Borries and Ingeborg Brandies, Frankfurt/M. 1970; Rudolf Krämer-Badoni, *Anarchismus. Geschichte und Gegenwart einer Utopie*, Vienna 1970; George Woodcock, *Anarchism. A History of Libertarian Ideas and Movements*, Harmondsworth 1970; Justus F. Wittkop, *Unter der schwarzen Fahne. Aktionen und Gestalten des Anarchismus*, Frankfurt/M. 1973.

59 EM 18 (1967), 111–39.
60 *Enquiry Concerning Political Justice and its Influence on Morals and Happiness*, ed. by F. E. L. Priestley, vol. II, Toronto 1946, p. 508.
61 *News from Nowhere*, in *Collected Works*, vol. XVI, London 1912, pp. 52ff.
62 *The Quintessence of Ibsenism*, p. 22.
63 'A Chinese Sage', in *Reviews*, pp. 528–38.
64 Ibid., p. 536.
65 Woodcock, *The Paradox of Oscar Wilde*, p. 152.
66 Roditi, *Oscar Wilde*, p. 150.
67 Pater, *Appreciations*, London 1915, p. 62. See also Günther Debon's detailed study, *Oscar Wilde und der Taoismus. Oscar Wilde and Taoism*, Bern and Frankfurt/M. 1986. (euro-sinica.2).
68 'Oscar Wilde's Absorption of "Influences". The Case History of Chuang Tzu', DUJ 64 (1971), 4. Also rather unconvincing is Brian Nicholas's study of sources, 'Two Nineteenth-Century Utopias. The Influence of Renan's "L'Avenir de la Science" on Wilde's "The Soul of Man under Socialism" ', MLR 59 (1964), 361–70, esp. 369 where mention is made of Wilde 'borrowing heavily'.
69 *The Soul of Man under Socialism*, in *Complete Works*, p. 1102.
70 Ibid., p. 1104.
71 Ibid., p. 1084.
72 Ibid., p. 1100.
73 Herbert Spencer, *First Principles* [1862], in *The Works of Herbert Spencer*, vol. 1: *A System of Synthetic Philosophy*, Osnabrück 1966, p. 291.
74 *Why I am a Socialist*, London 1886, p. 3.
75 *The Soul of Man under Socialism*, in *Complete Works*, p. 1101.
76 Ibid., p. 1084.
77 Ibid., p. 1007.
78 Ibid., p. 24.
79 Ibid., p. 1039.
80 Lynd, *England in the Eighteen-Eighties*, p. 219.

5 Culture and corruption. *The Picture of Dorian Gray*

1 Introduction in *The Picture of Dorian Gray. A Moral Entertainment. Adapted from the Novel by Oscar Wilde*, London 1973, p. 11.
2 *Scots Observer*, 5 July 1890. Quoted in *Oscar Wilde. The Critical Heritage*, p. 75.
3 'A Novel by Mr Oscar Wilde', *Bookman* (Nov. 1891). Quoted in *Oscar Wilde. The Critical Heritage*, p. 86.
4 *Letters*, p. 270, note 1.
5 See *Oscar Wilde. A Collection of Critical Essays*, ed. by Richard Ellmann, Englewood Cliffs, N. J., 1969, pp. 39–40.

6 See the useful collection of press reviews and a survey of textual variations and translations of the novel in *Art and Morality. A Defence of 'The Picture of Dorian Gray'*, ed. by Stuart Mason, London 1908. The book appeared in 1912 in revised and extended form with the new sub-title: *A Record of the Discussion which followed the Publication of 'Dorian Gray'*. There is a smaller selection of reviews in *Oscar Wilde. The Critical Heritage*, pp. 67–86. More recently Wolfgang Maier, in his dissertation on *Oscar Wilde, 'The Picture of Dorian Gray'. Eine kritische Analyse der anglistischen Forschung von 1962 bis 1982*, Frankfurt/M. 1984, has analysed criticism of the novel since 1962.

7 'A Study in Puppydom', *St James's Gazette*, 20 June 1890. Quoted in *Oscar Wilde. The Critical Heritage*, p. 69.
8 *Oscar Wilde. The Critical Heritage*, p. 72.
9 Ibid., p. 77.
10 Ibid., p. 82.
11 Hesketh Pearson, *The Life of Oscar Wilde*, London 1946, p. 156.
12 See German translations by Johannes Gaulke (1901), Felix P. Greve (1902), W. Fred (1906), Bernhard Oehlschlägel (1907), J. Cassirer (*c.* 1908), Margarete Preiss (1908), Hedwig Lachmann and Gustav Landauer (1909), Hugo Reichenbach (1915), Wilhelm Cremer (1922), Ernst Sander (1924), Richard Zoozmann (1924), Martha Grusemann (1925), D. Mitzky (1926), Roderich Frh. von Ompteda (1947), Alastair [Hanns Henning van Voigt] (1948), Liese-Lotte Dorm (1949), Botho H. Elster (1950), Günter Günther (1951), Otto Schumann (1951), and Christine Hoeppener (1966).
13 'Oscar Wilde', in *The Mountain in the Sunlight. Studies in Conflict and Unity*, London 1958, p. 135. A recent and important study of the novel is Manfred Pfister's *Oscar Wilde, 'The Picture of Dorian Gray'*, Munich 1986. (UTB. 1388). This covers the reception of Wilde and his novel mainly in German-speaking countries, sketches the present state of research, and offers a cautious interpretation of the book which finally Pfister sets in its historical context.
14 The *New Encyclopedia of the Opera*, ed. by David Ewen, London 1973, mentions operatic versions by William Orchard and Hans Joachim Schaeuble. *Kindlers Literaturlexikon*, among the entries under *The Picture of Dorian Gray* includes a ballet by M. Lang, with choreography by W. Orlikowsky, which received its first performance in Basel in March 1966. According to the German Film Institute there have been seven film versions up to now: *Dorian Grays Portraet*, Denmark 1910 (dir. by Axel Strøm); *Portret Doriana Greja*, Russia 1915 (dir. by Vsevolod Mejerchol'd); *The Picture of Dorian Gray*, Great Britain 1916 (dir. by Fred W. Durrant); *Das Bildnis des Dorian Gray*, Germany 1917 (dir. by Richard Oswald); *Az élet tzirálya*, Hungary 1917 (dir. by Alfréd Deésy); *The Picture of Dorian Gray*, USA 1944 (dir. by Albert Lewin); *Das Bildnis des Dorian Gray/Il ritratto de Dorian Gray*, Federal Republic of Germany/Italy 1969 (dir. by Massimo Dallamano).
15 *Oscar Wilde. The Critical Heritage*, p. 75.
16 Walter Pater, 'A Novel by Mr Oscar Wilde', *Oscar Wilde. The Critical Heritage*, p. 84.
17 *Letters*, p. 257.
18 According to Gide, Wilde said the following: 'Elles [mes pièces] sont presque toutes le résultat d'un pari. *Dorian Grey* [sic] aussi; je l'ai écrit en quelques

jours, parce qu'un de mes amis prétendait que je ne pourrais pas écrire un roman.' [They [my plays] are nearly all the result of a bet. *Dorian Grey* [*sic*] as well; I wrote it in a few days, because one of my friends claimed that I would not be able to write a novel]. 'Oscar Wilde', *L'Ermitage* (June 1902), 415.

19 *Art and Morality* (1912), p. 63.
20 *Life of Oscar Wilde*, p. 149.
21 *The Picture of Dorian Gray (Urfassung 1890)* von Oscar Wilde. Critical new edition with an introduction by Wilfried Edener, Nuremberg 1964. (Erlanger Beiträge zur Sprach- und Kunstwissenschaft. 18). See esp. the Introduction, pp. xvii–xix where Edener traces the origin of this legend. There is a similar view expressed by Rupert Croft-Cooke, *The Unrecorded Life of Oscar Wilde*, New York 1972, p. 26.
22 Charles C. Nickerson, ' "Vivian Grey" and "Dorian Gray"', TLS, 14 Aug. 1969, p. 909. Nickerson also reproduces the 'Artist's Preface' from the Charterhouse Edition (1904).
23 Brasol, *Oscar Wilde*, London 1938, p. 215.
24 See also the critical survey of Wilde biography, 'The Biographers and the Legends', in Croft-Cooke, *Unrecorded Life*, pp. 1–29. The biographies by H. Montgomery Hyde (1976) and Richard Ellmann (1986) have gone a long way towards separating fact from fiction.
25 *Memories and Adventures*, Garden City, NY, 1930 [1924], p. 84.
26 Donald L. Lawler, 'Oscar Wilde's First Manuscript of "The Picture of Dorian Gray"', SB 25 (1972), 125–35. See also Lawler's unpublished Ph.D. thesis, 'An Enquiry into Oscar Wilde's Revisions of "The Picture of Dorian Gray"', University of Chicago 1969, to which I have not had access.
27 XIII, p. 122   Roman numerals indicate chapters, and Arabic indicate pages in the *Complete Works* (1966).
28 Textual notes in *Oscar Wilde. The Picture of Dorian Gray*, ed. with an introduction by Isobel Murray, London 1974, p. 230. (Oxford English Novels).
29 See 'Bemerkungen zur Urfassung von Wildes "The Picture of Dorian Gray"', DNS 65 (n.s. 15) (1966), 324–32.
30 Edener, Introduction in *Dorian Gray*, p. xxxiii.
31 *Oscar Wilde*, p. 122.
32 *Oscar Wilde*, p. 137.
33 *Oscar Wilde*, p. 297.
34 *Letters*, p. 260.
35 'Some Elements in the Composition of "The Picture of Dorian Gray"', DUJ 33 (1972), 231.
36 II, p. 29.
37 VIII, p. 86.
38 Ibid.
39 IV, p. 54.
40 VIII, p. 79.
41 It is particularly interesting to note that at this point the magazine version has a different time-scheme. Chapter X – which corresponds to Chapter XII in the book version – begins with the sentence: 'It was on the 7th of November, the eve of his own thirty-second birthday, as he often remembered afterwards.' Richard Ellmann regards this as a reference to Wilde's own 32nd birthday,

which was in 1886, the year that Robert Ross and others believe marked the beginning of Wilde's homosexual activities: 'Wilde evidently considered this sudden alteration of his life a pivotal matter, to be recast as Dorian's murder of Hallward'. 'The Critic as Artist as Wilde', in *Wilde and the Nineties*, ed. by Charles Ryskamp, Princeton 1966, p. 11. Ellmann's essay is reproduced as the introduction to *The Artist as Critic. Critical Writings of Oscar Wilde*, ed. by Richard Ellmann, New York 1968, pp. ix–xxviii.

42 XIX, p. 158.
43 III, p. 37.
44 V, p. 59.
45 XV, p. 134.
46 IV, p. 46.
47 IV, p. 49.
48 XI, p. 111.
49 I, p. 18.
50 X, p. 98.
51 VII, p. 76.
52 XVI, pp. 140–1.
53 XVI, p. 142.
54 V, p. 64.
55 XVI, p. 142.
56 XVI, p. 141.
57 V, p. 59.
58 V, p. 61.
59 III, p. 44.
60 Ibid.
61 VII, p. 71.
62 Philip Collins, 'Dickens and London', in *The Victorian City. Images and Realities*, ed. by H. J. Dyos and Michael Wolff, vol. 2, London and Boston 1973, p. 541.
63 *The Collected Works of Walter Bagehot*, ed. by Norman St John-Stevas, vol. II, London 1965, p. 87.
64 IV, p. 49.
65 VII, p. 76. The fact that Dorian's impressions of the East End both here and in Chapter XVI have more than a grain of truth in them may be gauged from comparison with Paul de Rousiers's description of this area:

A population in abject poverty, squalid, wan, and forbidding in appearance, seethes in the narrow, dirty, muddy, reeking streets ... About the doors of public-houses, especially on Saturdays, may be seen crowds of persons of whom a considerable number are women. Drink is a ceaseless cause of physical and moral degradation, poverty, and irremediable ruin. It is only necessary to enter any one of the lanes which branch off from the main streets to convince oneself that vice is in its element. On the doorsteps of the little, mean, narrow houses where families are crowded together higgedly-piggedly, many a wretched creature may be seen like those just described.

The Labour Question in Britain [*La Question ouvrière en Angleterre*, 1895]. Translated by F. L. D. Herbertson, London 1896. The passage is quoted in *British Economy and Society, 1870–1970. Documents – Descriptions – Statistics*, ed. by R. W. Breach and R. M. Hartwell, Oxford 1972, pp. 51–2.
66 XVI, p. 141.
67 XIX, p. 158.

68 On the cliché of town v. country in the Victorian novel, see U. C. Knoepflmacher, 'The Novel between City and Country', in *The Victorian City*, ed. by
   Dyos and Wolff, vol. 2, pp. 517–36. Also Raymond Williams's more general
   account, *The Country and the City*, London 1973.

69 IV, p. 49.

70 VII, p. 76.

71 XVI, p. 141.

72 For a modern view of this problem, see Alexander Mitscherlich, *Die Unwirt-
   lichkeit unserer Städte. Anstiftung zum Unfrieden*, Frankfurt/M. 1965.

73 U. C. Knoepflmacher, 'The Novel between City and Country', p. 532.

74 See also Epifanio San Juan's observation: 'Restriction of space in the novel
   entails a corresponding withdrawal of characters into intense self-awareness
   which initially affects plot, diction, spectacle, and thought.' *The Art of Oscar
   Wilde*, p. 56.

75 X, p. 99.

76 On the literary motif of the *doppelgänger*, see Otto Rank, *Der Doppelgänger.
   Eine psychoanalytische Studie*, Leipzig, Wien and Zurich 1925 [1914];
   Wilhelmine Krauss, *Das Doppelgängermotiv in der Romantik. Studien zum
   romantischen Idealismus*, Berlin 1930 (Germanische Studien. 99); Ralph
   Tymms, *Doubles in Literary Psychology*, Cambridge 1949; Natalie Reber,
   *Studien zum Motiv des Doppelgängers bei Dostojevskij und E. T. A. Hoff-
   mann*, Giessen 1964; Robert Rogers, *The Double in Literature*, Detroit
   1970; Carl F. Keppler, *The Literature of the Second Self*, Tucson 1972;
   Clifford Hallam, 'The Double as Incomplete Self. Toward a Definition of
   Doppelgänger', in *Fearful Symmetry. Doubles and Doubling in Literature and
   Film*. Papers from the fifth annual Florida State University Conference on
   Literature and Film, ed. by Eugene J. Crook, Tallahassee, Fla., 1981,
   pp. 1–31; Karl Miller, *Doubles. Studies in Literary History*, Oxford 1985.

77 *The Golden Bough. A Study in Magic and Religion*, New York 1958 [1890],
   pp. 223–4.

78 Sigmund Freud, *Gesammelte Werke*, vol. VIII, Frankfurt/M. 1969 [1945],
   p. 297. See also his two treatises *Die Libidotheorie und der Narzissmus*, in
   Gesammelte Werke, vol. XI, pp. 427–46, and *Zur Einführung in den Narzissmus*, in *Gesammelte Werke*, vol. X, pp. 137–70.

79 Rank, *Der Doppelgänger*, p. 105.

80 II, p. 35.

81 Ibid.

82 The Sibyl Vane plot greatly resembles Wilde's prose poem *The Actress*, which
   was first published in Gabrielle Enthoven's collection *Echoes* [1890?], and
   later reprinted in Vyvyan Holland's biography *Son of Oscar Wilde*, London
   1954, Appendix C, pp. 258–60. The poem also describes how a great actress
   falls in love with a man and thereupon renounces her art. But unlike Sibyl
   Vane she returns to the stage once the affair is over. William E. Portnoy,
   'Wilde's Debt to Tennyson in "Dorian Gray"', ELT 17 (1974), 259–61, sees a
   link between this episode and Tennyson's *Lady of Shalott*: 'Wilde was
   drawing fairly heavily upon "The Lady of Shalott" for the narrative structure
   and imagist technique of one of the central episodes of his novel.' p. 260.

83 IV, p. 53.

84 V, p. 58.

85 IV, p. 51.
86 VII, p. 75.
87 VII, p. 77.
88 VII, p. 79.
89 VIII, p. 81.
90 VIII, p. 82.
91 VIII, pp. 87–88.
92 VIII, p. 88.
93 XVI, p. 141.
94 XX, p. 166.
95 Albert J. Farmer, *Le Mouvement esthétique et 'décadent' en Angleterre (1873–1900)*, Paris 1931, p. 192. (Bibliothèque de la Revue de littérature comparée. 75).
96 Ibid., pp. 192–3.
97 XX, p. 165.
98 'A Tragedy of the Artist. "The Picture of Dorian Gray"', NCF 24 (1969), 350. According to Ernest Dowson, the character in the novel is based on the artist Charles H. Shannon (1863–1937). *The Letters of Ernest Dowson*, ed. by Desmond Flower and Henry Maas, London 1967, p. 169.
99 Baker, 'A Tragedy of the Artist', 353.
100 SNNTS 5 (1973), 63–70.
101 Ibid., 63.
102 Ibid., 66.
103 II, p. 34.
104 Robert Merle, *Oscar Wilde*, p. 306, calls him 'délégué de la Moralité Victorienne' [delegate of Victorian morality] – a judgment echoed, as so often, almost word for word by Epifanio San Juan, Jr, who calls Basil the 'spokesman of standard morality'.
105 XII, p. 118.
106 XII, p. 117.
107 I, p. 19.
108 II, p. 33.
109 IX, p. 90.
110 The text offers no evidence for Christopher S. Nassaar's contention that 'Basil's murder is not only the murder of one human being by another but is also the murder of Pre-Raphaelite art and the Ruskinian "Moral Aesthetic" by decadent art', *Into the Demon Universe. A Literary Exploration of Oscar Wilde*, New Haven and London 1974, pp. 66–7. He also offers a somewhat one-sided interpretation of the novel as 'a study of various Victorian art movements corresponding to different stages in the development of Victorian human nature, and the main characters are meant to be personifications of these art movements and psychological states' (ibid., p. 37).
111 Rogers, *The Double in Literature*, p. 23.
112 XII, p. 119.
113 XIII, p. 122.
114 Harris, *Oscar Wilde* (1959), p. 70.
115 IV, p. 55.
116 IV, p. 56. The 'experimental method' played an important part in nineteenth-century scientific theory. The French physiologist Claude

Bernard, *Introduction à l'étude de la médecine expérimentale* (1865), was one of its outstanding representatives in the field of medicine; in 1879 Wilhelm Wundt founded the institute for experimental psychology in Leipzig, making the method commonplace in this field, too. See also *Foundations of Scientific Method: The Nineteenth Century*, ed. by Ronald N. Giere and Richard S. Westfall, Bloomington and London 1973.

117 I, p. 23.
118 *Sincerity and Authenticity*, Cambridge, Mass., 1972.
119 'The brilliant and corrupt Wotton, in fact, plays the rôle of the devil', Ted R. Spivey, 'Damnation and Salvation in "The Picture of Dorian Gray"', BUSE 4 (1960), 162. Spivey also puts forward the somewhat doubtful thesis 'that the root cause of Dorian's damnation as well as the source of Harry's evil is an insatiable curiosity, a never-ending desire for knowledge', 163. See also Masao Miyoshi, *The Divided Self. A Perspective on the Literature of the Victorians*, New York and London 1969, p. 312: 'Lord Henry is the classic devil figure.' Lord Henry's strong influence on Dorian is one reason why Kerry Powell, 'The Mesmerizing of Dorian Gray', VN 65 (1984), 10–15, places the novel in the '"mesmeric" tradition in fiction', 10.
120 III, p. 41.
121 VI, p. 69.
122 See Madeleine L. Cazamian, *Le Roman et les idées en Angleterre. I: L'Influence de la science (1860–1890)*, Strasbourg and Paris 1923; Walter E. Houghton, 'Anti-Intellectualism', in Houghton, *The Victorian Frame of Mind, 1830–1870*, New Haven and London 1971 [1957], pp. 110–36; Konrad Gross, 'Die Gestalt des Intellektuellen im spätviktorianischen Roman. Studien zum Einfluss der Naturwissenschaft und Bibelkritik bei Hardy, Gissing, Butler und Wells', unpublished diss., Cologne 1970.
123 IV, p. 56.
124 II, p. 29.
125 VI, p. 69.
126 XI, p. 104.
127 II, p. 32.
128 Ibid.
129 One must distinguish between Lord Henry's (and therefore Wilde's) concept of the 'new Hedonism' and that of Grant Allen, the socialist and utilitarian nature of which prompted Holbrook Jackson to describe Allen's essay on 'The New Hedonism', FortR (n.s.) (1894), 377–92, as 'a veiled piece of Socialist propaganda', *The Eighteen-Nineties*, p. 28. On the goal of self-development, Allen writes: 'Self-development ... is an aim for all; an aim which will make all stronger, and saner, and wiser, and better. It will make each in the end more helpful to humanity. To be sound in wind and limb; to be healthy of body and mind; to be educated, to be emancipated, to be free, to be beautiful – these things are ends towards which all should strain, and by attaining which all are happier in themselves, and more useful to others. That is the central idea of the new hedonism'. p. 380.
130 XI, p. 104.
131 Bradley, *Ethical Studies*. Second revised edition, with additional notes by the author, Oxford 1927. Reprinted 1959, p. 64.
132 Ibid., p. 96.

133 Ibid., p. 124.
134 See Anthony Quinton, *Utilitarian Ethics*, London 1973, and Richard D. Altick, 'The Utilitarian Spirit', in Altick, *Victorian People and Ideas*, New York 1973, pp. 114–45.
135 Bentham, *A Fragment on Government* and *An Introduction to the Principles of Morals and Legislation*, ed. with an introduction by Wilfrid Harrison, Oxford 1948, p. 126.
136 Norbert Kohl, 'Memento Vivere. Walter Paters Philosophie des Augenblicks in der "Conclusion". *Eine Interpretation*', AntAb 20 (1974), 146.
137 XIX, p. 162.
138 XI, p. 103.
139 XI, p. 105.
140 XI, p. 115.
141 *Thought* 23 (1948), 114–28. See also Ernst Bendz, 'Notes on the Literary Relationship between Walter Pater and Oscar Wilde', NM 14, no. 5/6 (1912), 91–127; Bendz, *The Influence of Pater and Matthew Arnold in the Prose-Writings of Oscar Wilde*, Gothenburg and London 1914; Eduard J. Bock, *Walter Pater's Einfluss auf Oscar Wilde*, Bonn 1913. (Bonner Studien zur englischen Philologie. 8); Robert K. Martin, 'Parody and Homage. The Presence of Pater in "Dorian Gray"', VN 63 (1983), 15–18.
142 *Complete Works*, p. 922.
143 Billie A. Inman, 'The Organic Structure of "Marius the Epicurean"', PQ 41 (1962), 484. On *Marius the Epicurean* see also James Hafley, 'Walter Pater's "Marius" and the Technique of Modern Fiction', MFS 3 (1957), 99–109; Graham Hough, 'Marius the Latitudinarian', in Hough, *The Last Romantics*, London and New York 1961 [1947], pp. 134–57; Louise M. Rosenblatt, 'The Genesis of Pater's "Marius the Epicurean"', CL 14 (1962), 242–60; Martha S. Vogeler, 'The Religious Meaning of "Marius the Epicurean"', NCF 19 (1964), 287–99; U.C. Knoepflmacher, 'The "Atmospheres" of "Marius the Epicurean"', in Knoepflmacher, *Religious Humanism and the Victorian Novel*, Princeton 1965, pp. 189–223; Paul Goetsch, 'Paters "Marius the Epicurean"', in Goetsch, *Die Romankonzeption in England 1880–1910*, Heidelberg 1967, pp. 195–201; Lawrence F. Schuetz, 'Pater's "Marius". The Temple of God and the Palace of Art', ELT 15 (1972), 1–19; Michael Ryan, 'Narcissus Autobiographer: "Marius the Epicurean"', ELH 43 (1976), 184–208; Olivia C. Ayres, '"Marius the Epicurean". The Dialectic as the Mimetic Form of Truth', SEL 18 (1978), 693–702; William E. Buckler, '"Marius the Epicurean". Beyond Victorianism', VP 16 (1978), 147–66; Jerome Bump, 'Seeing and Hearing in "Marius the Epicurean"', NCF 37 (1982), 188–206. See also the *Marius* chapters in the Pater monographs by A. C. Benson (1906), Germain d'Hangest (1961), Wolfgang Iser (1961 and English translation, Cambridge 1987), A. Ward (1966), Gerald Monsman (1967 and 1976), and R. Crinkley (1970).
144 *Marius the Epicurean*. Introduction by Osbert Burdett, London and New York 1968, p. 87. (EL 903).
145 Ibid.
146 Ibid., p. 181.
147 XI, p. 103.
148 *De Profundis*, in *Complete Works*, p. 873.

149 XI, p. 112.
150 Goetsch, *Romankonzeption*, p. 202. Jacob Korg, 'The Rage of Caliban',
     UTQ 37 (1967), 75–89, also interprets the novel in terms of a split identity:
     'Dorian's identity is divided between the painting and his physical self; but it
     is divided again when he develops the double personality of the dandy',
     p. 76. Less convincing is Morse Peckham's suggestion that 'Dorian is the
     Dandy, the man of style. The point of the story is that such a man can
     maintain his identity while he investigates the most terrible pits of London's
     erotic and economic sub-world', *Beyond the Tragic Vision. The Quest for
     Identity in the Nineteenth Century*, New York 1962, p. 318. Equally
     dubious is Isobel Murray's assertion: 'What the novel amounts to ... in a
     wide sense, is the growth, education, and development of an exceptional
     youth', Introduction in *The Picture of Dorian Gray*, ed. Murray, p. ix. This
     statement seems more like a definition of the classic *Bildungsroman*. Charles
     Altieri, 'Organic and Humanist Models in Some English Bildungsroman'
     [*sic*], JGE 23 (1971), 220–40, actually regards *Dorian Gray* as an example of
     the 'organic ideal' (221) of the *Bildungsroman*, defining the latter as a genre
     'which insists that the self must be allowed to grow with as little interference
     as possible', 220. It is impossible to reconcile this definition with the massive
     influence that Lord Henry has on Dorian. For a more balanced judgment, see
     G. B. Tennyson, 'The "Bildungsroman" in Nineteenth Century English
     Literature', in *Medieval Epic to the 'Epic Theater' of Brecht. Essays in
     Comparative Literature*, ed. by Rosario P. Armato and John M. Spalek, Los
     Angeles 1968, pp. 135–46. (University of Southern California Studies in
     Comparative Literature. I).
151 Foreword in *Egoism and Self-Discovery in the Victorian Novel. Studies in
     the Ordeal of Knowledge in the Nineteenth Century*. Introduction by Walter
     Allen, New York 1974, p. v.
152 *Middlemarch*. With an introduction by Newton P. Stallknecht, New York
     1963, p. 814.
153 Ibid., p. 816.
154 *The Portrait of a Lady*, New York [*c.* 1950], p. 68. (The Modern Library).
155 With reference to this stylistic mode in the nineteenth-century English novel,
     see Lisa Glauser, *Die erlebte Rede im englischen Roman des 19. Jahrhun-
     derts*, Bern 1948. (Schweizer anglistische Arbeiten) and Albrecht Neubert,
     Die Stilformen der 'Erlebten Rede' im neueren englischen Roman, Halle
     (Saale) 1957.
156 On this theme, see Volkmar Sander, *Die Faszination des Bösen. Zur
     Wandlung des Menschenbildes in der modernen Literatur*, Göttingen 1968.
     (Schriften zur Literatur. 10).
157 See H. Lucius Cook, 'French Sources of Wilde's "Picture of Dorian Gray"',
     RR 19 (1928), 25–34; Hartley, *Oscar Wilde. L'Influence française dans son
     œuvre*, Paris 1935, pp. 282–309; Oscar Maurer, Jr, 'A Philistine Source for
     "Dorian Gray"?' PQ 26 (1947), 84–6; Schön, 'Französische Einflüsse in
     Oscar Wildes Werken', unpublished diss., Hamburg 1949, pp. 49–83; in an
     original essay incorporating new material, Kerry Powell, 'Tom, Dick and
     Dorian Gray. Magic-picture Mania in Late Victorian Fiction', PQ 62 (1983),
     147–70, places the novel in the tradition of late Victorian '"magic portrait"
     fiction'.

158 Johann Wolfgang Goethe, *Faust. Der Tragödie erster Teil*, in *Sämtliche Werke*, vol. 5, *Die Faustdichtungen*, ed. by Ernst Beutler, Munich 1977, line 1112, p. 177.
159 Richard Ellmann, Introduction in *Oscar Wilde. A Collection of Critical Essays*, p. 4. See also Choisy, *Oscar Wilde*, Paris 1927, p. 148; Buckley, *The Victorian Temper*, pp. 234–5; Alick West, 'Oscar Wilde', in *Mountain in the Sunlight*, p. 139; San Juan, *The Art of Oscar Wilde*, p. 63; Dominick Rossi, 'Parallels in Wilde's "The Picture of Dorian Gray" and Goethe's "Faust"', CLAJ 13 (1969), 188–91; Hans-Peter Gerhardt, 'Oscar Wildes "Dorian Gray" als Faustdichtung', *Faust-Blätter* 25 (1973), 669–75; Joyce Carol Oates, '"The Picture of Dorian Gray". Wilde's Parable of the Fall', in Oates, *Contraries. Essays*, New York 1981, p. 11: 'The *consequences* of a Faustian pact with the Devil are dramatized, but the Devil himself is absent, which suggests that the novel is an elaborate fantasy locating the Fall within the human psyche alone.'
160 Gerhardt, 'Oscar Wildes "Dorian Gray" als Faustdichtung', 674.
161 See Lewis J. Poteet, '"Dorian Gray" and the Gothic Novel', MFS 27 (1971), 239–48: '*Melmoth the Wanderer* does provide many of the larger patterns with which Wilde shapes his novel, so that Wilde in fact may be said to have written a version of Gothic novel, giving the form contemporary dimensions', 240.
162 *Letters*, p. 813.
163 *Melmoth the Wanderer. A Tale*, ed. with an introduction by Douglas Grant, London 1972, p. 26 (Oxford English novels).
164 Ibid., p. 540.
165 Ibid., p. 60.
166 See T. Brucauff, 'Oscar Wilde', DNS 23 (1915/16), 588; Hartley, *Oscar Wilde*, p. 187; Brasol, *Oscar Wilde*, p. 215; Harro H. Kühnelt, *Die Bedeutung von Edgar Allan Poe für die englische Literatur*, Innsbruck 1949, p. 173; Ojala, *Aestheticism and Oscar Wilde*, pt 1, p. 209.
167 See Richard Aldington, Introduction in *Oscar Wilde. Selected Works. With twelve unpublished letters*, ed. by Richard Aldington, London and New York 1946, p. 18; Roditi, *Oscar Wilde*, p. 117; Nickerson, '"Vivian Grey" and "Dorian Gray"', TLS, 14 Aug. 1969, p. 909. See also the subsequent discussion in the TLS, 21 Aug. 1969, p. 931; 28 Aug. 1969, p. 955; 11 Sept. 1969, p. 1003; 9 Oct. 1969, p. 1159.
168 *Tales, Poems, Essays*. With an introduction by Laurence Meynell, London and Glasgow 1966, p. 184 (Collins Classics. 592).
169 Aldington, Introduction in *Oscar Wilde*, p. 18.
170 *Vivian Grey*, vol. I, Leipzig 1859, p. 144.
171 'Edward Randolph's Portrait', in *The Complete Novels and Selected Tales of Nathaniel Hawthorne*, ed. with an introduction by Norman Holmes Pearson, New York 1965 [1937], p. 963. Carl Hagemann, *Oscar Wilde. Sein Leben und Werk*, Leipzig 1925, p. 175, draws attention to the tale 'The Prophetic Pictures' (1837), in which two portraits anticipate the fate of Walter Ludlow and his wife Elinor. From the very beginning, Elinor's features on the portrait express 'grief and terror' (p. 221) – an expression which she herself only assumes some years later, when her husband wants to murder her. Clearly the resemblance to *Dorian Gray* consists in the fact that

here, too, a portrait reveals the inner nature of the character. Kerry Powell, 'Hawthorne, Arlo Bates, and "The Picture of Dorian Gray"', PLL 16 (1980), 403–16, also points out similarities between Wilde's novel and the two Hawthorne stories mentioned above: 'enough evidence exists to conclude that the numerous and detailed resemblances between Hawthorne and Wilde's stories cannot be convincingly explained away as merely coincidental', p. 416. The Hawthorne quotation comes from *The Complete Works of Nathaniel Hawthorne*, with introductory notes by George Parsons Lathrop, vol. 1, *Twice-Told Tales*, London 1882 (Riverside edition).

172 *The Complete Novels and Selected Tales of Nathaniel Hawthorne*, p. 969.
173 See Roditi, *Oscar Wilde*, pp. 117–18. Balzac's novel is also referred to by Ingleby, *Oscar Wilde* (1907), p. 312; Choisy, *Oscar Wilde*, p. 136; Brasol, *Oscar Wilde*, p. 215; Winwar, *Oscar Wilde and the Yellow Nineties*, London 1940, 1958, p. 165; Aldington, Introduction, in *Oscar Wilde*, p. 17.
174 *Letters*, p. 122.
175 Sherard, *Life of Oscar Wilde* (1906), pp. 233–4.
176 *Tales, Poems, Essays*, p. 38.
177 *Ashes of the Future*, Chicago 1888, p. 48.
178 Ibid., p. 68.
179 The 'yellow book' in Chap. XI of *Dorian Gray* is the subject of source studies by Walter Fischer, '"The Poisonous Book" in Oskar [*sic*] Wildes "Dorian Gray"', ESt 51 (1917/18), 37–47; Bernhard Fehr, 'Das gelbe Buch in Oscar Wildes "Dorian Gray"', ESt 55 (1921), 237–56.
180 Fehr, 'Das gelbe Buch in Oscar Wildes "Dorian Gray"', 250ff., has shown in detail the extent to which the two penultimate paragraphs of chap. XI – in which Wilde conjures up images of imperial Rome and lists some of the decadent 'heroes' of the Renaissance – draw on corresponding passages in Sueton's *De vita Caesarum*, Gibbon's *The Decline and Fall of the Roman Empire*, and John Addington Symonds's *The Age of the Despots* (*Renaissance in Italy*, vol. I). R. D. Brown, 'Suetonius, Symonds, and Gibbon in "The Picture of Dorian Gray"', MLN 71 (1956), 264, repeats Fehr's findings without acknowledgment.
181 XI, p. 109.
182 Reprinted in *Miscellanies*, pp. 327–41.
183 'The Decay of Lying', in *Complete Works*, p. 974.
184 Ibid.
185 Ibid.
186 Ibid.
187 Ibid., p. 976.
188 Ibid., p. 975.
189 'The Critic as Artist', in *Complete Works*, pp. 1054–5.
190 *Letters*, p. 264.
191 'The Critic as Artist', in *Complete Works*, p. 1055.
192 III, p. 45.
193 IV, p. 56.
194 *Letters*, p. 259.
195 The aphorisms of the Preface originally appeared in the FortR, March 1891.
196 X, p. 101.
197 *Letters*, p. 266.

198 VIII, p. 81.
199 'Oscar Wilde. Sein Leben und Lebenswerk', in *Oscar Wilde. Werke in fünf Bänden*, vol. 1, Berlin 1922, p. 57.
200 *Oscar Wilde*, p. 160.
201 'Oscar Wilde and the Devil's Advocate', PMLA 59 (1944), 833–50.
202 *Aestheticism and Oscar Wilde*, pt 1, p. 213.
203 *Letters*, p. 352.
204 Barbara Charlesworth, 'The Solitary Prison of Oscar Wilde', *Spectrum* 6 (1963), 100–11. This article is incorporated in the 'Oscar Wilde' chapter of her *Dark Passages. The Decadent Consciousness in Victorian Literature*, Madison and Milwaukee 1965, pp. 53–80.
205 I, p. 25.
206 *De Profundis*, in *Complete Works*, p. 877.
207 See Jan B. Gordon, '"Parody as Initiation". The Sad Education of "Dorian Gray"', *Criticism* 9 (1967), 355–71.
208 On literary decadence, see Mario Praz's standard work *La carne, la morte e il diavolo nella letteratura romantica*, Florence 1930. See also Arthur Symons, 'The Decadent Movement in Literature', *Harper's New Monthly Magazine* 87 (June–Nov. 1893), 858–67; Ernst Robert Curtius, 'Entstehung und Wandlung des Dekadenzproblems in Frankreich', *Int. Monatsschrift f. Wissenschaft, Kunst und Technik* 15 (1921), 147–64; Walter Rehm, *Der Untergang Roms im abendländischen Denken. Ein Beitrag zur Geschichtsschreibung und zum Dekadenzproblem*, Leipzig 1930; Werner Wille, 'Studien zur Dekadenz in Romanen um die Jahrhundertwende', unpublished diss., Greifswald 1930; Cyril E. M. Joad, *Decadence. A Philosophical Inquiry*, London and New York 1948; A. E. Carter, *The Idea of Decadence in French Literature, 1830–1900*, Toronto 1958; George R. Ridge, *The Hero in French Decadent Literature* [Atlanta] 1961; Wendell V. Harris, 'Identifying the Decadent Fiction of the Eighteen-Nineties', ELT 5 (1962), 1–13; Koenraad W. Swart, *The Sense of Decadence in Nineteenth Century France*, The Hague 1964; Noël Richard, *Le Mouvement décadent. Dandys, esthètes et quintessents*, Paris 1968; Erwin Koppen, *Dekadenter Wagnerismus. Studien zur europäischen Literatur des Fin de siècle*, Berlin and New York 1973. (Komparatistische Studien. Beihefte zur 'arcadia'. Zeitschrift für Vergleichende Literaturwissenschaft); Laurence M. Porter, 'Literary Structure and the Concept of Decadence: Huysmans, D'Annunzio, and Wilde', CentR 22 (1978), 188–200; *Decadence and the 1890s*, ed. by Ian Fletcher, London 1979 (Stratford-upon-Avon Studies. 17); Richard Gilman, *Decadence. The Strange Life of an Epithet*, London 1979; Michel Décaudin, 'Définir la décadence', in Colloque de Nantes (21–24 Apr. 1976), *L'Esprit de décadence*, [Paris] 1980, pp. 5–12; Carlo Annoni, *Il decadentismo*, Brescia 1982; Jean Pierrot, *The Decadent Imagination: 1880–1900*, translated by Derek Coltman, Chicago 1982; Suzanne Nalbantian, *Seeds of Decadence in the Late Nineteenth-Century Novel. A Crisis in Values*, London 1983; R. K. R. Thornton, *The Decadent Dilemma*, London 1983.
209 Théophile Gautier, 'Charles Baudelaire' (1868), in Charles Baudelaire, *Les Fleurs du mal*, Paris 1900, p. 17.
210 XI, p. 107. See also 'The Critic as Artist', in *Complete Works*, p. 1029.
211 *Œuvres complètes*. Preface and notes by Marcel A. Ruff, Paris 1968, p. 517.

212 Koppen, *Dekadenter Wagnerismus*, p. 341.
213 See Thea von Seuffert, *Venedig im Erlebnis deutscher Dichter*, Stuttgart 1937 (Italienische Studien. 2); Walter Pabst, 'Satan und die alten Götter in Venedig. – Entwicklung einer literarischen Konstante', *Euphorion* 49 (1955), 335–59; Hellmuth Petriconi, *Das Reich des Untergangs. Bemerkungen über ein mythologisches Thema*, Hamburg 1958, esp. pp. 67–95.
214 *Emaux et Camées*, definitive text (1872) followed by *Poésies choisies*. With a biographical sketch and notes by Adolphe Boschot, Paris 1954, p. 17.
215 XIV, p. 127.
216 *Confessions of a Young Man*, London 1937, p. 62. (*The Works of George Moore*, Ebury edn, vol. 3).
217 Ibid., p. 34.
218 Ibid., p. 157.
219 Ibid., p. 162.
220 *Romankonzeption*, p. 140.
221 *Confessions of a Young Man*, p. 95.
222 Ibid., p. 159.
223 Quoted by Richard Hamann and Jost Hermand, *Impressionismus*, Munich 1972, p. 51 (Epochen deutscher Kultur von 1870 bis zur Gegenwart 3)).
224 *A Rebours*, with a preface by the author, written twenty years after the novel, Fasquelle edition 1974, p. 146.
225 Farmer, *Le Mouvement esthétique*, p. 123.
226 *The Stones of Venice, The Nature of Gothic*, in *The Works of John Ruskin*, ed. by E. T. Cook and Alexander Wedderburn, vol. X, London 1904, p. 196.
227 VI, p. 69.
228 *Culture and Anarchy*, in *The Complete Prose Works of Matthew Arnold*, ed. by R. H. Super, vol. V, Ann Arbor, Mich., 1965, p. 191.
229 Ibid., p. 165.
230 Ibid.
231 Richard Hamann and Jost Hermand, *Impressionismus*, p. 25.
232 XI, p. 113.
233 See, for example, I, p. 22; I, p. 24; II, p. 32; IV, p. 54; IV, p. 55; VI, p. 66; IX, p. 94; XVIII, p. 154.
234 There is no evidence that Wilde was familiar with Nietzsche's work, which was not translated into English until after 1896. Thomas Mann, however, noted a certain similarity in their moral views, and called them both 'Revoltierende, und zwar im Namen der Schönheit Revoltierende' [revolters, and that is to say revolters in the name of beauty] (p. 668); but elsewhere he also stresses the differences:

Natürlich hat die Zusammenstellung Nietzsches mit Wilde etwas fast Sakrilegisches, denn dieser war ein dandy, der deutsche Philosoph aber etwas wie ein Heiliger des Immoralismus. Und doch gewinnt durch das mehr oder weniger gewollte Märtyrertum seines Lebensendes, das Zuchthaus von Reading, Wildes dandyism einen Anflug von Heiligkeit, der Nietzsches ganze Sympathie erweckt hätte.

[Naturally there is something sacrilegious about putting Nietzsche together with Wilde, for the latter was a dandy, whereas the German philosopher was something like a saint of immoralism. And yet through the more or less deliberate martyrdom of his life's end, Reading Gaol, Wilde's dandyism takes on a tinge of sanctity which would have aroused all Nietzsche's sympathy.]

'Nietzsches Philosophie im Lichte unserer Erfahrung' (1947), in Thomas
Mann, *Adel des Geistes. Zwanzig Versuche zum Problem der Humanität*,
Berlin and Weimar 1965, pp. 653–4. The contrast between Wilde and
Nietzsche is also stressed by Janko Lavrin, *Aspects of Modernism. From
Wilde to Pirandello*, London 1935, p. 17; also David S. Thatcher, *Nietzsche
in England 1890–1914. The Growth of a Reputation*, Toronto 1970, p. 251,
who considers their positions to be 'vastly different'. Similarities, however,
are stressed by Norbert Loeser, 'Friedrich Nietzsche en Oscar Wilde', in
Nietzsche & Wilde en andere essays, Amsterdam 1960, pp. 133–82. Engel-
bert Weiser, *Die Kunstphilosophie Friedrich Nietzsches und Oscar Wildes*,
unpublished diss., Aachen 1977, deals both with differences and similarities.
An interpretation of *Dorian Gray* in the context of Nietzsche's *Geburt der
Tragödie aus dem Geiste der Musik* (1871) is offered by Frédéric Monney-
ron, 'Une lecture nietzschéenne de "Dorian Gray"', CVE 16 (1982),
139–45. For a general account of Nietzsche's reception in England and
America, see Patrick Bridgwater, *Nietzsche in Anglosaxony. A Study of
Nietzsche's Impact on English and American Literature*, Leicester 1972.
235 I, p. 24.
236 IV, p. 55.
237 VI, p. 69.
238 II, p. 36.
239 XIX, p. 161.
240 'The Critic as Artist', in *Complete Works*, p. 1023.
241 XI, p. 111.
242 'Anybody who studies the moods and thoughts of the Eighteen Nineties
cannot fail to observe their central characteristic in a widespread concern for
the correct – that is, the most effective, the most powerful, the most righteous
– mode of living', Jackson, *The Eighteen Nineties*, p. 14.
243 XI, p. 103.
244 See Steven Marcus, *The Other Victorians. A Study of Sexuality and
Pornography in Mid-Nineteenth Century England*, London 1966.
245 III, p. 44.
246 XV, p. 137.
247 XIX, p. 158.

6 Sensuality and suggestion. *Salomé* and *The Sphinx*

1 *Salome. Ihre Gestalt in Geschichte und Kunst. Dichtung – Bildende Kunst –
Musik*, Munich 1912. On the history and interpretation of the Salome story,
see also Reimarus Secundus, *Geschichte der Salome von Cato bis Oscar
Wilde, gemeinverständlich dargestellt*, 3 parts, Leipzig [1907]; Hédwige
Drwęska, 'Quelques interprétations de la légende de Salomé dans les littér-
atures contemporaines. Etude de littérature comparée', unpublished thesis,
Montpellier 1912; Isolde Lülsdorff, 'Salome. Die Wandlung einer Schöpfung
Heines in der französischen Literatur', unpublished diss., Hamburg 1953;
Helen G. Zagona, *The Legend of Salomé and the Principle of Art for Art's
Sake*, Geneva and Paris 1960; Franz Zaic, 'Zur Dramatisierung des Salome-
Stoffes in England', *Anglia* 78 (1960), 341–52. [Deals with the 1831 play *The
Daughter of Herodias* by Henry Rich]; Marilyn G. Rose, 'The Daughters of

Herodias in "Hérodiade", "Salomé", and "A Full Moon in March"',
CompD 1 (1967), 172–81; Helen O. Borowitz, 'Visions of Salome', *Criticism*
14 (1972), 12–21; Patricia R. Kellogg, 'The Myth of Salome in Symbolist
Literature and Art', unpublished Ph.D. thesis, New York University, 1975:
DA 36, no. 11, 1976, p. 7410-A; Rita Severi, 'Oscar Wilde e il mito di
Salomé', RLMC 34 (1981), 49–74.

2 *Oscar Wilde. The Critical Heritage*, p. 133.

3 Ingleby, *Oscar Wilde*, London 1907, p. 161; Drwęska, 'Quelques interprétations de la légende de Salomé', p. 75, where she refers to a letter from Robert
H. Sherard; Daffner, *Salome*, p. 309; *Salomé*, drawings by Alastair, Paris
1925, p. v; Cornelia O. Skinner, *Madame Sarah*, London 1967, p. 109;
Mario Praz, *Liebe, Tod und Teufel. Die schwarze Romantik* [*La carne, la
morte e il diavolo nella letteratura romantica*, 1930, *Romantic Agony*,
London 1933], vol. 2, Munich 1970, p. 265.

4 *Letters*, p. 336. Most critics have accepted this statement, e.g. Ransome,
Oscar Wilde, pp. 144–5; St John Ervine, *Oscar Wilde*, p. 134.

5 Very positive views of Wilde's French are to be found in André Gide,
Prétextes. Réflexions critiques sur quelques points de littérature et de morale,
Paris 1903, p. 169: 'Il [Oscar Wilde] savait admirablement le français, mais
feignait de chercher un peu les mots qu'il voulait faire attendre. Il n'avait
presque pas d'accent' [He had an admirable knowledge of French, but
pretended to search a little for the words he wanted to keep people waiting for.
He had practically no accent]; Sherard, *Life*, 1911, p. 85: 'French was so
familiar to him that, as he used to say, "he often thought in French"';
Henry-D. Davray, 'De quelques "poèmes en prose" inédits d'Oscar Wilde',
Mercure, 15 July (1926), 271: 'il possédait admirablement notre langue, dans
laquelle son vocabulaire était étonnement étendu' [he mastered our language
admirably, and had an astonishingly broad vocabulary]; Gustave Le Rouge,
'Oscar Wilde', NL (3 Nov. 1928), 5: 'Oscar Wilde s'exprimait en français sans
le plus léger accent et avec une pureté, un [*sic*] correction déconcertante'
[Oscar Wilde expressed himself in French without the slightest accent and
with a purity and a correctness that was disconcerting]. A more critical view is
expressed by Stuart Merrill, 'Souvenirs sur le symbolisme', in *Prose et vers.
Œuvres posthumes*, Paris 1925, p. 144:

Il [Oscar Wilde] écrivait le français comme il le parlait, c'est-à-dire avec une fantaisie
qui, si elle était savoureuse dans la conversation, aurait produit, au théâtre, une
déplorable impression. Un ami me racontait récemment qu'en sa présence, Oscar Wilde
termina le récit des aventures d'un roi (car les héros de Wilde étaient toujours des rois)
par cette phrase: 'Et puis, alors, le roi est mouru'.

[He wrote French as he spoke it, i.e. with a fantasy which, if it was to be savoured in
conversation, would have produced a deplorable impression in the theatre. A friend told
me recently that in his presence Oscar Wilde finished recounting the adventures of a king
(for Wilde's heroes were always kings) with this phrase: 'Et puis, alors, le roi est
mouru'].

This judgment, however, need not be taken as a total refutation of the others,
but simply shows that Wilde's French was not perfect.

6 Pearson, *Life of Oscar Wilde*, p. 226. Alfred Douglas appears to have
corroborated this statement during the Billing trial. The English dancer Maud
Allan, who danced the role of Salome, sued the MP Pemberton Billing on 29
May 1918 because she considered he had defamed her in a newspaper article.

Douglas, who appeared as a witness for Billing, remarked in connection with *Salomé* that: 'Ce drame, d'abord construit en anglais, traduit, pour être joué en France, avec l'aide d'écrivains français, alors que Wilde n'était pas encore très sûr de cette langue, fut remis en anglais par moi sous sa direction' [This play, first constructed in English, translated, so that it could be acted in France, with the help of French writers since Wilde was not yet very sure of that language, was put back into English by me under his direction]. Claude Cahun, 'La "Salomé" d'Oscar Wilde, le procès Billing et les 47,000 pervertis du "livre noir"', *Mercure* 128 (1918), p. 74.

7 Mason, *Bibliography of Oscar Wilde*, pp. 372–3.
8 Winwar, *Oscar Wilde and the Yellow 'Nineties*, London 1940, 1958, pp. 206–7; Pearson, *Life of Oscar Wilde*, pp. 225–6; Jullian, *Oscar Wilde*, Paris 1967, pp. 251–2.
9 'Oscar Wilde's "Salomé"', N&Q 204 (Feb. 1959), 56–7.
10 *Letters*, p. 305.
11 *My Diaries. Being a Personal Narrative of Events 1888–1914*, New York 1932 [1921], p. 58.
12 The passage is printed in *Letters*, p. 305. Adolphe Retté's claims are confirmed by Stuart Merrill, 'Souvenirs sur le symbolisme', in *Prose et vers*, pp. 144–5.
13 See Mason, *Bibliography of Oscar Wilde*, p. 370; Ross, Preface to 'La Sainte Courtisane. A Florentine Tragedy', in *Works*, London 1909, p. ix; Gerda Taranow, *Sarah Bernhardt. The Art within the Legend*, Princeton, N.J., 1972, pp. 201–2.
14 *Letters*, p. 317, note 1.
15 Ibid., pp. 324–5; Mason, *Bibliography of Oscar Wilde*, pp. 374–5.
16 Preface in 'La Sainte Courtisane', p. viii.
17 See also Lemonnier, *Oscar Wilde*, p. 162; Merle, *Oscar Wilde*, p. 328.
18 Wilde later criticised Douglas for 'schoolboy faults' in the English translation. *Letters*, p. 432.
19 All *Salomé* illustrations, including those not reproduced in the first English edition, are collected in *A Portfolio of Aubrey Beardsley's Drawings Illustrating 'Salomé' by Oscar Wilde*, London n.d. [1907]. See also the reproductions, some with commentaries, in *Aubrey Beardsley. Zeichnungen. Drawings*, Berlin 1964 and 1966; Brian Reade, *Beardsley*. Introduction by John Rothenstein, Stuttgart 1969; Eric T. Haskell, 'L'Interprétation figurée. Les illustrateurs de la "Salomé" de Wilde', unpublished Ph.D. thesis, University of California, Irvine 1980: DA 40, no. 12, pt. 1, 1980, pp. 6263–6264-A; Elliot L. Gilbert, '"Tumult of Images". Wilde, Beardsley, and "Salome"', VS 26 (1983), 133–59.
20 See William Rothenstein, *Men and Memories. Recollections, 1872–1900*, London and New York 1931, p. 184.
21 For example, see Brasol, *Oscar Wilde*, p. 243: 'In their indignant reception of Wilde's tone drama, the "peacock skirt", the "stomach dance" and "the dancer's reward" played an important role, although these drawings, to which Wilde himself disparagingly referred as "naughty scribbles of a precocious schoolboy", do not in the least interpret the spirit of the play. What really happened was that the perversions of Beardsley's brush were all too readily, and in some cases, intentionally, mistaken for the wickedness of Oscar's pen'; Merle, *Oscar Wilde*, p. 333: 'son [Beardsley's] œuvre, dans l'ensemble,

dénonce, caricature, plutôt qu'elle éclaire, l'œuvre de Wilde' [his work in its overall effect denounces and caricatures rather than illuminates the work of Wilde]; St John Ervine, *Oscar Wilde*, p. 135: 'The English translation was disfigured and made repellent by sixteen [*sic*] illustrations, drawn by Aubrey Beardsley, which insidiously increased Wilde's reputation as a moral degenerate'; Lewis Broad, *The Friendship and Follies of Oscar Wilde*, London 1954, New York 1955, p. 108: 'Beardsley's were not pictures that illustrated the text, they were productions of his own imaginings.'

22 *Salomé*, p. 77. Unless otherwise stated, quotations are from the French text of *Salomé* as published in the first collected works of 1908. The English translation is by Lord Alfred Douglas.

23 The production on 13 May in the Bijou Theatre, Bayswater, was reviewed by Max Beerbohm, who expressed doubts as to whether the play was suitable for the theatre:

Certainly, it is a good 'stage play' so far as the technique of its author is concerned. But, for all that, it is not a good play for the stage. It is too horrible for definite and corporeal presentment. It should be seen only through the haze of our imagination. The bitter triumph of Salomé's lust for John the Baptist, as she kneels kissing the lips of the severed head, is a thing that we can read of, and vaguely picture to ourselves, with no more than the thrill of horror which tragedy may rightly inflict on us. But when we see the thing – when we have it illustrated to us in sharp detail by a human being – then we suffer something beyond the rightful tragic thrill: we suffer qualms of physical disgust.

'Salome', in *Around Theatres*, vol. 2, London 1924, pp. 141–2; see also Graham Good, 'Early Productions of Oscar Wilde's "Salome"', NCTR 11 (1983), 77–92.

24 *Salomé*, p. 27.
25 Ibid., p. 32 and p. 33.
26 Ibid., p. 59.
27 Ibid., p. 78.
28 Ibid., p. 82.
29 Ibid., p. 69.
30 Ibid., p. 71.
31 Ibid., p. 73.
32 *Salomé en la literatura*, Madrid 1919, pp. 51–2.
33 *Salomé*, p. 29.
34 'Oscar Wildes Salome. Eine kritische Quellenstudie', unpublished diss., Münster 1913, p. 64.
35 *Into the Demon Universe. A Literary Exploration of Oscar Wilde*, New Haven and London 1974, pp. 100–1.
36 *Salomé*, p. 78.
37 *Into the Demon Universe*, p. 92. The sadism expressed in this play is particularly stressed by Isador N. Coriat, 'The Sadism in Oscar Wilde's "Salomé"', PsyR 1 (1914), 257–9. He calls it 'one of the finest examples of the portrayal of the sadistic impulse in literature', p. 259.
38 *Salomé*, p. 79.
39 Ibid., p. 43.
40 Ibid., p. 70.
41 Ibid., p. 7 and elsewhere.
42 Ibid., p. 27.
43 On the moon symbol, see the essay by Nicholas Joost and Franklin E. Court,

'Salomé, the Moon, and Oscar Wilde's Aesthetics. A Reading of the Play', PLL 8, suppl. (1972), 96–111.

44 Salomé, p. 5.
45 Ibid., p. 22.
46 Ibid., p. 31.
47 Ibid., p. 5.
48 Ibid., p. 22.
49 Ibid., p. 35.
50 Into the Demon Universe, p. 109.
51 See, for example, the witch Sycorax in The Tempest, V.i.269ff; also King Henry IV, Part I, I.ii.30ff.
52 'These images [of precious gems, of sophisticated jewels] cluster around the key motifs of the novel, and chiefly stress the natural phenomena, among which the most important is of course the Moon', Victor Brombert, The Novels of Flaubert. A Study of Themes and Techniques, Princeton 1966, p. 106. On the moon motif in this novel, see also the study by Heidi Suhner-Schluep, 'L'Imagination du feu ou la dialectique du soleil et de la lune dans Salammbô de G. Flaubert', unpublished thesis, Zurich 1970.
53 Salomé, p. 81.
54 Letters, p. 590.
55 Salomé, pp. 7, 12, 15, 20, 31, 52, 76.
56 Ibid., pp. 36, 53, 59, 64, 73.
57 Ibid., pp. 27, 39, 59, 61, 73.
58 Ibid., p. 80.
59 Lemonnier, Oscar Wilde, p. 166.
60 Salomé, p. 24.
61 Ibid., p. 27.
62 Ibid., pp. 29–30.
63 Letters, p. 589.
64 Charles Baudelaire, Œuvres complètes. Text annotated by Y.-G. Le Dantec. Revised edition by Claude Pichois, Paris 1961, p. 1037.
65 Edmund Wilson, 'Symbolism', in Wilson, Axel's Castle. A Study in the Imaginative Literature of 1870–1930, London and New York 1950 [1931], p. 22.
66 Le Trésor des humbles, Paris 1896, pp. 173–4. On the Symbolist plays of Maeterlinck, see also May Daniels, The French Drama of the Unspoken, Edinburgh 1953, and Marcel Postic, Maeterlinck et le symbolisme, Paris 1970.
67 Letters, p. 756.
68 Preface in 'La Sainte Courtisane', p. x. Shortly after the publication of Salomé, a French critic pointed out the 'manière dramatique de Maurice Maeterlinck' that was discernible in the play; Bernard Lazare, 'Salomé', Epl 3 (Jan.–June 1893), 383. See also Katharine Worth, 'Evolution of European "Drama of the Interior". Maeterlinck, Wilde and Yeats', MuK 25 (1979), 161–70.
69 Oscar Wildes Salome, p. 79.
70 'A propos de la Salomé d'Oscar Wilde', ESt 51 (1917/18), 61. For a general account of the French influences on Salomé, see Hartley, Oscar Wilde, pp. 151–68; Schön, 'Französische Einflüsse in Oscar Wildes Werken', unpublished diss., Hamburg 1949, pp. 84ff.

71 *Complete Works*, p. 559.
72 *Salomé*, in *Complete Works*, p. 574.
73 Ibid., p. 559.
74 Ibid.
75 Ibid., p. 574.
76 Z. Raafat, 'The Literary Indebtedness of Wilde's "Salomé" to Sardou's "Théodora"', RLC 40 (1966), 453–66, tries to prove Sardou's influence independently of the Salome story, but his arguments are none too convincing. The fact that both plays contain a discussion on the existence of angels, which both Théodora and Hérodias find boring, can scarcely be taken as proof of influence.
77 Mark 6:20.
78 See the interpretation of the biblical episode and its historical background in Jean Psichari, 'Salomé et la décollation de Saint Jean-Baptiste', Rhr 72, nos. 1–2 (1915), 131–58.
79 Heinrich Heine, 'Atta Troll. Ein Sommernachtstraum', in *Sämtliche Schriften*, ed. by Klaus Briegleb, vol. 4, chap. 9, verse 106.
80 Ibid., verse 92.
81 Ibid., verse 114.
82 The poem appeared originally in a collection by former students of Trinity College, Dublin, and was reprinted by Max Meyerfeld, 'Wilde-Nachlese', LitE 8, no. 17 (1 June 1906), 1229.
83 *Hérodias*, in *Trois contes*. Chronology and preface by Jacques Suffel, Paris 1965, p. 180. Brenda M. Livingston, 'Oscar Wilde and the Tragic Mode', unpublished Ph.D. thesis, University of California 1972, p. 195, points out the similarity between the characterisation of Salome together with her relationship with John, and that of Salammbô and Mâtho in Flaubert's novel.
84 Merle, *Oscar Wilde*, p. 329.
85 'A propos de la Salomé d'Oscar Wilde', 52.
86 'Comment Oscar Wilde rêva Salomé', *La Plume* 14 (1902), 1152. On Moreau's representations of Salome and their artistic conception, see Ragnar von Holten, 'Le Développement du personnage de Salomé à travers les dessins de Gustave Moreau', *L'Œil*, no. 78–80 (1961), 45–51 and 72; Jean Paladilhe, *Gustave Moreau*, Paris 1971.
87 'Leonardo da Vinci', in *The Renaissance. Studies in Art and Poetry*. With an introduction by Kenneth Clark, London and Glasgow 1961, p. 122.
88 *A Rebours* (1884), Poitiers 1974, p. 86.
89 See A. J. L. Busst, 'The Image of the Androgyne in the Nineteenth Century', in *Romantic Mythologies*, ed. by Ian Fletcher, London 1967, p. 75.
90 Edmund Bergler, '"Salome", the Turning Point in the Life of Oscar Wilde', PsyR 43 (1956), 100.
91 Kate Millett, *Sexual Politics*, New York 1970, p. 153.
92 H. Ernstmann, *Salome an den deutschen Hofbühnen. Ein Kulturbild*, Berlin 1906, pp. 14–15. Equally wide of the mark are the comments of J. Abraham, *Salome oder 'Über die Grenzen der Dichtung'. Eine kritische Studie*, Berlin 1907, who takes the text far too literally. He obviously has little feel for its literary qualities, and often comes to rather extraordinary conclusions. Thus for instance he comments as follows on Salome's comparison of Jokanaan's hair to 'grappes de raisins' and 'cèdres de Liban' (p. 28):

Die weintraubenähnlichen Haare sind möglicherweise dadurch zu erklären, dass Iochanaan [sic] sich in der Zisterne nicht gründlich gewaschen und dadurch eine Art Weichselzopf erworben hat; aber der Vergleich war auch für ihn jedenfalls so haarsträubend, dass sie ihm zu Berge stehen, wie die Zedern des Libanon' (pp. 10–11).

[The fact that the hair is like clusters of grapes is perhaps to be explained by Iochanaan [sic] not having washed himself properly in the cistern and thus having acquired a sort of elflock; but in any case even he found the comparison so hair-raising that his hair stands on end like the cedars of Lebanon].

93 *The Picture of Dorian Gray.* The Preface.
94 'Oscar Wilde: The Poet of "Salome"', in *Oscar Wilde. A Collection of Critical Essays*, ed. by Richard Ellmann, Englewood Cliffs, N.J., 1969, p. 60.
95 *Letters*, p. 144, note 3. See also Sherard, *The Life of Oscar Wilde*, p. 238, and *The Real Oscar Wilde*, pp. 271–6. Ransome, *Oscar Wilde*, p. 74, concurs with Sherard's view that the poem was finished in 1883.
96 *Bibliography of Oscar Wilde*, p. 398, 'portions of this poem were written as early as the author's Oxford days (1874–1878)'. He believes that the time reference in verse 9 ('I have hardly seen / Some twenty summers') is to the poet's age when the poem was begun. He also notes that verse 9 recurs almost word for word in the prize-winning 'Ravenna' (1878). Alfred Douglas, *Oscar Wilde and Myself*, p. 173, also says that the poem was begun in Wilde's Oxford days, as does Charles Ricketts, *Oscar Wilde*, Bloomsbury 1932, p. 58: '"The Sphinx", though this was issued in 1894, was written at Oxford, enlarged and retouched at the time of publication.'
97 Farmer, *Le Mouvement esthétique et 'décadent' en Angleterre*, p. 237: 'Le poème est manifestement d'une époque très postérieure à 1883 … L'atmosphère du Sphinx, toute chargés de suggestions macabres et pleine de cette sensualité ambiguë qui s'entoure d'un rutilement d'ors et de pierreries, nous ramène également à *Salomé*. Il y a lieu de conclure, en conséquence, que l'œuvre a été composée vers 1890 ou 1891' [The poem clearly dates from a period much later than 1883 … The atmosphere of *The Sphinx*, pregnant with macabre suggestions and full of that ambiguous sensuality that is surrounded by a glow of gold and precious stones, is equally reminiscent of *Salomé*. There is therefore reason to believe that the work was composed around 1890 or 1891]. Merle, *Oscar Wilde*, p. 190, is of the same opinion.
98 See Holland, *Oscar Wilde. A Pictorial Biography*, p. 91.
99 See BL ADD. Ms 37942–48. On the first page there is a handwritten note by Charles Ricketts, giving details of how the manuscript was found: 'This manuscript was entirely lost sight of & forgotten for years. It was found again at Richmond in a portfolio containing old Dial manuscripts, proofs, etc., put carefully away, & again forgotten, till it was found in sorting the lumber which had been carted here and put in the garret. How it escaped being burnt in the bonfires which are coincident with our changes of home, I am unable to say.'
100 *Oscar Wilde. The Critical Heritage*, p. 168.
101 For a general account of the mythology of the Sphinx, see John G. Wilkinson, *The Manners and Customs of the Ancient Egyptians*, vol. 1, Boston 1883, pp. 93–4; Selim Hassan, *The Great Sphinx and its Secrets*, Cairo 1953; A. Dessenne, *Le Sphinx. Etude iconographique*, Paris 1957; Hans Walter, 'Sphingen', AntAb 9 (1960), 63–72; also a comprehensive study by Heinz

Demisch, *Die Sphinx. Geschichte ihrer Darstellung von den Anfängen bis zur Gegenwart*, Stuttgart 1977.

102 *Miscellanies*, p. 295.

103 See Jackson, *The Eighteen Nineties*, pp. 138ff, and Lothar Hönnighausen, *Präraphaeliten und Fin de Siècle. Symbolistische Tendenzen in der englischen Spätromantik*, Munich 1971, esp. pp. 184ff. English translation, *The Symbolist Tradition in English Literature: A Study of Pre-Raphaelitism and 'Fin de Siècle'*, Cambridge 1988.

104 *Retrospective Reviews. A Literary Log*, vol. 1, *1891–1893*, London 1896, pp. 229–30.

105 'Pen, Pencil and Poison', in *Complete Works*, p. 1001.

106 The extravagant style lent itself to parody, as evinced by [Ada Leverson], 'The Minx. – "A Poem in Prose"', *Punch*, 21 July 1894, p. 33, and Y.T.O., *Aristophanes at Oxford. O.W.*, Oxford [1894]. The latter, a play in verse that satirises Wilde, contains a passage that is an unmistakable parody of *The Sphinx*:

But tell me, what means this? this strange-shaped tent,
Like some Konak of Kirghiz by the flood
Of shallow Tarim? Does it hide the wealth
Of Eastern realms; divans from Samarcand;
Curtains from Cashmere's vale; chibouques inlaid
With lapis-lazuli from rich Altai;
Deep silent carpets wrought for Usbeg Khans
By captive Persian dames? Or shall my eyes
Feast upon houris, such as stirred the blood
Of young Shiraz, what time immortal Hafiz
Discoursed of wine and beauty?   (pp. 20–1)

107 William Wordsworth, *Preface to the Second Edition ... of 'Lyrical Ballads'*, in *The Poetical Works of Wordsworth*. With introductions and notes, ed. by Thomas Hutchinson. A new edition, revised by Ernest de Selincourt, London 1961, p. 735.

108 See Frank Kermode, *Romantic Image*, London 1961 [1957], pp. 49–91, and Hönnighausen, *Präraphaeliten und Fin de Siècle*, pp. 348–59.

109 'Le Chat', in *Œuvres complètes*, p. 61.

110 Almut Pohle, 'Sphinx und Chimäre. Zu einer Episode der "Tentation de Saint Antoine"', in *Aufsätze zur Themen- und Motivgeschichte. Festschr. für Hellmuth Petriconi zum siebzigsten Geburtstag*, Hamburg 1965, p. 141.

111 *Oscar Wilde*, p. 74.

112 *Oscar Wilde*, p. 173. Also Merle, *Oscar Wilde*, p. 191; H. N. Fairchild, *Religious Trends in English Poetry*, vol. V, *1880–1920*, New York and London 1962, p. 151, and Frank Brennand, *Oscar Wilde*, London 1960, pp. 80–1.

113 See Harris, *Oscar Wilde* (1959), pp. 289ff.

114 On exoticism in the nineteenth century, see Friedrich Brie, *Exotismus der Sinne. Eine Studie zur Psychologie der Romantik*, Heidelberg 1920 (Sitzungsberichte der Heidelberger Akademie der Wissenschaften. Phil.-hist. Klasse. 3. Abhandlung); Pierre Jourda, *L'Exotisme dans la littérature française depuis Chateaubriand*, 2 vols., Paris 1938–56; Raymond Schwab, *La Renaissance orientale*, Paris 1950. On the concept of exoticism in literary history, see also Wolfgang Reif, *Zivilisationsflucht und literarische Wunsch-*

träume. Der exotistische Roman im ersten Viertel des zwanzigsten Jahrhunderts, Stuttgart 1975, esp. pp. 1–33.

115 Brie, *Exotismus der Sinne*, p. 5.

116 See Fehr, *Studien zu Oscar Wilde's Gedichten*, pp. 179–95; Farmer, *Le Mouvement esthétique et 'décadent'*, p. 235 and B. Ifor Evans, *English Poetry in the Later Nineteenth Century*, London 1966 [1933], p. 399, both stress the influence of a scene in Huysmans's *A Rebours*, in which Des Esseintes gets his mistress to quote the dialogue between Sphinx and Chimera in Flaubert's 'La Tentation de Saint Antoine'. Hartley, *Oscar Wilde*, pp. 63ff, opposes this thesis, and points to the influence of Baudelaire's 'Le Chat' and Maurice Rollinat's poem with the same title in *Les Névroses*, Paris 1904 [1883], pp. 103–6. On p. 106, in the last verse, the cat is described as 'Panthère du foyer, tigre en miniature'.

117 See Brasol, *Oscar Wilde*, p. 157.

118 *Tales, Poems, Essays*. With an introduction by Laurence Meynell, London and Glasgow 1966 [1952], p. 442.

119 Ibid.

120 Ibid.

121 Iser, *Walter Pater*, p. 62.

122 Ernest Dowson, 'Cynara', in *The Albatross Book of Living Verse*, ed. by Louis Untermeyer, London and Paris 1947, p. 516.

123 Hans H. Hofstätter, *Symbolismus und die Kunst der Jahrhundertwende. Voraussetzungen, Erscheinungsformen, Bedeutungen*, Cologne 1973 [1965], p. 109.

124 *Präraphaeliten und Fin de Siècle*, p. 348. Koppen, *Dekadenter Wagnerismus*, p. 98, calls the sphinx motif 'beliebte erotische Chiffre der europäischen Literatur der Décadence und Prädécadence' [favourite erotic figure in the European literature of decadence and pre-decadence].

125 Murray, *Oscar Wilde's Imaginative Work in the Light of his Literary Theory*, p. 297.

126 Ibid., p. 289.

127 Holland, *Oscar Wilde. A Pictorial Biography*, p. 91.

128 Hesketh Pearson, *The Life of Oscar Wilde*, p. 92.

7 Pathos and paradox. *Lady Windermere's Fan, A Woman of No Importance* and *An Ideal Husband*

1 *De Profundis*, in *Complete Works*, p. 877.

2 Ibid., p. 876.

3 André Gide, 'Oscar Wilde', *L'Ermitage* (June 1902), 415.

4 See the section on *Theaterstücke* in the bibliography of the German edition of this book.

5 'Neuere Aufsätze zu Oscar Wildes Dramen', LWU 1 (1968), 59–68. See also the useful collection of essays assembled in *Oscar Wilde, Comedies. 'Lady Windermere's Fan', 'A Woman of No Importance', 'An Ideal Husband', 'The Importance of Being Earnest'. A Casebook*, ed. by William Tydeman, London 1982.

6 'Oscar Wilde, Lady Windermere's Fan', in Cleanth Brooks and Robert B. Heilman, *Understanding Drama*, New York 1948, pp. 34–82.

7 'Oscar Wilde, Lady Windermere's Fan', in *Das englische Drama. Vom Mittelalter bis zur Gegenwart*, ed. by Dieter Mehl, vol. 2, Düsseldorf 1970, pp. 153–72. See also the history of the play's composition and performance in Ian Small's introduction to his highly recommended edition: *Lady Windermere's Fan. A Play about a Good Woman*, London 1980. (The New Mermaids).
8 'Oscar Wilde: An Ideal Husband', in *Das englische Drama im 18. und 19. Jahrhundert. Interpretationen*, ed. by Heinz Kosok, Berlin 1976, pp. 318–33.
9 Paul Goetsch, *Bauformen des modernen englischen und amerikanischen Dramas*, Darmstadt 1977, p. 1.
10 Roditi, *Oscar Wilde*, p. 137; Ojala, *Aestheticism and Oscar Wilde*, pt 1, p. 185, actually speaks of 'two kinds of plays in Wilde's drama: the comedy of conversation ... and the melodrama which dealt with some moral or intellectual problem of the day'.
11 Merle, *Oscar Wilde* (1948), p. 348.
12 'The Dandiacal Drama. A Study of the Plays of Oscar Wilde', unpublished Ph.D. thesis, Columbia University, 1957: DA 18, no. 4, 1958, p. 1429.
13 'The Divided Self in the Society Comedies of Oscar Wilde', MD 3 (1960), 16.
14 Ibid.
15 'Comedy and Oscar Wilde', SeR 74 (1966), 501–21.
16 Ibid., 501.
17 Ibid.
18 Wilde's plots have been universally dismissed by critics. Jacob T. Grein, *Dramatic Criticism*, vol. III, *1900–1901*, London 1902, p. 80: 'the plot is of secondary importance'. Hagemann, *Oscar Wilde* (1904), p. 56: 'Die Handlung seiner Stücke ist meist unsagbar läppisch' [the plots of his plays are mostly unspeakably silly]. David Daiches, *A Critical History of English Literature*, vol. IV, London 1969, p. 1104: 'The plots are ridiculous, sometimes degenerating into cheap farce.'
19 *Oscar Wilde*, p. 355. G. Wilson Knight, *The Golden Labyrinth. A Study of British Drama*, London 1962, p. 307, also detects an autobiographical reference: 'Wilde's plays can in parts be read as oblique expressions of his inner torment, using Lord Illingworth and Sir Robert Chiltern as masks.'
20 Merle, *Oscar Wilde* (1948), p. 86.
21 Patrick Byrne, *The Wildes of Merrion Square. The Family of Oscar Wilde*, London 1953, p. 203.
22 Edmund Bergler, '"Salome". The Turning Point in the Life of Oscar Wilde', PsyR 43 (1956), 101.
23 *The Second Mrs Tanqueray* (1893), London 1936, p. 17. (French's Acting Edition).
24 *Lady Windermere's Fan*, in *Complete Works*, p. 405.
25 Ibid., p. 418.
26 *An Ideal Husband*, in ibid., p. 545.
27 *Lady Windermere's Fan*, in ibid., p. 413.
28 Erik H. Erikson, *Identität und Lebenszyklus*, Frankfurt/M. 1971, p. 124. On the concept of identity, see also George H. Mead, *Mind, Self and Society. From the Standpoint of a Social Behaviorist*, University of Chicago 1934; Anselm L. Strauss, *Mirrors and Masks. The Search for Identity*, Glencoe, Ill. 1959; David J. de Levita, *The Concept of Identity*, The Hague 1965. On treatments of the

theme of identity in nineteenth- and twentieth-century English literature, see Masao Miyoshi, *The Divided Self. A Perspective on the Literature of the Victorians*, New York and London 1969, and Robert Langbaum, 'The Mysteries of Identity. A Theme in Modern Literature', in *The Modern Spirit. Essays on the Continuity of Nineteenth- and Twentieth-century Literature*, London 1970, pp. 164–84. This essay first appeared in ASch 34 (1965), 569–86.

29 *Lady Windermere's Fan*, in *Complete Works*, p. 404.

30 *An Ideal Husband*, in ibid., p. 501.

31 'The Collected Plays of Oscar Wilde', FortR 83 (n.s.) (1908), 802.

32 Maximilian Rieger, 'Die Technik der Dramen Oscar Wildes', unpublished diss., Vienna 1923, p. 93, believes that in this act the 'innere Unlauterkeit des Stückes festgelegt ist' [the inner insincerity of the play is established]. On the other hand, Percival P. Howe, *Dramatic Portraits*, London 1913, reprinted Port Washington and New York 1969, p. 99, declares: 'The third act of *An Ideal Husband* really is the "greatest" of "great" scenes.'

33 *Lady Windermere's Fan*, in *Complete Works*, p. 387.

34 Peter Pütz, *Die Zeit im Drama. Zur Technik dramatischer Spannung*, Göttingen 1970, p. 16.

35 William Archer, in his recollections of the première, lays particular stress on Lady Windermere's instructions to her butler: 'Parker, be sure you pronounce the names of the guests very distinctly to-night' as being especially conducive to tension. He adds: 'when the curtain fell on the first act, a five-pound note would not have bribed me to leave the theatre without assisting at Lady Windermere's reception in the second act'. *Play-Making. A Manual of Craftsmanship*, New York 1960 [1912], p. 116.

36 'Lady Windermere's Fan', in Brooks and Heilman, *Understanding Drama*, pp. 34–82.

37 Norman James, 'Oscar Wilde's Dramaturgy', unpublished Ph.D. thesis, Duke University, 1959, p. 128.

38 *Understanding Drama*, p. 56.

39 *Lady Windermere's Fan*, in *Complete Works*, p. 414.

40 On such inconsistencies, see also St John Ervine, *Oscar Wilde*, London 1951, pp. 211ff.

41 *Understanding Drama*, p. 65. See also Archer, *Play-Making*, p. 254: 'the scene of the five men in the third act of *Lady Windermere's Fan* is a veritable running-fire of epigrams wholly unconnected with the situation, and very slightly related, if at all, to the characters of the speakers'.

42 *Lady Windermere's Fan*, in *Complete Works*, p. 417.

43 Ibid., p. 393.

44 Ibid., p. 421.

45 Ibid., p. 423.

46 Lady Windermere is conscious of this irony when she says: 'How strange! I would have publicly disgraced her [Mrs Erlynne] in my own house. She accepts public disgrace in the house of another to save me ... There is a bitter irony in things, a bitter irony in the way we talk of good and bad women ... Oh, what a lesson!' Ibid., p. 420.

47 Ibid., p. 430.

48 Ibid., p. 421.

49 'Le Dandy', in Baudelaire, Œuvres complètes, ed. by Marcel A. Ruff, Paris 1968, p. 560. On dandyism, see also Thomas Carlyle, 'The Dandiacal Body' (1838), in Sartor Resartus, London 1903, pp. 235–47; Barbey d'Aurevilly, 'Du Dandysme et de G. Brummell', in Œuvres romanesques complètes, ed. by J. Petit, vol. 2, Paris 1966, pp. 667–733; Otto Mann, Der Dandy. Ein Kulturproblem der Moderne, rev. edn, Heidelberg 1962 [1st edn under title Der moderne Dandy. Ein Kulturproblem des 19. Jahrhunderts, Heidelberg 1925]; Friedrich Schubel, Das englische Dandytum als Quelle einer Romangattung, Uppsala 1950; Ellen Moers, The Dandy. Brummell to Beerbohm, London 1960; Emil H. Maurer, 'Dandy, Snob und Kleinbürger', in Der Spätbürger, Bern 1963, pp. 158–63; Der Dandy, ed. by Oda Schaefer, Munich 1964; Helmut Kreuzer, Die Boheme. Beiträge zu ihrer Beschreibung, Stuttgart 1968; James Laver, Dandies, London 1968. (Pageant of History); E. Carassus, Le Mythe du dandy, Paris 1971; Hans Hinterhäuser, 'Der Dandy in der europäischen Literatur des 19. Jahrhunderts', in Weltliteratur und Volksliteratur, ed. by Albert Schaefer, Munich 1972, pp. 168–93. Rev. new edn under title 'Der Aufstand der Dandies', in Hans Hinterhäuser, Fin de siècle. Gestalten und Mythen, Munich 1977. The French dandy tradition has been surveyed by Gustav Koehler, Der Dandysmus im französischen Roman des XIX. Jahrhunderts, Halle 1911. (Beih. ZRPh 33); On the Wildean dandy, see Alfred L. Recoulley III, 'Oscar Wilde, the Dandy–Artist. A Study of Dandyism in the Life and Works of Oscar Wilde', unpublished Ph.D. thesis, Chapel Hill, N.C., 1968; Klaus-Dieter Herlemann, 'Oscar Wildes ironischer Witz als Ausdrucksform seines Dandysmus', unpublished diss., Freiburg im Brsg. 1972; Giovanna Franci, Il sistema del Dandy. Wilde–Beardsley–Beerbohm. (Arte e Artificio nell'Inghilterra fin-de-siècle), Bologna 1977; Michel Lemaire, Le Dandysme de Baudelaire à Mallarmé, Montreal 1978; Der Dandy. Texte und Bilder aus dem 19. Jahrhundert, ed. by Hans-Joachim Schickedanz, Dortmund 1980; Andreas Höfele, 'Dandy und New Woman', in Die 'Nineties. Das englische Fin de siècle zwischen Dekadenz und Sozialkritik, ed. by Manfred Pfister and Bernd Schulte-Middelich, Munich 1983, pp. 147–63; Dandy – Snob – Flaneur. Dekadenz und Exzentrik. Kulturfiguren und Sozialcharaktere des 19. und 20. Jahrhunderts, ed. by Gerd Stein, vol. 2, Frankfurt/M. 1985.

50 Thorstein Veblen, The Theory of the Leisure Class. An Economic Study of Institutions, New York 1899. Reprinted London 1970, p. 41. (Unwin Books).

51 See Max Wildi, 'Künstler und Gesellschaft in England, 1850–1900', in Individuum und Gemeinschaft. Festschr. zur Fünfzigjahrfeier der Handels-Hochschule St Gallen 1949, St Gallen 1949, pp. 605–28.

52 Mann, Der Dandy, p. 45.

53 A Woman of No Importance, in Complete Works, p. 445.

54 An Ideal Husband, in ibid., p. 488. Lady Chiltern also implies that Lord Goring is a dandy, ibid., p. 511.

55 'Good-for-nothing young son', p. 483. Elsewhere he refers to him as one of the 'unemployed', ibid., p. 540. Sir Robert Chiltern introduces him to Mrs Cheveley as follows: 'allow me to introduce to you Lord Goring, the idlest man in London', ibid., p. 488.

56 'A Dandy is a Clothes-wearing Man, a Man whose trade, office and existence

consists in the wearing of Clothes ... he lives to dress'. 'The Dandiacal Body', in *Sartor Resartus*, p. 235.

57 *An Ideal Husband*, in *Complete Works*, p. 522.

58 'Le dandysme n'est même pas, comme beaucoup de personnes peu réfléchies paraissent le croire, un goût immodéré de la toilette et de l'élégance matérielle. Ces choses ne sont pour le parfait dandy qu'un symbole de la supériorité aristocratique de son esprit' [Dandyism is not even – as many somewhat unthinking people seem to believe – an immoderate taste for dress and material elegance. These things for the perfect dandy are nothing but a symbol of the aristocratic superiority of his spirit]. Baudelaire, 'Le Dandy', in *Œuvres complètes*, p. 560.

59 Mann, *Der Dandy*, p. 41.

60 *An Ideal Husband*, in *Complete Works*, p. 489.

61 See for example Lord Darlington in *Lady Windermere's Fan:* 'I think it shows rather a sweet and modest disposition to pretend to be bad.' *Complete Works*, p. 386.

62 John Ruskin, 'Of Queens' Gardens', in *Works*, ed. by E. T. Cook and A. Wedderburn, vol. 18, p. 122. Quoted by Walter E. Houghton, *The Victorian Frame of Mind 1830–1870*, New Haven and London 1971 [1957], p. 343.

63 *An Ideal Husband*, in *Complete Works*, p. 548.

64 Chap. 10. In the Tauchnitz edn, Leipzig 1851, p. 150. Reference in Houghton, *The Victorian Frame of Mind*, p. 352.

65 *An Ideal Husband*, in *Complete Works*, p. 501.

66 *Understanding Drama*, p. 77.

67 'What did Lady Windermere Learn?' CE 18 (1956), 11–14.

68 *Lady Windermere's Fan*, in *Complete Works*, p. 421.

69 Ibid., p. 430.

70 *An Ideal Husband*, in *Complete Works*, p. 486.

71 Ibid., p. 527.

72 Ibid., p. 529. Similarly, Aubrey Tanqueray calls his daughter Ellean 'Saint Ellean' and elsewhere says: 'I don't believe a purer creature exists out of heaven.' Arthur Wing Pinero, *The Second Mrs Tanqueray* (1893), London 1936, p. 28 and p. 31. (French's Acting Edition).

73 *An Ideal Husband*, in *Complete Works*, p. 523.

74 Ibid., p. 549.

75 Ibid., p. 501.

76 Robert H. Sherard, *The Real Oscar Wilde*, London n.d. [1916], p. 325.

77 C.3.3. was Wilde's number, denoting that he was imprisoned in Block C, Cell 3 on the 3rd floor of Reading Gaol. In a letter to Robert Ross, dated 13 May 1897, he says of Constance: 'From the very first she forgave me, and was sweet beyond words to me.' *Letters*, pp. 541–2. This impression is confirmed by a letter written on 9 September 1895 by Otho Holland Lloyd, Constance's brother, in which he says: 'Yesterday she wrote him a few lines to tell him that there was forgiveness for him.' *Letters*, p. 872.

78 *An Ideal Husband*, in *Complete Works*, p. 484.

79 *Lady Windermere's Fan*, in ibid., p. 430; *A Woman of No Importance*, in ibid., p. 459.

80 *Lady Windermere's Fan*, in ibid., p. 402.

81 Ibid., p. 390.

82 Ibid., p. 405.
83 *Letters*, pp. 331–2.
84 *Lady Windermere's Fan*, in *Complete Works*, p. 425.
85 Ibid.
86 Ibid., p. 423.
87 Ibid., p. 425.
88 Ibid.
89 *An Ideal Husband*, in ibid., p. 495.
90 Ibid.
91 Ibid., p. 519.
92 Ibid., p. 495.
93 Ibid., p. 487.
94 Ibid., p. 519.
95 Ibid., p. 533.
96 Ibid., p. 531.
97 Ibid., p. 533.
98 Ibid., pp. 535–6.
99 See also Erika Meier, 'Realism and Reality. The Function of the Stage Directions in the New Drama from Thomas William Robertson to George Bernard Shaw', unpublished diss., Bern 1967, esp. chaps. 1 and 2.
100 *An Ideal Husband*, in *Complete Works*, p. 550.
101 *A Woman of No Importance*, in ibid., p. 474.
102 Ibid., p. 459.
103 Ibid., p. 475.
104 *The Life of Oscar Wilde*, p. 248.
105 *A Woman of No Importance*, in *Complete Works*, p. 457.
106 Ibid., p. 475.
107 Ibid., p. 457.
108 Ibid., p. 474.
109 Ibid., p. 475.
110 *Oscar Wilde. The Critical Heritage*, p. 147.
111 *Victorian People in Life and in Literature*, New York 1970, p. 73.
112 *Journal, 1889–1939*, p. 848.
113 *Letters*, p. 353.
114 Gerhard Bauer, *Zur Poetik des Dialogs. Leistung und Formen der Gesprächsführung in der neueren deutschen Literatur*, Darmstadt 1969, p. 53.
115 Merle, *Oscar Wilde* (1948), p. 201.
116 *De Profundis*, in *Complete Works*, p. 913.
117 *Complete Works*, p. 43.
118 'Wilde's "The Importance of Being Earnest"', in *The Muse in Council*, London 1925, p. 225.
119 'The Unimportance of Being Oscar', PR 14 (1947), 302.
120 Ibid. See also Lemonnier, *Oscar Wilde*, p. 188: 'La monotonie même de l'invention met en garde contre les comédies de Wilde' [The monotony even of the invention puts one on one's guard against Wilde's comedies].
121 Peter Szondi, *Theorie des modernen Dramas*, Frankfurt/M. 1968 [1956], p. 88.

122 *The Importance of Being Earnest*, in *Oscar Wilde's Plays, Prose Writings, and Poems*. Introduction by Hesketh Pearson, London/New York 1967 [1930], p. 355.
123 *An Ideal Husband*, in *Complete Works*, p. 522.
124 *Lady Windermere's Fan*, in ibid., pp. 397–8.
125 In Dieter Mehl (ed.), *Das englische Drama*, vol. 2, p. 162.
126 *An Ideal Husband*, in *Complete Works*, p. 495.
127 Ibid., p. 505.
128 Ibid., p. 519.
129 *Lady Windermere's Fan*, in ibid., p. 387.
130 Ibid., p. 404.
131 Ibid., p. 387.
132 Ibid., p. 388.
133 Ibid., p. 404.
134 Goetsch, *Bauformen*, p. 15.
135 *The Playwright as Thinker*, New York 1967 [1946], p. 141.
136 *A Woman of No Importance*, in *Complete Works*, p. 460.
137 *An Ideal Husband*, in ibid., p. 490.
138 Ibid., p. 484.
139 Ibid.
140 Ibid., p. 497.
141 *A Woman of No Importance*, in *Complete Works*, p. 449.
142 *Lady Windermere's Fan*, in ibid., p. 413.
143 Ibid., p. 386. Mrs Erlynne's demands on Lord Windermere are accompanied by a similar word-play: 'You have a delightful opportunity now of paying me a compliment, Windermere. But you are not very clever at paying compliments.' Ibid., p. 407.
144 Ibid., p. 427.
145 LORD DARLINGTON: ... Most women, for instance, nowadays, are rather mercenary.   (Ibid., p. 388)

   DUMBY: Awfully commercial, women nowadays. Our grandmothers threw their caps over the mills, of course, but, by Jove, their granddaughters only throw their caps over mills that can raise the wind for them.   (Ibid., p. 415)
146 Ibid., p. 397.
147 Ibid., p. 387.
148 Ibid., p. 400.
149 *A Woman of No Importance*, in *Complete Works*, p. 447.
150 Ibid., p. 473.
151 Ibid., p. 479.
152 Ibid., p. 463.
153 *Über den physiologischen Schwachsinn des Weibes*, Halle a.S. 1900, p. 7.
154 *Théâtre complet de Emile Augier*, vol. 7, Paris 1890, p. 267.
155 *A Woman of No Importance*, in *Complete Works*, p. 457.
156 Ibid., p. 449. Many different reasons have been advanced for this double standard. H. R. Hays offers an interesting explanation: 'the male's insistence on a monopoly of his wife's sexual services and the requirement that she be intact at marriage is involved with his feelings about private property. In the Middle Ages ... marriage was combined with the acquisition of property and continued to be in later periods ... It seems likely that the stubbornly

persisting double standard is really largely dependent upon male anxiety. Even as property, a woman's person is an extension of the male ego.' *The Dangerous Sex. The Myth of Feminine Evil*, London 1966, p. 289.

157 George Rowell, *The Victorian Theatre. A Survey*, London 1956, p. 104. Marvin Mudrick compares the audiences of the Restoration with those of the late nineteenth century, and comes to the following somewhat questionable conclusion:

> The Restoration comic dramatists had the advantage of the last English audience; and it was an accomplished audience, for whom manners were graces, and wit an exercise of the mind upon things in the world. Talking into the dark, one learns – as Wilde learned – to talk to oneself, and at length ceases to believe in talk altogether except as a kind of cheerful whistling. Laughter becomes more and more improbable, because there is no longer anything substantial to laugh at; and the comic dramatist – deprived of audience, deprived of subject and motive, deprived of any acceptable ideal of manners and decorum, deprived of everything but his own wit whirling in a void has gone as far as possible toward writing about nothing at all. 'Restoration Comedy and Later', in *English Stage Comedy. English Institute Essays 1954*, ed. by W. K. Wimsatt, jun., New York 1955, p. 125.

158 *The Theatre* 23 (1894), 326. Quoted by Joseph W. Donohue, Jr, 'The First Production of "The Importance of Being Earnest". A Proposal for a Reconstructive Study', in *Essays on Nineteenth Century British Theatre*, ed. by Kenneth Richards and Peter Thomson, London 1971, p. 139.

159 See Lynton Hudson, *The English Stage, 1850–1950*, London 1951, pp. 80–1. On the English theatre in the late nineteenth century, see Victor Glasstone, *Victorian and Edwardian Theatres. An Architectural and Social Survey*, London 1975; Michael R. Booth, 'East End and West End. Class and Audience in Victorian London', ThR 2, no. 2 (1977), 98–103; Madeleine Bingham, *Henry Irving and the Victorian Theatre*. Foreword by John Gielgud, London 1978; George Rowell, *Theatre in the Age of Irving*, Oxford 1981; Walter Kluge, 'Das Theater der 'Nineties', in *Das englische Fin de siècle zwischen Dekadenz und Sozialkritik*, ed. by Manfred Pfister and Bernd Schulte-Middelich, Munich 1983, pp. 275–94; James Woodfield, *English Theatre in Transition 1881–1914*, London 1984.

160 *Modern Men and Mummers*, London 1921, pp. 80–1.

161 Ibid., p. 80.

162 Frank B. Hanson, 'London Theatre Audiences of the Nineteenth Century', unpublished Ph. D. thesis, Yale University, 1953, pp. 426–7.

163 Hesketh Pearson, *Beerbohm Tree. His Life and Laughter*, London 1956, p. 67.

164 According to George A. H. Sala, *Living London. Being 'Echoes' Re-echoed*, London 1883, p. 36, the first-nighters were a particularly elite circle of 'ladies and gentlemen of high social standing, literary and artistic eminence, or general intellectual culture, whom you are at liberty to call the "Upper Five Hundred", or "la Crème de la Crème", or "la Fine Fleur" but who in the *argot* of the Theatrical World are brutally but comprehensively styled "First Nighters".

165 Diana Howard, *London Theatres and Music Halls 1850–1950*, London 1970, p. 32.

166 W. Macqueen-Pope, *St James's. Theatre of Distinction*. With a foreword by Vivien Leigh, London 1958. See also Alfred E. W. Mason, *Sir George*

Alexander & the St James' Theatre, New York and London 1935. Reprinted 1969; Barry Duncan, *The St James's Theatre. Its Strange & Complete History 1835–1957*. With a foreword by Allardyce Nicoll, London 1964; Raymond Mander and Joe Mitchenson, *The Lost Theatres of London*, London 1968, pp. 451–84.

167 Macqueen-Pope, *St James's*, p. 124.

168 Ibid., p. 16.

169 Robert H. Sherard, *The Life of Oscar Wilde*, London 1911 [1906], p. 289; Pearson, *The Life of Oscar Wilde*, p. 223: 'Nothing to compare with it [the success of *Lady Windermere's Fan*] had been seen on the English stage since Sheridan's *The School for Scandal*, about 120 years before.' Charles Brookfield and J. M. Glover even wrote a musical satire on the play called *The Poet and the Puppets*.

170 Quoted by Pearson, *Life*, p. 224. The italicised words are particularly stressed, according to information given by George Alexander to Wilde's biographer Pearson.

171 *Miscellanies*, pp. 168–9.

172 *Letters*, p. 309. The change suggested by Alexander was also supported later by William Archer, one of the most renowned theatre critics of the time. In his book *Play-Making* he argues that it is pointless to preserve a secret which, when revealed, could only disappoint the audience by giving them the feeling that it was all a joke and their expectations as regards the genuineness of a problem had been ignored. He adds:

> It is not improbable (though my memory is not clear on the point) that part of the strong interest we undoubtedly felt on the first night arose from the hope that Lord Windermere's seemingly unaccountable conduct might be satisfactorily accounted for. As this hope was futile, there was no reason, at subsequent performances, to keep up the pretence of preserving a secret which was probably known as a matter of fact, to most of the audience, and which was worthless when revealed.' *Play-Making*, p. 202.

173 *Miscellanies*, pp. 164–6.

174 Anon., in *Oscar Wilde. The Critical Heritage*, p. 129.

175 Frederick Wedmore, in ibid., p. 129.

176 Arthur B. Walkley, in ibid., p. 119.

177 Justin H. McCarthy, in ibid., p. 131.

178 Walkley, in ibid., p. 120.

179 Anon., in ibid., p. 127.

180 Anon., in ibid., p. 130.

181 Anon., in ibid., p. 127 and p. 129.

182 Anon., in ibid., p. 130.

183 Anon., in ibid., p. 127.

184 Mason, *Sir George Alexander & the St James' Theatre*, p. 83.

185 According to Alan Harris, 'Oscar Wilde as Playwright. A Centenary Review', *Adelphi* 30 (1954), p. 223, Wilde earned about £7,000 from the play.

186 See W. Macqueen-Pope, *Haymarket. Theatre of Perfection*, London 1948, and Raymond Mander and Joe Mitchenson, *The Theatres of London*. Illustrated by Timothy Birdsall, London 1961, pp. 95–102. See also Douglas M. Berry, 'Her Majesty's Theatre. The Relationship of Playhouse Design and Audience', ThS (Ohio) 26/27 (1979/80 – 1980/81), 135–51.

187 Macqueen-Pope, *Haymarket. Theatre of Perfection*, London 1948.

188 Ibid., p. 336.
189 See *Letters*, p. 338, note 1; Mason, *Bibliography*, p. 403.
190 Pearson, *Beerbohm Tree*, p. 71.
191 See *Letters*, p. 320, note 5.
192 *Oscar Wilde. The Critical Heritage*, p. 154.
193 Ibid., p. 159.
194 *De Profundis*, in *Complete Works*, p. 875.
195 Ibid.
196 *Letters*, p. 352.
197 Ibid.
198 Mason, *Bibliography*, p. 438.
199 *Letters*, p. 669.
200 Ibid., p. 765, note 2.
201 Mason, *Sir George Alexander & the St James' Theatre*, pp. 90–1.
202 *The Speaker*, 12 Jan. 1895, in *Oscar Wilde. The Critical Heritage*, p. 179.
     Beckson's collection also contains the following reviews: H. G. Wells, *Pall
     Mall Gazette*, 4 Jan. 1895; William Archer, *Pall Mall Budget*, 10 Jan. 1895;
     George Bernard Shaw, *Saturday Review*, 12 Jan. 1895; Clement Scott,
     Illustrated London News, 12 Jan. 1895; Henry James, [letter of 2 Feb.
     1895]; William Dean Howells, *Harper's Weekly*, 30 March 1895.
203 Arthur B. Walkley, in *Oscar Wilde. The Critical Heritage*, p. 179. *Punch* said
     it was 'an unmistakable success', 2 Feb. (1895), 54. H. G. Wells commented
     on its excellent reception, *Pall Mall Gazette*, p. 3. Even Henry James had to
     agree that it had been a great success, though this led him to dark and, as it
     turned out, justified premonitions about how an audience that enjoyed such a
     play might react to his own, *Guy Domville*, whose première took place just
     two days afterwards at the St James's Theatre. In fact *Guy Domville* was a
     failure, running from 5 Jan. until 2 Feb., when it was replaced by *The
     Importance of Being Earnest*.
204 *Oscar Wilde. The Critical Heritage*, p. 173. Also in *The Theatrical 'World'
     of 1895*, London 1896, p. 14.
205 *Pall Mall Gazette*, p. 3.
206 *Oscar Wilde. The Critical Heritage*, p. 177.
207 Ibid., p. 181 and p. 178.
208 *The Theatrical 'World' of 1895*, p. 18.
209 *Oscar Wilde. The Critical Heritage*, p. 178.
210 *Athenaeum* 3507, 12 Jan. (1895), 57.
211 'The Play and the Problem', in *Oscar Wilde. The Critical Heritage*, p. 184.
212 Ibid., p. 176.
213 Mason, *Sir George Alexander & the St James' Theatre*, p. 31.
214 Also compare *A Woman of No Importance*, in *Complete Works*, pp. 436,
     437, 441, 458, 460, 463 with *The Picture of Dorian Gray*, in ibid., pp. 32,
     40, 43, 48, 137, 150.
215 *A Woman of No Importance*, in ibid., pp. 435–6.
216 *The Picture of Dorian Gray*, in ibid., p. 136.
217 *Oscar Wilde. The Critical Heritage*, p. 122.
218 Paris, n.d., p. 28.
219 'Oscar Wilde. L'Influence française dans son œuvre', unpublished thesis,
     Paris 1935, p. 130. As regards the influence of French drama on Wilde, see

also H. Stanley Schwarz, 'The Influence of Dumas fils on Oscar Wilde', FR 7 (1933), 5–25; Eduard Schön, 'Französische Einflüsse in Oscar Wildes Werken', unpublished diss., Hamburg 1949; Zeinab M. Raafat, 'The Influence of Scribe and Sardou upon English Dramatists in the 19th Century, with Special Reference to Pinero, Jones and Wilde', unpublished Ph.D. thesis, 2 vols., University of London, Birkbeck College, 1970, esp. chap. 8.

220 In *Théâtre complet de Emile Augier*, vol. 7, Paris 1890, p. 197.

221 *The Illustrated London News*, 12 Jan. 1895, p. 35.

222 *Oscar Wilde*, p. 337.

223 *An Ideal Husband*, in *Complete Works*, p. 493.

224 See André Siegfried, *Suez and Panama*. Translated from the French by Henry H. and Doris Hemming, New York 1940, p. 275.

225 Ibid., p. 277.

226 The fact that Wilde speaks of an 'Argentine' canal project may be connected with the critical development of economic relations between England and Argentina in the early 1890s, reaching a peak with the Baring crisis. See Henry S. Ferns, *Britain and Argentina in the Nineteenth Century*, Oxford 1960, esp. pp. 436ff.

227 On the theory and history of this genre see John R. Taylor, *The Rise and Fall of the Well-Made Play*, London 1967; William L. Taitte, 'The Structural Debt of the English Well-Made Play to the "pièce bien faite" and to Melodrama', unpublished Ph.D. thesis, Princeton University, 1975.

228 Szondi, *Theorie des modernen Dramas*, p. 89.

229 Ibid.

230 For a general account of this genre, see M. Willson Disher, *Melodrama. Plots that thrilled*, London 1954; Michael R. Booth, *English Melodrama*, London 1965; Frank Rahill, *The World of Melodrama*, University Park, Pa., and London 1967; Heinz Kosok, 'Drama und Theater im 19. Jahrhundert', in *Das englische Drama*, ed. by Josefa Nünning, Darmstadt 1973, pp. 362–71; James L. Smith, *Melodrama*, London 1973. (The Critical Idiom. 28); Kurt Tetzeli von Rosador, *Victorian Theories of Melodrama*, Anglia 95 (1977), 87–114; Michael R. Booth, *Victorian Spectacular Theatre, 1850–1910*, Boston 1981; Joachim Möller, 'Arrangierte Wirklichkeit. Viktorianische Melodramen als Lebenshilfe', GRM 34 (1984), 103–16.

231 *The Life of the Drama*, London 1969 [1965], p. 205.

232 *A Woman of No Importance*, in *Complete Works*, p. 469.

233 For a general account see Ramsden Balmforth, *The Problem Play and its Influence on Modern Thought and Life*, London 1928; Martin Ellehauge, 'The Initial Stages in the Development of the English Problem-Play', ESt 66 (1932), 373–401; Henry F. Salerno, 'The Problem Play. Some Aesthetic Considerations', ELT 11 (1968), 195–205; Paul Goetsch, 'Das englische Drama seit Shaw', in *Das englische Drama*, ed. by Josefa Nünning, esp. pp. 407–17; Elliott M. Simon, *The Problem Play in British Drama, 1890–1914*, Salzburg 1978

234 Ellehauge, 'Initial Stages', p. 373.

235 *Love's Labour's Lost*, v, ii. 406. Arden edition.

236 See Mary E. G. Marino, 'William Congreve and Oscar Wilde. A Comparative Study of their Social Comedy', unpublished Ph.D. thesis, Purdue University 1974: DA 35, no. 6, 1974, p. 3691 – A.

237 *A Woman of No Importance*, in *Complete Works*, p. 460.
238 'Ibsen discovered theatrical reality, and he made it so real that half the opposition to his drama was due to the discomfort most people experience when brought face to face with a new revelation of facts or ideas. Those who compromised achieved no such effect; they were merely illusionists, using reality to further illusion, rather than illusion to further reality.' Holbrook Jackson, *The Eighteen Nineties. A Review of Art and Ideas at the Close of the Nineteenth Century*. With an introduction by Karl Beckson, New York 1966 [1913], p. 213.
239 *Lady Windermere's Fan*, in *Complete Works*, p. 421.

8 Propriety and parody. *The Importance of Being Earnest*

 1 Ada Leverson, *Letters to the Sphinx from Oscar Wilde, with Reminiscences of the Author*, London 1930, p. 26. On relations between Ada Leverson and Wilde, see Charles Burkhart, 'Ada Leverson and Oscar Wilde', ELT 13 (1970), 193–200.
 2 *Dramatic Criticism*, vol. III, *1900–1901*, London 1902, p. 264. After Wilde's arrest, his name was covered over on the posters and made illegible on the handbills, although it may be assumed that all the theatre-goers knew who had written the play. There could scarcely have been a more vivid illustration of the Victorian hypocrisy which is so devastatingly satirised by the play itself. Pearson, *Life of Oscar Wilde*, p. 293, comments: 'the Victorians were quite willing to laugh so long as they could pretend that their laughter was not due to the man who had provoked it; and Alexander pandered to their hypocrisy'.
 3 Pearson, *Life of Oscar Wilde*, p. 257.
 4 James Agate, *The Dating of Plays*, in *The Amazing Theatre*, London 1939. Reprinted New York and London 1969, pp. 220–2.
 5 Oscar Wilde, Jean Anouilh, Claude Vincent, *Il est important d'être aimé*, Paris 1954. See also Franz Zaic, 'Zu Anouilhs Bearbeitung von Oscar Wildes "The Importance of Being Earnest"', DNS 8 (n.s.) (1959), 219–25. Zaic concludes that Anouilh's adaptation is a good deal cruder than the original (see 223).
 6 *Black and White*, 16 Feb. 1895, p. 210. See also Mason, *Bibliography*, p. 433, and Pearson, *Life of Oscar Wilde*, p. 258.
 7 One example is the anonymous review published in *Theatre*: 'Stripped of its "Oscarisms" – regarded purely as a dramatic exercise – it is not even a good specimen of its class. The story is clumsily handled, the treatment unequal, the construction indifferent, while the elements of farce, comedy, and burlesque are jumbled together with a fine disregard for consistency.' *Oscar Wilde. The Critical Heritage*, p. 200.
 8 *Pall Mall Gazette*, 15 Feb. 1895, p. 4, in *Oscar Wilde. The Critical Heritage*, p. 187.
 9 *New York Times*, 17 Feb. 1895, in *Oscar Wilde. The Critical Heritage*, p. 189.
10 *Truth*, 21 Feb. 1895, p. 464, in *Oscar Wilde. The Critical Heritage*, p. 191.
11 George Bernard Shaw, 'My Memories of Oscar Wilde', in Frank Harris, *Oscar Wilde*, 1959, pp. 332–3.
12 *Oscar Wilde. The Critical Heritage*, p. 195.
13 On the history of the play's composition, see H. Montgomery Hyde, '"The

Importance of Being Earnest". The "lost" scene from Oscar Wilde's Play', *The Listener*, 4 Nov. 1954, pp. 753–4. [Reprints a scene from the four-act version which was later cut]; Anon., 'Penultimate "Earnest"', BNYPL 60 (1956), 422–3; William W. Appleton, 'Making a Masterpiece', SatR, 12 May 1956, p. 21; Theodore Bolton, [review of] *Oscar Wilde, The Importance of Being Earnest. A Trivial Comedy for Serious People, in Four Acts as Originally Written, by Oscar Wilde*, ed. by Sarah A. Dickson, 2 vols., New York, 1956, in PBSA 50 (1956), 205–8; Sarah A. Dickson, Introduction, in *The Importance of Being Earnest. A Trivial Comedy for Serious People, in Four Acts as Originally Written, by Oscar Wilde*, vol. I, New York 1956; David V. Erdman, 'The Importance of Publishing "Earnest"', BNYPL 60 (1956), 368–72; Anon., 'Wilde's Comedy in its First Version', TLS, 1 March 1957, p. 136; Vyvyan Holland, Explanatory Foreword, in *The Original Four-Act Version of 'The Importance of Being Earnest'*, London 1957, pp. v–xiii; Paul C. Wadleigh, '"Earnest" at St James's Theatre', QJS 52 (1966), 58–62; E. H. Mikhail, 'The Four-Act Version of "The Importance of Being Earnest"', MD 11 (1968/69), pp. 263–6; Joseph W. Donohue, Jr, 'The First Production of "The Importance of Being Earnest". A Proposal for a Reconstructive Study', in *Essays on Nineteenth Century British Theatre*, ed. by Kenneth Richards and Peter Thomson, London 1971, pp. 125–43. See also the introduction to Russell Jackson's highly commended edition, *The Importance of Being Earnest. A Trivial Comedy for Serious People*, London 1980. (The New Mermaids). Ruth H. Berggren has recently compiled 'Oscar Wilde's "The Importance of Being Earnest". A Critical Edition of the Four-Act Version', 2 vols., unpublished Ph.D. thesis, University of Massachusetts, 1984 n: DA 45, no. 2, 1984, p. 524-A.

14 *Letters*, pp. 360, 364, 365.
15 Explanatory Foreword, in *The Original Four-Act Version of 'The Importance of Being Earnest'*, p. v.
16 *Letters*, p. 375.
17 Ibid., p. 376.
18 Explanatory Foreword, *The Original Four-Act Version of "The Importance of Being Earnest"*, p. vi.
19 'The First Production of "The Importance of Being Earnest"', in *Essays on Nineteenth Century British Theatre*, p. 133.
20 *Letters*, p. 734.
21 It is incomprehensible that the original four-act version should have been used in the popular single-volume student edition of Wilde's works first published in 1948 by Collins. In the 1966 edition, Vyvyan Holland gives the following explanation for this extraordinary decision: 'When ... Leonard Smithers published the play in book form, it was this three-act version that he had printed, and each subsequent edition has followed his pattern. Why this has been so is not clear, but the play as written by Oscar Wilde, with two extra characters in it, is the play as given in this volume. As Mr Philip Drake, who is responsible for this edition of Wilde's works, remarked, it seems a pity that George Alexander should have a permanent influence on the play.' Introduction, p. 13. This argument is untenable, because by his approval of the three-act version performed, and also by the publication which he supervised himself, Wilde clearly indicated that he had accepted George Alexander's

suggested cuts and had made them his own. Only the three-act version therefore corresponds to the author's final intentions. The irony of the title should not, perhaps, have had quite so much influence on the earnestness of the editor's work.

22 Robert Merle, *Oscar Wilde*, p. 344, believes that the play is 'une sorte de parodie' of Dumas Fils's *Fils naturel*: 'Les deux Jacques, en effet Jacques Vignot et Jack Worthing, le fils naturel et l'enfant trouvé, sont tous deux victimes d'un même préjugé social, et ne peuvent, à cause du mystère qui entoure leur naissance, épouser celle qu'ils aiment' [The two Jacks, that is, Jacques Vignot and Jack Worthing, the illegitimate son and the foundling, are both victims of a similar social prejudice and, because of the mystery surrounding their birth, are unable to marry the girl they love]. But the mere fact that two young men cannot marry the girl of their choice because of social prejudice is such a common literary theme that one really cannot take it as indicating a connection between two otherwise totally different plays. Werner Vordtriede, 'A Dramatic Device in "Faust" and "The Importance of Being Earnest"', MLN 70 (1955), 584–5, detects a similarity between the scenes in Marthe's house and garden in *Faust I* and Act 2 of *Earnest*.

23 'The Importance of Reading Alfred. Oscar Wilde's Debt to Alfred Musset', BNYPL 75 (1971), 506–42.

24 Ibid., 513.

25 *In ne faut jurer de rien. Comédie en trois actes* (1836), in *Œuvres complètes de Alfred de Musset*, vol. iv, Paris 1866, p. 340.

26 Paul and Pepper, 'The Importance of Reading Alfred', 520.

27 'Realism and Reality. The Function of the New Drama . . .', unpublished diss., Basel 1967, pp. 184–5.

28 *Engaged. An Entirely Original Farcical Comedy in Three Acts*, in *Original Plays by W. S. Gilbert*, 2nd ser., London 1920, p. 81.

29 Quotations in this chapter from the following edition: *Oscar Wilde's Plays, Prose-Writings, and Poems*. Introduction by Hesketh Pearson, London and New York 1967. (Everyman Paperback. 1858).

30 *Engaged*, pp. 81–2.

31 Act I, p. 354.

32 James M. Ware, 'Algernon's Appetite. Oscar Wilde's Hero as Restoration Dandy', ELT 13 (1970), 17, sees parallels to 'appetite-satisfaction motifs' in different Restoration comedies, esp. the character of Dorimant in Etherege's *The Man of Mode* (1676).

33 St. John Ervine, *Oscar Wilde*, London 1951, p. 287.

34 Act 1, p. 361.

35 Act 3, p. 399.

36 *Oscar Wilde. The Critical Heritage*, p. 191.

37 Ibid., p. 190.

38 *Past and Present* (1843), London 1897, bk III, chap. 13, p. 209. (Centenary ed).

39 *Ernest Pontifex or The Way of All Flesh*, ed. by Daniel F. Howard, London 1965, p. 69.

40 Names fascinated Wilde (*Letters*, p. 252). The characters in this play sometimes have names with meanings, such as Prism, Chasuble, and Merriman, or place-names such as Worthing or Bracknell (after the Marchioness of Queens-

berry's country estate). The name of Lane for Algernon's servant was possibly chosen with Wilde's publisher John Lane in mind – according to Pearson, Wilde did not like him. *Life of Oscar Wilde*, p. 229. William Green, *Oscar Wilde and the Bunburys*, MD 21 (1978), 67–80, discovered two models for Bunbury: 'In essence, I believe Wilde's Bunbury to be a composite of Henry Shirley [Bunbury] and Edward Herbert [Bunbury]. The imaginary Bunbury has something of both men in him', 74.

41 Act 1, p. 361.
42 Act 3, p. 390.
43 *De Profundis*, in *Complete Works*, pp. 880–1.
44 *Complete Works*, p. 982. The reversal of the man's role in relations between the sexes is also clear from Gwendolen's description of her father and his domestic life:

GWENDOLEN: Outside the family circle, papa, I am glad to say, is entirely unknown. I think that is quite as it should be. The home seems to me to be the proper sphere for the man. And certainly once a man begins to neglect his domestic duties he becomes painfully effeminate, does he not? (Act 2, p. 381).

45 Act 3, p. 393.
46 Act 1, p. 360.
47 Act 1, p. 361.
48 See Patrick Braybrooke, *Oscar Wilde. A Study*, London 1930, p. 24: 'Lady Bracknell is the type of person who would be quite sure that Bloomsbury was in London, and Heaven would be a bore to her if it did not contain Ascot week.'
49 Act 1, p. 355.
50 Act 1, p. 358.
51 Act 3, p. 394.
52 Act 3, p. 399.
53 See Arthur H. Nethercot, 'Prunes and Miss Prism', MD 6 Sept. (1963), 112–16. Nethercot believes that Wilde took the name of Miss Prism and her therewith associated attitude (prim, prissy) from book 2 of Dickens' *Little Dorrit* (1857). There the expression 'prunes and prism' occurs several times, once indeed in the chapter heading 'Mostly, Prunes and Prism'. This expression became quite common, referring to 'a prim and mincing manner of speech': SOED, under 'prune'. Nethercot also finds parallels between Miss Prism and Mrs General's style of upbringing. Less convincing is the attempt by E. B. Partridge, 'The Importance of not being Earnest', BuR 9 (1958), 153, to interpret the word through the dramatic function of the character herself: 'Since a prism is a transparent body used for decomposing light into its spectrum, "Prism" is as optically accurate a name for an agent of *anagnorisis* as even Aristophanes could invent.'
54 Act 2, p. 372.
55 Act 3, p. 400.
56 This recognition scene could also be regarded as a parody on the classical *anagnorisis*, which had been so common in Greek drama since the famous version of the motif in Homer's *Odyssey* (nineteenth canto), and which Aristotle treated theoretically in the fourteenth and sixteenth chapters of his *Poetics*.
57 'The Decay of Lying', in *Complete Works*, p. 975.

58 Act 2, pp. 381 and 383–4.
59 Act 2, pp. 380–1.
60 'The Courtship Dance in "The Importance of Being Earnest"', MD 1 (1959), 256. See a detailed analysis of the Gwendolen–Cecily dialogue (Act 2, pp. 381ff) in J. L. Styan, *The Elements of Drama*, Cambridge 1969 [1960], pp. 20–4 and 142–6.
61 Act 2, p. 384.
62 Act 2, p. 386.
63 *Le Rire*, Paris 1947, p. 29.
64 Act 3, p. 391.
65 Act 1, pp. 354–5.
66 The German translation 'aus Gram ganz erblondet' [quite blonde from grief] misses the witty point of the paradox. See Oscar Wilde, *Bunbury*, translated by Franz Blei and revised and supplemented by Kuno Epple, Stuttgart 1968, p. 13 (Reclam. 8498).
67 Act 1, p. 355.
68 Osbert Burdett, *The Beardsley Period. An Essay in Perspective*, London 1925, p. 40.
69 The original passage, translated, reads as follows:

This religious prudery often leads to hypocrisy. I know an important businessman in London who comes to Paris twice a year on business; there he is very gay and amuses himself on Sundays just as freely as anyone else. His Parisian host comes to his home in London, is very well received, and on Sunday, having come downstairs to the salon, pushes a ball on a little billiard table for ladies. And straight away there is the businessman, greatly alarmed, stopping the game: 'How scandalous! Supposing the neighbours heard!' – On his next trip he takes his wife and daughters to Paris; no more gaiety, no more letting down of the hair; no more entertainments on a Sunday; he is stiff, buttoned up, exemplary. His religion is an official costume. *Notes sur l'Angleterre*, Paris 1885 [1871], pp. 260–1.

70 Otto Reinert, 'Satiric Strategy in "The Importance of Being Earnest"', CE 18 (1956), 17, defines Bunburying as meaning 'to invent a fictitious character, who can serve as a pretext for escaping a frustrating social routine, regulated by a repressive convention'.
71 Act 1, p. 352.
72 Ibid.
73 Act 2, p. 387.
74 Act 2, p. 376.
75 See H. Montgomery Hyde, *Oscar Wilde. Famous trials*, seventh ser., Harmondsworth 1962 [1948], p. 60.
76 See Franz Zaic, 'Oscar Wilde: The Importance of Being Earnest', in *Das moderne englische Drama*, ed. by Horst Oppel, Berlin 1963, pp. 44–61; also Arthur H. Nethercot, 'Oscar Wilde and the Devil's Advocate', PMLA 59 (1944), 833–50.
77 Zaic, 'The Importance of Being Earnest', p. 45.
78 Ibid., p. 48.
79 Act 1, p. 352.
80 John Gielgud, *Stage Directions*, London 1963, p. 83. On production style for this play, see pp. 78–84. See also Max Beerbohm, '"The Importance of Being Earnest"', in *Around Theatres*, vol. I, London 1924, pp. 331–6.
81 Pearson, *Life of Oscar Wilde*, p. 254.

82 Such critics include, amongst many others: Mary McCarthy, 'The Unimportance of Being Oscar', PR 14 (1947), 303: 'Wilde's most original play';
W. H. Auden, 'A Playboy of the Western World. St Oscar, the Homintern
Martyr', PR 17 (1950), 394: 'the one work of Wilde's upon the excellence of
which we can all agree'; San Juan, *The Art of Oscar Wilde*, p. 180: 'his most
perfect play'. One exception is the astonishing judgment of Carl Hagemann.
He claims that the play is 'nichts wert' [worthless] and is nothing but a lame
farce of confusion, 'die breit, langweilig und witzlos an uns vorüberzieht'
[which long-windedly, boringly and witlessly passes us by]. *Oscar Wilde.
Studien zur modernen Weltliteratur*, Minden 1904, p. 79.
83 *Oscar Wilde*, London, 1907, p. 150.
84 *A Study of Oscar Wilde*, London 1930, p. 75.
85 Introduction, in *Oscar Wilde's Plays, Prose-Writings, and Poems*, p. xiv.
86 *Oscar Wilde*, p. 140.
87 Léon Lemonnier, 'Oscar Wilde et l'importance d'être sévère', RAA 10
(1932/33), 413; Robert J. Jordan, 'Satire and Fantasy in Wilde's "The
Importance of Being Earnest"', *Ariel* 1 (1970), 104.
88 Richard Foster, 'Wilde as Parodist. A Second Look at "The Importance of
Being Earnest"', CE 18 (1956), 18–23.
89 Partridge, 'The Importance of Being Earnest', 153.
90 Arthur Ganz, 'The Meaning of "The Importance of Being Earnest"', MD 6
(1963), 49.
91 Zaic, 'The Importance of Being Earnest', p. 45.
92 Harold E. Toliver, 'Wilde and the Importance of "Sincere and Studied
Triviality"', MD 5 (1963), 394.
93 'Serious Bunburyism. The Logic of "The Importance of Being Earnest"', EIC
26 (1976), 31: 'If the metalinguistic structure of the play and the characters is
not grasped, then not only is the nature of the play unrealized, but the play and
the characters *look* too fragile to handle, and consequently its beautiful
substructures – social and general human satire on food and power, religion,
death and resurrection, appearance and reality – have to be overlooked and
ignored and criticism creeps away in a flurry of embarrassed and misdirected
compliments', 41.
94 Sherard, *Life*, p. 332; Brasol, *Oscar Wilde*, p. 265; Archibald Henderson,
'Oscar Wilde', in *Interpreters of Life, and the Modern Spirit*, London 1911,
p. 91; Henry Ten Eyck Perry, *Masters of Dramatic Comedy and their Social
Themes*, Cambridge, Mass., 1939, p. 362; St John Ervine, *Oscar Wilde*,
p. 283; Norman James, 'Oscar Wilde's Dramaturgy', unpublished Ph.D.
thesis, Duke University, 1959, p. 190; David Parker, 'Oscar Wilde's Great
Farce "The Importance of Being Earnest"', MLQ 35 (1974), 173.
95 Eric Bentley, *The Playwright as Thinker*, New York 1967 [1946], pp. 140–5;
Reinert, 'Satiric Strategy', p. 14.
96 *Letters*, p. 369.
97 David Daiches, *Some Late Victorian Attitudes*. University of California at Los
Angeles, 1967, p. 66.
98 Alfred Douglas, *The Autobiography*, London 1929, p. 91 and p. 93. Harris,
Oscar Wilde, 1938, p. 113, describes Bosie's father, who is also called 'Black
Douglas', as follows: 'Queensberry was five feet seven in height, broad and
strong, with a plain, heavy, rather sullen face, and quick, hot eyes. He was a

mass of self-conceit, all bristling with suspicion, and in regard to money, prudent to meanness. He cared nothing for books, but had an athletic reputation as an ex-champion amateur boxer and a cross-country rider.' A detailed description is given by Francis A. K. Douglas and Percy Colson, *Oscar Wilde and the Black Douglas*, London 1949. See also the biographies of Brian Roberts, *The Mad Bad Line – The Family of Lord Alfred Douglas*, London 1981, and H. Montgomery Hyde, *Lord Alfred Douglas*, London 1984.

99 Pearson, *Life of Oscar Wilde*, p. 277.
100 *The Listener*, 4 Nov. 1954, p. 754. There is also an autobiographical reference in the scene with Jack's cigarette case, whose inscription 'From little Cecily, with her fondest love to her dear Uncle Jack' (Act 1, p. 351) betrays his friend's Bunburying to Algernon. Wilde made a habit of presenting to his homosexual friends silver cigarette cases inscribed with his name. Later, in the trial, they were produced as evidence against him, since the prosecuting counsel Carson did not heed Jack's protest: 'It is a very ungentlemanly thing to read a private cigarette case.' (Act 1, p. 350).

9 Apologies and accusations. *De Profundis* and *The Ballad of Reading Gaol*

1 Hyde, *Oscar Wilde. The Aftermath*, p. 1.
2 *De Profundis*, in *Complete Works*, p. 901.
3 *Letters*, p. 419.
4 On the history of the text, see Robert Ross, A Prefatory Dedication, in [*Works*], *De Profundis*, London 1908, pp. vii–xvi; *Letters*, pp. 423–4, 512–13, 564; Hyde, *Oscar Wilde. The Aftermath*, pp. 185–99; Hyde, 'The Riddle of "De Profundis". Who owns the Manuscript?' AntigR 54 (1983), 107–27.
5 See Hyde, *Oscar Wilde. The Aftermath*, p. 186, where he refers to a statement about this made by Ross in *The Library of William Andrews Clark, Jr.*, vol. 2, San Francisco 1922, p. 70.
6 See Alfred Douglas, *Oscar Wilde and Myself*, London 1914, p. 165; *The Autobiography of Lord Alfred Douglas*, London 1929, pp. 35, 132 and 134; *Without Apology*, London 1938, pp. 42, 114 and 218; *Oscar Wilde. A Summing-Up*, London 1940, reissued with an introduction by Derek Hudson, London 1950, p. 116.
7 Ransome, *Oscar Wilde*, p. 157. On the question of whether Douglas or Ross was the 'villain of the piece', and whether the unpublished section of *De Profundis* was read out in its entirety or only in extracts to the court during the Douglas v. Ransome trial, see the controversy in the columns of the TLS: Roy Harrod, TLS, 30 Aug. 1963, p. 657; James Lees-Milne, TLS, 6 Sept. 1963, p. 677; Martin Secker, TLS, 13 Sept. 1963, p. 693; H. Montgomery Hyde, TLS, 20 Sept. 1963, p. 711; C. H. Norman, TLS, 27 Sept. 1963, p. 745; H. Montgomery Hyde, TLS, 4 Oct. 1963, p. 787; C. H. Norman, TLS, 18 Oct. 1963, p. 827; H. Montgomery Hyde, TLS, 15 Nov. 1963, p. 933.
8 See a reprint of the review in Hyde, *Oscar Wilde. The Aftermath*, Appendix D, pp. 208–10.
9 Ibid., p. 208.
10 *Oscar Wilde and Myself*, p. 171.

11 *The Autobiography of Lord Alfred Douglas*, p. 135.
12 *Oscar Wilde. The Aftermath*, pp. 186–7.
13 *Letters*, p. 513. Robert Ross chose the title *De Profundis*, probably drawn from Psalm 130, verse 1.
14 See Mason, *Bibliography*, pp. 442ff.
15 The book was published under the title *The Suppressed Portion of 'De Profundis'. Now for the first time published by his literary executor Robert Ross*, New York 1913. Hyde, *Oscar Wilde. The Aftermath*, p. 196, contains a list of the people to whom Ross gave a copy.
16 *Letters*, p. 424.
17 Several times Wilde gives Douglas's silence during his two-year imprisonment as the reason for his writing the letter. *De Profundis*, in *Complete Works*, pp. 873 and 897.
18 *Letters*, p. 419.
19 This is the length of *De Profundis* in the one-volume *Complete Works* of 1966. According to Robert Ross, the manuscript consists of 'eighty close-written pages on twenty folio sheets'. A Prefatory Dedication, in *De Profundis*, p. xiii.
20 *Letters*, p. 514. See also *De Profundis*, in *Complete Works*, p. 912: 'I don't write this letter to put bitterness into your heart, but to pluck it out of mine.'
21 *De Profundis*, in *Complete Works*, p. 873.
22 '*There* was the one great psychological error of our friendship, its entire want of proportion.' Ibid., p. 948.
23 Ibid., p. 876.
24 Ibid., p. 875. The first part of this description recalls Matthew Arnold's definition of criticism as 'a free play of the mind on all subjects which it touches'. *The Function of Criticism at the Present Time*, in *The Complete Prose Works of Matthew Arnold*, ed. by R. H. Super, vol. III, Ann Arbor 1962, p. 269.
25 *De Profundis*, in *Complete Works*, p. 875.
26 Ibid., p. 874.
27 Ibid., p. 875. But see Alfred Douglas's very different account in *Oscar Wilde and Myself*, pp. 172–3.
28 *De Profundis*, in *Complete Works*, p. 877. Douglas called Wilde's account of their financial relationship 'monstrous lies'. *The Autobiography of Lord Alfred Douglas*, p. 41.
29 *De Profundis*, in *Complete Works*, p. 876.
30 Ibid., p. 877.
31 Ibid., p. 893.
32 Ibid., p. 895.
33 Ibid., p. 894.
34 Ibid., p. 878.
35 Ibid., p. 887.
36 Ibid., p. 896.
37 Ibid., pp. 878–9. See also *Letters*, p. 526.
38 *Letters*, p. 397.
39 Ibid., p. 393.
40 *De Profundis*, in *Complete Works*, p. 874.

41 *The Autobiography of Lord Alfred Douglas*, p. 41.
42 Douglas, *Oscar Wilde and Myself*, p. 177.
43 *De Profundis*, in *Complete Works*, pp. 874, 876, 877.
44 Ibid., p. 912.
45 Ibid., p. 881.
46 Ibid., p. 909.
47 Ibid., p. 879.
48 Ibid., pp. 912–13.
49 Ibid., p. 913.
50 Ibid.
51 Ibid., p. 947. In the letters he sometimes calls his life 'unworthy of an artist'. *Letters*, pp. 577, 581, 587.
52 *De Profundis*, in *Complete Works*, p. 913.
53 Ibid., p. 922.
54 Ibid.
55 Ibid., p. 914.
56 Ibid., p. 935.
57 Ibid., p. 919.
58 Ibid.
59 Ibid., p. 916.
60 'Wilde's characterization of himself is that of a neo-Christ capable of appreciating sorrow as well as pleasure. His declared intention is to change the past, not only in his own eyes but in the eyes of society and of God.' Meredith Cary, '"De Profundis" – Wilde's Letter to the World', TSL 16 (1971), 101.
61 *De Profundis*, in *Complete Works*, p. 923.
62 Ibid., p. 925.
63 Ibid., p. 933.
64 Ibid., p. 924.
65 Ibid., p. 929.
66 Ibid., p. 925.
67 See Hans Ording, 'Oscar Wildes estetiske Kristusbilde', KoK 54 (1949), 392–9.
68 See Frank P. Bowman, *Le Christ romantique*, Geneva 1973, esp. pp. 13ff and pp. 87ff.
69 *Vie de Jésus*, Paris 1965, p. 440. (Le Livre de poche. 1548/1549).
70 *De Profundis*, in *Complete Works*, p. 925, p. 930. On p. 925 Wilde para-phrases Renan, 'that Christ's great achievement was that he made himself as much loved after his death as he had been during his lifetime'. The original runs: 'S'être fait aimer "à ce point qu'après sa mort on ne cessa pas de l'aimer", voilà le chef-d'œuvre de Jésus et ce qui frappa le plus ses contemporains.' *Vie de Jésus*, p. 430.
71 Renan, *Vie de Jésus*, p. 433.
72 Ibid., p. 441.
73 *De Profundis*, in *Complete Works*, p. 926.
74 Ibid., p. 931.
75 Renan, *Vie de Jésus*, p. 431.
76 *De Profundis*, in *Complete Works*, p. 932.

77 Ibid., p. 934.
78 Ibid., p. 913.
79 D. *Martin Luthers Werke. Kritische Gesamtausgabe*, vol. 7, Weimar 1897, p. 562.
80 *De Profundis*, in *Complete Works*, pp. 936–7.
81 Ibid., p. 947.
82 Ibid.
83 Ibid., p. 937. Joseph Butwin, 'The Martyr Clown. Oscar Wilde in "De Profundis"', VN 42 (1972), 1–6, supports his thesis that Wilde was drawing himself as a 'martyr clown' by quoting this passage, amongst others.
84 From a review of *The Picture of Dorian Gray*, in *Daily Chronicle*, 30 June 1890, p. 7. Reprinted in *Oscar Wilde. The Critical Heritage*, p. 72.
85 *De Profundis*, in *Complete Works*, p. 917.
86 Most critics have been convinced of the sincerity of Wilde's confessions in *De Profundis*. For example, see Ingleby, *Oscar Wilde*, London 1907, p. 382; Ernst Bendz, 'Some Stray Notes on the Personality and Writings of Oscar Wilde. In Memoriam 30th November 1910', in *Minnesskrift. Göteborgs högre samskola 1910–1911. Minnesskrift utgiven av skolans lärare*, Göteborg 1911, p. 314; Braybrooke, *Oscar Wilde, A Study*, London 1930 (Studies Library 2), p. 131; Woodcock, *The Paradox of Oscar Wilde*, p. 92; John Sparrow, 'Oscar Wilde after Fifty Years', in *Independent Essays*, London 1963, p. 117: 'at all essential points the story it [*De Profundis*] contains rings true'.
87 Hugh Walker, 'The Birth of a Soul. (Oscar Wilde: the Closing Phase'), *Hibbert Journal* (July 1905), 756–68.
88 André Gide, 'Le "De Profundis" d'Oscar Wilde', L'Ermitage (15 Aug. 1905), 65–6.
89 Pearson, *The Life of Oscar Wilde*, p. 321.
90 St John Ervine, *Oscar Wilde*, p. 307. T. W. H. Crosland was especially polemical in the foreword to his pamphlet *The First Stone. On Reading the Unpublished Parts of 'De Profundis'*, London 1912: 'A blacker, fiercer, falser, craftier, more grovelling or more abominable piece of writing never fell from mortal pen', p. 6.
91 E. V. Lucas, in TLS, 24 Feb. 1905, pp. 64–5. Reprinted in *Oscar Wilde. The Critical Heritage*, pp. 247–8. Regenia Gagnier, '"De Profundis" as Epistola: in Carcere et Vinculis. A Materialist Reading of Oscar Wilde's Autobiography', *Criticism* 26 (1984), 335–54, refers to modern autobiographical research in showing that the convict Wilde's search for a new identity entails a degree of tension between a view of reality that was orientated by his imagination of what lay outside the prison walls, and a detailed realistic description of conditions within Reading Gaol. Her thesis is that 'The self in his [Wilde's] letter is a self constructed in a particular imaginative act of resistance against insanity and against the material matrix of prison space and time, that is, confined, segmented space and timelessness ... Romance and realism here are psychological – even survival – functions: romance dreams a future for the prisoner and resists the temporal regimentation of prison life; realism, in its patient enumeration of details, reconstructs the past obliterated by the sterile prison space', 335–6.

92 *De Profundis*, in *Complete Works*, p. 914.
93 *Letters*, p. 715.
94 *De Profundis*, in *Complete Works*, pp. 954 and 955.
95 *Letters*, p. 638.
96 'A Lord of Language', in *Vanity Fair*, 2 March 1905, p. 309. Reprinted in *Oscar Wilde. The Critical Heritage*, pp. 248–51. The passage quoted is on p. 250.
97 *De Profundis*, in *Complete Works*, p. 905.
98 Max Beerbohm, 'A Lord of Language', in *Oscar Wilde. The Critical Heritage*, p. 249.
99 Jan B. Gordon, 'Wilde and Newman. The Confessional Mode', *Renascence* 22 (1970), 183–91, finds similarities between Newman's *Apologia Pro Vita Sua* and Wilde's *De Profundis*: '*De Profundis* ... exhibits certain formal and stylistic features common to the *apologia* in general and Newman's in particular', p. 183.
100 Reprinted in *Reviews*, pp. 393–6. On the links between Wilde and Blunt see William T. Going's essay 'Oscar Wilde and Wilfrid Blunt. Ironic Notes on Prison, Prose, and Poetry', VN no. 13 (1958), 27–9.
101 Ibid., 393.
102 Ibid., 396.
103 *De Profundis*, in *Complete Works*, p. 918.
104 *Letters*, p. 715.
105 *De Profundis*, in *Complete Works*, p. 914.
106 *Letters*, p. 708.
107 Arthur Symons, '"The Ballad of Reading Gaol"', SatR, 12 March (1898), 365, in *Oscar Wilde. The Critical Heritage*, p. 219.
108 On the history of the ballad's composition, see Mason, *Bibliography of Oscar Wilde*, pp. 409–27, and Hyde, *Oscar Wilde. The Aftermath*, pp. 156–84.
109 *Letters*, p. 586.
110 Ibid., p. 684.
111 For details concerning the French translation of the poem, see Henry-D. Davray, *Oscar Wilde. La tragédie finale. Suivi d'épisodes et souvenirs et des apocryphes*, Paris 1928, esp. pp. 85–126.
112 *Oscar Wilde's 'Ballad of Reading Gaol'*, New York 1954.
113 Ibid., p. 67.
114 *Letters*, p. 691.
115 See Gottfried Sello, 'Heckels Holzschnitte zu Wildes "Zuchthausballade"', *Philobiblon* 7 (1963), 244–55.
116 *What to Read in English Literature*, London 1975.
117 Ibid., p. 127. Other Wilde critics have been equally positive, e.g. Ingleby, *Oscar Wilde*, 1907, p. 283: 'incomparably Wilde's finest poetic work'; A. Henderson, 'Oscar Wilde', in *Interpreters of Life, and the Modern Spirit*, London 1911, p. 64: 'his greatest poem'; Harris, *Oscar Wilde*, 1959, p. 230: 'beyond all comparison the greatest ballad in English; one of the noblest poems in the language'; Choisy, *Oscar Wilde*, p. 194: 'son chef-d'œuvre'; Lemonnier, *Oscar Wilde*, p. 243: 'son chef-d'œuvre poétique'; Woodcock, *The Paradox of Oscar Wilde*, p. 173: 'the best and most original of Wilde's

own poems'; Hyde, *Oscar Wilde. The Aftermath*, p. 184: 'perhaps the most moving denunciation of the inhumanity of capital punishment ever written in poetic form'.

118 See Rudolf Stamm, 'W. B. Yeats and Oscar Wilde's "Ballad of Reading Gaol"', in *Studies in English Language and Literature. Presented to Karl Brunner on the Occasion of his Seventieth Birthday*, ed. by Siegfried Korninger, Vienna and Stuttgart 1957, pp. 210–19. (WBEP. 65). An English version of this essay appeared under the title 'William Butler Yeats and "The Ballad of Reading Gaol" by Oscar Wilde', in Rudolf Stamm, *The Shaping Powers at Work. Fifteen Essays on Poetic Transmutation*, Heidelberg 1967, pp. 210–19.

119 W. B. Yeats, Introduction, in *The Oxford Book of Modern Verse 1892– 1935*, Oxford 1936. Reprinted 1960, p. vii.

120 Verse 80, in *Complete Works*, p. 855.

121 Verse 7, in ibid., p. 844.

122 *Shaping Powers*, p. 219.

123 *Oscar Wilde and Myself*, pp. 224–5. For further references to Hood's poem see Ingleby, *Oscar Wilde*, pp. 290–1; Richard Butler Glaenzer, 'The Story of "The Ballad of Reading Gaol"', *Bookman* (New York) 33 (1911), 379, and Holland, *Son of Oscar Wilde*, p. 178.

124 For a detailed study of links with Coleridge's *Ancient Mariner* see Burton R. Pollin's essay 'The Influence of "The Ancient Mariner" upon "The Ballad of Reading Gaol"', RLV 40 (1974), 228–34. According to Pollin, Wilde's poem suffers from 'a displacement of feeling, derived in part from the ill-digested absorption of powerful images and currents of dramatic force in the far greater ballad by Coleridge', p. 234. Bernhard Fehr, in his detailed *Studien zu Oscar Wilde's Gedichten*, comes to the conclusion that the *Ancient Mariner* was not a model for Wilde's ballad; see p. 205.

125 *The Ballad of Reading Gaol*, verse 50, lines 3–4, in *Complete Works*, p. 851.

126 *The Rime of the Ancient Mariner*, pt II, stanza 11, in *The Poems of Samuel Taylor Coleridge*. With an introduction by A. T. Quiller-Couch, London 1958, p. 285.

127 Ibid., pt III, stanza 12, in ibid., p. 287.

128 *English Poetry in the Later Nineteenth Century*, London 1966 [1933], p. 401.

129 Harris, *Oscar Wilde*, 1959, p. 227: 'I believe that Wilde owed most of his inspiration to "A Shropshire Lad"', and Hyde, *Oscar Wilde. The Aftermath*, p. 156: 'to some extent the metre he adopted, as well as the subject, was inspired by Housman's poem'.

130 *A Shropshire Lad*, Poem IX, in *Complete Works*. Centennial edition, with an introduction by Basil Davenport and a history of the text by Tom Burns Haber, New York 1959, p. 21.

131 Symons, *Oscar Wilde*, p. 35.

132 Verse 26, lines 2–4, in *Complete Works*, p. 847.

133 Verse 40, lines 1–2, in ibid., p. 849.

134 Verse 76, line 3, in ibid., p. 855.

135 Verse 90, lines 1–2, in ibid., p. 857.

136 Verse 101, lines 5–6, in ibid., p. 859.

137 Verse 96, line 6, in ibid., p. 858.

138 Mason, *Bibliography of Oscar Wilde*, p. 426. Of less significance is the fact that the uniform is described as 'scarlet' although Wooldridge belonged to the Royal Horse Guards (Blue). When this inaccuracy was pointed out to Wilde, he is said to have answered that he could hardly have written: '*He did not wear his azure coat, For blood and wine are blue*'. Pearson, *The Life of Oscar Wilde*, p. 345.

139 Verse 7, in *Complete Works*, p. 844. This basic motif of the poem runs like a variation on Bassanio's question to Shylock: 'Do all men kill the things they do not love?' *The Merchant of Venice*, Act 4, line 66.

140 See Merle, *Oscar Wilde*, 1948, p. 459.

141 Ibid., p. 456.

142 Verse 97, line 1, in *Complete Works*, p. 858.

143 Ibid., line 3.

144 Verse 96, line 2, in *Complete Works*, p. 858.

145 Verse 57, line 4, in ibid., p. 852.

146 Verse 94, lines 3–4, in ibid., pp. 857–8.

147 *Complete Works*, p. 966.

148 Ibid., p. 967.

149 Ibid., p. 960.

150 Ibid., p. 964.

151 Ibid., p. 958.

152 Verse 32, in *Complete Works*, p. 848.

153 Verse 36, in ibid., p. 848.

154 *Letters*, p. 676. Karl Beckson, 'Oscar Wilde and the "Almost Inhuman" Governor of Reading Gaol', N&Q 30 (1983) 315–16, has corrected two common errors in Wilde biography: Isaacson was not a Jew, as has generally been maintained, and he was neither a major nor a colonel, but a lieutenant-colonel.

155 Ibid., p. 574.

156 Hyde, *Oscar Wilde. The Aftermath*, p. 78.

157 *Letters*, p. 725.

158 *Complete Works*, p. 968.

159 Verse 34, lines 3–6, in *Complete Works*, p. 848.

160 '"The Ballad of Reading Gaol"', in *Oscar Wilde. The Critical Heritage*, p. 219.

161 *The Picture of Dorian Gray*. The Preface.

162 *Letters*, p. 654.

163 Verse 75, in *Complete Works*, p. 854.

164 Verse 38, line 3, in ibid., p. 849.

165 Verses 2 (lines 5–6) and 3 (lines 1–2); 6 (lines 5–6) and 7 (lines 1–2); 9 (line 6) and 10 (line 1); 17 (lines 5–6) and 18 (line 1–2), in *Complete Works*, pp. 843–5.

166 Verses 50–1, in ibid., pp. 850–1.

167 *Studien zu Oscar Wilde's Gedichten*, p. 200. Averil Gardner 'Oscar Wilde's Swansong', DR 54 (1974), p. 75, in her interpretation of the *Ballad*, also regrets the inclusion of these 'romantic' passages on the grounds that they 'add an unnecessarily "literary" quality to the poem'.

168 *Studien zu Oscar Wilde's Gedichten*, p. 200.

169 *Oscar Wilde*, p. 44.

170 Ibid.
171 *Letters*, p. 653.
172 'Pen, Pencil, and Poison', in *Complete Works*, p. 1008.
173 Verse 101, lines 5–6, in *Complete Works*, p. 859.

10 Plans, sketches and fragments

1 In *Miscellanies* (1908) Robert Ross published a fragment of the play which he reconstructed from parts of the first draft, commenting: 'At the time of Wilde's trial the nearly complete drama was entrusted to Mrs Leverson, who in 1897 went to Paris to restore it to the author. Wilde immediately left the manuscript in a cab. A few days later he laughingly informed me of the loss, and added that a cab was a very proper place for it.' Ibid., pp. xii–xiii.
2 'La Sainte Courtisane', in *Miscellanies*, p. 237.
3 Ibid., p. 238.
4 *The Portrait of Mr W. H.*, in *Complete Works*, p. 1196.
5 See, for instance, Hartley, *Oscar Wilde. L'Influence française dans son œuvre*, Paris 1935, p. 272; Schön, 'Französische Einflüsse in Oscar Wildes Werken', unpublished diss., Hamburg 1949, p. 119. On the Thaïs story and its various adaptations, see Oswald R. Kuehne, 'A Study of the Thaïs Legend with Special Reference to Hrotsvitha's "Paphnutius"', unpublished Ph.D. thesis, University of Pennsylvania, Philadelphia 1922.
6 Anatole France, *Thaïs*, Paris 1891 [1890], p. 290.
7 *La Tentation de Saint-Antoine*. Chronology and preface by Jacques Suffel, Paris 1967, p. 78.
8 According to Frank Harris, *Oscar Wilde* (1959), p. 85, Wilde told the basic story of 'A Florentine Tragedy' in the course of a lively conversation that took place before he had actually set it down in writing. The story is reproduced by L. G. M. Guillot de Saix under the title 'Le Marchand de Florence', in *Contes et propos d'Oscar Wilde . . .* Paris 1949, pp. 23–8.
9 The play was performed on television in March 1964. See 'Drama Handicapped by Wilde's Jewelled Verse', *The Times*, 12 March 1964, p. 16.
10 'A Florentine Tragedy', in *Complete Works*, p. 692.
11 Ibid., p. 695.
12 Ibid., p. 700.
13 Ibid., p. 697.
14 *Bibliography of Oscar Wilde*, pp. 583–5.
15 *Letters*, p. 649. According to André Gide, 'Oscar Wilde', *L'Ermitage* (June 1902), 425, Wilde intended to write this play and 'Ahab and Isabel' in Berneval-sur-Mer. 'C'est là qu'il veut écrire ses drames; son 'Pharaon' d'abord, puis un 'Achab et Jésabel' (Il prononce: Isabelle) qu'il raconte admirablement' [It's there that he wants to write his plays – his 'Pharaon' first, and then an 'Achab et Jésabel' (he pronounces it: Isabelle), which he narrates admirably].
16 *Oscar Wilde. La tragédie finale. Suivi d'épisodes et souvenirs et des apocryphes*, Paris 1928, p. 273. A highly imaginative 'Essai de reconstitution . . . de la dernière pièce imaginée et racontée par Oscar Wilde' was published by L. G. M. Guillot de Saix under the title 'Oscar Wilde et le théâtre. Jézabel. Drame inédit en un acte', *Mercure de France* 279 (1937), 513–49.

17 Holland, *Son of Oscar Wilde*, p. 264.
18 Ibid.
19 *A Collection of Original Manuscripts, Letters & Books of Oscar Wilde including his Letters Written to Robert Ross from Reading Gaol and Unpublished Letters, Poems & Plays formerly in the Possession of Robert Ross, C. S. Millard (Stuart Mason) and the Younger Son of Oscar Wilde*, London [1928]. See also L. G. M. Guillot de Saix, '"Une tragédie de femme" par Oscar Wilde', *Mercure de France* 286 (1938), 597–603. De Saix attempts to reconstruct the plot of the play, but this operation is highly speculative.
20 Shewan (ed.), 'A Wife's Tragedy', pp. 75–131. See also Rodney Shewan, 'Oscar Wilde and "A Wife's Tragedy". Facts and Conjectures', ThR 8, no. 2 (1983), 83–95.
21 Shewan, 'Oscar Wilde and "A Wife's Tragedy"', 91.
22 The first draft of this play dates from 1894 according to a letter Wilde wrote to George Alexander in August of that year (*Letters*, pp. 360–62). Harris's final version of the play was published for the first time in 1956 by H. Montgomery Hyde, with an informative introduction (pp. 7–43). See also T. H. Bell, 'Oscar Wilde's Unwritten Play', *Bookman* (New York), 71 (1930), 139–50.
23 Cora Brown-Potter bequeathed the scenario to L. G. M. Guillot de Saix, who together with Henri de Briel 'reconstructed' the play under the title *Constance, Comédie en quatre actes*. Edited by Henri de Briel and Guillot de Saix, in *Les Œuvres libres*, new series, no. 101, Oct. (1954), 201–302.
24 See Introduction, in *Mr and Mrs Daventry*, ed. by H. Montgomery Hyde, London 1956, p. 21. Also *Letters*, p. 762, pp. 813–14 and p. 830.
25 Harris, *Oscar Wilde* (1959), p. 313.
26 *The Sunday Special*, 28 Oct. 1900. Reprinted in *Dramatic Criticism*, vol. III: *1900–1901*, London 1902, pp. 42–6.
27 *The Saturday Review*, 3 Nov. 1900.
28 J. T. Grein, *Dramatic Criticism*, vol. III, p. 42.
29 *Mr and Mrs Daventry*, p. 56.
30 Ibid., p. 62.
31 Ibid., p. 113.
32 Ibid., p. 42.

Conclusion

1 *Letters*, p. 352.
2 Wolfgang Koeppen, 'Der Dichter, der ein Kunstwerk war. Die Bildnisse des Oscar Wilde', FAZ (5 June 1976), appendix.
3 *De Profundis*, in *Complete Works*, p. 939.
4 *Letters*, p. 512.
5 *Das neue Drama*, Berlin 1905, p. 280.
6 'The Decay of Lying', in *Complete Works*, p. 982.
7 'The Critic as Artist', in ibid., p. 1048.
8 *De Profundis*, in ibid., p. 937.
9 'On Translating Homer', in *The Complete Prose Works of Matthew Arnold*, vol. I, *On the Classical Tradition*, ed. by R. H. Super, Ann Arbor, Mich., 1960, p. 140.

10 Hoxie N. Fairchild, *Religious Trends in English Poetry*, vol. V, *1880–1920*, New York and London 1962, p. 142.
11 W. B. Yeats, *The Trembling of the Veil* [1922], in *Autobiographies*, London 1955 [1926], p. 138.
12 *De Profundis*, in *Complete Works*, p. 938.
13 Paul Goetsch, *Die Romankonzeption in England 1880–1910*, Heidelberg 1967, p. 202.
14 *The Importance of Being Earnest*, in *Oscar Wilde's Plays, Prose Writings, and Poems*. Introduction by Hesketh Pearson, London 1967 [1930], p. 390 (EL 1858).
15 Richard Ellmann, 'Romantic Pantomime in Oscar Wilde', PR 30 (1963), 342.
16 Pearson, *Life of Oscar Wilde*, p. 368.
17 *De Profundis*, in *Complete Works*, p. 922.
18 Ibid., p. 913.
19 W. S. Gilbert and Arthur Sullivan, *Patience, or Bunthorne's Bride!* London n.d. [1881], p. 13.
20 'A Satire on Romantic Drama', SatR (8 Dec. 1900). Reprinted in Max Beerbohm, *More Theatres 1898–1903*. With an introduction by Rupert Hart-Davis, London 1969, p. 333.
21 'Nietzsches Philosophie im Lichte unserer Erfahrung' [1947], in *Adel des Geistes. Zwanzig Versuche zum Problem der Humanität*, Berlin and Weimar 1965, p. 652.
22 *Aussenseiter*, Frankfurt/M. 1975, esp. pp. 260–7.
23 *Tout compte fait. Essai*, Paris 1972, p. 168.
24 'Romantic Pantomime in Oscar Wilde', p. 342.
25 'The Poet's eye, in a fine frenzy rolling, / Doth glance from heaven to earth, from earth to heaven'. *A Midsummer Night's Dream*, V.i.12–13.
26 *Hamlet*, V.i.185.

Select bibliography

For a detailed and annotated bibliography of works written by and about Oscar Wilde, the reader is referred to the German edition of this book: *Oscar Wilde. Das literarische Werk zwischen Provokation und Anspassung*, Heidelberg: Carl Winter Universitätsverlag 1980, pp. 521–686.

A   Bibliographies and reviews of research

Mason, Stuart [Christopher S. Millard], *A Bibliography of the Poems of Oscar Wilde. Giving particulars as to the original publication of each poem, with variations of readings and a complete list of all editions, reprints, translations, & c. With portraits, illustrations, facsimiles of title-pages, manuscripts, etc.*, London 1907.

— *Bibliography of Oscar Wilde.* With a note by Robert Ross, London 1914. [Privately printed: Edinburgh 1908]. New edition. Intro. by Timothy d'Arch Smith, London 1967. Repr. Boston 1972.

411

Horodisch, Abraham, *Oscar Wilde's 'Ballad of Reading Gaol'. A Bibliographical Study*, New York 1954.
Riege, Helmut, 'Bibliographie der Werke Oscar Wildes', in Oscar Wilde, *Briefe*, ed. by Rupert Hart-Davis. Transl. by Hedda Soellner, vol. 2, Reinbek b. Hamburg 1966, pp. 321–71.
Fletcher, Ian and John Stokes, 'Oscar Wilde', in *Anglo-Irish Literature. A Review of Research*, ed. by Richard J. Finneran, New York 1976, pp. 48–137. Suppl. 1983, pp. 21–47.
Dowling, Linda C., *Aestheticism and Decadence. A Selective Annotated Bibliography*, New York and London 1977.
Mikhail, Edward H., *Oscar Wilde. An Annotated Bibliography of Criticism*, London 1978.
Kohl, Norbert, 'Oscar Wilde-Bibliographie', in *Oscar Wilde. Das literarische Werk zwischen Provokation und Anpassung*, Heidelberg 1980, pp. 521–686.

B Editions

I COLLECTED WORKS

[*Works*, ed. Robert Ross], 14 vols., London 1908. Vol. 15: *For Love of the King*, London 1922. Repr. *The First Collected Edition of the Works of Oscar Wilde, 1908–1922*, 15 vols., London and New York 1969.
Complete Works of Oscar Wilde. With an introd. by Vyvyan Holland, London and Glasgow 1966 [1948].

II SELECTED WORKS

Plays, Prose-Writings, and Poems. Introd. by Isobel Murray, London and New York 1975 [1930]. (EL. 1858).
The Portable Oscar Wilde. Rev. edn, selected and edited by Richard Aldington and Stanley Weintraub, New York 1981 [1946].
Plays, Harmondsworth 1954.
'De Profundis' and other Writings. [Originally published as *Selected Essays and Poems*]. With an introd. by Hesketh Pearson, Harmondsworth 1984 [1954]. (PEL).
Selected Writings. With an introd. by Richard Ellmann, London 1961. (WC. 584).
The Artist as Critic. Critical Writings of Oscar Wilde, ed. Richard Ellmann, New York 1968.
Literary Criticism of Oscar Wilde, ed. Stanley Weintraub, Lincoln, Nebr. 1968.
Selected Writings, edited with an introd. by Russell Fraser, Boston [1969]. (Riverside editions. B 114).
The Illustrated Oscar Wilde, ed. by Roy Gasson, London 1977.
Fong, Bobby, 'The Poetry of Oscar Wilde. A Critical Edition', unpublished Ph.D. thesis, Univ. of California at Los Angeles, 1978: DA 39 no. 9, 1979, p. 5523–A.
The Complete Shorter Fiction of Oscar Wilde, ed. by Isobel Murray, Oxford 1979.
White, Nanci J., 'An Annotated Edition of the Poems of Oscar Wilde', unpublished Ph.D. thesis, York Univ. (Canada), 1980: DA 41, no. 10, 1981, P. 4397–A.
The Annotated Oscar Wilde, ed. by H. Montgomery Hyde, London 1982.
Two Society Comedies. A Woman of No Importance. An Ideal Husband, ed. by

Ian Small and Russell Jackson, London and New York 1983. (The New Mermaids).

III LETTERS

The Letters of Oscar Wilde, ed. by Rupert Hart-Davis, London 1962.
Selected Letters, ed. by Rupert Hart-Davis, London 1979.
More Letters of Oscar Wilde, ed. by Rupert Hart-Davis, London 1985.

IV SINGLE WORKS

The Picture of Dorian Gray (Urfassung 1890), ed. by Wilfried Edener, Nürnberg 1964. (Erlanger Beiträge zur Sprach- und Kunstwissenschaft. 18)
The Picture of Dorian Gray, ed. by Isobel Murray, Oxford 1974. (OEN).
The Importance of Being Earnest. A Trivial Comedy for Serious People, ed. by Russell Jackson, London and New York 1980. (The New Mermaids).
Lady Windermere's Fan. A Play about a Good Woman, ed. by Ian Small, London and New York 1980. (The New Mermaids).
Reed, Frances M., 'Oscar Wilde's "Vera; or, The Nihilists". A Critical Edition', Ph.D. thesis, University of California, Los Angeles, 1980: DA 41: no. 4, 1981 p. 1617–A.
'"A Wife's Tragedy." An Unpublished Sketch for a Play by Oscar Wilde', ed. Rodney Shewan, in ThR 7 (1982), 75–131.
Berggren, Ruth H., 'Oscar Wilde's "The Importance of Being Earnest"'. A Critical Edition of the Four-Act Version', 2 vols., unpublished Ph.D. thesis, Univ. of Massachusetts, 1984: DA 45: 2, 1984, p. 524–A.

C Biographies

Sherard, Robert H., *The Life of Oscar Wilde*. London 1906, 1911. Repr. New York 1928.
Douglas, Alfred, *Oscar Wilde and Myself*, London 1914, Repr. 1919.
Sherard, Robert H., *The Real Oscar Wilde*. To be used as a supplement to, and in illustration of 'The Life of Oscar Wilde', London 1916.
Harris, Frank, *Oscar Wilde. His Life and Confessions*, 2 vols., New York 1916. New edition: Together with memories of Oscar Wilde by Bernard Shaw, 1918. Reiss.: With a pref. by Bernard Shaw, London 1938. Repr. East Lansing (Mich.) 1959. Repr. London 1965.
Lemonnier, Léon, *La Vie d'Oscar Wilde*, Paris 1931. (Essais critiques. 24.)
Lewis, Lloyd and Henry J. Smith, *Oscar Wilde Discovers America [1882]*, New York 1936. Repr. New York 1967.
Douglas, Alfred, *Oscar Wilde. A Summing-Up*. With an introd. by Derek Hudson, London 1950 [1940], 1962.
Pearson, Hesketh, *The Life of Oscar Wilde*, London 1946. Rev. edn. 1954. Repr. London 1975. Reissued Harmondsworth 1985. (Penguin Literary Biographies.)
Hyde, H. Montgomery, *The Trials of Oscar Wilde*. With a foreword by Travers Humphreys, London 1948. American edition under the title *The Three Trials of Oscar Wilde*, New York 1956. New and enl. edition *Oscar Wilde*, Harmondsworth 1962, repr. London 1974.
Holland, Vyvyan, *Son of Oscar Wilde*, London 1954.

Holland, Vyvyan, *Oscar Wilde. A Pictorial Biography*, London 1960. American
    edition under the title *Oscar Wilde and his World*, New York 1960.
Auden, W. H., 'An Improbable Life', *The New Yorker*, 9 March, 1963,
    pp. 155–77. Repr. in *Oscar Wilde. A Collection of Critical Essays*, ed.
    Richard Ellmann, Englewood Cliffs, N.J. 1969, pp. 116–37.
Hyde, H. Montgomery, *Oscar Wilde. The Aftermath*, London 1963.
Jullian, Philippe, *Oscar Wilde*, Paris 1967.
White, Terence de Vere, *The Parents of Oscar Wilde. Sir William Wilde and Lady
    Wilde*, London 1967.
Fido, Martin, *Oscar Wilde*, London 1973. Pbk. 1976.
Hyde, H. Montgomery, *Oscar Wilde. A Biography*, London 1976.
Kronenberger, Louis, *Oscar Wilde*, Boston and Toronto 1976. (The Library of
    World Biography).
Morley, Sheridan, *Oscar Wilde*, London 1976.
Oscar Wilde. Leben und Werk in Daten und Bildern, ed. by Norbert Kohl,
    Frankfurt/M. 1976. (insel taschenbuch. 158). Rev. edn Frankfurt/M. 1986.
Wilde, Oscar, *Interviews and Recollections*, ed. by Edward H. Mikhail, 2 vols.,
    London 1979.
Pine, Richard, *Oscar Wilde*, Dublin 1983. (Gill's Irish Lives).
Hyde, H. Montgomery, *Lord Alfred Douglas. A Biography*, London 1984.
Ellmann, Richard, *Oscar Wilde*, London 1987.

D Criticism
I GENERAL STUDIES
Ransome, Arthur, *Oscar Wilde. A Critical Study*, London 1912, rev. 1913, repr.
    New York 1971.
Aronstein, Philipp, 'Oscar Wilde. Sein Leben und Lebenswerk', in *Oscar Wilde,
    Werke in fünf Bänden*, vol. 1, Berlin 1922, pp. 7–132.
Choisy, Louis-Frédéric, *Oscar Wilde*, Paris 1927.
Symons, Arthur, *A Study of Oscar Wilde*, London 1930.
Brasol, Boris, *Oscar Wilde. The Man – the Artist*, London 1938.
Lemonnier, Léon, *Oscar Wilde*, Paris [1938].
Roditi, Edouard, *Oscar Wilde*, Norfolk, Conn. 1947.
Merle, Robert, *Oscar Wilde*, Paris 1948, rev. edition, Paris 1984.
Woodcock, George, *The Paradox of Oscar Wilde*, New York 1949.
Ervine, St John, *Oscar Wilde. A Present Time Appraisal*, London 1951, New York
    1952.
Ojala, Aatos, *Aestheticism and Oscar Wilde*, 2 pts., Helsinki 1954–1955.
    (Annales Academiae Scientiarum Fennicae. Ser. B. 90, 2; 93, 2). Repr. 1980.
Merle, Robert, *Oscar Wilde*, Paris 1957. (Classiques du XIXe siècle. 4).
San Juan, Epifanio, Jr, *The Art of Oscar Wilde*, Princeton, N.J. 1967.
Funke, Peter, *Oscar Wilde in Selbstzeugnissen und Bilddokumenten*, Reinbek b.
    Hamburg 1969. (rowohlts monographien. 148).
Nassaar, Christopher S., *Into the Demon Universe. A Literary Exploration of
    Oscar Wilde*, New Haven and London 1974.
Chamberlin, J.E., *Ripe Was the Drowsy Hour. The Age of Oscar Wilde*, New
    York 1977.
Ericksen, Donald H., *Oscar Wilde*, Boston 1977. (TEAS. 211).
Shewan, Rodney, *Oscar Wilde. Art and Egotism*, London 1977.

Cohen, Philip K., *The Moral Vision of Oscar Wilde*, London 1978.
Omasreiter, Ria, *Oscar Wilde. Epigone, Ästhet und 'wit'*, Heidelberg 1978.
Stokes, John, *Oscar Wilde*, London 1978.
Kohl, Norbert, *Oscar Wilde. Das literarische Werk zwischen Provokation und Anpassung*, Heidelberg 1980.
Miller, Robert K., *Oscar Wilde*, New York 1982. (Modern Literature Series).
Gagnier, Regenia, *Idylls of the Marketplace. Oscar Wilde and the Victorian Public*, Stanford, Calif. 1986.

II SPECIAL STUDIES

Bock, Eduard J., *Walter Pater's Einfluss auf Oscar Wilde*, Bonn 1913. (Bonner Studien zur englischen Philologie. 8).
Bendz, Ernst, *The Influence of Pater and Matthew Arnold in the Prose-Writings of Oscar Wilde*, Gothenburg and London 1914.
Chauvet, Paul, 'Oscar Wilde' (1928), in *Sept essais de littérature anglaise*, Paris 1931, pp. 79–113.
Eichbaum, Gerda, 'Die persönlichen und literarischen Beziehungen zwischen Oscar Wilde und James MacNeill Whistler', ESt 65 (1931), 217–52.
Schnapp, Luise, 'Oscar Wilde und die Bibel', GRM 21 (1933) 360–73.
Defieber, Rudolf, 'Oscar Wilde. Der Mann und sein Werk im Spiegel der deutschen Kritik und sein Einfluss auf die deutsche Literatur', unpublished diss., Heidelberg 1934.
Cazamian, Madeleine L., 'Oscar Wilde', in *Le Roman et les idées en Angleterre*, vol. II, *L'Anti-intellectualisme et l'esthétisme (1880–1900)*, Paris 1935, pp. 150–204.
Charbonnier, J., 'L'intellectualisme d'Oscar Wilde', RAA 12 (1935), 508–19.
Hartley, Kelver, *Oscar Wilde. L'Influence française dans son œuvre*, Paris 1935.
Lavrin, Janko, *Aspects of Modernism. From Wilde to Pirandello*, London 1935. Repr. 1968, pp. 13–33.
West, Alick, 'Oscar Wilde', in *The Mountain in the Sunlight. Studies in Conflict and Unity*, London 1958, pp. 123–53.
Loeser, Norbert, 'Friedrich Nietzsche en Oscar Wilde', in *Nietzsche & Wilde en andere essays*, Amsterdam 1960, pp. 133–82.
Ellmann, Richard, 'Romantic Pantomime in Oscar Wilde', PR 30 (1963), 342–55.
Breugelmans, René, 'Stefan George and Oscar Wilde. A Confrontation', PPNCFL 15 (1964), 40–59; 17 (1966), 60–74.
Charlesworth, Barbara, 'Oscar Wilde', in *Dark Passages. The Decadent Consciousness in Victorian Literature*, Madison and Milwaukee 1965, pp. 53–80.
Dyson, A.E., 'Oscar Wilde. Irony of a Socialist Aesthete', in *The Crazy Fabric*, London 1966, pp. 138–50.
Borelius, Birgit, *Oscar Wilde, Whistler and Colours*, Lund 1968. (Scripta Minora Regiae Societatis Humaniorum Litterarum Lundensis 67, no. 3).
Oscar Wilde. A Collection of Critical Essays, ed. by Richard Ellmann, Englewood Cliffs, N.J. 1969.
Oscar Wilde. The Critical Heritage, ed. by Karl Beckson, London 1970.
Rieff, Philip, 'The Impossible Culture. Oscar Wilde & the Charisma of the Artist', *Encounter* 35 (Sept., 1970), 33–44.
Fernandez, Diane, 'Oscar Wilde et le masque', LetN (March 1971), 129–54.

Herlemann, Klaus-Dieter, 'Oscar Wildes ironischer Witz als Ausdrucksform seines Dandysmus', unpublished Diss., Freiburg/Brsg. 1972.
Davis, Lisa E., 'Oscar Wilde in Spain', CL 25 (1973), 136–52.
O'Brien, Kevin, *Oscar Wilde in Canada. An Apostle for the Arts*, Toronto 1982.
Debon, Günther, *Oscar Wilde und der Taoismus. Oscar Wilde and Taoism*, Bern 1986. (euro-sinica. 2).

III POETRY
(1) GENERAL STUDIES
Fehr, Bernhard, *Studien zu Oscar Wilde's Gedichten*, Berlin 1918. (Palaestra. 100).
Richter, Helene, 'Oscar Wildes Persönlichkeit in seinen Gedichten', ESt 54 (1920), 201–76.
Eichbaum, Gerda, 'Die impressionistischen Frühgedichte Oscar Wildes unter besonderer Berücksichtigung des Einflusses von James MacNeill Whistler', DNS 40 (1932), 398–407.
Roditi, Edouard, 'Oscar Wilde's Poetry as Art History', *Poetry* 67 (1945/46), 322–38.
Thomas, J. D., 'Oscar Wilde's Pose and Poetry', *Rice Institute Pamphlet* 42 (1954), 32–52.
Lombardo, Agostino, 'La poesia di Oscar Wilde', in *La poesia inglese dall'estetismo al simbolismo*, Roma 1950, pp. 115–54.
Gardner, Averil, '"Literary Petty Larceny". Plagiarism in Oscar Wilde's early poetry', ESC 8 (1982), 49–61.

(2) SINGLE POEMS
THE HARLOT'S HOUSE
Fehr, Bernhard, 'Oscar Wildes "The Harlot's House"'. Eine kritischästhetische Untersuchung', Archiv 134, 1916, pp. 59–75.
Thomas, J. D., 'The Composition of Wilde's "The Harlot's House"', MLN 65 (1950), 485–8.

THE BALLAD OF READING GAOL
Davray, Henry-D., 'L'Histoire de la Ballade de la Geôle de Reading', *Mercure* 195, (1 April 1927), 68–101.
Horodisch, Abraham, *Oscar Wilde's 'Ballad of Reading Gaol'. A Bibliographical Study*, New York 1954.
Stamm, Rudolf, 'W. B. Yeats und Oscar Wildes "Ballad of Reading Gaol"', in *Studies in English Language and Literature*. Presented to Karl Brunner on the occasion of his seventieth birthday, ed. Siegfried Korninger, Wien/Stuttgart 1957, pp. 210–19. (WBEP. 65). English version under the title: 'William Butler Yeats and "The Ballad of Reading Gaol" by Oscar Wilde', in Rudolf Stamm, *The Shaping Powers at Work. Fifteen Essays on Poetic Transmutation*, Heidelberg 1967, pp. 210–19.
Gardner, Averil, 'Oscar Wilde's Swansong', DR 54 (1974), 65–80.
Southerton, Peter, *The Story of a Prison*. With a foreword by Lord Wolfenden, Reading 1975, esp. pp. 109–15.
Lodge, David, 'Oscar Wilde: "The Ballad of Reading Gaol"', in *The Modes of*

Modern Fiction. Metaphor, Metonymy, and the Typology of Modern Literature, London 1977, pp. 17–22.

IV   FAIRY-TALES AND STORIES
(1)   GENERAL STUDIES

Herzog, Alice, 'Die Märchen Oscar Wildes', unpublished diss., Mulhouse 1930.

Gordon, Jan B., '"The Wilde Child". Structure and Origin in the *fin-de-siècle* Short Story', ELT 15 (1972), 277–90.

Monaghan, David M., 'The Literary Fairy-Tale. A Study of Oscar Wilde's "The Happy Prince" and "The Star-Child"', CRCL/RCLC 1, no. 2 (1974) 156–66.

Briggs, Julia, *Night Visitors. The Rise and Fall of the English Ghost Story*, London 1977, esp. pp. 81–95.

Quintus, John A., 'The Moral Prerogative in Oscar Wilde. A Look at the Fairy Tales', VQR 53 (1977) 708–17.

Apel, Friedmar, *Die Zaubergärten der Phantasie. Zur Theorie und Geschichte des Kunstmärchens*, Heidelberg 1978, esp. pp. 247–56.

Klotz, Volker, 'Wie Wilde seine Märchen über Andersen hinweg erzählt', in *Der zerstückte Traum. Für Erich Arendt zum 75. Geburtstag*, ed. by Gregor Laschen and Manfred Schlösser, Berlin and Darmstadt 1978, pp. 219–28.

Spelman, Marlyn K., 'The Self-Realization Theme in "The Happy Prince" and "A House of Pomegranates"', unpublished Ph.D. thesis, Univ. of Colorado at Boulder, 1978. – DA 39, no. 5, 1978, pp. 2959–2960 – A.

Petzold, Dieter, *Das englische Kunstmärchen im neunzehnten Jahrhundert*, Tübingen 1981, esp. pp. 303–12 (Buchreihe der Anglia. 20).

D'Alessandro, Jean M. Ellis, *Hues of Mutability. The Waning Vision in Oscar Wilde's Narrative*, Florence 1984.

Klotz, Volker, *Das europäische Kunstmärchen. Fünfundzwanzig Kapitel seiner Geschichte von der Renaissance bis zur Moderne*, Stuttgart 1985. 'Oscar Wilde', pp. 311–323.

(2)   SINGLE TALES AND STORIES
'THE CANTERVILLE GHOST'

Fischer, Walther, 'Über eine angebliche Quelle von Oscar Wildes Erzählung "The Canterville Ghost"', Nph 10 (1924), 42–9.

Schroeder, Horst, 'Oscar Wilde, "The Canterville Ghost"', LWU 10 (1977), 21–30.

'LORD ARTHUR SAVILE'S CRIME'

Klein, Alfons, 'Motive und Themen in Oscar Wildes "Lord Arthur Savile's Crime"', in *Motive und Themen in Erzählungen des 19. Jahrhunderts. Bericht über Kolloquien der Kommission für literaturwissenschaftliche Motiv- und Themenforschung 1978–1979, T.I*, ed. Theodor Wolpers, Göttingen 1982, pp. 66–87.

'THE HAPPY PRINCE'

Griswold, Jerome, 'Sacrifice and Mercy in Wilde's "The Happy Prince"', ChL 3 (1974), 103–6.

Martin, Robert K., 'Oscar Wilde and the Fairy Tale. "The Happy Prince" as Self-Dramatization', SSF 16 (1979), 74–7.

'*THE SELFISH GIANT*'

Kotzin, Michael C., '"The Selfish Giant" as Literary Fairy Tale', SSF 16 (1979), 301–9.

V   ESSAYS AND CRITICAL WRITINGS
(I) GENERAL STUDIES

Risse, Ursula, 'Kunstanschauung und Kunstschaffen bei Oscar Wilde', unpublished diss. Freiburg im Brsg. 1951.

Grabig, Liselotte, 'Gesellschaftsschilderung und Gesellschaftskritik bei Oscar Wilde', unpublished diss. Halle 1954.

Glur, Guido, 'Kunstlehre und Kunstanschauung des Georgekreises und die Ästhetik Oscar Wildes', unpublished diss., Bern 1957.

Rhodes, Robert E., 'The Literary Criticism of Oscar Wilde', unpublished Ph.D. thesis, Univ. of Michigan, 1964: DA 25, no. 6, 1964/65, p. 3582.

Ellmann, Richard, '*The Critic as Artist as Wilde*', in *Wilde and the Nineties. An Essay and an Exhibition*, ed. Charles Ryskamp, Princeton, N.J. 1966, pp. 1–21.

Weintraub, Stanley, 'The Critic in Spite of Himself', in *Literary Criticism of Oscar Wilde*, ed. Stanley Weintraub, Lincoln, Nebr. 1968, pp. ix–xxxvi.

Harris, Wendell V., 'Arnold, Pater, Wilde, and the Object as in Themselves They See It', SEL 11 (1971), 733–47.

Murray, Isobel, 'Oscar Wilde's Absorption of "Influences"'. The Case History of Chuang Tzǔ, DUJ 64 (1971), 1–13.

Yaffe, Ann R., 'Oscar Wilde as Critic', unpublished Ph.D. thesis, Univ. of London, 1972.

Green, R. J., 'Oscar Wilde's "Intentions". An Early Modernist Manifesto', BJA 13 (1973), 397–404.

Sussman, Herbert, 'Criticism as Art. Form in Oscar Wilde's Critical Writings', SP 70 (1973), 108–22.

Bashford, Bruce, 'Oscar Wilde, his Criticism and his Critics', ELT 20 (1977), 181–7.

Stavros, George, 'Oscar Wilde on the Romantics', ELT 20 (1977), 35–45.

Bashford, Bruce, 'Oscar Wilde and Subjectivist Criticism', ELT 21 (1978), 218–34.

Helfand, Michael S. and Philip E. Smith II, 'Anarchy and Culture. The Evolutionary Turn of Cultural Criticism in the Work of Oscar Wilde', TSLL 20 (1978), 199–215.

Quintus, John A., 'The Moral Implications of Oscar Wilde's Aestheticism', TSLL 22 (1980), 559–74.

Daruwala, M. H. 'Good Intentions. The Romantic Aesthetics of Oscar Wilde's Criticism', VIJ 12 (1984), 105–32.

(2) SINGLE ESSAYS AND CRITICAL WRITINGS
'*THE CRITIC AS ARTIST*'

Watson, Edward A., 'Wilde's Iconoclastic Classicism: "The Critic as Artist"', ELT 27 (1984), 225–35.

'THE DECAY OF LYING'

Schiff, Hilda, 'Nature and Art in Oscar Wilde's "The Decay of Lying"', E & S 18 (n.s.) (1965), 83–102.

'THE PORTRAIT OF MR W. H.'

Poteet, Lewis J., 'Romantic Aesthetics in Oscar Wilde's "Mr. W. H."', SSF 7 (1970), 458–64.
Kershner, R. B., Jr, 'Artist, Critic and Performer. Wilde and Joyce on Shake-speare', TSLL 20 (1978), 216–29.
Dowling, Linda, 'Imposture and Absence in Wilde's "Portrait of Mr. W. H."', VN 58 (1980), 26–9.
Schroeder, Horst, Oscar Wilde, 'The Portrait of Mr. W. H.' – Its Composition, Publication and Reception, Braunschweig 1984. (Braunschweiger anglisti-sche Arbeiten. 9). Annotations to Oscar Wilde, 'The Portrait of Mr. W. H.', Braunschweig 1986. Privately printed.

THE SOUL OF MAN UNDER SOCIALISM

Nicholas, Brian, 'Two Nineteenth-Century Utopias. The Influence of Renan's "L'Avenir de la science" on Wilde's "The Soul of Man under Socialism"', MLR 59 (1964), 361–370.
Thomas, J.D., '"The Soul of Man under Socialism". An Essay in Context', RUS 51 (1965), 83–95.
D'Amico, Masolino, 'Oscar Wilde between "Socialism" and Aestheticism', EM 18 (1967), 111–39.

VI THE PICTURE OF DORIAN GRAY

Pater, Walter, 'A Novel by Mr Oscar Wilde', Bookman, Nov. 1891, Repr. in Oscar Wilde. The Critical Heritage, ed. by Karl Beckson, London 1970, pp. 83–6.
Art and Morality. A Defence of 'The Picture of Dorian Gray', ed. by Stuart Mason [Christopher S. Millard], London 1908. Rev. and enl. as Art and Morality. A Record of the Discussion which followed the Publication of "Dorian Gray", London 1912. Repr. New York 1971.
Farmer, Albert J., 'Oscar Wilde, "Le Portrait de Dorian Gray" (1890)', in Le Mouvement esthétique et "décadent" en Angleterre (1873–1900), Paris 1931, pp. 170–208. (Bibliothèque de la Revue de littérature comparée. 75).
Spivey, Ted R., 'Damnation and Salvation in "The Picture of Dorian Gray"', BUSE 4 (1960), 162–70.
Goetsch, Paul, 'Bemerkungen zur Urfassung von Wildes "The Picture of Dorian Gray"', DNS 15 (n.s.) (1966), 324–32.
Gordon, Jan B., '"Parody as Initiation". The Sad Education of "Dorian Gray"', Criticism 9 (1967), 355–71.
Korg, Jacob, 'The Rage of Caliban',UTQ 37 (1967), 75–89.
Baker, Houston A., Jr, 'A Tragedy of the Artist. "The Picture of Dorian Gray"', NCF 24 (1969), 349–55.
Lawler, Donald L., 'An Enquiry into Oscar Wilde's Revisions of "The Picture of Dorian Gray"', unpublished Ph.D. thesis, Univ. of Chicago, 1969.
Rossi, Dominick, 'Parallels in Wilde's "The Picture of Dorian Gray" and Goethe's "Faust"' CLAJ 13 (1969), 188–91.

420   Select bibliography

Altieri, Charles, 'Organic and Humanist Models in some English Bildungsroman [sic]', JGE 23 (1971), 220–40.
Haefner, Gerhard, 'Elemente der Prosa Oscar Wildes in "The Picture of Dorian Gray". Ein Beitrag zur ästhetischen Bewegung in England', NsM 24 (1971), 31–8.
Poteet, Lewis J., '"Dorian Gray" and the Gothic Novel', MFS 27 (1971), 239–48.
Murray, Isobel, 'Some Elements in the Composition of "The Picture of Dorian Gray"', DUJ 33 (1972), 220–31.
Pappas, John J., 'The Flower and the Beast. A Study of Oscar Wilde's Antithetical Attitudes toward Nature and Man in "The Picture of Dorian Gray"', ELT 15 (1972), 37–48.
Stephenson, Muriel L., 'A Critical Examination of Oscar Wilde's "The Picture of Dorian Gray"', unpublished Ph.D. thesis, Univ. of North Dakota, 1972: DA 33, no. 7, 1972/73, P. 3675 – A.
Donnelly, William F., 'The Other Dorian Grays', unpublished Ph.D. thesis, Univ. of Wisconsin, 1973. – DA 34, no. 3, 1973/74, pp. 1237–38.
Gerhardt, Hans-Peter, 'Oscar Wilde's "Dorian Gray" als Faustdichtung', Fbl, no. 25 (1973), 669–75.
Itschert, Hans, 'Oscar Wilde: "The Picture of Dorian Gray"', in Der englische Roman im 19. Jahrhundert. Interpretationen. Zu Ehren von Horst Oppel, ed. by Paul Goetsch, Heinz Kosok and Kurt Otten, Berlin 1973, pp. 273–87.
Keefe, Robert, 'Artist and Model in "The Picture of Dorian Gray"', SNNTS 5 (1973), 63–70.
Lawler, Donald, 'The Revisions of "Dorian Gray"', VIJ 3 (1974), 21–36.
Mayer, Hans, 'Oscar Wilde, "Das Bildnis des Dorian Gray"', in: Aussenseiter, Frankfurt/M.1975, pp. 260–7.
Lawler, Donald L. and Charles E. Knott, 'The Context of Invention. Suggested Origins of "Dorian Gray"', MP 73 (1976), 389–98.
Briggs, Julia, Night Visitors. The Rise and Fall of the English Ghost Story, London 1977, esp. pp. 83–94.
Delabroy, Jean, 'Platon chez les dandies. Sur "Le portrait de Dorian Gray" d'Oscar Wilde', Littérature, no. 25 (Feb. 1977), 42–63.
Meyers, Jeffrey, 'The Picture of Dorian Gray (1891)', in Homosexuality and Literature 1890–1930, London 1977, pp. 20–31.
Ziolkowski, Theodore, Disenchanted Images. A Literary Iconology, Princeton 1977, pp. 128–32.
Hart, John E., 'Art as Hero: "The Picture of Dorian Gray"', RS 46 (1978), 1–11.
Powell, Kerry, 'Oscar Wilde "Acting". The Medium as Message in "The Picture of Dorian Gray"', DR 58 (1978), 104–15.
Powell, Kerry, 'Massinger, Wilde, and "The Picture of Dorian Gray"', ELN 16 (1979), 312–15.
Oates, Joyce Carol, '"The Picture of Dorian Gray". Wilde's Parable of the Fall', CritI 7, no. 2 (1980), 419–28. Repr. in Contraries. Essays, New York 1981, pp. 3–16.
Powell, Kerry, 'Hawthorne, Arlo Bates, and "The Picture of Dorian Gray"', PLL 16 (1980), 403–16.
Dickson, Donald R., '"In a Mirror that Mirrors the Soul". Masks and Mirrors in "Dorian Gray"', ELT 26 (1983), 5–15.

Manganiello, Dominic, 'Ethics and Aesthetics in "The Picture of Dorian Gray"',
  CJIS 9 (1983), 25–33.
Martin, Robert K., 'Parody and Homage. The Presence of Pater in "Dorian
  Gray"', VN no. 63 (1983), 15–18.
Powell, Kerry, 'Tom, Dick, and Dorian Gray. Magic-Picture Mania in Late
  Victorian Fiction', PQ 62 (1983), 147–70.
Maier, Wolfgang, Oscar Wilde, 'The Picture of Dorian Gray'. Eine kritische
  Analyse der anglistischen Forschung von 1962 bis 1982, Frankfurt/M. 1984.
  (Aspekte der englischen Geistes- und Kulturgeschichte. 1).
Powell, Kerry, 'The Mesmerizing of Dorian Gray', VN, no. 65 (1984), 10–15.
Pfister, Manfred, Oscar Wilde: 'The Picture of Dorian Gray', München 1986.
  (UTB. 1388).
Cohen, Ed, 'Writing gone Wilde. Homoerotic desire in the closet of represen-
  tation', PMLA 102 (1987), 801–13.

VII PLAYS
(I) GENERAL STUDIES
Hankin, St John, 'The Collected Plays of Oscar Wilde', FortR 83 (n.s.) (Jan.–June,
  1908), 791–802.
Harris, Alan, 'Oscar Wilde as Playwright. A Centenary Review', Adelphi 30
  (1954), 212–40.
Ganz, Arthur F., 'The Divided Self in the Society Comedies of Oscar Wilde', MD 3
  (1960), 16–23.
Hopper, Vincent F. and Gerald B. Lahey, 'The Playwright', in Lady Windermere's
  Fan, ed. by Vincent F. Hopper and Gerald B. Lahey. With a note on the
  staging by George L. Hersey, Great Neck, N.Y. 1960, pp. 9–39. (Barron's
  Educational Ser.).
Pearson, Hesketh, 'Oscar Wilde and his Actors', ThA 45 (1961), 63–75.
Duncan, Barry, The St. James's Theatre. Its Strange & Complete History
  1835–1957. With a foreword by Allardyce Nicoll, London 1964, esp.
  pp. 223–29 and pp. 242–4.
Gregor, Ian, 'Comedy and Oscar Wilde', SeR 74 (1966), 501–21.
Gocke, Rainer, 'Dramenfiguren zwischen Paradoxie und Pathos. Ein Versuch
  über Oscar Wildes Gesellschaftskomödien', unpublished diss., Münster
  (Westf.) 1973.
Matlock, Kate, 'The Plays of Oscar Wilde', JIL 4, no. 2 (1975), 95–106.
Bird, Alan, The Plays of Oscar Wilde, London 1977.
Catsiapis, Hélène, 'Ironie et paradoxes dans les comédies d'Oscar Wilde. Une
  interprétation', Thalia 1 (1978), 35–53.
Gagnier, Regenia, 'Stages of Desire. Oscar Wilde's comedies and the consumer',
  Genre 15 (1982), 315–36.
Wilde, Oscar, Comedies. 'Lady Windermere's Fan', 'A Woman of No Impor-
  tance', 'An Ideal Husband', 'The Importance of Being Earnest'. A Casebook,
  ed. by William Tydeman, London 1982.
Worth, Katharine, Oscar Wilde, London 1983. (Macmillan Modern Dramatists).
Johnson, Wendell S., 'Fallen Women, Lost Children. Wilde and the Theatre of the
  Nineties', TSL 27 (1984), 196–211.

422   Select bibliography

(2) SINGLE PLAYS
VERA; OR, THE NIHILISTS

Reed, Frances M., 'Oscar Wilde's "Vera; Or, The Nihilist"' [*sic*]. The History of a
Failed Play' *Theatre Survey* 26 (1985), 163–77.

LADY WINDERMERE'S FAN

Brooks, Cleanth and Robert B. Heilman, 'Oscar Wilde, "Lady Windermere's
Fan", in *Understanding Drama*, New York 1948, pp. 34–82.
Peckham, Morse, 'What did Lady Windermere Learn?', CE 18 (1956), 11–14.
Hopper, Vincent F. and Gerald B. Lahey, 'The Play', in *Lady Windermere's Fan*,
ed. by Vincent F. Hopper and Gerald B. Lahey. With a note on the staging by
George L. Hersey, Great Neck, N.Y. 1960, pp. 40–70. (Barron's Educational
Ser.)
Geraths, Armin, 'Oscar Wilde, "Lady Windermere's Fan"', in *Das englische
Drama*, ed. by Dieter Mehl, vol. II, Düsseldorf 1970, pp. 153–72.
Small, Ian, Introduction, in *Oscar Wilde, Lady Windermere's Fan. A Play about a
Good Woman*, ed. by Ian Small, London and New York 1980, pp. ix–xxx
(The New Mermaids).
Davidson, David, 'The Importance of Being Ernst. Lubitsch and "Lady Winder-
mere's Fan"', LFQ 11, no. 2 (1983), 120–31.

SALOMÉ

Daffner, Hugo, *Salome. Ihre Gestalt in Geschichte und Kunst. Dichtung –
Bildende Kunst – Musik*. With an etching by Wilhelm Thöny, with 2
supplements, 26 plates and 200 illustrations, München 1912.
Brass, Friedrich Karl, 'Oscar Wildes Salome. Eine kritische Quellenstudie',
unpublished diss., Münster 1913.
Praz, Mario, *La carne, la morte e il diavolo nella letteratura romantica*, Milano/
Roma 1930. Transl. from the Italian by Angus Davidson as *The Romantic
Agony*, London 1933, *passim*.
Bergler, Edmund, '"Salome". The Turning Point in the Life of Oscar Wilde',
PsyR 43 (1956), 97–103. Repr. in *Selected Papers, 1933–1961*, New York
1965, pp. 433–41.
Zagona, Helen G., 'Oscar Wilde's "Salomé". Sensationalism and enigma', in *The
Legend of Salomé and the Principle of Art for Art's Sake*, Geneva and Paris
1960, pp. 121–32.
Ellmann, Richard, 'Overtures to "Salome"', YCGL 17 (1968), 17–28. Slightly
rev. and reiss. in *Oscar Wilde. A Collection of Critical Essays*, ed. by Richard
Ellmann, Englewood Cliffs N.J., 1969, pp. 73–91; *Tri-Quarterly* 15 (1969),
45–64; *Golden Codgers. Biographical Speculations*, London and New York
1973, pp. 39–59.
D'Astorg, Bertrand, 'Le Mystère de Salomé', Rddm (Apr. 1971), 93–109.
Joost, Nicholas and Franklin E. Court, 'Salomé, the Moon, and Oscar Wilde's
Aesthetics. A Reading of the Play', PLL 8, suppl. (Fall 1972), 96–111.
Marcus, Jane, 'Salomé. The Jewish princess was a new woman', BNYPL 78
(1974), 95–113.
Schmidgall, Gary, 'Salomé', in *Literature as Opera*, New York 1977, esp. pp.
247–86.
Haskell, Eric T., 'L'Interprétation figurée. Les illustrateurs de la "Salomé" de

Wilde', unpublished Ph.D. thesis, Univ. of California, Irvine, 1980: DA 40, no. 12, pt. I, 1980, pp. 6263–4–A.
Rose, Marilyn G., 'The Synchronic Salome', in Ortrun Zuber (ed.), *The Languages of Theatre. Problems in the Translation and Transposition of Drama*, Oxford 1980, pp. 146–52.
Gilbert, Elliot L., '"Tumult of Images". Wilde, Beardsley, and "Salomé"', VS 26 (1983), 133–59.
Good, Graham, 'Early Productions of Oscar Wilde's "Salome"', NCTR 11 (1983), 77–92.
Shewan, Rodney, 'The Artist and the Dancer in Three Symbolist "Salomés"', BuR 30 (1986), 102–30.

A WOMAN OF NO IMPORTANCE

Guralnick, Elissa S. and Paul M. Levitt, 'Allusion and Meaning in Wilde's "A Woman of No Importance"', *Eire–Ireland* 13, no. 4 (1978), 45–51.

AN IDEAL HUSBAND

Mikhail, E. H., 'Self-Revelation in "An Ideal Husband"', MD 11 (1968/69), 180–6.
Kohl, Norbert, 'Oscar Wilde: "An Ideal Husband"', in *Das englische Drama im 18. und 19. Jahrhundert. Interpretationen*, ed. by Heinz Kosok, Berlin 1976, pp. 318–33.

THE IMPORTANCE OF BEING EARNEST

Bentley, Eric, *The Playwright as Thinker*, New York 1967 [1946], pp. 140–5.
Foster, Richard, 'Wilde as Parodist. A Second Look at "The Importance of Being Earnest"', CE 18 (1956), 18–23.
Reinert, Otto, 'Satiric Strategy in "The Importance of Being Earnest"', CE 18 (1956), 14–18
Partridge, E. B., 'The Importance of Not Being Earnest', BuR 9 (1958), 143–58.
Hopper, Vincent F. and Gerald B. Lahey, 'The Play', in *The Importance of Being Earnest*, ed. by Vincent F. Hopper and Gerald B. Lahey. With a note on the staging by George L. Hersey, New York 1959, pp. 40–52. (Barron's Educational Ser.).
Ganz, Arthur, 'The Meaning of "The Importance of Being Earnest"', MD 6 (1963), 42–52.
Toliver, Harold E., 'Wilde and the Importance of "Sincere and Studied Triviality"', MD 5 (1963), 389–99.
Zaic, Franz, 'Oscar Wilde, "The Importance of Being Earnest"', in *Das moderne englische Drama. Interpretationen*, ed. by Horst Oppel, Berlin 1963, pp. 44–61.
Meier, Erika, '"The Importance of Being Earnest"', in 'Realism and Reality'. The Function of the Stage Directions in the New Drama from Thomas William Robertson to George Bernard Shaw, unpublished diss., Basel 1967, pp. 182–95.
Jordan, Robert J., 'Satire and Fantasy in Wilde's "The Importance of Being Earnest"', *Ariel* 1, no. 3 (1970), 101–9.
Ware, James M., 'Algernon's Appetite. Oscar Wilde's Hero as Restoration Dandy', ELT 13 (1970), 17–26.

424   Select bibliography

Donohue, Joseph W., Jr, 'The First Production of "The Importance of Being Earnest". A Proposal for a Reconstructive Study', in *Essays on Nineteenth Century British Theatre*, ed. by Kenneth Richards and Peter Thomson, London 1971, pp. 125–43.

Poague, L. A., '"The Importance of Being Earnest". The Texture of Wilde's Irony', MD 16, nos. 3–4 (1973), 251–7.

Parker, David, 'Oscar Wilde's Great Farce "The Importance of Being Earnest"', MLQ 35 (1974), 173–86.

Spininger, Dennis, 'Profiles and Principles. The Sense of the Absurd in "The Importance of Being Earnest"', PLL 12 (1976), 49–72.

Stone, Geoffrey, 'Serious Bunburyism. The Logic of "The Importance of Being Earnest"', EIC 26 (1976), 28–41.

Green, William, 'Oscar Wilde and the Bunburys', MD 21 (1978), 67–80.

Barth, Adolf, 'Oscar Wilde's "Comic Refusal". A Reassessment of "The Importance of Being Earnest"', *Archiv* 131 (216. vol.) (1979), 120–8.

Jackson, Russell, Introduction, in *Oscar Wilde, The Importance of Being Earnest. A Trivial Comedy for Serious People*, edited by Russell Jackson, London and New York, 1980, pp. xi–xlv. (The New Mermaids).

'A WIFE'S TRAGEDY'

Shewan, Rodney, 'Oscar Wilde and "A Wife's Tragedy". Facts and Conjectures', ThR 8, no. 2 (1983), 83–95.

VIII *DE PROFUNDIS*

Beerbohm, Max, 'A Lord of Language', VF (2 March 1905). Repr. in *A Peep into the Past and other Prose Pieces*. Coll. and introd. by Rupert Hart-Davis, London 1972, pp. 37–41.

Gordon, Jan B., 'Wilde and Newman. The Confessional Mode', *Renascence* 22 (1970), 183–91.

Cary, Meredith, '"De Profundis" – Wilde's Letter to the World', TSL 16 (1971), 91–102.

Butwin, Joseph, 'The Martyr Clown. Oscar Wilde in "De Profundis"', VN 42 (1972), 1–6.

Hyde, H. Montgomery, 'The Riddle of "De Profundis". Who Owns the Manuscript?', AntigR 54 (1983), 107–27.

Gagnier, Regenia, '"De Profundis" as Epistola: in Carcere et Vinculis. A Materialist Reading of Oscar Wilde's Autobiography', *Criticism* 26 (1984), 335–54.

Bashford, Bruce, 'Oscar Wilde as Theorist. The Case of "De Profundis"', ELT 28 (1985), 395–406.

IX SOCIAL AND CULTURAL BACKGROUND. HISTORY OF IDEAS

Hamilton, Walter, *The Aesthetic Movement in England*, London 1882.

Symons, Arthur, 'The Decadent Movement in Literature', HarpNMM 87 (June–Nov. 1893), 858–67.

Jackson, Holbrook, *The Eighteen Nineties. A Review of Art and Ideas at the Close of the Nineteenth Century*, London 1913, 1922. Pbk. edn, New York 1966.

Egan, Rose Frances, 'The Genesis of the Theory of "Art for Art's Sake" in Germany and England', SCSML, pt. I, vol. 2, no. 4 (July 1921), 5–61; pt. II, vol. 5, no. 3 (Apr. 1924), pp. 1–33.

Mann, Otto, *Der Dandy. Ein Kulturproblem der Moderne*, Heidelberg 1962 [1925].

LeGallienne, Richard, *The Romantic '90s*. Introd. by H. Montgomery Hyde, London 1951 [1926].

Praz, Mario, *La carne, la morte e il diavolo nella letteratura romantica*, Milan and Rome 1930. Transl. from the Italian by Angus Davidson as *The Romantic Agony*, London 1933. Repr. 1951.

Farmer, Albert J., *Le Mouvement esthétique et 'décadent' en Angleterre (1873–1900)*, Paris 1931. (Bibliothèque de la Revue de littérature comparée. 75).

Rosenblatt, Louise, *L'Idée de l'art pour l'art dans la littérature anglaise pendant la période victorienne*, Paris 1931. (Bibliothèque de la Revue de littérature comparée. 70).

Guérard, Albert L., *Art for Art's Sake*, New York 1936. Repr. 1963. (Schocken Book. 65).

Joad, Cyril E. M., *Decadence. A Philosophical Inquiry*, London 1948.

Wildi, Max, 'Künstler und Gesellschaft in England, 1850–1900' in *Individuum und Gemeinschaft. Festschr. zur Fünfzigjahrfeier der Handels-Hochschule St Gallen 1949*, St Gallen 1949, pp. 605–28.

Robinson, James K., 'A Neglected Phase of the Aesthetic Movement: English Parnassianism' PMLA 68 (1953), 733–54.

Singer, Irving, 'The Aesthetics of Art for Art's Sake', JAAC 12 (1954), 343–59.

Kermode, Frank, *Romantic Image*, London and Glasgow 1971 [1957].

Ryals, Clyde de L., 'Toward a Definition of "Decadent" as Applied to British Literature of the Nineteenth Century', JAAC 17 (1958), 85–92.

Gerber, Helmut E., 'The Nineties. Beginning, End, or Transition', in *Edwardians and Late Victorians*. (English Institute Essays 1959), ed. by Richard Ellmann, New York 1960, pp. 50–79.

Moers, Ellen, *The Dandy. Brummell to Beerbohm*, London 1960. Repr. Lincoln, Nebr. 1978.

Goldfarb, Russell M., 'Late Victorian Decadence', JAAC 20 (1961/1962), 369–73.

Beckson, Karl, Introduction, in *Aesthetes and Decadents of the 1890s. An Anthology of British Poetry and Prose*, ed. by Karl Beckson, New York 1966, pp. xvii–xl.

Lester, John A., Jr, *Journey through Despair 1880–1914. Transformation in British Literary Culture*, Princeton, N.J. 1968.

Johnson, R.V., *Aestheticism*, London 1969. (The Critical Idiom. 3).

Hönnighausen, Lothar, *Präraphaeliten und 'Fin de siècle'. Symbolistische Tendenzen in der englischen Spätromantik*, München 1971. Translated as *The Symbolist Tradition in English Literature: A Study of Pre-Raphaelitism and 'Fin de siècle'*, Cambridge 1988.

Fin de siècle. Zu Literatur und Kunst der Jahrhundertwende, ed. by Roger Bauer *et al.*, Frankfurt/M. 1977). (Studien zur Philosophie und Literatur des neunzehnten Jahrhunderts. 35).

Franci, Giovanna, *Il sistema del Dandy. Wilde, Beardsley, Beerbohm*. (Arte e Artificio nell'Inghilterra fin-de-siècle), Bologna 1977.

Hinterhäuser, Hans, *Fin de siècle. Gestalten und Mythen*, München 1977.

Pierrot, Jean, *L'Imaginaire décadent (1880–1900)*, Paris 1977. Transl. by Derek Coltman as *The Decadent Imagination: 1880–1900*, Chicago 1982.

Kohl, Norbert, '"L'Art pour l'art" in der Ästhetik des 19. Jahrhunderts', LiLi 8, nos. 30/31 (1978), 159–74.

Wuthenow, Ralph-Rainer, *Muse, Maske, Meduse. Europäischer Ästhetizismus*, Frankfurt/M. 1978. (edition suhrkamp. 897).

Decadence and the 1890s, ed. by Ian Fletcher, London 1979. (Stratford-upon-Avon Studies. 17).

Gilman, Richard, *Decadence. The Strange Life of an Epithet*, London 1979.

Annoni, Carlo, *Il decadentismo*, Brescia 1982.

Horstmann, Ulrich, *Ästhetizismus und Dekadenz. Zum Paradigmakonflikt in der englischen Literaturtheorie des späten 19. Jahrhunderts*, München 1983.

Die 'Nineties'. Das englische Fin de siècle zwischen Dekadenz und Sozialkritik, ed. by Manfred Pfister and Bernd Schulte-Middelich, München 1983. (UTB. 1233).

Thornton, R.K.R., *The Decadent Dilemma*, London 1983.

Gardiner, Bruce, 'Decadence. Its Construction and Contexts', SoRA 18 (1985), 22–43.

Haley, Bruce, 'Wilde's "Decadence" and the Positivist Tradition', VS 28 (1985), 215–29.

Harris, Wendell V., 'An Anatomy of Aestheticism', in *Victorian Literature and Society. Essays Presented to Richard D. Altick*, ed. James R. Kincaid and Albert J. Kuhn, Columbus, Ohio 1985, 331–47.

Reed, John R., *Decadent Style*, Athens, Ohio 1985.

Dowling, Linda, *Language and Decadence in the Victorian Fiction Fin de Siècle*, Princeton 1986.

Rasch, Wolfdietrich, *Die literarische Décadence um 1900*, München 1986.

Index